BOOMS AND BUSTS

An Encyclopedia of Economic History
from Tulipmania of the 1630s to the
Global Financial Crisis of the 21st Century

Volume 2

James Ciment, Editor

SHARPE REFERENCE

an imprint of M.E. Sharpe, Inc.

SHARPE REFERENCE

Sharpe Reference is an imprint of M.E. Sharpe, Inc.

M.E. Sharpe, Inc.
80 Business Park Drive
Armonk, NY 10504

Cover photos (background; left to right) provided by Getty Images and the following: Mario Tama; Popperfoto; Yoshikazu Tsuno/AFP; Kean Collection/Hulton Archive; Melanie Einzig.

Library of Congress Cataloging-in-Publication Data

Booms and busts : an encyclopedia of economic history from Tulipmania of the 1630s to the global financial crisis of the 21st century / James Ciment, editor.
   v. ; cm.
Includes bibliographical references and index.
ISBN 978-0-7656-8224-6 (hardcover : alk. paper)
1. Financial crises—Encyclopedias. 2. Finance—Encyclopedias. I. Ciment, James.

HB3722.B67 2010
330.03—dc22   2010021272

Printed and bound in the United States

The paper used in this publication meets the minimum requirements of American National Standard for Information Sciences—Permanence of Paper for Printed Library Materials,
ANSI Z 39.48.1984.

CW (c) 10 9 8 7 6 5 4 3 2 1

Publisher: Myron E. Sharpe
Vice President and Director of New Product Development: Donna Sanzone
Vice President and Production Director: Carmen Chetti
Executive Development Editor: Jeff Hacker
Project Manager: Angela Piliouras
Program Coordinator: Cathleen Prisco
Assistant Editor: Alison Morretta
Text Design and Cover Design: Jesse Sanchez
Typesetter: Nancy Connick

Contents

Galbraith, John Kenneth

A widely read Post Keynesian economist of the post–World War II era, John Kenneth Galbraith was a major figure in the institutionalist school, a historically oriented school of economic thinking that examined the role of institutions—both social and economic—in shaping how economies operated. While Galbraith is best known for his work on income disparities, private wealth, and corporate power, he also examined the role of speculation in financial crises, most notably in his books *The Great Crash*, 1929 (1955) and *A Short History of Financial Euphoria* (1993).

Galbraith was born in a small town in Ontario, Canada, in 1908. Befitting his rural upbringing, his education focused on farming issues. He received his bachelor's degree from the Ontario Agricultural College and his doctorate from the University of California, the latter in 1934, and both in agricultural economics. He became a U.S. citizen in 1937. Combining academics, public service, and journalism, Galbraith had a variegated career, teaching economics at Harvard University from the 1930s onward, editing *Fortune*, a business magazine, in the mid-1940s, serving as deputy head of the Office of Price Administration, a price-setting federal agency, during the first half World War II, and then taking up the post of ambassador to India in the John F. Kennedy administration.

Galbraith had the rare knack of making economics accessible to ordinary readers, and several of his books—most notably, *The Great Crash*, *The Affluent Society* (1958), and *The New Industrial State* (1967)—topped nonfiction best-seller lists. While not as widely read as the above, his book *American Capitalism: The Concept of Countervailing Power* (1952) contended that the economic power of big business was increasingly held in check by countervailing institutions, such as government regulatory agencies and unions. In *The Affluent Society*, Galbraith bemoaned the danger of an American society in which increasing private wealth and an increasingly impoverished public sector perpetuated disparities in income and wealth. *The New Industrial State* argued how large corporations used sophisticated marketing and advertising techniques to shape demand, thereby distorting the ordinary workings of the marketplace. A 1973 work, *Economics and Public Purpose*, offered solutions to corporate power in the form of nationalizing the health and defense industries and putting in place wage, price, and profit controls.

Two of Galbraith's books focused primarily on the boom-and-bust cycle. In *The Great Crash*, he examined the worst financial crisis in the history of capitalism, laying the blamed for the catastrophe on out-of-control speculation in the corporate securities market, as crowd psychology replaced rational economic calculation, leading otherwise sane investors—both big and small—to conclude that wealth could be accumulated quickly and without any increase in productive output, and that share prices would consistently go up, outpacing real economic growth.

In *A Short History of Financial Euphoria*, Galbraith expanded his study of speculative episodes across centuries of capitalist history, noting that psychological factors make price-asset bubbles an intrinsic element of free-market economies. Moreover, he argued that investors participating in such bubbles have a "vested interest in error," that is, in perpetuating the illusion that wealth can be created out of nothing, since that illusion is what serves to send asset prices and investor returns upward. Presciently, Galbraith also used *A Short History* to deride the value of new and more exotic financial instruments, pointing out the dangers of using excessive debt to finance speculation, and noting how these developments could lead to disastrous collapses in asset prices that could drag down whole economies.

James Ciment

See also: Institutional Economics; Post Keynesian Theories and Models.

Further Reading

Galbraith, John Kenneth. *A Short History of Financial Euphoria.* New York: Whittle Books, in association with Viking, 1993.
———. *The Great Crash, 1929.* Boston: Houghton Mifflin, 1955.
Keaney, Michael, ed. *Economist with a Public Purpose: Essays in Honor of John Kenneth Galbraith.* New York: Routledge, 2001.
Parker, Richard. *John Kenneth Galbraith: His Life, His Politics, His Economics.* New York: Farrar, Straus, and Giroux, 2005.
Sharpe, Myron E. *John Kenneth Galbraith and the Lower Economics.* 2nd ed. White Plains, NY: International Arts and Sciences, 1974.
Williams, Andrea D., ed. *The Essential Galbraith.* Boston: Houghton Mifflin, 2001.

Geithner, Timothy (1961–)

Timothy F. Geithner was named secretary of the Treasury by President-elect Barack Obama in November 2008, barely three weeks after Obama won the election and in the midst of the national economic crisis. Geithner's nomination won prompt confirmation by the Senate, and he was sworn in on January 26, 2009. Geithner previously had served as undersecretary of the Treasury (1999–2001) in the Bill Clinton administration and later as director of the Federal Reserve Bank of New York (2003–2008). In the latter capacity, he worked with then Treasury secretary Henry Paulson and Federal Reserve chairman Ben Bernanke in 2007–2008 on managing the early stages of what would become the global financial crisis.

Timothy Franz Geithner was born on August 18, 1961, in New York City. As the son of an international development expert for the Ford Foundation, he was raised in the United States, Asia, and Africa. After graduating from the International High School in Bangkok, Thailand, he attended Dartmouth College, where he was a double major in government and Asian studies, with a concentration in Chinese. After graduating from Dartmouth in 1983, Geithner attended the School of Advanced International Studies at Johns Hopkins University and earned a master's degree in international economics and Asian studies in 1985. In the course of his academic career, he studied both Chinese and Japanese.

Before joining the Treasury Department, Geithner joined Kissinger and Associates, a leading policy consultancy in Washington, D.C., as an Asia expert and research assistant. In 1988, he took a position in the International Affairs division of the Department of the Treasury, serving as an attaché at the American Embassy in Tokyo and witnessing firsthand the onset of a decade of economic stagnation in Japan. Geithner rose to assistant secretary and then under secretary for International Affairs (1997–2001) in the Clinton administration, serv-

In February 2009, barely two weeks after being sworn in, Treasury Secretary Timothy Geithner introduced a financial stability plan aimed at unfreezing U.S. credit markets. Geithner had been involved in the financial crisis as president of the Federal Reserve Bank of New York. *(Win McNamee/ Getty Images)*

ing under Treasury secretaries Robert Rubin and Lawrence H. Summers, both of whom have been identified as mentors. Rising through the ranks of the International Affairs division, Geithner was at the heart of U.S. financial policy making in the bailout of Mexico (1995), the Asian financial crisis of 1997–1998 (Thailand, Korea, and Indonesia), and the 1998–1999 currency crisis in Brazil. In 2001, with the end of the Clinton administration, Geithner moved to the International Monetary Fund, where he served as director of policy development and review. In November 2003, he was named president and chief executive of the Federal Reserve Bank of New York, serving as vice chairman and a permanent member of the Federal Open Market Committee, which formulates the nation's monetary policy.

As the credit crisis broke out in 2007, Geithner found himself at the epicenter of the rapidly worsening financial turmoil. Along with Treasury Secretary Paulson and Federal Reserve chairman Bernanke, he agreed to handle the crisis at the investment bank Bear Stearns by providing emergency funding and then a $30 billion credit line to enable a rescue takeover by JPMorgan Chase. In September 2008, Geithner and Paulson attempted to make a stand against any additional government bailouts by allowing the troubled investment banking firm Lehman Brothers to file for bankruptcy. The failure of Lehman had a tsunami-like effect on the insurance-reinsurance giant AIG (American International Group) and the brokerage firm Merrill Lynch, among others, because of their heavy exposure in derivative markets. With fear spreading that other major firms—and much of the U.S. financial sector in general—were at risk, global capital markets began to seize up. And with the collapse of the global financial system considered a very real possibility, Paulson, Geithner, and Bernanke pushed through a buyout of insurance giant AIG with taxpayer money and the emergency sale of Merrill Lynch to Bank of America. Timothy Ryan, chief executive of the Securities Industry and Financial Markets Association, echoed the observation of many that Geithner was "one of a core group of government executives who's been part of every decision [in the current crisis]."

Immediately after taking office in January 2009, President Obama officially nominated Geithner as the new secretary of Treasury, declaring, "he will start his first day on the job with a unique insight into the failures of today's markets and a clear vision of the steps we must take to revive them." Geithner's vision clearly echoed the reformist approach declared by candidate Obama in March 2007: "[W]e need to regulate institutions for what they do, not what they are." Speaking to the Economic Club of New York in June of that year, Geithner stated that regulators needed to make it "more difficult for institutions [such as investment banks, hedge funds, and private equity firms] with little capital and little supervision to underwrite mortgages." As Treasury secretary, Geithner has promoted increased supervision and examination of such entities, as well as other banklike regulations, such as capital requirements, liquidity requirements, and leverage limits in exchange for government capital infusions to investment companies amounting to almost $2 trillion. In early 2009, he directed the allocation of the second tranche of money, totaling $350 billion, from the $700 billion bank bailout passed in October 2008 and administered under the Troubled Asset Relief Program, and addressed such other major issues as government support for the U.S. automobile industry, executive bonuses in financial companies, bolstering the mortgage and housing industries, tax policy, and foreign trade.

Frank L. Winfrey

See also: Federal Reserve System; Recession and Financial Crisis (2007–); Stimulus Package, U.S. (2009); Troubled Asset Relief Program (2008–).

Further Reading

Guha, Krishna, and Gillian Tett. "Man in the News: Timothy Geithner." *Financial Times*, March 21, 2008.

Kuttner, Robert. "Meet the Next Treasury Secretary." *American Prospect*, September 22, 2008.

Labaton, Stephen. "The New Team: Timothy F. Geithner." *New York Times*, November 7, 2008.

Landler, Mark, and Jackie Calmes. "Geithner, Rescue-Team Veteran, Has Head Start in Seizing Reins." *New York Times*, November 24, 2008.

"Timothy F. Geithner." *New York Times*, March 24, 2009.

General Motors

The world's largest automobile manufacturing corporation for most of the twentieth century, General Motors (GM) was also a leading innovator in the engineering and marketing of motor vehicles for much of its history. For years it dominated the global automobile industry, building up to half of all passenger cars in the world shortly after World War II. But with the rise of European and Japanese auto manufacturing beginning in the 1950s, GM saw its market share erode significantly, despite aggressive expansion into Europe and Asia. At home in the United States, just one in five cars sold was built by GM by the mid-2000s. The decline left the Detroit-based firm especially vulnerable to the global financial crisis and recession of the late 2000s, forcing GM to close plants and furlough workers, plead for billions of dollars in government loans, and ultimately place itself under the protection of U.S. bankruptcy laws in 2009.

Origins and Rise

Founded in 1908 by horse-carriage manufacturer William Durant—as a holding company for Buick—General Motors expanded through the 1910s and 1920s, acquiring or starting a number of other motor vehicle manufacturing companies in the United States and Europe, including Chevrolet, Oldsmobile, Pontiac, Cadillac, Opel (Germany), Vauxhall (Great Britain), and companies that would later be incorporated into GMC, GM's truck and bus manufacturing division.

Under its visionary chief, Alfred P. Sloan, General Motors developed a number of innovative strategies for marketing automobiles in the first half of the twentieth century. First, it created the model year, upgrading its cars annually to spur consumers to replace their automobiles before they broke down. Second, with its many divisions, GM could offer a range of automobiles for every budget, so that as customers' incomes rose and they upgraded their vehicles, they would remain GM customers. The company was often the first to introduce attractive amenities and moved early into credit financing, offering potential customers a way to make what for most was the second most expensive purchase (after a house) of their lives. Such innovation helped GM surpass rival Ford in the 1920s to become the largest automobile manufacturer in the United States and the world.

General Motors also became one of the most vertically integrated companies in American manufacturing, having developed a number of subsidiaries to provide parts, such as ACDelco, and financing, through the General Motors Acceptance Corporation (GMAC). GM also branched out into non-automobile-related businesses, most notably its Frigidaire line of household appliances.

After retooling for defense during World War II, GM continued its upward trajectory in the early postwar era. After briefly resisting unionization in the late 1930s, the company came to an understanding with the United Automobile Workers (UAW) following a long and costly strike in 1945–1946. In exchange for giving up its demand to have a seat on

GM's board—and a say in the way the company was run—the UAW won some of the highest wages ever earned for unskilled manufacturing workers along with generous health and pension packages. With other American automobile manufacturers forced to meet the GM/UAW terms—and with little competition from foreign carmakers—GM could afford such largesse. By the mid-1950s, it had the largest private workforce in the world, and its U.S. market share peaked at more than 50 percent.

Gradual Decline

While the company faced setbacks in the 1960s and early 1970s—including a devastating exposé on the safety of one its most popular vehicles and rising environmental protests about its failure to engineer less polluting cars—GM continued to thrive. Its first real stumble came with the oil crises of the 1970s, when political upheaval in the Middle East—the world's largest oil exporting region—sent crude prices skyrocketing from less than $4 a barrel in 1973 to more than $40 a barrel in 1980 (from $19 to $100 in 2008 dollars). Like other American automobile manufacturers, GM emphasized comfort and horsepower over fuel economy, leaving itself vulnerable to high gasoline prices. Making things worse, both European and Japanese manufacturers, having fully recovered from World War II, aggressively moved into the U.S. market with their fuel-efficient and reliable small vehicles.

While GM responded with small cars of its own—until plummeting oil prices in the 1980s and 1990s led it to reemphasize big cars, pickups, and a whole new type of large vehicle, the sports utility vehicle (SUV)—it failed to reverse its decline in market share. American customers increasingly came to see foreign cars, especially Japanese ones, as better built and better styled, even as those same foreign manufacturers took a page from GM's playbook and began introducing a line of cars to fit every budget.

Aside from increased foreign competition, GM's problems were also of its own making. GM's corporate structure—with each division largely running its own affairs—created independent fiefdoms that resisted efforts by corporate management to streamline the company in the face of growing competition; divisions resisted consolidating their operations and cannibalized each other's sales. The UAW also contributed to GM's decline, opposing changes in work rules that would allow assembly lines to work more efficiently, and threatening—or occasionally calling—strikes to resist cutbacks in wages or benefits, even as Japanese and European manufacturers opened nonunion plants in the United States that paid their workers less.

Despite such problems, GM continued to do well, aided by a booming economy and low gas prices from the mid-1980s through the late 1990s. While its U.S. market share shrank, GM was successful in Europe and aggressively moved into emerging markets, particularly in East Asia.

By the early 2000s, a new problem emerged. With a growing population of retirees eligible for generous pension and health care benefits, GM found itself saddled with enormous financial obligations. Combined with its declining U.S. market share, such costs devastated the corporate bottom line, as GM posted a record $10.6 billion in losses for 2005. GM responded by divesting its stakes in several foreign auto firms, reducing its annual dividends, and selling off much of its GMAC financing arm. Meanwhile, for some time, GM had been reducing its manufacturing capacity and workforce, especially in the United States. While GM employed nearly 900,000 workers worldwide in 1979, its peak year, the payroll had shrunk to roughly 300,000 workers in the mid-2000s.

Financial Crisis, Bailout, and Bankruptcy

In short, GM was in a weak position when a series of crises hit the entire U.S. auto industry in 2007 and 2008. The new challenges included a sudden spike in oil prices—reaching a record high of nearly $150 a barrel in the summer of 2008—which did the most damage to companies with big inventories of larger, less fuel-efficient

A General Motors dealership in Creedmoor, North Carolina, survived a major cutback in May 2009. The automaker announced that 1,100 dealerships would be dropped from its retail network—with more cuts to come. GM filed for bankruptcy protection on June 1. *(Bloomberg/Getty Images)*

vehicles, such as GM. But even when gas prices came down later in the year, GM faced two new problems: the economic recession and the global financial crisis. With consumer demand undermined and credit hard to come by, U.S. new light-vehicle sales plunged from more than 16 million in 2006 to fewer than 11 million in 2008.

While every automaker, both domestic and foreign, suffered in the face of these problems, GM's sales declines outpaced those of the industry overall. In 2007, GM lost its standing as the world's largest auto manufacturer—to Toyota—for the first time since 1926. Worse, collapsing sales and continued high costs produced record losses for GM—$38.7 billion in 2007 and $30.9 billion in 2008. Meanwhile, the company's stock price plummeted from a high of more than $80 a share in the late 1990s to less than $3 a share in November 2008, representing a more than sixty-year low. By May 2009, the share price would fall below $1.

As the financial crisis deepened in late fall 2008—and as the George W. Bush administration established the $700 billion Troubled Asset Relief Program for ailing financial institutions—General Motors, along with equally distressed Chrysler, announced that it was almost out of cash and would be forced into bankruptcy in 2009 unless it received aid from the government. Despite some popular and media outrage, especially after auto executives flew to Washington, D.C., on private

jets to plea for taxpayer aid, the outgoing Bush administration—supported by President-elect Barack Obama—agreed to provide $9.4 billion in loans to GM.

But there were strings attached, including a provision that the company come up with a restructuring plan by March 31, 2009, that would allow it to repay the debt and return to profitability. As the deadline loomed, the Obama administration pressured GM chief executive officer Rick Wagoner to resign and then offered the company a further sixty days to come up with a plan. Despite substantial cost-cutting efforts, the downturn in the automobile industry proved too strong and GM was unable to avoid collapse. On June 1, it filed for federal bankruptcy protection under Chapter 11, becoming the fourth-largest U.S. corporation in history to do so.

With the swift bankruptcy organization of Chrysler as a model—the smaller auto manufacturer had filed at the end of April and emerged from bankruptcy in early June—GM and the Obama administration worked to achieve what they called a "surgical bankruptcy" for GM, hoping that a swift emergence from bankruptcy would reassure potential automobile buyers that GM would continue as a going concern that could stand by the warranties on its automobiles.

During the course of the bankruptcy proceedings, GM was split into two entities: the General Motors Company, which purchased most of the old GM's assets and emerged from bankruptcy on July 10, an amazingly fast forty days after filing; and the Motor Vehicles Company, which remained in bankruptcy in order to settle the liabilities of the old GM with bondholders and others.

James Ciment

See also: Chrysler; Manufacturing; Troubled Asset Relief Program (2008–).

Further Reading

Chandler, Alfred D., ed. *Managerial Innovation at General Motors.* New York: Arno, 1979.

Farber, David. *Sloan Rules: Alfred P. Sloan and the Triumph of General Motors.* Chicago: University of Chicago Press, 2002.

General Motors Web site: www.gm.com.

Langworth, Richard M., and editors of *Consumer Guide. GM: 100 Years.* Lincolnwood, IL: Publications International, 2008.

German Historical School

Emerging in the nineteenth century, the German historical school was a school of economic thinking that emphasized empiricism rather than theory to explain how economies operate. German historical school thinkers, who utilized a cross-disciplinary approach in their research, argued that economic behavior and laws grow out of specific historical, social, and institutional contexts. Overshadowed by the more theoretical Austrian school and the classical economics of Britain, the German historical school had little influence on subsequent economic theory, though its approach was widely taken up by historians and sociologists.

The origins of the German historical school are based in German Romanticism, which questioned abstract theorizing, and the philosophy of GeorgW.F. Hegel, who emphasized the historicity of philosophical thought and discounted theoretical systems that applied in all places and times. Among the first practitioners of what would later be known as the German historical school was Wilhelm Roscher, a disciple of Hegel's. Producing his most influential work in the mid-nineteenth century, Roscher argued that one can understand economies only by closely examining historical and sociological evidence. Following Hegelian ideas about the cyclical nature of history, Roscher argued that economies also go through stages, which he likened to the human life cycle: youth, adulthood, and old age, and then, as with a new generation, back to youth again.

Roscher and other early German historicists were, by definition, modest in their claims and aspirations. Since they did not believe in universal economic laws, they were careful not to apply historical lessons to current economic situations, and they offered little in the way of advice to policy makers. Not so the next generation, or the so-called young historical school. Led by Gustav von Schmoller, this new generation of historical thinkers maintained that economics is by nature a normative, or prescriptive, discipline, drawing general rules about economic behavior from historical examples. Unlike Roscher, Schmoller and other young historical school thinkers were not shy about offering advice to economic policy makers and opened the Verein für Sozialpolitik (Association for Social Politics) in 1872 to do just that.

Despite the establishment of the Verein, most practitioners did not define themselves as members of a distinct school of economic thinking until forced to defend themselves when attacked by Carl Menger and his Austrian school followers. Contrary to the Germans, Menger argued for a deductive, rather than inductive, approach to economic theorizing, developing abstract principles that applied in various historical and national contexts. Known as the *Methodenstreit*, or Methods Debate, the late-nineteenth-century struggle of ideas ended with most economic departments at German universities falling under the influence of the Austrians.

Many of the German historicists then immigrated to the United States, where they found a conducive atmosphere for their kind of thinking in a country that emphasized a pragmatic and problem-solving approach—rather than theoretical approach—to the social sciences. Out of the German historical school and its related English historical school grew the American institutional school of the early twentieth century, with its emphasis on empirical research and its belief that economic behavior is shaped by specific historical situations.

James Ciment

See also: Austrian School; Institutional Economics.

Further Reading

Roscher, Wilhelm. *Principles of Political Economy.* New York: Arno, 1972.

Schmoller, Gustav von. "The Idea of Justice in Political Economy." In *Annals of the American Academy of Political and Social*

Science, vol. 4 (1893–1894). Available at http://socserv2.socsci .mcmaster.ca/~econ/ugcm/3113/schmoller/justice. Acccessed January 2010.

Germany

The modern German economy displays a variant of capitalism that is deeply shaped by its historical experiences of the twentieth century, and it is distinct from American-style capitalism. The three most significant events of Germany's twentieth-century economy are dramatic examples of the ways in which an advanced industrial power descended into the deep recessions of the business cycle. These events were World War I and the hyperinflation of the 1920s; World War II and the accompanying hidden inflation; and more recently, reunification, federal deficits, and the recession in 1992. The events were accompanied by government deficits that led to harmful inflation and currency reform, and their effect was to foster a cautious attitude toward monetary and fiscal policy. Today in Germany, there are institutional as well as historical impediments to running large federal deficits. However, the financial crisis of 2008–2009 has proven serious enough that these restrictions are gradually falling by the wayside.

The German Economy Before 1945

With its unification in 1871, Germany became a leader in the global market and by 1914 had become the world's second-largest industrial economy after the United States. During the second industrial revolution of the late nineteenth century in the steel, engineering, machinery, electrical, and chemical industries, Germany laid the institutional foundations for a coordinated market economy. With its large social insurance system, strong unions and trade associations, large and influential cartels, and the production of high-quality specialized products, Germany developed a style of capitalism that differed from that of the United States.

The next three decades, from 1918 to 1948, were traumatic ones that deeply shaped the attitude of Germany's post–World War II leaders toward economic policy. Massive government spending during World War I, financed primarily by the printing of money, and political conflicts after 1918, led to hyperinflation in Germany in 1923 and the need for a new currency in 1924. The Great Depression, beginning in Germany in 1929, reached its height in a wave of bank failures across central Europe in 1931. Only the suppression of wages and a huge fiscal stimulus under Germany's National Socialist (Nazi) regime, through public works and above all military spending, led Germany to a quicker recovery than the United States or Great Britain. Yet this military spending before and during World War II led to a new round of inflation, currency depreciation, black markets, and ultimately to another currency reform in 1948.

The Social Market Economy

After World War II, the West German state, under the guidance of Economics Minister Ludwig Erhard, developed the theory of the social market economy (SME) as a way to promote stability and growth. This aimed to guarantee long-term economic growth by establishing proper ground rules for competition and industrial organization and by providing state assistance in infrastructure investment, redistribution of wealth, and social welfare. The SME ushered in the *Wirtschaftswunder*, a period of impressive economic growth during the 1950s and 1960s that reestablished West Germany as a capital-intensive, export-oriented economy that sent automobiles, high-end machinery, and chemical products around the globe.

The institutions and characteristics of the SME—strong unions, cooperation between employers and employees, the representation of workers in management, rigid labor markets, vocational education, a direct and long-term relationship between banks and firms, and a tendency toward

Residents of Berlin line up at the state loan office in 1924. The introduction of the gold-backed reichsmark that year ended Germany's post–World War I inflation crisis, but the savings of a whole generation were lost. *(The Granger Collection, New York)*

diversified and flexible quality production—distinguish Germany's economy from that of the United States. The latter has historically been characterized by weaker unions, more flexible labor markets, less cooperation between workers and management, banks that look more for indirect and short-term relationships with firms, and mass production that, at least until the rise of flexible manufacture and mass customization, adapted less quickly to changes in market demand.

German leaders believed that the institutions of the SME would enable the market to correct itself during swings in the business cycle. The state would stabilize production over the long term, but would not provide economic stimuli in the short term through tax breaks and public works projects. Direct involvement in the business cycle was to be more the purview of monetary rather than fiscal policy. The two experiences with inflation and currency reform in 1924 and 1948, both of which resulted from large fiscal deficits and devastated the savings of many Germans, led Erhard and the German central bank to emphasize currency stability and, whenever possible, to avoid deficit spending to manage the business cycle. Germany's earliest post–World War II economists saw the SME as an alternative to the Keynesian approach of using fiscal and budgetary policy to influence business cycles.

This outlook changed in 1967 in the face of West Germany's first real post–World War II recession, when the federal government changed course in Keynesian fashion and invested in infrastructure and unemployment benefits to combat the downturn. Thus, a new belief in managing the business cycle persisted throughout the 1970s, spearheaded by Economics Minister Karl Schiller and bolstered by his relative success in overcoming the 1967 recession. However, the 1970s proved to be a decade of slower growth, higher unemployment, higher inflation, and lower profits. In 1982, after a decade of "stagflation," low productivity growth, two oil crises, and a burgeoning federal debt, the new government under Helmut Kohl moved away from Keynesian demand management, refocused on stabilizing production, and called for a reduction in the federal debt. This return to the core tenets of the SME remained the guiding principle behind economic policy throughout the 1980s.

Reunification and Lessons Learned from the Past

In the early 1990s, the reunification of East with West Germany presented a unique situation that required deficit spending on a large scale. In 1991 and 1992, in hope of raising the productivity of former East German workers, the newly united Germany ran large federal deficits in transfer payments and infrastructural investment in the former East. High expectations for a quick convergence of East Germany's economy with that of West Germany were not met. Instead, overinvestment in the construction sector, rising prices, high interest rates, the recession in 1992, and the threat all of this posed to monetary unification with the European Union (EU) left a bad taste for fiscal stimulus among many German economic thinkers.

What lessons were learned from Germany's deviation into using fiscal stimuli and undertaking demand management during the late 1960s and 1970s and its reunification experience? By and large, the majority of German economists in the 1990s and early 2000s concluded that demand management was ineffective and even harmful.

In commenting on Germany's fiscal policies in the 1970s, Peer Steinbrück, Germany's finance minister from 2005 to the present, remarked that "government debt rose, and the downturn came anyway." The fiscal deficits of the 1970s and the 1990s left Germany with a large federal debt, which rose from roughly 20 percent of gross domestic product (GDP) in 1970 to 60 percent in 2008, or 1.5 trillion euros. And although Germany ran a budget surplus in 2007, it was the first one in nearly two decades; until 2006 there had been an erosion of confidence in the government's ability to run a balanced budget during periods of economic growth. Many German economists continue to maintain that long-term growth requires long-range planning to cultivate production, not short-term stimulus to create demand.

In addition, Germany's membership in the EU places institutional constraints on the size of its deficits and its ability to pursue short-term fiscal stimuli. Under the Stability and Growth Pact of 1997, the EU penalizes its member states for deficits in excess of 3 percent of GDP. While this has not been strictly enforced, it illustrates how much the EU and the European Central Bank are concerned that national debts could grow large enough to negatively impact future growth by crowding out private investment.

The Financial Crisis of 2008–2009

Throughout the first phase of the financial crisis, during October and November 2008, German chancellor Angela Merkel and Finance Minister Steinbrück showed reluctance toward any large tax breaks or public spending, believing that Germany's traditional variety of capitalism was less vulnerable to a recession than that of either the United States or Great Britain. Both resisted calls for a Europe-wide fiscal stimulus package. This reflected fears in Germany that such a package would endanger the EU's Stability and Growth Pact, and that the potential for a large deficit and high interest rates would outweigh any immediate benefits.

Yet by January 2009, the financial and economic crisis had become severe and global enough for German leaders to act. As the world's leading exporter, Germany is highly dependent on the rest of the world—and Europe in particular—to buy its products: exports account for roughly one-third of German GDP. The vulnerability of Germany's banking sector, alongside predictions of negative growth and rising unemployment in Germany and across Europe, led Merkel and Steinbrück to pass Germany's largest postwar stimulus package of public investment and tax breaks. While many criticize this as too small, it nevertheless represents a break with Germany's post-1945 reluctance to engage in Keynesian demand management.

Stephen Gross

See also: European Central Bank; France; Italy; United Kingdom.

Further Reading
Abelshauser, Werner. *The Dynamics of German Industry: Germany's Path Towards the New Economy and the American Challenge.* Oxford, UK: Berghahn, 2005.
Braun, Hans-Joachim. *The German Economy in the Twentieth Century: The German Reich and the Federal Republic.* New York: Routledge, 1990.
Eichengreen, Barry. *The European Economy Since 1945.* Princeton, NJ: Princeton University Press, 2007.
Hall, Peter A., and David Soskice, eds. *Varieties of Capitalism: The Institutional Foundations of Comparative Advantage.* New York: Oxford University Press, 2001.
Siebert, Horst. *The German Economy: Beyond the Social Market.* Princeton, NJ: Princeton University Press, 2005.

Glass-Steagall Act (1933)

An early component of Franklin Roosevelt's New Deal agenda, the Glass-Steagall Act—officially the Banking Act of 1933—was legislation aimed at addressing failures in the nation's banking system that many economists and policy makers of the day believed contributed to the financial crisis of the early 1930s. It was named after its authors, Senator Carter Glass (D-VA), a former secretary of the Treasury, and House Committee on Banking and Currency chairman Henry Steagall (D-AL).

A complex bill, the measure included provisions that established the Federal Deposit Insurance Corporation (FDIC), creating deposit insurance for bank deposits, and separated commercial banking from riskier brokerage and investment bank services, as well as insurance underwriting. The latter provision was largely overturned with passage of the Gramm-Leach-Bliley Act of 1999, a repeal that many contemporary economists say contributed to the financial crisis of the late 2000s. (The Glass-Steagall Act of 1933 should not be confused with a similarly named act of 1932 expanding the powers of the Federal Reserve, or "Fed.")

Origins

The prelude to the act was the great 1920s bull market on Wall Street. Between 1927 and 1929, the New York Stock Exchange experienced one of the greatest percentage run-ups in securities values in its history, with average share prices climbing by 50 percent and such high-flying stocks as RCA seeing their values go up by 600 percent. Overall, the Dow Jones Industrial Average climbed from about 125 in 1925 to over 380 at the peak of the market shortly before the crash of October 1929.

While there had been solid gains in productivity, production, and profits during much of the 1920s, the economy weakened after 1927, making the spectacular gains of the late 1920s largely a speculative bubble. Pumping air into the bubble was the practice of buying equities on margin. Investors could take out loans from brokers and investment bankers to purchase stock, putting as little as 10 percent of their own money down. Brokers offered such loans because stock prices continued to rise, meaning that investors could pay back the hefty interest rates and fees with gains they made in the value of the shares they sold.

But when prices fell in the crash of 1929, a vicious cycle ensued. First, investors could not meet margin calls. For example, say an investor put down $100 on 100 shares valued at $10 each, for a total stock purchase price of $1,000, of which $900 was paid for with a loan from a broker. If the value of the shares fell by more than 10 percent, then the investor now owed more than the stock was worth, triggering a margin call by the lender. As many investors found themselves in this position, brokers and investment bankers, in turn, could not pay back the loans they had taken out from other financial institutions to lend out to investors.

According to many economic historians, the margin call contagion might have been confined to the relatively small pool of stock market investors—less than one in ten Americans had money invested in securities in 1929—had it not been for the fact that many commercial banks had gone into the brokerage and investment banking businesses. This meant that the money of ordinary depositors had disappeared in the great bear market that followed the crash of 1929. At first, only the largest institutions in New York were affected. As those banks began to tighten credit, however, the crisis spread to large and small banks across the country. Panicky depositors began to pull out their money, forcing more than 2,000 financial institutions into bankruptcy in 1929 and 1930 together.

The mass withdrawal of funds, along with the bankruptcies, froze the nation's credit markets, drying up the funds available for investment. This inevitably led to dramatic falls in production, corporate revenues, output, and employment. The deepening economic gloom only created more fear, which prompted more depositors to withdraw their money from banks. By early 1933, as the country waited for President-elect Roosevelt to take office—in those days, the inauguration was held in March—the nation's banking system was on the verge of collapse, a situation made worse by the Fed's decision to hike the interest rate it charged on loans to member banks.

Upon taking office in early March, Roosevelt promptly declared a bank holiday, closing the nation's lending institutions for several days. During the hiatus, Congress passed the Emergency Banking Relief Act, which allowed solvent banks to reopen with a Treasury Department license, while nonsolvent banks were reorganized under the department's aegis. These measures halted the panic but did nothing to address the underlying problems that had led to the crisis in the first place.

That's where the Glass-Steagall Act came in. Signed into law on June 16, 1933, the law established the FDIC, which provided federal insurance on bank deposits up to a specified amount ($2,500 at the time, raised to $100,000 in 1980 and to $250,000 in 2008—the latter temporarily, to the end of 2013). The FDIC was intended to reassure depositors that they would not lose their money if a commercial bank should fail.

In the decades since, the FDIC has been one of the most successful agencies created by the federal government. Not a single cent of insured deposits has ever been lost, and depositors find almost no delay in accessing their money. This was evident during the financial crisis of 2008–2009, when such major institutions as the California-based IndyMac Bank and Washington State–based Washington Mutual (WaMu), among other smaller ones, failed. In both cases, the FDIC put the banks in receivership, reorganizing IndyMac as OneWest Bank and selling off Washington Mutual's commercial banking operations to the holding company JPMorgan Chase. Note that in the case of IndyMac Bank, depositors with deposits above the insurance limit did lose some of their deposits. Since Washington Mutual's commercial banking operations were sold to JPMorgan Chase, rather than reorganized by the FDIC, depositors with deposits above the insurance limit did not lose.

The other key provision of the Glass-Steagall Act prohibited commercial banks from engaging in investment bank and brokerage services. Although there were a number of reasons for this, the main one was that investment banking and brokerage services are inherently speculative activities, as they entail the underwriting of corporate securities whose value can rise and fall precipitously in a short period of time, thereby putting bank depositors' money at risk. Supporters of the Glass-Steagall Act argued that it was necessary to prevent a repeat of the crisis that had hit the nation's banks following the crash of 1929. Moreover, if the federal government was going to insure depositors' money, then it had an interest in making sure those deposits were not put at inordinate risk, thereby requiring taxpayer money to cover for speculative losses.

Repeal of Provisions

The Glass-Steagall Act remained in effect and largely untouched through the 1970s. By that time, much of the financial industry was chafing under the restrictions of the legislation, a discontent that received a sympathetic ear in an increasingly conservative political environment, where government regulation was seen as hampering private industry. In the early 1980s, two pieces of federal legislation—the Depository Institutions Deregulation and Monetary Control Act of 1980 and the Garn-St. Germain Depository Institutions Act of 1982—began to whittle away at some of the provisions of the act. The former removed the Fed's power to regulate interest rates at savings and loans, and the latter removed many other regulations on savings and loans.

But the major repeal legislation was the Gramm-Leach-Bliley Act of 1999 (officially the Financial Services Modernization Act)—named after its sponsors, Senator Phil Gramm (R-TX), Representative Jim Leach (R-IA), and Representative Thomas J. Bliley, Jr., (R-VA)—which allowed for the formation of bank holding companies that could simultaneously engage in commercial banking, investment banking, brokerage services, and insurance. The reasons for the repeal were both immediate and long term. As to the former, it allowed for the merger of Citicorp, a bank holding company, and Travelers Group, an insurance company that owned the brokerage company Smith Barney, to form the conglomerate Citigroup, which would offer commercial and investment banking services, as well as brokerage and insurance businesses.

The longer-term factors behind the repeal were based on the idea that, with financial information made more accessible by innovations in technology and communications, investment banking and brokerage services were not nearly as risky as they once had been. Moreover, conservative economic thought held that the market could sort out the risk better than blanket government restrictions, as depositors and investors would stay away from institutions with unsound reputations. Finally, it was argued, allowing banks to diversify actually moderated risk.

The repeal of restrictions on commercial banking led to mergers throughout the financial industry and seemed to be working as the new holding companies became enormously profitable in the early and mid-2000s. With the financial crisis of 2008, however, many economists and policy makers began to rethink Gramm-Leach-Bliley. The fact that Citigroup received some $50 billion in Troubled Asset Relief Program (TARP) money in 2008—the largest amount given to a single institution under the aegis of the program (insurance giant AIG received more, but only $40 billion of it came from TARP)—led many commentators to conclude that some financial institutions had grown "too big to fail." In other words, by allowing giant bank holding companies to engage in both commercial banking and riskier investment banking and brokerage services, the repeal had created institutions whose failure so threatened the global financial system that the government would inevitably be forced to rescue them should they approach insolvency. Despite such reservations, the Barack Obama administration and Democratic-controlled Congress were silent on the prospect of reinstituting the old Glass-Steagall restrictions on bank holding company activities.

James Ciment

See also: Banks, Commercial; Banks, Investment; Great Depression (1929–1933); New Deal; Regulation, Financial.

Further Reading

Benston, George J. *The Separation of Commercial and Investment Banking: The Glass-Steagall Act Revisited and Reconsidered.* New York: Oxford University Press, 1999.

Kaufman, Henry. *The Road to Financial Reformation: Warnings, Consequences, Reforms.* Hoboken, NJ: John Wiley & Sons, 2009.

Peláez, Carlos M., and Carlos A. Peláez. *Regulation of Banks and Finance: Theory and Policy After the Credit Crisis.* New York: Palgrave Macmillan, 2009.

Goldman Sachs

Until its restructuring as a bank holding company in late 2008, Goldman Sachs—usually referred to in the industry as simply Goldman—was one of the oldest, wealthiest, and most influential investment banks in the United States. Many of its top executives have served in high-level government economic positions in both Republican and Democratic administrations, including Treasury secretaries Robert Rubin of the Bill Clinton administration and Henry Paulson of the George W. Bush administration.

Founded just after the Civil War and based in New York City, the company offers a wide variety of financial services, including the facilitation of corporate mergers and acquisitions, asset management, financial underwriting, securities trading, private equity deals, and the marketing of U.S. Treasury securities.

While not as hard hit as other financial institutions by the financial crisis and recession of 2007–2009, Goldman nevertheless found itself in need of billions of dollars in federal bailout money under the Troubled Asset Relief Program (TARP). The crisis also prompted the decision to reorganize as a bank holding company, which would allow it to open a commercial bank, giving it access to borrowing at the discount window and in the fed funds market, but also subjecting it to increased regulation and government oversight.

Goldman was founded by German immigrant Marcus Goldman in 1869. When his son-in-law

Samuel Sachs joined the firm in 1882, the current name was adopted. Goldman Sachs was a pioneer in the private bond market and was among the first Wall Street firms to conduct initial public offerings (IPOs) in the early twentieth century, including those of Sears, Woolworth, and later Ford. Having set up a kind of early mutual fund in 1928, the company was hard hit by the market crash of the following year.

The company survived the Great Depression and thrived in the bull market of the 1950s and 1960s and began establishing offices in other financial centers, beginning with London in 1972. The company also branched out into other businesses, including commodities trading and asset management in the 1980s. In 1999, the firm went public, though it only offered up 12 percent of its equity in its first IPO. At the same time, the company made huge profits managing the IPOs of other companies, particularly in the tech sector. Still, Goldman had its stumbles along the way, most notably during the collapse of Penn Central railroad in 1970. Holding tens of millions of dollars of the company's bonds, Goldman was nearly driven into bankruptcy itself.

It looked in far better shape during the initial months of the subprime mortgage market collapse of 2007, having gone "short" on mortgage-backed securities, meaning it bet on their market values going down, which they indeed did, making Goldman some $4 billion in profit in the process. This was at a time when other investment banks and financial institutions were teetering on the brink of insolvency because of their exposure to subprime mortgage-backed securities.

While revenues were down significantly during the first three quarters of 2008, the firm was still posting a modest profit, even as the financial crisis saw investment banks Lehman Brothers go bankrupt and Merrill Lynch bought out at fire sale prices by Bank of America. By September, however, the contagion of investor fear finally hit Goldman Sachs, especially after insurance and financial services giant American International Group (AIG) took $85 billion in bailout money from the federal government. The company was still highly respected and

in the black, but investors nevertheless feared no stand-alone investment bank could thrive or even survive in the current crisis. As its stock price went into freefall and its assets diminished, Goldman stepped up to receive some $10 billion in government bailout money under TARP.

At the same, the company decided to radically restructure. On September 21, 2008, it reorganized itself as a bank holding company. A bank holding company can control one or more commercial banks or other bank holding companies when it owns 25 percent or more of the other companies. As with any major change, there were benefits and costs. On the plus side, Goldman could now enter commercial banking, allowing it access to a whole new revenue stream and potentially vast assets. On the downside, at least as far as its stockholders, executives, and traders were concerned, as a bank holding company Goldman would be subject to greatly increased government scrutiny and regulation. The freewheeling investment banking days, in which the company could take greater risks for greater profits, were now in the past. Goldman's decision—along with a similar move by rival Morgan Stanley—ended the era of stand-alone giant investment banking firms on Wall Street.

Still, investors retained their faith in Goldman's legendary ability to make money in good times and bad; just after their reorganization announcement, widely watched investor Warren Buffett put $5 billion in the firm. The company raised an additional $5 billion in a stock offering.

After suffering a major loss in the last quarter of 2008, the company posted more than $1.6 billion in profit in the first quarter of 2009, a result more related to rebounding markets and a lack of competition than to commercial bank operations, which had yet to commence in earnest. In early 2009, the company also announced that it planned to raise capital in the securities markets to allow it to pay back the federal bailout money before the end of the year.

Goldman Sachs continued to profit as the financial markets and the economy as a whole recovered, posting $3.5 billion in profits in the first quarter of 2010. But troubles also continued to plague the firm, including outrage at its continued bonuses to executives—some $5 billion for the first quarter of 2010—and, more seriously, a decision by the Securities and Exchange Commission to charge the company with fraud in April. The regulators alleged that Goldman, in league with a hedge fund, sold mortgage-related financial instruments to investors that it knew were designed to fail. Goldman denied the allegations.

James Ciment

See also: Banks, Investment; Troubled Asset Relief Program (2008–).

Further Reading

Ellis, Charles D. *The Partnership: The Making of Goldman Sachs.* New York: Penguin, 2008.

Endlich, Lisa. *Goldman Sachs: The Culture of Success.* New York: A.A. Knopf, 1999.

Taibbi, Matt. "The Great American Bubble Machine." *Rolling Stone,* 1082–1083. Available at www.rollingstone.com/politics/story/28816321/the_great_american_bubble_machine. Accessed August 24, 2009.

Goodwin, Richard Murphy (1913–1996)

Richard Murphy Goodwin was an American economist and mathematician. He is best known for having developed models of endogenous economic cycles, the Goodwin class struggle model, and Goodwin's nonlinear accelerator.

Goodwin was born in Indiana in 1913. He received a Bachelor of Arts and a doctorate degree from Harvard University, where he taught from 1942 until 1950. He taught next at Cambridge University (England) until 1979, then at the University of Siena (Italy) until his retirement in 1984. He died on August 13, 1996, while vacationing in Siena.

Goodwin's class struggle model was first proposed in 1967. Drawing on the work of Michal Kalecki, "the Marxist Keynes," and on the math used to model the relationship between predators and prey in biology, Goodwin constructed a nonlinear model of the cyclical relationship between wage share and employment. According to this model, high levels of employment lead to wage inflation (through supply and demand), which increases workers' wage share. This, in turn, reduces profits and demotivates future investment. Lowered investment reduces output, thus reducing labor demand, employment, and wages. A reduction in employment and wages leads to increased profits, investment, and employment, thereby completing the cycle, which begins again. The exogenous growth components in Goodwin's model are productivity growth and labor supply growth. The two classes of income recipients (predators and prey, in essence) are profit-earning capitalists (business owners) and wage-earning workers. A Phillips curve, described as an inverse relationship between the rate of unemployment and the rate of inflation, determines the growth of wages. The Goodwin model proved popular and enduring both among Keynesians and Marxists, and has had the benefit of functioning without fixed floors or ceilings, and without exogenous shocks.

Another of Goodwin's contributions to Keynesian economics is his nonlinear accelerator, first illustrated in a 1951 article. Accelerators are a key to the theory of investment (the change to capital stock over time). The Keynesian answer to the question "What is investment?" is "Investment is what capitalists do." Investors purchase stocks and other items for their portfolios. Business owners invest in their companies by funding such areas as business activity or expansion, workers' wages, and equipment improvements and purchases. Keynesians tend to focus on investment as a type of behavior.

In the accelerator theory of investment, investment behavior is seen as a response to changing conditions of demand. For example, when there is greater demand for a product, a business will invest in accelerating production in order to increase supply. In this case, as in the field of physics, the term "accelerate" means "to *change* speed" ("decelerate" is a neologism coined by those who understood accelerate to mean "to *increase* speed"). Thus, the accelerator theory of investment says that accelerating demand results in accelerating supply, through the mechanism of investment.

Goodwin's nonlinear accelerator consisted of an investment function, an accounting identity, and a consumption function. One result of the nonlinear accelerator was that, once proved valid, it demonstrated that very little could be done to the system to affect the timing of the business cycle. In other words, the severity of an economic boom or bust had almost no relationship to how long it would last. In the July 1953 issue of *Econometrica*, a team of economists confirmed this theory by computer.

Bill Kte'pi

See also: Endogenous Growth Models; Kalecki, Michal; Keynesian Business Model; Marxist Cycle Model.

Further Reading

Flaschel, Peter, and Michael Landesmann, eds. *Mathematical Economics and the Dynamics of Capitalism: Research in Honor of Richard M. Goodwin.* New York: Routledge, 2008.

Goodwin, Richard M. *Chaotic Economic Dynamics.* New York: Oxford University Press, 1990.

Goodwin, Richard M., and Lionello F. Punzo. *The Dynamics of a Capitalist Economy.* New York: Westview, 1987.

Landesmann, Michael, and R. Stehrer. "Goodwin's Structural Economic Dynamics: Modelling Schumpeterian and Keynesian Insights." *Structural Change and Economic Dynamics* 17:4 (2006): 501–526.

Strotz, R.H., J.C. McAnulty, and J.B. Naines, Jr., "Goodwin's Nonlinear Theory of the Business Cycle: An Electro-Analog Solution." *Econometrica* 21:3 (July 1953): 390–411.

Government Accountability Office

The Government Accountability Office (GAO) advises Congress and the heads of executive branch agencies about ways to make government more efficient, effective, ethical, equitable, and responsive. In recent years, "about four out of five GAO recommendations" over a range of public policy trends, challenges, and opportunities likely to affect the United States and the federal government have been implemented.

The GAO has played an important role in analyzing the major events in and causes of U.S. and international economic downturns over the past eight decades. It has been especially active in analyzing the many facets of the financial crisis of 2007–2008. In doing so, it provides critical data and insights to economists who investigate business cycles.

The GAO was authorized by the Budget and Accounting Act of 1921. Originally called the General Accounting Office, its name was changed in 2004 to better reflect its "accountability" functions and activities. The agency that works for the U.S. Congress is independent and nonpartisan with a broad mandate to provide information and recommendations to control of government expenditures, Originally the agency was charged with checking the legality of government expenditures by auditing and reviewing fiscal records and vouchers. Today, financial audits represent only about 15 percent of the agency's workload.

The contemporary mission of the GAO is to support the Congress "to help improve the performance and ensure the accountability of the federal government for the benefit of the American people" by "providing timely information that is objective, fact-based, nonpartisan, non-ideological, fair, and balanced" over "a broad range of financial and performance audits and program evaluations." The GAO currently organizes its resources in support of three broad external strategic goals: helping to address the challenges to the well-being and economic security of the American people, U.S. national and homeland security efforts, and modernizing government to meet current and emerging issues. The GAO's basic work products are reports, testimonies, correspondence, and legal decisions and opinions to provide "oversight, insight, and foresight."

The GAO is headquartered in Washington, D.C., and has eleven field offices in major cities around the country. It employs approximately 3,200 career civil servants whose knowledge, training, and skills cover a wide range of academic, professional, and scientific disciplines. The comptroller general of the United States is the leader of the GAO, and its staff is organized around thirteen research, audit, and evaluation teams that support the three strategic goals. The teams are (1) Education, Workforce, and Income Security; (2) Financial Markets and Community Investment; (3) Health Care; (4) Homeland Security and Justice; (5) Natural Resources and Environment; (6) Physical Infrastructure; (7) Acquisition and Sourcing Management; (8) Defense Capabilities and Management; (9) International Affairs and Trade; (10) Applied Research and Methods; (11) Financial Management and Assurance; (12) Information Technology; and (13) Strategic Issues.

GAO Foresight and Oversight

The GAO Strategic Plan (2007–2012) identified and described seven key themes that will affect the United States over the next several decades: (1) safety and security threats requiring attention in a number of areas—terrorism, violent crime, natural disasters, and infectious disease; (2) fiscal sustainability concerns as government spending on social insurance programs create a potential tax gap and environmental sustainability concerns as economic growth puts stress on air and water quality and induces climatic change; (3) economic growth and competitiveness because the saving and investment behavior of U.S. citizens is inadequate to provide sufficient capital for investment in research, development, and productivity enhancements from domestic sources; (4) global interdependency that requires reducing impediments to the exchange of people, ideas, goods, and capital while simultaneously requiring secure borders for the safety of the nation; (5) stresses from societal change due to an aging population and an increasingly diverse population, which will strain social programs; (6) threats to the quality of life raised from perceptions of increasing income insecurity and the gap between the "haves" and the "have-nots"; and (7) the ethical and moral questions that so-

ciety must confront due to advances in science and technology. The Strategic Plan outlines key efforts, potential outcomes, and suggested government performance goals to address each of the themes.

The GAO has played an important role in analyzing the 2007–2009 financial crisis and reporting its findings to Congress and the public. These findings include testimony before congressional committees as well as written reports on mortgage-based financial activities, unregulated participants in the financial system, the bailout of American International Group (AIG), the execution of the Troubled Asset Relief Program, assessing current regulatory oversight and necessary reforms, and developing evaluation criteria for the process of disbursing economic relief funds to state and local governments. In a July 2007 report, the GAO concluded that improved federal oversight of the leveraging of assets by key financial institutions—as well as leveraging issues for the financial system as a whole—was necessary to prevent similar financial crises in the future.

Frank L. Winfrey

See also: Congressional Budget Office; Council of Economic Advisers, U.S.; Fiscal Balance; Fiscal Policy; National Economic Council.

Further Reading
Government Accountability Office Web site: www.gao.gov.

United States Government Accountability Office. "Financial Markets Regulation: Financial Crisis Highlights Need to Improve Oversight of Leverage at Financial Institutions and Across System." Report to Congressional Committees, GAO-09-739. Washington, DC: United States Government Accountability Office, July 22, 2009.

Great Depression (1929–1933)

The worst economic catastrophe in modern human history, the Great Depression devastated the United States and other industrialized countries in the early 1930s and beyond. Triggered by the sudden and dramatic collapse in the American stock market in late 1929, the Great Depression actually originated in a "perfect storm" of underlying economic problems and, according to economic historians, was worsened and perpetuated by misguided government policies.

The Depression wreaked havoc on virtually every sector of the global economy, hitting the United States especially hard by bankrupting small businesses, wiping out farmers, freezing credit markets, erasing corporate profits, and sending unemployment rates soaring to more than 25 percent. Between the Wall Street crash of October 1929 and the inauguration of President Franklin Roosevelt in March 1933, at the depths of the downturn, the U.S. gross domestic product fell by nearly one-third—the steepest decline in the nation's history.

The impact of the Depression on subsequent American and world history is almost incalculable. In the United States and other industrialized countries, it led to a dramatic expansion in the power and scope of central governments, as they took a more hands-on approach to their respective economies and became far more involved in the everyday lives of ordinary citizens. The Depression—or, more accurately, the responses of the Herbert Hoover and Franklin Roosevelt administrations to it—forged a general consensus among a generation of policy makers that the countercyclical fiscal policies advocated by English economist John Maynard Keynes—whereby governments should borrow and spend to stimulate the economy during downturns in the business cycle—offered the best way to fight recession and maintain growth.

Apart from economics, the Great Depression had profound political and geopolitical ramifications. In the United States, it led to a far-reaching political realignment, as Roosevelt built a coalition of low-income workers, white ethnics, Northern blacks, and Southern whites into a left-of-center Democratic Party majority that would hold through the 1970s. Overseas, the Depression contributed to the rise to power of the Nazis in Germany and the onset of World War II.

For economists and economic historians, the Great Depression remains the benchmark against which all subsequent economic downturns are measured, offering lessons and warnings about how to avoid them and how to deal with them if they do occur.

Origins

In the popular imagination, the era that preceded the Great Depression was a time of great economic prosperity. The image of the Roaring Twenties—in reality fostered amid the gloom of the 1930s—did carry some truth. After a brief but sharp recession in 1921–1922, U.S. economic growth was substantial and sustained for much of the rest of the decade. Corporate profits were up, construction boomed, stock prices soared, and unemployment held steady at historically low levels of 4 percent or under.

Yet the prosperity—unequally distributed and unregulated—was superficial. First, there was the prosperity gap between urban and rural America. The roughly one in four U.S. households that still supported themselves primarily by farming did not prosper during the boom years of the 1920s. Having expanded production during World War I—often by going into debt for new land and machinery—American farmers were unprepared for the dramatic and sustained drop in agricultural prices that occurred after the conflict ended. Between 1919 and 1930, U.S. farm income as a percentage of national income fell by almost half, from 16 percent to 8.8 percent. As some economic historians maintain, American agriculture was in a state of depression a full ten years before the rest of the country. Nor was farming the only sector that lagged during the 1920s; textiles, the railroad industry, and coal mining were also hurting. Even prosperous industries were weaker than they appeared, as a wave of corporate mergers left many companies saddled with large debts.

Nevertheless, broad swaths of the economy prospered through much of the 1920s, fueled by rapid growth in consumer durables—such as appliances and radios—and motor vehicles, along with supporting industries like steel, rubber, and petroleum refining. The decade also brought significant increases in productivity, as advances in communication, transportation, and electrification increased worker output. Still, the gains were not equally distributed. Weak labor unions and falling tax rates for corporations and the wealthy meant that most of the income gains of the decade accrued to the upper reaches of the economy. By 1929, the bottom 40 percent of the population received just 12.5 percent of aggregate personal income, while the top 5 percent received 30 percent, the most acute inequality in the twentieth century. With their incomes rising by 75 percent between 1920 and 1929, and the marginal tax rates falling, the top 1 percent put much of their gains into speculative activities.

Such activities helped hide the underlying weaknesses in the economy, as speculation-fueled rises in real-estate values and especially stock prices became vertiginous in the latter half of the decade. Between 1924 and 1929—the peak years of the bull market—the Dow Jones Industrial Average (DJIA) increased fivefold, climbing above 381 in early September of the latter year. Some of the upswing was based on legitimate gains in productivity and profit, but most of it was speculative, fueled by both the public and private sectors, especially after key industries like automobiles and consumer durables saw slower growth after 1927. The newly created Federal Reserve Board (Fed) contributed to the speculation by keeping interest rates low, which enabled individuals and corporations to borrow money more cheaply and easily—often, in the case of the former, for speculative purposes and, for the latter, to finance a wave of corporate mergers. Only in 1928 did the Fed begin to tighten credit and warn about the dangers of stock speculation. By then, however, the bubble was self-perpetuating.

Other government policies—or the lack of them—contributed to the precariousness of the nation's economy. In an age of pro-business Republican Party ascendancy in the White House and on Capitol Hill, there was little inclination or will to impose government regulation or even oversight of the financial sector. Corporations routinely misrepresented their finances to obtain loans, while investment banks and brokers encouraged margin buying. Loans were extended for up to 90 percent of the value of equities purchased on the stock market, with lenders and borrowers sharing the assumption that values would continue to rise. Indeed, by 1929, many Americans had come to believe that the country had achieved sustained prosperity. On the eve of the crash, observed the noted economist Irving Fisher, "stock prices have reached what looks like a permanently high plateau."

Stock Market Crash and Banking Crises

In retrospect, it is clear that America had entered a recessionary period by mid-1929, as construction and consumer spending—two key growth sectors—went into decline and businesses cut back on production and employment to reduce their growing inventories, further depressing demand. By early September, stock prices had begun to sag. On October 28, "Black Tuesday," they fell precipitously. Literally overnight, the paper value of stocks sank from $87 billion to $55 billion. And with that drop, the inherent perils of buying equities on margin began to be realized. In the previous environment, with brokerage houses and investment banks extending credit to clients, an investor had needed to put down just $100 to buy $1,000 worth of stock; if the value of the stock went from, say, $10 to $20 per share, the investor made a 1,000 percent profit. But if the stock should fall from $10 to $5, the investor had to come up with $400 to pay back the loan, in addition to the $100 investment that had now vanished. Now, suddenly, overextended brokers and investment bankers were making margin calls—demanding that investors pay back their loans. With stock prices falling, however, they could not do so. This set off new panic selling and further drops in stock prices. By mid-November, the DJIA had fallen by a third, to under 200. By mid-1932, the index sank to 41 points, a level not seen since the nineteenth century and down a staggering 89 percent from its peak on September 3, 1929.

As devastating as these losses were to investors, the impact of the crash might have been contained had the underlying economy not been riddled with the weaknesses outlined above. After all, just one in ten American households owned stock shares; of these, just one in three had substantial investments on Wall Street. But the inherent weaknesses of the economy proved fatal, as most households—having experienced few of the productivity gains made during the 1920s—had little discretionary income to sustain demand. The problem was compounded by the fact that American industry had expanded capacity dramatically during the previous boom period. Thus, the vicious cycle that had begun in the summer of 1929—declining demand leading to layoffs, leading to further drops in consumer demand—sent the U.S. economy into free fall through 1930 and early 1931. A brief recovery then set in, as businesses began to rebuild inventories and low prices fueled renewed demand. The stock market recovered, too, regaining most of its postcrash losses by April 1931.

But it was a false dawn. The Depression—a term popularized by Hoover, who thought it was less ominous-sounding than "crisis" or "panic"—was still on in earnest, perpetuated by four key forces. One was rising unemployment and its devastating impact on consumer demand. During 1930, the national unemployment rate averaged 8.7 percent; for 1931, the figure was 15.9; by 1932 and 1933, it hovered around 25 percent. A second factor was the continuing weakness in the agricultural sector, as crop prices reacted to falling demand and plummeted even more steeply through 1930 and 1931. Heavily in debt and with their income falling, many farmers were pushed into bankruptcy; hundreds of thousands of farms were foreclosed by rural banks, many of which fell into bankruptcy as well. Since many rural banks borrowed money from their larger urban counterparts, the crisis soon spread to the entire banking system as frightened depositors began to withdraw their savings.

Adding to the nation's economic woes were the Fed's monetary policies. In retrospect, economists from across the political spectrum generally agree that the Fed's policies had disastrous effects. First, the Federal Reserve Bank of New York, the most important of the regional banks in the system, significantly increased its discount rate—the rate it charges member banks to borrow money—and cut back the amount of money it put into circulation through the purchase of government bonds. The Federal Reserve Bank of New York believed that the most critical problem was industrial overcapacity rather than consumer underdemand, and that making credit harder to come by would reduce capacity and thereby lift prices and profits. To be fair, the bank was hamstrung by federal legislation that required it to maintain a certain level of gold deposits before it could issue credit. At the time, gold deposits were shrinking, as domestic and foreign holders of gold-backed U.S. currency demanded payment in the precious metal, leaving the Fed unable to loosen credit. Whatever the reason, the Fed's efforts to shrink the money supply exacerbated an already bad situation as depositors withdrew their money from the banking system, preferring to hide it under their figurative mattresses instead. From August 1929 to March 1933, the money supply in the United States fell by fully one-third, driving down prices and drying up funds available to businesses for investment and hiring.

The Hoover administration's response also proved inadequate to the problem. Steeped in ideas of "rugged individualism" and encouraged by conservative Treasury secretary Andrew Mellon, who advocated a laissez-faire approach to the crisis, the president refused to increase government spending or launch jobs programs, fearful that they would create a dependency among ordinary citizens. Meanwhile, he hoped the private sector would take up the slack and tried to win pledges from industrial leaders to maintain wages and production. Finally realizing that such voluntary measures were not

On his first full day in office, March 5, 1933, President Franklin D. Roosevelt announced bold emergency measures to rescue the U.S. financial system. Relief, recovery, and reform—in that order—were the goals of his New Deal program. *(The Granger Collection, New York)*

enough, Hoover in 1932 set up the Reconstruction Finance Corporation, which provided loans to big business in the hope that they would use them to invest, extend credit, and hire the jobless. Hoover also launched some limited works programs, commissioning such projects as the Hoover Dam on the Arizona-Nevada border. Most economic historians agree, however, that it was too little, too late.

Finally, there was the international dimension to the crisis. The global economic order of the 1920s had been built on a precarious foundation. Determined both to punish Germany—which they blamed for the war—and to force it to pay for the rebuilding of the their war-wracked infrastructure, the victorious Allies imposed vast reparations on Berlin. When Germany proved unable to pay the

required amounts in the early 1920s, the United States—which had emerged from the war as the world's largest creditor nation—stepped in, providing loans to Germany to pay the Allies so that they, in turn, could pay their loans to the United States. Complicating the equation, the United States maintained high tariffs, making it difficult for countries to sell in the United States and obtain the dollars they needed to pay back their loans to the U.S. government and U.S. financial institutions.

The economic crisis of the early 1930s only exacerbated the situation. With the crash on Wall Street, U.S. foreign investment dried up, further depriving other economies of the dollars they needed to repay their loans. Declining consumer purchasing power and corporate profits shrank America's appetite for imports, a trend that hit Latin American economies with particular ferocity. As American investors came to fear the ability of foreign governments and industries to pay dividends and repay loans, they began to divest themselves of foreign holdings, pulling back virtually all of the foreign investment made during the boom years of the 1920s (about $11 billion in all). Policies out of Washington, D.C., only added to the woes. In a move aimed to protect American industries and jobs, Congress passed the Smoot-Hawley Act in 1930, imposing some of the highest tariffs in U.S. history and further undermining the ability of foreign industries to sell in the United States. The tariff also triggered retaliatory moves by other countries, putting a new crimp in international trade.

All of these problems came to a head in the crisis affecting the international gold standard in 1931. Pegging national currencies to gold had been a sacrosanct economic principle for hundreds of years, as nations based the value of their currency on the gold reserves held in their vaults. During the 1920s, the system caused problems for many countries, ranging from inflation in Germany to unemployment in Great Britain. In September 1931, Great Britain went off the gold standard, followed by more than forty countries in late 1931 and 1932. Hoover refused to follow suit, though most international investors were convinced that it was only a matter of time before the United States did the same. In any event, Hoover monetary policy caused a massive outflow of gold from the United States. One of President Roosevelt's first moves after taking office was to take the United States off the gold standard in June 1933.

In the long run, the decision to abandon the gold standard was a smart one. Indeed, according to some economists, it was the single most important factor in ending the global depression, as it allowed governments to increase the supply of money more easily and thereby stimulate economic activity. It also removed one of the main impetuses for raising tariffs and imposing exchange controls, since countries no longer had to fear runs on their gold reserves. In the short term, however, abandoning the gold standard created uncertainty in the value of various currencies, thereby disrupting trade and international finance.

By 1933, the world economy had hit bottom, with economists estimating a total drop in output of 38 percent since 1929. Unemployment had skyrocketed in virtually every industrialized economy, bank failures had become widespread, and international trade had fallen dramatically. As in the United States, many governments worsened the situation by raising taxes and decreasing spending to balance their budgets, in the hope that lower government borrowing would free up capital for private investment. Fearing social unrest at home, many governments also turned inward, passing tariffs and exchange controls in the hope of saving businesses and jobs, and thereby placating angry citizens. This beggar-thy-neighbor approach underscored what some economists regard as the single most important factor in turning what might have been a sharp economic downturn into a prolonged global depression—the lack of international leadership. In previous economic crises, Great Britain had repeatedly stepped up to impose order on chaotic global markets. Now, however, Britain was weakened by World War I, deeply in debt, and no longer in a position to do so. Its obvious successor as a global power, the United States, facing its own grim economic outlook and gripped by isolationist politics, declined the role.

While 1933 marked the low ebb of the global economy, it also represented a turning point, as the abandonment of the gold standard and new stimulative measures began to kick in. No longer fearing that a run on gold reserves would undermine its currency, the Bank of England, for example, was able to lower interest rates, promoting investment and consumption at home. Under its new National Socialist (Nazi) regime, Germany launched a major government spending program—including a huge military buildup—that put millions of citizens back to work. In the United States, Roosevelt's New Deal policies helped stabilize the financial

Only the massive military buildup of World War II provided the economic stimulus that finally ended the Great Depression, according to most economic historians. *(Gordon Coster/Time & Life Pictures/Getty Images)*

markets and banking sector with new regulations and protections for investors and depositors and pumped funds into the economy through new spending and jobs programs, although only World War II expenditures would be sufficient to pull the economy back to its prior level.

All of these measures represented the triumph of what would become known as Keynesian economics, which advocated that in a time of high unemployment and underutilized industrial capacity, the government had to step in and stimulate the economy when private industry would not or could not. Government, the Keynesians said, had to abandon the time-honored idea that the best means for lifting an economy out of a downturn was constricting the money supply and balancing the budget. Instead, governments had to act countercyclically—"priming the pump," as the American expression went—growing the money supply and investing in the economy, even if it meant borrowing to do so. This new Keynesian

consensus would dominate economic policy in the industrialized, noncommunist world through the 1970s, when another downturn, this one marked by an unprecedented combination of high inflation and slow growth, once again tested the premises of the existing economic policy paradigm.

James Ciment

See also: Boom, Economic (1920s); New Deal; Recession, Roosevelt (1937–1939); Stock Market Crash (1929).

Further Reading

Aldcroft, Derek H. *The European Economy, 1914–2000.* London: Routledge, 2001.

Bernanke, Ben. *Essays on the Great Depression.* Princeton, NJ: Princeton University Press, 2000.

Bernstein, Michael A. *The Great Depression: Delayed Recovery and Economic Change in America, 1929–1939.* Cambridge, UK: Cambridge University Press, 1989.

Eichengreen, Barry. *Golden Fetters: The Gold Standard and the Great Depression, 1919–1939.* New York: Oxford University Press, 1992.

Feinstein, Charles H., Peter Temin, and Gianni Toniolo. *The*

European Economy Between the Wars. Oxford, UK: Oxford University Press, 1997.

Friedman, Milton, and Anna Jacobson Schwartz. *The Great Contraction, 1929–1933.* Princeton, NJ: Princeton University Press, 2009.

Galbraith, John Kenneth. *The Great Crash, 1929.* Boston: Houghton Mifflin, 1997.

Kindleberger, Charles P. *The World in Depression, 1929–1939.* Berkeley: University of California Press, 1973.

Shlaes, Amity. *The Forgotten Man: A New History of the Great Depression.* New York: Harper Perennial, 2008.

Temin, Peter. *Lessons from the Great Depression.* Cambridge, MA: MIT Press, 1989.

Greece

One of the birthplaces of Western civilization, Greece is a small country of roughly 11 million people located at the extreme southern end of the Balkans, consisting of a mainland, the large Peloponnese Peninsula, and dozens of inhabited islands in the Aegean, Ionian, and Mediterranean seas.

Despite its geographic location in Eastern Europe, Greece remained outside the Soviet orbit during the cold war and was considered part of Western Europe. Its economy, one of the weakest in Western Europe, traditionally relied on two main industries—shipping and tourism—though the industrial and agricultural sectors remain significant as well. Although it has one of the highest rates of institutional and household borrowing in the European Union (EU), and although its banking sector was heavily exposed to financially turbulent markets in the Balkans, the Greek economy weathered the global financial crisis that began in 2007 relatively well at first, according to economists, though a heavy public debt left the government little room to employ countercyclical economic stimulus policies and the country nearly experienced default in 2010.

Historical Foundations

Divided into often mutually antagonistic city-states in ancient times, Greece emerged as a cultural center in the middle of the first millennium BCE, when philosophers and artists laid the cultural foundations of Western civilization. Because of its fragmented geography, however, the inhabitants of Greece were rarely able to unite politically, leaving the region vulnerable to conquest by larger civilizations. After being taken over by the Romans in the second century BCE, Greece fell under the political hegemony of that empire and its successors until the fall of the Byzantine Empire in the mid-fifteenth century CE. For the next 300 years, the country was ruled by the Ottoman Turks, who were finally ousted in the Greek War of Independence in the 1820s.

While retaining its independence, except for a brief period of occupation by the Nazis during World War II, Greece remained one of Europe's poorer countries through the first half of the twentieth century. Aided by the United States, Greece's government was able to defeat a communist insurgency after World War II. This allowed the country to defy its geography and join the Western Europe community of capitalist democracies, even though it was ruled by a military dictatorship in the late 1960s and early 1970s.

Postwar Industrial Economy

Whether under democratic or military rule, Greece participated in the postwar economic boom in Western Europe, achieving one of the highest growth rates in the world during the 1950s and 1960s. Several factors contributed to what became known as the "Greek economic miracle." First was the country's participation in the Marshall Plan, a massive influx of U.S. capital aimed at jump-starting Western European economies in the wake of World War II and preventing leftist revolutions.

The Greek government also instituted a number of policies to lure foreign investment, largely from Western Europe, including a dramatic devaluation of the Greek currency, the drachma. With the infusion of capital, Greece developed a major chemical manufacturing sector and built up its infrastructure. Concurrently, the prosperity of Western Europe led to a massive influx of tourist money that further aided development and lifted the standard of living. Whereas the Greek per capita income stood at about 40 percent of France's just after World War II, it had reached about 80 percent by the time Greece entered the European Community (later the European Union, or EU) in 1981.

As in much of Western Europe, Greece's economy stagnated in the 1970s. Productivity gains began to lag, and the country was hit by rapidly rising oil prices. To lift itself out of the economic doldrums, the government significantly increased public spending in the 1980s, paying for the expansion by borrowing from abroad. But all the borrowing and spending led to high inflation and high public debt, the latter climbing above total gross domestic product (GDP) by the early 1990s, which in turn triggered several currency crises during the 1990s.

To curb inflation, which peaked at nearly 25 percent in the early 1990s, the Greek government instituted a number of fiscal reforms: reductions in government spending, limits on public borrowing, wage and price controls, and a bolstering of the drachma. All of these policies were instituted not just to lower inflation—which they did, to about 2 percent by decade's end—but to bring the country into line with public spending and inflation mandates set by the EU for membership in the new eurozone. Greece became a member of that monetary union in 2001, converting its currency to the euro and turning over interest-rate-setting authority to the European Central Bank.

Fiscal restraint and renewed European economic growth in the early and middle years of the twenty-first century's first decade helped revive the Greek economy, as did infrastructure development and other preparations for the Olympic Games of 2004, held in and around Athens. That year, the country achieved a near 5 percent growth rate, one of the highest in the European Union. By 2007, just before the global financial crisis, Greece's per capita

GDP had achieved parity with the average for the EU as a whole, though the latter had been weighed down by the entry of several relatively poor former Eastern bloc countries in 2004 and 2007.

Still, the Greek economy was not as strong as the numbers suggested. Household, business, and public borrowing remained high, and low interest rates had fueled an unsustainable run-up in real-estate prices during the middle of the new century's first decade. In addition, many Greek banks had loaned substantial amounts to rapidly growing but volatile economies in the Balkans, especially since the end of large-scale civil conflict in the former Yugoslavia in 1999. In short, the Greek banking system was highly leveraged by the close of 2000's first decade. Thus, when the global financial crisis hit in 2008, the Greek government responded forcefully by becoming the second EU country, after Ireland, to guarantee savings in its domestic banks. With this move, the government sought to reassure skittish foreign depositors and investors that the nation's banking sector was secure.

At the same time, the high levels of public debt made it difficult for the government to engage in economic stimulus spending. In 2009, the Greek government's deficit was running at 12.7 percent of GDP while its overall debt was 113 percent of GDP; of the latter figure, roughly two-thirds was owed to foreigners. With such a huge debt load and worker unrest in the country making it seem that the government would not be able to impose the austerity measures debt holders would like to see to bring down the deficit, fears began to spread in the bond markets that Greece would be unable to refinance bonds worth some $23 billion and that the government would go into default.

Ordinarily this would be a problem for Greece alone but, of course, Greece was part of the eurozone and was not alone among eurozone members in having shaky finances. Spain, Portugal and Ireland faced similar circumstances. Thus, Greece's default might shake confidence in the eurozone's ability collectively to deal with a serial default.

Germany and France, the largest economies in

Shareholders of the National Bank of Greece, the country's largest commercial banking group, met in Athens in January 2010. The government had just announced a three-year plan to reduce a runaway budget deficit—the highest in the European Union. *(Bloomberg/Getty Images)*

the eurozone, were at first reluctant to help Greece but, as many economists pointed out, Greece's membership in the eurozone had come with the implicit assumption—at least to those buying its bonds—that it would never be allowed to default, that it would be saved by the European Central Bank. This allowed Greece to borrow money at much cheaper rates, and the country had binged for a time on this cheap credit. Now the bills were coming due.

By early 2010, it was becoming clear that Greece would be rescued by the stronger eurozone economies, but only if Athens took the necessary measures to rein in government spending. In March, the Socialist Party government of Prime Minister George Papandreou did impose tough austerity measures as well as substantive tax hikes, though how effective the latter would be in rais-

ing revenue was open to question. Greece had the lowest level of tax collection and the highest level of tax avoidance of any country in the eurozone.

Nevertheless, the moves were enough to convince French president Nicholas Sarkozy and German chancellor Angela Merkel to arrange a financial rescue of the country, though Merkel in particular imposed tough conditions and insisted that much of the bailout package would come not from the European Central Bank but from the International Monetary Fund, which is well known for imposing tough austerity measures on countries that come looking for funding in times of fiscal crisis. The agreement allowed Greece to borrow money in the bond markets but only by offering significantly higher interest rates, some 3 percent above what Germany paid on its bonds. The money helped Greece avoid default, but whether the country was on the long and painful road to fiscal recovery—as opposed to merely postponing default—would depend upon whether the austerity measures and enhanced tax collection truly took hold.

Meanwhile, much of the financial world continues to hold its breath. Greece is a tiny economy, and a default there, in and of itself, would hardly shake global financial markets. But, increasingly, economists had come to see Greece as merely the shakiest of a whole row of sovereign dominoes waiting to fall. If Greece collapsed, it could trigger a panic that might cause much of the international edifice of sovereign debt financing to collapse.

James Ciment

See also: Ireland; Portugal; Spain.

Further Reading

Dimitrakopoulos, Dionyssis G., and Argyris G. Passas. *Greece in the European Union.* New York: Routledge, 2004.

Kalaitzidis, Akis. *Europe's Greece: A Giant in the Making.* New York: Palgrave Macmillan, 2010.

Organisation for Economic Co-operation and Development (OECD). "Economic Survey of Greece 2009." Available at www.oecd.org/document/38/0,3343,en_33873108_3387 3421_43349670_1_1_1_1,00.html. Accessed September 21, 2009.

Greenspan, Alan (1926–)

One of the most influential Federal Reserve Board (Fed) chairs in history, Alan Greenspan was a key decision maker during the unprecedented expansion of the U.S. economy in the 1990s. Widely credited with policies that helped America prosper, Greenspan came under criticism both before and after he left office in 2006, with many economists and others blaming his loose monetary policies and failure to enforce bank regulations as key reasons for the dot.com bubble of the 1990s and early 2000s, and the housing bubble of the early and mid-2000s, contributing to the financial crisis that crippled the global economy beginning in 2007.

Greenspan was born in New York City in 1926. An accomplished musician in his younger years, he became interested in economics in his teens and enrolled in New York University (NYU), earning bachelor's and master's degrees. Forced to leave the economics PhD program at Columbia University in 1951 because he could not afford the tuition, he eventually earned his doctorate from NYU more than a quarter century later.

Meanwhile, upon graduation from NYU, Greenspan joined the National Industrial Conference Board, a nonprofit business research group, and then opened his own economic consulting firm, Townsend-Greenspan & Company, in 1954. He served as director of policy research for the 1968 presidential campaign of Richard Nixon and then was appointed chair of the Council of Economic Advisers by Nixon's successor, Gerald Ford, in 1974. Thirteen years later, President Ronald Reagan appointed Greenspan chairman of the Fed, where he would serve until 2006, the second longest tenure in the institution's history. He was reappointed five more times, by Republican and Democratic presidents alike.

Greenspan faced a test of fire within months of his appointment when, on October 19, 1987, the Dow Jones Industrial Average posted its greatest one-day drop in history, both in absolute and percentage terms to that time. The new chair's forceful statement that the Fed would provide a source of liquidity to the financial markets is widely credited for preventing the stock market crash of 1987 from triggering a full-blown recession.

Although willing to expand the money supply in times of crisis, Greenspan saw himself primarily as an inflation fighter. Heavily influenced by his mentor, former Fed chairman Arthur Burns, with whom he studied at Columbia, Greenspan pursued tight money policies during the recession of the early 1990s and has been blamed by his fellow Republicans for bringing about the defeat of incumbent George H.W. Bush in the presidential election of 1992.

Half a decade later, however, Greenspan pursued a diametrically opposed policy during the Asian financial crisis of 1997, when he flooded the world's financial markets with dollars in an effort to slow the capital flight from affected economies in that part of the world. Greenspan also took an activist role in the 1998 collapse of Long-Term Capital Management, a major U.S. hedge fund. Fearing its bankruptcy could have a chilling effect on global financial markets, Greenspan orchestrated a bailout of the firm by commercial and investment banks.

Despite such disruptions, the U.S. economy boomed in the 1990s and Greenspan's stewardship of the money supply was often credited with sustaining the expansion. Thus, while Fed chairmen always have enormous influence over the economy, Greenspan seemed to exert more than most, more even than the presidents under whom he served. Investors worldwide heeded and hung on his carefully parsed—and some would say, cryptic—pronouncements on the economy. When, in one of his most famous utterances, he mentioned in 1996 that an "irrational exuberance" had inflated share valuations too high, stock markets around the world tumbled. Nonetheless, Greenspan did not propose regulations that might have tempered the dot.com stock bubble that collapsed finally in 2001.

Federal Reserve Board chairman Alan Greenspan testifies before the Senate Banking Committee in July 2005. Greenspan's comments on economic trends were closely parsed in the financial community and often had a direct effect on markets. *(Mark Wilson/Getty Images)*

But in the wake of that collapse the U.S. economy entered recession, Greenspan reversed course, lowering the fed funds rate to just 1 percent, a historic low. The rate would remain at or below 3 percent through the middle of 2005.

This lengthy run of historically low rates not only made it cheaper for banks to borrow money but to lend it as well. Many economists cite Fed policy as contributing to the mortgage lending boom of the early and mid-2000s, which sent house prices soaring across the country, as banks and other financial institutions began to devise ever-riskier loans—including adjustable rate mortgages—and to offer mortgages to ever-riskier borrowers, with so-called subprime mortgages. At the same time, there was an ever-increasing trade in mortgage-backed securities, as lenders bundled the mortgages and sold them to investors, for the purpose of spreading risk around.

Even as housing prices soared, some critics began to argue that Greenspan's loose monetary policies were contributing to the deterioration in lending practices and thus inflating a housing bubble. Greenspan argued that unlike overvalued securities, housing prices had never collapsed on a national scale and thus there was little danger of a major crisis in the housing markets.

In the wake of the collapse, other critics such as Nobel Prize–winning economists Joseph Stiglitz and Paul Krugman have argued that Greenspan failed to use his powers to rein in deceptive and dangerous lending practices. For his part, Greenspan has said that he did seek tighter regulation of Freddie Mac and Fannie Mae, the government mortgage insurers that back a large portion of the nation's mortgages. But he has also admitted fault. In 2008, he agreed with some of his critics and said that he could have done more to push for regulation of derivatives such as mortgage-backed securities. It is the collapse in the value of those derivatives that was the prime cause of the financial crisis that began in 2007.

In the wake of his departure from the Fed, Greenspan has served as an economic adviser to a number of financial institutions.

James Ciment and John Barnhill

See also: Banks, Central; Federal Reserve System; "Irrational Exuberance"; Monetary Policy.

Further Reading

Andrews, Edmund L., "Greenspan Concedes Error on Regulation." *New York Times,* October 23, 2008.

Fleckenstein, William A., and Frederick Sheehan. *Greenspan's Bubbles: The Age of Ignorance at the Federal Reserve.* New York: McGraw-Hill, 2008.

Greenspan, Alan. *The Age of Turbulence: Adventures in a New World.* New York: Penguin, 2007.

Woodward, Bob. *Maestro: Greenspan's Fed and the American Boom.* New York: Simon & Schuster, 2000.

Gross Domestic Product

Gross domestic product (GDP) is the sum of the monetary value of all final goods and services produced within a country (or region) during a specified period of time, usually a year but sometimes a quarter. It does not matter who produces the goods and services—citizens or foreign workers, private companies or government institutions, local or foreign-owned enterprises. Goods and services are included in the calculation of GDP simply if they are produced within the particular territory and time frame.

GDP measures the final production, or the value of products and services bought by end users. Thus, for example, the value of a jacket as the final product is counted once; the value of the fabric, buttons, and other components that are included in the jacket are not counted a second time. According to the production approach, GDP is the sum of added value—total output minus intermediate products—at all stages of production (from a piece of wood or plastic to a button, and from a button to a jacket), plus taxes but minus production subsidies. According to the income approach, GDP equals the sum of profits, specifically firms' operating profits—minus rent, interest on debt, and employee compensation; interest income of households through their loans to business firms; rental income households receive from property, as well as royalties from patents and copyrights and income received by employees, including salaries wages, and fringe benefits, plus unemployment and Social Security payments. The methodology for calculating GDP and its components is established by an internationally agreed-upon framework known as the System of National Accounts.

GDP is a widely used measure of the economic size of a country, and per capita GDP is calculated as a measure of the economic welfare of its population. Economists, policy makers, and business leaders rely on GDP, per capita GDP, and GDP growth for several purposes: comparing different countries and regions (assuming they use the same definitions and methodologies for calculating GDP and that the same currency is used and fluctuations in exchange rates and prices are eliminated); formulating economic policy; and making private business decisions about where to invest, export, or locate production facilities.

GDP measures the value of the goods and services at the time they were sold. Thus, if the prices increase by 5 percent but the production level remains the same, nominal GDP also increases by 5 percent—the inflation rate. Real GDP (or GDP in current prices) is equal to nominal GDP adjusted for changes in prices. Thus, if only prices change but the production level does not, real GDP remains the same. For example, if the overall price level doubles and nothing else changes, nominal GDP doubles but real GDP stays the same.

Economic growth is often measured by the growth rate of real GDP (real GDP growth). Growing real GDP is a sign of increasing output; declining real GDP is a sign of economic recession or even depression.

According to the expenditure approach, GDP can be also measured as the sum of private consumption expenditures or household consumption (C), private investment expenditures including gross capital formation, changes in inventories, and newly constructed residential housing (I), government expenditures on goods and services excluding transfers (G), and exports of goods and services (EX) minus imports of goods and services (IM): GDP = C + I + G + EX − IM. This does not mean that countries should restrict imports in order to increase their GDP. Total imports are subtracted from GDP because the other components already include imports—the consumption totals include both goods and services imported from abroad, as well as those produced domestically—and GDP measures only the value of goods and services produced at home and used for private consumption or investment, government purchases of goods and services, or exports.

GDP is linked to a country's balance of payments because it is the sum of private consumption and investment expenditures, government consumption expenditures, and the goods and services account. Moreover, gross national disposable income is the sum of GDP and the balances of the income and current transfers account. The four latter accounts also form the current account.

There is also a link between GDP and welfare. If welfare is expressed as the sum of domestic spending—private consumption plus investment expenditures plus government purchases of goods and services $(C + I + G)$—one can say that GDP is the sum of welfare and net exports $(EX - IM)$. Thus, in countries with trade deficits, welfare is larger than GDP; in countries with trade surpluses, GDP exceeds welfare. This does not mean that all countries should strive for large trade deficits. They may run out of funds for financing them, and their ability to import may decrease in the future. Moreover, if they take large loans for financing their foreign trade deficits, they will have to repay those loans, including principal and interest, in the future. The composition of imports is another important factor: current imports of machinery, for example, may increase future exports and future GDP. If an economy grows very rapidly, its welfare does not have to decrease in the future when it has a foreign trade surplus and when it pays back its loans. But if it grows slowly, or if its economy declines, it may face substantial decreases in welfare.

If one country has a GDP twice as large as that of another country, this does not mean that personal income or purchasing power is twice as high in the first country. If the former country has a much larger population than the latter country, GDP on a per capita basis may actually point to a lower average income. For example, if the GDP of Country A is $200 million and the GDP of Country B is $100 million, but Country A's population is 400,000 and Country B's population is only 100,000, then Country A's per capita GDP is $500 and Country B's per capita GDP is $1,000. Moreover, there may be differences in price levels as well. Because a cup of coffee, or an automobile, or a taxi ride does not cost the same in every country, an equal per capita real GDP in two countries does not mean that it is possible to buy the same goods and services in those two countries on the same income.

It is also important to note that GDP does not measure the value of goods produced in previous years even though some products—such as buildings, cars, and computers—are used for several or many years. Nor does GDP reflect the distribution of income among the population (income is distributed more evenly in some economies than in others, lowering the overall poverty rate) or government spending (some countries spend more on health and education, for example, while others invest more heavily in their military). Various forms of labor (services) are excluded entirely from GDP, including volunteer work, raising one's family, and illegal activities. GDP also takes no measure of the amount of pollution, environmental degradation, or depletion of natural resources caused by economic activity—all of which reduce human welfare in the long run. And finally, GDP tends to increase in the aftermath of armed conflicts and natural disasters, as large construction projects may have to be launched to rebuild facilities that were destroyed.

Tiia Vissak

See also: Growth, Economic.

Further Reading

Gutierrez, Carlos M., Cynthia A. Glassman, J. Steven Landefeld, and Rosemary D. Marcuss. *Measuring the Economy: A Primer on GDP and the National Income and Product Accounts.* Washington, DC: Bureau of Economic Analysis, U.S. Department of Commerce, 2007.

International Monetary Fund. *Balance of Payments and International Investment Position Manual.* 6th ed. Washington, DC: International Monetary Fund, 2010.

System of National Accounts. Brussels: Commission of the European Communities, International Monetary Fund, Organisation for Economic Co-operation and Development, United Nations and World Bank, 1993. Available at http://unstats.un.org/unsd/sna1993/toctop2.asp. Accessed December 2009.

Growth Cycles

A growth cycle tracks the change of the economy, often measured by gross domestic product (GDP), with respect to a long-term trend. In other words, as the economy grows along an expected path, the growth cycle shows how the economy may, at times, grow a bit faster or a bit slower. Growth cycles are often confused with business cycles, because they are closely related. The business cycle shows expansions (increases) and contractions (decreases) of a variable such as GDP over a designated period of time. Growth cycles, by contrast, reflect the fluctuations that occur within the expansion phase of a business cycle, when the average trend line is rising. The "peaks" and "troughs" of the growth cycle are defined only relative to the general upward trend line.

Cycles and Phases

Business cycles and growth cycles in a nation's economy are determined by examining the fluctuations in several variables, indicating whether overall business conditions are expanding or contracting. For the purposes of the present explanation, however, gross domestic product is used as a single measure of overall U.S. economic activity.

Consider the time period between the second quarter of 2006 and the first quarter of 2007, when the business cycle showed the economy still in an expansionary phase. The growth cycle, however, showed that the economy was in a "growth recession." During this period, the U.S. economy grew at rates of 2.7 percent, 0.8 percent, 1.5 percent, and

0.1 percent, respectively—all positive, but below trend. Because growth cycles are characterized by changes in the *rate* of economic growth, not just whether the economy is expanding or contracting, they can indicate important phases in the cycle.

Determining the Trend: Moving Averages

One of the major difficulties in analyzing the growth cycle is that the underlying trend to which growth is compared is not constant, but continually changing. Economists used the concept of a moving average to measure the trend. For example, in 2007, GDP grew at an average rate of 2.38 percent. Thus, in the fourth quarter of 2007, when GDP fell by 0.2 percent, growth was 2.58 percent below average (0.2 percent plus –2.38 percent). Moving on to the first quarter of 2008, economists compute a new moving average, adding one new observation (0.9 percent for the first quarter of 2008) and dropping the oldest data point (0.1 percent for the first quarter of 2007). Thus, the average growth rate for the year ending the first quarter of 2008 was 2.58 percent (4.8 percent + 4.8 percent – 0.2 percent + 0.9 percent, divided by 4). For the purpose of studying the growth cycle, growth in the first quarter of 2008 was 1.68 percent below average (0.9 percent – 2.58 percent).

To calculate moving averages, economists often use more complex mathematical methods called "filters." This more sophisticated technique enables them to better isolate the difference between a long-run trend line and the short-run fluctuations around it.

Short-Run Fluctuations

An important concept in understanding growth cycles is the so-called output gap, which is the deviation from the potential level of output in an economy at any point in time. The output gap can either be positive or negative. A negative output gap does not necessarily mean a recession, but merely slower growth than the average within a growth cycle.

Analysis of growth cycles leads to an understanding of the relationship between the output gap and the cyclical unemployment rate. Okun's law, named for mid-twentieth-century U.S. economist Arthur Okun, connects the output gap and the cyclical unemployment rate. Cyclical unemployment occurs when workers lose their jobs because of poor business conditions and a weak overall economy. According to Okun's law, when the output gap is 2.0 percent below potential, the cyclical unemployment rate rises by 1.0 percent. Increases in cyclical unemployment are typical during recessions in both the business cycle and the growth cycle.

The Phillips curve—named for New Zealand economist Alban William Phillips—is a theoretical relationship between the change in the rate of inflation and the short-term output gap. The Phillips curve shows that when an economy is producing at an above-average rate with a positive output gap, inflation will increase. Another implication of the Phillips curve is that a negative output gap will reduce the rate of inflation. This implies that peaks within the growth cycle will likely lead to inflation; by the same token, troughs in the growth cycle will help reduce the rate of inflation. It also means that the study of growth cycles can help predict when inflation will be on the rise in an economy and suggest ways in which it can be minimized or avoided altogether. While the Phillips curve has been a hotly debated theory among economists, most agree that there are short-run trade-offs between the output gap and inflation.

Andre R. Neveu

See also: Growth, Economic.

Further Reading

Burns, Arthur F., and Wesley C. Mitchell. *Measuring Business Cycles.* New York: National Bureau of Economic Research, 1946.

Jones, Charles I. *Macroeconomics.* New York: W.W. Norton, 2008.

Klein, Philip A., and Geoffrey H. Moore. *Monitoring Growth Cycles in Market-Oriented Countries: Developing and Using International Economic Indicators.* Vol. 26, Studies in Business Cycles. Cambridge, MA: Ballinger, 1985.

Moore, Geoffrey H., and Victor Zarnowitz. "Appendix A: The Development and Role of the National Bureau of Economic Research's Business Cycle Chronologies." In *The American Business Cycle: Continuity and Change,* ed. Robert J. Gordon. Chicago: University of Chicago Press, 1990.

Growth, Economic

Economic growth is defined as an increase in the output of goods and services in an economic system. For nations, it is usually measured by changes in gross domestic product (GDP). The term "gross" is used to indicate that the value of the capital that was used up in producing the GDP was not accounted for. Net domestic product (NDP) is GDP minus the value of the capital that was used in the process of producing the GDP.

Economic growth and productivity are two separate but related measures. Economic growth can come from increases in productivity (technological change) or from increases in the quality and amount of labor and capital that are used to produce the output. Economists are most interested in the growth of per capita GDP (also called "intensive growth"), but the growth in GDP itself (or aggregate GDP, also called "extensive growth") is also a closely followed statistic.

Despite the close relationship between economic fluctuations and economic growth, economists have tended to study these separately and in quite different ways. Most theories of booms and busts stress the demand side: Why do consumers and investors change how much they want to spend from year to year? Theories of economic growth instead tend to stress the supply side: Why are firms producing more this year than last year? Nevertheless, it is possible to outline several ways in which growth and business cycle fluctuations interact.

Effects of Economic Growth on Business Cycles

One might expect that there would be little or no economic fluctuation in a world without economic growth. If everyone earned the same income year after year, they would—at least on average—make similar expenditures year after year. Producers would thus know the total market for the goods and services they produce. In such a world, one might expect all producers and consumers to continue happily from year to year producing and consuming what they did the year before. In such a scenario, governments would have little reason to change the annual money supply or government budget, in which case these sources of economic cycles would disappear as well. The "cycle" would be nothing more than a *nearly* flat line.

Small fluctuations might still persist. Competition among firms for an unchanging market sometimes might lead to a bunching of investment expenditures. Likewise, consumer expenditures on expensive durable goods that are purchased only occasionally (such as houses and cars) might not occur evenly through time. In the absence of growth, however, one could anticipate that these booms and busts would be relatively small and inconsequential.

Intensive economic growth occurred slowly if at all before the early nineteenth century, though there were certainly economic fluctuations. The oscillations are often referred to as "harvest cycles," as they tended to be driven by variations in agricultural output from year to year. Now that agriculture has come to comprise only a small percentage of GDP in developed countries, annual changes in the harvest alone are not likely to cause booms and busts.

Scholars of economic growth increasingly recognize that the output of individual goods and services does not expand at the same rate. Economic growth is associated with innovation: firms develop new goods and services through innovations in technology or firm organization, or

by forging new ties with other firms. Sometimes the impact on other sectors is positive, as when increased production of automobiles is associated with increased purchase of oil or rubber for tires. Often, though, the impact is negative, as when the automobile displaced the manufacture of carriages, buggy whips, and horseshoes.

Such changes in the output of goods and services mean that employment and output expand rapidly in some sectors of the economy while contracting in others. Even within sectors, the successful development of new goods or services by some firms may squeeze other firms out of the market. Since these changes both across and within sectors are difficult to predict, neither capital investment nor workers are likely to flow quickly from declining firms to growing firms. As a result, the process of economic growth creates periods of unemployment.

Medium-Term Growth Cycles

Economists have begun to connect their theories of growth with their theories of cycles in discussing the idea of a "medium term." That is, economists expect that there will be periods of a decade or more in which economies either grow fast and have mild and short business downturns, or grow slowly (or decline) and have severe and long business downturns. The 1950s and 1960s were characterized in most developed countries by rapid growth and mild business cycles; conversely, the 1930s and 1970s were characterized by limited or negative growth and severe cycles. In studying economic fluctuations, economists have tended to emphasize the shorter business cycles rather than the arguably more important medium-term fluctuations. Because of this emphasis, they have treated all business cycles as essentially the same despite the fact that they appear to be quite different in length, intensity, and the nature of constituent phases.

In terms of the argument above—that fluctuations are largely a result of growth—one might well expect that periods of rapid growth would also be periods of severe fluctuation. Recall, however, that the link from growth to booms and busts depends on the uncertainties surrounding the different experiences across firms and sectors. One might therefore expect that periods in which investors and workers are able to identify with some accuracy the firms and sectors that can grow quickly will be characterized by both growth and limited fluctuations. If, on the other hand, there are difficulties in achieving expansion in some sectors or firms, perhaps because workers need to move geographically or receive extensive training, then a lengthy period of sluggish growth and severe cycles may result.

It may be that the relative balance between growing sectors and declining sectors differs across the medium term. If many sectors are growing at once, rapid growth with limited fluctuations results. If few sectors are growing but many are declining, the reverse occurs.

Long Growth Cycles

The idea that the medium term merits specific study has existed on the fringes of economic science for some time. The question then arises if a longer cycle—the one beyond the medium term—also deserves special examination. For example, if "good" decades of economic expansion are observed to alternate with "bad" decades, then one begins to wonder if there is some regular, long cycle at work. Accordingly, the Russian economist Nikolai Kondratieff developed the idea of long waves (Kondratieff cycles) in the early twentieth century. Long waves are generally believed to be about half a century in duration. Long wave theory has been little discussed in recent decades, with interest in the phenomenon tending to peak during periods of poor economic performance, such as the 1930s and 1970s. Thus, with the global financial crisis of 2008–2009, it may stage a comeback.

Long wave theory is challenged on both empirical and theoretical grounds. Theoretically, economists wonder what forces could drive regular cycles of such a length. Empirically, modern eco-

nomic growth has occurred only long enough to generate a handful of such cycles, complicated by such shocks to the global economy as two world wars. In other words, at least some of the "good" and "bad" of the past century may have been caused by such unusual events.

Technological innovation has been a particular area of emphasis in many long wave theories. One might reasonably expect that a wave of innovations would encourage both investment and consumption. But why would technological innovation be more likely to occur when the boom generated by the previous cluster of innovations had turned to bust? At such times, money is scarce as firms struggle to finance innovative activity. According to one argument, firms are then more willing to take chances, making radical innovations more likely. Examining the historical evidence, however, it is not at all clear that technological innovations (radical or otherwise) are more common during periods of stagnation or decline.

Other long wave theorists talk of cycles in resource prices (of energy, for example), investment rates (interest rates), or credit availability (available cash for expansion). In all of these cases, however, both the theoretical arguments and empirical evidence are viewed with grave suspicion by the vast majority of economists. In fact, economists have come up with no compelling or widely accepted explanation of even medium-term cycles, let alone a cogent explanation for the more elusive and difficult to understand long wave patterns.

Sectoral Interactions and Growth Cycles

Standard economic theory suggests that workers and investment will flow quickly from declining sectors to growing sectors. In reality, much can be learned about booms and busts by looking at how sectors (and firms) differ in their growth performance. For most of the twentieth century, though, economists tried to understand economic fluctuations only in terms of the movements of a handful of economy-wide variables such as consumption, investment, and money supply. Only within the last several years have some experts in economic fluctuations examined how varying performance across sectors can cause booms and busts. If many sectors are declining but few are growing, unemployment will be a likely result. Moreover, even if certain growth sectors are able to absorb workers from declining sectors, this will not happen overnight. Workers will face many barriers—retraining and relocation, most obviously—in moving from one industry another, making a smooth, quick transition unlikely.

Standard economic theory suggests that wage rates will fall in the face of unemployment and that, as wages do fall, more workers will be hired. Again, this logic ignores the challenges of moving across sectors. Empirically, there is a further puzzle: during bad periods, wages often do not fall even when unemployment is high. During the Great Depression, for example, real wages (that is, wages adjusted for changes in the price level) actually rose.

Savings, Investment, and the Growth Cycle

If the amount that people save exceeds the amount that people invest, then an economic downturn will result. Of course, classical economic theory suggests that interest rates will fall in such a situation, thereby discouraging saving (the reward for which would decrease) and encouraging investment (because the cost of borrowing would fall). As with falling wage rates, though, this mechanism does not seem to work fast enough in real life to prevent busts.

Personal savings decisions generally reflect an individual's expectations regarding the future. A person is most likely to save if he or she is worried about the future. Investment decisions are even more future oriented. A person is most likely to invest if he or she is confident about the future. Investment decisions also depend on the rate of innovation: investment is often called forth because new technology must be embodied in new equipment. Thus, savings are more likely to exceed

investments if expectations of future growth falter, and/or the rate of innovation slows. (Note also that a declining rate of innovation might itself lead to low expectations.)

Savings and investment are connected by financial institutions of various sorts. Rates of investment depend on both the institutional structure and the level of trust and confidence within the financial system. Financial innovations such as hedge funds or derivatives trading may support growth by increasing the supply of funds to investors. Yet if lenders lose confidence in these instruments, the result may be a financial crisis that triggers a broad economic contraction.

Effects of Booms and Busts on Growth

Although booms and busts are largely a result of the process of economic growth, the cycle affects that process in many ways as well. There have been several analyses of the effect of business cycle volatility on growth. The empirical results are diverse and seem to depend a great deal on the precise specification of the equations employed. This may be because different sources/types of volatility—changes in government policy, trends in technology—have different effects. Moreover, if cycles are different during medium-term upswings than during medium-term downswings, analyses that lump the two types together are likely to generate misleading results.

Theoretically, though, it is not hard to imagine a variety of connections between fluctuations and growth. On the positive side, there remains the possibility that certain types of innovation may be more likely during economic downturns or upswings. Then, too, it is often suggested that economic fluctuations serve a kind of cleansing function: weaker firms are put out of business, and surviving firms are forced to make tough decisions and thus jettison their least productive workers. Such a shaking-out process could then lead to a period of economic growth. There is evidence for both of these scenarios. More controversially, firms may introduce productivity-enhancing innovations under the pressure to reduce costs during periods of poor economic performance. In all of these ways, then, busts serve the longer-term process of growth by rooting out unproductive practices. The effect, though, should not be exaggerated: some very productive firms and workers may also suffer during economic downturns.

It would seem natural to expect that booms and busts have a negative rather than positive impact on economic growth. Lengthy periods of unemployment can lower GDP—the most common measure of economic growth—below what it could have been. Moreover, to the extent that learning by doing is an important component of productivity advance—such as when workers develop better methods of production in the course of producing a good or service—then any reduction in output reduces economic growth.

Levels of investment are also affected by interest rates. During boom periods, central banks generally raise interest rates in order to discourage investment and restrain inflationary pressures. Before the 1930s, economists tended to urge low interest rates to foster growth. Since then, economists and central banks have focused primarily on stabilizing business cycles.

Some economists have urged an emphasis on fiscal policy (government spending and taxation) rather than on monetary (interest rate) policy during boom times. Tax increases that are clearly temporary might cause consumption rather than investment to fall. If these taxes were used to finance government expenditure during the next recession, the government would not have to borrow (and thereby help avoid rising interest rates).

The hardest link to establish is possibly the most important: cycles affect expectations. Investors (and innovators) must worry that a future recession will cause their otherwise sensible investment plans to become unprofitable. If investors need to borrow, they may find that banks are unwilling to lend if they fear a severe economic downturn is just around the corner. It is not clear how important these cyclically related expectations are. Investors have a host of other things

to worry about: the future prospects of technology, institutions, tastes, and competitor behavior. But fears regarding cycles may nevertheless cause some dampening of the long-term trend in investment.

The Demand Side in Growth

Business cycle theory to date has tended to emphasize the demand side, while growth theory has tended to stress the supply side. The discussion of expectations should serve as a reminder that the two are closely linked. Thus, under at least some circumstances, increases in demand may stimulate increases in supply. Moreover, growth can be sustained in the long run only if demand and supply expand at similar rates: firms that produce more will suffer rather than prosper if consumers are not willing to buy their output. Economists as yet understand poorly how demand and supply interact through time.

Double-digit inflation adds a great deal of uncertainty to investment decisions. It increases the cost of negotiating business deals, as one cannot easily specify a future delivery price. It also instigates financial speculation, which tends to destabilize the economy. Empirical studies have suggested that lowering inflation from 50 percent to 5 percent increases growth by 1–2 percent. However, this result is largely taken from a small sample of countries that experienced both very high inflation and very slow growth. While the negative impact on growth of high inflation seems fairly clear, it is not at all clear that moderate rates of inflation (below, say, 5 percent) have any negative impact on growth.

Indeed, some economic theories suggest a possible positive impact of moderate levels of inflation: Workers may be fooled by rising wages into taking high-productivity jobs that they otherwise would have rejected, even though the real wage (the purchasing power of a worker's income) is unchanged. In addition, producers may be fooled by rising output prices, which they believe will result in higher profits. Not realizing that wage and other costs are going up as much as prices, producers might respond by expanding production. All in all, the effects of moderate inflation can lead to greater economic growth overall.

Economists worry about deflation as well. The Great Depression was a time of rapid deflation, which likely contributed to its severity by encouraging people and businesses to hoard money rather than invest it. The deflation also increased the real value of debts, which were denominated in dollars, forcing many businesses into insolvency. The much lower levels of deflation observed in the late nineteenth century (likely driven by technological innovation) had little or no negative consequences. The lesson seems to be that, as in the case of inflation, moderate levels of deflation pose no great danger.

Rick Szostak

See also: Gross Domestic Product; Growth Cycles.

Further Reading

Blanchard, Olivier. *Macroeconomics.* 5th ed. Upper Saddle River NJ: Prentice Hall, 2009.

Pasinetti, Luigi L. *Structural Change and Economic Growth: A Theoretical Essay on the Dynamics of the Wealth of Nations.* Cambridge, UK: Cambridge University Press, 1981.

Szostak, Rick. *The Causes of Economic Growth: Interdisciplinary Perspectives.* Berlin: Springer, 2009.

Weil, David N. *Economic Growth.* Boston: Addison-Wesley, 2005.

Haberler, Gottfried von (1900–1995)

Economist Gottfried von Haberler was a member of the intellectual group known as the Mises Circle (Mises-Kreis) led by Austrian economist and philosopher Ludwig von Mises. The group was influenced by the Austrian or Vienna school of economics (also known as the psychological School), which flourished from the late 1800s until the early 1930s.

Austrian school economists believed and taught that the price level is key to understanding economic phenomena in free markets. Because prices are determined by people making subjective decisions in dynamically changing markets, Mises maintained, prices are thus determined by human psychology. Mises's influence on Haberler led the latter to propose policies in keeping with Mises's free-enterprise ideas. Haberler, however, eventually came to reject some aspects of the Austrian school's views, such as the use of the gold standard as the measure for the value of currency. Because of this and other positions, Haberler is sometimes labeled a right-wing Keynesian.

Gottfried von Haberler was born in Austria on July 20, 1900. He was educated at the University of Vienna, where he earned PhD degrees in economics and law and in 1928 joined the faculty. Haberler left Vienna for Switzerland in 1934, and two years later he emigrated to the United States, where he became a professor of economics at Harvard University. At Harvard, he worked closely with Joseph Schumpeter, another Austrian émigré. The two economists had been influenced by the Austrian school and both opposed Keynesian support of government intervention in the economy.

Haberler's most influential economic theories pertained to international trade and business cycles, as presented in his major published works, *Theory of International Trade* (1936) and *Prosperity and Depression* (1937). While in Vienna, he had argued for a policy of free trade to allow the development of an international division of labor. In Haberler's view, such a policy would lead to greater productivity and a greater abundance of goods for all. His argument, while based on classical economic theories, was strengthened by his belief in the Austrian school theory of value and price.

Haberler made a strong case for allowing businesses to engage in free enterprise as a way to promote economic growth. He also developed a method of analyzing the business cycle based on older economic theories. He was opposed to the Keynesian reliance on political manipulation of the money supply, especially where such policies would lead to inflation. He was also opposed to protectionism and to mixing capitalist, socialist, and communist polices in free-market economic systems.

In the 1950s and 1960s, Haberler rejected the gold standard for currencies and argued for the trading of national fiat currencies in exchange programs, thereby joining with Milton Friedman and other monetarists. In the 1970s he studied the problem of stagflation and the role of labor unions in causing inflationary recessions. In 1971, Haberler retired from his position at Harvard and became a resident scholar at the American Enterprise Institute for Public Policy Research, a free-enterprise think tank based in Washington, D.C. Haberler died on May 6, 1995, in Washington.

Andrew J. Waskey

See also: Austrian School; Mises, Ludwig von; Schumpeter, Joseph.

Further Reading

Baldwin, Robert E. "Gottfried Haberler's Contributions to International Trade Theory and Policy." *Quarterly Journal of Economics* 97:1 (February 1982): 141–148.

Gillis, Malcolm. "Gottfried Haberler: Contributions upon Entering His Ninth Decade." *Quarterly Journal of Economics* 97:1 (February 1982): 139–140.

Haberler, Gottfried. *Prosperity and Depression: A Theoretical Analysis of Cyclical Movements.* 5th ed. New York: Atheneum, 1963.

———. *The Theory of International Trade: With Its Applications to Commercial Policy.* Trans. Alfred Stonier and Frederick Benham. New York: Augustus M. Kelley, 1968.

Hansen, Alvin Harvey (1887–1975)

Economist Alvin Hansen was the leading American interpreter of Keynesian theory in the 1930s and 1940s. He spearheaded important advances in the exposition of Keynesian theory, enabling widespread acceptance of Keynesian public policy.

Alvin Harvey Hansen was born in Viborg, South Dakota, on August 23, 1887. He graduated from Yankton College in 1910 and, after working for several years in South Dakota public schools, received his PhD in 1918 from the University of Wisconsin. He taught at Brown University in Providence, Rhode Island, and the University of Minnesota in Minneapolis before joining Harvard University in 1937 to fill the Littauer chair in political economy.

When he arrived at Harvard, Hansen was considered part of the older generation that supported the political economy of John Maynard Keynes. Hansen's teaching on fiscal policy influenced a rising generation of important economists, many of whom helped transform Keynesian economic ideas into public policy. Initially, Keynes's *General Theory of Employment Interest and Money* (1936) was not well received in the United States, but Hansen expounded, defended, and modified Keynesian thought to meet the demands of the U.S. economy. His future writings were developments of Keynesian thought.

By 1938, Hansen had focused his efforts on the pressing problem of economic stagnation. Three years later, he published *Fiscal Policy and Business Cycles*, in which he gave his full support to Keynes's analysis of the causes and cures for the Great Depression. Because the book was written by an economist and past president of the American Economic Association, it gained the attention of a wide audience. According to Keynes, without government intervention, the business cycle would eventually turn upward but would not do so quickly, nor would it rise to its previous heights. While Hansen was not fully convinced that all of Keynes's ideas were correct, he believed that underemployment made government intervention necessary.

In 1953, Hansen published *A Guide to Keynes*, a chapter-by-chapter exposition of Keynes's *General Theory of Employment Interest and Money*, which provided American students with a clear understanding of Keynes's theories. Hansen also continued to address the problem of full employment for decades to come.

Hansen generally ignored the views of the Austrian school economists, but he agreed with the Austrian-American economist Joseph Schumpeter, who also taught at Harvard, that the Great Depression marked a confluence of several economic cycles, including the long Kondratieff cycle (40 years), the mid-range Juglar cycle (about 10 years), and the shorter Mitchell-Persons cycle (about 40 months). Hansen hypothesized that these cycles followed a long-term price decline that had been caused by a shortage of gold that could be used for exchange.

During the course of about three decades, from about 1935 to 1965, Hansen's views found practical application in U.S. economic policy. He held several positions in the Franklin Roosevelt administration, playing a key formative role in the creation of the Social Security system and the Council of Economic Advisers. A prolific writer, popular professor, and frequent testifier before Congress, Hansen was once called "the American Keynes." *A Guide to Keynes* was vital in advancing Keynesian theory in the United States and throughout the world. In the economic community, Hansen is perhaps best known for his IS-LM model, or Hicks-Hansen synthesis, regarding the effect of fiscal and monetary policies on national income (where I stands for investment, S for savings, L for liquidity, and M for money supply). The model combined elements of both Keynesian and neoclassical theories in a single economic framework. Alvin Hansen died on June 6, 1975, in Alexandria, Virginia.

Andrew J. Waskey

See also: Boom, Economic (1920s); Great Depression (1929–1933); Keynesian Business Model; Neoclassical Theories and Models.

Further Reading

Breit, William, and Roger L. Ransom. *The Academic Scribblers.* 3rd ed. Princeton, NJ: Princeton University Press, 1998.

Hansen, Alvin Harvey. *Guide to Keynes.* New York: McGraw-Hill, 1953.

Metzler, Lloyd Appleton. *Income, Employment and Public Policy: Essays in Honor or Alvin H. Hansen.* New York: W.W. Norton, 1948.

Rosenof, Theodore. *Economics in the Long Run: New Deal Theorists and Their Legacies, 1933–1993.* Chapel Hill: University of North Carolina Press, 1997.

Harrod, Roy Forbes (1900–1978)

Roy Forbes Harrod, a follower of the British economist John Maynard Keynes—particularly Keynes's theory of economic expansions and contractions—added significantly to the field of economics with his investigations into the interactions between so-called dynamic versus stable economic systems.

Harrod was born on February 13, 1900, in Norfolk, England. He was educated at Westminster School, attended Oxford University's New College, and briefly studied economics at King's College, Cambridge University, under Keynes. In 1922, Harrod was named a fellow and tutor in economics at Christ College, Oxford, and from 1938 to 1947, he was a fellow at Oxford's Nuffield College. During World War II, he served in a variety of posts on behalf of the prime minister and in the admiralty. Following the war, Harrod returned to Christ College until 1952, when he was appointed Nuffield Reader of International Economics. He was a founder of the Oxford Economics Research Group.

Among Harrod's important contributions to the discipline of economics was his view that economics is "dynamic," or continually unstable and changing, rather than "static," or stable and unchanging. (His views, formed at Oxford, were later adopted by the Cambridge University economists.) In his dynamic model, Harrod showed that economic expansions (booms) and contractions (busts) were deviations from the equilibrium rate of growth. Therefore, his theory included both a stable (nondynamic) trend line—the average long-run growth in the economy—and unstable (dynamic) localized and short-term deviations from the trend line.

Harrod presented his thoughts in *The Trade Cycle: An Essay* (1936), which he further developed in "An Essay in Dynamic Theory." Independent of the economist Evsey Domar, he developed an economic model now known as the Harrod-Domar model (he would have received full credit for this insight—as well as for others of his ideas—had the publication of his works not been delayed). The Harrod-Domar model shows that the economy does not naturally have a balanced rate of growth, nor does it naturally find full-employment equilibrium.

In his later work, *Towards a Dynamic Economics* (1948), Harrod explained that an economy can grow generally over time, but does so in unstable ways—owing, for example, to inflation or too rapid an expansion. Such instability results in a failure of that cycle of the economy to reach its potential.

By the time *Towards a Dynamic Economics* was published, Harrod's model of economic growth incorporated the concept of warranted rates of growth. Harrod defined the term *warranted rates of growth* as the satisfaction that all producers have produced exactly what is needed for the market, a condition in which inventories and output are in perfect balance; it also includes the satisfaction that all households have saved at the desired level. Harrod showed that when these conditions are not met and imbalances occur, unstable cycles form around the general trend line, thus slowing overall growth.

By the late 1940s and early 1950s, Harrod had begun researching the life and work of Keynes. He became Keynes's biographer, publishing *The Life of John Maynard Keynes* in 1951. In addition to John Richard Hicks and James E. Mead, Harrod corresponded with Keynes until the end of Keynes's life. Harrod continued teaching, researching, and writing until his death on March 8, 1978, in Norfolk.

Andrew J. Waskey

See also: Keynesian Business Model.

Further Reading

Harrod, Roy Forbes. *Collected Interwar Papers and Correspondence of Roy Harrod*. Northampton, MA: Edward Elgar, 2003.

———. *Trade Cycle: An Essay*. Cranbury, NJ: Scholar's Bookshelf, 1965.

Rampa, Giorgio, A. P. Thirlwall, and Luciano Stella. *Economic Dynamics, Trade and Growth: Essays on Harrodian Themes*. Port Washington, NY: Scholium International, 1998.

Young, Warren. *Harrod and His Trade Cycle Group*. New York: New York University Press, 1989.

Hawtrey, Ralph George (1879–1975)

Ralph George Hawtrey was a follower of the Alfred Marshall neoclassical economic tradition of free markets. He is best known for developing the "overconsumptionist" monetary theory of business cycles, as well as the concept that became known as the multiplier, which showed the effect of a change in total national investment on the amount of total national income.

Hawtrey was born on November 22, 1879, in Slough, Buckinghamshire, England. He studied at Eton College before attending Cambridge University, from which he graduated in 1901 with honors in mathematics. From 1928 to 1929, he was a visiting professor at Harvard University. Hawtrey spent most of his career with the Treasury of Great Britain. He also studied and wrote about economics for much of his life. After World War II, he became Price Professor of International Economics at the Royal Institute for International Affairs (now Chatham House). He was knighted in 1956 for his work in economics.

Hawtrey's first book on economics, *Good and Bad Trade* (1913), focused on the trade cycle. He developed a theory that variations in the money supply, or the amount of currency, in an economy cause the cycle of growth, peak, recession, and bottom in economic expansions and contractions. His ideas differed from those of the Continental (French, German) economists, who believed that the factors driving the phases of the business cycle were so-called real (that is, non-monetary) phenomena.

In contrast to the Continental economists, Hawtrey followed the Anglo-American tradition, which emphasized psychological and other factors as the causes of economic cycles. This view was built on the teachings of Alfred Marshall, who argued that economic as opposed to monetary factors such as business confidence and credit can cause disequilibrium in an economy, which in turn drives the business cycle.

Hawtrey's next and very influential book, *Currency and Credit*, was published in 1919 (revised 1927, 1950). It presented a purely monetary theory of the economic cycle. The most important of its several distinctive features was its stress on "effective demand," meaning the total of both consumption spending and investment spending. Hawtrey linked changes in effective demand with changes in the money supply and showed how this relationship caused changes in credit availability and production output within business cycles. He also noted that expansions and contractions in available credit within an economy did not generally occur at the same time as changes in prices and wages. Such time differences created lags in the economy, which caused the phases of the business cycle.

Hawtrey's ideas had a great deal of influence in the United States, especially during the Great Depression, when American economists applied his monetary theory to the actions of the Federal Reserve. He died in London on March 21, 1975.

Andrew J. Waskey

See also: Classical Theories and Models; Financial Modeling of the Business Cycle; Marshall, Alfred; Neoclassical Theories and Models.

Further Reading

Capie, Forrest, Geoffrey Edward Woods, and R.G. Hawtrey. *The Development of Monetary Theory, 1920 & 1930.* Vol. 1 [1938]. London: Routledge, 2000.
Davis, E.G. "R.G. Hawtrey (1879–1975)." In *Pioneers of Modern Economics in Britain*, 203–233, ed. D.P. O'Brien and J.R. Presley. London: Macmillan, 1981.
Deutscher, Patrick. *R.G. Hawtrey and the Development of Macroeconomics.* Ann Arbor: University of Michigan Press, 1990.
Saulnier, Raymond Joseph. *Contemporary Monetary Theory: Studies of Some Recent Theories of Money, Prices, and Production.* New York: Columbia University Press, 1938.

Hayek, Friedrich August von (1899–1992)

An Austrian-born economist who spent much of his working life in Great Britain, the United States, and West Germany, Friedrich August Hayek is best known in economic circles for his critique of socialism and his advocacy of free-market economics. The Nobel Prize–winning economist was also something of a Renaissance man, making important contributions to the fields of political theory and psychology over a career that spanned most of the twentieth century. His most famous work, *The Road to Serfdom* (1944), which argued that collectivist economics inevitably lead to political tyranny, was a major influence on the thinking of libertarians and such later free-market conservatives as Ronald Reagan and Margaret Thatcher.

The son of a doctor, Hayek was born in Vienna on May 8, 1899. After serving in the Austro-Hungarian army in World War I, he attended the University of Vienna, where he earned doctorates in both law and political science in the early 1920s. His first academic publications came in the field of psychology, but he gradually drifted toward economics, influenced by the strongly free-market, antisocialist theories of Ludwig von Mises, a leading light of the Austrian school of economics. He moved to the London School of Economics in 1931 and became a British subject in 1938 after Austria merged with Nazi Germany. Twelve years later, he moved to the University of Chicago, where he helped make the economics department a major force in free-market theory. In 1962, Hayek returned to Europe, becoming professor of economics at the University of Freiburg, West Germany, and the University of Salzburg, Austria. He died in Freiburg on March 23, 1992.

Hayek began his professional career amid a great debate in Europe over the ability of a socialist economy to allocate resources as effectively as a capitalist economy. Those on the left side of the political spectrum argued that governments could create and run large and efficient enterprises by incorporating capitalist-style pricing mechanisms while avoiding the free market's tendency to concentrate too much power in the hands of wealthy capitalists. Building on the work of Austrian school economists, who emphasized subjective individual decision making in setting market prices, Hayek argued that many of the factors that went into investment decisions were beyond the ken of individuals and individual firms. Only through the unfettered free market as a whole—consisting of individuals driven by the profit motive and fear of business failure—could resources be effectively allocated. These insights have provided the foundation for modern economists' understanding of the key role of information—how it is dispersed and how some economic agents may know more than others—in economic decision making.

Like other economists, Hayek also had to contend with what appeared to be a failure of the free market in the 1930s—why, during the Great Depression, the marketplace seemed so ineffective in allocating resources efficiently, as evidenced by the widespread idling of factories and workers. In his 1931 book *Prices and Production*, Hayek laid the blame on central banks, such as the U.S. Federal Reserve, for driving interest rates to artificially low levels. This led businesses to over-invest—especially in long-term projects where interest rates played a greater role in the decision making—leading to an artificial boom. Eventually, the boom could not be sustained and a bust ensued. This was not necessarily bad, in Hayek's view, as it would reallocate resources to more efficient activities. In effect, Hayek said that the way to avoid recessions was to avoid policies that led to economic booms. In other words, governments should use monetary policy to smooth out the business cycle. Hayek also came to

A proponent of the unfettered free market and a principal rival of John Maynard Keynes, Austrian-born economist Friedrich August von Hayek blamed economic downturns on government interference in the market system. He won the Nobel Prize in 1974. *(Hulton Archive/Stringer/Getty Images)*

disagree with John Maynard Keynes's argument that governments can help lift economies out of recession by borrowing and spending to stimulate demand. That, Hayek maintained, would increase the money supply and lead to runaway inflation.

Hayek also had to contend with pro-socialist critics of capitalism who gained increasing legitimacy as the Great Depression persisted. Socialists argued that government planners could effectively run an economy by collecting and analyzing data and then making appropriate decisions. But like other members of the Austrian school, Hayek maintained that such mathematical modeling of the economy was an illusion, since the data were so extensive and largely based on subjective decision making as to evade analysis by experts. Only the free market, in his opinion, could utilize such data effectively.

With the *The Road to Serfdom*, Hayek pursued another tack in his assault on socialist thinking. In that work, he argued that government control of the economy is a form of totalitarianism, since the ability to make money and provide for oneself is the central pillar of freedom. Moreover, he said, while democratic socialists, like those in Britain, might have good intentions, they were embarking on a slippery slope by trying to regulate and control the free market. Such tinkering, he wrote, inevitably leads to political tyranny and the gross inefficiencies that were a hallmark of centrally planned economies, such as that of the Soviet Union.

In the first decades after World War II, Hayek became a kind of voice in the wilderness as Keynesian economics came to be adopted, in various forms, in most of the world's major noncommunist industrial economies. Nevertheless, he was awarded the Nobel Prize for Economics in 1974, along with the Swede Gunnar Myrdal, for his work on the role of money in the business cycle. With the persistent recession of the 1970s, which seemed to defy Keynesian nostrums, and the triumph of conservative politics in Britain and the United States during the late 1970s and early 1980s, Hayek was restored to influence and widely celebrated. And while the recession of 2007–2009 revived interest in Keynesian economics, Hayek's work on how central banks can, by excessively loose monetary policy, trigger wild swings in the business cycle seemed as pertinent as ever.

James Ciment

See also: Austrian School; Mises, Ludwig von.

Further Reading
Caldwell, Bruce. *Hayek's Challenge: An Intellectual Biography of F.A. Hayek.* Chicago: University of Chicago Press, 2004.

Feser, Edward. *The Cambridge Companion to Hayek.* New York: Cambridge University Press, 2006.

Hayek, Friedrich. *The Road to Serfdom.* Chicago: University of Chicago Press, 1980.

Hedge Funds

Like a mutual fund, a hedge fund is an open-ended investment fund in which various parties pool their money and turn it over to a manager who places it in a portfolio of investments. In both cases, investors typically pay management fees, though with hedge funds these are often tied to performance as well as to the net asset value of the fund. As hedge funds are private endeavors, largely outside government purview, it is difficult to precisely gauge how much money they control. Estimates in late 2009 put that sum at about $2 trillion worldwide. Economists disagree about the role hedge funds play in the business cycle. Some say their emphasis on speculation drives up asset prices to unsustainable levels while others argue that because the funds are so heavily leveraged, they contribute to financial instability.

Hedge funds differ from mutual funds in several key ways. First, hedge funds, which are usually limited partnerships rather than general funds, involve smaller pools of investors and have minimum investment amounts far higher than those of mutual funds, putting them out of reach of most middle-class investors. In addition, since 2004, hedge fund investors must be accredited by the government as having a certain amount of income, wealth, and investment experience. Third, hedge funds can engage in certain types of investments, such as buying derivatives and options and short-selling stocks, which mutual funds are prohibited from by law.

Investors choose hedge funds over mutual funds for two basic reasons. First, because hedge funds can engage in more speculative investment, they potentially offer far higher returns over a shorter period of time. Second, because hedge funds can engage in short-selling, they offer the potential to make money in a down market, thereby hedging against the rest of the portfolio, which consists of ordinary purchases of securities. In a short sale, the investor, or hedge fund manager, sells a security he has purchased from a third party, promising to buy it back at a later date. If the price goes down, the short-seller pays less money than he sold it for, making a profit on the deal.

Like mutual funds, various hedge funds engage in different kinds of investment strategies. Some focus on regular corporate securities; others on derivatives. Some are global in scope; others focus on a given national market. There are hedge funds that engage in commodity and currency speculation, while others focus on securities in particular economic sectors. In addition, some hedge funds pursue event-driven strategies, others attempt to gauge the direction of markets, and still others engage in arbitrage, attempting to capitalize on price differentials between markets. Some seek to become actively involved in the management of the companies they buy into, while others simply invest.

Hedge funds generally engage in riskier investment activity than mutual funds. Not only does this involve short-selling, purchases of volatile derivatives, and investment in riskier corporate equities—sometimes even buying whole companies—but hedge funds also typically leverage their assets. That is, they borrow large amounts of money against the assets they own, allowing them to engage in even more investment activity. Of course, in leveraging their assets, they become even more exposed should those investments lose money. That is, a hedge fund that borrows $10 against $1 in assets can lose all of its initial assets if the investments fall just 10 percent in value. In 1998, the Connecticut-based hedge fund Long Term Capital Management (LTCM), which was leveraged by a factor of more than 30, nearly failed after suffering losses stemming from the Russian financial crisis. Fearful that the failure of the fund, which invested in all kinds of major financial institutions and financiers, might cause a panic in the credit markets, the Federal Reserve Bank of New York organized a $3.6 billion bailout by various financial institutions. Many financial experts feared that as LTCM sold off its assets, particularly its corporate securities, to pay off its debts, it would lead to a dramatic sell-off of such securities, a subsequent collapse in prices that would force other investors to sell their stocks. Ultimately, said some, the collapse of LTCM could have resulted in a stock market crash of such scope as to trigger a recession in the larger economy.

Since hedge funds are private entities and investors in them are presumed to be wealthier and more sophisticated, there is far less government oversight and regulation of the funds and those who manage them, thereby adding to the risk investors sustain. Specifically, mutual funds are regulated by the Securities and Exchange Commission (SEC), while hedge funds are not. In addition, hedge funds lack the transparency of mutual funds, often making it difficult for investors to divine the reasoning behind the investment decision making of managers.

The origin of the modern hedge fund dates back to 1948. It was the brainchild of Australian-born U.S. financial journalist and sociologist Alfred Jones, who realized that the risk associated with long-term stock positions could be mitigated through short-selling. Four years later, Jones reorganized his fund along lines similar to current hedge funds, turning it into a limited partnership and adding incentive fees for the managing partner.

But Jones's business remained unique until profiled by *Fortune* magazine in 1966, which noted that his fund significantly outperformed every mutual fund on the market. Two years later, there were well over 100 hedge funds in the United States alone. Losses during the economically volatile 1970s kept the hedge fund market small until a new journalistic profile in 1986 once again touted the phenomenal returns of some funds. By this time, many hedge funds had diversified far beyond Jones's original strategy of balancing long-term corporate equities with short-sold stocks. By the 1990s, hedge funds were employing leading portfolio managers, many of them lured from the mutual fund industry by the huge incentives hedge funds offered.

While hedge funds have won plaudits from

the many investors who have made money from them, they have also come under heavy criticism from several sectors of society. Many economists and financial experts fear that their leveraging activity adds undue risk to financial markets, while labor leaders complain that hedge funds, in pursuit of fast profits, often take over companies only to strip them of their assets—including lucrative pension funds—and then liquidate them, costing jobs.

More recently, like many other financial institutions, hedge funds have been implicated in—and have suffered large losses from—the financial crisis of 2008–2009 and accompanying recession. Many hedge funds had invested heavily in the subprime mortgage–backed securities that were at the vortex of the crisis. As a result, losses and withdrawals from hedge funds have reduced the industry from its estimated $2.5 trillion peak in late 2007 to about $2 trillion by the end of 2009.

Still, say those who support seeing more regulation of hedge funds, including many officials in the Barack Obama administration, hedge funds are of such size as to collectively pose a systemic risk. To rein in what is seen as too free-wheeling an industry, Secretary of the Treasury Timothy Geithner has spoken of requiring larger hedge funds to register with the SEC, as mutual funds are required to do. Hedge funds would then have to disclose their investor positions to regulators, on a confidential basis, allowing the latter to assess whether those investments pose a risk to the financial system as a whole. But hedge fund managers have argued that no such regulation is needed because, unlike huge commercial banks, no single hedge fund is large enough to pose a systemic risk and those who invest in hedge funds are sophisticated and wealthy individuals who can look after their own interests and do not need government regulators to do so. With the Obama administration experiencing increasing headwinds in Congress against more financial industry regulation, it remains open to question whether new controls on hedge funds can be imposed.

James Ciment

See also: Banks, Investment; Long-Term Capital Management; Recession and Financial Crisis (2007–).

Further Reading
Agarwal, Monty. *The Future of Hedge Fund Investing: A Regulatory and Structural Solution for a Fallen Industry.* Hoboken, NJ: John Wiley & Sons, 2009.
Altucher, James. *SuperCash: The New Hedge Fund Capitalism.* Hoboken, NJ: John Wiley & Sons, 2006.
Bookstaber, Richard. *A Demon of Our Own Design: Markets, Hedge Funds, and the Perils of Financial Innovation.* Hoboken, NJ: John Wiley & Sons, 2007.
Burton, Katherine. *Hedge Hunters: How Hedge Fund Masters Survived.* New York: Bloomberg, 2010.
Snider, David, and Chris Howard. *Money Makers: Inside the New World of Finance and Business.* New York: Palgrave Macmillan, 2010.
Temple, Peter. *Hedge Funds: Courtesans of Capitalism.* New York: John Wiley & Sons, 2001.

Hicks, John Richard (1904–1989)

Nobel laureate John Hicks is considered one of the preeminent economists of the twentieth century. Among his many contributions to economic theory, Hicks resolved the fundamental conflicts between business cycle theory and equilibrium theory, which views macroeconomic forces as balancing out one another to establish a steady-state (that is, noncyclical) condition.

John Richard Hicks was born on April 8, 1904, in Warwick, England. He attended Clifton College from 1917 to 1922, and completed his education in 1926 at Balliol College, Oxford, where he studied mathematics, philosophy, politics, and economics. Hicks's specialty during these years was mathematics, and his education was supported by scholarships in that field. In the early 1930s, Hicks was a temporary lecturer in economics at the London School of Economics. Beginning as a labor economist, undertaking qualitative analysis on industrial relations, he soon gravitated toward his passionate interest in the application of quantitative methods to economic theory. His first major work, *The Theory of Wages in 1932* (1932), was followed in 1934 by the publication in *Economica* of "A Reconsideration of the Theory of Value," with R.G.D. Allen.

From 1935 to 1936, Hicks was a fellow of Gonville and Caius College at Cambridge University, where he worked on a manuscript that would be published in 1939 as *Value and Capital* (a second edition was issued in 1946). The book was based on research he had done in London, examining the close interrelationships between markets. His central thesis posits that economic equilibrium, or a balanced economy, is the product of the interaction between mutually canceling forces and that the establishment of such an equilibrium does not preclude—and may be used to help forecast—the cyclical development of an economy. In the book, which helped introduce the notion of general equilibrium theory to English-speaking audiences, Hicks refined general equilibrium theory to accommodate mathematical modeling. As a consequence, he greatly influenced the direction that general economic theory would take, and how it would be taught in the United States and internationally.

Between 1938 and 1946, Hicks taught at Victoria University in Manchester, where he did groundbreaking research on welfare economics and social accounting. In 1939, he and Nicholas Kaldor developed the Kaldor-Hicks measure for economic efficiency. With Kaldor-Hicks, an economic outcome is deemed more efficient if a Pareto optimal outcome (in which at least one person is better off and nobody is worse off) can be reached through a "fairness" compromise. This takes place when compensation is taken from those who have fared better from a particular outcome and given to those who have fared worse. Hicks's work in this area has been applied to a wide range of issues, including assessments of damages for victims of environmental pollution.

Hicks returned to Oxford, first as a research fellow of Nuffield College (1946–1952), then as Drummond Professor of Political Economy (1952–1965), and finally as a research fellow of All Souls College from 1965 until his retirement

in 1971. Knighted in 1964, he was a co-recipient with American economist Kenneth Joseph Arrow of the 1972 Nobel Prize in Economics for his numerous contributions to general economic equilibrium theory and welfare theory. Hicks died in Blockley, England, on May 20, 1989.

Important works by Hicks include *The Social Framework: An Introduction to Economics* (1942), *A Contribution to the Theory of the Trade Cycle* (1950), *A Revision of Demand Theory* (1956), "The Measurement of Real Income," in *Oxford Economic Papers* (1958), *Essays in World Economics* (1959), *Capital and Growth* (1965), and *A Theory of Economic History* (1969).

Andrew J. Waskey

See also: Kaldor, Nicholas; Keynes, John Maynard.

Further Reading
Hamouda, O.F. *John R. Hicks: The Economist's Economist.* Oxford, UK: Blackwell, 1993.
Hicks, John Richard. *Collected Essays on Economic Theory. Vol. 1, Wealth and Welfare.* Cambridge: Harvard University Press, 1981.
———. *Collected Essays on Economic Theory. Vol. 2, Money, Interest, and Wages.* Cambridge: Harvard University Press, 1982.
———. *Collected Essays on Economic Theory. Vol. 3, Classics and Moderns.* Cambridge: Harvard University Press, 1983.

Hoarding

A natural instinct in humans and some animals, hoarding refers to a behavior in which an organism gathers and stores up supplies—usually food—to meet future perceived needs. In this context, hoarding may be seasonal or, in the case of humans, triggered by social or environmental catastrophe or fear of such catastrophe. In humans, hoarding may also reflect compulsive behavior divorced from real-world circumstances. Such pathology aside, hoarding is seen by economists as essentially rational behavior by individual human beings, even if the collective effects can be socially and economically disruptive.

Hoarding has an important role in economics, though it can mean different things in different contexts. The hoarding of goods such as food and other necessities in anticipation of a catastrophe, such as a hurricane, can distort the normal functioning of supply and demand dynamics. Not only can it lead to shortages but, by dramatically increasing the demand side of the equation over a short duration—too short for expansion of manufacturing or distributing to meet the increased need—mass hoarding can drive up prices, leading to intense but usually short-term bouts of inflation. Because such hoarding often occurs in the context of a disaster, governments often impose emergency regulations that make it a crime, or an act subject to civil penalties, to profit unduly from the situation by price gouging. Retailers may also act to limit the impact of emergency hoarding by imposing limits on the amount of critical goods individuals are allowed to buy during the emergency. In addition, during times of war, when certain scarce goods are necessary for defense, governments may impose rationing to limit the amount of those goods an individual can buy over a certain period of time.

Money and Gold

Hoarding may also be triggered by economic crisis. Under these circumstances, the items usually hoarded are money or a commodity, such as gold, that can serve as a substitute for it. The hoarding of money or gold almost always occurs during times of great economic uncertainty, though there are usually opposing factors for hoarding one or the other. Gold is frequently hoarded as a hedge against inflation. During periods in which the money supply is expanding too rapidly—or because social unrest, war, or some other circumstance has led to supply shortages—prices rise quickly as the value of money declines. For thousands of years, gold has possessed a value beyond its intrinsic worth as a metal. If individuals expect money to become less valuable, they may hoard gold as a hedge against inflation, particularly the

virulent and rapid form of inflation known as hyperinflation. In times of inflation, people may also hoard goods as a hedge against future price increases, a process that can feed upon itself as more and more consumers chase fewer and fewer goods, thereby accelerating the inflationary process. Such a situation occurred during the oil crises of the 1970s.

While most individuals recognize inflation as an economic threat, fewer understand the dangers of deflation. Indeed, in some ways, deflation can be more dangerous for an economy than inflation, as long as the latter is kept in relative check. During periods of deflation, the value of money goes up as prices go down. At first glance, deflation sounds like a good thing—commodities, products, and services get cheaper. Indeed, say economists, if it remains moderate, deflation (like inflation) is not necessarily a terrible thing. However, with deflation, the real value of debt increases because the debt is denominated in the nominal currency. The real increase in debt can lead to numerous bankruptcies and an economic crisis.

On the other hand, inflation means that those who owe money can pay it back with funds not worth as much as they were lent in real terms. While this helps borrowers, it can prove disastrous for lenders and for the economy generally, since banks and others lenders may freeze credit if they believe every loan will create a loss on their balance sheets. This, in turn, can choke off the investments businesses are willing and able to make—investments that would lead to growth and employment. As for deflation, it can also disarm the most important tool central banks have for lifting an economy out of recession—that is, lowering interest rates—since deflation may render nominal positive interest rates negative in real terms.

As the economy shrinks in an economic downturn, consumers stop spending and start putting money into savings as a hedge against future needs. During such periods, if there is no deposit insurance, there may be a common perception that banks and other financial institutions are insecure places to put money. If lending institutions are no longer able to offer attractive returns on deposited money, this further encourages customers to take their money out of banks—sometimes quite suddenly. Banks, of course, traditionally earn most of their profit on the spread between the lower interest rate they pay depositors and the higher interest rate they charge lenders. If they do not see profitable lending opportunities, however, then they cannot pay depositors any return and may eventually find themselves insolvent. Moreover, if interest rates are very low, money may just be "hoarded" as it sits in a checking account where it earns no interest and does not serve as a basis for new lending.

Such situations lead to hoarding, that is, keeping money under the proverbial mattress in a noncirculating, nonperforming state. Individuals may also hoard money in anticipation of further drops in prices, making it cost-effective to hold onto money and buy nonessential goods in the future. Such actions, if widespread, can drive down aggregate demand and starve the economy of funds needed for lending and investment.

This was the situation that gripped the United States and many other industrialized economies in the early years of the Great Depression and led British economist John Maynard Keynes to develop his critique of the equilibrium theory of classical economics. According to the latter view, the forces of supply and demand always lead to an equilibrium of high output and low unemployment. Keynes, instead, argued that aggregate demand can fall so precipitously—in part, because of hoarding—that an equilibrium may be reached in which output is low and unemployment is high. Keynes then argued that only the government has the capacity in such a circumstance to lift aggregate demand by the central bank pumping money into the economy or through fiscal policy, which Keynes preferred.

"Cornering Markets"

Finally, hoarding can also refer to the effort by investors to capture a market in a critical commodity. The idea here is that, by buying up all or most of some commodity and hoarding it for a time, a supplier of goods or an investor in them can corner the market on a particular item, thereby driving up its price and gaining a windfall profit. Efforts to corner a market can be successful in local situations or in exceptional circumstances.

THE "BOY OF THE PERIOD" STIRRING UP THE ANIMALS.

In an 1869 political cartoon, financier Jay Gould (left) attempts to corner the gold market, represented by bulls and bears in a cage. President Ulysses Grant (rear) carries a bag of federal gold stores released on the open market to counter Gould's ploy. (*The Granger Collection, New York*)

In the early 2000s, for example, energy companies such as Enron were able to create a situation in California's newly deregulated electricity market in which they were able to hold back the flow of electrons—in a sense, hoarding it—thereby compelling utilities and other consumers to pay highly inflated rates for electricity. This cornering effort was particularly effective since electricity is essential and cannot be effectively stored. Enron ended up generating huge windfall profits from the episode, though not enough to save the company when its huge debt load and poor accounting practices drove it into bankruptcy shortly thereafter, in late 2001.

In general, however, efforts to corner markets are usually futile in the long run, for two basic reasons. First, because cornering the market drives up prices, it spurs those not otherwise economically motivated to make an extra effort to produce or find the cornered commodity. Second, since cornering a market on a vital commodity can cause social or economic disruption, it may lead to collective or governmental action to prevent the effort from succeeding. Such was the case in 1869, when American financiers Jay Gould and Jim Fisk attempted to corner the gold market, triggering a decision by the federal government to release part of its gold stores for sale on the open market.

Ulku Yuksel

See also: Confidence, Consumer and Business; Consumption; Savings and Investment.

Further Reading

Burdekin, Richard C.K., and Pierre L. Siklos, eds. *Deflation: Current and Historical Perspectives.* New York: Cambridge University Press, 2004.

Friedman, Milton, and Anna Jacobson Schwartz. *The Great Contraction, 1929–1933.* Princeton, NJ: Princeton University Press, 2009.

Jarrow, Robert A. "Market Manipulation, Bubbles, Corners, and Short Squeezes." *Journal of Finance and Quantitative Analysis* 27:3 (September 1992): 311–336.

McLean, Bethany, and Peter Elkind. *The Smartest Guys in the Room: The Amazing Rise and Scandalous Fall of Enron.* New York: Portfolio, 2004.

Renehan, Edward. *Dark Genius of Wall Street: The Misunderstood Life of Jay Gould, King of the Robber Barons.* New York: Basic Books, 2005.

Siklos, Pierre L., ed. *The Economics of Deflation.* Northampton, MA: Edward Elgar, 2006.

House Financial Services Committee

The U.S. House Committee on Financial Services (or House Banking Committee) is the second-largest committee in the House of Representatives. It oversees the entire financial services industry, including the securities, insurance, banking, and housing industries. The committee also oversees the work of the Federal Reserve (Fed), the Department of the Treasury, the Securities and Exchange Commission, and other financial services regulators.

History and the Committee System

The House Committee on Financial Services (HFSC) was created in 1865 as the Banking and Currency Committee, which assumed responsibilities spun off from the Ways and Means Committee (which still has responsibility for tax, tariff, and revenue raising–related issues). It assumed its current name in 1968. Such congressional committees are legislative subunits of their respective branches of Congress, and especially since the early twentieth century they have acted with increasing autonomy. President Woodrow Wilson famously said that "Congress in session is Congress on public exhibition; Congress in its committee rooms is Congress at work." The jurisdiction of the American legislature is so broad that no one can be well versed on every issue, nor does the legislative process permit time for all representatives to become well versed on the issues underlying each bill as it is introduced; this is especially true in the House, where terms are only two years. Committees meet to review legislative matters pertaining to their area of focus. The current structure of congressional committees dates from the 1946 Legislative Reorganization Act, making the HFSC one of 21 House committees; there are 20 Senate committees and 4 joint committees with members from both branches.

The HFSC and Its Subcommittees

The HFSC, then, is extremely influential in legislation dealing with the financial services industry, which includes banking, housing, insurance, and securities, as well as oversight of regulators and federal bodies related to that industry, including the Securities and Exchange Commission (SEC), the Treasury Department, and the Federal Reserve. Committee members generally serve on more than one subcommittee—for example, a congressman might chair the Subcommittee on Oversight and Investigations and also serve on the Subcommittee on Financial Institutions and Consumer Credit. As of the 111th Congress (2009–2011), there are six subcommittees:

The Subcommittee on Capital Markets, Insurance, and Government-Sponsored Enterprises reviews matters related to the securities industry and capital markets (as well as bodies like the SEC and the New York Stock Exchange), the insurance industry apart from health insurance, and government-sponsored enterprises like Fannie Mae and Freddie Mac (though not Ginnie Mae).

The Subcommittee on Financial Institutions and Consumer Credit oversees financial regulators like the Federal Deposit Insurance Corporation (FDIC) and the Federal Reserve (Fed), the banking system and its health and efficiency, and all matters related to consumer credit.

The Subcommittee on Housing and Community Opportunity oversees the Department of Housing and Urban Development (HUD), matters related to housing, government-sponsored insurance programs, and Ginnie Mae (the Government National Mortgage Association, a government-sponsored enterprise within HUD).

The Subcommittee on Domestic Monetary Policy and Technology handles domestic monetary policy and those bodies related to it or that impact it, as well as matters related to currency (including the Bureau of the Mint).

The Subcommittee on International Monetary Policy and Trade oversees international monetary policy and matters related to international trade and institutions, like the International Monetary Fund (IMF) and the World Bank.

The Subcommittee on Oversight and Investigations conducts the oversight of all matters within the HFSC's jurisdiction.

The Housing Bubble of 2002–2007

The previous chair of HFSC, from 2001 to 2007 and thus during the housing boom and the early stages of the financial crisis, was Mike Oxley (R-ID), best known as the cosponsor of the Sarbanes-Oxley Act of 2002, which strengthened the oversight of public companies in response to the massive accounting fraud scandals of the first few years of the century. The HFSC is the body before which investigations into such cases take place; in the summer of 2002 the HFSC regularly made the news because of the WorldCom hearing. Like other committees, the HFSC has the power to subpoena individuals to appear to testify before the committee; earlier in 2002, Enron chief executive officer Kenneth Lay was compelled to appear before both the HFSC and the Senate Commerce Committee during the Enron hearings that helped inspire Sarbanes-Oxley.

At other times, testimony may be given to the committee in writing. That same summer, Fed chairman Alan Greenspan submitted written testimony to the HFSC stating that the accounting scandals had done no serious harm to the "remarkably efficient and productive economy," and that though they had temporarily undermined investor confidence, that confidence would be regained thanks to the natural economic health of the country.

The Financial Meltdown of 2007–2008

Barney Frank (D-MA) became the chairman of the HFSC in 2007, having previously been the ranking Democrat on the committee. Frank has been criticized for his possible contribution, through his leadership on the HFSC, to the conditions that led to the global financial meltdown of 2007–2008. For instance, he opposed a proposal to create a new administrative agency within the Treasury Department that would have overseen HUD, Fannie Mae, and Freddie Mac. Frank's opposition was on the grounds that the troubles faced by Fannie Mae and Freddie Mac were exaggerated, and that putting them under greater scrutiny would reduce the availability of affordable housing. A few years later, of course, those companies were hit hard by the subprime mortgage crisis and in September 2008 put into receivership by the U.S. government.

On the other hand, Frank did show concern with policies that he felt were leading to economic troubles. For example, he has been critical of the Fed, and was one of the few Democrats to openly criticize Alan Greenspan during the housing boom. Since Greenspan's departure from the Fed in 2006 and the subsequent deflation of the housing market, many economists have joined Frank in assigning some of the blame for the bubble to Greenspan's decisions, including an overly expansive monetary policy.

As chairman of the HFSC, Frank was also instrumental in winning passage of the American Housing Rescue & Foreclosure Prevention Act of 2008 (AHRFPA). Unlike the Troubled Asset Relief Program (TARP), which provided billions in aid to leading financial institutions that were exposed to mortgage-backed securities, the new legislation provided mortgage refinancing assistance to homeowners threatened with foreclosures. Like many on the political left, Frank and members of the Democratic majority on the committee believed that direct aid to mortgagees was the best way to address the critical issue in the financial crisis—the failure of ordinary borrowers to make their mortgage payments for a variety of reasons.

Bill Kte'pi

See also: Regulation, Financial.

Further Reading

House Financial Services Committee Web site: http://financialservices.house.gov.

Weisberg, Stuart E. *Barney Frank: The Story of America's Only Left-Handed, Gay, Jewish Congressman.* Amherst: University of Massachusetts Press, 2009.

Housing

No sector of a nation's economy is more important than housing. Not only are vast amounts of a nation's wealth tied up in housing stock and residential real estate but also housing supports huge industries, including construction, finance, real-estate sales, home improvement, and consumer durables (such as appliances and furniture). For most individuals and households, the purchase of a home is the single-largest investment they will make in their lifetime, and the equity contained in their home represents their greatest asset.

Private homeownership generally is considered to be a positive in most societies, as it is seen as contributing to economic prosperity and social stability. Not surprisingly, many governments, including that of the United States, attempt to promote homeownership through a variety of means, including tax breaks, monetary policy, financial regulation, and transportation policy. In many countries, this has led to a vast expansion of homeownership, particularly since the end of World War II. Moreover, there is a general political consensus that government *should* play a role in homeownership. A minority view, however, holds that government efforts to promote homeownership can have negative consequences, distorting markets and encouraging individuals for whom renting might be a wiser economic choice than purchasing homes.

Housing, of course, is a necessity of life; everyone has to live somewhere. But housing also represents an investment opportunity. Throughout much of modern history, housing has been seen as a sure and steady, though not particularly rapid, means of amassing wealth. That is because housing prices are related to incomes and rents. Generally, when homes become too expensive or when the monthly costs of financing a home far outstrip rents, people refrain from purchasing homes, bringing down their prices. However, when credit becomes loose (easy to obtain), as it did during the mid-2000s, individuals can pay more for homes than their incomes normally would permit. During such periods, housing prices tend to rise more rapidly, leading to a housing "bubble" that inevitably deflates when credit tightens again.

Types and Value

Housing comes in several varieties. The most common form is the residential home for a single household, situated on land that is held in fee simple ownership. These may be detached homes, physically disconnected from other homes, or attached or semi-attached homes, such as townhouses. Condominiums and co-ops represent another form of housing. Condominiums are housing units that are owned by individual households, while the common areas, including the land, are owned collectively by all of the unit owners. In a cooperative, all of the units are owned by a legal entity—typically, a corporation—that is under the ownership of the residents of the co-op. Another major category of housing is manufactured, or mobile, homes. While these may be situated on private parcels of land, most are located in mobile home parks, where the mobile homeowner leases land on which his or her manufactured home sits. A final category of housing—a form of nonprimary residence—is the time-share. Here, a group of owners collectively purchase a residence, usually a condominium, with their shares representing the amount of time they may occupy it.

In the United States, these forms of housing together represented roughly $20 trillion in value in 2010, about 150 percent of annual gross domestic product. Of this total, slightly less than half, or $9.6 trillion, represented equity held by homeowners, while $10.4 trillion consisted of mortgage debt.

Finance

As these figures indicate, to pay for their homes, most people must obtain financing. Typically, most households do not have enough cash on hand to pay the full price of the home, and even when they do, they may choose to keep some of their wealth in more liquid forms than housing. This requires home purchasers to obtain mortgages, which banks offer on different terms.

A traditional mortgage—the kind that dominated housing finance until the 1990s—is a fixed rate, thirty-year mortgage. Usually, the mortgagor must put down 20 percent of the value of the home, which is determined by a government-licensed assessor, at the time of purchase. The mortgagor makes a monthly payment on the loan, which remains the same throughout the thirty-year life of the mortgage. That payment covers the interest—which remains at the same rate for the life of the mortgage—and a portion of the principal. Over time, the percentage of the payment that goes toward paying the interest decreases, and the amount that goes toward paying down the principal increases. Most banks offer variations on the traditional mortgage, such as a fifteen- or twenty-year fixed rate mortgage, which allows the borrower to pay off the mortgage more quickly and usually at a slightly lower rate of interest, though at the cost of a higher monthly payment.

Beginning in the early 1980s, variable rate mortgages were introduced. With these loans, the interest rate is reset periodically based on a margin above an index that represents the cost to the lender of obtaining the borrowed funds. These loans are made at lower initial rates, but the borrower assumes the risk that the interest rate will adjust upward, increasing the payment, at a later date. Variable rate loans are attractive to home buyers who do not expect to own the property for an extended period of time and expect to resell the property before the interest rate adjusts upward.

To encourage homeownership and to increase the number of mortgagors—and, of course, to expand their markets and profitability—financial institutions, including banks as well as monoline institutions specializing in mortgage financing—began to develop new, hybrid forms of mortgages in the 1990s, although many did not become widespread until the 2000s. The most common of these loans is the interest-only adjustable rate mortgage (ARM). With an interest-only ARM, the mortgagor pays a low initial interest rate for a fixed period of time, typically one to five years. For that period of time, the mortgagor is required to pay only the interest on the loan—no payments are made on the principal—allowing for a substantially lower monthly payment. At the end of the introductory period, two things happen. First, the mortgagor is required to begin paying a portion of the principal each month. Second, the interest rate adjusts, usually upward, in relation to an index that reflects the cost of funds to the lender. What this means for the mortgagor is a much higher monthly payment. During the housing boom of the early and mid-2000s, many of these ARM loans were subprime mortgages, that is, mortgages offered to borrowers with little or bad credit history—individuals who traditionally would not have been able to obtain a mortgage.

Another hybrid mortgage that was offered during the 2000s was the Alt-A, or "stated income" mortgage, which was intended for borrowers who had good credit but could not document their income (such as self-employed workers and employees who work on commission). The loan was made on the basis of the borrower's stated income, with no verification. The number of Alt-A loans increased dramatically during the housing price run-up of 2005–2007, leading many to suspect that these loans were really "liar" loans. These mortgages contributed to the housing boom and its later bust.

Homeowners, of course, can refinance their homes, and many choose to do so, especially when interest rates are falling or when the amount of equity in the home as a result of rising value allows the owner to secure a lower interest rate. In other words, because the mortgagee is taking on less risk—the mortgagor now may be taking out a loan for 50 percent of the home's value as opposed to 90 percent—it can offer a lower rate. This offers two benefits to the mortgagor: a lower monthly payment and/or cash in hand, if the mortgagor decides to take out a loan for a larger amount than is owed. Such a transaction is known as a cash-out refinancing.

Finally, a homeowner may take out a second mortgage, or home equity loan. That is, as the mortgagor pays down the principal or as the value of the home rises, the owner's equity (share of ownership) in the home grows. Equity represents collateral that a mortgagor can use to borrow more money from a lender. With a second mortgage, the borrower usually pays a fixed interest rate. But a second mortgage is "second" in more ways than one. Not only does it come after a first mortgage, but also it is second in line should the mortgagor default. That is, if a mortgagor cannot make the payment on either of the mortgages, the holder of the first mortgage is first in line to secure its exposure through seizure of the property. Because of the greater risk involved with second mortgages, they usually come with a higher interest rate. The same risk to the lender applies to home equity loans, though in this case, the interest rate usually is tied to an index that reflects the cost of funds to the lender and requires the borrower to make interest payments as long as he or she owns the property securing the home equity loan.

Historically, mortgagees, or mortgage originators, such as commercial banks and savings and loan institutions, held onto mortgages for the life of the loan, earning their profit from the margin between interest payments and their cost of funds. Of course, this exposes to them default risk. That is, when a mortgagor cannot make his or her monthly payment, the holder of the mortgage can pursue legal means to seize the property, which the mortgagor offered as security to obtain the loan in the first place. When the mortgagee moves to seize the property, the property is said to be in foreclosure. Upon obtaining title to the property, the mortgagee usually sells the property to recoup whatever funds it can to cover the unpaid loan.

Another risk that lenders face in offering long-term, fixed rate mortgages is the risk that the interest rate will go up, meaning that the cost of funds to provide the mortgage exceeds the interest rate the lender is earning on the mortgage. This is called interest rate risk, and the longer the term of the loan, the greater the risk. Thus, it would be advantageous to lenders to be able to sell the mortgages in secondary markets or to a government agency to reduce the interest rate risk and to get more funds to originate more mortgages. (Lenders earn income from fees, such as underwriting and processing fees, that they charge to mortgagors.)

Beginning in the early 1980s, Fannie Mae (Federal National Mortgage Association) and Freddie Mac (Federal Home Loan Mortgage Corporation), government-sponsored enterprises launched by the federal government, started buying mortgages from lenders and developing mortgage-backed securities of various types. This allowed banks and other mortgagees to bundle mortgages and sell them to investors, thereby spreading out the default and interest rate risk. The idea behind mortgage-backed securities was that this process would lower the level of exposure and hence the risk taken on by mortgagees. And, as basic economics dictate, where there is a lower risk, there are lower returns. In other words, by lowering their risk, mortgage originators would lower the returns, based on interest rates, that they were willing to accept from mortgagors.

Government Homeownership Policies

The U.S. government actively encourages homeownership. But repurchasing mortgages and securitizing them, as Fannie Mae and Freddie Mac do, is just one of the many direct and indirect means by which the government does so. Because most homeowners finance their homes, interest rates are crucial to homeownership. By lowering those rates through the monetary policy tools at its disposal, the Federal Reserve and other central banks around the world can make financing a mortgage less costly, thereby expanding the number of individuals who can buy homes and, as most mortgagors are primarily concerned with the monthly payment they are required to make on their mortgage, increasing the value of the home that a given borrower can afford.

Tax policy also comes into play in encouraging homeownership. Since the income tax was introduced in 1913, it has included a home mortgage deduction. That is, a mortgagor can deduct the interest payments made on a primary residence from his or her taxable income. (The United States is not alone in offering a mortgage interest deduction, but it offers some of the most generous terms.) In 1986, changes to the tax code enhanced the value of the mortgage interest deduction, thereby encouraging mortgage lending and hence homeownership. Prior to that year, the interest paid on all personal loans—from student loans to credit card bills—was deductible. By limiting the deduction to mortgage interest only, the government influenced borrowing practices, prompting many people to take out larger mortgages, with greater interest payments, and using the cash saved to pay for other purchases or pay down other loans.

The U.S. government has been especially active over the past fifty or so years in encouraging homeownership. Since the 1960s, the government has instituted a number of fair housing laws—for example, forbidding racial covenants that allow home sellers or real-estate agents to discriminate against individuals to whom they sell or offer homes. In addition, with the Community Reinvestment Act of 1977, the government put in place penalties on financial institutions that engage in redlining—that is, limiting or refusing loans in so-called high-risk areas, usually minority neighborhoods in the inner city.

Finally, there are a variety of indirect means by which governments can encourage homeownership. Chief among these in the United States is transportation policy. By providing massive financing for limited-access, high-speed roadways through the Interstate Highway System from city centers to outlying areas in the decades after World War II, the federal government allowed for the development of new suburbs, where detached, residential homes were both cheaper and more easily available.

Economic Impact

Like that other great consumer purchase, the automobile—which generates economic activity in the steel, rubber, and other industries—housing has a major ripple effect throughout the economy. Mortgages sustain a significant portion of the financial sector in most countries. There is also the real-estate industry—that is, the marketing and selling of homes—which accounts for roughly 500,000 jobs in the United States.

Of course, there is more to housing than finance and sales. The houses people live in have to be built by someone, as does the infrastructure of streets, utilities, and other services that support those homes. Revenues in the residential construction industry amounted to roughly $300 billion in 2007, with the total number of individuals working in the industry estimated at 800,000, although most economists believe these numbers have come down significantly as the decline in the housing market has deepened. In addition, housing remodeling remains a major industry, with roughly $32 billion in annual revenue and 280,000 workers. Finally, there are all of the furniture and consumer durables, such as refrigerators and washers and dryers, with which people fill their homes. Electronic and appliance stores did roughly $110 billion in sales in 2007, while furniture and furnishing establishments did roughly $33 billion in sales.

Beyond these specific industries, housing has a broader impact on national economies and societies. Most sociologists confirm that homeownership has a positive impact on neighborhoods and communities—that is, when people have a vested economic interest in maintaining the property value of their homes, they work harder to ensure that their neighborhoods remain clean and safe. This is one reason why governments encourage homeownership—particularly in lower-income areas—through the many programs and policies noted earlier.

In terms of the economy, housing equity represents a vast pool of wealth. When housing prices are rising and equity is accumulating, people tend to spend more and save less because they feel that their financial situation is more secure. As consumer spending generates roughly two-thirds of all economic activity in most advanced economies, the effect of rising house prices ripples throughout the economy. Falling house prices, of course, can have the opposite effect. Moreover, many economists point out that housing plays a major role in the labor market as well. Exceedingly high house prices make it difficult for communities to attract workers, while falling house prices may discourage workers from moving to new locales to find jobs or better-paying work because they fear losing the money they have invested in their homes. Such phenomena can produce labor market rigidity that dampens economic growth or recovery. For these reasons, some economists argue that homeownership is not an unalloyed good for economies and societies and that governments should rethink the incentives they provide to homeowners and potential homebuyers.

James Ciment

See also: Housing Booms and Busts; Mortgage Markets and Mortgage Rates.

Further Reading

Floyd, Charles F., and Marcus T. Allen. *Real Estate Principles.* 9th ed. Chicago: Dearborn Real Estate Education, 2008.

Guttentag, Jack. *The Mortgage Encyclopedia: An Authoritative Guide to Mortgage Programs, Practices, Prices, and Pitfalls.* New York: McGraw-Hill, 2004.

Morris, Charles R. *The Trillion Dollar Meltdown: Easy Money, High Rollers, and the Great Credit Crash.* New York: PublicAffairs, 2008.

Shiller, Robert J. *Subprime Solution: How Today's Global Financial Crisis Happened and What to Do About It.* Princeton, NJ: Princeton University Press, 2008.

Housing and Urban Development, Department of

The federal government of the United States has undertaken efforts to provide housing assistance to those with low incomes since the 1930s. In the 1960s, however, most federal efforts toward housing were brought under the administration of the newly formed U.S. Department of Housing and Urban Development (HUD). A cabinet-level agency, HUD was created as part of the Department of Housing and Urban Development Act of 1965 and was given the broad charter to develop and coordinate U.S. government policy toward housing and urban concerns.

Upon its creation in 1964, HUD took over the operation and coordination of the many existing federal government housing programs. Thus HUD adopted the missions of the departments that came under its control, such as the Federal Housing Administration (FHA), which was created in 1934 to provide a uniform system of mortgage insurance. Since the creation of HUD did not interrupt many of the programs that existed prior to 1965, scholars often treat the pre-1965 programs as HUD programs, although HUD was not yet in existence.

HUD's initial focus in the mid-1960s was on three key areas: (1) increasing homeownership rates for all Americans, (2) assisting low-income renters in finding and affording safe and adequate housing, and (3) improving the condition of U.S. cities. Fighting racial discrimination would later be added to HUD's mission as part of the Civil Rights Act of 1968. Title VIII of the act prohibited any form of housing discrimination based on race, religion, or national origin, and gave HUD the duty to investigate violations of the law. Finally, in 1987 Congress made HUD responsible for assisting homeless individuals with housing and support services.

HUD has approached the objective of increasing homeownership in a variety of different ways.

Homeownership was encouraged through the creation of mortgage insurance (first started as part of the FHA in 1934). By insuring private mortgages against the risk of default, the federal government created an incentive for lenders to extend more loans to a larger pool of potential homeowners. This likely contributed in part to the homeownership rate's rise from almost 44 percent in 1940 to nearly 63 percent in 1970, although a much larger factor was probably the tremendous increase in household incomes during the 1960s.

Today, HUD still promotes homeownership through its management of the FHA and its mortgage insurance programs. In addition, HUD has regulatory oversight of Fannie Mae and Freddie Mac, the two government-sponsored enterprises (GSEs) that exist to help expand homeownership opportunities. Fannie Mae was established in 1938 to help provide mortgages to low-income households, while Freddie Mac was created in 1970 to broaden the secondary mortgage market and thus increase the amount of funding available for new mortgages.

Assistance for low-income renters was initially provided through public housing. Public housing is housing that is owned and operated by the government. Prior to the creation of HUD, public housing in the United States was the primary way that the federal government provided housing assistance to the poor. Beginning with the creation of HUD, however, the link between low-income subsidies and government ownership began to be severed. Through the Section 23 Leased Housing Program, HUD began in the early 1960s to lease housing units from private landlords and rent them out to low-income individuals at a subsidized rate.

The health and vibrancy of U.S. cities was also addressed, in part, through the public housing program. In the 1960s, much of what critics would call "substandard" housing was in cities. Through HUD and its various departments, grants were provided to cities for so-called slum clearance and redevelopment. Public housing units for low-income city residents were typically part of the redevelopment. More recently, however, urban redevelopment programs have become more decentralized and have tried to provide incentives for private redevelopment in certain areas of cities, typically known as Empowerment Zones.

As HUD is the manager of public housing in the United States, criticism of this public policy often falls on the department itself. Much of the research investigating the theoretical benefits of such projects has concluded that the magnitude of provision is probably unwarranted, and perhaps even counterproductive. Many of the health, environmental, economic, and social problems that public housing was intended to help resolve have been linked to the nature of public housing projects. In a 2006 ranking of New York City's ten worst landlords published in *The Village Voice*, HUD topped the list. Furthermore, the success stories of urban revitalization programs have been marred by accusations that they gentrify urban areas, causing the poor to be displaced rather than becoming long-term beneficiaries.

HUD's regulatory responsibility over Fannie Mae and Freddie Mac has come under fire for helping cause the 2008 financial panic. In trying to meet its mission of expanding homeownership to minorities and low-income households, HUD required these GSEs to purchase more of the loans made to subprime borrowers. To do this, HUD allowed the GSEs to count mortgage-backed securities for subprime loans toward their affordable housing credits. As a result, the GSEs ended up holding the securities instead of the loans, which was problematic because of the increased risk associated with these securities. Note that Fannie Mae and Freddie Mac were put into conservatorship by the federal government on September 7, 2008. Critics have also accused HUD of inadvertently encouraging lax mortgage lending and underwriting standards, a charge that HUD officials deny.

Joshua Hall and Justin Ross

See also: Fannie Mae and Freddie Mac; Federal Housing Administration; Housing; Housing Booms and Busts.

Further Reading

Bachhuber, Jay, and Samara Smith. "HUD." *The Village Voice*, June 27, 2006.

Department of Housing and Urban Development Web site: www.hud.gov.

Hall, Joshua, and Matt Ryan. "The Economics of Government Housing Assistance for the Poor." In *Housing America: Building Out of a Crisis*, ed. R. Holcombe and B. Powell. New Brunswick, NJ: Transaction, 2009.

Leonnig, Carol D. "How HUD Mortgage Policy Fed the Crisis." *Washington Post*, June 10, 2008.

"63 Years of Federal Action in Housing and Urban Development." *Cityscape: A Journal of Policy Development and Research* 1:3 (1995): vi–ix.

Thompson, Lawrence. *A History of HUD.* http://mysite.verizon.net/hudhistory/. Accessed March 2009.

Housing Booms and Busts

In ordinary economic times, housing represents a relatively staid market, with prices rising steadily but gradually over the years. Prices are kept in check by incomes—when prices rise too much, people cannot afford to buy homes—and by rents—if monthly mortgage payments rise too much in relation to rents, people will choose the latter option for their housing needs. In addition, the housing market has built-in "frictions" (an economic term for things that slow or hamper business and trade) that limit speculation. That is, buying and selling a house involves large expenses—broker's commissions, fees, moving costs—hassles—packing, finding new schools for one's children—and sentiments—neighborhood friends, memories—that slow people's propensity to buy and sell their homes to cash in on market trends.

But there are periods when housing prices fluctuate dramatically, when speculation in homes and other forms of residential real estate influences the market more than usual, and when housing valuations go up rapidly and then fall off suddenly. While there have been a number of housing booms and busts in modern economic history, none has involved more money and none has been more widespread than the boom and bust that occurred during the first decade of the twenty-first century. As with any other episode of speculation, economists debate the causes of this most recent housing bubble, but most agree that excessive financial leveraging was the critical factor. Money for investment in housing, the argument goes, simply was too cheap and easy to obtain, creating a sudden upsurge in demand that drove up prices and led to more speculative investment in housing. When credit became tighter, as is inevitable, prices dropped just as rapidly.

Historical Ups and Downs

With its abundant land, rapidly growing population, and entrepreneurial spirit, the United States has experienced many speculative real-estate episodes in its history. Indeed, many of the great booms and busts of the country's first century of existence—including those of the 1790s, 1810s, and 1830s—were driven largely by people engaged in the rapid buying and selling of lands on the urban fringes of major cities, in lots proposed for new towns in the West or for farmland. Inevitably, the booms led to busts. With much of the financing coming from European and particularly British banks—through the U.S. financial system—the booms inevitably turned to busts when overseas bankers became concerned about financial leveraging.

By the early twentieth century, with the United States emerging as the world's largest creditor nation, financial bubbles were generated by excesses of domestic capital flowing into the housing market. A stunning example of a speculative bubble occurred in coastal Florida during the 1920s, as middle-class investors from around the country, prospering from a booming economy, poured capital into residential land in Miami and other growing Florida cities. Land prices skyrocketed, leading more speculators to move in, and sending prices up further still—until infrastructure problems, weather catastrophes, and exceedingly high prices began to scare away new investors, causing prices to plummet.

Still, for all of these episodes, owning one's own home remained within the financial reach of only a minority of Americans through World War II. In 1940, just 44 percent of all families lived in houses that they owned. Prior to and during the Great Depression, mortgages were expensive, often requiring down payments of as much as 50 percent of the price of the home, short repayment periods, and a balloon payment at the end. To expand homeownership, the federal government established the Federal National Mortgage Association (Fannie Mae) in 1938. The agency bought mortgages from banks, allowing those institutions to offer more mortgages and on easier terms—often with just 20 percent down, a thirty-year payment period, and no balloon payment at the end. In 1944, the Servicemen's Readjustment Act, or GI Bill, offered low-interest loans to veterans for the purchase of homes. These programs worked: by 1970, homeownership had expanded to 65 percent, even amid a rapidly growing population, and remained at that level through the early 2000s.

Despite the increasing demand created by the growing prosperity of middle-class families, house prices in the 1950s and 1960s grew steadily but unspectacularly. The median price climbed from about $55,000 in 1950 to about $80,000 in 1970 (figures in 2009 dollars), a gain of 54 percent, or an average of 2.7 percent per year. House prices continued to climb steadily over the next few decades, reaching $150,000 in 2000, a rise of about 87 percent, or 2.9 annually. This steady rise, however, disguises a number of spikes in the mid-1970s and mid- to late 1980s, as well as some significant declines, including those associated with the high interest rates and recessionary economy of the late 1970s and early 1980s and the economic downturn of the early 1990s. However, during the period from 2000 to 2007—the height of the most recent housing bubble—the median home price rose from $150,000 to $266,000.

Origins of the Housing Boom

A number of factors, originating in both the public and private sectors, explain this spectacular run-up in prices. All of these forces contributed to a significant increase in financial leveraging—that is, a huge increase in the amount of credit available for home financing and in the amount of borrowing—which led to a dramatic drop in the cost of that credit. With so much cheap money pouring into the housing market, economists argue, it was all but inevitable that home prices would rise quickly and dramatically.

The origins of the housing boom and bust of the 2000s go back roughly forty years to the federal government's decision in 1968 to turn Fannie Mae into a private shareholder-owned, government-sponsored enterprise. At the same time, the government created the Government National Mortgage Association (Ginnie Mae), a government-owned corporation that continued to guarantee mortgages for new and low-income homebuyers. This assured those holding the mortgages that they would be paid their principal and interest, allowing issuers to offer mortgages on better terms.

In 1970, the federal government created a new government-sponsored enterprise, the Federal Home Loan Mortgage Corporation (Freddie Mac), to provide competition for Fannie Mae. Around the same time, Fannie Mae expanded the range of mortgages it could buy. Then, in 1977, Congress passed the Community Reinvestment Act, which penalized financial institutions that failed to provide mortgages in low-income, minority neighborhoods. All of these actions were designed to increase the number of homeowners, especially among those sectors of the population—the working class and minorities—who previously had been unable to obtain mortgages. Together, these agencies helped expand the secondary mortgage market, including the market for bundled mortgage-backed securities. Over subsequent decades, both Fannie Mae and Freddie Mac expanded the types of mortgages they bought and marketed as securities, including, by the 1990s and 2000s, mortgages given to borrowers with less than sterling credit. These would come to be known as subprime mortgages.

The secondary mortgage market is critical to housing around the world because it allows mortgage originators, such as banks, savings and loan institutions, and monoline companies (those specializing in mortgage lending), to offer more mortgages by selling existing ones. It also ensures that the risk inherent in the primary mortgage market—specifically, default and foreclosure risk—is spread among a broad array of investors, lowering the risk for the originator and allowing mortgagees to offer loans with lower interest rates and more affordable terms.

In the 1990s and 2000s, however, successive presidential administrations—that of both Democrat Bill Clinton and Republican George W. Bush—pursued policies aimed at expanding homeownership. Fannie Mae and Freddie Mac began to ease credit requirements on the mortgages they bought from mortgage originators, including many subprime and adjustable rate mortgages (ARMs). The latter offered low initial, or "teaser," interest rates, as well as interest-only payments, that expired after a certain period of time, whereupon the rate would become adjustable, usually in relation to some kind of index reflecting the cost of funds to the lender. With an ARM loan, if the lender's costs of funds go up, the interest rate charged to the borrower (and hence the mortgage payment) also will rise.

This lowering of standards by the government-sponsored enterprises had a major impact on both the primary and secondary mortgage markets. Mortgage originators began to lower their own standards for verifying the creditworthiness of mortgagors. They began to offer so-called NINA (no stated income, no asset) mortgages, which required no documentation of the mortgagor's income or assets, and NINJA (no income, no job or assets) loans, for which the mortgagor could simply attest that he or she had a job. Mortgage originators, or mortgagees, felt comfortable doing this because they did not hold on to the mortgages—and with them, the risk of default—for very long, instead quickly selling them to one of the government-sponsored enterprises or on the greatly expanded secondary mortgage market. Indeed, the market for mortgage-backed securities exploded in the early 2000s, from roughly $60 billion annually in 2000 to $570 billion in 2006, an increase of more than 800 percent. Many of these mortgage-backed securities were made up of NINA, NINJA, and other subprime mortgages.

The monetary policy of the Federal Reserve (Fed) also helped inflate the mortgage credit markets. To help lift the economy out of the recession of 2001 and 2002—a downturn triggered by the collapse of technology stock prices and, to a lesser extent, the terrorist attacks of September 11, 2001—the Fed, under the leadership of Alan Greenspan, lowered interest rates dramatically by mid-2003. By taking actions to lower rates, the Fed makes it easier for people to borrow money— for mortgages, among other things—thereby stimulating the economy, albeit at the risk of spurring inflation. Many economists argued, both at the time and in retrospect, that the Fed kept rates too low for too long, even after the economy had revived and even after it had become clear that housing prices were rising too rapidly.

Such criticisms aside, both the Fed's monetary policy and the loose credit markets were doing what policy makers wanted: increasing home-ownership, which rose from the 65 percent rate that held from the 1960s through the 1980s to 70 percent by the mid-2000s.

Housing Boom of the Early and Mid-2000s

Meanwhile, housing prices were going through the roof. Between 2000 and 2007, the median home price in the United States rose from about $150,000 (2009 dollars) to $266,000, a gain of roughly 77 percent, for an average year-over-year increase of 11 percent—this at a time when the overall inflation rate was averaging about 3 percent annually. The increases were even more spectacular in "hot" real-estate markets of the Southwest and Florida. In Los Angeles and Phoenix, home prices nearly doubled between 2003 and 2007; in Las Vegas and Miami, they more than doubled. The United States was not alone in experiencing a housing price bubble. The easy credit made possible by the monetary policies of

In the heady days of the U.S. housing boom, which peaked in early 2005, many new homes were sold while still under construction. Mortgages rates were artificially low, and prices were at an all-time high. *(Dave Einsel/Stringer/Getty Images)*

the world's central banks and the international market in mortgage-backed securities were pushing up housing prices in markets from Australia to Great Britain to Spain. The global housing bubble, however, was not universal; there were major exceptions, particularly in countries where credit standards did not fall and financial leveraging did not increase substantially, including France, Germany, and—in the aftermath of a massive collapse in property prices in the 1990s—Japan.

But in buoyant markets, like that of the United States, the bubble became self-sustaining. With housing prices continuing to rise, credit became even easier to obtain and lenders dropped their underwriting standards, giving out larger and larger loans with smaller and smaller down payments. After all, if house prices continued to rise and demand remained strong, the holder of the mortgage could sell the property for a profit should the borrower default. Meanwhile, with low monthly payments—a result of low interest rates or ARMs—homeowners could buy more and more expensive homes, even beyond what their income justified. And, even if the ARM threatened to adjust the monthly payment upward, the homeowner could refinance on perhaps even better terms, as now he or she had more equity.

Housing Bust of the Late 2000s

Of course, house prices could not go up forever, nor could interest rates remain low and credit terms easy. Economists debate the exact cause of the housing price crash that began in late 2006 and accelerated in 2007 and 2008. (The timing of the crash varied from market to market.) Some contend that it had to do with increasing interest rates in the mid-2000s, while others argue that it had to do with a weakening of the overall economy and rising unemployment. Still others point to housing market fundamentals—housing prices in many markets rose so high that potential buyers were priced out of the market, or they rose too high in relation to rents, making homeownership less attractive. In either case, the result was lowered demand. In addition, in many areas,

particularly the lower-cost urban fringes of major metropolitan areas, developers had built too many homes, creating a glut that falling demand could not meet. Contributing to the problem on the exurban fringe was a spike in gas prices in 2008, which made the long commutes from such areas that much more expensive.

The fall in prices was more precipitous than the rise had been. The median price for a home fell from its peak of $266,000 in 2007 to roughly $165,000 by early 2009, a decline of about 38 percent, before recovering somewhat by the end of the latter year. In particularly frothy markets, the fall was even steeper. In California, the median home price fell from just under $500,000 at the height of the market in early 2007 to less than $250,000 at the trough in early 2009—fully a 50 percent drop, unprecedented in the modern history of the state's housing market.

Once housing prices began to fall, the engine that had driven them up in the first place—easy credit terms and the expanding secondary mortgage market—went into reverse. As credit became more expensive and more difficult to obtain, fewer people were able to buy homes, causing prices to drop further and wiping out vast amounts of equity. This, in turn, made it more difficult for homeowners to refinance as the monthly payments on their ARMs shot up. This forced more homeowners into foreclosure, putting more properties on the market and exerting further downward pressure on prices, especially as the mortgage holders tried to unload them at prices below falling market rates. Many homeowners found themselves "underwater"— that is, owing more than their newly depreciated home was worth, causing many to put their credit standing at risk and walk away from their homes. By 2009, roughly one-fourth of all homeowners in the United States were "upside down," owing more than the value of their property.

Meanwhile, in the secondary mortgage market, another crisis emerged. With foreclosure rates skyrocketing beyond those normally factored into the risk profiles of mortgage-backed securities, investors became wary of these financial instruments.

Real-estate brokers lead prospective buyers on a tour of foreclosed properties in Las Vegas, Nevada, in 2009. The number of foreclosures skyrocketed—there and across America—as more and more homeowners failed to keep up with monthly mortgage payments. *(Ethan Miller/Getty Images)*

Because many banks had a lot of mortgage-backed securities in their portfolios, their financial health was put in jeopardy. And with nobody able to ascertain what these securities were worth, nobody could ascertain the depth of the problems facing financial institutions. Banks stopped lending to one another, threatening a global meltdown in the credit markets—the primary reason for the $700 billion federal government bailout of late 2008. While the bailout stabilized the banks, banks became increasingly hesitant to lend money, either for mortgages or for business investment. This dearth of credit helped plunge the United States and much of the global economy into the worst economic downturn since the Great Depression, putting millions of people out of work in many countries. With no jobs, homeowners could not afford their mortgage payments, leading to more foreclosures. Overall, foreclosures soared from 1.2 million in 2006, or 1 in 150 homes, to 3.1 million in 2008, or 1 in 53 homes; in the third quarter of 2009 alone, 937,000 went into foreclosure, or 1 in 136 homes. The pain was felt strongest in markets where the bubble had inflated the most. In 2009, for example, California and Florida accounted for no less than 40 percent of all foreclosures.

The epidemic of foreclosures and rapidly falling home prices exerted a major drag on the economy—and not just because the housing market crash dried up credit throughout the financial markets. Buoyant home prices keep the economy active, as homeowners tend to spend more when they believe they are enjoying rising equity in their homes. Homeowners either do cash-out refinancing, allowing them to make purchases, or spend more because they believe that the rising equity in their homes will allow them to save less for retirement. Indeed, at the height of the housing market boom, U.S. saving rates were near zero and sometimes even negative, meaning that people were spending more than they earned, with homeowners financing the difference through low-interest home equity lines of credit. Overall, the value of residential real estate in the United States fell from $24 trillion in 2007 to about $20 trillion in 2009, while home equity fell from $16 trillion to $9.6 trillion. The difference between the former and latter figures represents total mortgage amounts.

Obama Administration's Efforts to Stabilize the Market

The danger of rising foreclosures to home values and to the housing market generally—and the overall importance of the housing market to the U.S. economy—prompted the incoming administration of President Barack Obama to launch a program that would offer government guarantees to lenders that allowed mortgagors owing up to 105 percent of the value of their homes to refinance at lower interest rates, thereby lowering their monthly housing bill. The program, according to President Obama, would help as many as 4 million homeowners stay in their homes. But the program was voluntary, lenders proved slow to take up the offer, and the extensive paperwork slowed down the process, so that only a small fraction of the 4 million were getting relief by the end of the year. In early 2010, the administration proposed a new, more aggressive plan, called the Homeowner Stability Initiative, funded with $75 billion in bailout money repaid to the federal government by major financial institutions. The administration estimated that the program could save between 7 million and 9 million American homes from foreclosure.

Critics of the plan pointed out its flaws and dangers. Some, particularly on the conservative side of the political spectrum, argued that it was not fair to help some homeowners with their mortgages—especially those who had taken out mortgages they could not really afford—while leaving more responsible borrowers to subsidize them with their tax dollars. In addition, some feared that the relief would go to speculators as well as to homeowners who were threatened with losing their primary residence, increasing moral hazard—the possibility that people will behave in a more risky fashion in the future if past experience leads them to believe they will be bailed out. To these arguments, President Obama countered that foreclosures threatened not only the people losing their homes but also all homeowners as foreclosures put downward pressure on overall housing prices.

More progressive critics argued that the rising foreclosure rates were not attributable to excessive mortgage payments, but to a lack of income. That is, President Obama's plan to provide mortgage relief in the form of lower interest rates, lower monthly mortgage payments, and even lower principal would not matter to a person who was out of a job and could not pay his or her mortgage no matter how much it was reduced. Instead, these critics argued that the administration needed to be more aggressive in lowering the unemployment rate through tax cuts and stimulus spending, which would accelerate economic growth. Only then, they said, could the avalanche of foreclosures be halted, housing prices be stabilized, and the drag that the housing bust was having on the overall economy be overcome.

James Ciment

See also: Florida Real-Estate Boom (1920s); Housing; Mortgage Lending Standards; Mortgage Markets and Mortgage Rates; Mortgage, Subprime; Real-Estate Speculation; Recession and Financial Crisis (2007–).

Further Reading

Barth, James R. *The Rise and Fall of the U.S. Mortgage and Credit Markets: A Comprehensive Analysis of the Market Meltdown.* Hoboken, NJ: John Wiley & Sons, 2009.

Bitner, Richard. *Confessions of a Subprime Lender: An Insider's Tale of Greed, Fraud, and Ignorance.* Hoboken, NJ: John Wiley & Sons, 2008.

Fox, Justin. *The Myth of the Rational Market: A History of Risk, Reward, and Delusion on Wall Street.* New York: HarperBusiness, 2009.

Gramlich, Edward M. *Subprime Mortgages: America's Latest Boom and Bust.* Washington, DC: Urban Institute, 2007.

Krugman, Paul R. *The Return of Depression Economics and the Crisis of 2008.* New York: W.W. Norton, 2009.

Muolo, Paul, and Mathew Padilla. *Chain of Blame: How Wall Street Caused the Mortgage and Credit Crisis.* Hoboken, NJ: John Wiley & Sons, 2008.

Posner, Richard A. *A Failure of Capitalism: The Crisis of '08 and the Descent into Depression.* Cambridge, MA: Harvard University Press, 2009.

Shiller, Robert J. *Irrational Exuberance.* 2nd ed. New York: Currency/Doubleday, 2005.

———. *The Subprime Solution: How Today's Global Financial Crisis Happened and What to Do About It.* Princeton, NJ: Princeton University Press, 2008.

Spotgeste, Milton R., ed. *Securitization of Subprime Mortgages.* Hauppauge, NY: Nova Science, 2009.

Thornton, Mark. "The Economics of Housing Bubbles." In *America's Housing Crisis: A Case of Government Failure,* ed. Benjamin Powell and Randall Holcombe. Edison, NJ: Transaction, 2009.

Zandi, Mark M. *Financial Shock: A 360° Look at the Subprime Mortgage Implosion, and How to Avoid the Next Financial Crisis.* Upper Saddle River, NJ: FT Press, 2009.

Iceland

Iceland, a tiny Scandinavian country of roughly 300,000 people, situated in the North Atlantic, experienced one of the most dramatic boom-and-bust cycles in world history in the 1990s and 2000s. The Icelandic boom began in the early 1990s, as the government ended the post–World War II economic and capital controls that had lasted from June 1944 independence from Denmark until the 1980s. The boom led to one of the world's highest levels of gross domestic product (GDP) per capita ($63,830 in 2007); adjusted for purchasing power parity, this put Iceland fourth in the world after Luxembourg, Norway, and the United States. Iceland also had one of the highest levels of economic and political freedom in the world, and the world's third-highest score on the 2009 Human Development Index. In 2008, however, the Icelandic economy collapsed, producing a major political crisis.

Foreign Capital–driven Boom

Until the 1980s, Iceland's economy centered on fishing and was notable primarily for its extensive state involvement; the country was experiencing the beginnings of economic decline by the late 1980s. Under the leadership of the Independence Party and its leader, Davíð Oddsson, Iceland embraced the global market in the early 1990s, opening its domestic economy and joining in the European Economic Area. As a result, Iceland's economy soared. Oddsson's government privatized state enterprises and cut subsidies and taxes dramatically (corporate tax rates dropped from 45 percent to 18 percent, individual rates from over 30 percent to under 23 percent). Iceland embraced European Union (EU) regulatory standards with respect to financial markets, allowing capital mobility and giving foreign investors confidence in Icelandic assets. Inflation, which had been over 50 percent in the early 1980s, fell to close to zero by the mid-1990s. Unemployment also declined to levels well below the Organisation for Economic Co-operation and Development (OECD) average in the late 1990s and early 2000s.

This economic liberalization occurred at a time when world interest rates were low and world capital markets were highly liquid. Thus, when the Icelandic government privatized the country's banking system in the early 2000s, the banks were able to borrow heavily abroad. Rising

Residents of Reykjavik, Iceland, take to the streets in 2008 to call on the government to resign and banks to be more open about the nation's economic plight. The currency and banking system both collapsed, and the government resigned in early 2009. *(AFP/Stringer/Getty Images)*

interest rates in Iceland, introduced by the Central Bank of Iceland to ward off a return to inflation, brought a rapid influx of foreign capital invested in Glacier Bonds, fueling a soaring Icelandic Stock Exchange. Icelandic bank assets grew from 96 percent of GDP at the end of 2000 to eight times GDP at the end of 2006, as the banks bought financial firms outside Iceland and established foreign branches (including Internet banks). Icelandic entrepreneurs such as Bakkavor Group, FL Group, and Baugur—often styled "Viking Raiders" in the press—used the capital available from Icelandic banks to purchase foreign assets. For example, among the British firms bought by Icelandic investors were Singer, Hamleys, and easyJet. Icelanders also bought "trophy assets" such as the British West Ham United soccer team. The boom produced multiple Icelandic tycoons, including Bjorgolfur Thor Bjorgolfsson, who at age forty in 2007 had assets estimated at more than $3 billion, and Lydur Gudmundsson and Agust Gudmundsson, who together founded Bakkavor, which operated 55 factories in 8 countries and was the largest provider of fresh prepared foods and produce in Britain.

Financial Crisis and Economic Collapse

By 2005 Iceland had the highest current account deficit in the OECD, and, in a "mini-crisis" in 2006 that foreshadowed later problems, the Icelandic stock market and exchange rate fell sharply, causing inflation to hit 8 percent. The economy briefly recovered when the banks brought in foreign deposits through international subsidiaries like Icesave, Edge, and Save & Save, and the boom continued until the world financial crisis hit in 2008 and liquidity dried up globally.

By March 2008, markets recognized that the outstanding Glacier Bonds were unlikely to be rolled over and that Icelandic firms would face a liquidity crisis as the foreign capital invested in the bonds (an amount equal to nearly 100 percent of GDP) flowed out of the country. Anticipating a fall in the krona, Icelandic banks hedged the currency, which contributed to the krona's collapse in March 2008. Like the rest of the world, Iceland's banks and political system were unprepared for the global credit crisis that began in 2008. When interest rates began to rise and asset prices to fall, the highly leveraged Icelandic debtors were unable to adequately roll over their loans and began to come under stress. As the credit crunch drove investors to seek safety, Icelandic borrowers found their situation rapidly deteriorating.

The political response to the crisis, both in Iceland and abroad, exacerbated the problem. The Icelandic government moved hesitantly at first, and then suddenly nationalized Glitner, one of the three large Icelandic banks. This produced an immediate collapse of the krona and stock prices, and it led international credit agencies to downgrade Icelandic debt. This in turn pushed the other two banks, Landsbanki and Kaupthing, into insolvency in early October and led to their nationalizations. In desperation, the Icelandic government attempted to secure a loan from Russia, but this fell through.

IMF Rescue

The Icelandic government then sought assistance from the International Monetary Fund (IMF) to deal with the liquidity crisis, but the British government blocked IMF assistance as a means of obtaining bargaining power in their efforts to force the Icelandic government to guarantee the savings of British depositors in Icelandic banks. Since these depositors included British local governments' funds, as well as individuals who had been drawn by the high returns, the foreign governments had a strong incentive to attempt to shift the problem to the Icelandic government. British prime minister Gordon Brown even invoked an antiterrorism law against the Icelandic banks, seizing both Icelandic government and many private assets in the UK. This prompted an Internet petition featuring "postcards" of ordinary Icelanders holding signs with sentiments

like "[Prime Minister] Gordon [Brown], We Are Not Terrorists." When the Icelandic government agreed to Britain's terms, the IMF assistance began to flow. It proved too little, too late, to save the Icelandic economy, however, and the collapse produced a political crisis that was only partially resolved with the ouster of the Independence Party, in power for 18 years and steward of the country's transition to a finance-oriented economy—and its replacement by a left-of-center coalition of the Social Democratic Alliance and the Left-Green Movement.

Andrew P. Morriss

See also: Finland; Norway; Sweden.

Further Reading

Boyes, Roger. *Meltdown Iceland: How the Global Financial Crisis Bankupted an Entire Country.* New York: Bloomsbury, 2009.

OECD. *Economic Survey of Iceland 2006: Policy Challenges in Sustaining Improved Economic Performance.* Paris: Organisation for Economic Co-operation and Development, 2006.

Portes, Richard, and Friorik Már Baldursson. *The Internationalization of Iceland's Financial Sector.* Reykavijk: Icelandic Chamber of Commerce, 2007. Available at www.vi.is/files/15921776Vid4WEB.pdf.

Immigration and Migration

A part of the human experience since prehistoric times, immigration and migration have played a major role in the economic destiny of regions and nations in the modern era—both in places that tend to receive immigrants and migrants and in those that send them. In the modern era, migration and immigration have tended to flow in two basic directions—from rural to urban areas and from economically developing countries or regions to developed ones.

According to the International Organization for Migration, there are more than 200 million international migrants—that is, people migrating between countries—in the world today, with Europe accounting for more than 70 million (both sending and receiving), North America for some 45 million, and Asia for another 25 million. But experts say that the greatest mass migration in history has occurred within a single country, as China has seen more than 100 million people move from rural areas to urban ones since the advent of economic modernization in the late 1970s.

Causes

While migration and immigration can be induced by noneconomic factors such as war, social chaos, environmental degradation, and political, ethnic, or religious persecution, large-scale, sustained movement tends to be rooted in economics. And here, there are both push and pull factors, specifically, the lack of opportunity in the sending region or nation and the perceived economic vitality of the receiving place. (Slave trading, while usually economic in nature, was, of course, an involuntary form of migration or immigration and is therefore outside the scope of this article.)

Throughout much of human history, immigration and migration have tended to be either local or to have taken place gradually, over long spans of time. This was due to the technological limitations of pre–industrial revolution transportation systems and the slow pace of economic change. In the modern era, improved transportation systems as well as the faster pace of economic change have greatly accelerated the numbers of people who migrate and immigrate as well as condensing the time frame in which they do so. As immigration scholars have long noted, socially disruptive economic developments—for good and bad—are a more important impetus for immigration and migration than poor but stable economic conditions. In other words, mere poverty alone is not as critical a factor in sending people away as is economic transformation.

For example, southern Italy has been an economically disadvantaged region for centuries. But it was only with the changes economic modernization set in motion—specifically, nineteenth-century changes in agriculture and land law that

made thousands of peasants economically redundant—that large-scale immigration and migration both to Italian cities and to foreign countries, largely in the Western Hemisphere, began to occur. Similarly, Mexico has been a less developed nation than the United States for virtually all of these two countries' histories. And while there has been substantial immigration from Mexico to the United States for much of the twentieth century, it was the increased pace of their economic integration in the last two decades of the century—as well as in the early years of the twenty-first—that greatly accelerated the process, as large numbers of Mexican farmers found it increasingly difficult to compete with low-cost agricultural imports from the United States.

Over a shorter time frame, economic cycles can have a major impact on levels of migration and immigration. For example, immigration to the United States stood at roughly 300,000 annually in the prosperous late 1920s—even after strict quotas were imposed in the early years of the decade—but fell to less than 50,000 in the depths of the Great Depression in the early and mid-1930s. More recently, during the economic boom times of the 1990s and early 2000s, over 1 million immigrants entered the United States each year. In economically troubled 2008, however, the foreign-born population of the country grew by just half that number. Economic downturns have particularly harsh effects on immigrants. According to a 2008 Pew Hispanic Center study, tens of thousands of Hispanic immigrants withdrew from the U.S. labor market since the recession began in late 2007. Between 2007 and 2008, the number of illegal immigrants declined by about 11 percent, from 12.5 million to 11.2 million.

Impact

Migration and immigration can have positive and negative economic effects on both sending and receiving regions and countries. For the former, the positive effects can include the relief of population pressures as well as the input of capital in the form of remittances or investments by immigrants. On the negative side of the ledger is the loss of productive people. Migrants and immigrants tend to be young, healthy, and ambitious, exactly the kind of people an economy needs to prosper. Moreover, sending countries have invested in the upbringing and education of emigrants, investments that accrue to the receiving country. This is especially the case with the phenomenon known as "brain drain," in which educated people from the developing world or rural areas immigrate or migrate to countries and regions where their skills or learning are better remunerated. Shortages of engineers, health care professionals, financial experts, and other highly skilled and educated people can significantly retard economic growth and modernization in many developing world countries and regions.

Still, migration and immigration can have a positive effect on the national social ledgers of sending countries and regions. In places of high unemployment or population density, emigration can relieve social pressures that often lead to unrest and even civil war. Moreover, modern technology has made it much easier in recent years for emigrants to send remittances home, or to return home and invest money made while abroad.

The World Bank reports that migrant workers send back $600 billion a year to their home countries worldwide. This sum can represent up to three times the money sent by governments as overseas aid and by businesses as foreign direct investment, and is very critical to the developing economies. During the global economic recessions of 2007–2009, the growth of remittances globally fell to close to zero for the first time since these money flows have been tracked.

The case of El Salvador illustrates the importance of remittances. Approximately 2.5 million legal and illegal Salvadoran immigrants, equivalent to more than one-third of the population of El Salvador, live in the United States and remit an estimated $2.5 billion annually, or 17.1 percent of the country's gross domestic product (GDP), to their family members. The remittances have

grown at the rate of over 6 percent per year since the late 1990s and as of early 2010 almost one in four households receives money from relatives in the United States, the most of any Latin American country. Three-quarters of the money goes to paying for household expenditures; hence, along with a 13 percent sales tax, the remittances in many ways subsidize the Salvadoran government's budget.

For other countries, such as Yemen and Gambia, remittances amount to more than 5 percent of GDP. However, remittances have the greatest overall impact in Asia, with China and India being the top recipient countries. The Center for Global Development noted that a Mexican male in his mid-thirties with nine years of education is likely to make 132 percent more working in the United States than in his home country. For a Bolivian and a Haitian, the increases would be close to 270 percent and 740 percent, respectively.

There are also benefits and liabilities for the countries and regions that take in immigrants. These places reap the benefits of young, healthy, ambitious workers—as well as skilled technicians and professionals and entrepreneurs—without having paid for some or all of their upbringing, education, and training. Approximately four in ten PhD scientists working in the United States, for instance, were born abroad. The Kauffman Foundation's index of entrepreneurial activity is nearly 40 percent higher for immigrants than for U.S. natives. In the last three decades, the Chinese and Indian immigrants have grown in importance as drivers of U.S. innovation. Chinese immigrants contributed to just 2 percent of the innovations in 1975, and that figure has grown to over 8 percent today, while the Indian immigrants' innovation figure has grown to almost 5 percent during the same time period. Still, the contributions of these two immigrant groups has begun to level off in the past few years, raising concerns about the ability of the United States to innovate in the future.

While the United States has been a draw for immigrants since its founding, for other developed-world countries the phenomenon of mass immigration has more recent origins. After World War II, many European countries were desperate to rebuild and were experiencing labor shortages; many used immigration to continue the pace of development. Britain, for one, passed the Nationality Act of 1948, which gave all citizens of Commonwealth countries and colonial subjects the right of unrestricted entry into the United Kingdom and led to a dramatic upturn in immigration through the rest of the twentieth century and into the twenty-first.

Moreover, immigration can help balance out demographic imbalances. As the population in developed-world countries ages in coming decades, the immigration of younger workers from the developing world could help contribute to the tax base necessary to support the generous public pension and health care systems in Europe. Conversely, many experts say that Japan's restrictive immigration rules might hamper its ability to fund pensioners, who could account for as many as one in three citizens by mid-century.

Still, immigration does not come without costs. Many residents of developed-world countries—including already settled immigrants—resent newcomers, whom they see as competitors, cultural threats, and sources of crime, though statistical evidence does not support the latter fear, as newly arrived immigrants in the United States tend to have lower crime rates than the rest of the population. Illegal immigrants are especially seen as a problem, particularly in the United States, where many people believe—and some studies bear out—that they end up costing more in terms of education, health care, and criminal justice than they contribute in taxes.

Whatever the costs or benefits—and in spite of temporary immigrant-reducing downturns such as the financial crisis and recession of the late 2000s—immigration from the developing world to the developed world, as well as internal migration from farms to city in such places as China, is expected to continue accelerating into the foreseeable future, as economic globalization and the increased environmental stresses of climate change spur tens of millions of people to pick up stakes and move about the planet.

James Ciment and Abhijit Roy

See also: Labor Market; Wages.

Further Reading

Borjas, George. *Heaven's Door: Immigration Policy and the American Economy.* Princeton, NJ: Princeton University Press, 1999.

Ciment, James, ed. *Encyclopedia of American Immigration.* Armonk, NY: M.E. Sharpe, 2001.

Council of Economic Advisers. *Economic Report of the President*, Chapter 9, "Immigration." Washington, DC: U.S. Government Printing Office, 2007.

Lee, Ronald, and Timothy Miller. "Immigration, Social Security, and Broader Fiscal Impacts." *American Economic Review* 90 (May 2000): 350–354.

Panayiotopoulos, Podromos. *Immigrant Enterprise in Europe and the USA.* New York: Routledge, 2006.

Parson, Craig A., and Timothy M. Smeeding. *Immigration and the Transformation of Europe.* Cambridge, UK: Cambridge University Press, 2006.

Income Distribution

Income is the amount of money received by an individual over a given period of time, usually measured in yearly increments. It includes wages and other forms of compensation to labor, such as tips, commissions, and bonuses, as well as earnings from the ownership of real and financial assets, including interest payments, dividends, rents, capital gains, and profits. In addition, income includes government compensation in the form of Social Security, welfare, unemployment payments, and, in the United States, earned income tax credits. Nations also can be said to have incomes. A nation's income is the total of all wages (labor income) and all interest, dividends, rents, capital gains, and profits (capital income).

Distribution refers to the way in which that income is apportioned among different groups of people within a particular geographic area, usually a nation. These groups may be based on race, gender, or age, though the most commonly used distribution group is socioeconomic class. When income is distributed fairly evenly across socioeconomic groups, a society is said to be more egalitarian; when income disparities between groups are large, a society is said to be less egalitarian. Income distribution varies widely among countries—and even within different parts of the same country—and among regions of the world. Within a given country, income distribution tends to shift over time, sometimes trending toward greater equality and sometimes toward greater inequality. Income distribution and the business cycle affect one another, although economists disagree over what degree of inequality is opportune for sustained economic growth.

It is important to note the distinction between income and wealth. The latter refers to the net value of assets owned by an individual (or a nation) at a given point in time. Wealth can be distributed unevenly as well. In fact, wealth tends to be distributed more unevenly than income, as discrepancies in wealth represent, in part, the accumulation of unequal distributions of income over many years and even generations. Other than labor income such as wages and salaries, income flows such as interest payments, rents, and capital gains result from the ownership of real or financial assets that are included in wealth.

Economists use two tools to measure income distribution—one graphical and one statistical. The former is the Lorenz curve, which illustrates how national income (vertical axis) is distributed among households (horizontal axis). A perfectly straight diagonal line from bottom left to top right would represent a perfectly even distribution of income, with the degree of sag in the line representing the level of income inequality.

In the following figure, if income is distributed equally, every quartile of households (representing one-quarter of the population) would receive 25 percent of total income. This is shown by the dotted lines converging on the 45-degree line in the bottom-left corner. The actual distribution of income is shown by the curved line, which indicates that the bottom quartile of households

The Concept of Income Distribution

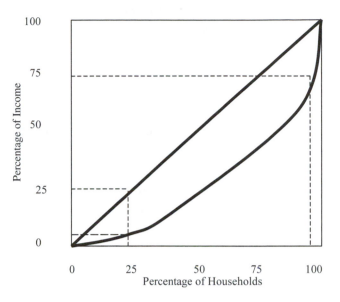

receives only about 5 percent of total income, while the top 5 percent of households receive about 25 percent of total income.

Statistically, income distribution is measured by the Gini coefficient. Here, perfect equality—all people receive the same amount of income—is represented by 0, and perfect inequality—one person makes all the money—is represented by 1. Thus, a lower Gini coefficient represents greater income equality, and vice versa. For example, the Gini ratio for the United States increased from 0.408 to 0.443 between 1997 and 2007, indicating a long-term increase in income inequality.

Causes of Income Inequality

Income inequality occurs for a variety of reasons. Primary among these is the matter of birth. Inheriting a great fortune all but assures an individual of a steady income of interest, dividends, rents, and capital gains. But entrepreneurial activity may be just as important, as successful entrepreneurs tend to have very large incomes. For all but the very wealthy, however, income comes largely in the form of wages. Here, several factors come into play. Higher-skilled occupations tend to pay more because there are fewer workers with those skills, allowing them to command higher pay. Even within a profession, those with greater talent and skills—or a willingness to work longer hours—tend to earn more than their colleagues.

While most people would agree that higher levels of skill, talent, and work ethic should be rewarded, other—less equitable—factors also come into play, such as racial and gender discrimination and, of course, the accident of birth. Even excluding the very wealthy—who derive a large proportion of their wealth from capital income—those who are born into higher-income families are more likely to receive the kinds of education and training that lead to higher incomes from labor.

As noted earlier, income distribution can be measured across different groups. In the United States, whites tend to earn more than other ethnic groups—with the exception of some Asian-American groups—and men tend to earn more than women, although in both cases, the gap has been shrinking gradually over the last several decades. In addition, people tend to earn more as they get older until, reaching retirement, their income falls off as they become more dependent on capital income from retirement accounts and from Social Security payments.

Income distribution also differs among countries. In general, less developed countries have greater levels of income inequality because there are fewer professionals and skilled workers per capita, and because income derived from wealth tends to be distributed even more unequally. But even within the developed world, income distribution varies widely. Income redistribution policies are the chief reason this is so. While the market may decide that the heir to a great fortune deserves a much greater income than the hardworking offspring of a manual laborer, society may disagree and institute policies to redress the inequality through such means as progressive taxation, educational subsidies, and social welfare payments. Thus, countries with general social welfare programs and highly progressive income taxes tend to see income distributed more evenly than those without.

At the same time, as American economist Arthur Okun argued in his classic 1975 work *Equality and Efficiency,* a dollar taken from the rich does not always translate into a dollar received by the poor. The "leaky bucket," as Okun called it, means that increasing income equality often comes at the price of economic efficiency and lower overall national income because it may lead to lowered incentives to work and earn money—as more of it is taken in taxes—and contributes to labor shirking, as people accept a lower standard of living from unemployment or social welfare benefits but more leisure time.

Income distribution also can change over time in a given country. For example, the United States saw income distribution begin to equalize during the first few decades after World War II, a result of rising education levels, government social welfare policies, strong labor unions, and a steeply progressive income tax. By the mid-1970s, however, the trend had begun to reverse, with rising levels of income inequality. This, most economists agree, resulted from lowered taxes on the wealthy, less government assistance to poor families, a rise in the number of households headed by single mothers, and a growing discrepancy in the level of income earned by college-educated versus non-college-educated workers.

The last factor can be accounted for, say many economists, by globalization. As manufacturing moved increasingly to the developing world, this contributed to a decline in manufacturing jobs in the United States—jobs that paid relatively well but did not require high levels of education. But globalization was not the only factor. Important, as well, was the decline in unionization rates; rising levels of immigration, which brought in more low-wage labor competition; and the computer revolution, which increased the number of jobs requiring higher levels of education.

Income Distribution and the Business Cycle

Economists vigorously debate the impact of income distribution on the business cycle, and vice versa. While all agree that extremes of income distribution (too much equality or too much inequality) have a deleterious effect on economic growth, they do not agree on what level of inequality is optimal. Liberal economists in the Keynesian tradition argue that because those who earn lower incomes tend to spend more of their income, greater income equality creates greater aggregate demand, leading to higher levels of economic growth and more economic stability. Thus, they advocate measures and policies that tend to make income distributions less unequal, such as income redistribution and progressive income taxes. Conservatives, on the other hand, argue that government policy should emphasize supply-side factors—that is, create the conditions for capital accumulation that allow for higher levels of investment, which stimulates higher employment and, in turn, contributes to higher wage levels. In other words, greater income inequality leads to a faster-growing economy, which leads to higher income levels for all, even if the distribution becomes more skewed.

As for the effect of the business cycle on income distribution, the picture is equally mixed. On the one hand, periods of rapid growth contribute to greater equality in income distribution, as low unemployment levels give wage earners a stronger bargaining position in the marketplace, thereby ensuring that more of the national income goes to wages as opposed to profits, which generally accrue to wealthier individuals. Recessions, on the other hand, tend to worsen the bargaining positions of wage earners, lowering how much they earn. In addition, recessions are marked by higher levels of unemployment, further depressing the amount of income earned, especially among low-wage workers, who often are the first to be laid off.

Of course, periods of economic growth also see increases in corporate profits, which largely accrue to high-income individuals, while recessions see decreased profits and capital income. Moreover, wages tend to be, in Keynesian terms, "sticky"—that is, both employees and employers are unwilling or unable, because of contracts, to lower wages as profits decline. And because higher-income individuals tend to derive more of their income from interest, dividends, rents, profits, and capital gains than from wages, their share of national income tends to go down more quickly during recessions than those whose primary source of income is wages. Indeed, this seems to be the case for the very worst of economic contractions, as income equality in the United States rose during the Great Depression and, as preliminary findings seem to reveal, rose during the "Great Recession" of 2007–2009 as well.

James Ciment and Derek Bjonback

See also: Poverty; Wages; Wealth.

Further Reading

Frank, Robert H. *Falling Behind: How Rising Inequality Harms the Middle Class.* Berkeley: University of California Press, 2007.

Kelly, Nathan J. *The Politics of Income Inequality in the United States.* New York: Cambridge University Press, 2009.

Okun, Arthur M. *Equality and Efficiency: The Big Tradeoff.* Washington, DC: Brookings Institution, 1975.

Pontusson, Jonas. *Inequality and Prosperity: Social Europe vs. Liberal America.* Ithaca, NY: Cornell University Press, 2005.

Ryscavage, Paul. *Rethinking the Income Gap.* New Brunswick, NJ: Transaction, 2009.

Wolff, Edward N. *Poverty and Income Distribution.* 2nd ed. Malden, MA: Wiley-Blackwell, 2009.

India

Located in South Asia, India is the second-largest nation in the world by population (with an estimated 1.2 billion people in 2009). Home to some of the oldest civilizations in human history, it is a multi-ethnic democratic state with a free market emerging from decades of centralized planning.

Until the eighteenth century, India had one of the most vibrant economies in the world, before being gradually absorbed into the British Empire from that period through independence in 1947. India's economy, like that of many other colonies, was restructured by its European conquerors to serve the needs of the colonizing power. In India's case, this meant a gradual weakening of its once-dominant textile industry, which was seen by British manufacturers as a serious source of competition.

After achieving independence, India's government pursued a policy common in newly emerging nations in Africa and Asia of centralized planning, import substitution, and poverty alleviation through subsidies on basic commodities and other measures. The result of such policies was stability, but slow economic growth. Beginning in the early 1990s, the country embarked on free-market reforms that, according to many economists, have helped spur more rapid growth and turned India into one of the most powerful emerging markets in the world.

As of December 2009, India's gross domestic product (GDP) growth of 6.1 percent ranked second only to China's, among major developing world countries, and surpassed the growth rates of the United States and all other developed countries in the third quarter of 2009. India's economic growth, especially in the last two decades, has been remarkable. The nation has gone through several phases of economic expansion in its history, going back to the Middle Ages and earlier. The colonization process, which lasted about 200 years, was not beneficial for India, and it emerged weak and poverty-stricken when it gained independence in 1947. But changes soon followed. Today, the Indian economy is growing at a significant rate and seems poised for further growth.

It is sometimes assumed that India, prior to colonization, represented a region caught in a population trap that prevented it from growing economically. The bulk of its population merely subsisted. However, there is evidence that, prior to the middle of the eighteenth century, southern India was a dynamic hub of economic activity. There was significant growth in the agricultural sector, with more modest expansion in manufacturing and trading. According to some reports, the Indian subcontinent accounted for fully a quarter of world manufacturing output in 1750.

Some Indian nationalist writers noted that the nation underwent a process of deindustrialization during the period of colonization in the late eighteenth and nineteenth centuries. This is said to have occurred in two stages. In the first stage, the collapse of the Mughal Empire drove down grain productivity, which hurt India's competitiveness in terms of manufactured textiles. In the second stage, productivity advances stemming from the adoption of the factory system in England drove down the price of one of India's main exports, textiles, which caused further deindustrialization.

India After Independence

Independence from the British in 1947 was regarded throughout India as a triumph of the Gandhian strategy of nonviolence. Yet the fruits of independence were bittersweet, since the freedom was tied to the partition of the country along communal lines. The Republic of India was established on January 26, 1950, with a bicameral parliament representing one of the world's largest electorates. The two legislative houses were the Rajya Sabha, or Council of States, and the Lok Sabha, or House of the People.

India has witnessed sweeping changes since independence. In 1947, the national literacy rate was only 18 percent, the investment rate about 9 percent of GDP, life expectancy at birth around 32 years, and the annual economic growth rate about 3 percent. Within 50 years, the nation's literacy rate had risen to 60 percent, the investment rate had grown to 30 percent of GDP, life expectancy at birth had climbed to about 63 years, and the annual GDP growth rate stood at about 8 percent.

At the time of independence, India's per capita annual income was extremely low (US$95 in 1974 prices). Achieving economic growth following independence was a priority for political leaders, whose model for success was the Soviet Union. The result was a reluctance to rely on private entrepreneurship and the free markets. Instead, India adopted a development strategy that has been referred to as "import substitution industrialization," which relied on tariffs and quotas to protect new domestic industry.

In the political sphere, India faced several threats in the initial period after independence. The hostility between India and Pakistan escalated from the time Pakistan achieved independence, also in 1947. And India entered into conflict with China during the 1950s over land in its northeast region. The dispute escalated into a full-fledged attack by Chinese forces in 1962 and came to an end with a Chinese declaration of a cease-fire only after India appealed to the Western world, particularly the United States, for involvement and military aid.

India's economic development projects in the 1950s, 1960s, and 1970s were characterized by heavy state involvement, again following the Soviet model. There was relatively strong agricultural growth, mainly due to the success of the Green Revolution movement launched in the 1970s, but the public sector seemed to become increasingly inefficient and tainted by corruption, both political and bureaucratic. Yet, in some sense, the strategy proved successful. India did establish a growing industrial base, there was a moderate increase in savings, and from 1950 to 1980, growth rates for real GDP and per capita GDP were 3.7 percent and 1.5 percent, respectively. Although these were dramatic increases from colonial times, they were extremely weak compared with the economic performance of other East Asian nations. For the most part, India remained poor and largely dependent on agriculture, regional inequality mounted, and the global oil crisis of 1973 created inflationary pressures as well as balance-of-payment difficulties.

While the annual growth rate in the 1950s, 1960s, and early 1970s fluctuated right around 3.5 percent, there was steady growth from the mid-1970s to the 1980s, and annual increases of about 6 percent between 1980 and 2005. India's shift to a pro-market economy—heralding the growth it enjoys today—is generally considered to have begun in the early 1990, but many economists point to the start of real growth somewhat earlier,

during the 1980s. Indeed, several major economic reforms were instituted in the 1980s. Although basic restrictions were not eliminated and the market forces were not set free, the state regulatory apparatus was fundamentally reoriented. Rather than being aimed at boosting production for the domestic market, the new reforms promoted export production. This shift in attitude, according to some economists, was responsible for the first spurt of economic growth, even though the results were somewhat nebulous. India's economy did show a healthy increase in growth of 5.6 percent between 1980 and 1985, but the fiscal deficit reached 12 percent of GDP and the current accounts deficit, as a share of GDP, expanded from 1.7 percent to 3 percent in the latter part of the 1980s. These macroeconomic problems were occurring at a time of escalating political and social unrest in different parts of the country and increased tension with Pakistan. Additionally, internal and international borrowing funded most of the policy reforms, which created a fiscal crisis that left India on the verge of bankruptcy in 1991.

Globalization

India witnessed some sweeping economic changes during the 1990s, with export-led growth seen as the preferred course for the economy, along with increased foreign direct investments to reduce the trade deficit. At about the same time, the decline of the Soviet Union and the collapse of communism in Eastern Europe led to a drop in trade with these markets. Thus, India had no choice but to enter the world market, bringing a marked uptick in the GDP growth rate during the early 1990s—to 6.7 percent.

The dramatic policy shift and trend toward globalization brought fundamental changes to the structure of the Indian economy. Among these were the increasing importance of external trade, external capital flows, and a remarkable growth in the service sector. By the early 2000s, the nation's information technology (IT) industry had made huge leaps into the world market, bringing in

White-collar employees enter Technopark, the home of forty-five hardware and software companies, in India's Karnataka state. With Bangalore and other areas, Karnataka is a center of the nation's burgeoning IT service sector—a source of increasing foreign revenue. *(EyesWideOpen/ Getty Images)*

billions of dollars from foreign firms outsourcing IT jobs. India's foreign exchange reserves also grew at a rapid rate, exceeding $100 billion annually by 2004. The economy as a whole grew at rates of 5.2 percent and 4.6 percent for 2001 and 2002.

And the trend continued. From 2003–2004 to 2007–2008, the share of merchandise trade to GDP increased from 23.7 percent to more than 35 percent; including trade in services, the latter figure was 47 percent of GDP. Meanwhile, net foreign capital inflows grew from 1.9 percent of GDP in 2000–2001 to 9.2 percent by 2007–2008. India's capital markets also flourished, with a strong trend in outbound direct investment flow as Indian capitalists invested heavily in foreign countries. The largest growth by far, however, was seen in the service sector. This was partly due to the globalization process and partly due to India's demographic dividend through a large, young, well-educated labor force.

Financial Crises of the 1990s and 2000s

Since India's entry into the global economy, two major crises have rocked the developed and developing world. The first was the Asian financial crisis of 1997, which affected mostly countries in East Asia. The second was the subprime crisis that began in the United States and Europe in 2006–2007 and eventually spread to other countries as well.

In the crisis that swept the so-called Asian tiger nations and others in 1997, exchange rates tumbled, output fell, and unemployment rates increased—with political instability inevitably ensuing. The crisis was relatively short-lived, however, and most of the affected countries bounced back relatively quickly. India, in spite of its geographic proximity to several of the affected countries, escaped relatively unscathed. Its growth rate dipped marginally in 1997, primarily due to domestic factors rather than regional ones. The economy had not yet made the full transition to exports, which accounted for only about 8 percent of GDP at the time. Moreover, only 13 percent of its exports were with the Asian countries affected by the crisis. Thus, India's balance of payments was not greatly affected by the 1997 downturn in these economies. Capital controls that were still in place helped to shield India from abrupt changes in short-term capital.

India was much more closely integrated with the global economy by the time the subprime mortgage crisis began to surface. Initially, at least, India did not seem to be greatly affected by the crisis. As the global financial markets began to be affected, however, the net flow of capital to India turned negative, as foreign institutional investors began selling their assets in an attempt to salvage overseas cash balances. By the end of 2008, India's current account felt the impact of the slowdown in its exports, a direct result of recessionary trends in developed countries. In 2008–2009, exports to the United States—India's largest buyer—fell by 1.6 percent. The impact of the global recession was relatively smaller on India's service exports, mainly due to the growth in software and financial services.

Prior to the crisis, India's central bank, the Reserve Bank of India (RBI), was more intent on controlling money supply growth in its attempt to reduce inflationary tendencies in the economy. However, RBI shifted toward an expansionary policy to deal with the liquidity crunch and near freezing of international credit. Fiscal measures were also undertaken to deal with the impact of the crisis on the Indian economy by increasing the fiscal deficit, much like stimulus packages introduced in the United States and elsewhere. The overall balance-of-payments situation remained quite steady in spite of strains on the capital and current accounts. FDI flows began to increase in 2008–2009 and crude oil prices were low, in part a function of reduced imports.

The end of 2009 brought good news—a return to economic growth—even though a crisis in the Dubai market in late 2009 threatened prospects for the 4.5 million Indians living in the Persian Gulf as well as India's exports to the region. All in all, India was generally less affected by the financial crisis and global recession of the late 2000s than most other countries. Reasons included its large and diversified consumption base, a relatively moderate trade-to-GDP ratio, the relative insulation of India's financial markets, a healthy balance of external reserves, and less than complete capital account convertibility. Nevertheless, India continues to face some chronic economic problems: widespread poverty; economic, regional, and social inequality; lack of infrastructure; poor education for the masses; corruption; and inadequate employment opportunities for a large and growing labor force.

Sharmistha Self

See also: BRIC (Brazil, Russia, India, China); Emerging Markets; Transition Economies.

Further Reading

DeLong, J. Bradford. "India Since Independence: An Analytical Growth Narrative." In *Modern Economic Growth: Analytical Country Studies*, ed. Dani Rodrik. Princeton, NJ: Princeton University Press, 2003.

Grabowski, Richard, Sharmistha Self, and Michael P. Shields. *Economic Development: A Regional, Institutional, and Historical Approach.* Armonk, NY: M.E Sharpe, 2006.

Panagariya, Arvind. "India in the 1980s and 1990s: A Triumph of Reforms." IMF Working Paper no. WP/04/43. International Monetary Fund, 2004.

Parthasarathi, P. *The Transition to a Colonial Economy: Weavers, Merchants, and Kings in South India 1720–1800.* New York: Cambridge University Press, 2001.

Prasan, A., and C.P. Reddy. "Global Financial Crisis and its Impact on India." *Journal of Social Science* 21:1 (2009): 1–5.

Indicators of Financial Vulnerability

Recent financial crises, such as the Asian currency crisis of 1997–1998, the stock market downturn of the early 2000s, and the global financial meltdown of 2008–2009, have refocused the attention of economists on determining how to predict future problems. To do this, they examine what are known as indicators of financial vulnerability. The basic idea is that if economists can identify problematic trends, they can provide early warning signals to government officials who would in turn implement policy changes so as to avoid a crisis.

As the crisis of 2008–2009 indicated, systemic financial problems can affect any size or kind of economy, from those in the developing world, to emerging markets, to advanced industrialized economies like the United States. Nevertheless, emerging market economies tend to be more vulnerable to crises because of their greater reliance on external funding and other capital inflows for economic growth.

As the premier global institution for dealing with financial crises, the International Monetary Fund (IMF) has outlined vulnerability factors in government policy, financial sector activities, corporate policy, and household behavior. The IMF has also set up a system for monitoring the contagion of crises across economic sectors, tracking whether a country's fiscal deficit is having an impact on currency exchange rates, whether the country's banking sector is vulnerable because it holds a large amount of government debt, and other economic trends.

The four key indicators that the IMF monitors are levels of external and domestic debt; monetary reserve adequacy; financial sector strengths and weaknesses; and the soundness of corporate finances. External and domestic debt issues include repayment schedules and interest rate and currency fluctuations. The ratio of external debt to exports, and of external debt to GDP, are especially helpful indicators of trends in debt and repayment capacity. The ratio of debt to tax revenue is particularly critical when gauging a country's repayment capacity. Indicators of reserve adequacy are instrumental in determining a country's ability to avert liquidity crises. Specifically, the ratio of reserves to short-term debt is important in assessing the vulnerability of countries with significant but uncertain access to capital markets. Strengths and weaknesses in a nation's financial sector include the quality of assets, profitability and liquidity, and the pace and quality of credit growth. Other market risk factors, such as changes in interest rates and exchange rates, are also monitored. Corporate sector indicators pertaining to leverage, profitability, cash flow, and financial structure are also important considerations.

British economist E. Philip Davis has identified a set of seven generic indicators derived from the theory of financial instability and empirical studies of financial crisis incidents. His leading indicators approach is used in predicting turn-ing points of the business cycle, primarily in industrialized countries, and has been effective in detecting early warning signs of a financial crisis. That is, when a particular indicator exceeds a critical threshold, a warning signal is given. Davis's indicators include corporate and household indebtedness relative to assets and income; prices of equities of various kinds; how much money is in the economy; the health of financial institutions, as measured by capital adequacy, the amount of nonperforming loans, and other indicators; external financial indicators, such as trade flows and balance of payments; overall macroeconomic indicators, including GDP growth, business investment, and inflation; and qualitative social and political indicators, such as easing of financial regulations, removal of entry barriers to markets, health and coverage of the social safety net, and perceptions of the government and central bank's willingness to make sound fiscal and monetary decisions.

In recent decades, great advances have been made in incorporating vulnerability assessments into the financial surveillance systems. As the global financial crisis of 2008–2009 showed, such indicators are as important for emerging market economies as they are for developed economies. Early warning system (EWS) models incorporating the above indicators are used by international financial institutions such as the IMF and World Bank and by national central banks in predicting the likelihood of impending crises. But these models have their limits. While they offer a systematic, objective, and consistent method of predicting crises, they have a mixed record of forecasting accuracy. Economists and policy makers use them alongside other inputs in their surveillance programs.

But developing-world economies are not the only ones that benefit from effective analysis of indicators of financial vulnerability, as shown by the failure to foresee recent crashes in asset prices in the United States, and the degree of economic chaos they can produce. Some economists, for example, were warning of overly inflated corporate equity prices, particularly in the technology sector, during the late-1990s run-up in stock prices known as the dot.com bubble. Indeed, it was in reference to this phenomenon that Alan Greenspan uttered his famous "irrational exuberance" remark in a 1996 speech.

Just over a decade later, however, Greenspan himself was coming under criticism for not heeding the warnings of some economists, notably Robert Shiller and Dean Baker, that the low interest rate policy of the Federal Reserve, which Greenspan headed through 2006, was contributing to a housing bubble that was leaving the U.S. economy vulnerable to a sudden collapse in housing prices. In fact, there were other indicators of financial vulnerability during the mid-2000s housing bubble beyond overly inflated asset values, including high levels of household indebtedness and large numbers of questionable loans and securities on the balance sheets of financial institutions—most notably, collateralized debt obligations. But few in policy-making positions appeared to take heed of the warnings. Thus, as it became clear during the financial crisis beginning in late 2008, and the deep recession that accompanied it, indicators of financial vulnerability are only useful if they are heeded.

Abhijit Roy

See also: Asian Financial Crisis (1997); International Monetary Fund.

Further Reading

Athukorala, Prema-chandra, and Peter G. Warr. "Vulnerability to a Currency Crisis: Lessons from the Asian Experience." *World Economy* 25:1 (2002): 33–57.

Davis, E. Philip. "Financial Data Needs for Macro-prudential Surveillance: What Are the Key Indicators of Risks to Domestic Financial Stability?" *Center for Central Banking Studies* London: Bank of England, 1999.

Grabel, Ilene. "Predicting Financial Crisis in Developing Economies: Astronomy or Astrology?" *Eastern Economic Journal* 29:2 (2003): 243–250.

Hardy, Daniel C., and Ceyla Pazarbasioglu. "Determinants and Leading Indicators of Banking Crises: Further Evidence." *IMF Staff Papers* 46:3 (1999): 247–258.

International Monetary Fund (IMF). "Vulnerability Factors." Available at www.imf.org/external/np/exr/facts/vul.htm. Accessed November 2009.

Indonesia

The fourth most populous nation in the world, with an estimated 240 million people, Indonesia consists of an archipelago of thousands of large and small islands stretching from west of the Malay Peninsula in Southeast Asia to the Arafura Sea north of Australia. It is a polyglot nation, with a variety of ethnic, linguistic, and religious constituencies, though ethnic Javanese and practitioners of Islam predominate. The country's geographic expansiveness and cultural diversity have fueled a number of armed separatist movements over the years, though most have become quiescent in recent times.

A longtime colony of the Netherlands, Indonesia won its independence just after World War II and has been either democratically or autocratically ruled ever since. Economically underdeveloped during its first decades of independence, Indonesia is now considered a middle-income country with a significant industrial base and large oil reserves, though it is still home to many people living below the poverty line.

The Jakarta government has opened up the economy to foreign investment, which has contributed to growth but exposed the country to fluctuations in the world financial system. Indonesia was hard hit by the Asian financial crisis of 1997–1998 and has seen its growth rate drop significantly as a result of the global financial crisis and recession of 2008–2009.

Economic History

Indonesia's archipelagic geography stifled political unity until the modern era, though the various islands have conducted extensive trade with other parts of Asia for thousands of years. Indeed, it was traders who brought the major religions to the islands—first Hinduism and Buddhism before the common era, and then Islam in the eleventh century CE.

European explorers began to arrive in the islands—known at the time as the East Indies—in the sixteenth century, largely in pursuit of exotic and lucrative spices. By the early seventeenth century, the Dutch came to dominate trade in the islands. At first ruled by a private trading concern, the Dutch East India Company, the islands were turned into a nationalized colony of the Netherlands at the beginning of the nineteenth century.

Indonesia remained in Dutch hands, aside from a brief Japanese occupation during World War II, until 1949, when the colonial power was thrown out after several years of armed struggle by nationalist insurgents. Among the leaders of the independence movement was Sukarno (many Indonesians go by a single name), who served as the country's first president from 1945 through 1967. (He declared Indonesia independent in 1945, but the Netherlands did not concede until four years later.)

Sukarno was a leftist who pursued a statist path to economic development, with the government emphasizing industrial development for the purpose of economic self-sufficiency. Although he succeeded in establishing a heavy industrial base, the economy stagnated, with gross domestic product (GDP) standing at just $70 billion by the end of his reign. Sukarno's politics had grown increasingly radical, becoming more hostile to the West and friendlier with China, his rule becoming increasingly autocratic. He was finally ousted in 1965 by Suharto, the head of Indonesia's military, who had initiated a bloody, anti-leftist coup two years earlier that resulted in the deaths of hundreds of thousands of Communists, trade unionists, and others.

Under Suharto, the Indonesia government pursued its "New Order" economic policy. To curb the rampant inflation of the Sukarno era, Suharto instituted tight fiscal policies and backed a strong rupiah, Indonesia's national currency. Aided by the spike in oil and raw material prices in the 1970s—Indonesia also has significant timber, rubber, and mineral resources—the economy flourished for a time. The dramatic decline in oil prices during the 1980s, however, led to a 20 percent drop in per capita GDP.

To compensate for the lost oil revenues, the Suharto government instituted free-market reforms, opening the country to greater foreign investment outside the oil sector and promoting tourism. Overall, Suharto's more open policies led to economic gains, as per capita GDP climbed to about $1,000 by the mid-1990s.

But there were problems with the Suharto regime as well. Aside from being even more authoritarian than his predecessor, Suharto presided over an extremely corrupt political and economic system, in which insiders, including many members of his own family, gained control of strategic businesses and made fortunes siphoning money from foreign investments. The commercial legal system was flawed as well, making it difficult for people to enforce contracts and collect debts. And despite economic reforms, there were other distortions in the marketplace, including a vari-

Sales promotion representatives await customers at the Sharia Finance Exhibition in Jakarta, Indonesia, in 2009. The government launched its first retail Islamic bond to help fund a $6 billion economic stimulus package and offset a mounting budget deficit. (Adek Berry/Stringer/AFP/Getty Images)

ety of nontariff barriers to free trade, subsidies to inefficient state-owned enterprises, export restrictions, and domestic subsidies on basic goods. The financial sector was extremely weak, with little regulatory oversight and a great deal of government corruption leading to the manipulation of banking balance sheets by politically connected insiders.

Financial Crises

With the Asian financial crisis that began in Thailand in July 1997, the weakness of Indonesia's financial sector soon became apparent. With its huge foreign reserves (largely from petroleum exports) and low inflation, Indonesia at first seemed immune from the panic in other regional economies that had caused vast outflows of foreign capital. But the contagion soon spread, sending the rupiah spiraling downward, despite government efforts to bolster it by raising interest rates. Ultimately, Indonesia was forced to go to the International Monetary Fund (IMF) for an emergency $23 billion loan, but this did little to stop the rupiah's devaluation. In all, Indonesia's GDP fell by some 13 percent following the onset of the Asian financial crisis.

Meanwhile, as the rupiah fell and the economy tumbled, inflation flared, unemployment rose, and poverty became widespread. Under IMF dictates, the government tried to put its fiscal house in order by cutting subsidies on food and fuel, which triggered massive rioting in a number of cities. While angry with the government, many of the rioters also turned on ethnic Chinese, who controlled much of the nation's business.

In spring 1998, the economic crisis and political turmoil led to Suharto's ouster and Indonesia's emergence as the world's third-largest democracy. Under various administrations from the late 1990s through the mid-2000s, the nation worked to put its economic and legal house in order. The government cut back on subsidies, reduced government debt, and instituted much-needed regulatory oversight of the financial system, thereby reassuring foreign investors. All of these reforms contributed to robust economic growth, which averaged between 5 and 10 percent annually. Also assisting Indonesia's recovery were steadily rising commodity prices through the mid-2000s, though these hurt the nation's poor by raising fuel and food prices.

Indonesia was not hit as hard by the global financial crisis of the late 2000s as some other Asian nations, its economy growing by more than 6 percent in 2008 and more than 4 percent, annually adjusted, in the first quarter of 2009. Nevertheless, foreign investment fell as investors remained skittish about emerging markets and the prices of critically important natural resources declined. To counteract the impact of the global financial crisis, the Indonesian government instituted a $6.9 billion stimulus package in the first half of 2009.

James Ciment

See also: Emerging Markets; Southeast Asia; Transition Economies.

Further Reading
Ariff, Mohamed, and Ahmed M. Khalid. *Liberalization, Growth and the Asian Financial Crisis: Lessons for Developing and Transitional Economies in Asia.* Northampton, MA: Edward Elgar, 2000.
"Indonesia Upgraded: A Brightening Outlook of Indonesia's Economy." *The Economist*, May 22, 2009.
"Indonesia's Economy and the Election: So Far So Good." *The Economist*, January 8, 2009.
Ricklefs, M.C. *A History of Modern Indonesia Since c. 1200.* Palo Alto, CA: Stanford University Press, 2008.
Taylor, Jean Gelman. *Indonesia: People and Histories.* New Haven, CT: Yale University Press, 2003.

Industrial Policy

Industrial policy is the set of plans, policies, and programs initiated by a national government to enhance industrial output and strengthen the economy. The term implies that government should play an active, participatory role in guiding the direction of a nation's industrial economy.

In the United States, an earnest debate over a national industrial policy—and whether there should even be one—began in the early 1980s. Robert Reich, then a Harvard University professor and later U.S. secretary of labor, advocated the need for a comprehensive industrial policy in his book The Next American Frontier (1983) as did left-leaning economists Barry Bluestone and Bennett Harrison in their influential and widely read *The Deindustrialization of America* (1982). In the aftermath of the 1981–1982 economic recession, Reich and other industrial policy proponents argued that many of the nation's most important industries, such as steel, textiles, and rubber, had failed and that the U.S. economy had been deindustrializing since the 1960s. This, they say, had resulted in increasing unemployment, mounting business failures, and declining labor productivity. Furthermore, they argued, other basic industries were no longer competitive in the global economy due to overemphasis by management on short-term profitability rather than long-term innovation.

Critics of industrial policy, on the other hand, present a less optimistic view. During times of economic crisis, as in the 1930s, the 1980s, and the financial meltdown of 2007–2008, these economists strongly opposed the bailing out of troubled companies and industries. They argued, basically, that government only makes matters worse and that the free market should be left alone to do its job. However painful this may be in the short term, the result in the long run will be a better, sounder economy.

Definition

Industrial policy can be defined either broadly or narrowly. The broad definition focuses on the public policies and private sector strategies that affect the nation's economic development and international competitiveness. In the United States, this perspective encompasses large-scale economic policies, labor-management relations, education and scientific research, production technology, and business and civic cultures. However, be-

cause of the sheer breadth of topics and issues it covers, the broad definition of industrial policy in the United States loses much of its usefulness as a basis of policy discussion.

A narrower definition is often more useful. From this perspective, industrial policy focuses on measures taken by the government to improve the country's economic health through the industrial sector in general or through specific industries. The narrower definition, which has gained wide acceptance among scholars, business executives, and public policy makers, focuses on selective government policies that stimulate the development of newly emerging technology industries; the transference of new knowledge and industry "best practices" to enhance the competitiveness of mature, slow-growth industries; and efforts to maintain employment and existing companies in declining industrial sectors. In the United States during the twentieth century, the narrow definition of industrial policy has found expression in several examples of public policy application. Such policies generally focus on direct subsidies, tax credits and deductions, and other incentives for a range of industry sectors, including agriculture, automobiles, steel, telecommunications, and synthetic fuels, with varying degrees of long-term, economic success.

International Industrial Policy

Outside the United States, industrial policy has been common practice for many decades in Europe and Asia. In Great Britain, industrial policies were designed to improve declining productivity and market share of global trade through coordination between government and industry, consolidation of existing industries, special preference to domestic firms on government contracts, and direct subsidies and tax credits for declining and emerging industries. In Germany, the federal government has provided significant subsidies and a guaranteed domestic market to existing industries, such as coal, steel, and shipbuilding. Moreover, the German government has supplied a policy "basket" of subsidies, project grants, and tax incentives to emerging biotechnology, computer, aerospace, and nuclear energy industries. In Japan, the powerful Ministry of International Trade and Industry (MITI) targeted its post–World War II policies at a number of industries whose advancement was deemed critical to the nation's economic success. The Japanese government assisted firms in narrow segments of these targeted industries in capturing market share through tax incentives, special depreciation rules, government-funded research assistance, and direct financial subsidies.

Pros and Cons

Proponents of industrial policy generally believe that national governments should be directly involved in establishing and achieving national goals for high-growth industries and increasing employment. Relying solely on the free market and large-scale economic policies, they argue, fails to address the specific problems of important sectors in American society and does not fully recognize the involvement of foreign governments in international economic competition. Finally, proponents maintain, if major corporations and key industrial sectors are allowed to fail, the economic disruption to the American economy will cause panic in the financial markets and raise the costs of unemployment assistance, employment re-training, and corporate pension bailouts.

Opponents of industrial policy argue that government management of specific industry sectors—that is, picking "winners and losers"—is a recipe for long-term economic failure. Reliance on "corporate welfare," in the form of billions of dollars in short-term aid, will not cure the long-term, structural problems of ailing corporations and industries. Because politicians and government bureaucrats lack the experience and knowledge to properly manage private sector organizations, they are likely to channel scarce public resources to inefficient but politically influential industries, while increasing costs to the beleaguered taxpayer. As economist Charles Schultze, chairman of the

Council of Economic Advisers under President Jimmy Carter, argued in 1983:

> One does not have to be a cynic to forecast that the surest way to multiply unwarranted subsidies and protectionist measures is to legitimize their existence under the rubric of industrial policy. The likely outcome of an industrial policy that encompasses some elements of both "protecting the losers" and "picking the winners" is that the losers would back the subsidies for the winners in return for the latter's support on issues of trade protection.

Since 1995, international industrial policy has been subordinated to tax, tariff, and trade rules of the General Agreement on Tariffs and Trade and other free-trade pacts. As a result of the global financial crisis of 2008–2009, however, the United States, Great Britain, France, Japan, Korea, and other national governments have provided hundreds of billions in their respective currencies for public bailouts of failing financial sectors, with the U.S. government also providing multi-billion-dollar direct loans to its flagging auto industry—all public policy decisions heralding a new era in industrial policy.

Thomas A. Hemphill

See also: Manufacturing.

Further Reading

Lehne, Richard. "15 Industrial Policy and High-Tech Industries." In *Government and Business: American Political Economy in Comparative Perspective.* New York: Seven Bridges Press, 2001.

Johnson, Chalmers, ed. *The Industrial Policy Debate.* San Francisco, CA: ICS Press, 1984.

Norton, R.D. "Industrial Policy and American Renewal." *Journal of Economic Literature* 24:1 (March 1986): 1–40.

Reich, Robert B. *The Next American Frontier.* New York: New York Times Books, 1983.

Schultze, Charles. "Industrial Policy: A Dissent." *Brookings Review* 2 (October 1983): 3–12.

IndyMac Bancorp

The IndyMac Bancorp was the parent company of IndyMac Bank, the largest savings and loan as-

Customers line up in front of an IndyMac branch in Southern California after the bank was shut down and placed under FDIC control in July 2008. The failure of IndyMac, following a wave of mortgage defaults, was one of the largest in U.S. banking history. *(Gabriel Bouys/AFP/Getty Images)*

sociation (S&L) serving the Los Angeles area, and the seventh-largest mortgage lender in the United States in the mid-2000s. IndyMac Bank closed down its retail lending and wholesale divisions in July 2008—constituting the fourth-largest bank failure in U.S. history—and was placed under conservatorship by the Federal Deposit Insurance Corporation (FDIC). The holding company filed for Chapter 7 bankruptcy. As of mid-2009, Indy-Mac Federal Bank existed for the sole purpose of managing IndyMac accounts until they can be redistributed.

IndyMac was spun off from Countrywide Mortgage Investment in 1997. "Mac" was a contraction of "Mortgage Corporation," paralleling the designation Freddie Mac for the Federal Home Loan Mortgage Corporation. Countrywide itself had been founded in 1985 to collateralize mortgages originating with Countrywide Financial. The age

of the collateralized mortgage obligation—which backed bonds with pools of mortgage debts—had just begun, and Countrywide was eager to participate. After twelve years as part of Countrywide, IndyMac had come into its own and was launched as an independent company just as the subprime mortgage market was exploding.

The Pasadena-based bank prospered, operating as both a savings and loan and a mortgage lender, primarily for residential mortgages. The holding company made a number of acquisitions over the next decade, including SGV Bancorp, Financial Freedom, the New York Mortgage Company, and the Barrington Capital Corporation. Many economic analysts, including those at the U.S. Treasury Department, have argued in retrospect that the company may have been too aggressive in its acquisitions. Moreover, they say, the company was not diligent enough when it came to ensuring that its investments were safe and its borrowers were able to repay their debts.

By early 2008, IndyMac was reeling from the wave of defaults on home mortgages it had financed—especially subprime mortgages. Thus, the institution was on shaky ground when, on June 26, 2008, Senator Chuck Schumer (D-NY) released letters he had written to federal regulators calling into question IndyMac's ability to remain solvent. Some commentators have argued that Schumer's comments sealed the bank's fate; Treasury Department officials later concluded that his disclosure was a minor factor compared to the debt IndyMac had accrued in its acquisitions and the lax lending practices it engaged in to help finance that debt, both of which left it vulnerable when the housing market collapsed in 2007.

The bank took severe losses throughout the fourth quarter of 2007 and into 2008, as the subprime mortgage crisis made it impossible to securitize most of IndyMac's mortgage loans. (Nearly all of them were issued for single-family residences, with few safer commercial mortgages to balance the risk.) The bank sought large infusions of capital but proved unsuccessful in finding investors. Nonperforming loans rose 40 percent in a single quarter, and the company admitted that it expected further losses. Hastening the bank's demise, the ratings of $160 million worth of mortgage-backed securities issued by IndyMac were downgraded in April 2008. This brought the bank's risk-based capital below the 10 percent required by federal regulations to qualify an institution as "well-capitalized"; now at the 8–10 percent level, it was designated as "adequately capitalized," meaning that it would cost the bank even more to borrow.

Investigators later discovered that, in order to maintain appearances of health, IndyMac had backdated an $18 million contribution from IndyMac Bancorp. The holding company had transferred the money to the bank shortly before IndyMac disclosed information about its performance in the first quarter of 2008 health; the transaction was backdated to make it appear the funds had been received during that quarter in order to stay above that "well-capitalized" minimum. Darrel Dochow, western regional director of the Treasury Department's Office of Thrift Supervision (the regulatory agency for S&Ls), had permitted the deceptive backdating and was forced to resign in February 2009.

In the meantime, beginning in July 2008, depositors rapidly began withdrawing their money from IndyMac accounts, as bad news about the company began to leak out to the public. Job cuts came just as rapidly, and the company's stock price plummeted to 44 cents a share—down from $50 two years earlier. IndyMac's credit rating was downgraded to CCC, one of the lowest available without being in default. On July 11, the Federal Deposit Insurance Corporation (FDIC) put IndyMac Bank in conservatorship and established IndyMac Federal Bank to manage its assets until they were transferred to the new OneWest Bank in March 2009. Meanwhile, several lawsuits were filed alleging fraud and other wrongdoing connected with IndyMac's accounting and lending practices.

Bill Kte'pi

See also: Banks, Commercial; Panics and Runs, Bank; Recession and Financial Crisis (2007–).

Further Reading

Krugman, Paul. *The Return of Depression Economics and the Crisis of 2008.* New York: W.W. Norton, 2009.

Shiller, Robert J. *The Subprime Solution: How Today's Global Financial Crisis Happened, and What to Do About It.* Princeton, NJ: Princeton University Press, 2008.

Soros, George. *The New Paradigm for Financial Markets: The Credit Crisis of 2008 and What It Means.* Jackson, TN: PublicAffairs, 2008.

Inflation

Inflation refers to an overall rise in the average level of prices of goods and services in an economy over a period of time. During periods of inflation, currency decreases in value—that is, each unit of currency buys fewer goods and services. The opposite of inflation is deflation, when the average level of prices falls and each unit of currency buys more.

Mainstream economists point to the fundamentals of supply and demand as the source of inflation, either through increased costs of production at the supply end or through increases in aggregate demand that are not compensated for by an increasing supply of goods and services. Monetarists, however, insist that inflation is brought on by increasing the amount of money in circulation and that it is a purely monetary phenomena.

In the mainstream view, inflation usually, but not always, accompanies periods of economic expansion because demand is rising faster than supply. In the monetarist view, however, inflation is a result of government policy, and thus it is somewhat independent of the business cycle, although governments often expand the money supply as a means to lift economies out of recession. Economists disagree as to the effects of inflation. Keynesians even argue that modest inflation can be good for an economy. Regardless, all agree that high rates of inflation are harmful because they create uncertainty about future prices that discourages saving and investment, among other effects. In periods of extreme inflation, known as hyperinflation, entire economies can be wrecked, leading to political and social turmoil.

Measuring Inflation

Economists use a number of indices to measure inflation. The most widely known measure in the United States is the consumer price index (CPI), maintained by the Bureau of Labor Statistics, which measures the prices of some 80,000 goods and services. Although this measure is followed closely by economists and policy makers, the CPI has its faults, as it does not take into account the quality of goods. For example, cars today are far more expensive than they were twenty years ago, but they are also more reliable and longer lasting. Is the level of inflation in automobile prices

offset, either partially or wholly, by the fact that people now spend less on maintenance and replacement costs? The CPI does not address such questions. In addition, the CPI includes products in highly volatile sectors such as food and energy. As a result, the Federal Reserve (Fed), which sets monetary policy in the United States and thus exerts a major influence on inflation rates, prefers to look at "core inflation," or core CPI, a measure that excludes products in the sectors that the Fed has no control over. Thus, the Fed monitors the core CPI to determine whether inflation in commodity markets (food and energy) is spilling over to produce inflation in the broader economy.

In addition to the CPI, economists analyze the producer price index, also maintained by the Bureau of Labor Statistics, which tracks changes in wholesale prices, and the gross domestic product (GDP) deflator, maintained by the Bureau of Economic Analysis, which tracks price changes in everything that is included in gross domestic product—a far broader array of goods and services. By using the GDP deflator, economists can determine real GDP, that is, the growth in the economy adjusted for changes in overall prices. Nominal GDP measures overall growth, or shrinkage, without taking into account inflation or deflation. Looking at nominal GDP, growth may come from either higher prices or expanded output. Likewise, changes in real GDP come from an expansion or contraction of actual output, not just changes in prices.

Causes

Economists disagree as to the causes of inflation. Mainstream economists argue that inflation is caused by rising production costs, rising aggregate demand, or both. Production costs may rise for a number of reasons, including increases in the price of raw materials, the cost of borrowing money, labor costs, energy costs, and other factors. When these costs rise, producers tend to pass the increase on to consumers in the form of higher prices, in order to maintain revenue and profits. In classical economics, this reduces the quantity of goods and services demanded, which, in turn, brings down input prices as supply and demand adjust to a new equilibrium. However, producers often reduce production as their costs rise, leading to a shortage of supply. If the money supply stays the same as the supply of goods drops, this produces a phenomenon that economists call "cost-push" inflation. Conversely, increases in aggregate demand also may cause inflation. If spending by households, businesses, and/or government increases—and supply fails to keep up—this results in what economists call "demand-pull" inflation.

Monetarists differ from mainstream economists in that they lay the blame for inflation largely or even exclusively on monetary policy. Milton Friedman, perhaps the most famous monetary economist, once observed that inflation "is always and everywhere a monetary phenomenon." In other words, if governments increase the total amount of money that people have to spend, entrepreneurs will find that they do not have as many goods to sell as people can afford to buy. Because entrepreneurs make more profit by raising prices, they will react to increased consumer spending by raising their prices. As all or most prices begin to rise, the price level increases, and the economy experiences inflation.

According to monetarists, central banks, such as the Federal Reserve in the United States, cause inflation. Central banks increase the money supply through open market operations. In the United States, open market operations refer to the buying or selling of Treasury securities by the Fed. When the Fed buys Treasury securities from the U.S. Department of the Treasury or from the public, it pays for them using newly created money. This newly created money enters and circulates in the economy, chasing too few goods and causing prices to rise.

A small minority of economists take a slightly different position on the monetary causes of inflation. They argue that inflation can be caused by increases in the money supply within the private banking system. This view is called the endogenous theory—that is, internally created—money by the private sector. An example of this theory in operation is the housing price bubble of the mid-2000s, which was created, these economists say, by the financial industry's overly lenient credit policies that inflated the amount of money chasing the supply of homes. According to this theory, even if the Fed takes action to decrease the amount of money and credit, the private sector will find ways around the tightening and continue to increase credit despite central bank restraint. An example would be banks increasing their use of eurodollar borrowings to fund domestic loans. There are many other instances in which the private sector has found ways to work around regulations that could restrict lending.

Inflation and the Business Cycle

Inflation usually occurs in periods of economic expansion, when aggregate demand rises faster than producers can meet it. In this way, inflation can become self-generating: as prices rise, workers demand wage increases, which businesses accept because they are earning solid revenues. In other times, however, inflation may accompany periods of economic stagnation or even contraction. The best-known episode of so-called stagflation occurred in the 1970s when rapidly rising energy costs slowed the U.S. economy even as they sent the prices of energy-dependent goods and services upward. As prices rose, so did the demands of labor, furthering the inflation cycle even as overall economic growth remained anemic. To get out of this vicious cycle, the Fed dramatically hiked interest rates and tightened credit, setting off a recession so deep that it cooled inflationary pressures as producers were forced to rein in costs to meet lowered demand and workers resisted calls for higher wages for fear of risking layoffs.

All economists agree that excessive inflation is bad for the economy. The reason for this is simple: when households believe that money is declining in value, they lower their saving rate, as the money they put away will have less value in the future. Businesses feel the pinch, too. Lower saving rates make borrowing money costlier, discouraging investment. And without investment, production lags, which can fuel inflation. In extreme cases of inflation, consumers may even begin to hoard goods for fear of extreme price increases, creating shortages that bring on or worsen the very hyper-inflation they fear.

There is less consensus among economists about the positive effects of inflation. Some argue that there are no positive effects, while others say that inflation can be used to pull economies out of recession. If an economy is being dragged down by excessive debt, for example, inflation can help reduce that debt load. That is, because debt usually is paid back over time, the real level of debt goes down as the value of money decreases. Inflation also raises nominal interest rates, giving central banks the opportunity to lower the rates they charge commercial banks; lower rates make borrowing cheaper and encourage the kind of investment that helps lift economies out of recession. Keynesian economists argue that because nominal wages are "sticky"—that is, slow to adjust to economic changes—inflation allows for the lowering of real wages—that is, wages adjusted for inflation—thereby bringing labor markets into equilibrium faster than would occur without infla-tion. Finally, American economist James Tobin has theorized that because inflation has a greater impact on monetary assets, it encourages invest-ment in capital goods over financial products, which also can lead to economic recovery.

James Ciment and D.W. MacKenzie

See also: Deflation; Price Stability.

Further Reading
Friedman, Milton. "Unemployment Versus Inflation? An Evaluation of the Phillips Curve." Occasional Paper no. 44, Institute of Economic Affairs, 1975.
Frisch, Helmut. *Theories of Inflation.* Cambridge, UK: Cambridge University Press, 1983.
Hayek, Friedrich A. *Prices and Production.* 1931. New York: A.M. Kelley, 1967.
Okun, Arthur. *Prices and Quantities: A Macroeconomic Analysis.* Washington, DC: Brookings Institution, 1981.
Palley, Thomas I. "Competing Theories of the Money Supply: Theory and Evidence." *Metroeconomica* 45:1 (February 1994): 67–88.
Phelps, Edmund S. "Anticipated Inflation and Economic Welfare." *Journal of Political Economy* 73:1 (February 1965): 1–17.
———. "Phillips Curves, Expectations of Inflation and Opti-mal Unemployment over Time." *Economica* 34:135 (August 1967): 254–281.
Samuelson, Paul, and Robert M. Solow. "Analytical Aspects of Anti-Inflation Policy." *American Economic Review* 50:2 (May 1960): 177–194.
Tobin, James. "Inflation and Unemployment." *American Economic Review* 62:1 (March 1972): 1–18.

Information Technology

Information technology (IT), a term first coined in the 1980s, refers to the software and hard-ware of computer information systems, either in stand-alone form or linked in networks. Informa-tion technology incorporates the design, develop-ment, application, support, and management of computer information systems.

The economic impact of information tech-nology is varied and immense. First, since the widespread adoption of user-friendly, personal computers in the 1980s and the Internet in the 1990s, information technology has emerged as a vast economic sector in and of itself. Second, information technology has reshaped the way the world does business, as there is virtually no in-dustry, no job, and no sector of the economy that has been unaffected by the revolution in informa-tion technology, allowing for enormous gains in productivity, on the one hand, but disruptions of old business models, on the other.

Finally, information technology has trans-formed the relevance of economic theory. Informa-tion, of course, is crucial to the decisions made by economic players. Some schools of classical econom-ics presume that buyers and sellers have access to all pertinent information about transactions before they make their economic decisions. By amassing more information and making it more widely available, computer technology puts economic theory and practice more in line with each other.

IT Sector

The modern computer era began in the 1940s, with the development of so-called electronic brains, huge and expensive vacuum tube–driven machines. Transistor technology in the 1950s and integrated circuit technology in the 1960s made computers smaller and cheaper. By the 1970s, this process, along with developments in software, allowed for the desktop computer to emerge. Over the course of the 1980s and 1990s, such computers became ubiquitous in households and businesses throughout the developed world. At the same time, the development of computer networks and the Internet allowed for the transfer of information from one computer to another. The first development allowed for huge amounts of information to be amassed, while the latter allowed for its dispersion.

Defining what constitutes the information technology sector—and therefore its size—is difficult. Moreover, much economic activity related to information technology occurs within companies that primarily are devoted to other activities. That is, companies as diverse as automobile manufacturers and coal mining may have large IT departments. But looking at just one part of the IT sector gives a sense of its overall size. According to the U.S. Census Bureau, in the late 2000s, computer design and related services—including software development and support, the design of computer systems, and on-site management and operation of client computer systems and data processing facilities—generated roughly $275 billion in annual revenues, or 2 percent of U.S. gross domestic product (GDP). Most economists, however, take such figures with a grain of salt. The constantly falling cost of IT infrastructure—as well as the exponential gains in output with each new generation of IT systems—makes it difficult to measure the relative share of IT in GDP and in productivity.

San Jose, California—seen from a bird's-eye view, through a fish-eye lens—is the self-proclaimed capital of the Silicon Valley, the epicenter of the Internet dot.com boom of the 1990s. (David McNew/Getty Images)

Productivity and "Creative Destruction"

Information technology has transformed virtually every sector of the economy. Among the most important effects has been the increased productivity that IT allows through reductions in coordination costs within companies, between companies, and between companies and customers. An analysis of just one period of the IT revolution in the United States—1995 to 2000—reveals the kinds of productivity gains made possible by IT. Many economists point to these years as the period in which the spread of computers over the previous two decades finally made its impact on productivity, as companies and workers began to make full use of their potential. Thus, while productivity gains averaged about 1.35 percent annually between 1973 and 1994, they jumped to 2.87 percent between 1995 and 2000. Moreover, economists note that industries that incorporated IT more readily—or simply were more suited to implement IT—made productivity gains far in excess of industries that did not or could not incorporate it as readily.

One of the industries that made the most of the new technology was finance. By the 1980s, many large institutional investors had developed complex computer programs to oversee their portfolios and automate their trading decisions. That is, investors allowed computers to automatically sell or buy shares in response to market trends. The stock market crash of 1987 made the dangers of that approach apparent, as a sell-off in corporate equities triggered a cascade of computer-generated selling orders that caused the Dow Jones Industrial Average to plunge from 2,246 to 1,739—the largest single-day percentage loss in the index's history. In the aftermath of the crash, the New York Stock Exchange and other exchanges instituted rule changes to prevent such an occurrence in the future.

Like all new technologies and the entrepreneurial activity that makes use of them, IT has had a disruptive effect as well, serving as a major force in what twentieth-century economist Joseph Schumpeter called the "creative destruction" of capitalism. Online retailing, for example, has had a major impact on traditional "brick and mortar" stores, particularly in industries with vast arrays of different products, such as bookselling. While major chain bookstores have seen sales remain flat since the late 1990s, the Internet bookselling giant Amazon.com increased sales from less than a $1 billion in North America in 2000 to well over $6 billion in 2009. Content providers also have felt the "creative destruction" of IT. The music industry, for example, saw revenues decline by roughly one-third between 1999 and 2008, a result, most experts agree, of the free and largely illegal practice of sharing and downloading, a development made possible by IT. Newspapers have seen such huge losses in circulation, as readers access their content for free on online, and advertising revenues—as customers stop buying classified ads and sell their goods and services at online sites such as eBay and Craigslist—that some experts talk of an industry-wide collapse.

By the 1990s, these transformations had led many investors to conclude that IT had changed the very nature of modern capitalism. To get in early on the economic revolution promised by IT and the Internet, many began to put their money into firms developing these new technologies and firms utilizing them to pursue other businesses. By the end of the decade, vast sums of money were pouring into these businesses, either in the form of venture capital or purchases of equity shares once the companies became publicly listed, leading to an asset price bubble in the IT sector. The Nasdaq stock market—where many of these firms were listed—soared from roughly 800 at the beginning of 1995 to nearly 4,700 at its peak just after the turn of the millennium, an increase of nearly 600 percent. But the revolution wrought by IT was slower in coming than many had anticipated; traditional market forces—in the form of poor earnings reports and tighter credit policies implemented by the Federal Reserve—soon exerted themselves, leading to many IT bankruptcies and a crash in the overall value of IT equities. By mid-2002, the Nasdaq index had fallen to under 1,200, as the dot.com bubble burst.

IT and the Markets

More long lasting is the IT revolution's impact on how financial markets operate. Information, say economists, is critical to the smooth functioning of the financial marketplace, as buyers and sellers determine how much they will pay for and charge for financial instruments, respectively. First conceived in the early twentieth century, efficient market theory—which argues that the prices of traded assets reflect all available information—was given new credence by the IT revolution at the end of the century. With computers and the Internet, economic agents now truly had access to all information available, guaranteeing that they would act in a more rational fashion. Because buyers and sellers had access to all of this information and acted rationally, there was no need for government regulation, said proponents of the theory. However, in the aftermath of the financial crisis of 2008–2009, many economists have abandoned the theory, noting that psychology and behavioral habits undermine the notion that perfect access to information guarantees that economic agents will act rationally. The IT revolution may be a game changer as far as markets are concerned, these economists said, but it still could not change human nature.

James Ciment

See also: Dot.com Bubble (1990s–2000); Technological Innovation.

Further Reading

Cassidy, John. *Dot.con: The Greatest Story Ever Sold.* New York: HarperCollins, 2002.

Metz, Tim. *Black Monday: The Catastrophe of October 19, 1987, and Beyond.* New York: William Morrow, 1988.

Samii, Massood, and Gerald Karush, eds. *International Business and Information Technology: Interaction and Transformation in the Global Economy.* New York: Routledge, 2004.

Turban, Efraim, Dorothy Leidner, Ephraim McLean, and James Wetherbe. *Information Technology for Management: Transforming Organizations in the Digital Economy.* Hoboken, NJ: John Wiley & Sons, 2007.

Innovation, Financial

Financial innovation is generally recognized as a response on the part of the financial industry to regulatory and environmental challenges. Financial institutions, like other businesses, attempt to respond to challenges to the environment and regulatory framework. But financial institutions face far greater challenges than most other businesses, as the financial services industry has traditionally been one of the most heavily regulated in the United States and most other capitalist economies despite three decades of deregulation.

Many instruments in the financial marketplace that are now regarded as ordinary or standard were in fact the result of financial innovation. For example, the market for the eurodollar—that is, a U.S. dollar deposited in a European Bank and a frequently used international currency—was established as a way to circumvent Regulation Q, instituted in 1933 to restrict the maximum interest rate that a bank could pay on deposits. Similarly, off-balance-sheet financing/lending (assets or debts not on a firm's balance sheet) and offshore banking (in which the branch of a bank is located in a less regulated offshore financial center, such as the Cayman Islands)—now common practices—developed in response to the tight regulatory capture by federal banking regulators. Indeed, a great many innovations have been devised by financial institutions in recent times in response to regulatory challenges and decreasing earning margins. According to some economists, the variety of innovative instruments and practices provides a strong indication that the current regulatory structure is obsolete and in need of overhaul.

Innovation has been a vital factor in the modern financial system of the twentieth and twenty-first centuries. It might be said, in fact, that a basic loan is the only true, classical banking product and that all other offerings have been the result of financial innovation. According to the industry, modern banking is driven by financial innovations and their ability to meet customers' needs and fuel the economy at large. Central bankers and financial regulators take a somewhat more cautious view, pointing out that financial innovations tend to weaken the effectiveness of monetary policy.

Although the conflict between modern economic reality and rigid, obsolete regulations often gives rise to financial innovation, the emergence of new instruments and practices also has been triggered by different kinds of challenges. Changes in the macroeconomic environment—the economy as a whole—induce financial institutions to seek innovative products and the processes to support them, such as adjustable rate mortgages (ARMs). ARMs—in which a low initial interest rate readjusts with shifts in a pegged index, such as the federal funds rate, after a given period of time—were designed, in theory at least, to offer lower rates to first-time homebuyers and those with poor or little credit history. Likewise, changes in the macroeconomic environment—such as high interest rates, high inflation, and increases in government deficit financing—often give rise to financial innovations as well. Indeed, ARMs were first created during a period of high interest rates in the 1990s, to make mortgages more affordable to middle-income homebuyers.

Technology is another major force that drives innovation. Responding to technological challenges may lead to the modification not only of financial instruments, but also of delivery channels and the way the financial institutions relate to the customer. Regulatory environments in particular have been made obsolete by technical innovations such as electronic funds transfers. Changes in perceived market conditions have also traditionally contributed to the innovative behavior of financial institutions and the development of financial innovations such as ARMs after the inflation of the 1970s and early 1980s. Financial institutions, being primarily established as profit-making entities, are, in a modern economy, market driven. Firms at the micro level design, develop, and launch new or modified products because they are

thought to be more profitable; and as there is no competition, the company launching them can reap the (usually short-term) benefits of being a market leader. In a competitive market, market participants are in constant search of new, innovative ways to make greater profits; financial innovations arise as a result of that drive.

Financial innovations can be classified in a number of categories, and a distinction can be drawn between product innovations and process innovations. Product innovations appear when a financial institution launches a new product in the market that bears similarities with existing products but in fact falls outside the current regulatory capture and opens new market potential for the institution launching it. For example, the financial derivative—a financial instrument whose value is "derived" from another financial product or index—is related to the much older futures contract on a commodity, in which an investor agrees to purchase a certain quantity of a commodity in the future at a fixed price. In both cases, the value of the instrument is derived from something else. Process innovation, by contrast, changes the way the institution manages an existing financial product or performs a particular financial process so as to increase efficiency, expand the market, and improve profitability. Process innovations often focus on transaction costs and how they can be reduced. Debit cards, for example, offer banks, merchants, and consumers a much less expensive and time-consuming method of paying for goods and services than the traditional written check.

Other analysts recognize another general category of financial innovation—system or institutional innovations. This type affects the financial sector as a whole, generating a wave of changes that affects the entire financial sector. System innovations in the financial industry tend to take hold quickly and become difficult if not impossible for a single institution to resist implementing.

Some economists have pointed out that a significant financial innovation can provide a shock, or series of sustained shocks, to an economy. According to Benjamin Graham and David Dodd, a financial innovation can be understood as a "deviation from the normal patterns." Although financial innovations generally arise in response to market imperfections, such as taxes, regulations, moral hazard, and the like, they are not entirely driven by them. Instead, financial innovations are more directly dictated by the profit-maximizing principle that drives the institutions as businesses. Concern over transaction costs is often underplayed in the analysis of financial innovation and of what triggers such costs. Although transaction costs arise in response to regulatory limits, the ultimate goal of financial institutions is to increase profitability and to control these costs.

Globalization, liberalization, and deregulation, which marked the years of expanded American banking from the mid-1980s to early in the new century's first decade, have created a particularly conducive climate for financial innovation. The demand for a new round of financial regulation after the crisis of 2007–2009 was generally expected to limit the innovative behavior of banks, who fully expected the regulator authorities to resist new instruments and processes. This is not to say, however, that financial innovation will come to a stop—only that it might not be in the forefront for the time being.

Željko Šević

See also: Collateralized Debt Obligations; Collateralized Mortgage Obligations; Credit Default Swaps; Debt Instruments; Financial Markets; Liberalization, Financial; Regulation, Financial.

Further Reading

Allen, Franklin, and Douglas Gale. *Financial Innovation and Risk Sharing.* Cambridge, MA: MIT Press, 1994.

Geanuracos, John, and Bill Millar. *The Power of Financial Innovation.* New York: HarperCollins Business, 1991.

Graham, Benjamin, and David Dodd. *Security Analysis.* New York: Whittlesey House, 1934.

Miller, M.H. "Financial Innovation: Achievements and Prospects." *Journal of Applied Corporate Finance* 4:4 (1992): 4–11.

———. "Financial Innovation: The Last Twenty Years and the Next." *Journal of Financial and Quantitative Analysis* 21:4 (1986): 459–471.

Šević, Željko. "Financial Innovation." In *Encyclopaedia of Political Economy*, ed. P. O'Hara. London: Routledge, 1999.

Institutional Economics

Institutional economics was a school of economic and political thought embraced by U.S. scholars in the early twentieth century that focused on the role of institutions—social as well as economic—in shaping how economies operate. Emerging out of the German historical school, it eschewed the theoretical, mathematical modeling of mainstream classical and neoclassical economics, instead emphasizing that the economic behavior of people and institutions was rooted in specific historical circumstances. Practitioners of institutional economics looked for pragmatic solutions to real-life, time- and place-specific economic problems, rather than formulating concepts that, in theory, applied to all situations. Many institutional economists—among them Adolf Berle and Wesley Mitchell—took up policy-making or influential positions in government or the private sector.

The three major practitioners of institutional economics were Thorstein Veblen, a founder of the New School for Social Research in New York City; John Commons, a labor studies pioneer at the University of Wisconsin; and John Kenneth Galbraith, a widely read and influential writer on American capitalism in the immediate post–World War II era.

In his most famous work, *The Theory of the Leisure Class* (1899), Veblen argued that consumer behavior is not purely rational and utilitarian, but is shaped by social institutions and traditions. Specifically, he said, those with disposable incomes tend to spend their money in ways that publicly display their wealth. Thus, people might spend their money on flashy clothes rather than paying the rent, thereby distorting the smooth running of the economy. Moreover, people might borrow to sustain a particular lifestyle, which could have a negative effect on financial markets. In making such arguments, Veblen was critiquing the work of the classical economists, whose mathematical models depended on consumers behaving in predictable ways across class, time, and space. Moreover, Veblen contradicted mainstream economists—who insisted that government interference in the economy only distorted markets and led to inefficiencies—by arguing that government had a role in making sure that more of society's resources went toward providing for the basic needs of the less fortunate than toward the "conspicuous consumption" of the well-off and those aspiring to appear well-off.

Not a major economics thinker, Commons is best known for two accomplishments. First is the establishment of labor history as discipline; in doing so, Commons emphasized that members of the working class were not purely economic actors, always seeking the highest remuneration for the least possible effort, but rather had other interests and values—including dignity and security—that were shaped by their involvement in institutions such as labor unions and factories. Second, Commons put institutional economic thinking into practice by pushing for government regulations and agencies—and helping to create them—that would provide a counterbalance to the power of private economic institutions such as corporations. Commons believed that economies could provide the highest standard of living to the largest number of people when they operated not by purely antagonistic, market-driven forces, but by negotiation and compromise among institutions, such as corporations, unions, and government.

Galbraith's writings focused on the workings of the huge corporations that dominated economic and social life in the years after World War II. According to Galbraith, the power of these vast institutions was more likely to shape the operation of the market than vice versa, as classically trained economists insisted. Their advertising shaped consumer behavior; their control of the production process distorted the normal workings of supply and demand; and their huge bureaucracies sought long-term stability rather than immediate profit, as mainstream economists argued.

No longer influential, institutional economic thinking lives on in the work of behavioral economists, who share their predecessor's belief that economic agents do not always act in purely rational and utilitarian ways, but often make economic decisions based on psychological and sociological factors.

James Ciment

See also: Behavioral Economics; Galbraith, John Kenneth; German Historical School; Veblen, Thorstein.

Further Reading

Commons, John R. *Institutional Economics: Its Place in Political Economy.* New York: Macmillan, 1934.

Galbraith, John Kenneth. *The New Industrial State.* Boston: Houghton Mifflin, 1967.

Veblen, Thorstein. *The Theory of the Leisure Class: An Economic Study in the Evolution of Institutions.* New York: Macmillan, 1899.

Yonay, Yuval P. *The Struggle over the Soul of Economics: Institutionalist and Neoclassical Economists in America Between the Wars.* Princeton, NJ: Princeton University Press, 1998.

Insull, Samuel (1859–1938)

A celebrated business leader of the 1920s, Samuel Insull built a vast utilities empire that by the end of that decade was valued at more than $2 billion, making its money by providing electricity to more than 4 million customers in 32 states. But the assets of the interlocking web of companies he created were over-leveraged and when the credit markets froze up after the Wall Street crash of 1929, the empire collapsed, wiping out the savings of millions of small investors and leaving Insull himself impoverished.

Born in London in 1859, Insull went to work for inventor and entrepreneur Thomas Edison's British representative at the age of twenty-one. His business acumen soon caught the attention of the famed inventor, who made Insull his personal secretary and brought him to the United States in 1881. Insull rose through the ranks of Edison's wide-ranging business, helping to build power stations around the United States and participating in the formation of Edison General Electric (later General Electric).

In 1892, Insull left General Electric and Edison's employ and moved to Chicago, where, taking out a personal loan for $250,000—then a small fortune—he launched Chicago Edison and purchased one of the city's many independent power-generating plants. (Although the company bore the famed inventor's name, it was not owned by him.) Unlike in later years when utilities became a highly regulated and stable business, electrical generation at the dawn of the electrical age was a highly speculative enterprise with lots of competition. Insull prospered through aggressive acquisition and innovation, of both the technical and entrepreneurial variety. When it became clear that the alternating current (AC) system pioneered by George Westinghouse was superior to the direct current (DC) advocated by Edison, Insull abandoned his former employer's technology and became among the first to adopt AC for his power systems.

In 1894, he built the Harrison Street Power Station, then the largest in the world. It was a gamble. Electricity, of course, cannot be stored, so supply and demand have to be evenly matched. Build too large a station and much of it can sit idle; build too small a station and risk losing customers when the power supply fails. Insull came up with an idea to make sure that his station ran as close to capacity as possible. By charging lower prices for electricity at off-peak hours, he could even out usage and lower prices even for peak use hours. To spur demand further, Insull offered a low-cost home-wiring service and even gave away appliances for free.

Insull realized that economies of scale applied to electricity as they did to other businesses and, from the 1890s through the 1920s, he built numerous power stations or purchased those of competitors. In 1907, he amalgamated his largest holdings into a new company known as Commonwealth Edison and, by the middle of the next decade, possessed a virtual monopoly over the Chicago electricity business. Insull also bought major interests in urban and inter-urban electric train systems in the Midwest.

By the 1910s and 1920s, Insull was starting or purchasing utilities across the Midwest and around the country, creating a web of companies linked together into five separate electricity-generating and -distributing systems. Insull became the major figure in a burgeoning business; between 1919 and 1929, electrical production went from 38.9 million kilowatt hours to 97.4 million. By the latter year, Insull controlled roughly one-eighth of the country's electricity-generating capacity.

While Insull's electricity-generating empire was real, the legal and financial framework for it was of more questionable value. Insull set up holding companies that owned other holding companies that owned still other holding companies; there were sometimes four or five levels of ownership between Insull and the firm that actually supplied electricity to consumers. The reason for this complicated ownership pattern was to get around rules established by local and state governments to make sure that these natural monopolies did not charge customers excessive fees for electricity. The strategy worked. By 1930, Insull's assets were valued at a then-staggering $2.5 billion and "Insullism" became a byword for conglomerate-style corporations.

But to build this empire, Insull borrowed heavily, using the assets of one company as collateral to buy others. This worked as long as the economy was expanding, credit was free-flowing, and his customer base was growing and able to pay its bills. But with the stock market crash of 1929 and subsequent economic depression, all of that came to a halt. Unable to pay his many creditors, Insull saw his empire begin to collapse while he himself was removed by the boards of many of the various holding companies he had created.

Indicted on charges of embezzlement and investor fraud, Insull fled to Europe in 1932, returned voluntarily to the United States, and eventually stood trial. Acquitted, he returned to Europe a virtually penniless man and died in Paris in 1938. To prevent such utilities empires from arising again, Congress passed the Public Utility Holding Act of 1935, limiting utilities to specific geographic regions and subjecting them more thoroughly to state regulations. The act was eventually repealed and replaced by a weaker law, the Public Utility Holding Company Act of 2005.

James Ciment

See also: Boom, Economic (1920s); Corporate Corruption; Great Depression (1929–1933).

Further Reading

McDonald, Forrest. *Insull.* Chicago: University of Chicago Press, 1962.

Platt, Harold L. *The Electric City: Energy and the Growth of the Chicago Area, 1880–1930.* Chicago: University of Chicago Press, 1991.

Wasik, John F. *The Merchant of Power: Samuel Insull, Thomas Edison, and the Creation of the Modern Metropolis.* New York: Palgrave Macmillan, 2006.

Integration, Financial

The term "financial integration" refers to the synthesis or unification of a country's financial markets with the markets of other countries, whether located in the same or another geographic region. Financial integration may therefore be understood as the homogenizing process of a given financial area.

As the global economic crises of recent years have shown, financial integration resulting from the force of globalization can be a double-edged sword: on the one hand, it can bring great efficiencies into regional financial operations; on the other hand—as evidenced by the Asian financial crisis of 1997–1998 and the global financial meltdown of 2008–2009—it can also accelerate the spread of a financial crisis from one country to another.

Financial integration results from the removal of the barriers to financial transactions through deregulation and privatization (the transfer of companies from public to private ownership), and through the elimination of barriers preventing foreign institutions from offering cross-border financial services. Financial integration has also been facilitated through technological progress (especially digital processing and the Internet), which has allowed financial transactions between countries to be performed almost instantaneously. Moreover, the adoption of a single currency in economic regions (such as portions of the European Union) has made cross-border transactions much easier to achieve through increased competitiveness and financial transparency.

In these various ways, financial integration is achieved through the enactment of formal agreements between countries, as when Chile and Mexico concluded a series of agreements in the wake of the North American Free Trade Agreement (NAFTA, signed 1994), or when China signed trade agreements with countries gathered at an Association of Southeast Asian Nations (ASEAN) summit meeting in 2004. Financial integration can also be the result of less formal arrangements between countries. Even broad coordination of standards, rules, and regulations provides efficient support for financial integration.

Europe and the United States

A good example of financial integration can be found in Europe, with the adoption of the Markets in Financial Instruments Directive (MiFID) in 2004 and its implementation in 2007. MiFID promotes harmonized regulation of firms dealing in securities markets and offering investment services to clients in other European countries. Thirty European countries have adopted MiFID. Home countries supervise the standarized regulations. Nevertheless, MiFID raised a number of concerns—as efforts at financial integration often do—regarding the fragmentation of markets. According to theory, financial integration tends to increase competition between countries. And indeed, the greater trade efficiency resulting from MiFID and other integration measures has raised the level of competition.

In the United States, a greater degree of financial integration emerged with the Riegle-Neal Interstate Banking and Branching Efficiency Act of 1994. The legislation repealed earlier legal restrictions, namely the McFadden Act of 1927, that prohibited interstate branching—that is, prevented banks from operating in more than one state. The Riegle-Neal Act allowed lending institutions to acquire other banks or to set up branches in other states. It promoted financial integration by allowing banks to operate "cross-border" (interstate) accounts. Likewise, the Gramm-Leach-Bliley Financial Modernization Act of 1999 allowed banks, securities firms, and insurance companies to merge, thus permitting greater integration of financial services by a single firm. This legislation repealed the Glass-Steagall Act of 1933, which had separated commercial and investment banking.

Africa, Latin America, and Asia

African countries have encountered greater obstacles in the pursuit of financial integration. Even the agreements that they do reach often do not fully deliver their benefits. Political cohesion and stability—which are critical to financial integration—are all too rare on the African subcontinent. On the positive side, countries in eastern and southern Africa signed a treaty of economic cooperation in 1993, opening the way toward greater financial integration. The Southern African Development Community was established in 1996 and the East African Community in 1999. If falling short of fully integrated common markets, such initiatives held promise for greater regional cooperation in trade and finance.

Latin America has witnessed a de facto kind of financial integration, primarily as a result of foreign investments beginning in the 1990s. A liberalization process initiated in the 1990s led to the listing of financial instruments on foreign stock markets. In the Caribbean, financial integration has taken the form of cross-border ownership involving both financial and nonfinancial firms in the tourism and leisure industries.

In Asia, a measure of financial integration came as a result of the globalization movement that began in the 1990s, but the extent and effects of the changes are debated. According to some observers, Asian financial integration lags far behind that of Europe before 1993, relying more on the development of global markets and foreign investments in the nations of the region. For large-scale financial integration to occur in Asia, many agree, major political, economic, and social obstacles have to be overcome.

Marc Lenglet

See also: Asian Financial Crisis (1997); Business Cycles, International.

Further Reading

Bowden, Roger J., and Vance L. Martin. "International Business Cycles and Financial Integration." *Review of Economics and Statistics* 77:2 (1995): 305–20.

European Commission. *European Financial Integration Report 2008* (January 2009). Available at http://ec.europa.eu/internal_market/finances/fim/index_en.htm. Accessed May 2009.

Galindo, Arturo, Alejandro Micco, and César Serra. "Financial Integration." In *Beyond Borders: The New Regionalism in Latin America. Social Progress in Latin America.* Washington, DC: Inter-American Development Bank, 2002.

World Bank. *Global Development Finance: The Role of International Banking.* Vol. 1: *Review, Analysis and Outlook.* Washington, DC: World Bank, 2008.

Interest Rates

The interest rate is the amount, expressed as an annual percentage, that a borrower pays in addition to the principle (the amount borrowed in a loan), for the privilege of borrowing money. Generally, the interest rate both protects against inflation—so that the amount the lender gets back is still worth as much as the amount lent (the real interest rate)—and guarantees the lender a profit, in lieu of, or perhaps in addition to, other fees. (A credit card company, for instance, receives penalty fees and possible membership fees, as well as fees from the vendors that use their services, on top of the interest the cardholder pays; this helps ensure that the card issuer earns a profit even if the cardholder pays off the balance every month in order to avoid interest.) Depending on the loan, interest can be compounded annually, monthly, daily, or at other frequencies.

Nominal and Real Interest Rates

The nominal—or payable—interest rate is the one defined in the appropriate contract or other formal agreement. For example, a credit card that charges 16.9 percent on the balance has a 16.9 percent nominal interest rate. The real interest rate does not show up anywhere in the literature pertaining to the debt. It represents the purchasing power of the interest payments received—that is, the nominal interest rate adjusted for inflation over the period of time in which the interest is paid.

Interest rates that are compounded at different frequencies can be converted to a "common denominator," called the effective interest rate or annual equivalent rate (AER), so named because it restates the nominal interest rate as an interest rate with annual compounding. The AER is similar to the APR, or the annual percentage rate, the terms in which credit card rates, mortgage rates, and other loans rates are usually expressed. The Truth in Lending Act requires that loan and credit card paperwork disclose the APR of the loan, as the periodic interest rate times the frequency with which the interest is compounded during the year. Various finance charges are taken into account in determining the APR so as to make the cost of borrowing as transparent as possible. However, the APR does not include the possibility of high penalty fees for late or missed payments, with the risk of a permanent increase in the interest rate, and thus may understate the true cost of borrowing.

Federal Funds Rate and the Discount Window

One of the most important interest rates in the U.S. financial system is the federal funds rate. One of the essential monetary policy targets of the Federal Reserve (Fed), the fed funds rate is the interest rate paid on federal funds. These are loans (usually one-day, "overnight" loans) made among banks for the purposes of maintaining the minimum reserve required by regulation (up to one-tenth of the bank's demand accounts, such as checking accounts). Banks that have more reserves on hand than they need to meet that minimum can make a small profit on loans to banks that come up reserve-short for the day. Institutions involved in the federal funds system, and affected by this interest rate, include not only federal agencies and government-sponsored enterprises, but also commercial banks, savings and loans, many investment banks, and foreign banks that operate branches in the United States. By extension, most transactions in the U.S. economy "touch" the federal funds system through some degrees of separation—every dollar in circulation passes through hands participating in this system.

When the media reports the Federal Reserve raising or lowering interest rates, it is the fed funds rate they are referring to—specifically the nominal rate, which is a target range determined twice per quarter by the Federal Open Market Committee (FOMC). A committee within the Federal Reserve, the FOMC consists of the seven members of the Federal Reserve Board, the president of the Federal Reserve Bank of New York, and four other presidents of Federal Reserve banks, filled by one-year rotating terms. Raising the rate contracts the money supply, discouraging institutions from borrowing from other banks; lowering the rate encourages such borrowing.

The discount window is similar to the fed funds rate. It is the interest charged on loans made by the Federal Reserve to banks and can take any of three forms: the primary credit rate and, for less sound banks, the secondary credit rate for overnight loans, and the seasonal credit rate for loans of up to nine months. All three interest rates are somewhat higher than the fed funds rate.

During the 2008–2009 global financial crisis, one of the ways the Fed responded was to reduce the discount window—lowering it in small increments, from 6.25 percent in July 2007 to 0.50 percent in December 2008—and to extend the length of primary credit loans to ninety days. The goal was to drastically increase the availability of funds to institutions in order to prevent insolvency and the need for further bailouts by an already taxed federal government.

Interest rates, particularly those set by central banks like the Fed, can both affect and be affected by the business cycle. High rates increase the cost of borrowing, thereby stifling investment; low rates do the opposite. Central banks will often raise rates during periods of rapid economic expansion, since inflation becomes a concern at such times. By making loans more expensive, they can put a check on price and wage increases. During times of economic contraction or, more rarely, during deflationary episodes, the bank will lower the rates, making loans cheaper, with the goal of increasing economic output, employment, and mild inflation.

The size and direction of the interest rate hike or decrease, as well as its timing, can be critical in averting inflation or recession. Many economic historians have cited the Fed's high interest rate policy as a key factor in deepening and prolonging the Great Depression in the 1930s. Conversely, the Fed has been blamed for contributing to the housing bubble of the early 2000s by maintaining historically low interest rates even when it was clear to many economists that the housing market was overheated, a key factor in the crisis that struck the world financial system in 2008.

Bill Kte'pi and James Ciment

See also: Banks, Central; Debt; Federal Reserve System; Monetary Policy; Mortgage Markets and Mortgage Rates; Savings and Investment.

Further Reading

Bernstein, Peter L. *A Primer on Money, Banking, and Gold.* Hoboken, NJ: John Wiley & Sons, 2008.

Brigo, Damiano, and Fabio Mercurio. *Interest Rate Models: Theory and Practice: With Smile, Inflation, and Credit.* New York: Springer Finance, 2007.

Gali, Jordi. *Monetary Policy, Inflation, and the Business Cycle: An Introduction to the New Keynesian Framework.* Princeton, NJ: Princeton University Press, 2008.

Homer, Sidney, and Richard Sylla. *A History of Interest Rates.* Hoboken, NJ: John Wiley & Sons, 2005.

Langdana, Farrokh K. *Macroeconomic Policy: Demystifying Monetary and Fiscal Policy.* New York: Springer, 2009.

Intermediation, Financial

Contemporary financial markets are complex structures that bring together many different players and allow the exchange of financial instruments representing shares, debt, commodities, and other underlying financial objects and contracts, which are thereby made negotiable. Essential to these markets are financial intermediaries between suppliers and users of capital. Suppliers are institutions such as central banks, the Federal Reserve, commercial banks, insurance companies, credit unions, pension funds, real-estate investment trusts, and mortgage pools, which distribute capital to users through investment in loans, bonds, and stocks; the users, in turn, use these financial resources to fund their economic activity. Such users include businesses, which use the funds for investments, expansion, and operating; consumers, who use capital for things like home purchases and higher education costs; and governments, which use the capital for infrastructure improvements and other public needs.

Intermediation occurs in a variety of ways, through such devices as checks, credit cards, stocks, and financial contracts. Although all of these are recognized mediums of exchange, it is important to distinguish between different forms of financial intermediation—specifically, those closely related to markets (such as the buying and selling of corporate securities) and those directly related to the transformation of corporate balance sheets (through direct lending). Both relate to credit, but while intermediation markets transform credit over time, banks create new money.

Among the different groups of participants

in capital markets, banks are generally viewed as intermediaries through which money is created, distributed, and stored. They act as intermediaries between lenders and depositors, managing assets funded by deposits (liabilities) and redistributing those assets through lending. As a result, banks offer payment services to their customers. Banks can follow a generalist strategy, offering a full array of financial services, from deposit accounts to diversified loans, to real estate or life insurance at the wholesale or retail level ("universal banks"). Banks can also take a more restrictive approach, focusing on high-net-worth individuals (private banks), mergers and acquisitions, syndication, or other specialized activities (investment banks). All of these institutions differ from central banks, which serve as creditors to both private banks and governments. Central banks (such as the U.S. Federal Reserve) play a major role in regulating a nation's money supply.

Brokerage houses such as Morgan Stanley or the largely online firm Charles Schwab constitute another class of intermediaries, facilitating exchanges within financial markets. Brokers, as defined in the United States, are entities other than banks that are in the business of buying and selling securities for others. They do not necessarily need to be in direct contact with customers, though this is usually the case. They conduct research on issuers and offer order-routing, order-taking, and execution services to their retail, corporate, and institutional clients (asset managers, hedge funds, proprietary trading desks, or third brokers). In addition, they may develop a whole range of ancillary services, such as trading algorithms packages, facilitation services, clearing or prime brokerage services that are marketed to clients who need them in order to conduct their businesses in financial markets. Brokerage houses may also provide their customers with administrative support, such as regulatory reporting. For all the services they deliver, brokerage houses usually take a commission—the expression of intermediation service. Because their business is at the heart of the financial markets, they are often exposed to

conflicts of interest. In fact, brokers may be full subsidiaries of investment banks working with issuers. In this case, brokers implement policies and procedures known as "Chinese walls" to prevent private information from being used by analysts or traders to perform their duties, whether writing or making transactions for customers.

Marc Lenglet

See also: Savings and Investment.

Further Reading

Allen, Franklin, and Douglas Gale. "Financial Intermediaries and Markets." *Econometrica* 72:4 (2004): 1023–1061.

Bond, Philip. "Bank and Non-Bank Financial Intermediation." *Journal of Finance* 59:6 (2004): 2489–2529.

De Goede, Marieke. *Virtue, Fortune and Faith: A Genealogy of Finance.* Minneapolis: University of Minnesota Press, 2005.

Heffernan, Shelagh. *Modern Banking in Theory and Practice.* Hoboken, NY: John Wiley & Sons, 1996.

Mizruchi, Mark S., and Linda Brewster Stearns. "Money, Banking and Financial Markets." In *Handbook of Economic Sociology*, ed. Neil J. Smelser and Richard Swedberg. Princeton, NJ: Princeton University Press, 1994.

Spencer, Peter D. *The Structure and Regulation of Financial Markets.* New York: Oxford University Press, 2000.

International Development Banks

International development banks provide loans to developing countries from resources contributed by both developing and developed countries. The loans provided come in two varieties: long-term loans charging market rates of interest and long-term loans charging below-market rates of interest. They also provide financial resources in the form of grants. The purpose of these loans and grants is to increase the level of development, or rate of growth, of developing countries. These banks generally come in two varieties: multilateral and subregional. Some examples of the former are the World Bank, African Development Bank, European Bank for Reconstruction and Development, and the Inter-American Development

Bank Group. Examples of subregional banks include the West African Development Bank, East African Development Bank, and the Caribbean Development Bank.

Rationale

Poor countries face a number of barriers to growth and development. Most suffer from a lack of savings. Economists generally argue that capital—man-made means of production (machinery)—is a critical input in the production process. In order to increase labor productivity and growth, the labor force must be better equipped with capital. To create capital, firms must invest, and this investment must be financed by savings. A lack of savings will dramatically reduce investment, which, in turn, will reduce capital formation. Workers will be ill equipped with machines, and growth (at least in the short run) will be reduced.

Many developing countries are also lacking a highly developed physical infrastructure such as roads, communication systems, and so on. In order to build these critical components, public investment must occur and this will have to be financed via savings. Without savings, these investments will not occur. Overall growth will be lowered if producers find it difficult to transport products or to communicate with each other.

Many developing countries also lack social infrastructure, an important component of which is the educational system. In the long run, it is the rate of technical innovation that is the key component of long-term growth. In order to be able to innovate or borrow technology from elsewhere, it is essential for the labor force to rapidly accumulate human capital via education. This requires investment and savings.

In light of the above, development banks can play an important role. They can augment the savings available to poor countries such that investment in capital, physical infrastructure, and social infrastructure can be increased. In addition, these banks can provide the resources and information

necessary to increase the efficiency of government bureaucracy in developing countries. As a result, economic growth can be increased and economic development enhanced.

There are, however, critics of development banks and their policies. Some scholars have argued that the impact of investments by development banks has been meager. One of the reasons for this is that there is often little follow-up work accompanying projects funded by these banks. In other words, once projects are completed there is little attempt to see or calculate the actual benefits generated by such activity. Did the investment actually succeed in raising educational standards, enhancing productivity, and so on? Without this kind of evaluation the banks are likely to continue some projects that generate very little economic and social return to society.

Some have also argued that the activities of development banks often create systems of incentives that are inimical to long-term economic growth. Ruling groups in developing countries and the bureaucracies that implement policy have their own interests in mind when making and implementing policy. Their interests include expanding the power and influence of their particular parts of the government as well as their long-term political survival. The interests of society in general are important only to the extent that the survival and success of the political elite depends upon the general well-being of society. If the political elite has to extract revenue from society at large in order to generate the revenue necessary for political survival, then the former will be interested in promoting the interests of the latter. If, instead, members of the political elite can get the revenue they need from external sources, then their political prospects are not dependent on the well-being of their own society, and they are unlikely to engage in socially productive policies.

The above argument is generally made with respect to foreign aid. Foreign aid represents a flow of revenue into a developing country. This eases the constraint on the receiving government and allows it to reduce its dependence upon the savings of its own population for development. This is likely to create an environment inimical to good policy. To the extent that loans from development banks incorporate an element of aid, they may very well undermine the foundations for good governance.

There are, of course, reforms in lending practices that can be utilized to minimize these negative effects. The more successful these reforms, the more likely the activities of development banks will be successful in promoting growth and development.

Development Banks and Financial Crises

In the past, developing countries in various parts of the world have been subject to periodic financial crises that were devastating to their growth process. Generally, such crises have led to the collapse of the domestic banking system and foreign exchange crises, characterized by dramatic falls in currency values and increasing difficulty in making international payments. This in turn has caused dramatic declines in domestic and foreign investment accompanied by declines in growth, and rising unemployment and inflation. Latin America, in particular, has been subject to a series of crises resulting in a "stop-and-go" pattern of economic growth.

The financial crisis of 2008–2009 originated in the developed world and initially had little or no impact on the developing world. The financial sectors in most developing countries were not exposed to the type of toxic assets that undermined the financial systems in the United States and much of Europe. Nonetheless, the significant economic downturn in the United States and Europe had a negative impact on developing countries. Export markets for developing nations shrank as growth in the developed world slowed down. In addition, remittances to developing countries by their workers who have migrated to the developed world fell dramatically. Finally, capital inflows into developing countries from the developed countries declined.

The Asian Development Bank, with sixty-seven member nations and headquarters in Manila, the Philippines, is one of a number of global and regional institutions that promote economic and social development through loans, grants, and other assistance programs. *(Bloomberg/Getty Images)*

Development banks can play an important role in limiting these negative effects. These organizations are intent upon increasing the flow of loans and investments into developing countries, with a focus on programs aimed at the poorest countries. This will ensure that infrastructure and technology projects in developing countries continue, as they are likely to be especially important in terms of providing employment opportunities. The resources currently available to the development banks are limited, however. But coordination of programs across banks can enhance their impact.

One further point needs to be made. The current financial and economic crisis will certainly have a negative impact on growth prospects in developing countries, but this negative impact is likely to be dampened by a number of factors. First, the extent to which capital markets in developing countries were linked to those in developed countries was limited, thus limiting the impact of the crisis. Second, growth rates in the developing world have increasingly become decoupled from those in the developed world. The trade linkages for the former have been shifting away from the United States and Europe and toward rapidly growing Asia. Third, the prospects for rapid growth in India and China remain high. This will partially affect the negative consequences of economic slowdown in the developed countries. Fourth, the institutional structure and policy mechanisms in many developing countries have improved significantly. Finally, significant countercyclical fiscal packages have been implemented not only in the developed world, but also in rapidly growing economies such as China, India, and Brazil.

Richard Grabowski

See also: International Monetary Fund; World Bank.

Further Reading

Griffith-Jones, S., and J.A. Ocampo. "The Financial Crisis and Its Impact on Developing Countries." United Nations Development Program Working Paper, 2009.

Nandé, W. "The Financial Crisis of 2008 and the Developing Countries." UNU-Wieder. Discussion Paper No. 2009/01, January 2009.

Overseas Development Institute. "The Global Financial Crisis and Developing Countries." Background Note, October 2008. Available at www.odi.org.uk/resources/download/2462.pdf. Accessed April 2010.

World Bank. "Swimming Against the Tide: How Developing Countries Are Coping with the Global Crisis." Background Paper for the G20 Finance Ministers and Central Bank Governors Meeting. Horsham, UK, March 13–14, 2009.

International Economic Agreements

An international economic agreement establishes reciprocal conditions between two or more nations for trade, investment, currency and exchange policy, labor mobility and working conditions, economic relief, environmental regulation, or common management of waterways and resources.

Narrowly defined, an international agreement is a treaty with bilateral principles for trade in which the designation of "most-favored-nation" status introduces a commercial advantage over tariff reductions among reciprocal transactions. Historically, this type of positive economic discrimination has evolved from the architecture of strategic international alliances, with enforcement clauses being strictly secured by national government's oversight.

From another perspective, an international economic agreement represents a shared commitment to a cluster of principles or related international policies—covering trade, investment, currency, and economic relief—signed on a multilateral basis and enforced by specific international regulatory institutions. Whereas simple bilateral trade accords played a key role in most international relations during the nineteenth and early twentieth centuries, extended multilateral and regional agreements, broader in scope, became the mainstay of international economic relations after 1947.

Trade agreements come in many varieties within the two basic bilateral and multilateral frameworks. In free trade area agreements, like the North American Free Trade Agreement (NAFTA), signers pledge to reduce or eliminate tariffs and other barriers to trade between them, but leave up to individual countries control over tariffs on goods from nonsignatory countries. In a customs union, all internal tariffs are removed and a single tariff structure is created for trade with nonsignatory nations. A common market agreement, like that of the predecessor organizations to the European Union (EU), differs from a customs union in that barriers to the movement of capital and labor are lowered or removed along with tariffs on trade goods. With a monetary union, such as the EU's eurozone, a single currency and monetary policy is adopted, usually run by a common central bank. Finally, with an economic union, like the EU, all kinds of economic policies—from regulations to taxation—are harmonized.

These various forms of trade agreements have their benefits and their drawbacks. On the plus side, trade agreements allow for the freer movement of goods, services, capital, and even labor, so as to

402 International Economic Agreements

create greater efficiencies of production, distribution, and marketing. More comprehensive agreements, such as monetary and economic unions, offer the opportunity to coordinate economic and other policies across a broad area, as well as enhance the power of unions vis-à-vis nonmember states and trading blocs. But trade agreements also have their critics, particularly in cases where one signatory is seen to have some economic advantage over another. Many people in the United States and Canada, especially in the labor community, for example, criticized NAFTA out of fear that Mexico's substantially lower labor costs would deplete jobs north of the border. On the other side, some in Mexico have noted that the availability of cheaper American grains have driven thousands of less-efficient Mexican farmers off the land.

Interwar Period: Failure of International Agreements

With the Treaty of Versailles in 1919, the turmoil of World War I was settled, if not fully resolved. The agreement proved not entirely satisfactory, as some European leaders realized that further negotiations would be needed if the European markets, destroyed by war, revolution, and the collapse of empires, were to be rebuilt. What ensued was an attempt to promote new international forums, such as the League of Nations, and to sponsor a series of international conferences that would resolve economic problems and disputes. But as these initiatives faltered, one after another, governments began to back away from their international commitments. Suspicions, misgivings, and military rivalry became the driving forces of international relations.

The failure of economic diplomacy during the interwar period sheds light on some factors that have magnified short-term conflicting interests rather than the commitment to general cooperation. First and foremost, the political margins of negotiators became narrow, both internally and externally, when governments yielded to the pressure of economic and social crisis—as seen in the

traumatic inflationary cycle of 1918–1924 and, later, in the Great Depression of 1929–1933.

Second, agreements also became increasingly difficult when no clear leadership became evident on the international scene. In that regard, the 1920s revealed a widening political gulf among the core winning powers, together with the decline of British authority and the withdrawal of the United States from the European political "mess."

Third, and finally, agreements became more problematic when no international organization existed to frame the arrangements, either through long-term goals for economic relations, a legal framework of liability, or compliance and enforcement through oversight and information gathering. The League of Nations, created in 1919, soon backtracked from this direction and became known as a political forum that strived for peacekeeping rather than an intervening power in the sensitive area of policy making. When it came to trade and monetary policy, every nation envisaged that the strong hand should belong to the independent central banks of the world's major economies, not to a scattered diplomatic institution.

Recurring economic crises, a lack of leadership, and a lack of international institutions thus constituted three main factors that thwarted the prospects for overarching agreements. In this context, the international architecture that surfaced in the 1920s and 1930s was one of imperial and regional trade preferences and bilateral protectionist trade agreements. The Customs Union formed by France with members of its empire in 1928, and the Commonwealth system established by Great Britain in 1932, are paramount examples of the former. The bilateral commercial treaties signed by the United States, mostly with Latin American countries, and the bilateral trade blocs forged by Nazi Germany, exemplify the latter.

Post–World War II Period: Multilateral Relations and Trade Liberalization

In the eyes of many observers, the trade discrimination of the 1930s led to the armed aggression of World War II. Import quotas, imperial and regional trade preferences, currency controls, and other discriminatory practices were perceived as the harbingers of war. And if preferential trade unleashed the evil of world conflicts, the best way to safeguard a peaceful future was through the promotion of free trade and multilateral relations. This view, particularly entrenched in the U.S. State Department, paved the way for postwar reconstruction plans based on the nondiscrimination of third partners, indivisibility of agreements, and reciprocity of treatment.

Two pillars of the new world order—the International Monetary Fund and the World Bank—emerged from the Bretton Woods Conference of 1944 with the mission of backing up currency stability, financial integration, and multilateral aid among the adherent countries. The third pillar was a common agreement signed by twenty-three nations in 1947, called the General Agreement on Tariffs and Trade (GATT), which covered 60 percent of world trade.

Central to this agreement was the restoration of the world's international trade on a nondiscriminatory basis: concessions granted by each country to a single partner were henceforth extended to all signatories of GATT accords. In this manner, GATT set the stage for a trade-off between reductions in import restrictions, on the one hand, and reciprocal market access to other trading countries, on the other. The conventional approach of mutual commitment to a fixed set of rules also underwent significant change, being replaced by the more flexible and cooperative principle of periodical multilateral negotiations, or the so-called GATT rounds.

The historical agreement signed in 1947 benefited mostly from the combination of export boom and strong economic growth that followed World War II. This resulted in broadening the scope of international economic accords along a double path: more goods and trade issues included on the agenda and more countries brought into the GATT fold.

The first phase of the GATT rounds consisted of negotiations over tariff reductions on industrial products, following an item-by-item approach. After that, the Kennedy Round (1963–1967) pioneered a formula for gross average cuts on imported goods and extended the agenda to antidumping, agriculture, subsidies, technical barriers to trade, and countervailing duties. The Tokyo Round (1974–1979) reinforced the previous tariff cuts and adjoined the issues of public procurement, safeguard, and revision of GATT articles.

The Uruguay Round (1986–1993) debated nontariff barriers, intellectual property, services, and trade-related investments. The previously neglected sectors of agriculture and textiles, in which the developing economies had clear advantages, also came to occupy a central place in negotiations. The full membership of GATT rose to 113 countries, accruing the representation of less-developed economies. To tap the mounting inclusiveness, GATT became a permanent institution, renamed the World Trade Organization (WTO), in 1995.

Late Twentieth and Early Twenty-First Centuries: Regionalism and Globalization

Despite the unprecedented height of multilateral openness, other tendencies were also wending their way, particularly among the less-developed countries. A first wave of preferential trade agreements occurred in the 1960s and early 1970s, in an attempt to liberalize commerce between regional trading partners, while discriminating against third parties. This was a defensive move to counteract worldwide multilateralism led by the United States, and to draw up a network of neighboring alliances. By forming preferential trade agreements, the less-developed economies could reduce the cost of achieving any given level of import-competing industrialization, improve the member's terms of trade vis-à-vis the rest of the world, benefit from local economies of scale, and cope with political isolationism.

The second surge of preferential trade agreements arose in the early 1990s, part and parcel of the ongoing changeover of the world order. Rather than being simply opposed to multilateral initiatives, regional integration arrangements forged complementary networks that strengthened national participation in the overriding multilateral environment.

In a period marked by burgeoning economic interdependence—the end of the cold war, the technological revolution in telecommunications, and a growing share of the less-developed economies in world trade—the forging of regional trade preferences became the flip side of increasing the scope of GATT/WTO. Moreover, the wave of preferential trade agreements did not curtail the path of export growth, but actively contributed to its enhancement. Even though the long-term welfare consequences of this economic "regionalism" are still unclear, its role remains undisputed.

The most important preferential economic agreements today govern such free-trade regions and customs unions as the European Community, NAFTA, MERCOSUR, Association of Southeast Asian Nations (ASEAN), Andean Pact, and the Caribbean Community (CARICOM). Beyond such regional security measures, multilateralism still persists as an inescapable path to solving international problems. The decision of the 1997 Climate Convention in Kyoto, at which industrialized nations committed themselves to reducing their emissions of greenhouse gases by an average of 5 percent compared with 1990 emissions, is the best example of ongoing international agreements that require inclusive cooperation on a world scale.

Nuno Luis Madureira

See also: International Policy Coordination.

Further Reading

Goldstein, Judith, and Joanne Gowa. "U.S. National Power and the Post-War Trading Regime." *World Trade Review* 1:2 (2002): 153–170.

Goldstein, Judith L., Douglas Rivers, and Michael Tomz. "Institutions in International Relations: Understanding the Effects of the GATT and the WTO on World Trade." *International Organization* 61:4 (2007): 37–67.

Mansfield, Edward D., and Eric Reinhardt. "Multilateral Determinants of Regionalism: The Effects of GATT/WTO on the Formation of Preferential Trading Arrangements." *International Organization* 57:4 (2003): 829–862.

McCarthy, Dennis. *International Economic Integration in Historical Perspective.* New York: Routledge, 2006.

International Monetary Fund

An international financial institution established just after World War II, the International Monetary Fund (IMF) studies national economies, provides technical assistance and training to governments, and, most importantly, lends money to nations in need, particularly in the developing world. Like its sister institution the World Bank, the IMF is funded chiefly by member states, with the bulk of its money coming from developed nations. While the World Bank generally focuses on long-term development, IMF aid is typically extended at times of crisis in a nation's economy. Since the late 1940s, the IMF has played an important and often controversial role in business cycles around the world by responding to banking and currency crises of great magnitude and consequence.

The "intellectual founding fathers" of the IMF were two economists, John Maynard Keynes of the United Kingdom and Harry Dexter White of the United States. The idea of the fund was discussed by delegates from forty-five countries attending the Bretton Woods Conference in New Hampshire in July 1944. The IMF was officially founded on December 27, 1945, when representatives of twenty-nine countries signed the Articles of Agreement. Operations got under way in May 1947. As of 2009, the ever-expanding organization had 185 member states.

Structure and Operations

Although the IMF is a specialized agency of the United Nations, it has its own charter, finances, and governing structure. The IMF is funded by member countries, whose annual payment, called a "quota," depends on the size and strength of the member country's economy. The same factors also determine a country's voting power and the maximum sum it can receive from the organization in loans. The IMF also borrows money from international lending institutions such as the central banks of member countries. The IMF has three main functions: (1) economic surveillance, (2) lending, and (3) providing technical assistance and training. Toward those ends, the IMF publishes compilations of research bulletins, staff papers, working papers, economic outlooks, policy papers, financial market updates, manuals, guides, and reports; it organizes conferences, seminars, and workshops; and it combats money laundering and terrorism. The IMF headquarters is located in Washington, D.C., with additional offices in Paris, Warsaw, Tokyo, and New York. The organization has approximately 2,500 employees from more than 140 countries. Its managing director since November 2007 has been Dominique Strauss-Kahn of France.

The IMF was created to promote global growth by overseeing the international monetary system. As such, it seeks to ensure the stability of exchange rates between national currencies, to encourage member states to remove exchange restrictions that hinder foreign trade, and—especially in the first decade of the twenty-first century—to facilitate financial transactions between countries. By creating the IMF, the founding members sought to avoid a repetition of the situation in the 1930s, when several countries devalued their currencies and raised foreign trade barriers to increase their export competitiveness. These steps brought a dramatic decline in world trade, increased unemployment, and deepened the economic recession in many countries. Financial isolationism and worldwide recession, in turn, helped pave the road to World War II.

Although the Articles of Agreement have been amended several times, the IMF's main goals—the stability of exchange rates and removing exchange restrictions—have remained unchanged through the years. In addition, the organization has taken on new tasks. Until 1971, the IMF supervised a system of fixed exchange rates tied to the U.S. dollar (which in turn was pegged to the value of gold). However, the aftermath of the Vietnam War, the oil shocks of the 1970s, and the printing of money to pay for President Lyndon B. Johnson's Great Society triggered a period of uncontrolled inflation in the United States, which in turn caused a precipitous devaluation of the dollar against other currencies. Neither the central banks of other industrialized countries nor the IMF itself could stop the decline of the dollar. First Canada and then the European industrial nations, no longer seeing the dollar as a stable currency, let their own currencies float freely.

With the breakdown of the dollar-based international monetary system, the role of the IMF was expanded. During the oil crisis in the 1970s, the IMF increased institutional lending and began helping poor countries by providing emergency financing to solve their balance-of-payments difficulties. Again in the 1980s, the IMF increased lending in reaction to a global financial crisis. In the 1990s, it helped the former Soviet bloc countries in the transition to market-driven economies by providing financial support, policy advice, and technical assistance. The organization proved highly successful in the latter efforts, as several of these countries joined the European Union in 2004. Meanwhile, in 1996, the IMF began coordinating efforts with the World Bank to help poor countries reduce their debt burden to manageable levels.

Loans granted by the IMF are typically provided under special arrangement. If a country wants to borrow money from the IMF, it has to agree to institute prescribed economic policies and austerity measures. The IMF's twenty-four-member executive board (large economies like the United States have their own seats, while smaller ones are grouped) must approve the country's Letter of Intent and a Memoranda of Economic and Financial Policies listing these measures.

The IMF employs several different loan instruments, called "facilities." The Poverty Reduction and Growth Facility, established in 1999, is a low-interest (0.5 percent annually) lending mechanism for low-income countries. Those with a per capita income of less than US$1,095 are eligible for these loans; 78 such countries were eligible in 2008. Such loans are used for reducing poverty, strengthening governance, and spurring economic growth. Another instrument, the Exogenous Shocks Facility, supports low-income countries that face unexpected and uncontrollable emergencies, such as a natural disaster or declining global commodity prices. Again, the annual interest rate is low (0.5 percent). In addition to these two types of loans, Stand-by Arrangements are geared to countries with short-term balance-of-payments problems, such as reduced exports. Extended Fund Facilities were established for helping countries with long-term balance-of-payments problems. Supplemental Reserve Facilities provide short-term financing for countries with sudden crises, as in the case of massive capital outflows. Compensatory Financing Facilities assist countries with sudden decreases in exports or sudden increases in the price of imported cereals. Finally, additional emergency assistance is offered to countries recovering from armed conflicts and natural disasters.

Controversies and Criticisms

The policies and requirements of IMF loans have come under criticism among some economists and public policy officials. Indeed, critics maintain, the IMF can actually hurt an already troubled economy through the imposition of inappropriate "one-size-fits-all" policies. IMF policy prescriptions that impose tight spending restrictions on a country to which it lends money, for example, may be more effective for economies suffering from excessive government spending and inflation rather than for economies that are going through a severe debt crisis and declining prices. The issue was debated in the mid-1990s, for example, when the IMF demanded that the government of South Korea undertake what appeared to be inappropriately tight financial policies given the particular nature of its economic troubles. Advocates of the IMF counter such criticism by pointing out that the economy of South Korea did recover relatively quickly, arguing for the IMF approach.

During the financial crisis of 2008–2009, the IMF provided loans valued at more than $50 billion to emerging countries—though the largest loan, $39 billion, went to Greece in 2010—to help them cope with declines in capital inflows, exports, and local demand, and to support banks

Delegates of the International Monetary Fund and World Bank convene in Singapore for the annual joint meeting of the two groups in September 2006. The fall event has been a focal point of antiglobalization demonstrations. *(Bloomberg/ Getty Images)*

with financial difficulties. It also offered advice to advanced countries in designing more effective stimulus packages and provided all members with economic analyses and forecasts.

Tiia Vissak

See also: International Development Banks; World Bank.

Further Reading

Andersen, Camilla. "Changing IMF Works Hard to Combat Global Crisis." *IMF Survey Magazine*, February 26, 2009. Available at www.imf.org/external/pubs/ft/survey/so/2009/INT022609A.htm. Accessed November 2009.

"Articles of Agreement of the International Monetary Fund." Available at www.imf.org/external/pubs/ft/aa/index.htm. Accessed November 2009.

Boughton, James M., and Domenico Lombardi, eds. *Finance, Development, and the IMF*. New York: Oxford University Press, 2009.

Driscoll, David D. "The IMF and the World Bank: How Do They Differ?" Available at www.imf.org/external/pubs/ft/exrp/differ/differ.htm, August 1996. Accessed November 2009.

Hill, Charles. *International Business: Competing in the Global Marketplace*. 7th ed. New York: McGraw-Hill/Irwin, 2009.

Humphreys, Norman K. *Historical Dictionary of the International Monetary Fund*. Lanham, MD: Scarecrow, 1999.

International Monetary Fund Web site: www.imf.org.

Pauly, Louis W. *Who Elected the Bankers? Surveillance and Control in the World Economy*. Ithaca, NY: Cornell University Press, 1997.

International Monetary Fund Mortgage Market Index

The International Monetary Fund (IMF) Mortgage Market Index is a composite index conceived and compiled by the IMF, published for the first time in the April 2008 issue of *World Economic Outlook*. The index quantifies the institutional features of mortgage markets and the ease with which the mortgage credit can be accessed in eighteen industrial countries. Some have argued that the index has been signaling the deterioration of risk conditions in housing markets and rising volatility in deregulated credit markets, especially in the United States, since the mid-2000s.

The Mortgage Market Index (MMI) is a simple mathematical average of five important institutional indicators of the housing markets: mortgage equity; the existence of early payment fees; loan-to-value ratio; average mortgage term; and the level of development of secondary mortgage markets. Mortgage equity measures the amount of money a homeowner can borrow against the net current value of the property, or the difference between the current market value of the property minus the outstanding principal of the mortgage. The higher the current value, the higher the equity build-up and the higher the amount one can borrow. Fee-free repayment enables the homeowner to refinance the existing mortgage at a lower rate, thereby reducing the mortgage payment without paying a prepayment penalty. The loan-to-value ratio indicates the percentage of the value of the property financed by mortgage. The length of the mortgage term, whether it is for 15 or 30 years, for instance, affects the debt-service-to-income ratio, or the ease with which one repays the mortgage; the shorter the mortgage term, the higher the debt-service-to-income ratio and the higher the financial burden of the mortgage. The level of development of secondary mortgage markets affects the lenders' ability to refinance the mortgage. The higher the level of development, the easier it is for the originators of the mortgages to sell them in the secondary markets where they are repackaged and sold to hedge funds, pension funds, or other secondary investors.

Even though industrial countries are generally characterized by well-developed financial markets, the institutional features of national mortgage markets as measured by the MMI differ significantly. Whereas mortgage markets are easily accessible in the United States, they are not in such countries as Germany, Italy, and France. In these and other countries, homeowners can neither borrow against accumulated equity nor refinance without paying extra fees. In addition, the average mortgage term in these countries is fifteen years, with a loan-to-value ratio of 75 percent. The result is a relatively high debt-service-to-income-ratio. In the United States, by contrast, a home mortgage term is typically thirty years (or adjustable) and the loan-to-value ratio is 80 percent, lowering the debt-to-income-ratio significantly and enabling more homeowners to finance their mortgage. In addition, whereas secondary mortgage markets are nonexistent in most European countries, they are well developed in the United States; in 2008, mortgage-backed security issues in the United States constituted about 20 percent of outstanding residential loans. In France and Germany in the years leading up to the financial crisis of 2008, mortgage-backed security issues constituted roughly 1 and 0.2 percent of outstanding residential mortgage loans, respectively. Accordingly, the United States ranks highest among the eighteen nations for which the IMF calculates the Mortgage Market Index, followed by the Scandinavian and non-U.S. Anglo-Saxon countries such as Australia and Canada (see table below).

According to IMF data, countries with a high MMI also show strong positive correlations between consumption and housing wealth, and between housing prices and consumption. Thus, appreciation in housing prices and subsequent rises in equity appear to have facilitated higher household consumption. Under the assumption that higher future income and/or increasing housing wealth can make the repayment of debt relatively easier, homeowners have accumulated more and more debt to finance

present consumption. Not surprisingly, data for the United States support these findings. Between 1995 and 2006, homeownership in the United States jumped to 69 percent, a significant increase of about 6 percent. With home equity constituting a large portion of the total wealth held by middle-income groups, the bursting of the housing bubble beginning in 2007 left homeowners with unprecedented debt but without the inflated housing wealth to fall back on. All in all, the housing bubble undermined consumer discipline in borrowing and spending, which contributed to untenable levels of debt.

As a simple mathematical average, the IMF Mortgage Market Index treats each indicator in the index with equal weight. It might be argued, however, that the relative importance of each indicator may be different in individual countries and that the weights should be adjusted accordingly. Nevertheless, the MMI remains a useful and informative economic index that may provide an early alarm for future volatility in the housing market.

Mehmet Odekon

See also: International Monetary Fund; Mortgage Markets and Mortgage Rates.

Further Reading

Carderelli, Roberto, Deniz Egan, and Alessandro Rebucci. "Press Points for Chapter 3: The Changing Housing Cycle and Its Implications for Monetary Policy." Available at www.imf.org/external/pubs/ft/weo/2008/01/pdf/3sum.pdf (April 2008). Accessed November 2009.

International Monetary Fund (IMF). *World Economic Outlook: Housing and the Business Cycle.* Washington, DC: International Monetary Fund, 2008.

Mortgage Market Index Ranking of Industrial Countries, 2007

Country	Mortgage Market Index (MMI)
United States	0.98
Denmark	0.82
Netherlands	0.71
Australia	0.69
Sweden	0.66
Norway	0.59
United Kingdom	0.58
Canada	0.57
Finland	0.49
Spain	0.40
Ireland	0.39
Japan	0.39
Greece	0.35
Belgium	0.34
Austria	0.31
Germany	0.28
Italy	0.26
France	0.23

International Policy Coordination

Globalization and its close cousin, regionalization, have increasingly linked the economies of the world so that the rise and fall of a business cycle in one country more readily induces similar movements in the cycles of other countries.

Again and again during the course of the twentieth century, it became clear that the nations of the world were bound more and more closely by trade, finance, migration, and environmental issues. This is not to say that what happens to one happens to all, nor that what is good for one is good for all. What it does say is that, increasingly, what happens to one affects all. There have been a variety of responses to this, from protectionist impulses as nations seek to build a shell around themselves and prevent the impact, to internationalist efforts to eliminate or change the relevance of national borders. Somewhere in between lies international policy coordination, or the open discussion and collective debate of national policies in an international context, not with the goal of making all nations adopt the same policies, but simply to encourage them to develop their policies with an awareness of their potential impact elsewhere. Even when national governments have different goals, it is possible to negotiate so that various national policies can be designed to fit together more or less harmoniously.

The Twentieth Century

The Great Depression and World War II were two key events in the development of economic policy competition and coordination among nations.

The severe economic downturn of the 1930s set in motion the forces of economic nationalism as various nations erected higher and higher trade barriers in order to protect national industries and to bring down politically destabilizing levels of unemployment. But many economic histories argue that this protectionism only deepened the Depression while increasing international tensions, contributing to the outbreak of the most destructive war in human history.

The end of World War II saw a more urgent desire for international cooperation and coordination, not only in the political and legal contexts that were the main focus of the United Nations, but in economic and other areas as well. Even during World War II, delegates from all forty-four Allied nations met at the Mount Washington Hotel in Bretton Woods, New Hampshire, to hammer out the details of what has since been called the Bretton Woods system—an international economic system requiring each country to maintain a fixed exchange rate for its currency relative to the only currency considered at the time sufficiently stable to act as an anchor for the international monetary system, the U.S. dollar, itself to be fixed to the price of gold. The International Monetary Fund and the World Bank were established by the conference as well. By the early 1970s, in the face

In July 1944, at the United Nations Monetary and Financial Conference in Bretton Woods, New Hampshire, delegates of the forty-four Allied nations of World War II laid the foundations of the postwar international monetary system and open trade. *(Alfred Eisenstaedt/Time & Life Pictures/ Getty Images)*

of high inflation brought on by the costs of the Vietnam War, the Great Society, and the energy crisis, and suffering from a widening and unprecedented trade deficit, the United States could not protect the dollar from a steep decline in value. As a consequence, it was the United States that broke the Bretton Woods accord by abandoning the dollar/gold standard in 1971. The decision was made by President Richard Nixon—without consulting with the other Bretton Woods nations or even the U.S. State Department—in response to the dollar's rapid depreciation with respect to other currencies and gold and the increasing demands of other nations for the United States to make good on its debts in gold. Within five years, none of the world's major currencies was fixed anymore, either to gold or to the U.S. dollar.

Supranational Unions

Various supranational unions, also known as regional trade blocs, have provided their member nations with the opportunity to coordinate their policies or have required a certain amount of coordination as a prerequisite for membership. The European Union (EU) is the best-known example, consisting in 2009 of twenty-seven member states with a common trade policy, various international bodies governing interactions between member states, and a common currency used by sixteen of the member states. More than just an economic union, the EU also guarantees the freedom of movement of people, goods, services, and capital among its member states, and helps to guide the foreign policies of its member states. As of 2009, the members of the EU are Austria, Belgium, Bulgaria, Cyprus, the Czech Republic, Denmark, Estonia, Finland, France, Germany, Greece, Hungary, Ireland, Italy, Latvia, Lithuania, Luxembourg, Malta, the Netherlands, Poland, Portugal, Romania, Slovakia, Slovenia, Spain, Sweden, and the United Kingdom. Croatia, Macedonia, and Turkey are official candidates for membership. To join the EU, a candidate state must be a stable, function-

ing democracy; must demonstrate a respect for human rights and the rule of law; and must have an economy that can participate competitively in that of the EU.

Other supranational unions are less developed than the EU, which has spent decades working toward the unity it currently enjoys. The North American Free Trade Agreement (NAFTA), an economic agreement between Canada, Mexico, and the United States, and in effect since 1994, provides an example of less integrated economic policy. While NAFTA has lowered numerous trade barriers and tariffs and helped coordinate industrial and financial policy among the three nations, its goals are more modest than those of the EU and do not include efforts to develop a common currency or eliminate barriers to the free movement of workers.

Nevertheless, agreements such as NAFTA promote social and economic progress among member states and encourage coordination of regional development and various spheres of policy among those members. The Association of Southeast Asian Nations (ASEAN) includes the nations of Brunei, Cambodia, Indonesia, Laos, Malaysia, Myanmar, the Philippines, Singapore, Thailand, and Vietnam. The African Union includes fifty-three African states, with the possibility of moving toward an EU-like unity. The Union of South American Nations (USAN) is specifically modeled after the EU and integrates two regional customs unions, the Andean Community and Mercosur (Mercado Común del Sur). Member states include Argentina, Bolivia, Brazil, Chile, Colombia, Ecuador, Guiana, Paraguay, Peru, Suriname, Uruguay, and Venezuela. A paper entity only at the time of this writing, the hope is for USAN to eliminate tariffs among member states by 2019, integrate infrastructure such as highways and pipelines, and move toward an EU-style political-economic community that coordinates the development of foreign policy and trade with entities outside the union.

Economists and political scientists wonder how great economic stresses, such as the financial crisis and global recession of the late 2000s, have affected and will continue to affect international policy coordination. Given the vulnerabilities the crisis revealed, and the protectionist pressures the recession has presented, many world leaders would agree with French president Nicolas Sarkozy's sentiments that, "We must rethink the financial system from scratch, as at Bretton Woods."

Bill Kte'pi and James Ciment

See also: International Economic Agreements.

Further Reading

Branson, William H., Jacob A. Frenkel, and Morris Goldstein, eds. *International Policy Coordination and Exchange Rate Fluctuations.* Chicago: University of Chicago Press, 1990.

Haas, Peter M. *Knowledge, Power, and International Policy Coordination.* Columbia: University of South Carolina Press, 1997.

Krasner, Stanley, ed. *International Regimes.* Ithaca, NY: Cornell University Press, 1983.

Ruggie, John. *Constructing the World Polity: Essays on International Institutionalization.* New York: Routledge, 1998.

Inventory Investment

In a company, inventories are stored quantities of raw material, work in progress, or finished products. Raw materials are goods bought from a supplier that must be transformed during the production cycle in order to create finished products that may then be sold. Works in progress are unfinished products. A good is not a raw material, a finished product, or a work in progress by virtue of its inherent properties, but by nature of the company's business. Thus, coffee may be a finished product for a producer or retailer, but a raw material for a company like Starbucks. Inventory investment generally turns back into cash in the short term through the sale of finished products. Inventory may become a permanent investment if the production cycle requires more than one year, or because the company is not able to sell finished products within one year. The latter case may be the result of strong competition, a product's obsolescence, or economic recession.

Inventory investment also plays a role in macroeconomic analysis, as inventories represent a key bellwether for national economies. Companies generally tend to accumulate inventory during economic downturns, while maintaining optimal levels of inventory, or even experiencing shortages, during prosperous periods. Collectively, these changes are referred to as "inventory cycles" and represent the shortest of the major business cycles the economy experiences. Aggregate inventory levels are also a leading indicator that economists use to ascertain in which direction the economy is likely to move in the short term.

For example, between November of 2008 and November of 2009, U.S. business inventories fell roughly 11 percent, from $1.476 trillion to $1.313 trillion, indicating that companies were selling off goods and that the economy was coming out of recession. However, the figures also help to explain why employment figures were slower to respond to the recovery, as companies chose to sell off the goods they already had on hand rather than hire new workers to make more. As a general rule, a company is successful if it is able to generate good returns using minimal resources, including inventories. Resources invested in inventories may increase or decrease. An increase in inventories, however, may be a result of good news (an increase in sales), a change in inventory policy (a larger inventory may increase customer satisfaction), or a negative event (a reduction in sales). While rises in inventory can sometimes bode ill for a company or the economy for a while—indicating slackening demand—this is not always the case. Companies may expand inventory if they expect the economy to turn around and demand to increase.

Inventory investment includes carrying costs such as insurance, warehousing, handling, goods deterioration, and/or theft. Despite the costs, however, inventories are necessary in order to avoid interruptions in output, to maintain sales, and to ensure consumer trust. Moreover, placing orders is costly because of the shipping and time required to manage the order. Finally, like any other investment, inventories must be financed with capital, either in the form of debt or equity—that is, by borrowing money thorough the issuance of bonds *and* by taking out loans from banks or through issuing shares.

But capital is costly. With this in mind, companies must identify their optimal inventory level, which depends primarily on the industry. A retailer needs inventories, for example, while an insurance company does not. Additionally, inventory depends on the kind of policy companies wish to implement. If a company prefers an aggressive management policy, it will minimize inventories, otherwise it will accept higher levels of inventory with higher carrying costs but usually fewer lost sales.

Traditionally, an optimal inventory level could be identified by means of the economic order quantity (EOQ) model, which takes into consideration carrying costs (which increase with higher quantities in stock) and restocking costs (which decrease with higher quantities), in order to identify the quantity of inventory that minimizes the total cost.

More recently, beginning in the 1980s, a new and innovative approach in inventory management called "just in time" (JIT) was implemented by Japanese companies. This approach, which seeks to reduce inventories to the very minimum level (zero if possible), is based on a new kind of relationship with suppliers, with whom a high level of coordination is needed. In the new relationship, suppliers are expected to provide raw materials only for immediate need—thus, the number of orders is at the maximum level and inventory turnover is at a maximum. This policy is not easy to implement, but highly efficient and profitable. To take one of many examples, JLG Industries, a Pennsylvania-based manufacturer of aerial work platforms, was able to reduce inventory from 40 percent of sales in 1990 to 9 percent in 1998, with a net income that increased from $3.2 million in 1991 to $ 46.5 million in 1998, largely through the use of just-in-time inventory management.

Companies with low inventory levels may react faster to unexpected drops in product demand. They may immediately reduce orders for raw materials, for example, and thus have less unsold product. Moreover, such companies generally have

fewer debts with suppliers in the short term, reducing the risk of becoming low on cash.

Companies with a high level of inventory (or with long-term purchasing contracts for fixed quantities) are less flexible. If the economy slows down, they may experience cash stress. A drop in sales implies a reduction in cash proceeds. If, in the meantime, they have a lot of raw materials and, consequently, outstanding payables, it may be difficult to meet their obligations.

An increase in inventory always leads to cash absorption because of the increase in purchasing costs that must be paid to suppliers. When this increase also corresponds to an increase in sales, the cash absorption is offset by an increase in cash generated by collected sales. Otherwise, the company has less cash available for new investments, meeting debt obligations, and paying shareholders.

A useful performance indicator for inventory management is inventory turnover, or the ratio of cost of goods sold to inventory level. The ratio represents the number of times inventories are renewed in one year: the higher the ratio, the more efficient the management.

The following formula determines the number of days of sales that can be covered with current inventories:

$$\frac{\text{Inventories}}{\text{Cost of goods sold}} \times 365$$

The higher the ratio, the more relaxed the inventory management. Comparing the ratio of one company with that of others can help management determine if the inventory level is typical for the industry, what the market trends are, and whether or not the company is being efficiently managed. With respect to the latter, there might be a chance to improve profitability by reducing inventory stock. Generally speaking, a company should keep inventories low, except when a more aggressive management policy negatively affects profitability instead of improving it.

Laura Peressin, Giorgio Valentinuz,
and James Ciment

See also: Savings and Investment.

Further Reading

Arvan, L., and L.N. Moses, "Inventory Investment and the Theory of the Firm." *American Economic Review* 72:1 (1982): 186–193, and 73:1 (1983): 251.

Followill, R.A., M. Schellenger, and P.H. Marchard. "Economic Order Quantities, Volume Discounts and Wealth Maximization." *Financial Review* 25:1 (1990): 143–152.

Johnson, H. Thomas, and Robert S. Kaplan. *Relevance Lost: The Rise and Fall of Management Accounting.* Cambridge, MA: Harvard Business School Press, 1991.

Sadhwani A.T., M.H. Sarhan, and D. Kiringoda. "Just in Time: An Inventory System Whose Time Has Come." *Management Accounting* 67 (December 1985): 36–44.

Schonberger, Richard L. *Japanese Manufacturing Techniques.* New York: Free Press, 1982.

Treml, H.E., and K. Lehn. "Decentralization, Incentives, and Value Creation: The Case of JLG Industries." *Journal of Applied Corporate Finance* 13:3 (2000): 60–70.

Investment, Financial

Financial investment is the acquisition of instruments such as corporate stock, government and private bonds, foreign exchange, bank deposits, and other forms of loans by financial firms, businesses, organizations, and individuals. Financial assets such as these are often referred to as "cash instruments" because their values are determined in markets where they can be bought and sold relatively easily for cash. Also included among financial investments are derivative instruments, also known as "derivatives," such as options, futures, swaps, and other instruments whose values are derived from such other assets as cash and real estate. Derivative instruments are acquired in order to reduce risk, to provide insurance against certain losses and negative events, or for sheer speculation. They may be bought and sold, but not as readily as cash instruments.

The proliferation of ever more exotic and complicated financial instruments over the past decade or so—such as the aforementioned derivative instruments—has been widely blamed for the financial crisis that gripped world markets in late 2008. Because the risks associated with these instruments were poorly understood—or miscalculated—many investors, including institutional ones, found themselves in financial difficulty when the market for these complicated instruments crashed. Moreover, burdened by having these instruments on their balance sheets and unable to determine their value or to sell them, many financial institutions were forced to rein in the credit they offered businesses and households, a phenomenon that helped turn the financial crisis into a global recession.

Uncertainty and Expectations

The prices of financial instruments generally depend on expectations of uncertain future outcomes. For example, stock prices depend on the expected future performance of corporations, and a derivative such as a forward foreign exchange contract depends on expected future exchange rates. Information about the future is incomplete, and prices of financial instruments and their derivatives therefore may be driven by heuristics (simple rules of thumb) or emotional sentiments. Price movements can be volatile when there is uncertainty about the future and may diverge from long-run trends for extended periods of time.

Financial investment is distinct from what economists define as investment, which is the direct creation of physical capital such as a factory, a machine, or a bridge. The purchase of newly issued stock or bonds may, of course, end up funding the building of the factory or the purchase of tools, but this type of financial investment and economic investment are different concepts. Much financial investment has a relationship to economic investment, as when someone buys stock issued years ago or opens a savings account at a bank that uses the money to provide revolving credit to consumers. In these latter cases, no new productive capital is created when the financial investment is made.

The Financial Sector

Purchases and sales of financial instruments and derivatives occur in the economy's financial sector.

When the financial sector consists of mostly private firms, the term "financial industry" may be used in place of financial sector. In most countries, the financial sector consists of intermediaries, formal exchanges, and over-the-counter markets.

Intermediaries are institutions that offer one set of financial arrangements to those contributing funds and another set of arrangements to those borrowing the funds. For example, commercial banks offer depositors a variety of checking and savings accounts and certificates of deposit with different interest rates and maturities, and they offer borrowers a variety of loans of different lengths, methods of payment, and charges. Intermediaries channel funds from one set of financial assets to another set of financial assets, usually deposits to business and consumer loans, and in the process they assume risks and incur costs.

Exchanges such as stock markets, options markets, and some futures markets are centralized markets in which large numbers of buyers and sellers interact directly and set asset prices through a process of supply and demand. Over-the-counter markets are dealers who link buyers and sellers one transaction at a time. Most bonds, foreign exchange, and financial derivatives are traded in over-the-counter markets. These are less transparent than exchanges because they reveal little information about prices and trading volumes; buyers and sellers only see the price of one particular transaction.

Economic Purposes

The fundamental economic purpose of the financial sector, and thus of financial investment, is to channel savings to economic investment. The financial sector's role in channeling funds to new projects and research activities is critical to the economy's long-run rate of growth. For example, without financial intermediaries to connect savers and investors, there would be less investment and innovation, all other things being equal, because investors and innovators would also have to be savers.

Financial investment also channels funds to cash-constrained consumers, a process that is economically beneficial if it permits consumers to better allocate their purchases over time. For example, without mortgage loans people would have to build their homes gradually as their income flows permit the purchase of building materials and construction services. Also, financial investment reduces life's risks because it permits people to save for contingencies and borrow during emergencies.

Costs

Financial intermediaries, exchanges, and markets are costly to operate, and they may introduce risks and uncertainties when investments are bought and sold. In today's high-income countries these sectors have a direct cost of several percent of gross domestic product to operate and even more if regulatory costs are included. Banks earn a spread between deposit rates and borrowing rates, and brokers, dealers, and financial firms charge high fees for their services.

Modern financial sectors are also prone to systemic instability. For one thing, all intertemporal transactions, or those that take place over time, such as mortgages, are subject to default. In addition, the complexity of today's financial instruments and derivatives makes it impossible for any one investor, financial firm, or government regulatory agency to fully grasp the risks of every financial investment. The many levels of derivative instruments available in the modern financial sector imply that any one default or market failure can trigger many more defaults and failures throughout the system. From an economic perspective, when the financial sector falters in its role of channeling savings to investment, innovations, and consumption, there are very real economic consequences.

Instability in financial intermediaries, exchanges, and markets also results from the divergence in purposes of sellers and purchasers of financial assets. In explaining the financial collapse during the Great Depression, British economist

John Maynard Keynes observed in his pathbreaking 1936 book, *The General Theory of Employment, Interest and Money*, that before the development of modern financial systems,

> enterprises were mainly owned by those who undertook them or by their friends and associates, investment depended on a sufficient supply of individuals of sanguine temperament and constructive impulses who embarked on business as a way of life. . . .

Today, however,

> as a result of the gradual increase in the proportion of the equity in the community's aggregate capital investment which is owned by persons who do not manage and have no special knowledge of the circumstances, either actual or prospective, of the business in question, the element of real knowledge in the valuation of investments by those who own them or contemplate purchasing them has seriously declined.

Keynes feared that "when the capital development of a country becomes a by-product of the activities of a casino, the job is likely to be ill-done." Although Keynes focused on the stock market as a source of instability, the same problem exists in all financial markets. For example, in government bond markets, prices are determined by savers, speculators, financial firms, gamblers, and business firms that have no interest in the underlying government agency that issued the bond.

Financial investment has thus become a major contributor to the booms and busts observed in modern economies. It has proved difficult to find the optimal balance between the need for larger financial sectors to facilitate the flow of funds from savers to investors, innovators, and consumers on the one hand, and the increasing complexity that seems to generate occasional economic crises on the other.

Why Financial Transactions Fail

There are several basic difficulties in carrying out a financial investment; all are related to asymmetric information, which describes a situation in which one side of a financial transaction has more information about future profits and the likelihood of repayment than the supplier of the savings.

There are two factors that play into the problem of asymmetric information situations, including:

1. Adverse selection in which persons who take out an insurance policy are likely to be those people who may need it, undermining the actuarial statistical analysis insurance companies make to spread out risk; and
2. Moral hazard in which persons are likely to engage in risky behavior when they know the costs of that risky behavior.

Information asymmetries point to a role for government policy. In a developed economy such as that of the United States, the Securities and Exchange Commission (SEC) was created to oversee financial markets. Among other things, it requires firms that issue stock or bonds to provide financial information to prospective buyers. In most countries the government agencies that supervise banks require that financial statements be public so that depositors and other holders of bank liabilities can judge the bank's ability to meet its obligations. Government-mandated information permits financial transactions to be completed where the fear of default, adverse selection, or moral hazard would otherwise cause prospective buyers or sellers to shy away.

Financial intermediaries introduce a "principal–agent problem." Banks, money managers, and hedge funds (the agents), among other intermediaries, effectively play with other people's (the principals') money, and there may be incentives that lead them to treat funds differently from what financial investors would prefer. For example, a profit-maximizing bank might be tempted to invest in excessively risky assets because if things work out, the bank owners stand to enjoy high profits, but if things do not work out, it is the depositors who suffer most of the losses. The fear of bank failures has led many countries to provide depositors with deposit insurance. But unless banks and other intermediaries are closely regulated, such insurance can worsen the principal–agent problem because principals have less motivation to monitor agent activity.

The U.S. savings and loan (S&L) crisis, which occurred after a weakening of banking regulations in the early 1980s, illustrates some of the weaknesses of financial intermediaries. S&Ls were suddenly permitted to freely determine interest rates on deposits and to make commercial loans after decades of regulated interest rates and lending restricted to home mortgages. The deregulated S&Ls began expanding deposits by offering higher interest rates on government-insured accounts and making risky commercial loans even though they had no experience in assessing business risks. In a few cases, corrupt individuals acquired savings and loans to channel the savings of depositors protected by deposit insurance to their business friends. U.S. taxpayers paid more than $100 billion to cover the bank losses and the stolen deposits.

Explaining the Variety

The problems of moral hazard, adverse selection, asymmetric information, fraud, and contract enforcement explain why intermediaries, exchanges, and over-the-counter markets coexist: each has its advantages and disadvantages in dealing with these problems. For example, relatively inexpensive financial markets such as bond and stock markets can exchange the stocks and bonds of well-known corporations, whose value can be easily judged by most savers. Less-well-known borrowers rely on banks, which devote resources to investigating and monitoring small business firms and their projects. Financial intermediaries such as banks, pension funds, mutual funds, and insurance companies are good at pooling risk.

The creation of new financial institutions and instruments is called "financial innovation." An economy that has experienced a large amount of financial innovation and thus has a variety of intermediaries and markets is said to have a "deep" financial sector.

Problems of Financial Depth

A recent example of financial innovation is the collateralized debt obligation (CDO), a derivative that is a claim to some share of a large bundle of financial instruments. For example, a CDO is created when a bank originates mortgages or auto loans, puts them together into one large bundle, and then sells shares in the earnings from the mortgages or auto loans to investors, pension funds, hedge funds, and other banks. But CDOs are not simple shares. To make them as profitable as possible for the loan originators, CDOs are split into separate "tranches," each with a different rate of return and a different priority for receiving the returns on the underlying mortgages. Purchasers of a share in the top tranche are the first to get paid from the returns on the whole bundle of mortgages, and the purchasers of the other tranches are paid only after the higher tranches receive payment. The bottom tranche, sometimes referred to as "toxic waste," stands to earn a relatively high stated interest rate but only after all the other tranches are paid. The tranches are carefully structured to gain the highest possible ratings for each one. The top tranche is normally awarded an AAA rating, given only to financial instruments with no risk. Its share of the total bundle must be small enough to make it highly unlikely that the total returns on the whole bundle will not be large enough to fully service that upper tranche.

The AAA tranche can be quite large even when the underlying instruments are risky. For example, the top tranche of U.S. CDOs of subprime mortgages, home loans to relatively risky borrowers, issued during 2005–2007 included about 80 percent of all the mortgages in the total CDO. Only if more than 20 percent of subprime borrowers stopped servicing their debt would the AAA-rated tranche no longer earn full returns, which was considered highly unlikely during the optimistic early 2000s.

CDOs of subprime mortgages played a central role in causing global financial markets to collapse in 2007 and 2008. It turned out that many banks that originated subprime mortgages had enticed borrowers with easy introductory interest charges for the first two or three years, while U.S. housing prices were clearly in a bubble in many parts of the country. Securitization also led banks to encourage loan officers to issue mortgages with little concern for borrowers' ability to service the debt, since the bank would not have any risk once the loans were bundled and sold as CDOs. Regulators and the banks themselves should have become suspicious when loan officers openly began to refer to the subprime mortgage market as "the liar's market." When the housing price bubble burst, defaults became much more likely than the ratings suggested.

Complexity and Risk

There was a second financial innovation meant to enhance the safety of CDOs that also failed: credit default swaps (CDSs). CDSs covering CDOs were options that paid out the full value of the CDO in the case of default. Interestingly, these derivative instruments were not only purchased by investors in CDOs, but also by hedge funds, speculators, and plain old gamblers who did not own any CDOs but just wanted to place a bet that the CDOs would default in the future. Such gambles are comparable to the purchase of a fire insurance policy on a neighbor's house; if the neighbor's house burns down, the policy holder receives a windfall equal to the value of the house without actually owning and losing it. Of course, the neighbor also might have purchased insurance, in which case the insurance company has to pay out twice the value of the house. CDSs worth many times the value of the underlying CDOs were sold, exposing the sellers to huge potential payments in the case of the default of specific CDOs.

The over-the-counter CDS market is another example of Keynes's point about the divergence of interest in the financial instruments and the economic activities that underlie those financial instruments. By 2007, it is estimated, more than $50 trillion in credit default swaps had been contracted by investors, hedge funds, banks, and other assorted gamblers throughout the global financial industry.

One of the largest sellers of CDSs for tranches of the subprime mortgage CDOs was the U.S. insurance firm AIG, which sold the CDSs through its London-based Financial Products Division. Britain did not require AIG to hold reserves on the CDOs as long as the firm's own financial models showed reserves were not necessary. While AIG's customers clearly thought there was risk, since they paid billions of dollars in premiums for the CDSs, the company's London office set no reserves aside and booked all premiums as pure profit. AIG's management paid the 400 employees in its London office yearly bonuses equal to about one-third of the premiums collected on the CDSs, or more than $1 million per year per employee.

By 2008, the AAA-rated tranches of the subprime mortgage CDOs had proved to be risky after all, and AIG was called on to pay out the losses. Since there were no reserves to cover the losses, the U.S. government had to channel over $180 billion to AIG to keep the firm solvent. With its widespread life insurance, fire insurance, auto insurance, and other insurance businesses, the firm was deemed to be too important for the U.S. economy to fail and leave millions of people and businesses uninsured.

In some instances the innovations raised incomes of bankers and financial executives at the long-run expense of taxpayers, duped investors and pensioners, and foreclosed homeowners. Overall, rather than spreading risk and permanently increasing homeownership, financial innovation created a global financial system that threatened the stability of the world's economy.

The Future

In the aftermath of the 2008–2009 financial crisis, many governments grappled with the need for financial regulation and reform. Should financial markets and intermediaries be more close-ly regulated to prevent excesses like subprime mortgages and the derived CDOs and CDSs that spread the losses throughout the world? Should certain instruments or markets simply be prohib-ited? At the time of this writing, it was not yet clear where each national government would set the balance between the further financial innova-tion favored by the financial industry and the eco-nomic stability favored by most savers, workers, and pensioners.

Hendrik Van den Berg

See also: Financial Markets; Savings and Investment.

Further Reading

Greenlaw, D., J. Hatzins, A. Kashyap, and Y.S. Shin. "Lever-aged Losses: Lessons from the Mortgage Market Meltdown." Proceedings of the U.S. Monetary Policy Forum, 2008.

Keynes, John Maynard. *The General Theory of Employment, Interest and Money.* London: Macmillan, 1936.

Minsky, Hyman P. *Can "It" Happen Again?* Armonk, NY: M.E. Sharpe, 1982.

Ireland

Once one of the economically backward countries in Western Europe—a nation whose poverty sent millions of inhabitants abroad in search of op-portunity—Ireland emerged in the 1990s as one of the world's fastest-growing economies. It was a mecca for high-tech and other foreign compa-nies seeking a well-educated, English-speaking, low-cost workforce with access to the European Union market. Between 1990 and 1995, the Irish economy grew at an impressive 5.14 per-cent annually. In the second half of the decade, it expanded at rates unseen outside the developing dynamos of Asia, earning Ireland the nickname "Celtic Tiger" (after the fast-growth Asian Tigers of the 1980s).

As it turned out, however, the rapid growth of the Irish economy in the 1990s and early 2000s was fragile and unsustainable, dependent on a prosperous world economy and pumped up by

a bubble in property values. When the world's credit markets seized up in late 2008, Ireland was particularly hard hit, experiencing such an enormous drop in economic output and rise in unemployment that some economic analysts began speaking of an "Irish Depression."

The Transformation

How was the Irish economy transformed from a sleepy economic backwater into the Celtic Tiger in the first place? Part of the story is explained by convergence—the idea that it is easy for coun-tries that are behind to "catch up" by adopting the latest technology and production methods developed by more economically advanced coun-tries. Convergence was certainly part of the story in Ireland's case, as the country was able to catch up with the rest of the industrialized world by implementing cost-saving technology developed elsewhere.

Yet the extraordinary growth of the 1990s and early 2000s cannot be explained entirely by convergence, since Ireland not only converged on other developed countries; it also surpassed many of them. In per capita terms, Ireland's gross do-mestic product (GDP) rose to at least 20 percent higher than that of Germany, France, Italy, and the United Kingdom. In just two decades, Ireland not only caught up with other Western industri-alized giants, but also became a frontrunner. To understand the economic growth in Ireland, one must look at how the institutional framework or "rules of the game" have changed there over the past several decades.

The roots of Ireland's transformation began in the 1950s, when it experienced poor economic performance relative to other European countries. While the Continent profited by a postwar eco-nomic boom, average annual growth rates were an anemic 2 percent in Ireland. As a result, about one-seventh of the entire national population emi-grated to other countries between 1950 and 1960. Beginning in the mid-1960s, however, the Irish government began a series of policy changes that lowered trade barriers and made the country more attractive for direct foreign investment. These policy changes included the lowering of tariffs starting in 1964 and the signing of the Anglo-Irish Trade Agreement in 1965. As a result of these changes, annual growth rates rose to comparable levels with the rest of Western Europe. In the 1960s, Ireland increased GDP by an average of 4.2 percent each year. And although Irish growth rates from 1950 to 1973 were not high enough to catch up with countries like France and Belgium, an institutional foundation was laid that would lead to greater growth in subsequent years.

Following the 1973 oil shock, the Irish government attempted to boost overall demand in the country by implementing a series of policies aimed at jump-starting aggregate demand and, according to Keynesian theory, the economy as well. National pay agreements forced wages and salaries to rise, government agencies hired workers in an effort to fight unemployment, transfer payments swelled, and public infrastructure projects increased capital expenditures. In the end, however, these macroeconomic policies were not effective at stimulating the Irish economy. The nation's average annual growth rate was a meager 2.2 percent from 1973 to 1992. To make matters worse, efforts to boost consumer demand in the country led to a financial crisis. To finance its expansionary fiscal policy, the Irish government had borrowed heavily, which in turn led to a high debt-to-GDP ratio. The government was facing a serious budget deficit problem and had to cut spending drastically.

Crisis Creates Opportunity

Irish policy makers aggressively cut government spending in nearly all areas during the late 1980s. Outlays for agriculture, roads, housing, education, and the military all were cut by at least 5 percent; and in 1987, the entire operating budget was cut by 3 percent. In addition, the scope of the government was shrunk, as numerous agencies were eliminated and thousands of government employees were forced to return to the private sector. As a result of these sweeping changes, the federal deficit was eliminated by 1987 and the debt-to-GDP ratio fell to manageable levels by the early 1990s.

Ireland was poised for its economic takeoff. With government spending under control, policy makers were able to create a more competitive tax system. From 1989 to 2000, the standard income tax rate was cut from 35 percent to 24 percent. Perhaps even more important was a reduction in corporate taxes, from 40 percent in 1996 to 12.5 percent in 2003. The latter cut helped spur capital investment, especially in high technology.

Combined with Ireland's new openness to trade in the 1960s and its entry into the European Community (now European Union, EU) in 1973, the new tax policies proved highly effective in spurring economic growth. According to the Fraser Institute's economic freedom index—which measures the degree of competitiveness in national economies—Ireland rose from the sixteenth freest economy in the world in 1980 to seventh in 2000. Many analysts point to this as the foundation of Ireland's newfound prosperity, as policies consistent with economic freedom—steady taxation, responsible government spending, and minimal barriers to trade—allowed entrepreneurial activity to thrive. Other factors in the economic boom included the effects of EU subsidies on education and infrastructure spending and the role of industrial policy. For example, the availability of an educated workforce, combined with low corporate taxes and access to European markets through the EU, gave Irish state development organizations such as the Industrial Development Agency the ability to lure high-tech firms such as Dell and Microsoft to the country.

From Boom to Bust

The dramatic economic growth achieved by Ireland between the mid-1990s and the mid-2000s was followed by an equally dramatic economic collapse, with many of the gains in employment

Construction projects stand idle along the River Liffey in downtown Dublin in 2009. After a decade of spectacular growth beginning in the mid-1990s, Ireland suffered one of the worst economic collapses of any developed nation since the Great Depression. *(Bloomberg/Getty Images)*

and GDP nearly wiped out. Unemployment nearly doubled, to more than 11 percent by the end of 2008, while the overall GDP shrank by 7.1 percent during the fourth quarter of that year alone. In September 2008, the government of Ireland officially declared the country to be in a recession. So bad were the indices and forecasts, however, that many economists referred to conditions as the Irish Depression.

Some of this catastrophe was, no doubt, a result of the global economic downturn. Heavily dependent on exports, Ireland suffered mightily as demand for its products shrank and as foreign and domestic manufacturers cut production. At the same time, some of the forces that made Ireland among the hardest hit of European Union economies in the 2007–2009 recession were home-grown. As in the United States—and, closer to home, Spain—the main domestic source of the trouble was a bubble in the housing market that had been inflated by rising incomes and employment, a growing population of young people

eager to buy their own homes, loose credit standards, and speculative frenzy. Land and property values in Dublin, its suburbs, and even far-flung agricultural areas of the country had seen enormous increases in the early 2000s. Developers built thousands of new homes and millions of square feet of commercial space to capitalize on the nation's growing prosperity—to which all the construction contributed further. Irish banks contributed to the speculative frenzy by offering mortgages equal to 100 percent of the value of a home and loosening standards on who could obtain a mortgage. In addition, interest rates fell on the heels of the Irish economy's linking to the economy of the EU with the introduction of the euro in 2002. This encouraged more people to borrow money, both to buy homes and to borrow against them.

By 2007, the tide in the property market began to turn. With too many housing units on the market and with the ratio of home prices to income at an all-time high, prices began to drop.

Many who had speculated in real estate, as well as all those who purchased homes too expensive for their budgets, now proved unable to meet their mortgage obligations—which forced even more property onto the market. Nor was the crisis confined to homeowners and speculators. At the height of the property boom, the construction sector had an outsized role in the national economy, accounting for some 10 percent of GDP and more than 12 percent of employment. With the bust in the property market, many construction workers suddenly found themselves unemployed (though some were foreigners who left the country when the work dried up).

The bursting of the property bubble escalated into a broad-based financial crisis as lending institutions were left with massive bad loans on their books. The crisis worsened with the freezing up of the international financial system in 2008, as Irish financial institutions, operating in a relative small national economy, had been heavily dependent for their liquidity on international monetary transfers. When that liquidity dried up, the banks found themsleves heavily exposed, which forced the government to bail out some institutions with multibillion-euro loans and to nationalize others. Although the infusion of money temporarily halted the crisis, it did little to lift Ireland out of its economic morass. Indeed, economic forecasters predicted even worse times to come, with some forecasting as much as a 25 percent drop in GDP by the end of 2010—a rate of contraction not experienced by other industrialized economies since the Great Depression of the 1930s.

Joshua C. Hall and William J. Luther

See also: Greece; Portugal; Spain; United Kingdom.

Further Reading

Crafts, N. "The Golden Age of Economic Growth in Western Europe, 1950–1973." *Economic History Review* 48:3 (1995): 429–447.

Gwartney, J., and R. Lawson. *Economic Freedom of the World: 2008 Annual Report.* Vancouver, Canada: Fraser Institute, 2008.

Powell, B. "The Case of the Celtic Tiger." *Cato Journal* 22:3 (2003): 431–448.

"Irrational Exuberance"

The phrase "irrational exuberance" has come to be associated with any unexplained (at least in pure economic terms) major upturn in the stock market or, indeed, any other real or financial market, or the economy as a whole. An implied warning, the term was coined by Federal Reserve chairman Alan Greenspan in a dinner speech at the American Enterprise Institute in Washington, D.C., during a stock market boom in late December 1996. The phrase almost immediately gained popularity in the financial markets, serving as a wake-up call for investors at the time. The run-up taking place in the stock market, Greenspan implied, did not make sound economic sense. Either the comment was prescient or it had a direct effect on market perceptions—perhaps both. In any event, financial markets around the world underwent a significant decline in value in the days that followed. Although the run-up resumed and even accelerated shortly thereafter, Greenspan's term had become a catchphrase among market analysts and commentators to describe steep, unexpected, unexplained increases in the price of any real or financial assets.

"Irrational" refers specifically to investor decisions that are not rooted in logic or sound economic theory. "Exuberance" refers to the high levels of positive emotion—specifically, enthusiasm and excitement—that attend a run-up in prices of real or financial assets. In conjunction, the words were applied in some quarters to the dot.com bubble of the late 1990s, when Internet start-up companies and technology stocks in general were finding hordes of investors and attracting rampant speculation. Amid talk of a "new economy"—in which value would be measured not in terms of production or even profits, but online traffic and the potential it implied—traders became unduly excited about and inordinately invested in vague financial prospects. Economic fundamentals generally did not support this view and, according to some analysts (especially in retrospect), may have actually pointed in the opposite direction. In short, stock market traders and investors in general were being irrationally exuberant about the pricing of these stocks at the time. Once this realization set in, a different psychology took hold and stock market prices dropped sharply.

Notable among the follow-up voices invoking Greenspan's phrase was that of Yale University economist Robert Shiller, who used it as the title of his 2000 book about the dot.com phenomenon. Published at the peak of that boom in March 2000, Shiller's book presented a series of arguments for why stocks—of technology companies in particular—were overvalued at the time. His work like Greenspan's 1996 dinner speech, proved prescient, as the dot.com bubble burst in the weeks and months that followed.

In the first decade of the twenty-first century, economists and journalists began invoking "irrational exuberance" in reference to another kind of bubble—this time in the housing market. Shiller, for example, issued a second edition of his book in 2005 predicting the collapse in home prices that began the following year. In another expression of irrational exuberance in the financial marketplace, the price of houses across the country rose to untenable levels. Fueled by easy credit, median housing prices in certain areas of the country were six to nine times higher than median annual income. This was just one of a multitude of measures reflecting the fact that property values were no longer conforming to sound economic theory. Inevitably, when prices began to plummet in the most inflated areas, the ripple effect was felt throughout the economy.

Irrational exuberance invariably results in asset pricing bubbles like those in the dot.com and housing markets during the late 1990s and mid-2000s. Yet the phenomenon is hardly new and hardly confined to the United States. Indeed, it has recurred throughout the world since the advent of the market economy in the Middle Ages. A manic surge in the price of tulips in Holland during the 1630s was perhaps the first example of an asset price bubble and the irrational exuberance that gave rise to it.

At the height of the tulip craze, speculators were trading small fortunes in gold, jewelry, and land for a single bulb. Indeed, the term "tulipmania" came to be used for the very phenomenon later encapsulated in the phrase "irrational exuberance." In the interim—and into the twenty-first century—the phenomenon became increasingly frequent and widespread. As early as 1841, the Scottish journalist and poet Charles Mackay reflected on such episodes of human folly in a classic book titled *The Extraordinary Popular Delusions and the Madness of Crowds*. It might have been titled *Irrational Exuberance*.

Some analysts and economic experts refer to such episodes as essentially rational "mistakes"—that is, that traders who fuel the run-ups are, in fact, acting rationally based on the information they have at the time. Only in hindsight, it is argued, can their decisions be characterized as irrational. According to the countervailing view, however, many of these episodes can be predicted to end badly—even *while* they are occurring. The use of the term "irrational exuberance" reflects the latter view. Those who invoke the phrase clearly imply the need for more careful and deliberate valuations and projections in the rise and fall of asset prices.

Omar J. Khan

See also: Asset-Price Bubble; Dot.com Bubble (1990s–2000); Greenspan, Alan.

Further Reading

Dash, Mike. *Tulipomania: The Story of the World's Most Coveted Flower and the Extraordinary Passions It Aroused.* New York: Random House, 2001.

Mackay, Charles. *The Extraordinary Popular Delusions and the Madness of Crowds.* Amherst, NY: Prometheus, 2001, reprint.

Shiller, Robert J. *Irrational Exuberance.* 2nd ed. Princeton, NJ: Princeton University Press, 2005.

Israel

A geographically small nation located at the eastern end of the Mediterranean, Israel—with a population of approximately 7.3 million—was established as a homeland for the Jewish people in 1948. With its network of kibbutzim, or producer cooperatives, Israel began its existence as a semi-socialist state. Economic stagnation in the 1970s and 1980s led the government to liberalize the economy, and by the 1990s the country had emerged as one of the most dynamic economies in the Middle East, with a vigorous agricultural, tourism, and manufacturing sector, the latter including world-class defense, medical technology, and software sectors. Israel has also benefited from the Jewish Diaspora, which has provided much-needed capital throughout the country's history.

Home to the ancient Hebrew tribes in the second and first millennium BCE, Israel was occupied by the Romans in the second century BCE, who eventually expelled many of the Jews after a series of unsuccessful revolts. For the next roughly 2,000 years, Jews lived in exile, largely in Europe, Southwest Asia, North Africa, and eventually North and South America. Their religious tradition, however, spoke of a return to the "promised land." Ironically, however, it was secular Jews, influenced by the nationalist currents sweeping Europe in the nineteenth century, who developed Zionism, the political movement for a modern Jewish state in the historical land of Israel.

Zionists' efforts to encourage Jews to return to move to Palestine were given a tragic boost by the Holocaust, and by the late 1940s, hundreds of thousands of Jews had settled in British-controlled Palestine, a development that antagonized local Arabs. Unable to reconcile the two groups, the British abandoned Palestine in 1948 but not before the Jewish population declared an independent state. War between the Jews and surrounding Arab states ensued, leading to a Jewish victory and the exile of hundreds of thousands of Palestinian Arabs. Relations with both the Palestinians and surrounding Arab states have remained tense, with periodic wars and rebellions occurring through the present day.

Many of the Zionist leaders who founded Israel were influenced by socialist ideals, and the economy they established in Israel included a major role for the state in directing economic development, along with the above-noted network of kibbutzim and a powerful union sector. Emerging from war, with a large population of refugees, Israel in its early years was forced to implement strict austerity measures, rationing, and price controls. By the early 1950s, however, the government was able to ease restrictions while the economy benefited from U.S. aid, large transfers of capital from the Jewish Diaspora, German reparations for the Holocaust, and the sale of Israel bonds abroad, largely to Jews living outside Israel. All of this capital allowed for massive investment in infrastructure and education.

The government also instituted a policy of import substitution, which included high tariffs on imported goods, and state support for critical industries and subsidies to the export sector, including agriculture. Between 1950 and 1965, Israel enjoyed one of the fastest gross domestic product (GDP) growth rates in the world, averaging 11 percent per annum, though with the huge influx of immigrants this only amounted to GDP per capita growth of about 6 percent. Despite these gains, Israel was hampered by one critical drawback—its need to spend large amounts on defense. In the wake of the 1967 and 1973 wars, Israel's defense budget amounted to an astonishing 30 percent of gross national product, though much of this was offset by military aid from the United States.

In 1977, Israel decided to replace a fixed exchange rate for its national currency, the shekel, with a floating one. The result was a crippling inflationary spiral that dramatically reduced growth rates through the mid-1980s and required the government to put into place restrictions on capital movements into and out of the country. At the same time, the government moved to liberalize the economy, deregulating many industries, privatizing some government enterprises, and allowing more market forces to determine the allocation of economic resources. But while reducing its role in directing economic development, the government expanded its social welfare obligations, introducing a national health system and increasing social security–style payments to the elderly and disabled, thus helping to ease the dislocations and growing income inequality resulting from economic liberalization.

The policies were a major success. By the late 1990s, Israel had emerged as a high-tech leader, as well as a leading exporter of defense and medical technology, cut diamonds, and winter and citrus crops. At the same time, the country also came to attract much foreign investment, particularly in its software and Internet sectors, which drew large amounts of venture capital from the United States, though this left the country exposed to the dot.com bust of the early 2000s. In 2003, for example, the Israeli economy shrunk by more than 1 percent.

As for the global recession of the late 2000s, Israel has weathered it relatively well, posting GDP growth of roughly 5 percent in 2008 and a contraction of 0.3 percent in 2009, relatively small by developed-world standards for that troubled year in the global economy. Economists cite several reasons for this success, including the government's conservative macroeconomic policies and its tight regulation of the financial sector, which meant that Israeli banks did not engage in the kinds of risky investment decisions that brought so much grief to financial institutions in the United States and several countries in Europe. By 2009, Israel was ranked fifty-first in the world in terms of total GDP, a remarkable achievement for such a small nation, and forty-eighth by GDP per capita, putting the country at the lower end of industrialized nations.

James Ciment

See also: Middle East and North Africa.

Further Reading

Ben-Bassat, Avi, ed. *The Israeli Economy, 1985–1998: From Government Intervention to Market Economics.* Cambridge, MA: MIT Press, 2002.

Nitzan, Jonathan, and Shimshon Bichler. *The Global Political Economy of Israel.* Sterling, VA: Pluto, 2002.

Senor, Dan, and Saul Singer. *Start-Up Nation: The Story of Israel's Economic Miracle.* New York: Twelve Publishers, 2009.

Italy

Home to the Roman Empire and birthplace of the Renaissance, Italy has been central to the development of Western civilization for more than two thousand years. Beginning in the late Middle Ages, various city-states in Italy established trade links throughout the Mediterranean region and as far away as India and even China. Early Italian bankers, particularly in Venice, pioneered modern accounting, bookkeeping, and business finance—innovations that later spread to other parts of Europe and led to the birth of modern capitalism.

For all of these innovations, Italy lagged behind Northern Europe both politically and economically in the eighteenth and nineteenth centuries. It remained divided among various states until unification in the latter half of the nineteenth century and was far poorer than much of the rest of the Continent. The post–World War II economic boom, however, lifted Italy to the front ranks of industrialized countries—today it ranks seventh worldwide by gross domestic product (GDP), with an economy based on manufacturing, services, tourism, and the production of high-end artisan goods.

The Italian economy has several structural weaknesses, including a stark division in wealth between the northern and southern halves of the country and a rapidly aging population whose pensions are eating up an ever-larger share of the national budget. Since the 1990s, the country has experienced stagnant growth, a situation compounded by the financial crisis of the late 2000s. Nevertheless, because of its general economic conservatism—practiced by both households and financial institutions—Italy has not experienced the same economic tumult as the United States and a number of other European economies.

A History of Division

Inhabited since Paleolithic times, the Italian Peninsula was the center of the Roman Empire, which ruled the Mediterranean world and much of the Middle East from the second century BCE through the fifth century CE. After the fall of the Roman Empire, Rome itself became the home of the Roman Catholic Church, one of the only pan-European institutions to survive imperial collapse. At the same time, however, Italy went into a prolonged period of conflict and stagnation, divided politically among warring city-states.

From the 1400s through the 1600s, the peninsula underwent an economic and cultural rebirth, known as the Renaissance. In this period, Italian artists created some of the greatest masterpieces of Western civilization even as their more commercially minded countrymen developed the foundations of the modern capitalist economic order.

After centuries of political division and occasional conquest by outsiders, Italy was unified under royal rule in the 1860s. But the country remained economically divided between an industrializing and modernizing North and an agriculturally based South, where landownership was consolidated in the hands of a small landlord class and feudal economic relations persisted. Hundreds of thousands of impoverished peasants fled the region in the late nineteenth and early twentieth centuries, either for the cities of northern Italy or across the Atlantic to the Americas.

Economic and political chaos in the wake of World War I led to the rise of an Italian fascist regime. Under dictator Benito Mussolini, Italy pioneered a corporatist economic and political order in which society was organized into economic interest groups controlled by the state. While promising prosperity and liberation from class struggle, corporatist fascism as developed under Mussolini largely benefited the interests of the state and its business elite allies.

Modern Industrial Democracy

With the end of World War II and the defeat of fascism, Italy was established as a democratic republic and incorporated into the emerging Western European economic and political order. It was an original member of the European Economic Community (later the European Union), whose founding documents were known as the Treaties of Rome, after the Italian capital, where they were signed.

Italy also became an integral part of the transatlantic political and economic system that emerged in the wake of World War II. The nation's rapid

The Italian automobile industry, known for some of the world's most popular brands and stylish designs, helped fuel the nation's "economic miracle" of the post–World War II era. Fiat has bought several major domestic manufacturers and a stake in Chrysler. *(Damien Meyer/ AFP/Getty Images)*

economic growth during that period—often referred to as the "Italian economic miracle"—saw per capita GDP rise from $3,800 in 1950 to $10,400 in 1973. As for other Western European nations, Italy's recovery was aided in the late 1940s by the U.S. Marshall Plan, which included massive U.S. economic aid aimed at jump-starting war-torn economies and preventing the spread of leftist and communist governments. Italy's extraordinary growth in the first several decades after World War II was assisted as well by the extraordinary economic performance of much of Western Europe and North America, which was a boon to Italian exports.

Rapidly rising oil prices and widespread recession in much of the industrialized world led to stagnant growth in the 1970s. But with the return of global economic prosperity and falling oil and natural resource prices in the 1980s, Italy prospered, for a time reaching GDP per capita parity with Great Britain.

During the postwar era as a whole, Italy developed a unique form of industrial capitalism. Unlike those of other major European countries, Italy's economy was dominated by small and medium-sized companies, many of them family-owned and -run. While Italy was home to a variety of mass-production industries—everything from cars to tires to household appliances—it specialized in the production of high-end consumer goods, including clothes, shoes, and other leather products.

By the late 1990s, however, Italy was once again stagnating economically, dragged down by the impoverished South (or Mezzogiorno), corruption, massive government debt (reduced somewhat before Italy's conversion to the euro at the beginning of 1999), political paralysis, and an aging population. While much of Europe was experiencing modest growth from the late 1990s

to the mid-2000s, Italy saw almost none, averaging well under 2 percent per year for most of that period.

Economists point out, however, that the Italian economy is often in better shape than statistics suggests because of its large informal sector, which may account for as much as 15 percent of national economic activity. In addition, Italian households tend to save more and spend less than those in the United States and many other advanced industrialized countries. Credit card and household debt remain a fraction of that in the United States, for instance. Italian homeowners also tend to carry smaller mortgages than those in many other countries, which helped the country avoid the housing bubble experienced in the United States, Spain, and the British Isles in the early and mid-2000s.

All of these factors helped Italians weather the financial crisis and recession of 2008–2009 better than citizens of the United States and other European countries. In addition, Italy's conservative bankers largely stayed away from the more exotic financial instruments, such as mortgage-backed securities, which brought down financial institutions in the United States and other Western European countries during the 2008–2009 financial crisis.

James Ciment

See also: France; Germany; United Kingdom.

Further Reading

Hearder, Harry, and Jonathan Morris. *Italy: A Short History.* 2nd ed. New York: Cambridge University Press, 2001.

Organisation for Economic Co-operation and Development (OECD). "Economic Survey of Italy 2009." Available at www.oecd.org/document/48/0,3343,en_2649_33733_42987824_1_1_1_1,00.html. Accessed September 22, 2009.

Schioppa, Fiorella P. *Italy: Structural Problems in the Italian Economy.* New York: Oxford University Press, 1993.

Japan

An island nation of roughly 125 million people, Japan has the third-largest economy in the world with a gross domestic product (GDP) of roughly $4.3 trillion annually in the late 2000s. An ethnically homogenous country with a history stretching back thousands of years, Japan emerged onto the world stage as a rising industrial power in the late nineteenth century, the first non-European (or non-European-settled) nation to achieve such a status.

After a period of militaristic rule and imperial expansion in the first half of the twentieth century, and defeat in World War II, Japan emerged as a thriving capitalist democracy in the second half of the century, even challenging U.S. economic hegemony for a time in the 1980s. But the boom led to speculative excess, particularly in real estate, setting off a financial crisis and a period of long-term stagnation in the 1990s and early 2000s.

Just when the Japanese economy began to recover, it was hit by the global financial crisis and recession of the late 2000s. While the Japanese financial sector has not been as deeply affected as its counterparts in the United States and some European countries, the economy as a whole—deeply dependent on exports—has been hard hit by falling demand, sinking it into a new slump.

Economic History up to the Meiji Restoration

Human habitation of the Japanese archipelago stretches back to the Paleolithic Era. Heavily influenced by Chinese civilization, with peoples and ideas arriving via the Korean Peninsula, Japanese civilization and the first Japanese state emerged around the third century CE, with Buddhism following several hundred years later. Another import was the Chinese form of bureaucratic government—which laid out codes for private landownership, granting equal land plots to all adult males, and a taxation system to finance the imperial government—under Prince Shotuku in the seventh century.

By the eighth and ninth centuries, however, the equal land allotment system had broken down, as the central government weakened. Monasteries, imperial retainers, and local landlords, or daimyo, began consolidating more and more land and forcing peasants to work for them, though these peasants never became serfs like their European counterparts in the same period. To maintain order, local landlords organized armies of warriors known as *samurai*.

During this period, there was often great tension between the centralizing efforts of the shogunate, or imperial household, and local landlords, leading to periodic strife that further impoverished the peasantry. Japan's feudal order of powerful landlords, a weak central government, and a cowed peasantry persisted for centuries after it had disappeared in Europe. Under the Tokugawa Shogunate, which emerged in the late 1500s, there was some effort to curb the power of the daimyo, though most avoided taxation and other forms of control from the central government, with the burden of supporting that government falling on the peasantry.

But there were also countervailing forces at work during the Tokugawa Shogunate, which lasted until the Meiji Restoration of 1867. While the economy largely rested on agriculture, especially rice, trade in other goods—cloth, cooking oil, sugar, paper, and iron—emerged. Urbanization also accelerated, with the commercial center of Osaka boasting a population of roughly 1 million people by 1750 while the imperial capital of Kyoto and the administrative center of Edo (later Tokyo) each had populations of about 400,000. Manufacturing and a financial sector also became key ingredients of the growing Japanese economy in these years.

Europeans first arrived in the islands in the early 1500s, but after a period of growing influence they were restricted to a few tiny islands where they could conduct only limited commerce with licensed Japanese traders. By these means, Japan largely isolated itself from the outside world until the mid-nineteenth century, when American naval ships and traders forced its doors open. This opening up was part of a long tradition whereby Japan periodically adopted foreign technologies and ideas—usually from China and Korea—and then closed itself off again.

Emergence as Leading Industrial Power

In 1867, the feudal Tokugawa Shogunate was overthrown and replaced by a new imperial order, an event known as the Meiji ("enlightened") Restoration. The new imperial government based in Tokyo recognized that to avoid the fate of other Asian countries, such as China and India, which were either colonized by Europeans outright or had their economies dominated by them, Japan would have to adopt the political, economic, and military practices of the West if it was to remain independent and achieve prosperity.

With its long tradition of borrowing innovations from China, the Japanese were highly successful in adapting themselves to the modern capitalist and imperialist world order of the late nineteenth and early twentieth centuries. The old feudal order was replaced by a modern bureaucratic state endowed with great powers to set economic policy. A modern legal framework was established, abolishing a system that subjected people of different classes to different rules, and the rudiments of democracy were put into place.

With the government providing various forms of economic stimulus, many of the old daimyo turned themselves into industrialists, building factories, railroads, and corporations, some of which survive to the present day. The Japanese also built a modern army and embarked on imperial expansion, seizing Korea and Formosa (modern-day Taiwan), establishing a "sphere of influence" in Mainland China, and even defeating Russia in a war for influence in East Asia, the first time in the modern era that a non-European country had beaten a European one in a major conflict.

Japan prospered mightily, joining the front ranks of industrialized countries by World War I. But the expansion created problems. Poor in natural resources, Japan found itself having to export more and more to pay for the resources it needed, fueling fears among the elite and the larger electorate that unless it continued its overseas expansion its fortunes would be reversed. As in other newborn democracies, such as Germany and Italy, many Japanese came to question whether a democracy could secure Japan's rightful place as a leading power, a fear that became fused with an ultra-nationalist ideology that endorsed the notion of the Japanese people's innate racial superiority over others.

By the 1930s, the militarists had captured

power in Japan and embarked on a massive expansion of the armed forces and the defense industry while launching an invasion of China. Japan's rising power and belligerency raised tensions with another great power of the Pacific, the United States. When Washington attempted to restrict Japanese militarism by limiting key exports, the Japanese military determined that it had to neutralize U.S. power in the western Pacific. In late 1941, it launched a surprise attack against American forces in Hawaii, triggering the United States' entry into World War II. At the same time, Japan launched a massive invasion of Southeast Asia, seizing the territory from European colonizers, all under the banner of creating the "Greater Co-Asian Prosperity Sphere," a euphemistic title for an East Asian and western Pacific economic community, free of Western powers but utterly dominated by Tokyo.

The Japanese militarists' decision to go to war with China and the United States proved disastrous in the end. Bogged down in the vast reaches of China, Japan was overwhelmed by the greater industrial resources and population of the United States. Its cities and industrial centers were bombed to annihilation, with the aerial attack culminating in two atomic bomb blasts that forced Japan to surrender unconditionally to Washington in late 1945. Occupied by the U.S. military after World War II, Japan adopted a democratic constitution written for it by U.S. authorities.

Postwar Economic "Miracle"

While the country lay in ruins, it did enjoy certain advantages even in the immediate postwar era of inflation, unemployment, and shortages of consumer goods. Its populace was highly educated and highly skilled, it had centuries of manufacturing experience behind it, it had a host of major corporations that had been highly profitable before the war, and it had a seventy-five-year tradition of effective economic policy making by the central government. Determined to prevent a leftist takeover of Japan in the early years of the cold war, the United States did much to bol-

ster the Japanese economy. Especially during the Korean War from 1950 to 1953, U.S. military procurement provided a much-needed boost to manufacturing and agriculture, at one point accounting for more than a quarter of all exports.

Unlike the United States, however, the Japanese were not reluctant to employ central planning to direct the economy. Central to this effort was the establishment of the Ministry of International Trade and Industry (MITI) in 1949. MITI not only developed the economic blueprint for Japan's economic recovery from war but also it made sure that the nation's banking and manufacturing sectors cooperated with government in developing key heavy industries. The government also encouraged the importation of the latest manufacturing technologies, which forced industry to modernize. MITI set import and export policies to make sure that nascent domestic industry was protected and the exports that had long been essential to Japan's economic prosperity were promoted.

The Japanese central bank contributed as well, providing easy credit so that industry could grow, while the legislature eased up on antimonopoly rules. Huge, vertically integrated conglomerates in shipbuilding, steel, and consumer goods production known as *keiretsu* emerged. Industrial peace was achieved, largely by reining in the power of unions while guaranteeing workers steadily rising wages and lifetime employment, though this only applied to major corporations that, in turn, relied on a network of smaller suppliers and subcontractors hiring people without such benefits.

The result of all this was the so-called Japanese miracle of the 1950s and 1960s, when the country consistently ranked at the top of the world nations in GDP growth. By the early 1970s, Japan had emerged as the second-largest noncommunist economy in the world. And while the country faced setbacks in the 1970s—a result of rapidly rising oil prices and economic stagnation in much of the industrialized world that undermined exports—it roared back to life in the 1980s.

Adopting technologies from the West and then improving on them—as well as developing some of its own under MITI's guidance—Japan's export-driven economy became a world manufacturing leader in such fields as shipbuilding, steelmaking, electronic consumer goods, and automobiles. So successful was the Japanese model of manufacturing that U.S. firms looked to the country for inspiration. The American automobile industry, for one, tried to re-create the team-oriented production techniques of Japanese assembly lines while that industry and others adopted Japan's "just-in-time" inventory control methods, which streamlined the supply process. For the Japanese people, the success was registered in rising standards of living, with per capita income rising to 80 percent that of the United States by 1990.

Stagnation and the "Lost Decade"

But there was a darker side to the boom as well—speculative excess and overcapacity. With so much capital on hand, Japanese individuals and businesses began to speculate in securities and real estate, driving up both, especially the latter, to unsustainable levels. At one point in the late 1980s, it was estimated that the paper value of real estate in the greater Tokyo area surpassed that of the entire United States. Ultimately the bubble burst, wiping out the assets and portfolios of individuals and businesses alike. A nation of savers became even more frugal as a result, undermining consumer demand.

Meanwhile, having overbuilt industrial capacity, Japanese companies found themselves saddled with debt, forcing some to abandon traditional guarantees of lifetime employment for their workers. Rising Asian economies were also eating into Japanese overseas markets for consumer goods, though these same economies were also becoming customers for Japanese exports of machinery and other industrial goods.

The Japanese banking system was overleveraged as well and suffering from a lack of liquidity. But rather than root out the weaker institutions, the Japanese central bank and financial authorities did everything they could to keep them limping along, creating uncertainty in the financial markets and undermining credit. Moreover, the central bank was slow to lower interest rates, say many economists, further contributing to the stagnation in the Japanese economy through the early 1990s.

The Japanese government tried to compensate for the slump in other ways, embarking on a mas-

Government integration of manufacturing, finance, and labor for targeted industries—such as consumer electronics—led Japan's emergence as a major industrial power in the 1950s and 1960s. Matsushita epitomized the conglomerates known as *keiretsu*. (*Bill Ray/Time & Life Pictures/Getty Images*)

sive public building project. But it was not enough to overcome the slowdown in the private sector, which was also suffering the effects of lowered demand from a shrinking and ageing population. Finally, in the late 1990s and early 2000s, the government embarked on the "structural reforms" international economists and institutions had been advising for years, in an effort to dispose of the many toxic assets on the books of financial institutions. But such efforts only contributed to more deflation and a further bout of zero and negative growth.

Gradually, however, demand began to revive, reducing the problem of overcapacity, and the banks started to purge their books of bad assets. Some of this reversal was achieved by a central bank policy known as "quantitative easing." While the Bank of Japan had already overcome its reluctance to lower interest rates in the 1990s, bringing down the rate it charged banks to zero or near-zero, this had failed to stimulate credit, investment, and spending. In the early 2000s, it employed the new "quantitative easing" strategy, pumping new money into the economy by buying up corporate and government debt. The idea was to stimulate inflation—though not too much—thereby getting consumers to spend and businesses to invest. The strategy appears to have worked. By 2005, the economy had returned to sustained growth, even coming to surpass the rate of economic expansion in the United States and the European Union.

The "lost decade," as the period of stagnation from the early 1990s to the early 2000s is sometimes called, did have one positive side-effect, strengthening Japan's financial institutions by requiring them to reduce their exposure to debt and increase their capital. With banks holding far less debt than their Western counterparts, not only did they weather the financial crisis of the late 2000s better, but also they were able to take advantage of the turmoil in the United States and certain European banking sectors by snapping up financial assets at reduced prices.

For a time, in the first months of 2008, it appeared that Japan might even be able to sustain positive economic growth despite the global financial crisis. But, inevitably, its export-driven economy felt the impact of the global recession engulfing the United States and European Union, though exports to the still buoyant Asian economies helped offset some of the losses in exports to the West. By 2009, Tokyo was experiencing its first trade deficit in more than thirty years while major corporations began to report significant losses. In the last quarter of 2008, even the iconic Japanese automaker Toyota posted a loss, its first since before World War II.

James Ciment

See also: China; Korea, South.

Further Reading

Bank of Japan. "Financial System Report (September 2009): The Current State of Japan's Financial System and Challenges: An Overview." Available at www.boj.or.jp/en/type/ronbun/fsr/fsr09b.htm. Accessed September 24, 2009.

Hirschmeier, Johannes, and Tsunehiko Yui. *The Development of Japanese Business, 1600–1980.* Boston: G. Allen & Unwin, 1981.

Koo, Richard C. *The Holy Grail of Macroeconomics: Lessons from Japan's Great Recession.* Hoboken, NJ: John Wiley & Sons, 2008.

Mosk, Carl. *Japanese Industrial History: Technology, Urbanization, and Economic Growth.* Armonk, NY: M.E. Sharpe, 2001.

Wood, Christopher. *The Bubble Economy: Japan's Extraordinary Boom of the '80s and the Dramatic Bust of the '90s.* New York: Atlantic Monthly, 1992.

Jevons, William Stanley (1835–1882)

Studies by the English neoclassical economist and statistician William Stanley Jevons on the causes of rapid fluctuation in the value of British currency added significantly to the understanding of business cycles in the nineteenth century. Along with Leon Walras of France and Carl Menger of Austria, Jevons was also a major contributor to the theory of marginal utility, which hypothesizes that utility determines value.

Jevons was born on September 1, 1835, in Liverpool, England. He graduated from the University of London in 1852 and then spent five years in Australia as an assayer at the Sydney Mint. In that capacity, he collected extensive data on the Australian climate, which began his interest in statistics. He was also fascinated with the economic impact of the Victoria gold rush and its effects in Sydney, which led to his booklet *Remarks on the Australian Goldfields*, published in 1859. Returning to England, Jevons attended University College, London, receiving a bachelor's degree in 1860 and a master's degree in 1863. From 1866 to 1875, he served as a professor at Owens College, Manchester, and for the next five years as professor of political economy at University College, London.

Jevons's research on the fluctuating value of the British currency compared to gold, for which he collected and collated statistics, helped form the basis of his 1862 paper for the British Association, "On the Study of Periodic Commercial Fluctuations." This was followed by the book *A Serious Fall in the Value of Gold, Ascertained, and Its Social Effects Set Forth* (1863), which earned the admiration of fellow economists. Its success encouraged Jevons to write "On the Variation of Prices and the Value of Currency Since 1782," which he read to the London Statistical Society in May 1865.

By this time, Jevons's work had started to attract widespread attention, especially when economist John Stuart Mill cited his statistics to explain why Britain's national debt should be systematically reduced. British prime minister William Gladstone also drew from Jevons's ideas in his plans to reduce the country's national debt over thirty-nine years.

While at Owens College, Jevons had written his best-known work, *The Theory of Political Economy* (1871), which integrated the various strands of his research on money supply, currency fluctuations, and business cycles. Jevons believed that business cycles were not random events but influenced by seasonal variables. For example, he argued, sunspots affect the weather, which in turn has an impact on agricultural production and the economy.

On August 13, 1882, two years after retiring from University College, London, Jevons drowned while swimming near Hastings. His eldest son, Herbert Stanley Jevons (1875–1955), a respected economist, geologist, and educator, edited his father's papers.

Justin Corfield

See also: Seasonal Cycles; Sunspot Theories.

Further Reading

Jevons, H.A. *Letters and Journals of W.S. Jevons.* London: Macmillan, 1886.

Keynes, John Maynard. *Essays in Biography.* London: Hart-Davis, 1951.

Peart, Sandra. *The Economics of W.S. Jevons.* London and New York: Routledge, 1996.

———. *W.S. Jevons: Critical Responses.* London and New York: Routledge, 2003.

Robbins, L.C. "The Place of Jevons in Economic Thought." *Manchester School* 50 (1982).

JPMorgan Chase

JPMorgan Chase was an active, and successful, player in the global financial crisis of 2008–2009. The firm showed the other side of a serious recession: the bargains to be made, and the long-term strategic advantages to be gained by those properly positioned during unstable economic times.

As a bank, JPMorgan Chase traces its origins back to 1799, and was formed through a series of mergers and takeovers. The name comes from the J.P. Morgan & Co. bank and the Chase Manhattan Bank, and as such it is one of the oldest financial services companies in the world, with total assets of $1.78 trillion (as of June 30, 2008) and 228,452 employees.

The Bank of the Manhattan Company was established in 1799 and was founded by Aaron Burr, U.S. vice president under Thomas Jefferson. In 1955, it merged with the Chase National Bank (founded 1877) to become the Chase Manhattan Bank, which emerged during the 1970s as one of the best-known and most widely respected banking houses in the United States. However, its exposure to "toxic" real-estate mortgages resulted in its purchase by the Chemical Bank of New York (founded in 1823 as the New York Chemical Manufacturing Company), although it continued to trade as the Chase Manhattan Bank.

Drexel, Morgan & Co. was established in 1871. It helped finance a number of financial institutions during the depression of 1895 and in that same year was renamed J.P. Morgan & Company under the leadership of J. Pierpont Morgan (1837–1913), who helped finance the career of Andrew Carnegie. J.P. Morgan & Company emerged from the crisis as one of the biggest and most powerful banking institutions on Wall Street (New York City). Its headquarters, built in 1914 at 23 Wall Street, was known as the "House of Morgan." By that time J.P. Morgan had established extensive political links in Western Europe and helped finance British and French war bonds during World War I.

The Twentieth Century

The first decade following the war was a busy one for both banks as the economy expanded for most of the 1920s. Then came the most important—and disastrous—event in the banks' history. On what is known as "Black Thursday," October 24, 1929, the U.S. stock market underwent the biggest crash in history. After the fall in share prices in the morning, J.P. Morgan himself tried to reverse the slide. He attempted to inject some confidence, albeit only in the short term, back into the market through cash infusions and continued assurances to the financial community of more help to come. But a larger crash in share prices took place the following week that sent his bank reeling. The Great Depression had begun and, in a few years, Morgan's bank found itself at a crossroads in its history. In 1935 it had no choice but to separate its investment banking operations from the main company and overall reduce its level of operations. This was the case as well for Chase Manhattan and other banking operations.

On to the Twenty-first Century

The post–World War II decades of expansion saw banks grow again and attempt diversification. The impressive growth in the U.S. economy during the 1990s instilled even greater confidence in the banking community. By this decade, many banks had once again joined investment banking with their regular banking operations. In order to continue growing and become more efficient over a wide range of business activities, banks began to merge. In 1999 J.P. Morgan & Co., merged with the Chase Manhattan Bank to become JPMorgan Chase.

By the first decade of the twenty-first century, JPMorgan Chase completed its acquisition of other banks, notably the Bank One Corporation, which had only been formed six years earlier from a merger of Banc One of Ohio (formerly the City National Bank & Trust Company and the Farmers Savings & Trust Bank) and the First Chicago NBD (created from a merger of First National Bank of Chicago, and the NBD Bancorp, formerly the National Bank of Detroit).

The Financial Meltdown of 2008

While the financial crisis of 2008 is most often associated with contracting and failed firms, it also provided opportunities to more well-positioned companies for accelerated expansion and market control. Eager to continue to expand, JPMorgan Chase took advantage of the collapse in the share price of Bear Stearns to take over what had been the fifth-largest investment bank in the United States in March 2008. The takeover came after Bear Stearns had suffered major problems. On March 14, 2008, the company lost 47 percent of its market value as rumors spread about investors desperate to withdraw their capital. With the realization that Bear Stearns might well be insolvent, on Sunday, March 16, JPMorgan Chase announced that it was prepared to buy Bear Stearns and two days later offered 0.05472 of their shares for one in Bear Stearns, valuing Bear Stearns shares at $2

James Dimon (left), the chairman and chief executive officer of JPMorgan Chase, and Alan Schwartz, the president of Bear Stearns, answer questions before Congress about the $236 billion acquisition of Bear Stearns in March 2008. *(Mark Wilson/Getty Images)*

each. Six days later the offer was revised to $10 a share, with the merger formally completed on June 2, 2008. The collapse of Bear Stearns was one of the first major signs of the impending economic downturn in the U.S. financial system, but it was far less dramatic than that of many other companies, as it was absorbed into another institution.

The takeover of other banking institutions continued, and on September 25, 2008, JPMorgan Chase bought the Washington Mutual Bank from Washington Mutual Inc. Founded in 1889 as the Washington Mutual Building Loan and Investment Association, the Washington Mutual Bank was the largest savings and loan bank in the United States.

Implications

The case of JPMorgan Chase shows an important distinction between the stock market crash and Great Depression of the early 1930s and the financial meltdown of 2008–2009. The capital destruction in the earlier disaster was so deep and widespread, there were very few pockets of economic activity that could take advantage of falling prices. This was not the case in the more recent crisis. Financial institutions that had steered relatively clear of the more toxic assets, and that had slowly and methodically expanded

operations over the previous half century, like JPMorgan Chase, were in a perfect position to absorb operations that they could get on the cheap and use to their advantage in the years to come. On the other hand, this situation often results in a less competitive industry, which has consequences for consumers.

Justin Corfield

See also: Banks, Investment; Bear Stearns; Recession and Financial Crisis (2007–); Troubled Asset Relief Program (2008–); Washington Mutual.

Further Reading

Chernow, Ron. *The House of Morgan: An American Banking Dynasty and the Rise of Modern Finance.* New York: Simon & Schuster, 1991.

Crisafulli, Patricia B. *The House of Dimon: How JPMorgan's Jamie Dimon Rose to the Top of the Financial World.* Hoboken, NJ: John Wiley & Sons, 2009.

McDonald, Duff. *Last Man Standing: The Ascent of Jamie Dimon and JPMorgan Chase.* New York: Simon & Schuster, 2009.

Juglar, Clément (1819–1905)

Clément Juglar was a French physician turned economist who came to be regarded as a founder of modern business-cycle theory. Indeed, he is credited with being one of the first economists to recognize the existence of business cycles and to describe them based on collected data.

Juglar was born on October 15, 1819, in Paris, France. Trained as a physician, he wrote a thesis on the pulmonary effect of heart disease. His studies in epidemiology and demographics prompted in him an interest in economics during the national recession of 1847 and the revolution of 1848. While researching the effects of catastrophe (such as war and famine) on the size of the French population from the early eighteenth to the mid-nineteenth century, Juglar expanded his inquiry to determine their impact on trade. Based on his findings, he began writing a series of articles on economics during the early 1850s.

In 1857, Juglar published an article titled "Des crises commerciales et monétaires de 1800 à 1857" (Business and Monetary Crises from 1800 to 1857) in the *Journal des Économistes*, articulating his theory of the cyclical nature of economic growth and decline. He elaborated his findings in the book *Des crises commerciales et de leur retour périodique en France, en Angleterre et aux Etats-Unis* (Periodic Business Crises in France, England, and the United States) (1862). Juglar's thesis, which he expanded and refined significantly in succeeding years, suggested that business goes through regular and repeatable cycles that can be described and predicted. According to Juglar, business cycles occur at intervals of eight to eleven years, and comprise three distinct phases—prosperity, crisis, and liquidation. Within these longer cycles are shorter cycles, which explains why there are temporary reverses during economic recoveries. Juglar's cycles are sometimes compared to Kondratieff cycles, which are considerably longer. The Norwegian economist John Akerman later hypothesized shorter sets of cycles that combine to form Juglar cycles, which he then combined into longer cycles of sixteen years.

Yet Juglar was an empiricist more than a theorist, much as such later economists as Frederick Mills, Wesley Clair Mitchell, and other statisticians. His approach was to draw conclusions from masses of data collected over long periods of time. This approach was applauded in some circles and criticized in others as an effort to produce results that could be defended rather than advancing a theory that was open to dispute. As a result, *Des crises commerciales* was a seemingly convincing, albeit difficult, book to read.

While Juglar was acknowledged as having made substantial contributions to the understanding of economic panics and crises, his work was not universally accepted. One reviewer of *Des crises commerciales* accused him of overestimating the importance of banking. Indeed, Juglar posited a strong relationship between banking activity and business cycles without offering a full explanation or analytical proof. His view was rooted in empirical data, such as banking statistics, and was based on the notion that banking crises generally precipitated commercial crises.

Clément Juglar died on February 28, 1905. Although his investigations into the business cycle remained influential, the importance of his work may have been exaggerated by a later misunderstanding. In the 1930s, the great economist and political scientist Joseph Schumpeter, referring to a contemporary edition of Juglar's writings, cited the Frenchman's contributions without realizing—or perhaps choosing not to state—that the publication incorporated work by later economists as well.

Robert N. Stacy

See also: Kondratieff Cycles; Schumpeter, Joseph.

Further Reading

Groenewegen, Peter D. *Physicians and Political Economy: Six Studies of the Work of Doctor-Economists.* London: Routledge, 2001.

Juglar, Clement. *A Brief History of Panics: And Their Periodical Occurrence in the United States.* 3rd ed. New York: Forgotten Books, 2008.

Kaldor, Nicholas (1908–1986)

British economist Nicholas Kaldor's most significant work concerned the relationship between national economic growth and the way in which capital and labor resources are used and distributed in an economy. His wide-ranging interests included trade cycles, the causes of the Great Depression, welfare economics, and public finance. He is regarded as one of the most original and innovative economists of the post–World War II era.

Kaldor was born on May 12, 1908, and educated in Budapest, Berlin, and London. In 1930, he earned his doctorate from the London School of Economics, where he lectured from 1932 to 1947. It was there that he made his greatest contributions to trade cycle theory, at first under the influence of Friedrich Hayek and the Austrian school of economics, and then as a convert to Keynesian theory.

Early in his career, Kaldor published articles on regional problems in economic development, the first of which examined the Danube region of Europe. In 1947, Kaldor left academia to work for Swedish economist and politician Gunnar Myrdal as director of the Research and Planning Division of the Economic Commission for Europe (a predecessor of the European Union). Kaldor served as an economic adviser to a number of governments, including those of Great Britain, India, Iran, Mexico, Turkey, and Venezuela. His advisory work proved largely ineffectual, however, because the nations he counseled often did not follow through on his proposals, usually for political rather than economic reasons. Nevertheless, Kaldor's research during this period was important to his later work in theoretical economics.

In 1950, after serving for two years on the Economic Commission, Kaldor took a teaching position at King's College, Cambridge University, where he became a full professor in 1966 and taught until his death in 1986. There, Kaldor enhanced his already strong reputation as a supporter of Keynesian theories and an expert on growth and resource distribution. His application of Keynesian principles to the study of trade cycles and interest rates, presented in several published works, drew widespread interest in the economics community. However, it was in the study of wealth accumulation and distribution that Kaldor made his most important contributions. His initial research on wealth focused on capitalist countries, but he later expanded his research to include developing nations as well.

Beginning with a groundbreaking essay published in 1932, Kaldor examined the effects of technical progress on the economy, challenging the position of many economists at the time who claimed that technical advancements had created a disturbance in the economic equilibrium that had contributed to the Great Depression. Like the Austrian School economist Joseph Schumpeter, Kaldor believed that when technical progress caused a disturbance or "disequilibrium" in an economy, this often produced economic expansion in the long run. Kaldor believed investment, especially in innovation, to be a critical factor in determining profits. In what became known as Kaldor's law, he maintained that the primary requirement for economic growth is full employment and that the manufacturing sector is usually the most critical to economic growth—a point of view that sparked debate and criticism among many economists, including American Nobel laureate Paul Samuelson.

Described as one of the last of the great economic generalists in an age of increasing specialization, Kaldor collaborated with a number of other influential economists, including Piero Sraffa and Joan Robinson. Made a life peer, or baron, in 1974, Kaldor died on September 30, 1986, in Cambridgeshire, England.

Robert N. Stacy

See also: Hicks, John Richard; Keynesian Business Model.

Further Reading

Kaldor, Nicholas. *Essays on Economic Stability and Growth.* 2nd ed. New York: Holmes & Meier, 1980.

King, John Edward. *Nicholas Kaldor.* Basingstoke, UK: Palgrave Macmillan, 2008.

Lawson, Tony, J. Gabriel Palma, and John Sender, eds. *Kaldor's Political Economy.* London: Academic, 1989.

Nell, Edward J., and Willi Semmler, eds. *Nicholas Kaldor and Mainstream Economics: Confrontation or Convergence?* New York: St. Martin's, 1991.

Skott, Peter. *Kaldor's Growth and Distribution Theory.* New York: Peter Lang, 1989.

Turner, Marjorie S. *Nicholas Kaldor and the Real World.* Armonk, NY: M.E. Sharpe, 1993.

Kalecki, Michal (1899–1970)

The Polish economist Michal Kalecki has been accurately characterized as a Keynesian. In fact, Kalecki published many of the ideas for which John Maynard Keynes became known before the release of Keynes's *General Theory of Employment, Interest and Money* (1936). But Kalecki's work was published in Polish and French rather than English, and consequently went largely unnoticed. It was not until the 1990s, with the publication of *The Collected Works of Michal Kalecki*, that much of his work became available in English.

Kalecki was born in Lodz, Poland, on June 22, 1899. He attended Warsaw Polytechnic Institute and, following several years in the Polish armed forces, attended Gdansk Polytechnic but did not receive a degree. He worked for the Institute of Studies of Economic Conditions and Prices in Warsaw from 1929 to 1936, during which time he produced much of his important work and writing on business cycles.

Kalecki's theories were based on the premise that political factors are as important as economic ones, especially where there is imperfect competition or conflict between management and the working class. In his writings, Kalecki maintained that the level of investment coupled with consumption played a key role in business cycles. If, for example, during a depression the rate of investment were to increase, the corresponding increase in demand for consumer goods would exceed that of the investment. This situation would come about when workers producing investment goods eventually spent their money on consumer goods. Workers making consumer goods would also buy more consumer goods. In this way Kalecki, like Keynes, believed that government deficit spending on public works—that is, investment and the creation of investment goods—would stimulate the economy.

Although Keynes and Kalecki shared similar views, they came from very different backgrounds.

Keynes's frame of reference was the generally thriving capitalist economy of Great Britain. While Kalecki had lived and worked in Britain from 1936 to the end of World War II—first at the London School of Economics and later at Cambridge University—his earliest work was shaped by his experience in Poland, which had been part of Prussia, Russia, and Austria before briefly gaining independence after World War I. When Kalecki returned to Poland after the war, its economy was a state-run socialist system based on the Soviet model.

Like Keynes, Kalecki believed that saving money was not an unalloyed virtue because if everyone saved—rather than spent—it would impede economic growth. Thus, what is good for the individual is bad for the whole. Similarly, both men argued that cutting wages, while possibly good for an individual company, would be bad for the economy as a whole since it would decrease consumer demand for goods.

Kalecki, who died in Warsaw on April 18, 1970, greatly influenced such Cambridge economists as Joan Robinson and Nicholas Kaldor. It has been suggested that among the reasons the COMECON (Council for Mutual Economic Assistance) nations of Eastern Europe began to suffer economic problems by the late 1960s and early 1970s was that the older generation of economists was dying, leaving no adequate successors. Whether or not that is true, Kalecki, sometimes known as the "left-wing Keynes," left a conspicuous void after his death.

Robert N. Stacy

See also: Burchardt, Fritz; Goodwin, Richard Murphy; Keynesian Business Model.

Further Reading

Bhaduri, Amit, and Kazimierz Laski. "Relevance of Michal Kalecki Today." *Economic and Political Weekly* 29:7 (February 12, 1994): 356–357.

Blaug, Mark. *Michal Kalecki.* Brookfield, VT: Edward Elgar, 1992.

Kriesler, Peter. *Kalecki's Microanalysis: The Development of Kalecki's Analysis of Pricing and Distribution.* New York: Cambridge University Press, 1987.

Sadowski, Zdzisław, and Adam Szeworski, eds. *Kalecki's Economics Today.* New York: Routledge, 2004.

Sawyer, Malcolm C., ed. *The Economics of Michal Kalecki.* Basingstoke, UK: Macmillan, 1985.

———. *The Legacy of Michał Kalecki.* Cheltenham, UK: Edward Elgar, 1999.

Steindl, Josef. "Personal Portrait of Michal Kalecki." *Journal of Post Keynesian Economics* 3:4 (Summer 1981): 590–596.

Kautsky, Karl (1854–1938)

Karl Kautsky was a prominent Marxist political and economic theorist whose work is most notable for linking long-term political, social, and historical forces with economic cycles. That link, he believed, is especially clear in particular economic contractions in capitalist systems, which he believed to be in unstoppable decay.

Kautsky was born on October 16, 1854, in Prague, then part of the Austrian Empire. His family moved to Vienna when he was a child, and he studied history and philosophy at the University of Vienna, where he joined the Social Democratic Party of Austria in the mid-1870s. He went to Zurich, Switzerland, in 1880 and, influenced by the German political theorist Eduard Bernstein, became a Marxist. Kautsky traveled to London the following year to meet Karl Marx and Friedrich Engels, and in 1883 he founded the Marxist journal *Die Neue Zeit* (The New Times), which he edited until 1917.

An orthodox Marxist regarded as the intellectual heir and successor to both Marx and Engels, Kautsky was also influenced by the work of the eighteenth-century British economist Thomas Malthus and was for many years prominent as a socialist intellectual. In his writings, Kautsky extended Marx's ideas and critiqued the ideas of others. His work on what Marx and Bernstein believed was the coming crisis of capitalism appeared in the 1890s and was favorably reviewed by Vladimir Lenin. By the time of the Bolshevik Revolution in 1917, however, Kautsky had become marginalized by the train of events and the direction of communism in the Soviet Union. He was labeled an apostate for his criticisms of the Communist Party.

In the years leading up to World War I, Kautsky was a political activist as well as an intellectual, favoring revolution rather than accommodation and opposed to any alliance with organizations that were not orthodox Marxist. He lobbied for the Socialist deputies of the German Reichstag to abstain rather than vote against Germany's entry into World War I in 1914. Although he changed his position months later, his support for the war was the kind of position that led Lenin to distance his party from other socialist organizations across Europe.

In his essay "Finance-Capital and Crises" (1911), Kautsky addressed the problem of periodic economic crises, emphasizing a distinction between industrial cycles, which he regarded as harmful to workers and beneficial to capitalists, and agricultural cycles, which he believed distributed benefits evenly regardless of one's position in the cycle. In his view, cyclical crises had not been addressed by early economists because they had not occurred before the advent of the industrial revolution. Contemporary economists, he maintained, were in a state of denial; what they called crises were actually part of the demise of capitalism.

Kautsky's view was opposed to that of economist Clément Juglar, who believed that the cycles of boom and bust would continue. Kautsky argued that the end of capitalism would begin with what he called the anarchy of the production of commodities—in other words, overproduction by and lack of coordination between individual producers unaware of the activities of others. That situation, combined with a rapidly growing labor force and the development of technology that could speed up production, would overload the system with goods and be followed by a drop in consumption. Supply and demand would eventually come into equilibrium, but at great cost to the laboring masses.

In 1922, Kautsky published an article in *Foreign Affairs* titled "Germany Since the War," in which he examined political and economic conditions in that country in the aftermath of World War I. In it he described in great detail the problems facing Germany as a result of the harsh terms of the Treaty of Versailles. Among the issues he identified were the Allied policy of holding an entire nation responsible for the mistakes of its government and, following comments by John Maynard Keynes, the reparations program. The vast sums Germany was forced to pay led to large budget deficits, disastrous inflation, and an unfavorable balance of payments, which made payment of the reparations all the more onerous. At the conclusion of the article, Kautsky predicted—eleven years before the rise of Adolf Hitler and the Nazis—that the misery of the German people resulting from Allied policies would eventually give rise to armed opposition and revenge. After living in Vienna since 1924, Kautsky and his family left the city upon Hitler's annexation of Austria in 1938. They traveled first to Czechoslovakia and then to Amsterdam, where Kautsky died on October 17 of that same year.

Robert N. Stacy

See also: Malthus, Thomas Robert; Marxist Cycle Model.

Further Reading

Kautsky, John H. *Karl Kautsky: Marxism, Revolution & Democracy.* New Brunswick, NJ: Transaction, 1994.

Salvadori, Massimo L. *Karl Kautsky and the Socialist Revolution, 1880–1938.* London: NLB, 1979.

Steenson, Gary P. *Karl Kautsky, 1854–1938: Marxism in the Classical Years.* Pittsburgh, PA: University of Pittsburgh Press, 1991.

Keynes, John Maynard (1883–1946)

One of the most influential economists of the twentieth century, John Maynard Keynes challenged the classical economic paradigm of self-regulating markets, arguing that during times of economic recession, aggregate demand lags behind aggregate supply. To encourage the former, he argued, government stimulus was needed, with each dollar authorities pumped into the economy having a multiple effect in creating demand as it is spent by successive individuals and businesses, minus that portion that is saved. Keynes called this phenomenon the multiplier. Hesitantly adopted by several governments, including that of Franklin Roosevelt in the 1930s, Keynes's ideas became the foundation of economic policy in much of the noncommunist industrialized world for several decades after World War II.

Keynes was born in Cambridge, United Kingdom, in 1883, his father a lecturer in economics at the university there. After attending Eton, the most prestigious English private boarding school—on a scholarship—Keynes enrolled at King's College, Cambridge University, as a mathematics major. While earning his bachelor's degree in 1904, Keynes also became interested in economic studies—encouraged by the then-dean of English economics, Alfred Marshall—and social philosophy. After a short stint in the civil service, Keynes returned to Cambridge University to study, and began publishing articles on economics. During these years, Keynes also became involved with the influential social and literary circle known as the Bloomsbury Group, which included such luminaries as E.M. Forster, Lytton Strachey, and Virginia Woolf.

During World War I, Keynes was recruited by the government to work out economic arrangements with Britain's allies and, at war's end, was appointed by the Treasury Department as a representative to the Versailles Peace Conference of 1919. Although British and French political leaders ignored Keynes's warning that large reparations payments from Germany would cripple that nation's economy, the conference—or, more precisely, its consequences—would establish his reputation as a major economic thinker. His book *The Economic Consequences of the Peace* (1919), reiterating the position he took at the conference, proved prescient later in the 1920s, when Ger-

In addition to charting a major new direction in macroeconomic theory, John Maynard Keynes advised the British and U.S. governments on economic policy and was a leading architect of the monetary system and global financial institutions for the postwar world. *(George Skadding/Time & Life Pictures/Getty Images)*

many was unable to meet its reparations quotas and descended into economic chaos.

Keynes became a successful investor during the 1920s even as he continued to research and write in the fields of mathematics and economics, publishing work on probability theory and the need for an inflationary monetary policy that would help reduce Britain's nagging unemployment problem. But his call in the acerbically titled *Economic Consequences of Mr. Churchill* for Britain not to go back on the gold standard—it had abandoned it at the outset of the war—went unheeded. The 1920s also saw Keynes begin his studies on the relationship between employment, money, and prices—a subject that he would continue to pursue into the 1930s and that would establish his reputation. In his *Treatise on Money*, published in 1930, Keynes argued that high personal savings rates—caused by tight money and high interest rates—could impede investment and lead to higher unemployment.

Personally affected by the Great Depression—his investments of the 1920s being wiped out by the stock market crash of 1929—Keynes turned from theory to advocacy with his 1933 work *The Means to Prosperity*, where he began to argue for countercyclical public spending, the hallmark of what would become known as the Keynesian economic model. It was in this book also that Keynes explained the multiplier effect for the first time, arguing that when government injected one dollar into the economy by hiring workers it produced a greater economic stimulus, as that worker might spend the money at a store, thereby aiding a storekeeper who might order more goods from a manufacturer, and so on.

In 1936, Keynes published the work for which he is best known—*The General Theory of Employment, Interest and Money*—a book that provided the theoretical underpinnings for the recommendations he first offered in *The Means to Prosperity*. In it, he dismissed the accepted wisdom of classical economics that economies tend toward a high-employment, high-output equilibrium where free wage and price competition produces a balance between supply and demand. That is, when demand is low, prices drop, which re-stimulates demand. Government efforts to stimulate demand, either by expanding the money supply or putting money directly into the economy, will only affect price, not output or employment, according to this school of thought. Indeed, such remedies will only make things worse, by distorting the natural workings of the marketplace.

Keynes argued quite the opposite. Focusing on the demand side of the equation, he insisted that aggregate demand worked independently of supply and was the result of millions of individual decisions. Thus, during downturns like the Great Depression, economies may find their equilibrium at a level of high unemployment and low output. It was at such times that outside stimulus was needed and that only the government could provide effective amounts of it. Although some of his ideas were adopted in Britain and the United States during the Great Depression, it was only after World War II that the Keynesian economic model became the new paradigm of academics and policy makers in the industrialized world.

As for Keynes himself, he was sidelined during the great debate around his ideas in the late 1930s as he recuperated from a 1937 heart attack. And with the outbreak of World War II, he focused his energies on practical solutions, such as those offered in his 1940 book *How to Pay for the War*, in which he called for higher taxes and compulsory savings, not only to pay for the war, but to control inflation by limiting the growth of aggregate demand. In 1944, he headed Britain's delegation to the Bretton Woods Conference, a meeting of various allied governments in the New Hampshire community of the same name where the postwar global economic order was to be planned. There, Keynes was a radical voice, calling for a common world currency and international financial regulatory bodies. But as representatives of the world's leading economy, more moderate U.S. delegates won the day. Still, Keynes was satisfied with the results of the conference, which included mechanisms for currency stabilization among countries and the establishment of financial institutions—notably, the International Monetary Fund and what is popularly known as the World Bank—designed to smooth out economic crises and aid development.

By this time, however, Keynes was not a healthy man. His work at the conference and his efforts to secure an American loan for Britain at war's end further exhausted him, leading to his death in 1946 at the age of sixty-two.

James Ciment

See also: Great Depression (1929–1933); Keynesian Business Model.

Further Reading

Clarke, Peter. *The Keynesian Revolution in the Making, 1924–1936.* New York: Oxford University Press, 1988.

Felix, David. *Keynes: A Critical Life.* Westport, CT: Greenwood, 1999.

Skidelsky, R.J.A. *John Maynard Keynes: A Biography.* London: Macmillan, 1983.

———. *Keynes: The Return of the Master.* London: Public Affairs 2009.

Keynesian Business Model

According to the Keynesian business-cycle model—named for its architect, the early-twentieth-century British economist John Maynard Keynes—economic downturns are due primarily to falling demand, which, in turn, reduces real output and employment, leading to a further fall in demand. In his influential and pathbreaking book of 1936, *The General Theory of Employment, Interest and Money*, Keynes asserted that this negative economic cycle can be mitigated and even reversed by large-scale government spending as well as reductions in interest rates on the part of central banks. The Keynesian model dominated the thinking of economic policy makers in much of the industrialized world from the late 1930s through the early 1970s, until a combination of stagnant growth and high inflation seemed to undermine its basic premises. In the wake of the 2007–2009 global financial meltdown and recession, however, Keynesian ideas have once again become the basis for government economic policy decisions in the United States and elsewhere.

Before Keynes, most economists and governments held to the basic tenets of classical economics, a body of macroeconomic theory first developed by British and French economists—including Adam Smith, David Ricardo, John Stuart Mill, and Jean-Baptiste Say—in the latter half of the eighteenth and first half of the nineteenth centuries. According to this model, economies tend toward a high-employment, high-output, supply-and-demand equilibrium. In the words of Say, "supply creates its own demand." In other words, where there is free wage and price competition, an increase in production will lower prices, which in turn increases demand and thus employment. Conversely, a decline in production will raise prices, which in turn increases production and also employment. According to classical economics, then, increasing aggregate demand, by expanding the money supply (via lower interest rates) or by direct infusions of government spending, affects only wage and price levels; it does not affect the level of unemployment or real economic output. Indeed, according to classical economic theory, these two government remedies will have a negative impact on the economy by drying up investment funds that could be better used by private industry. The policy implications of the classical model are clear: governments have little ability to effect overall economic output, and the measures they take are usually harmful. The Great Depression of the early 1930s, however, challenged the presumptions of classical economics, as the prolonged slump and the unprecedented levels of unemployment undermined the idea that economies tend toward a full-employment, high-output equilibrium.

Focus on Demand

Unlike classical economists, Keynes focused on the demand side of the equation or, more specifically, the aggregate demand that results from the spending decisions made by all players in an economy—consumers, businesses, and government. According to Keynes, reduced spending leads to reduced demand, which in turn leads to further reductions in spending and so forth. This cycle, he argued, was responsible for the prolonged economic slump of the 1930s. Most economists of Keynes's day asserted that reduced spending was caused by a tightened money supply as banks became more cautious in their lending, thereby making it hard for businesses to invest and hire. Expanding on the work of earlier business cycle theorists, Keynes contended that larger factors send economies into slumps. Specifically, he said, the millions of decisions made by consumers and businesses for any number of reasons lead to the reduced aggregate demand that is the primary cause of an economic downturn. Yet Keynes did not ignore the supply side of the equation, which lay at the heart of classical economics. Whereas the latter assumed price and wage flexibility, Keynes argued for their inflexibility. In other words, demand is not created by supply, as Say maintained; it works independently of it. Thus, Keynes maintained, an economy can find its supply-demand equilibrium far below the full-employment and high-output level insisted upon by classical economists.

Just as classical economic theory had important policy ramifications, so did the Keynesian business cycle model. Because it argued that expansion and contraction cycles are the economic norm—as opposed to the high-output, high-employment equilibrium asserted by classical economists—the Keynesian model held that government should intervene in the economy to flatten that cycle and the human misery it causes. He also argued that there are times when only government action can lift an economy out of a low equilibrium slump through fiscal policy. That is, by pumping expenditures directly into the economy—Keynes advocated direct employment on infrastructure projects as one way to do this—the government can increase demand. Moreover, every dollar spent would have a multiplier effect, as contractors buy supplies and the people who are hired spend more money in stores.

The Keynesian model had a dramatic impact on the economists who shaped government policy during the post–World War II era, even if his recommendations were only tepidly applied in the United States and other industrialized nations during the Great Depression itself. Moreover, there was nothing in the Keynes model that said increased government spending had to be on infrastructure. Military spending, he implied, would have much the same economic effect, even if the social consequences were not as positive. Indeed, the mass spending of World War II, which effectively lifted the United States out of the Great Depression, seemed to confirm this view. For the next few decades, national governments applied Keynesian ideas, effectively tempering the business cycle and, say proponents, contributing mightily to the West's postwar economic boom of the 1950s and 1960s.

Challenges

Keynesian economics immediately faced challenges both from the Left and the Right, and itself was split between competing interpretations in Cambridge, England, and Cambridge, Massachusetts. The most critical challenge to the model came with the persistent economic troubles of the 1970s, in which high inflation co-existed with sluggish growth. The Keynesian solution of pumping money into the economy—in the United States, through military spending on the Vietnam War and expanded social programs—only seemed to exacerbate inflation without easing stagnation. To address this problem, a number of governments, including that of the United States, shifted to an economic policy based on monetarist theories. According to these theories' most forceful proponent, American economist Milton Friedman, the money supply was the primary determinant of change in output and prices. Thus, increasing the money supply during economic downturns—by lowering interest rates or through government spending—had an inevitable inflationary effect that fed on itself. (Consumers tended to spend more before their dollars lost value, and workers demanded higher wages.) What the government should do instead, said the monetarists, was adhere to a stable and predictable monetary increase, so as to wring inflation out of the economy and produce stable growth. In fact, the monetarist approach of the U.S. Federal Reserve during the late 1970s and early 1980s did lower the inflation rate dramatically, if at the cost of temporarily high unemployment rates.

The monetarist approach was not entirely triumphant, however, as governments in the West continued to use both Keynesian and monetarist—or modified monetarist—approaches to effect stable growth. With the economic crisis of the 2000s, the pendulum began to shift back toward a Keynesian model in the United States and elsewhere, as governments began to increase spending to counteract the dramatic fall in aggregate demand and rising unemployment set off by a sudden contraction in the credit markets. Whether such measures—including President Barack Obama's unprecedented $787 billion Economic Stimulus Package of 2009—would have the effect assumed by the Keynesian model remained to be seen.

James Ciment

See also: Classical Theories and Models; Great Depression (1929–1933); Keynes, John Maynard; Neoclassical Theories and Models; New Deal.

Further Reading

Cate, Thomas, ed. *An Encyclopedia of Keynesian Economics.* Cheltenham, UK: Edward Elgar, 1997.

Clarke, Peter. *The Keynesian Revolution and Its Economic Consequences.* Cheltenham, UK: Edward Elgar, 1998.

Felix, David. *Biography of an Idea: John Maynard Keynes and the General Theory of Employment, Interest and Money.* New Brunswick, NJ: Transaction, 1995.

Keynes, John Maynard. *The General Theory of Employment, Interest and Money.* London: Macmillan, 1936.

Skidelsky, Robert. *John Maynard Keynes: A Biography.* London: Macmillan, 1983.

Kindleberger, Charles P. (1910–2003)

The American economist and economic historian Charles Kindleberger was a leading architect of the Marshall Plan, the U.S. economic and technical aid program to rebuild Europe after World War II, and a prolific writer. He authored more than thirty books, the best known of which is *Manias, Panics and Crashes: A History of Financial Crises* (1978). Revised editions of the work appeared after the burst of the dot.com bubble in 2001 and (posthumously, with updates by Robert Z. Aliber) amid the recession of 2007–2009. Kindleberger taught economics at the Massachusetts Institute of Technology (MIT) for thirty-three years.

Charles Poor Kindleberger II was born on October 12, 1910, in New York City. He graduated from the University of Pennsylvania in 1932 and received his master's degree from Columbia University in 1934, where he also completed his doctorate, under the monetary theorist James W. Angell, in 1937. His thesis, *International Short-Term Capital Movements*, was published that same year.

As a researcher in international trade and finance for the Federal Reserve Bank of New York from 1936 to 1939, Kindleberger spent a year in Switzerland with the Bank of International Settlements. He served as a research economist for the board of governors of the Federal Reserve System from 1940 to 1942, leaving that position for a naval commission in World War II. Dissatisfied with his desk job, he joined the Office of Strategic Services (OSS), the precursor to the Central Intelligence Agency, as an intelligence officer. He went on to become a major in the 12th Army Group in Europe, identifying enemy supply lines for Allied bombing missions.

With the end of the war, Kindleberger was appointed chief of the Division of German and Austrian Economic Affairs at the U.S. Department of State in Washington, D.C., where he played a key role in devising the European Recovery Program, or Marshall Plan. Returning to academia in 1948, Kindleberger joined MIT as an associate professor of economics and became a full professor in 1951; he was the Ford international professor of economics until his retirement in 1976, and maintained his ties with the university as a professor emeritus.

Unlike the many economists who seek to support their theories through statistical data and economic modeling, Kindleberger looked for historical parallels to explain his views. The first of his major works in the field of economic history to gain notice outside academia was *The World in Depression 1929–1939* (1973). In that book, he argued that the Great Depression of the 1930s resulted from the decline of British economic dominance after World War I and the failure of Republican administrations in the United States to take up the lead in global affairs. That reluctance, he maintained, was evidenced by the isolationist policies of the Warren G. Harding and Calvin Coolidge administrations, the lack of U.S. interest in maintaining foreign exchange rates, and the unwillingness of President Herbert Hoover to support failing banks at the start of the Depression. Kindleberger also criticized the work of economist Paul A. Samuelson and dismissed John Maynard Keynes's position that the Depression was caused by a lack of demand. The liberal economist John Kenneth Galbraith praised the book, though he found Kindleberger's conclusions about the difficulties in the New York Stock Exchange "cautious."

Kindleberger's next major work, *Manias, Panics, and Crashes* (1978), examined stock market crashes through history and the problems of rampant speculation. The book sold well when it was first published and was released in four new editions thereafter. Other notable works by Kindleberger include *Europe's Postwar Growth: The Role of Labor Supply* (1967), *American Business Abroad* (1969), and *World Economic Primacy: 1500–1990* (1996). He died in Cambridge, Massachusetts, on July 7, 2003.

Justin Corfield

See also: Great Depression (1929–1933); Panics and Runs, Bank.

Further Reading
Galbraith, John Kenneth. *Money: Whence It Came, Where It Went.* London: Andre Deutsch, 1975.

Kindleberger, Charles. *The Life of an Economist: An Autobiography.* Oxford: Basil Blackwell, 1991.

Kindleberger, Charles, and Robert Z. Aliber. *Manias, Panics, and Crashes: A History of Financial Crises.* 6th ed. Basingstoke, UK: Palgrave Macmillan, 2010.

Kondratieff Cycles

Kondratieff cycles—also known as supercycles, long waves, or k-waves—are long-term trade cycles affecting the global capitalist economy, each just over a half a century in duration, that follow a predictable pattern of expansion and stagnation and/or decline. Because they involve such profound economic change, Kondratieff cycles are also linked to political upheavals, such as war and revolution. The cycles are named for Soviet economist Nikolai Kondratieff (also spelled Kondratiev), who conceived of them in the 1920s as a way to explain the history of capitalism from the French Revolution of the late eighteenth century through his own time. In the decades since, other social science theorists have elaborated on Kondratieff's original concept, reconsidering the causal factors of the cycles and extending them to later time periods.

Foundations and Dynamics

Like many innovative theories, Kondratieff's was not entirely original. Earlier economists, such as the Frenchmen Clément Juglar in the 1860s, had suggested that capitalist economies operate in shorter expansion-contraction phases. Two Dutch economists of the early twentieth century, Jacob van Gelderen and Samuel de Wolff, had proposed somewhat longer phases as well. Still, the most widely circulated and influential articulation of the idea of long-term economic cycles was Kondratieff's.

His theory—first presented in a 1926 article titled "The Long Waves in Economic Life"—was based on an analysis of the economies of Great Britain, France, and, to a lesser extent, the United States. (These countries, he noted, offered the richest mine of economic data for that period.) Using these numbers, Kondratieff calculated that, in the previous 130 or so years, the three countries had experienced two-and-a-half long-term economic cycles: a broad upswing from 1789 to 1814, and a downswing from 1814 to 1849; another upswing from 1849 to 1873, and a downturn from 1873 to 1896; and an upswing from 1896 to the early 1920s, which Kondratieff predicted would soon turn to another downswing. He also asserted that, if the economic data were available, the era prior to

1789 would reveal the same pattern. Kondratieff did not insist that periods of upswing and downswing are uniform and consistent. He did say that, in the former period, years of growth outnumbered years of contraction, while recessions tend to occur more frequently during the downswing phase of the cycle.

Periods of economic expansion, according to Kondratieff's theory, are characterized by falling interest rates, increased wages, rising prices, and the increased production and consumption of basic commodities. (His analysis focused on data for coal, pig iron, and lead.) Other characteristics of upswing periods include the widespread introduction of new technologies and increased gold production. In downswings, the agricultural sector experiences long-term depression, new technologies are invented, and gold production falls. Finally, Kondratieff offered the paradoxical idea that political tensions rise during times of economic expansion and ease during times of economic contraction.

Kondratieff was most emphatic about the impact of economic cycles, arguing that they result in many phenomena that, in a mistaken logical order, often are identified as causes of the cycle. For example, he argued, while individual creativity certainly plays a role in technological innovation, the conditions that allowed for that creativity and, more importantly, the application of that technological creativity to the broader economy are a "function of the necessities of real life" as determined by long-term economic cycles. In other words, as a Marxist, Kondratieff emphasized the importance of great historical forces beyond the influence of individual economic agents. Similarly, political tensions typically do not trigger long-term upswings or downswings but tend to be caused by upswings. Thus, wars are a result of increased competition for resources and markets, and revolutions are produced by the "social shocks" associated with the "new economic forces" of upswing periods. Nor did the inclusion of new countries into the global economy, such as

Kondratieff Cycles

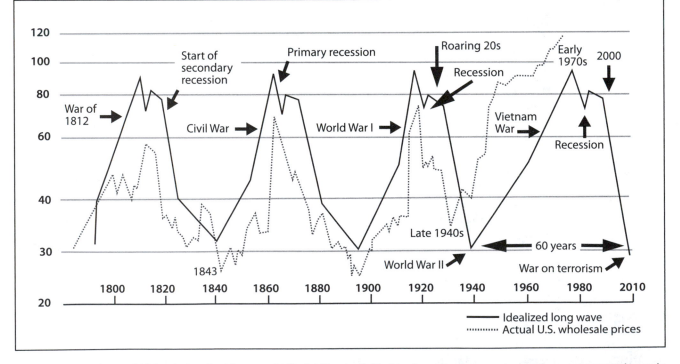

A comparison of actual U.S. wholesale prices and Nikolai Kondratieff's idealized long wave shows close correspondence in roughly half-century cycles: upwaves of inflation/expansion, price/growth peaks, downwaves of contraction, and recessionary troughs.

the United States in the mid-nineteenth century, produce upswings. Again, the long-term phases in the cycle, Kondratieff insisted, created the conditions for their inclusion.

Influences and Variations

As history would have it, Kondratieff's theories brought great personal misfortune to their author. Originally a proponent and architect of the five-year economic plans of the Communist Soviet Union, Kondratieff became convinced, as a result of his research into long-term cycles, that the plans were misguided and ineffective. This position put him at odds with Soviet dictator Joseph Stalin, who had him imprisoned and then executed during the political purges of the late 1930s.

Outside the Soviet Union, meanwhile, Kondratieff's theory was gaining adherents, among them Austrian-American economist Joseph Schumpeter. While accepting the existence of Kondratieff cycles—indeed he gave them their name as a homage to the recently executed Russian—Schumpeter argued in the late 1930s that the pivot between periods of economic decline and expansion is caused by the activities of entrepreneurs and business innovators. Usually these activities entail the introduction of technological innovation to the wider economy, such as the application of steam power in the late eighteenth century (corresponding to the Kondratieff upswing beginning in 1789) or the spread of railroads in the mid-nineteenth century (the upswing beginning in 1849).

In the years immediately following World War II, as advocates of the Keynesian economic consensus promoted government stimulus as a way to avoid or dampen the effects of market forces, Kondratieff cycles fell out of favor. In the mid-1960s, a Marxist economist named Ernest Mandel revived interest in them with his prediction that the latest upswing cycle, which began in the late 1940s, would come to an end within five years. Mandel was not far off the mark, as the early 1970s brought an end to the postwar global economic expansion.

Other economists have elaborated on Schumpeter's interpretation of Kondratieff's work. Shifting the focus from entrepreneurs to the large-scale industrial firms of the post–World War II era, Christopher Freeman of Great Britain and Carlota Pérez of Venezuela argued in the 1980s that the phases of the Kondratieff cycle are associated with new methods of business organization and management, themselves triggered by the constraints and opportunities brought by fundamental technological change.

Kondratieff's theory continues to intrigue economists to the present day, partly because it has accurately predicted long-term change in the global capitalist economy. The late 1920s did, indeed, usher in a lengthy downturn in the global economy, just as the late 1940s brought a turnaround that lasted until the early 1970s. Thus, according to Kondratieff's theory—and, specifically the Schumpeter-Freeman-Pérez reinterpretation—a new long-term expansion should have begun in the 1990s, following the introduction of new information technologies and the long-term managerial and organization responses to them. Other disciples of Kondratieff emphasize the inclusion of new economies—such as China's—as a factor in the new growth phase. By Kondratieff's reckoning, then, the deep recession of 2007–2009 did not signal an end to the long-term expansion of the global economy, as many feared, but rather a rough patch—albeit it a rocky and jarring one—on a quarter-century-long road of expansion that would come to an end in the 2020s.

James Ciment

See also: Juglar, Clément; Kondratieff, Nikolai Dmitriyevich; Seasonal Cycles; Sunspot Theories.

Further Reading

Barnett, Vincent L. *Kondratiev and the Dynamics of Economic Development: Long Cycles and Industrial Growth in Historical Context.* New York: St. Martin's, 1998.

Freeman, Chris, and Francisco Louçã. *As Time Goes By: From the Industrial Revolutions to the Information Revolution.* New York: Oxford University Press, 2001.

Mandel, Ernest. *Long Waves of Capitalist Development: A Marxist Interpretation.* New York: Verso, 1995.

Solomou, Solomos. *Phases of Economic Growth, 1850–1973: Kondratieff Waves and Kuznets Swings.* New York: Cambridge University Press, 1988.

Kondratieff, Nikolai Dmitriyevich (1892–1938)

The Russian economist Nikolai Dmitriyevich Kondratieff was one of the most influential thinkers on business cycles in the twentieth century, known for his work on a long-wave theory of growth. A prominent critic of Western capitalism and an active socialist revolutionary, Kondratieff applied his formidable research and theoretical acumen to the early economic planning agenda of Soviet Russia. One of the leading proponents of Soviet leader Vladimir Lenin's New Economic Policy (NEP), Kondratieff was to die in Joseph Stalin's Great Purge of the late 1930s at the age of only forty-six.

Born on March 4, 1892, north of Moscow, Kondratieff came from a peasant family but managed to secure tuition at the University of St. Petersburg from the Ukrainian economist Mikhail Tugan-Baranovsky, who got to know the boy and was impressed with his potential. Kondratieff initially specialized in agricultural economics and, as deputy minister of food, was involved in conducting studies of food shortages during World War I. The Russian Revolution of 1917 forced Russia to end its participation in that conflict and eliminated Kondratieff's position.

Because his political views were in agreement with those of the revolution, Kondratieff was allowed to return to academia. He began teaching at the Agricultural Academy of Peter the Great in 1919, and the following year became founding director of the Moscow Business Conditions Institute, which planned, monitored, and forecast economic and business activity in Soviet Russia; he served in that position until 1928. With the

Communist regime keen to introduce a five-year plan for the nation's economy, Kondratieff became integrally involved in establishing the underlying principles and theories. Toward that end, he traveled to Great Britain, Germany, and North America in the early 1920s to gain firsthand knowledge of Western business-cycle theory.

Kondratieff formulated his general thesis in works titled *The World Economy and Economic Fluctuations in the War and Post-War Periods* (1922), *On the Notion of Economic Statics, Dynamics and Fluctuations* (1924), and *The Great Economic Cycles* (1925), published in Russian. In them, he outlined his idea of what economists came to call "Kondratieff cycles" or "Kondratieff waves." Every fifty or sixty years, he showed, Western capitalist economies experienced periods of economic depression after periods of rapid growth. Although earlier economists had suggested a similar concept, Kondratieff devised and elaborated the theory independently, proving far more insightful and influential than any predecessors.

Kondratieff's research greatly impressed the Soviet regime, which adopted his ideas as the theoretical foundation for the nation's economic policy in the mid-1920s. The New Economic Policy that evolved from Kondratieff's work assumed the primacy of agricultural production over heavy industrial manufacture. But by the late 1920s, Vladimir Lenin, the founder of Soviet communism, was dead, and Joseph Stalin had taken control of the government. The new leader was suspicious of officials who had worked under his predecessor, and Kondratieff's political fortunes took a turn for the worse. His influence as a government economist greatly reduced, Kondratieff was fired as director of the Business Conditions Institute in 1928. The following year, the *Great Soviet Encyclopedia* declared his theory "wrong and reactionary."

Kondratieff was arrested in July 1930 and eventually charged with being a member of the Peasants Labor Party, an illegal organization that, according to some scholars, might have never even existed. He was sentenced to eight years in prison, but Stalin—who viewed him, like so many other intellectuals, as an enemy—wanted him executed. While in prison, Kondratieff managed to complete several more works on economic theory, which were published posthumously. On September 17, 1938, Kondratieff was tried for a second time, sentenced to ten years in prison, and barred from writing to anybody outside the prison. That same day, he was shot dead by a firing squad. It was not until July 1987 that Kondratieff was officially rehabilitated in the Soviet Union. Eleven years later, with the Soviet Union dissolved, his collected works were translated into English by Stephen S. Wilson and published in London by Pickering & Chatto.

Justin Corfield

See also: Kondratieff Cycles.

Further Reading

Barnett, Vincent L. *Kondratiev and the Dynamics of Economic Development: Long Cycles and Industrial Growth in Historical Context.* New York: St. Martin's, 1998.

———. "Which Was the 'Real' Kondratiev: 1925 or 1928?" *Journal of the History of Economic Thought* 24:4 (December 2002): 475–478.

Jasny, Naum. *Soviet Economists of the Twenties: Names to Be Remembered.* Cambridge, UK: Cambridge University Press, 1972.

Louca, Francisco. "Nikolai Kondratiev and the Early Consensus and Dissensions About History and Statistics." *History of Political Economics* 31:1 (1999): 169–206.

Koopmans, Tjalling Charles (1910–1985)

The Dutch-American economist Tjalling Charles Koopmans was a co-winner, with Leonid Kantorovich of the Soviet Union, of the 1975 Nobel Prize in Economic Sciences. The two were awarded the prize for their "contributions to the theory of optimum allocation of resources," or, according to the Royal Swedish Academy of Sciences, "how available productive resources can be used to the greatest advantage in the production of goods and services." Beginning with his work on the efficient use of shipping facilities, Koopmans was said to apply "brilliant mathematical techniques to develop the complicated equations in this field." His work in econometrics and mathematical programming helped open a new area of economic studies.

Tjalling Koopmans was born on August 28, 1910, at 's-Graveland, The Netherlands. At age seventeen, he entered the University of Utrecht, where he studied mathematics and theoretical physics. In 1933, after meeting the Dutch economist Jan Tinbergen, Koopmans moved to Amsterdam to work on mathematical economics and statistics. After completing his doctoral thesis at the University of Leiden in 1936, he served as a professor at the Netherlands School of Economics from 1936 to 1938, and as the specialist financial secretary at the League of Nations from 1938 to 1940.

Moving to the United States in 1940, Koopmans worked as an economic analyst for the Anglo-American Combined Shipping Adjustment Board. Near the end of World War II, he joined the Cowles Commission for Research in Economics at the University of Chicago, where he served as a professor from 1944 to 1955. He became a naturalized U.S. citizen in 1946. When the Cowles Commission moved to Yale University in 1955, Koopmans went with it; he was a professor there from 1955 until his death in 1985.

Koopmans's growing interest in the economics of transportation led to his study of optimal routing. At Yale, he devoted much of his research to the economics of optimal economic growth and the development of a comprehensive theory to determine the proper allocation of resources—labor, capital, and natural resources—to ensure optimum growth in an economic system. This led to his Nobel Prize–winning study of the optimum allocation of resources, in which he used his background in mathematics to provide a system of interacting equations that took into account the cost of materials at their source, then the cost of transporting them using alternative routes.

In addition to his research, Koopmans wrote extensively on economic theory and the major issues facing twentieth-century economists. His best-known book, *Three Essays on the State of Economic Theory* (1957), continues to be widely read. Koopmans received honorary doctorates in economics from the Netherlands School of Economics; the Catholic University of Louvain, Belgium; Northwestern University; and the University of Pennsylvania. He died on February 26, 1985, in New Haven, Connecticut.

Justin Corfield

See also: Growth, Economic.

Further Reading

Koopmans, Tjalling. *The Scientific Papers of Tjalling C. Koopmans.* New York: Springer-Verlag, 1970.

———. *Three Essays on the State of Economic Theory.* New York: McGraw-Hill, 1957.

Korea, South

South Korea, officially the Republic of Korea, is a geographically small nation of about 48 million people, located in the southern half of the Korean Peninsula, east of China and west of Japan. Inhabited by an ethnically homogenous people with a civilization going back thousands of years and heavily influenced by China, the Korean Peninsula was largely isolated from the outside world until the late nineteenth and early twentieth centuries, when it became a colony of Japan. Following the latter nation's defeat in World War II, the peninsula was divided into two countries—capitalist South Korea and communist North Korea.

In the wake of a brutal three-year war between the two countries (1950–1953), South Korea was left an impoverished, largely agricultural nation ruled by a repressive dictatorship. Beginning in the 1960s, however, the country began to industrialize, emerging as one of the world's largest economies and, in the 1980s, as a nascent democracy. While suffering a major setback with the Asian financial crisis of the late 1990s, the South Korean economy continued to grow at breakneck speed until slowed by the global financial crisis and recession of 2008–2009.

Economic History to the Korean War

Korean history dates back to the migration of people from China in the early Neolithic Era, with the first agricultural settlements appearing around 6,000 BCE. Koreans date the beginning of a distinct Korean civilization to the founding of the Gojoseon state in 2333 BCE. Chinese social, cultural, and economic influences remained strong—particularly Buddhism, which arrived in the fourth century CE—though various Chinese efforts to conquer the peninsula in the first millennium CE were repulsed by temporary confederations of Korean kingdoms. Despite such invasions, Korea became a center of manufacturing, especially known for its ceramics, and the seeds of a national commercial system emerged.

Following a period of civil conflict and chaos, much of Korea was united under the Koryo dynasty from the tenth through fourteenth centuries. Korean society became increasingly stratified during this period, with a wealthy and powerful aristocracy largely situated in the capital and an impoverished peasantry, consisting of serfs and large numbers of privately held and government-owned slaves, in the countryside. There were no cities other than the capital, Songdo (now Kaesong); the use of money waned and commerce nearly died out.

In the late fourteenth century, the Koryo dynasty was overthrown (with the help of the Ming dynasty in China) and replaced by the Choson (or Yi) dynasty, which would rule the country until 1910, when the Japanese occupied the peninsula and made it an imperial colony. Choson rulers, employing Confucian bureaucratic methods, imposed a strong centralized government on the peninsula from its capital Seoul. They replaced the system of tributes paid by local landlords—who imposed them on peasants—to a universal tax on agricultural harvests. Such reforms eased the financial burden of peasants and brought a measure of prosperity to the countryside. Choson bureaucrats also granted merchants the freedom to accumulate and invest capital, though it required them to be licensed by the government.

Korea prospered in the seventeenth and eighteenth centuries with the adoption of new, more productive agricultural methods, new crops from the Americas, and a merchant-led commercial system that expanded trade domestically and with China and Japan, exporting tobacco, cotton, ginseng, ceramics, and paper. Seoul emerged as a major manufacturing center, with more than a thousand markets by 1800.

Politically, however, the Choson dynasty increasingly came under the control of China, becoming a mere vassal by the 1700s. At the same time, Korea became closed off to the world, earning the title "hermit kingdom." By the 1800s, the country's economy began to slide into stagnation and its people into poverty. Not until the Sino-Japanese War of 1894–1895 was Korea finally liberated from Chinese rule, with the nation declared an independent republic.

Liberation proved limited and short-lived, however, as Japanese political and economic interests came to dominate the peninsula, culminating in Korea's formal annexation as an imperial colony in 1910. While the Japanese did much to develop the country, building the beginnings of a modern industrial and transportation infrastructure and opening it up to outside trade, the effort was largely to serve the colonizers' interests. Korean nationalists remained harshly opposed to Japanese rule, especially during World War II, when the Japanese used Korean males as slave laborers and Korean females as sex slaves for imperial troops.

With Japan's defeat in 1945, the Korean Peninsula was divided at the 38th parallel, with areas to the north under the Soviet sphere and areas to the south within the U.S. sphere. The division was supposed to be temporary, until elections could be held to choose a government for a unified Korea.

But the two superpowers and the two governments of Korea could not be reconciled, and the division was formalized in 1948.

Two years later, North Korea, under the leadership of Kim Il Sung, invaded the South in the hope of unifying the country under communist rule. Nearly successful, Kim's troops were driven back by South Korean, U.S., and other allied forces. After a newly communist China entered the fray on behalf of the North, the war settled into a stalemate, finally halting with an armistice (not a formal peace treaty) in 1953. To this day, the two countries remain technically at war and the border between them highly militarized.

Economy Since the Korean War

South Korea emerged from the war with its infrastructure decimated and its people impoverished. It was among the poorest nations in the world, with a per capita gross domestic product (GDP) on par with much of Africa. It did not stay that way for long. Using massive amounts of U.S. aid, dictator Syngman Rhee, while ruthlessly repressing political dissent of any kind, built a broad-based educational system and a modern transportation and communications infrastructure that unified the mountainous country. South Korea also received significant amounts of aid from Japan during this period, as reparations for the years of exploitative colonial rule.

Like the Japanese government, the South Korean regime engaged in strategic economic planning for the country, working with major family-owned industrial conglomerates known as *chaebol* to develop key heavy industries and a strong export sector. It was a smart strategy, according to economic historians, since South Korea had to export to pay for the natural resources it lacked and had a high savings rate among its still low-income citizenry, which lowered domestic demand. Starting in areas such as textiles and clothing, Korea moved into the production of steel, ships, cars, and electrical and electronic items and components. The government assisted companies by intervening to maintain quiescent workforces, protecting them from competition and granting financial aid to promote *chaebol*.

Chaebol are large business groups with a plethora of diversified subsidiaries, including chemicals, heavy industry, electronics, and services. They are family founded, owned and supported by complex cross shareholdings, subsidies, and loan guarantees. Much of the large business sector was part of a *chaebol* network and the network exerted widespread, ingrained, and deep influences on society. Practices included lifetime employment, "seniorityism," and extensive in-house inculcation in company history, vision, and songs. *Chaebol* dominated some localities, leading to the emergence of company towns such as Woolsan (Hyundai) and Pohang (POSCO) to house and serve the needs of employees.

There were more than sixty *chaebol* in all, although a few dominated. By the 1990s, the top five (Hyundai, Daewoo, Samsung, LG, and SK) accounted for about 9 percent of South Korea's GDP; the top 30 accounted for 15 percent of GDP and spread across over 800 subsidiaries and affiliates. Some became major global companies engaging in production, acquisitions, and investments.

The emphasis on industrialization created a growing disparity in wealth between the countryside and city, causing a mass exodus from the former to the latter. But the policy paid off, as South Korea experienced GDP growth consistently around 10 percent annually from the 1960s through the 1980s, rising from about $30 billion in 1960 to $340 billion in 1989. During the same period, the per capita GDP climbed from $1,200 to more than $8,000, one of the fastest increases in human history and one that pulled South Korea—one of the four economic "tigers" of East and Southeast Asia—into the ranks of the developed world.

Cultural Factors

Culture and custom aided the government in its efforts to make Korea an economic powerhouse. Today it is currently the ninth-largest economy in the world. Deeply influenced by Confucian attitudes about work and education, South Koreans are known to put in extraordinarily long hours at work and at school, and to save their money assiduously.

The nation's economic system and success were also influenced by cultural heritage. Especially influential were Buddhism (from 372 CE, and especially 935 to 1392) and Confucianism, the state religion for more than 500 years, to the early twentieth century. The Confucian code of personal and social behavior was maintained by a hierarchical, authoritarian structure. Social values included an emphasis on family, close relationships between father and son, differential gender roles, precedence of elders, and mutual trust among friends. Also held in high regard was educational attainment, one of the best and shortest ways to social status and *jasusungga* (making one's own fortune).

In addition, Korean society was resistant to foreign peoples, countries, and cultures for several reasons. First, the population was ethnically and linguistically homogeneous to a strong degree. Second, the prevalent agrarian society was characterized by passive, closed, and insular perspectives. The climate favored rice cultivation, which was labor-intensive, time-intensive, and centered along rivers and deltas in isolated communities. These communities fostered close-knit, interdependent groups that emphasized collectivism and inter-group responsibilities. Third, antagonistic memories and feelings toward foreign interventionist powers were deeply entrenched.

The historical and cultural legacy has influenced the modern South Korean economy through the predominant corporate culture, management values, and organizational structures and practices. One long-standing expression of that legacy has been a group-oriented approach to business. Traditionally, Korean workers have tended to sacrifice their personal goals for collective ones, in return for which they have been taken care of by the business or community. In-group harmony (*inhwa*) was important, with mutual independence making out-group boundaries more salient. Commercial enterprises were highly centralized and vertically organized, with family-style hierarchical principles and relationships making for more predictable behavior, obligations, and indebtedness.

Authoritarianism and paternalism have been much in evidence in Korean culture, with companies assuming the role of parents and employees the role of family members. Important positions traditionally were filled by kinship-based recruiting from extended clans (*chiban*) or regions, dominated by kinship-based relationships with owners (*hyulyon*). Ideas of harmony and family-oriented management had seniority as the primary factor. Thus, Korean organizations were, according to Korea scholars Y.H. Cho and J.K. Yoon, "like families as well as armies."

Such influences have continued into contemporary society, guiding daily life and social mores, values, ways of thinking, and modes of conduct, with family, hierarchy, seniority, and traditions paramount. Nevertheless, cutting against these cultural elements are more contemporary developments and trends, such as Western approaches to education and employment, globalization, the internationalization of business, and opening up to other cultures. Indeed, from the early 1990s,

South Korean governments explicitly employed a policy of globalization (*segyewha*) that facilitated more communication and interaction with other countries. Companies adopted similar policies, sending employees abroad for exposure to different cultures.

Government

While the Seoul government was highly successful in promoting industrial development, it was not always as disciplined with its own finances. It ran up major budget deficits in the 1970s—exacerbated by the sudden rise in global energy and raw material prices—which forced the government, under pressure from international financial institutions, to put its fiscal house in order. A conservative monetary policy helped rein in inflation but also triggered widespread unrest, which eventually forced the regime to democratize (the desire to present its best face to the world for the 1988 Seoul Olympics was also a factor). By the late 1980s and early 1990s, the country was once again achieving remarkable levels of growth, with *chaebol* such as Samsung, Daewoo, and Hyundai establishing themselves as globally

Union employees of a debt-burdened South Korean bank protest IMF policies during the Asian debt crisis of 1997. As a result of conditions imposed by the IMF in exchange for its bailout package, Koreans feared foreign domination of the nation's financial system. (*Choo Youn-Kong/AFP/Getty Images*)

recognized brand names in consumer electronics, shipbuilding, and automobiles, respectively.

In 1997, however, the Korean economy stumbled as a result of the Asian financial crisis that began in Thailand. As foreign investors pulled their money out of high-growth Asian economies, such as South Korea's, the national currency, the won, began to depreciate rapidly. The situation was made worse by the fact that Korean banks were saddled with large portfolios of nonperforming loans. In addition, some of the *chaebol* found themselves unable to meet their own debt obligations. One of the largest, Daewoo, was ultimately dismantled and sold off in pieces by government regulators. By the end of 1997, South Korean leaders were forced to go to the International Monetary Fund for a bailout, which ultimately amounted to nearly $60 billion. Contributing to the problem, according to some Korea experts, was the nepotism and "crony capitalism" inherent in the country's close political-business connections, opaque structures, and corporate governance characterized by circular investments and complicated inter-company relations.

The troubles and humiliation the Asian financial crisis brought to South Korea were relatively short-lived. With new sources of foreign and domestic capital pouring in, the nation's merchants and manufacturers once again began to expand operations, contributing to a GDP growth rate of nearly 10 percent in 2000. Meanwhile, the government embarked on an extensive restructuring of the financial sector, imposing new rules that made the cozy and often corrupt relationships between bankers and industrialists more difficult to sustain.

Despite such restructuring, the South Korean economy and its financial sector were especially hard hit by the global financial crisis of 2008–2009 and the recession that grew out of it. Fearing a repeat of 1997, foreign investors pulled massive amounts of capital out of Korean securities and banks, triggering a 40 percent drop in the country's main stock index and a more than 25 percent decline in the value of the won. Heavily dependent on exports, the South Korean economy was disproportionately hurt by the global recession, forcing the government to bolster bank reserves and pump money into the economy through aggressive stimulus measures. Still, economic experts expected South Korea to come out of the crisis more quickly than the United States and the European Union, since so much of its economy was now connected to China's (which continued to surge).

James Ciment and Chris Rowley

See also: Asian Financial Crisis (1997); China; Japan.

Further Reading

Buzo, Adrian. *The Making of Modern Korea.* New York: Routledge, 2007.

Cho, Y.H., and J. Yoon. "The Origin and Function of Dynamic Collectivism: An Analysis of Korean Corporate Culture." *Asia Pacific Business Review* 7:4 (June 2001): 70–88.

Cumings, Bruce. *Korea's Place in the Sun: A Modern History.* New York: W.W. Norton, 2005.

Rowley, C. "The Credit Crunch and Impacts in Asia." *Professional Manager* 14:7 (2008).

Rowley, C., and J. Bae, eds. Korean Businesses: Internal and External Industrialisation. London: Frank Cass, 1998.

Rowley, C., and Y. Paik, eds. *The Changing Face of Korean Management.* London: Routledge, 2009.

Rowley, C., T.W. Sohn, and J. Bae, eds. *Managing Korean Businesses: Organization, Culture, Human Resources and Change.* London: Frank Cass, 2002.

Stiglitz, Joseph E., and Shahid Yusef, eds. *Rethinking the East Asian Miracle.* New York: Oxford University Press, 2001.

Kuznets, Simon Smith (1901–1985)

The Russian-American economist Simon Smith Kuznets was awarded the 1971 Nobel Prize in Economics in recognition of "his empirically founded interpretation of economic growth." Kuznets is credited with revolutionizing the field of econometrics and developing the concept of gross national product (GNP). His research also had a profound impact on economists' understanding of how business cycles work.

Kuznets was born on April 30, 1901, in Pinsk, Russia (now Belarus), to Abraham and Pauline Friedman Kuznets. When his father immigrated to the United States in 1907, he changed the family name to Smith; Kuznets, who remained in Russia, retained his original surname. After beginning his higher education in 1922 at Kharkov (now Kharkiv), Ukraine, he moved to the United States and completed his bachelor of science degree at Columbia University in 1923, his master's the following year, and his doctorate in 1926. Kuznets then became a research fellow with the Social Science Research Council, where his research on the cyclical pattern in prices led to his first book, *Secular Movements in Production* (1930).

Kuznets taught at the University of Pennsylvania from 1930 to 1954. He then became a professor of political economy at Johns Hopkins University, where he remained until 1960. He was the Frank W. Taussig research professor in economics at Harvard University from 1960 until his retirement in 1971.

Heavily influenced by economist John Maynard Keynes, much of Kuznets's early work concerned the study of prices. His book *Commodity Flow and Capital Formation* was published by the National Bureau of Economic Research (NBER) in 1938; three years later he completed *National Income and Its Composition, 1919–1938* (1941), which described trends in gross national product (GNP) during the years between World War I and II. From this work, Kuznets developed the model of the business cycle known as the Kuznets curve, which identifies increases or acceleration in GNP during boom periods and declines or slowdowns in GNP during downturns.

Studying Keynes's Absolute Income Hypothesis (1936), Kuznets found that Keynes's predictions did not hold up under careful examination. Expanding Keynes's empirical work on the subject to cover the period from the 1870s until the 1940s, Kuznets showed that in spite of very large changes in income, the savings ratio remained constant throughout the seventy years in question. This became the basis of Kuznets's book *Uses of National Income in Peace and War* (1942) and influenced Milton Friedman's later work on the relationship between income and savings.

Kuznets's extensive research on the national income accounts of the United States—calculating national income back to 1869 broken down by industry, product, and usage, and measuring the distribution of income between the rich and the poor—earned widespread academic acclaim. *Capital in the American Economy* was published in 1961, and *Economic Growth of Nations: Total Output and Production Structure* appeared ten years later. By this time, Kuznets had convinced the U.S. Department of Commerce to standardize its measurement of GNP. At the same time, he argued in print and before a U.S. Senate hearing that GNP was not the sole indicator of economic health in the United States or, especially, developing nations.

Although much of his work was devoted to the study of U.S. economic health, during the 1960s Kuznets began to study developing countries and concluded that the problems facing most of them were the same as those faced by countries in the industrialized world before they had become economically developed. His concern that less developed nations would be left behind the economically developed world led to a major study in which Kuznets examined empirical data on income disparity in developing nations and identified a rising middle class as those countries became industrialized.

In his last years, Kuznets enjoyed a flurry of recognition for his achievements. He was awarded the Robert Troup Paine Prize in 1970, followed by the Nobel in 1971, and the Francis A. Walker Medal in 1977. Simon Kuznets died in Cambridge, Massachusetts, on July 8, 1985.

Justin Corfield

See also: Friedman, Milton; Gross Domestic Product; Keynesian Business Model.

Further Reading

Abramovitz, M. "The Nature and Significance of Kuznets Cycles." *Economic Development and Cultural Change* 9 (1961): 225–248.

Bird, R.C., M.J. Desai, J.J. Enzler, and P.J. Taubman. "Kuznets Cycles in Growth Rates: The Meaning." *International Economic Review* 6 (1965): 229–239.

Kuznets, Simon S. *Capital in the American Economy: Its Formation and Financing.* Princeton, NJ: Princeton University Press, 1961.

———. *Economic Change: Selected Essays in Business Cycles, National Income, and Economic Growth.* New York: W.W. Norton, 1953.

Labor Market

The labor market is the theoretical "place" where the supply of and the demand for labor determine compensation and employment levels, usually measured by the number of hours worked.

Modern economies have many labor markets, varying in size, with a host of geographic and political factors coming into play. Labor markets are also highly segmented. While many unskilled jobs can be filled by almost any adult, most professions require skills and education, which means that only a certain segment of the labor market can work in them.

The supply of labor is determined by a host of factors, including population, demographics, education, immigration, and labor participation rates. In the United States, the working population is defined as all adults over the age of sixteen. And while mandatory retirement age has largely been outlawed or discontinued in the United States, elderly persons are generally less likely to work than younger persons. Thus, all things being equal, as America's population ages, its labor market shrinks. Immigration also plays a role in two ways. First, relatively more immigrants than native-born

citizens tend to be of working age, so that a country with high immigration levels tends to have a faster-growing labor market than a country with low immigration. In addition, immigrants tend to cluster in certain occupations, leading to greater labor market segmentation.

Labor market participation rates are subject to a host of variables beyond age. Wages are a critical factor; as they go up, labor market participation tends to rise. Economists refer to this relationship as "labor elasticity." The more likely workers are to join the labor market in response to higher wages, the more "elastic" the market is. But demographic factors also play a role. Adult males, because most have to support themselves or a family, tend to have higher participation rates and are less likely to be affected by wage levels. In other words, male adult labor participation is highly "inelastic." Before the 1960s and the mass influx of women into the labor force, the women's labor market participation was more elastic, as many chose—or were compelled by social factors to choose—unpaid wifely or motherly activities and were less likely to join the labor force in response to higher wages. Today, with more women supporting themselves or contributing to the support of their families, their labor elasticity has decreased. For the young, who are supported by their parents, and the old, who may receive income from various forms of pension or feel they are too old to work, labor elasticity is also higher.

Thus, labor supply is subject to a host of factors, making determination of the labor supply a complex science. Similarly, labor demand is affected by a number of factors, most importantly labor's productivity and the economy's demand for the goods and services produced in a particular labor market. Finally, both labor supply and demand are affected by laws and institutions that determine how work is done and how much workers are paid.

Consider first productivity, for which capital equipment is critical. Workers today are far more productive than their counterparts of a century ago, in large part because of new technologies and infrastructure. For example, a truck driver on modern superhighways can haul far more goods, farther and faster, than a wagon master on dirt tracks could in 1900. Likewise, an economist working with computers and having access to whole databases of information can be more productive than one ensconced in a library using pencil and paper. Moreover, workers in the twenty-first century are generally better educated and more skilled than their counterparts at the turn of the twentieth century, contributing to higher productivity.

When workers are more productive, they are generally in higher demand. This also means that, all things being equal, they can command higher wages. Such differences are a function of places as well as time. Workers in the United States are in higher demand and can command higher wages than their counterparts in Mexico because of the skills they possess and the technologies and infrastructure available to them. Of course, with the spread of high technology and improving education in developing countries, the comparative advantages enjoyed by American workers are shrinking by the decade.

Occupation is another fundamental factor in determining labor demand. Occupations that require higher skill levels and more education usually pay better, since fewer people spend the time and money necessary to obtain them. Moreover, it is not easy for workers to shift from one occupation to another; a coal miner cannot simply switch to nursing because the coal industry is shrinking and the health care industry is expanding. Economists divide labor markets into two segments: a primary market in which skilled and therefore difficult-to-replace workers have better pay, and a secondary market in which unskilled, replaceable workers are paid less.

Labor markets differ from other markets for a number of reasons. Most importantly, because labor is not owned by the purchaser as with traditional goods, the employer must encourage the laborer to work with a certain level of effort, skill, and honesty. As a result, labor's price may be somewhat higher at what economists call an "efficiency wage." Furthermore, labor markets are affected by social norms and government regulations on issues such as the rights of workers to organize in unions, to receive the minimum wage, and to certain protections under rules regarding racial, sexual, or other forms of discrimination.

Upturns and downturns in the economic cycle can also affect the labor market. When aggregate demand drops (for any number of reasons), the economy enters a period of diminished growth or outright contraction, also known as a recession. Diminished demand causes businesses to reduce production, and hence employment, in an effort to cut inventories or reduce output. Economists refer to this phenomenon as "cyclical unemployment."

Two examples, one from economic history and one from the 2007–2009 recession, illustrate that any number of factors can come into play during economic crises. A dramatic drop in aggregate demand during the Great Depression led to unprecedented levels of unemployment—up to one-fourth of the U.S. workforce at the trough of the downturn in early 1933. In the classical economic model, the lower demand for labor would bring down wages and increase employment. As Keynes argued, however, wages sometimes did not fall for a variety of social and economic reasons—including employment contracts, collective bargaining agreements, worker morale, and others—and when wages did fall, they further reduced aggregate demand, thus worsening the Depression. To get out of this economically crippling situation, Keynes advocated government spending to increase aggregate demand and, thus, output and employment.

The 2007–2009 recession, while nothing on the scale of the Great Depression, showed a similar pattern of persistent unemployment even as the economy recovered. The drop in aggregate demand resulted in higher unemployment, and while companies were shedding workers, wage inelasticity appeared to ease as companies and governments chose—and got workers to accept—reduced pay and shorter hours (the latter often in the form of unpaid furloughs). A series of federal government stimulus packages attempted to ease unemployment by maintaining aggregate demand, but were offset by reductions in state and local government spending and ongoing decline in the key auto and housing sectors.

James Ciment

See also: Employment and Unemployment; Unemployment, Natural Rate of; Wages.

Further Reading

Ashenfelter, Orley C., and David Card, eds. *Handbook of Labor Economics.* Amsterdam: North-Holland, 1999.

Head, Simon. *The New Ruthless Economy: Work and Power in the Digital Age.* New York: Oxford University Press, 2005.

Killingsworth, Mark R. *Labor Supply.* New York: Cambridge University Press, 1983.

Mincer, Jacob. *Studies in labor supply.* Aldershot, UK: Edward Elgar, 1993.

Lachmann, Ludwig Maurits (1906–1990)

Ludwig Maurits Lachmann was a German economist who was profoundly influenced by the work of Friedrich Hayek and the Austrian school, of which he became an important, if somewhat unorthodox, member. Lachmann, who helped revive interest in the Austrian school in the 1980s, is perhaps best remembered for his ideas about economic expectations, which he viewed as neither hard data nor mathematical variables but as subjective interpretations.

Born on February 1, 1906, in Berlin, Germany, Lachmann studied at the Askanisches Gymnasium and the University of Berlin, where he completed his doctorate in economics in 1933. While at the University of Zurich, Switzerland, in the summer of 1926, he was influenced by Hayek's work and by the Austrian school, which would have an impact on the rest of his life.

With Adolf Hitler's rise to power in Germany, Lachmann moved to England and studied at the London School of Economics under Hayek. As a student, he traveled to the United States from November 1938 to April 1939, completing his master of science degree upon his return to London. After completing a research fellowship at the University of London, he served from 1943 to 1947 as acting head of the Department of Economics and Commerce at the University College of Hull (later the University of Hull). With his wife, the former Margot Wulff, Lachmann moved in 1949 to South Africa, where he joined the University of Witwatersrand, Johannesburg, as a professor and remained there until his retirement in 1972. From 1961 to 1963, he also served as president of the Economic Society of South Africa.

Throughout his academic career, Lachmann had been intrigued with the ideas of Austrian school economist Carl Menger. Indeed he believed that the school had, from the mid-twentieth century, deviated from Menger's original ideas about the construction of a marginal utility theory of value. In his writings, Lachmann prominently supported the use of hermeneutic methods in the study of economic phenomena. He was dubbed a "fundamentalist Austrian" for his opposition to the neoclassical school, his research and writing on economic subjectivism, imperfect knowledge, methodological individualism, and strong support for the "radical subjectivist" strand of Austrian economics.

As a professor at the University of Witwatersrand, Lachmann traveled regularly to New York City, where, from 1974 to 1987, he collaborated on research with Israel Kirzner to reinvigorate the Austrian school. The revival of that movement was evident during the Austrian Economics Seminar at New York University from 1985 until 1987, which Lachmann helped organize.

Lachmann had formed his own views on the business cycle, arguing for radical subjectivism, a concept he traced back to Menger, and discarding the "elaborate formalism" of what was then regarded as orthodox economics. Following Lachmann's death on December 17, 1990, his widow established the Ludwig M. Lachmann Research Fellowship at the London School of Economics.

Justin Corfield

See also: Austrian School; Hayek, Friedrich August von.

Further Reading

Lachmann, Ludwig Maurits. *Capital and Its Structure.* London: Bell and Sons, 1956.

———. *Capital, Expectations, and the Market Process: Essays on the Theory of the Market Economy,* ed. W. Grinder. Kansas City, MO: Sheed, Andrews, and McMeel, 1977.

———. "From Mises to Shackle: An Essay." *Journal of Economic Literature* 14 (1976): 54–62.

Lange, Oskar R. (1904–1965)

Oskar Richard Lange was a Polish economist who believed in the possibility, and indeed necessity, of incorporating aspects of free-market principles into socialist governing systems to ensure the economic success of socialism. The major goal of this theoretical work was to help avoid disastrous upswings and downturns in a socialist government's business cycles.

He was born Tomaszow Mazowiecki in central Poland on July 27, 1904, to Arthur Julius Ros-

Polish-born economist Oskar Lange taught at the University of Chicago, became a diplomat back in Poland, and returned to the United States in 1945 as ambassador. He advocated flexible market pricing in socialist economic systems. *(Howard Sochurek/Time & Life Pictures/Getty Images)*

ner, an affluent textile manufacturer, and Sophie Albertine Rosner. He completed his bachelor's degree at the University of Krakow (Poland) in 1926; two years later he earned a master's of law. After briefly working at the Ministry of Labor in Warsaw, he became a research assistant at the University of Krakow, where he worked from 1927 until 1931. Winning a Rockefeller fellowship in 1934, he went to Great Britain and then to the United States in September 1935. He was named a professor at the University of Chicago in 1938 and became a U.S. citizen five years later, changing his name to Oskar Richard Lange.

It was during his time at Chicago that Lange developed his most important ideas on economics. Although he was a socialist, Lange disagreed with the economic theories of Karl Marx, the father of socialist thought. In his first major work, *On the Economic Theory of Socialism,* published in 1938, Lange argued that the centralized control of an economy must be flexible and realistic, otherwise countries like the Soviet Union would decline as economic powers. Lange believed that it was important for socialist countries to relax their grip on the economy and let the free market dictate policy.

For example, he believed that fixing prices artificially through centralized control (as done in the Soviet Union) would damage the general economic welfare of a country. Rather, he thought there had to be flexible pricing that would actually reflect increased production or demand, or shortages. In this way, a socialist economy could automatically deal with shortages in products and goods and also eliminate surplus production for the optimal economic benefit of society. Lange argued that such a socialist market economy could operate more effectively than capitalist economies because the latter often feature business monopolies that create artificial shortages in order to raise prices, or cut prices to increase market share and eliminate competition. As a result of more flexible control, market socialism would be able to triumph and avoid the boom-and-bust cycle that occurred with uncontrolled capitalism, such as existed in the United States.

Lange's work attracted the attention of Joseph Stalin, then leader of the Soviet Union. In March 1944, with World War II still raging, Stalin, then a U.S. ally against Nazi Germany, asked President Franklin Roosevelt to allow Lange to visit the Soviet Union to brief him on his economic ideas.

At the end of World War II, Lange played an increasingly important role as a government official in Poland, then under Soviet control. He renounced his U.S. citizenship, and the pro-Soviet Polish government appointed him as its first ambassador to the United States. He also served as the Polish delegate to the United Nations Security Council. From August 7 to August 12, 1964, following the death of Polish president Aleksander Zawadzki, Lange was one of the four acting chairmen of the Council of State. That year, as a tribute to Lange, the University of Warsaw published a special volume of academic economics papers containing contributions by forty-two leading economists and statisticians. Lange died following a long illness on October 2, 1965, in London, England. In 1974, Warsaw's University of Economics was named in his honor.

Justin Corfield

See also: Marxist Cycle Model.

Further Reading

Friedman, Milton. "Lange on Price Flexibility and Employment: A Methodological Criticism." *American Economic Review* 36:4 (1946): 613–631.

Hull, Cordell. *The Memoirs of Cordell Hull,* Vol 2. London: Hodder & Stoughton, 1948.

Sadler, Charles. "Pro-Soviet Polish-Americans: Oskar Lange and Russia's Friends in the Polonia, 1941–1945." *Polish Review* 22:4 (1977): 25–39.

Latin America

A vast region, defined as much by history and ethnicity as it is by geography, Latin America stretches southward from the Mexican border with the United States to the tip of South America, encompassing that continent, Central America, and much of the Greater Antilles in the Caribbean basin.

Most of the roughly 570 million people in the region can trace their descent to one or more of three ethnic groups: Europeans, initially from colonial powers Portugal and Spain beginning in the sixteenth century and later from many other countries; African slaves, who were forcibly brought to the region in significant numbers from the sixteenth to nineteenth centuries; and indigenous peoples, who first settled in the region in Paleolithic times. Many of the countries have large ethnically distinct populations of so-called mestizos, or persons of mixed European and indigenous heritage.

With the exception of isolated pockets where indigenous languages predominate, the inhabitants of Latin America speak either Spanish or Portuguese and participate in a culture that is an amalgam of European, African, and indigenous American elements. The majority of Latin Americans practice Catholicism, though significant numbers are Protestants or followers of indigenous or Afro-Christian hybrid religions. (This shared Iberian-influenced linguistic and cultural heritage does not apply to those inhabitants of countries or territories of the region colonized by the English, Dutch, and French, such as Haiti, Jamaica, Belize, or Suriname.)

Inhabited by a variety of indigenous cultures at first contact with Europe in 1492—including high civilizations of the Andes, Central America, Mexico, and possibly the Amazon basin—much of the region was conquered over the course of the sixteenth century by Spain and Portugal. Contact led to the mass extermination of indigenous peoples and the influx of colonizers from Europe and slaves from Africa. The Spanish and Portuguese built an economy based on commercial crop production, including sugar, tobacco, grains, and livestock, much of it exported to Europe.

Vast plantations and ranches predominated, with a small, largely European elite ruling over a vast peasantry of indigenous and mestizo workers or African slaves, with gross inequalities in wealth between the two classes. Such patterns persisted even after much of the region achieved independence from Spain and Portugal in the early nineteenth century. With power in the hands of commercial agricultural interests, Latin America was slow to develop a significant middle class and was late to industrialize, its economy largely geared to the production and export of minerals or agricultural commodities.

Only in the twentieth century did some areas—such as Argentina, Brazil, and Mexico—see the development of an industrial base, though the region's economy continued to rely on the export of raw materials. Such reliance—as well as ill-considered fiscal policies by various governments—resulted in uneven economic development and a series of financial crises. By the end of the century, however, some of the more advanced economies of the region had developed a significant middle class and a substantial industrial sector, though large inequalities in wealth persisted.

Conquest, Colonialism, and Mercantilist Economics

It is generally believed that the region was first inhabited between roughly 15,000 and 12,000 BCE by peoples who migrated across the Bering Strait from East Asia and then down the spine of the Western Hemisphere. The first civilizations emerged in eastern Mexico in the second millennium BCE and, by the time of first contact with Europeans in 1492, there were major civilizations in the Andes (Inca), the Valley of Mexico (Aztec), and the Yucatan region of Mexico and Central America (Maya), and perhaps also the Amazon basin. While the difficult geography of the region made intra-American contact difficult, there were wide-scale trading networks that tied various ethnic groups to the centers of civilization. The civilizations of the Valley of Mexico, for example, traded as far

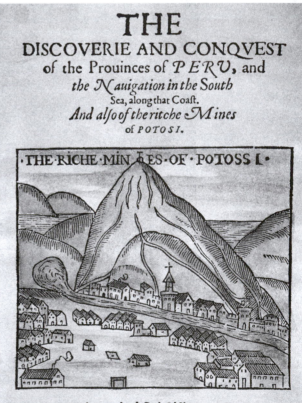

Precious metals from Latin American mines—such as the Potosí silver mine in Upper Peru (now Bolivia)—brought a windfall to sixteenth-century Spain. The new wealth increased demand for products and raised prices, ultimately leading to economic decline. *(The Granger Collection, New York)*

away as the present-day U.S. Southwest, Central America, and even the islands of the Caribbean.

The coming of Spanish and Portuguese (and later Dutch, English, and French) colonizers beginning in the late fifteenth century CE utterly transformed the region and its economy. First, with the colonizers came European diseases, which wiped out large portions of the indigenous population. It is estimated that the number of indigenous people living in the Valley of Mexico, for example, fell from 25 million in 1519, when the first Spanish conquistadores, or conquerors, arrived, to just 1 million by the early seventeenth century. Contributing to this "Native American holocaust" was the *encomienda* system the Spanish set up in their American colonies, whereby by the conquistadores were given huge land grants or mines and the right to tax or employ the local indigenous peoples. While enslaving the latter was formally outlawed, the *encomienda* system operated as a kind of legalized form of slavery, since the natives could not look for other work and were legally bound to the land.

Second, to compensate for a rapidly declining population of indigenous people, the Spanish and Portuguese imported millions of Africans, largely to work on plantations in the Caribbean, coastal regions of mainland Spanish America, and Portuguese Brazil. Finally, the conquerors brought new crops, such as wheat and sugar, and new livestock, primarily cattle and sheep, which transformed farming in the region. (There was also a transfer of Native American crops, such as potatoes and corn, that transformed agriculture in the Eastern Hemisphere as well.)

The conquest also had a profound effect on European economies. The flood of precious metals from American mines created high inflation in Spain and Portugal, raising the cost of production and thereby undermining the manufacturing sectors in those countries. At the same time, rising prices helped traders in all parts of Europe, laying the foundations for a middle class, especially in Northern Europe. The influx of precious metals also provided Europe with the currency to purchase goods from China, helping to spur international trade.

While indigenous peoples and African slaves suffered, the Latin American economy slowly grew and diversified through the sixteenth and seventeenth centuries, producing crops and minerals not only for export but for domestic consumption as well. By the early 1700s, Latin Americans had built a thriving local economy based on intercolonial trade in foodstuffs, textiles, and manufactured goods, in spite of the mercantilist policies of Spain. Under mercantilism, colonial powers attempted to direct all benefits to themselves by restricting their colonies' trade with other powers and by stifling the production of manufactured goods there, the latter in order to turn the colonies into captive markets for goods from the mother country.

This mercantilist policy was largely honored in the breach until the eighteenth century, when Madrid initiated reforms intended to direct more trade to Spain. As a result, the value of exports soared but domestic manufacturing collapsed, as cheaper and better-made European goods flooded local markets. By the latter part of the century, Spain had created a functioning mercantilist system, but when war came to Europe and the transatlantic sea lanes were closed around 1800, it could not sustain it.

And just as the Latin American economy began to shrink, Spain imposed new taxes to help pay for defenses against other European powers eyeing the rich colonies for conquest and trade. The result was widespread dissatisfaction among colonial elites, which by the early nineteenth century had led to a wave of national revolutions that saw Spain driven from South and Central America in the early nineteenth century, though it retained control of its Caribbean territories. Brazil, too, achieved independence from Portugal in this period.

From Neocolonialism to Economic Nationalism

While many of the independence leaders dreamed of a unified and free Spanish America, the region soon came to be divided into more than a dozen small and medium-sized states. Equally disappointing for Latin Americans was the political turmoil that enveloped most of the nations through much of the nineteenth century, until put down by military strongmen, or caudillos, after the 1870s. The turmoil also contributed to economic stagnation through much of the century even as the *encomienda* system and its postcolonial avatars discouraged the rise of a prosperous peasantry, while the power of landowners stifled the rise of an independent merchant and manufacturing sector.

With Europeans largely interested in their own internal development or the development of their colonies in other parts of the world, and the United States preoccupied with settling and developing its vast internal markets, there was little foreign capital to be invested in the region. But as Europe and the United States grew richer, there was more excess capital to invest in the late nineteenth century; Latin America, with its vast mineral and agricultural resources, seemed an excellent place to do so, especially after the return of domestic peace to the region in the late nineteenth century.

What ensued was a new form of outside exploitation, one economic historians refer to as neocolonialism, whereby political sovereignty is maintained in a country but the heights of the economy come under the control of foreign interests, along with a small local elite. In Mexico and Central America, the dominant power in the late nineteenth and early twentieth centuries came to be the United States, which developed sugar, rubber, and banana plantations as well as Mexican oil fields. And while Americans made substantial investments in South America as well, Europeans—especially the British—predominated here, developing sugar, coffee, and cotton plantations in Brazil, mining in the Andean countries, livestock raising and meatpacking in Argentina and Uruguay, and transportation and communications infrastructure throughout the continent.

While the economies of the region prospered and attracted millions of immigrants from South-

ern and Eastern Europe, the development of more commercialized forms of plantation agriculture resulted in even more concentrations of wealth and land in the hands of local elites, resulting in more peasants forced off their lands and into the status of an agricultural proletariat. The state, controlled by landed elites, helped facilitate the process by passing laws that favored the rich and by sending in the military whenever the poor rose up to challenge the system. Meanwhile, in the growing cities of Latin America, the influx of European immigrants and capital—and the infrastructure that capital financed—led to the development of an industrial base, particularly in the south of Brazil and the nations of the "southern cone" of South America—Argentina, Chile, and Uruguay.

By the early years of the twentieth century, then, Latin American economies had become somewhat modernized and integrated into the global trading network. While such integration fostered continued growth of the middle class, it also exposed the region to the fluctuations in the global economy. With its economy built on exports, Latin America was hard hit by the dramatic drop in world demand during the Great Depression, which especially affected the middle class. The result was a strong shift to economic nationalism in many Latin American countries, most of which tried to gain more control over their resources—most notably, Mexico's nationalization of its oil industry in the late 1930s—and to expand their industrial base to meet the domestic need for both consumer and capital goods. World War II aided this effort, as demand for Latin American resources soared and competition from European and U.S. manufacturers was sidelined either by the conflict itself or, in the case of the United States, for meeting defense needs.

Much of this economic nationalism was forwarded by authoritarian regimes, such as that of Juan Perón in Argentina, and was continued in the immediate postwar era. While much of Latin America thrived in the 1950s and 1960s, as governments attempted to jump-start heavy industry and a booming global economy soaked up Latin

American natural resource exports, the wealth continued to accrue largely to the upper reaches of society. This triggered a period of political turmoil that saw major guerrilla movements develop in several countries, though most were eventually crushed by the military.

Debt Crisis, Neoliberalism, and Beyond

While the industrialized world went into a prolonged period of stagnation in the 1970s and early 1980s, many Latin American countries thrived. The differing fates were related, as the soaring cost of natural resources produced both high inflation and unemployment in the West while pouring capital into resource-rich Latin American countries. With many experts concluding that a period of sustained high prices for natural resources was part of the world's economic future, many of the authoritarian regimes in the region were able to borrow large sums of capital for internal development and consumption. The result was a greatly rising debt load in many Latin American countries that became unsustainable when resource prices fell in the early 1980s, and resulted in what came to be known as the "debt crisis." During this time, many countries in the region—most notably, Mexico—teetered on the edge of bankruptcy. The crisis forced many countries to turn to loans from multilateral financial institutions, which imposed harsh austerity measures that deeply affected workers and consumers and required governments to curtail the economic nationalist policies of high tariffs and nationalization of industries and finance.

The new economic policies of the 1980s and 1990s went by a number of names: one was the "Washington Consensus" (since much of it was pushed by the United States and the Washington-based multilateral financial institutions of the International Monetary Fund and the World Bank); another was "neoliberalism." (The latter was used in the European sense of the term, meaning more laissez-faire–oriented economics.) Whatever the term, the policies called for industries and banks to be privatized, subsidies on basic consumer products removed, and tariffs designed to protect local industries eased or ended. To supporters of these policies, the process was a painful but necessary step toward greater economic efficiency and profitability and a fuller integration of Latin American economies into the world economy, all of which would eventually benefit Latin Americans of all classes. To detractors, the policies allowed wealthy local elites and foreign investors to seize control of formerly publicly held properties for a song and to repatriate billions in profits out of the country.

Whether a period of necessary adjustment or plunder, the 1980s and 1990s saw Latin America go into a period of slow and uneven negative economic growth, increasing inequities in wealth and income, and periodic financial crisis. The worst of these came in 1998 and 1999, in the wake of the Asian financial crisis, when panicky foreign investors began to pull out massive amounts of capital from Latin American financial institutions and stock markets, causing local currencies to collapse and setting off widespread recession in much of the region.

By the early 2000s, many Latin American governments had turned away from neoliberalism, either because they believed it had failed or because they held the political costs to be too high. In some countries, such as Venezuela, the government completely repudiated the policies, embarking instead on massive spending schemes and subsidies, paid for by oil revenues, to bolster development and ease poverty. But in other countries, the move away from neoliberalism was more deliberate, with the rebuilding of social welfare safety nets, targeting of key industries for development, and attempts to build intraregional trading networks, all the while fostering increased economic integration with the world. Whether bolstered by these policies alone or aided by a growing world economy and new demand for raw materials from rising powers like China, Latin American economies generally prospered in the early and middle 2000s, with countries like Brazil and Mexico emerging onto the international scene as rising economic powers invited into such clubs of major industrialized and industrializing countries as the G-20.

While the Latin American financial sector was not heavily exposed to the exotic financial instruments—such as mortgage-backed securities—that led to the crisis in the financial sector of the United States and a number of European countries, nor did the region experience a housing bubble as inflated as that of the United States and some other regions of the industrialized world, Latin America was hard hit by the global financial crisis of 2008–2009 and subsequent recession nonetheless. As investors around the world panicked, they pulled out of markets that were deemed riskier, such as those in Latin America. The result was capital flight and a major drop in securities valuations on local stock markets. This led to drops in currency values, which increased debt loads in several countries, though nations that relied on natural resource exports were cushioned from the impact for a time by high prices. But the global recession that followed the crisis has pulled down those prices, with the result that most of the economies of the region have experienced negative growth since late 2008.

James Ciment

See also: Argentina; Brazil; Central America; Chile; Colombia; Emerging Markets; Mexico; Tequila Effect.

Further Reading

Chasteen, John Charles. *Born in Blood and Fire: A Concise History of Latin America*. New York: W.W. Norton, 2006.

Council on Foreign Relations. "Latin America: Not So Insulated After All." November 17, 2008. www.cfr.org/publication/17786/latin_america.html?breadcrumb= percent2Fregion percent2F243 percent2Fsouth_america. Accessed September 25, 2009.

Eakin, Marshall C. *The History of Latin America: Collision of Cultures*. New York: Palgrave Macmillan, 2007.

Langley, Lester D. *The Americas in the Modern Age*. New Haven, CT: Yale University Press, 2003.

O'Brien, Thomas F. *Making the Americas: The United States and Latin America from the Age of Revolutions to the Era of Globalization*. Albuquerque: University of New Mexico Press, 2007.

Skidmore, Thomas E., Peter H. Smith, and James N. Green. *Modern Latin America*. 7th ed. New York: Oxford University Press, 2010.

Topik, Steven, Carlos Marichal, and Zephyr Frank, eds. *From Silver to Cocaine: Latin America Commodity Chains and the Building of the World Economy, 1500–2000*. Durham, NC: Duke University Press, 2006.

Law, John (1671–1729)

An economist before economics was an established discipline, Scotsman John Law wrote about and studied the relationship between money, real goods, and wealth. Today he is best remembered for creating one of the first financial bubbles in history, the so-called Mississippi Bubble of 1716–1720, which led to a major financial crisis in France.

Law was born into a family of bankers on April 21, 1671, in Edinburgh, Scotland. It was assumed that he would go into the family business, but following his father's death in 1688, with inheritance money in his pocket, Law chose a path that involved gambling, romance, and violence. In 1694, he killed a rival in a duel over a woman, for which he narrowly escaped the death penalty and was fined on charges of manslaughter. He then moved to the Netherlands, the financial center of Europe, where he saw firsthand fortunes being made (and lost) through financial speculation.

From the Netherlands, Law moved permanently to France, where the economy was in a severe crisis due to the cost of its role in the War of Spanish Succession. Philippe, Duke of Orleans, who was effectively in control of the French government at the time, appointed Law controller-general of finances. Law had impressed the duke with his argument that the only way to improve France's economic situation was to end the private tax farms, abolish minor monopolies, and establish a central bank to oversee government finances. He also proposed the institution of a large state trading company to generate profits to pay off the national debt. This led to the creation, in May 1716, of the Banque Générale Privée (General Private Bank), which was financed by government-printed paper money. Legally it was a private bank, but 75 percent of its capital came from the government in the form of bills and notes.

The General Private Bank would prove to be Law's undoing. In August 1717, he used the institution to fund the so-called Mississippi Company and start a French colony in North America's Louisiana Territory. The aim was to establish a business venture that would rival the British East India Company by taking control of the lands around the Mississippi, Ohio, and Missouri rivers.

The Duke of Orleans granted Compagnie d'Occident (Company of the West) a trade monopoly in North America and the West Indies, prompting speculation in shares of the new enterprise. Law combined the Banque Royale with the trading company and issued more and more shares to raise capital, which was then used to pay off government debt. A significant portion of the money also found its way into the pockets of government officials, and, some believed, Law himself. Share prices more than tripled by 1720, and the scheme finally collapsed when investors realized that the business ventures in America were not as successful as originally thought and graft had depleted the profits. As word spread, the bubble burst and the value of the stock plummeted to virtually nothing.

Law left France in disgrace. He received an official pardon from the British courts in 1719 and spent four years in England before finally settling in Venice, Italy, where he died, destitute, on March 21, 1729.

Justin Corfield

See also: Classical Theories and Models; Mississippi Bubble (1717–1720).

Further Reading

Gleeson, Janet. *Millionaire: The Philanderer, Gambler, and Duelist Who Invented Modern Finance.* New York: Simon & Schuster, 2000.
Minton, Robert. *John Law, The Father of Paper Money.* New York: Association, 1975.
Montgomery Hyde, H. *John Law: The History of an Honest Adventurer.* London: W.H. Allen, 1969.
Murphy, Antoin E. *John Law: Economic Theorist and Policy-Maker.* New York: Oxford University Press, 1997.

Leads and Lags

Leads and lags refer to the expediting and delaying, respectively, of the settlement of debts in international business trade. Specifically, the premature payment for goods purchased in another country is known as a "lead," while the delayed payment for such goods is known as a "lag."

The basic concept behind leads and lags is simple. If a purchaser of goods in Country A expects the value of his currency to rise in the coming days or weeks, he may choose to delay payment for the goods manufactured in Country B, since such a delay will make purchasing the goods less costly. Conversely, he may choose to pay ahead of time if he thinks Country A's currency is going to decline in value, thereby making the cost of the goods more expensive in the future.

Obviously, betting on leads and lags is a highly speculative activity that can hurt the purchaser financially should currency exchange rates take an unexpected turn. For the seller, there is much less risk, since he will be paid the agreed-upon amount in his own currency regardless of fluctuations in the exchange rate.

Whether or not a purchaser engages in lead or lag payments depends on several factors. First, it generally has to be agreed upon by both the purchaser and the seller. Even though the risk accrues to the purchaser alone, the seller might have cash-flow problems and need prompt payment for goods sold. Second, the use of leads and lags is usually confined to big-ticket items—such as aircraft, expensive machine tools, and military hardware—since only then do the savings of leads and lags become large enough to make it worth the purchaser's while (or offset the special fees or interest costs that a delayed payment may entail).

Leads and lags also require a fluctuating exchange-rate system. Leads and lags were relatively rare during the period from the end of World War II through the beginning of the 1970s, when the fixed exchange rates of the Bretton Woods international economic system were in effect. Thus, during that period, extreme fluctuations in currency exchange rates were quite rare. With the decline of the Bretton Woods system in the 1970s, currencies began to float in value against one another, rising and falling with increasing volatility. Under those conditions, lead and lag payments became more common. In the decades since, technological innovations have made exchange rate information more widely available, making it possible to calculate fluctuations more rapidly—again contributing to an increase in lead and lag payments.

Leads and lags can affect the business cycles of a particular country in a number of ways. If too many foreign consumers are holding back on payments to Country A, for example, then businesses in that country can suffer financially from the disruption of cash flow. Just such a situation arises when the currency of a particular country has been weakening, or even if it is expected to weaken. The result is a snowballing of the economic downturn. A similar kind of vicious cycle can be caused by government action. If Country A's economy is softening due to an expected weakening of the currency, the government might decide to devalue the currency even further in order to spur exports and bolster manufacturing. Such a move, however, could then encourage the consumers in other countries to delay payments, resulting in cash-flow problems for sellers in Country A and hastening economic contraction.

Justin Corfield and James Ciment

See also: Exchange Rates.

Further Reading

Chipman, John S. *The Theory of International Trade*. Cheltenham, UK: Edward Elgar, 2008.

Kemp, Murray C. *International Trade Theory*. London: Routledge, 2008.

Williams, John Burr. *International Trade under Flexible Exchange Rates*. Amsterdam: North-Holland, 1954.

Lehman Brothers

As one of the oldest and largest investment banks on Wall Street—its origins dating back to before the Civil War—Lehman Brothers' filing for Chapter 11 bankruptcy protection was the largest bankruptcy in U.S. history and a key triggering event for the fall 2008 meltdown in the global financial markets. It was also the largest failure of an investment bank since the collapse of Drexel Burnham Lambert in 1990.

The firm Lehman Brothers was founded in 1850 when Mayer Lehman emigrated to the United States from Bavaria (in present-day Germany) to join his brother Henry Lehman, who had arrived six years earlier to run a store in Montgomery, Alabama. The two went into the business of trading in cotton and, in 1858, moved their operation to New York. They were so prosperous that they were able to loan money to the state government of Alabama to help pay for reconstruction.

In 1887 the firm gained a seat on the New York Stock Exchange, and from 1906 it became involved in underwriting the flotation of companies on the stock market. Although hit by the Great Depression, Lehman Brothers nevertheless made a small fortune from carefully investing in the venture capital market in the late 1930s. The last member of the Lehman family to control the company was Robert Lehman, who died in 1969.

Under the management of Peter Peterson from 1973, the firm grew, acquiring other investment banking companies. They bought Kuhn, Loeb & Co. in 1977, and were soon the fourth-largest investment bank in the United States, after Salomon Brothers, Goldman Sachs, and First Boston. Following the economic downturn of the early 1980s, Peterson was ousted and Lewis Glucksman took

An employee of Lehman Brothers carries a box of his possessions from company headquarters in New York City on September 15, 2008, the day the investment firm filed for Chapter 11 protection in bankruptcy court. *(Chris Hondros/ Getty Images)*

over after a power struggle that began in 1983 when Glucksman was appointed as a co-CEO.

The company was not in very good financial shape after the battle, and Glucksman decided to sell it for $360 million to Shearson, an electronic transaction firm backed by American Express. In 1994, however, Lehman Brothers Kuhn Loeb was spun off into a separate entity and finally sold publicly on the stock market as Lehman Brothers Holdings, with Richard S. Fuld as the chairman and CEO. The company then grew rapidly. Although it had left asset management in 1989, in 2003 it decided to reenter the field and before long it had a vast sum of assets under management. In 2007 this generated the company $3.1 billion in net revenue, and just before it went bankrupt, it had $275 billion in assets under management.

In 2003, the Securities and Exchange Commission became concerned about what it saw as undue influence by the company's investment banking section over reports put together by the firm's research analysts. Regulators found that the firm had published improper financial advice as had many other companies, which together paid out $1.4 billion in fines, of which Lehman had to contribute $80 million to settle conflict-of-interest charges.

By mid-2007, economic problems resulting from the collapse of the collateralized debt obligation market had begun to plague the company, which in response axed its subprime lender, BNC Mortgage in August, shedding 1,200 employees. At the same time, it quickly moved to reduce its exposure to the subprime market. But problematic loan debts remained on its balance sheets and during the first part of 2008 it was clear that the company was still heavily exposed to the subprime loan market. In early 2008, it sold $6 billion in assets, creating losses in the second quarter of $2.8 billion. As this news went public, the stock in Lehman Brothers fell dramatically, losing 73 percent of its value between January and June 2008. In August 2008, Lehman Brothers initiated new cost-cutting measures, laying off 1,500 people just ahead of the deadline for reporting for the third quarter in September. With the share slide, some companies started to consider buying Lehman Brothers. The Korea Development Bank was seriously interested but then decided against it; the same was true for Bank of America and Barclays Bank.

The collapse of the bank came in September 2008. On September 13, the president of the Federal Reserve Bank of New York, Timothy F. Geithner, called a meeting with Lehman Brothers to try to work out a financial solution to prevent bankruptcy. The efforts came to naught, and on Monday, September 15, 2008, the company sought bankruptcy protection. At the time, it had assets of $639 billion but had incurred a bank debt of $613 billion and bond debt of $155 billion. That same day had seen Lehman shares fall by 90 percent of their remaining value. On the following day, Barclays PLC announced that it was prepared to buy sections of Lehman Brothers for $1.75 billion.

The collapse of Lehman Brothers caused share prices to plummet across the board on the New York Stock Exchange, particularly for financial sector stocks. Some economic analysts argue that the company's collapse was perhaps the single most important triggering event of the financial crisis and the seizing up of the international credit market in the early fall of 2008, itself a major contributing factor to the deep global recession of that same year. In retrospect, say some analysts, the government's decision not to bail out Lehman Brothers helped precipitate the crisis, forcing a much bigger bailout of the banking industry several weeks later. Others, however, counter that the problems in the financial sector were systemic and that Lehman Brothers' collapse was more a symptom than a cause of that weakness.

Justin Corfield and James Ciment

See also: Banks, Investment; Recession and Financial Crisis (2007–).

Further Reading

Auletta, Ken. *Greed and Glory on Wall Street: The Fall of the House of Lehman.* New York: Random House, 1986.

A Centennial: Lehman Brothers 1850–1950. New York: Lehman Brothers, 1950.

McDonald, Lawrence G., with Patrick Robinson. *A Colossal Failure of Common Sense: The Inside Story of the Collapse of Lehman Brothers.* New York: Crown Business, 2009.

Lerner, Abba P. (1903–1982)

The Russian-American economist Abba Ptachya Lerner was one of the most influential theorists in the field during the twentieth century. While he did not contribute directly to the literature of business cycles, his work in such areas as general equilibrium and international trade theory influenced the thinking of several prominent economists in the area of cycles. Although he was a socialist, Lerner championed free markets and opposed the minimum wage and any sort of price controls.

Lerner was born in Bessarabia (then part of the Russian Empire) on October 28, 1903, and his family migrated to London's East End three years later. After holding a variety of jobs during the 1920s, Lerner enrolled at the London School of Economics in 1929. He studied there under Austrian economist Friedrich Hayek, who influenced much of his later work. Lerner distinguished himself as a student, though it took until 1944 to complete his doctoral thesis, titled "The Economics of Control: Principles of Welfare Economics." He also attended Cambridge University for a period in 1936, where he was influenced by John Maynard Keynes. The following year he moved to the United States and became something of an academic nomad, teaching economics at the University of Kansas City (1940–1942), the New School for Social Research in New York City (1942–1946), Roosevelt University in Chicago (1947–1959), Michigan State (1959–1965), the University of California at Berkeley (1965–1971), Queen's College, City University of New York (1971–1978), and Florida State University (1978 until his death on October 27, 1982).

While best remembered for developing a model of market socialism, Lerner was a master at tackling a broad variety of economic issues and concepts with a fresh eye. He cogently revised such controversial economic theories as Wilhelm Launhardt's representation of the dynamics of international trade, and those of Alfred Marshall. His work on the latter led to the Marshall-Lerner principle, which linked elasticity conditions, exchange rates, and fluctuations in the balance of trade.

A prodigious writer, Lerner published many important papers on economic theories, even as a student. His doctoral thesis, for example, expanded on Marshall's work. In the 1940s and 1950s, Lerner addressed a dizzying array of economic and social issues and ideas. Notable books include *The Economics of Control* (1944), *The Economics of Employment* (1951), and *Essays in Economic Analysis* (1953). He also contributed to the Lange-Lerner-Taylor theorem, which used a trial-and-error approach to analyze levels of public ownership and determine levels of output and equilibrium.

Lerner's socialist leanings were a source of opposition by the political right, including many in the field. Nevertheless, he became a friend of Republican senator from Arizona Barry Goldwater and economist Milton Friedman—though he and Friedman had disagreed about Lerner's use of the "equal ignorance" assumption to support his argument that equal distribution of income is optimal.

Justin Corfield

See also: Hicks, John Richard; Keynes, John Maynard; Marshall, Alfred.

Further Reading

Bronfenbrenner, Martin. "Abba Lerner, 1903–1982." *Atlantic Economic Journal* 11 (March 1983).

Lerner, Abba. *Selected Writings of Abba Lerner*, ed. David Colander. New York: New York University Press, 1983.

Samuelson, Paul A. "A.P. Lerner at Sixty." *Review of Economic Studies* 31:3 (1964): 169.

Scitovsky, Tibor. "Lerner's Contribution to Economics." *Journal of Economic Literature* 22:4 (1984): 1547–1571.

Leveraging and Deleveraging, Financial

Financial leverage is the use of borrowed money to finance an investment. The larger the proportion of funds contributed by creditors relative to that by owners in the enterprise, the greater the financial leverage. An investment financed with 100 percent of owners' equity is unleveraged. Individuals, corporations, and governments all use financial leverages when they borrow. Consequently, financial leverage is a necessary practice in modern economies without which long-term investment would be impossible. At the same time, however, financial leverage increases return volatilities and bankruptcy risk. It is one of the main causes of many financial crises in history. Recent examples include the Asian currency crisis of 1997–1998 and the subprime mortgage crisis in the United States. Financial deleverage refers to the attempt or process of reducing existing debt.

Benefits and Costs

Financial leverage magnifies investment gains and losses. On the one hand, financial leverage increases returns of equity. When equity holders borrow to invest, they pay fixed obligations to creditors regardless of investment outcomes. If the return earned on an investment is greater than the cost of borrowing, the return to equity holders will be proportionally higher after the fixed interests are paid. On the other hand, financial leverage can escalate losses. It increases financial distress and bankruptcy risk of equity holders. When an investment is highly leveraged, payments to creditors become burdensome. Fixed interests will be paid even if an investment is at a loss. The more loss occurs, the more equity holders have to use their own capital to fulfill debt payments. Default on a debt will cause bankruptcy of the borrowing parties.

Financial deleverage reduces the total amplifying effect of volatility, both its potential upside gains and downside losses. Involuntary financial deleverage—that is, selling assets to repay debt when refinancing of debt is difficult during financial distress—will cause asset prices to decline steeply. If such deleverage happens at a broader economic scale, it may cause a financial crisis or deepen an existing one.

Types

Individuals, companies, and governments all engage in financial leverage. Individuals who use borrowed funds to invest are leveraged. Real-estate investment is a well-known example; properties are purchased with the lender's capital so that borrowers can use real estate at the same time it is being paid for. Another example is when individuals engage in financial transactions using margins. They borrow cash from the counterparty to buy securities in order to boost returns. Investors also invest in various leveraged financial instruments such as options and futures to increase potential gains. In the United States, credit scores measure probabilities of individuals' defaulting on their loans and thus affect individuals' ability to borrow from financial institutions. However, government incentive policies or fraudulent mortgage practices may cause some to neglect this risk guideline.

Companies invest in assets by either selling equity or borrowing funds. A leveraged firm takes on debt to purchase assets while an unleveraged firm uses its equity. Leverage ratios measure a company's debt level; the best known are debt-to-equity ratios and debt ratios (total debt divided by total assets).

Firms use financial leverages to accelerate potential growth or returns. Certain tax policies also encourage debt financing. Interest payments are considered expenses of conducting business and are therefore exempt from corporate tax payments. This is similar to the situation in which individuals are encouraged to buy instead of rent houses because mortgage interest payments are exempt from personal taxes. Companies in certain industries—for example, utility companies or real-estate companies—borrow more than companies in other industries on average because they have more stable earnings or can provide more collateral for higher leverages.

Companies can borrow from corporate bond markets. Corporate bonds are standard debt securities traded at the over-the-counter market or through private placements where debt contracts are negotiated among private parties. Standard & Poor's, Moody's, and Fitch are rating agencies that assign letters ranging from AAA, AA, A, BBB, BB, B, CCC, CC, C, to D to various bonds. AAA is the highest rating. D is the lowest. Ratings of corporate bonds indicate their levels of default risk. An investment-grade bond is rated BBB or higher. A high-risk bond, which has a rating lower than BBB, is called a junk bond. It is also called a

high-yield bond because it offers a high return to compensate for its high risk.

Companies deleverage to reduce risks by using cash flows generated from operations or by selling off assets. Deleverage is considered a red flag to investors, who expect growth in the companies they invest in. It can be a warning signal of a company in financial distress.

Public sectors, such as municipal and federal governments, or government agencies, have been using financial leverage extensively to finance roads, education, and other public projects when tax revenues are not enough to cover expenses. A debt security issued by a city, county, state, or other local government entity is called a "municipal bond." Interests earned on municipal bonds are exempt from federal taxes and from most state and local taxes as well. A debt security issued by the U.S. government to meet federal expenditures is called a "treasury security." Treasury securities are categorized as bills, notes, or bonds based on their length of maturity. A national government may issue a debt security denominated in a foreign currency. This is called a "sovereign bond." A sovereign credit rating is the rating that indicates the risks of a country's investing environment. Debt-to-GDP ratio, in which total debt of a nation is divided by its gross domestic product (GDP), is commonly used in macroeconomics to indicate the degree of a country's ability to pay back its debt.

Financial Leverage and the Subprime Mortgage Crisis

Just as excessive borrowing led to the Asian currency crisis of 1997–1998, financial leverage was one of the major factors causing the subprime mortgage crisis in the United States that began in 2007. Both individual and corporate borrowing contributed to the crisis.

First, some homebuyers put little or no down payment to purchase homes that they could not afford, expecting to make profits when house prices continued to rise. The lower underwriting standards and nontraditional mortgages allowed many homebuyers with below prime credit scores to purchase homes with adjustable rate mortgages that are subject to higher interest rates and default risks later on. When house prices began to fall in mid-2006 and the Federal Reserve set higher benchmark interest rates, short sales, foreclosures, and loan defaults became widespread.

Second, many financial institutions in the United States were highly leveraged during the housing boom. For example, investment banks had an average debt-to-equity ratio of 25:1, which means that for every dollar of equity, investment banks borrowed $25 on average. Government-sponsored enterprises (GSEs) such as Fannie Mae and Freddie Mac also had high leverages. In 2008, Fannie's total assets to capital ratio was about 20:1, while Freddie's was about 70:1. GSEs could borrow at very low cost because many investors believed their debts were guaranteed by the federal government. During the housing boom of 2002–2005, many banks, hedge funds, insurance companies, and other financial institutions invested heavily in mortgage-backed securities with borrowed funds, which earned them high returns but caused them to become vulnerable to a downturn in the real-estate market.

When the house bubble began to burst in 2006, many homeowners were left in a situation where the value of their homes was lower than the mortgage they owed. Since many loans were highly leveraged with little equity, some homeowners simply defaulted on their loans and walked away. Failure of the mortgage market drove down values of financial firms' assets, which had been backed by the mortgage revenues. Companies' equities were quickly wiped out because the proportion of equity to debt was very low. Existing loans were unable to renew, forcing the companies to raise additional capital from the markets. Most firms were unable to obtain external funds in the midst of a crisis and had to sell assets to pay off debts. This involuntary financial deleverage caused steep declines in asset prices, which deepened the crisis even further.

The negative impact of financial leverage was severe. By the end of September 2008, there were no large investment banks left in the United States. Two of them (Morgan Stanley and Goldman Sachs) converted to bank holding companies so they could receive federal assistance, but then were subject to more regulations. Three of the five largest investment banks either went bankrupt (Lehman Brothers) or were bought out by other banks (Merrill Lynch and Bear Stearns). In an attempt to ease the crisis, the U.S. Treasury took over Fannie Mae and Freddie Mac in the same month.

Future Possibilities

Financial leverage magnifies investment gains. It can lead to excessive risk taking. Extreme borrowing usually occurs when there is an upward trend of asset pricing or during asset bubbles, when downside losses seem unlikely. Since the subprime crisis, the U.S. government has been fixing and establishing laws and regulations to restrict excessive leverages and to ensure that individuals and companies have enough equity or capital to cushion against potential negative shocks.

Consumers and corporations have been deleveraging starting in 2007. Deleveraging will improve financial health in the long run, but it can have detrimental effects in the short term. Household deleveraging reduces loans and consumer spending, which hurts banks and retail businesses. Corporate deleveraging reduces investments, which slows economic growth.

While the private sector has been deleveraging, the public sector in the United States has leveraged up. The national debt increased dramatically in the aftermath of the subprime crisis, passing $12.3 trillion in January 2010, or about 83 percent of GDP. A significant increase in national debt not only results in large interest payments, but also may have adverse effects on the economy. Higher interest rates lead to the possibility of higher taxes. If the government cannot make the payments, more borrowing has to be done. This will raise interest rates and slow the domestic economy. Furthermore, large increases in debt are often associated with a rise in inflation and a depreciation of the national currency. As the currency depreciates, demand for the country's debt will decrease, which drives up interest rates even more and causes further currency depreciation, ultimately risking a downward spiral. Despite these possible problems, some economists maintain that the U.S. government had little choice but to increase debt. In this view, less government spending would have worsened the recession and jeopardized the shaky financial system.

Priscilla Liang

See also: Corporate Finance; Financial Markets; Investment, Financial; Mortgage, Subprime; Recession and Financial Crisis (2007–).

Further Reading
Acharya, Viral, and Matthew Richardson, ed. *Restoring Financial Stability: How to Repair a Failed System.* Hoboken, NJ: John Wiley & Sons, 2009.
Antczak, Stephen, Douglas Lucas, and Frank Fabozzi. *Leveraged Finance: Concepts, Methods, and Trading of High-Yield Bonds, Loans, and Derivatives.* Hoboken, NJ: John Wiley & Sons, 2009.
Bernstein, William. *The Investor's Manifesto: Preparing for Prosperity, Armageddon, and Everything in Between.* Hoboken, NJ: John Wiley & Sons, 2009.
Brigham, Eugene F., and Michael C. Ehrhardt. *Financial Management: Theory & Practice.* San Diego, CA: South-Western, 2008.
Neftci, Salih. *Principles of Financial Engineering.* San Diego, CA: Academic, 2004.

Liberalization, Financial

Financial liberalization is the process of removing government regulations or restrictions on financial products, institutions, and markets. Through the early twentieth century, there was little regulation of the financial marketplace in the United States and most of the world. But economic downturns such as the Great Depression, many of which were triggered by financial upheavals, convinced economists and policy makers that rules and regulations were needed to rein in the kinds of speculative excess and malfeasance in the financial markets that could disrupt the rest of the economy. Beginning in the 1970s, however, the new consensus was that regulation stifled innovation and growth in financial markets, and this led to a wave of liberalization lasting into the early twenty-first century. While it is too soon to assess the full shakeout of the financial crisis of 2008–2009, it appears to have created a new policy consensus around the idea of re-regulation.

(A note on terminology: In a European context, "liberalization" signifies less government involvement in economic affairs. Thus, American conservatives—known as economic "liberals" in Europe—support liberalization while liberals, in the American sense of the term, oppose it.)

Pre-Twentieth-Century Regulation

Rules and regulations on financial dealings are as old as trade itself, with rules on usury, or excessive interest or even interest itself, going back to ancient times. During the Middle Ages, the Catholic Church regarded the charging of interest as a sin and forbade church members from engaging in interest-earning money lending. While the church gradually lifted such proscriptions in the early modern era—an early example of financial liberalization—other faiths, most notably Islam, maintain them to the present day.

Regulation of the financial markets fluctuated in nineteenth-century America. For much of the period through the mid-1830s, the country had a kind of central bank, known as the Bank of the United States, which acted to stabilize U.S. currency by collecting the notes issued by commercial banks—which were widely used as currency—and demanding payment in silver or gold. This made sure that commercial banks operated in a sound fashion, maintaining adequate reserves of specie against the notes they issued. Such restrictions, however, were not popular among many commercially active people outside the major cities of the East, since they saw it as restricting expansion of the money supply and hence economic growth.

Responding to such appeals, President Andrew Jackson vetoed the re-chartering of the bank in 1832—allowing it to close down four years later. This left the U.S. banking system largely unregulated through the early twentieth century.

Only during the Civil War did the national government attempt to regulate banks, mainly as a way to raise revenue for the war effort. With the National Banking Act of 1864, Congress offered state banks national charters—allowing them to issue national notes—but only if they sunk one-third of their capital into U.S. bonds. When few state banks took up the offer—most opposed the requirement and other federal regulations—Congress passed another law the following year, imposing a crippling tax on state bank notes, pushing many banks to re-charter as federal banks. However, the innovation of checkable deposits at this time allowed those state banks that did not re-charter as national banks to survive without issuing their own banknotes. Prior to checkable deposits, banks made loans by issuing their own banknotes. With checkable deposits, state banks that received deposits of national banknotes from other banks could hold reserve assets equal to a fraction of their deposit liabilities and make loans by creating checkable deposits rather than issuing their own currency. This has resulted in the dual banking system (a network of federally and state chartered banks) that exists today.

Early Twentieth-Century Regulation

The extreme economic volatility of the late nineteenth and early twentieth centuries led to new calls for financial regulation. In 1913, Congress responded with the Federal Reserve Act, which established the Federal Reserve System—also known as the Fed—America's decentralized version of European central banks. The Fed included twelve regional banks, to ensure that the financial interests of various parts of the sprawling republic were represented. Far more powerful than the earlier Bank of the United States, the Fed lent money to member banks—all fed-erally chartered banks and any state banks that wished to join—at varying interest rates, which allowed it to control the nation's money supply. It also regulated member banks by ensuring that they maintained adequate reserve assets against deposit liabilities.

Still, other aspects of the banking system went unregulated. Key among these was the ability of commercial banks to engage in investment bank activity—that is, the underwriting and trading of corporate securities, both inherently speculative activities. While such activities proved lucrative for banks in the bull stock market years of the late 1920s, they proved disastrous in the wake of the Wall Street crash of 1929. Losses on the stock exchange caused major commercial banks either to fail outright or cut back on the credit they offered regional and local banks. The result was a wave of bank runs and failures at financial institutions across the United States in the early 1930s.

The Emergency Banking Act of 1933 gave the Fed unprecedented power to certify solvent banks and reorganize insolvent ones. Later that year, Congress passed the Glass-Steagall Act, officially the Banking Act of 1933, prohibiting commercial banks from engaging in brokerage, investment banking, and insurance businesses. In addition, Glass-Steagall established the Federal Deposit Insurance Corporation (FDIC), providing federal guarantees on deposits up to a certain amount (originally $2,500, rising to $100,000 by century's end, and temporarily increased to $250,000 as a response to the financial crisis of 2008–2009). Together, the two measures helped stabilize the banking system, even as they placed new restrictions on how banks could operate and the reserves they were required to hold. With the Banking Act of 1935, the federal government extended its control over the nation's banking system. The legislation transferred power over interest rates from the regional banks of the Fed to a centralized board of governors appointed by the president. In addition, the act required large state banks to join the Fed in order to use the FDIC, subjecting them to its oversight.

Liberalization and Deregulation in the Late Twentieth Century

The financial regulatory system established by Franklin Roosevelt's New Deal of the 1930s held through the 1970s, assuring a stable banking system. But the galloping inflation and economic downturns of the latter decade created a need—and political consensus—for financial liberalization. Many banks and savings and loans (S&Ls) found themselves in a quandary as inflation rates rose above the interest rates they were permitted to charge on loans and offer on deposits. With depositors putting their money into other financial institutions—such as the higher-paying money market accounts being offered by brokerage houses—banks and particularly S&Ls found themselves short of liquidity.

The liberalization of the nation's financial system began with the passage of the Depository Institutions Deregulation and Monetary Control Act (DIDMCA) of 1980. Its numerous provisions reflect the compromises necessary to enact such an all-encompassing piece of legislation. As its title suggests, however, the major provisions of interest to us can be divided into two groups:

1. Deregulation: The remaining Regulation Q ceilings (interest-rate ceilings on the interest depositors could be paid) were phased out over a six-year period that ended in 1986. Asset and liability powers of banks and thrifts were expanded. S&Ls and savings banks were allowed to extend loans to businesses and offer more services to customers. All depository intermediaries were permitted to offer NOW accounts (interest-bearing checkable deposits) to households. State usury ceilings (maximum interest rates financial institutions are allowed to charge borrowers on certain types of loans) were suspended.

2. Monetary control: All depository institutions were subject to reserve requirements (so-called universal reserve requirements). Reserve requirements were to be the same on particular types of deposits across institutions (so-called uniform reserve requirements); this provision was phased in over an eight-year period that ended in 1987.

The liberalization of the nation's financial system continued with the S&Ls, which were granted "regulatory relief" by the Garn–St. Germain Depository Institutions Act of 1982. Under this law, S&Ls—originally restricted largely to home mortgages—were permitted to invest in riskier commercial real estate and businesses. With little oversight, such financial liberalization led to excessive speculation by S&Ls and a wave of bankruptcies by the late 1980s and early 1990s. In response, Congress created the Office of Thrift Supervision to oversee S&Ls.

Still, efforts at re-regulation paled in comparison to the continued push for financial liberalization. By the late 1990s, many large commercial banks were lobbying to end the provision of Glass-Steagall that barred commercial banks from engaging in investment banking activity. They offered two key arguments to make their case. First, they said, in a rapidly evolving financial marketplace, the distinctions between traditional deposits, loans, and securities were blurring, making it difficult for regulated commercial banks to operate and costing them business, as less regulated investment banks and brokerages took advantage of these new financial instruments. Second, they argued, there was greater safety in diversification.

The arguments of the commercial banks won the day and, in 1999, Congress passed the Gramm-Leach-Bliley Act, officially known as the Financial Services Modernization Act. The legislation repealed all provisions of Glass-Steagall that prevented commercial banks from engaging in investment banking, brokerage, and insurance activities, or from setting up bank holding companies that would allow them to do so.

Financial Crisis of 2008–2009

While such financial liberalization led to greatly enhanced profits for bank holding companies in the early twenty-first century, it also created new dangers and risks. As banks diversified, it became increasingly difficult for government regulators to figure out how to impose existing rules. In other words, engaging in so many financial activities allowed bank holding companies to choose from a host of competing agencies as to who should regulate them. Some turned to the Office of Thrift Supervision, which had a well-deserved reputation for imposing a light regulatory hand.

In addition, the new liberalization allowed bank holding companies to invest in a host of increasingly exotic financial instruments, most notably mortgage-backed securities, or mortgages bundled together and then sold to investors. Many financial institutions also began to invest in credit default swaps, essentially insurance policies on other securities. Much of this financial innovation was rooted in the booming housing market of the early and mid-2000s. But when housing prices collapsed in the latter years of the decade, these financial instruments lost their value. Worse, it became difficult to assess what these different securities were even worth.

Uncertain how many so-called toxic assets were on the books of other financial institutions—and hence, how solvent those institutions were—many banks stopped lending money to each other. Because lending between banks is a critical activity that keeps the credit markets operating, fear spread that the loan freeze could plunge the global economy into another Great Depression. As banks refused to lend to businesses as well, choking off investment and payrolls, the Fed and other central banks created vast bailout funds to rescue financial institutions of all sizes. At first, the main goal was to buy up the "toxic assets" and thereby bolster the solvency of financial institutions. That proved unrealistic, however, as it became hard to assess what was toxic and what was not, or how much the assets were worth. The Fed therefore shifted gears and began buying equity stakes in financial institutions.

Such intervention in the financial marketplace was unprecedented, especially in the relatively laissez-faire financial environment of the United States. It also raised questions about how much control the federal government—now a partial owner of major financial institutions—should have over their operations. Hewing to the line that financial institutions should be free of political control, the federal government took a relatively light hand, beyond restricting the bonuses that top executives of bailed out firms could receive.

Over time, a consensus began to build for a new set of regulations and regulatory institutions, especially after the Democratic landslide in the 2008 elections that put Barack Obama in the White House and gave the party even greater majorities in both houses of Congress. While such reform was still a work in progress a year after the election, two basic strands were becoming clear: a streamlining of the regulatory process that would make it difficult for financial institutions to play off one agency against another, and new means for assessing and responding to systemic risk such as speculative behavior by large, diversified institutions whose collapse could bring down the global financial system.

James Ciment

See also: Financial Markets; Innovation, Financial; Regulation, Financial.

Further Reading

Alexander, Kern, Rahul Dhumale, and John Eatwell. *Global Governance of Financial Systems: The International Regulation of Systemic Risk.* New York: Oxford University Press, 2006.

Barth, James. *The Rise and Fall of the U.S. Mortgage and Credit Markets: A Comprehensive Analysis of the Market Meltdown.* Hoboken, NJ: John Wiley & Sons, 2009.

Krugman, Paul. *The Return of Depression Economics and the Crisis of 2008.* New York: W.W. Norton, 2009.

Spencer, Peter D. *The Structure and Regulation of Financial Markets.* New York: Oxford University Press, 2000.

White, Lawrence J. *The S&L Debacle: Public Policy Lessons for Bank and Thrift Regulation.* New York: Oxford University Press, 1991.

Life Insurance

The life insurance industry plays an important role in the life of a business cycle. Through their large-scale investments, insurance companies have, at times, contributed to swings in the economic cycle. Moreover, when insurance companies raise or lower premiums as a result of gains or losses on the stock market, they may spur or decrease disposable income, employment, and, in turn, consumer spending within an economy, an important determinant of economic growth or contraction.

Background

Life insurance is essentially a contract between an insurer and a policyholder whereby the insurer agrees to pay a sum of money on the occurrence of the death of the individual, or in some cases upon the individual's sustaining a terminal or critical injury. To achieve this, the policyholder, or another person such as a family member or an employer, pays an amount known as a premium at regular intervals, or in some cases, a lump sum.

In some cases there are variations, which may include the funeral and burial expenses. In most cases, however, the life insurance policy calls for the payment of a single lump sum by the insurance company if various conditions in the policy have been met. Over time, actuaries working for insurance companies have been able to assess the risk of death to people of particular age groups and occupations with a high degree of accuracy, as well as the risk to people living in a specific area, people suffering from similar health complaints, or those involved in a particular lifestyle activity such as smoking.

This has led to policyholders often filling in specific application forms in which the individual risk is assessed by the insurer, and the premium or payout adjusted accordingly. Similarly, there are often exceptions to payout by the insurer, such as in cases of suicide, or where a person has been taking part in a specific high-risk activity prohibited by the policy or has provided misleading or inaccurate information.

Insurance companies assess the risk of the insured, and over time, as more and more statistics have been collected, actuaries have been able to assess a more and more specific level of risk.

People seeking insurance often contact a range of insurance companies, and generally start paying premiums to the company that offers the lowest premium level and/or the highest payout for their individual circumstance. Unlike choosing other kinds of insurance, such as car insurance, where people might prefer a company that advertises how easily it deals with problems, a person considering life insurance is not going to be the one submitting the claim, so other factors are considered. Most life insurance companies therefore focus on their ability to charge low premiums as their primary marketing strategy.

Insurance Companies and Economic Cycles

The nature of the life insurance business means that companies have vast sums of capital to invest, since they are collecting premiums well in advance of paying out benefits when a customer passes away or becomes incapacitated. Because of this, insurance companies run large investment divisions. With their vast assets, these companies can have a major impact on the valuation of securities and other traded assets and can, during times of speculative excess, contribute to rapidly rising bull markets. In periods of economic boom, such as the late 1990s and the early 2000s, life insurance companies (and other insurance companies) collected premiums and then were able to make large profits on their investments and speculation. Because of these profits, some companies were able to lower premiums for policyholders. The lower the premiums, the more people would take out policies with a specific company, thereby allowing the company to increase its market share.

This led to some insurance companies becoming involved in heavy speculation on the stock and commodity markets. For a time, when returns were good, this led to the lowering of premiums paid, as noted above, a situation welcomed—in the short term at any rate—by most consumers. However, when smaller profits were made in the investment or speculation, or when, on occasions, losses were accrued, this caused many problems for the insurance companies. At the depths of the bear market in late 2008, many insurance companies, including such giants as MetLife, reported huge hits to the corporate securities part of their portfolios. Nevertheless, most major life insurance companies maintain well-diversified portfolios overall and none came close to insolvency.

However, unlike an investment bank where people have invested sums of their own money, if a life insurance company does close down, except for those customers who have paid their policy in terms of a lump sum (which is unusual), the loss to the consumer, in the short term, is not as much. Yet, in the long term, this could result in life insurance companies significantly increasing their premiums charged, and this in turn costs the consumer much more. The increase in cost can be dramatic in the case of companies paying life insurance for their employees, when the life insurance is essentially factored into the cost of hiring labor. A rise in life insurance premiums translates into a rise in the cost of employment, and this in turn can effect underlying employment rates.

Justin Corfield

See also: AIG; Retirement Instruments; Savings and Investment.

Further Reading

Black, Kenneth, Jr., and Harold D. Skipper, Jr. *Life Insurance.* Englewood Cliffs, NJ: Prentice Hall, 1994.

"Financial Crisis Poses Greatest Threat to Insurance Industry, Study Says." *Insurance Journal,* June 23, 2009. Available at www.insurancejournal.com/news/national/2009/06/23/101637.htm. Accessed November 2009.

Rotman Zelizer, Viviana A. *Morals and Markets: The Development of Life Insurance in the United States.* New Brunswick, NJ: Transaction, 1983.

Vartabedian, Ralph, and Tom Hamburger. "AIG Crisis Could Be Tip of an Insurance Iceberg." *Los Angeles Times,* March 30, 2009. Available at http:// articles.latimes.com/2009/mar/30/nation/na-aig30. Accessed November 2009.

Linens 'n Things

Founded in 1975 and based in Clifton, New Jersey, Linens 'n Things, Inc., was a chain of retail stores that sold housewares, decorative accessories, and small appliances for the home. It quickly became popular throughout the United States and Canada, at its peak operating 589 stores in 47 U.S. states and 6 Canadian provinces. By the first decade of the twenty-first century, however, the company had fallen on hard times and finally went bankrupt in 2008.

Linens 'n Things was one of the first retail companies to provide, in one store, a wide range of low-priced, high-quality home products such as bedding, towels and other bathroom accessories, crockery and dinnerware, kitchen appliances and accessories, home electrical items (especially fans, air conditioners, and small kitchen items), curtains, and blinds. It also specialized in bridal registries.

In February 2006, Apollo Management, a private equity limited partnership run by Leon Black, bought Linens 'n Things for $1.3 billion, and as late as 2007 the home goods retailer was on the Forbes list as the 114th-largest private company in the United States. At that time, Robert J. DiNicola was the company's chief executive officer (CEO). It employed 19,000 people, held assets valued at $1.65 billion, and earned revenue in 2005 of $2.7 billion (an increase of 1.2 percent from the previous year). However, the company's net profits were only $36 million, or less than 1.4 percent of earnings—well below average for a large discount-based retail company.

The financial precariousness of Linens 'n Things became evident in the middle of the new century's first decade as the economic downturn kicked into gear and American consumers started cutting back on buying housewares and other company items, resulting in overstocked stores and declining sales. In March 2007, management began a series of layoffs that would reach the tens of

The home-products retail chain Linens 'n Things, which once operated 589 stores and employed 19,000 workers, liquidated its remaining outlets and ceased operations amid the economic recession in late 2008. *(Joe Raedle/Getty Images)*

thousands as the situation continued to deteriorate. On May 2, 2007, the company filed for Chapter 11 bankruptcy protection. In the petition made to a court in Delaware, the company said that it would have to close 120 stores, with the largest number in California (27) and Michigan (10), where the downturn in sales had been most severe. Michael Gries of the financial advisory firm Conway Del Genio Gries was then brought in as chief restructuring officer and interim CEO, with DiNicola becoming executive chairman. Gries closed 200 "underperforming" stores to slow financial hemorrhaging of the company's funds and to put what was left of the business up for sale.

The bankrupt company announced in October 2008 that it would hold a massive closeout sale of all products, fixtures, furniture, and equipment at its remaining 371 stores. The liquidation continued on the Linens 'n Things Web site until early 2009. According to retail analysts, the company's main downfall was that it had moved from its original mainstream business of stocking high-quality, low-priced items into the promotion of new products and large clearance sales. At the same time, it had started to face increased competition from similar chains, including Bed Bath & Beyond, at a time of economic downturn.

Justin Corfield

See also: Recession and Financial Crisis (2007–).

Further Reading

Bernfield, Susan. "Selling Out to the Bare Walls." *Businessweek*, March 16, 2009, p. 42.

Genoways, Ted. "The Hard Sell." *Mother Jones* 34:3 (May–June 2009): 71–74.

"Linens 'n Things Seeks to Speed Up Store Closings." *Los Angeles Times*, October 8, 2008, p. C2.

Linens 'n Things Web site: www.lnt.com.

Walker, Rob. "Cleaned Sheets." *New York Times Magazine*, August 30, 2009, p. 18.

Liquidity Crunch

In microeconomics (the economics of individuals, households, and firms), liquidity signifies the amount of cash on hand, or the existence of assets, such as stock shares, that can easily be converted into cash in order to meet expenses. A liquidity crunch, then, occurs when a company or household runs out of such assets or cash to meet expenses, and can no longer secure credit. In macroeconomics (the study of the economy as a whole), a liquidity crunch occurs when lenders in general become skittish about offering credit, choking off investment and payrolls and contributing to an economic downturn.

Most firms need credit to function—for investment, operating expenses, and payroll—especially because they are often awaiting payment from clients. When those payments do not come, or if a firm seeks to expand, it will turn to lenders for credit. But if lenders perceive that a company is having trouble meeting payments, it may be more demanding on the terms of the loan, requiring more collateral or higher interest rates to make up for the additional risk. The additional requirements are often so burdensome that a company may choose to reorganize under bankruptcy law rather than try to obtain credit under these conditions.

When such circumstances apply to an entire national economy, or sector of it, the ramifications of a liquidity crunch may become dire. Large-scale liquidity crunches often occur during times of economic recession, as many companies come to face their own shortages of cash or readily convertible assets, as customers disappear, as clients delay payment or fail to pay altogether, and as convertible assets drop in value. When this occurs, lending institutions often become more selective about whom they lend money to and how much they offer in credit, limiting loans to individuals and companies with substantial secured assets and better credit ratings. This phenomenon is known as a "flight to quality."

The subprime mortgage crisis that began in 2006 offers an extreme example of this kind of macroeconomic liquidity crunch. In the early part of the decade, credit was loose and mortgages were easy to obtain, fueling a run-up in housing prices. This eased credit even further, since homebuyers automatically found themselves with a secured asset in the form of rising equity in their property. Lenders worried less about the creditworthiness of their borrowers—even subprime borrowers with low income or uneven credit histories—since they could seize the property of anyone who failed to make their mortgage payments and sell the property at a profit.

But when housing prices peaked and then began to fall in 2007, the situation reversed itself. Lenders became more hesitant to offer mortgages to riskier customers and even to more creditworthy ones. As the housing crisis began to put a damper on consumer spending and the economy sank into recession, people began to lose their jobs and became increasingly unable to service their mortgages. This created a liquidity crunch for some financial institutions, forcing them to cut off credit. Even sound lenders became more wary of offering credit, not just to homebuyers but to other individuals and firms, leading to a liquidity crunch throughout the economy. With money becoming less available to finance mortgages, housing prices fell even further—a situation made worse by the many foreclosed properties coming onto the market.

In addition, many financial institutions had invested in securities that were backed by mortgages. As these securities dropped in value—or when the value of the securities became difficult to assess—banks further tightened credit, even to each other. Lenders began to fear that borrowers had too many mortgage-backed securities—which came to be called "toxic assets"—on their books and might be unable to pay back their loans. The investment bank Lehman Brothers became the best-known victim of the 2007–2009 liquidity crunch, collapsing in the late summer of 2008. Beyond the financial sector, companies found it increasingly difficult to borrow, limiting investment and hiring. Individuals, too, found it harder to obtain credit or saw their credit card limits shrink, dampening consumer demand.

While the liquidity crisis of the end of the century's first decade is just beginning to be studied, economists have long debated what triggers liquidity crises on a macroeconomic level and what measures should be taken to ease them. Most agree, however, that liquidity crunches are an inherent part of business cycles, providing short- and long-term corrections after periods of loose credit and rapid economic expansion.

James Ciment and Justin Corfield

See also: Corporate Finance; Credit Cycle; Debt; Financial Markets.

Further Reading

Cooper, George. *The Origin of Financial Crises: Central Banks, Credit Bubbles and the Efficient Market Fallacy.* New York: Vintage, 2008.

Elliott, Larry. *The Gods That Failed: How Blind Faith in Markets Has Cost Us Our Future.* New York: Nation Books, 2009.

Gold, Gerry, and Paul Feldman. *A House of Cards: From Fantasy Finance to Global Crash.* London: Lupus Books, 2007.

Spotton Visano, Brenda. *Financial Crises: Socio-economic Causes and Institutional Context.* New York: Routledge, 2006.

Turner, Graham. *The Credit Crunch: Housing Bubbles, Globalisation and the Worldwide Economic Crisis.* London: Pluto, 2008.

Liquidity Trap

Governments have a number of tools at their disposal to help the economy during recessionary periods. They can utilize tax policy to promote investment or initiate stimulus programs to increase demand for goods and services and put people to work. But the most readily available tool—and the one most commonly employed—is monetary policy.

Sometimes, however, monetary policy is ineffective, and the reason may be that the economy is in a liquidity trap. In this situation, efforts to increase the money supply have failed to encourage borrowing that could stimulate the economy, either because interest rates are so close to zero that they cannot fall any lower, or because banks do not want to make loans. In either case, the economy is awash in liquid assets and cash that are readily convertible into other assets. However, the increase in liquidity does not have the expected positive impact on lending, investment, and economic growth.

Thus, a liquidity trap can, in broad terms, represent a situation in which monetary policy is ineffective or, more narrowly, in which interest rates are at or near zero. Technically speaking, a liquidity trap occurs when increases in the money supply—as effected by a central bank's buying and selling of government bonds—do not reduce the interest rate. In other words, the central bank has expanded the money supply by providing additional cash reserves to commercial banks, but these same institutions do not lend the money to businesses and households, either because they are worried about the capacity of borrowers to repay or because businesses and households evince no demand for such credit.

During extreme periods of contraction, such as the recession of 2007–2009, the U.S. Federal Reserve reduced the nominal interest rate—that is, the interest rate not adjusted for inflation—to near zero as a way to stimulate investment, demand, and hiring. The United States then entered a liquidity trap because the Federal Reserve could not lower the interest rate any further even as the economy remained mired in slow or negative economic growth.

A liquidity trap occurs because commercial banks—though they are able to borrow money more cheaply from the central bank—remain hesitant in their own lending. They may be facing a liquidity crunch of their own due to bad loans on their books or because they question the creditworthiness of potential borrowers, a situation particularly acute during recessionary periods when households and businesses are experiencing higher rates of insolvency and bankruptcy. Moreover, a liquidity trap may also coincide with deflation and an economy-wide preference for liquidity, as households and firms choose to save the extra money in the economy rather than spend it, thereby increasing the value of the money in circulation. Deflation can often dampen investment, since the future returns on an investment are worth less. The Japanese economy of the late twentieth century—during the so-called lost decade of the 1990s—provides a classic example of a liquidity trap. Fueled by favorable trade balances and a booming economy, the Japanese went on a buying spree in the 1980s, driving up the prices of all kinds of assets—from corporate securities to commercial real estate to golf club memberships—to unsustainable levels. When the bubble burst in the early 1990s, financial institutions became hesitant to offer credit and the economy began to contract. With deflation setting in, Japanese households and firms hesitated to make long-term investments, fearing a loss in value. In addition, many banks held vast quantities of depreciated assets on their books, further reducing their willingness to lend. The result was an extended period of stagnation, with the economy failing to grow or diversify.

The Bank of Japan undertook the classic solution of lowering interest rates as a way of stimulating lending, investment, demand, and hiring. But because of the many bad assets on their books—and because of fears of deflation and continued economic stagnation—commercial banks failed to respond by making credit more available, even when they themselves were able to borrow money at a central bank interest rate of near zero. In addition, massive stimulus programs undertaken by the government also failed to lift the economy. Only when commercial banks began purging their books of bad assets did they begin to lend more freely, restoring modest growth to the nation's economy in the early 2000s.

The Japanese experience of the 1990s weighed heavily on the thinking of economic policy makers in the United States and other industrialized countries as they grappled with the financial crisis and recession of the late 2000s. Many came to recognize that the unwillingness of the Japanese government and commercial banks to write off bad loans contributed to the long period of stagnation, and that simply lowering central bank nominal interest rates to near zero was not sufficient to lift the economy out of recession. During the financial crisis of 2008–2009, the lessons from Japan prompted

government to take more aggressive steps to deal with "troubled assets" as a way for economies to avoid falling into the liquidity trap.

James Ciment and Justin Corfield

See also: Banks, Central; Federal Reserve System; Interest Rates; Monetary Policy.

Further Reading
Sevensson, Lars E.P. "Escaping from a Liquidity Trap and Deflation: The Foolproof Way and Others." *Journal of Economic Perspectives* 17:4 (Fall 2003): 145–166.
Tirole, Jean. *Financial Crises, Liquidity, and the International Monetary System.* Princeton, NJ: Princeton University Press, 2002.
Wilson, Dominic. *Is Shutting Krugman's Liquidity Trap the Answer to Japan's Problems?* Canberra: Australia-Japan Research Centre, 1999.

Loan-to-Value Ratio

The loan-to-value ratio (LTV) is the ratio of the amount of a loan to the value of the asset being purchased by that loan. Along with the creditworthiness of the borrower, the type of asset being purchased, and the overall credit situation in the economy at large, LTV is a critical factor in the assessment lenders make in deciding whether to offer a loan in a given situation. LTVs apply to all loan situations, whether the borrower is a firm or an individual, or whether the loan is for a car, a house, commercial real estate, corporate securities, a business, or business equipment.

All other factors being equal, low LTVs usually mean less risk for the lender and lower interest rates for the borrower. To take an extreme example, an LTV of 1:10 on a $20,000 loan means that the bank is lending $20,000 against a $200,000 asset. Unless the value of the asset falls by more than 90 percent—a highly unlikely scenario in most lending situations—the lender is unlikely to lose money on the deal, even if the borrower fails to service the loan. That is because the lender can take possession of the asset and sell it off for more than the loan was worth.

High LTVs reflect the creditworthiness of the borrower in several ways. First, by putting down a higher percentage of the asset's value in cash, the borrower has demonstrated sufficient assets to make a large down payment, indicating a strong financial situation. For many individuals, this means having made an effort to save and good financial habits. Moreover, a higher down payment commits the borrower to servicing the loan, since he or she risks losing that money in the eventuality of default.

For home mortgages, the most common type of loans, LTVs have fluctuated over the years, though the general trend has been toward higher ratios. In the United States, through the early part of the twentieth century, banks generally required substantial down payments on a home mortgage—in the range of 50 percent or more, keeping the LTV at 5:10 or less. This discouraged home buying and kept homeownership rates low. In the late 1930s, the federal government established Fannie Mae to provide support for mortgage. In the post–World War II era, generous loans to returning veterans and federal guarantees on home mortgages permitted commercial lenders, such as banks and, increasingly, savings and loans, to offer higher LTV ratios, prompting a surge in homeownership. Fannie Mae purchased, held, or sold to investors Federal Housing Administration (FHA) and Veterans Administration (VA) loans that provided liquidity in the mortgage and an expansion of mortgage debt and homeownership.

Still, through the 1970s, most lenders insisted on an LTV of no more than 8:10. In other words, they required borrowers to put down at least 20 percent of the value of the loan. With various reforms to savings and loan (S&L) regulations, which made it easier for the industry to provide loans not only on home mortgages but on commercial real estate as well, the LTV climbed higher. But the S&L crisis of the late 1980s, combined with declining real-estate values in the early 1990s, reversed that trend.

Even as the S&L crisis broke, however, innovations in the financial markets were beginning to send LTVs back up in the 1990s and early 2000s. Specifically, financial institutions began to bundle home mortgages into financial products that could be traded like any security. Aside from the profits to be made, the impetus for so-called mortgage-backed securities was that they spread the risk of default from the issuing institution to investors. For proponents of such securities, this meant that banks could offer loans to less creditworthy customers and raise the LTV ratio, since the issuer of the mortgage was not entirely liable in case of default.

By the early 2000s, the securitization of mortgages, along with historically low interest rates from the Federal Reserve, had led the financial industry to begin offering mortgages with LTVs of 10:10 and even higher. That is, they began offering loans in excess of the value of the home, giving the borrower money to make improvements or to spend the money on anything else he or she desired.

In retrospect, LTVs this high seem foolhardy. But at the time—during the housing boom of the early and mid-2000s—lenders believed that rising house prices provided adequate security against their loans. That is, if a borrower took out a $200,000 loan for a $180,000 house and defaulted, it did not matter because the price of the house was likely to rise above $200,000 over a relatively short time period. Of course, when housing prices began to fall in the late 2000s and the recession caused many people to default, many banks found themselves with assets worth less—sometimes far less—than the loans that had been extended. Indeed, many borrowers simply walked away from their homes when their mortgages came to exceed the value of their properties—a situation known as being "upside down" or "underwater."

With so many bad loans on their books, banks began to rein in their lending and to demand lower LTVs on the mortgages they offered. By the late 2000s, it was increasingly common for banks to insist on a traditional LTV of no more than 8:10 and sometimes, for less creditworthy customers, even lower than that. Lower LTVs put an additional damper on home sales and contributed to falling values in a vicious cycle that devastated the housing, real estate, and home construction industries.

James Ciment and Justin Corfield

See also: Collateral; Debt; Mortgage Lending Standards; Mortgage Markets and Mortgage Rates.

Further Reading

Goodhart, C.A.E., and Boris Hofmann. *House Prices and the Macroeconomy: Implications for Banking and Price Stability.* New York: Oxford University Press, 2007.

Shiller, Robert J. *Subprime Solution: How Today's Global Financial Crisis Happened and What to Do About It.* Princeton, NJ: Princeton University Press, 2008.

White, Lawrence J. *The S&L Debacle: Public Policy Lessons for Bank and Thrift Regulation.* New York: Oxford University Press, 1991.

Long-Term Capital Management

Long-Term Capital Management (LTCM) was a hedge fund that nearly went bankrupt in 1998. Its bailout by major U.S. banks—a bailout coordinated by the Federal Reserve (Fed)—is said, by some economists, to have contributed to the 2008–2009 financial crisis, as many financial institutions came to believe that even if their high-risk investment strategies should fail, they would see themselves rescued with the help of the federal government.

LTCM's Investment Strategies

A hedge fund is a nontraditional type of mutual fund formed as a partnership of up to ninety-nine investors. Partners in hedge funds are wealthy individuals and institutions with significant net worth. Minimum investments start at $1 million, and many hedge funds have much higher minimum requirements to participate. Hedge funds attempt to earn high or maximum returns regardless of whether prices in broader financial markets are rising or falling. The funds trade securities and other creative financial instruments and try to outperform traditional investment funds by employing novel trading strategies. Because of their limited number and the wealth of their participants, hedge funds are not regulated in the same way that traditional mutual funds are.

Some of the strategies employed by hedge funds include the following: selling borrowed securities (selling short) in the hope of profiting by buying the securities at a lower price on a future date; exploiting unusual price differences between related securities in anticipation of making a profit when the prices come into more traditional alignment; trading options and derivatives; and borrowing to invest so that returns are increased.

One of the best-known hedge funds, and ultimately an infamous type, was Long-Term Capital Management. It was founded in 1994 by John Meriwether, formerly of the investment bank Salomon Brothers, and Robert Merton and Myron Scholes, who shared the 1997 Nobel Prize in economics for their work in modeling financial risk. LTCM required investors to make a minimum investment of $10 million for three years. LTCM raised $3 billion over the course of a few months in 1994, as investors—drawn by the company's stellar management—clamored to be a part of this hedge fund.

They were well rewarded for doing so. In their first year, investors made a 20 percent return, followed by 43 percent in the second year, and 41 percent in the third. LTCM achieved these spectacular returns by using trading strategies that suggested that the prices of the different securities being invested in should be related to one another, based on risk, maturity, and liquidity. If rates among securities got out of alignment, LTCM would, in effect, place bets that rates would return to the traditional or historical alignment. In fact, the fund was purchasing bonds it believed to be overpriced and selling them short (that is, borrowing and selling, then buying them back later when, it was hoped, their price had dropped). Using such a strategy, LTCM made profits as long as the spread between the two types of bonds narrowed, regardless of the direction in which financial prices or interest rates moved. In addition, LTCM relied on short-term bank loans to leverage, or increase, the amount of investable funds.

Crisis

Although returns fell to 17 percent in 1997 (due, said the company, to increased competition as other funds copied its strategies), the strategies worked well until late summer 1998, when Russia defaulted on its debt, throwing global financial markets into turmoil. The default by Russia was related to the Asian financial crisis of 1997 and caused interest rates and financial prices to move in nontraditional ways. The prices of the securities that LTCM thought would rise relative to U.S. government securities did the opposite because of perceived increases in risk. In short, the spread between the financial prices widened rather than narrowing as expected. There was a "flight to quality" as funds flowed into U.S. government securities (pushing their prices up) and out of other securities (pushing their prices down). LTCM was particularly vulnerable because it had borrowed roughly 50 times its capital (investors' funds). When prices failed to move in the expected direction, the fund's capital base was swiftly depleted. Losses were magnified because of the high degree of leveraging (reliance on borrowed funds). With the value of LTCM's securities falling, banks suggested that the fund should liquidate its positions so that the bank loans could be repaid.

Bailout

To ward off the fund's certain bankruptcy, a consortium of sixteen leading U.S. banks agreed to a $3.6 billion loan package to bail out LTCM on September 24, 1998. Thus, the securities whose prices had fallen did not have to be sold at a loss but could be held until their prices moved into more traditional alignment. In an extremely unusual and controversial move at the time, the Federal Reserve (Fed) arranged the bailout. LTCM had tried to arrange a deal on its own for more than a month but had failed. The Fed brokered the deal to prevent the liquidation of LTCM's $200 billion in securities and avoid what it thought might be a frantic reaction in financial markets. It was alleged that LTCM was linked to about $1.25 trillion worth of positions in global financial markets. The liquidation of LTCM's positions would have exacerbated the price falls and led to losses by the banks that had loaned to the hedge fund.

There was also concern that if LTCM were forced to liquidate, a chain reaction could be set off. The dramatic drop in the prices of the securities that LTCM was liquidating could cause the crisis to spread to other hedge funds that employed similar strategies. In that event, other banks that had loaned to hedge funds could also experience major losses. By 1999, LTCM was able to repay the $3.6 billion bailout by the sixteen banks. When the loans were repaid, LTCM quietly closed.

As financial analysts note, the LTCM rescue was not exactly like the bailout of major financial institutions in 2008. In the LTCM case, the Fed merely "arranged" the bailout, unlike the 2008 bailouts of Bear Stearns, Fannie Mae, Freddie Mac, AIG, Citigroup, Bank of America, and many other of the nation's largest banks, where the Fed and Congress orchestrated and underwrote the bailouts.

The LTCM episode caused some analysts to call for more oversight and rules for the very lightly regulated hedge fund industry. But others argued that this was not a good solution because hedge funds would merely go "offshore" where they could escape regulation. The problem was—and continues to be—not so much that the wealthy investors in hedge funds might lose their money but that the banks that loan to the funds to enable them to leverage their bets would also lose, putting them and the financial system they buttress at risk. Perhaps, say some analysts, the solution would be for banks to be more judicious in lending to hedge funds and to more fully disclose their exposure to potential losses.

In 2009, some analysts argued that the collapse of LTCM was a harbinger of the later financial crisis of 2008–2009, with many suggesting the company's collapse should have been a wake-up call to the financial industry and regulators. Others wondered if the 2008–2009 crisis could have been avoided if the Fed had not orchestrated the 1998 bailout of LTCM, causing market participants to believe that the Fed would intervene if large in-situations got into trouble—a situation known as moral hazard. If regulators had let LTCM fail (and lived with the consequences), or if they had recognized lapses in the financial regulatory structure, perhaps the later crisis could have been avoided. One thing is certain: the $3.6 billion private sector bailout of LTCM, which seemed monumental at the time, was dwarfed by the later direct public sector bailouts of the crisis of 2008–2009, which total in the hundreds of billions of dollars.

Maureen Burton

See also: Hedge Funds.

Further Reading
Burton, Maureen, and Bruce Brown. *The Financial System and the Economy.* 5th ed. Armonk, NY: M.E. Sharpe, 2009.
Burton, Maureen, Reynold Nesiba, and Bruce Brown. *An Introduction to Financial Markets and Institutions.* 2nd ed. Armonk, NY: M.E. Sharpe, 2010.
Cowen, Tyler. "Bailout of Long-Term Capital: A Bad Precedent?" *New York Times*, December 26, 2008. Available at www.nytimes.com/2008/12/28/business/economy/28view.html. Accessed February 2010.
Dowd, Kevin. "Too Big to Fail? Long-Term Capital Management and the Federal Reserve." *Cato Institute Briefing Papers*, September 23, 1999. Available at www.cato.org/pubs/briefs/bp-052es.html. Accessed February 2010.
Lowenstein, Roger. *When Genius Failed: The Rise and Fall of Long-Term Capital Management.* New York: Random House, 2000.

Lowe, Adolph (1893–1995)

German economist and sociologist Adolph Lowe was a pioneer in elucidating and analyzing the dynamics of business cycles. He made significant contributions to understanding the ways in which socio-behavioral changes—in addition to purely economic factors—influence the rate and direction of business cycles.

Adolph Lowe was born on March 4, 1893, in Stuttgart, Germany, where he was also raised. He studied in Munich before becoming a student of political economist Franz Oppenheimer at the University of Berlin, where he focused on economics and sociology. He served in the German military during World War I, after which he became a financial adviser to the Weimar Republic.

Lowe joined the Ministry of Economics in 1922 and worked there for four years before leaving for a position at the Institut für Weltwirtschaft (World Economic Development Institute) in Kiel. At the Institute, he researched business cycles in collaboration with economists Fritz Burchardt, Gergard Colm, Hans Neisser, and Jacob Marschak. In 1926, he published his first major essay on business cycles, titled "Wie ist Konjunkturtheorie uberhaupt moglich?" (How Is Business Cycle Theory Possible at All?). The essay, in opposition to the prevailing economic thinking at the time, proved that there existed a vital, intricate connection between research on business cycles and that on the general equilibrium economic theory. It profoundly influenced Friedrich Hayek and later members of the Austrian school of economics and their thinking about business cycles.

In 1931, Lowe moved to the University of Frankfurt, where he was influenced by the philosophers Max Horkheimer and Theodor W. Adorno of the Frankfurt school. Two years later, however, with the rise to power of Adolf Hitler, Lowe was forced to leave his position because of his support for the Social Democratic Party, his previous membership in the Socialization Committee, and his Jewish background. He fled Germany with his family, living briefly in Geneva, Switzerland, before moving to England. There he worked at the London School of Economics and the University of Manchester. He remained in Britain until 1940, when he was interned as an enemy alien in spite of his opposition to Hitler. He moved to the United States at the invitation of Alvin Johnson, where he served as the director of the Institute of World Affairs at the New School for Social Research in New York City until 1983.

Although he was initially influenced by the work of John Maynard Keynes, at the New School Lowe remained faithful to his research at Kiel, which had provided the underpinnings for many of his theories on the nature of business cycles, the importance of changes in social and behavioral structures, and on pure economic forces—and had overturned some of the fundamental thinking on orthodox economic theory. Lowe attempted to restructure the Institute of World Affairs based on the Kiel model. Using what he termed "instrumental analysis," he combined research on behavioral patterns with economic analysis in his best-known book, *On Economic Knowledge* (1965). This was followed by the publication in 1969 of his influential article "Toward a Science of Economics," and, in 1976, with the publication of *The Path of Economic Growth*. These works did not immediately sit well with the academic establishment in economics, which was more comfortable with mechanistic views of economic theory. Additionally, because Lowe was a socialist and supported the use of government policy instruments to improve the economic well-being of the country, some of his ideas were unpopular during the cold war. Although he pointed out that the U.S. economy was already heavily regulated by such legislation as antitrust laws, it did not stop free-market economists and politicians from criticizing him. Lowe died on June 3, 1995, in Wolfenbüttel, Germany.

Justin Corfield

See also: Behavioral Economics; Keynesian Business Model.

Further Reading

Hagemann, H., and H.D. Kurz. "Balancing Freedom and Order: On Adolph Lowe's Political Economics." *Social Research* 57 (1990): 733–753.

Lissner, Will. "In Memoriam: Adolph Lowe 1893–1995, Economist." *American Journal of Economics and Sociology* (January 1996).

Lowe, Adolph. *Essays in Political Economics: Public Control in a Democratic Society.* New York: New York University Press, 1987.

———. *On Economic Knowledge: Toward a Science of Political Economics.* Armonk, NY: M.E. Sharpe, 1977.

———. *The Path of Economic Growth.* Cambridge, UK: Cambridge University Press, 1976.

Loyd, Samuel Jones (1796–1883)

Samuel Jones Loyd, First Baron Overstone, was a British financier, politician, and leading authority on the nation's banking during the mid-nineteenth century. An influential force in British government in the 1840s, he was responsible for the introduction of the Bank Charter Act of 1844, which strengthened and extended the power of England's central bank. Loyd was also an effective champion for the role of a national central bank in maintaining a healthy financial system.

Born in Lothbury, England, on September 25, 1796, Samuel Loyd was the only son of Lewis Loyd, a clergyman turned banker, and Sarah Jones Loyd, whose father owned the Manchester bank where Lewis worked. Samuel Loyd attended Eton College and Trinity College, Cambridge, from which he graduated in 1818. That same year he joined Jones, Loyd & Co. A member of the Liberal party, he was elected to Parliament in 1819 and continued to serve until 1826. He married the daughter of a Nottingham banker in 1829 and amassed a personal fortune over the course of the next twenty years.

In December 1832, Loyd was defeated for a parliamentary seat for Manchester but remained a powerful figure in the government because of his wealth, connections, and understanding of economic processes. A member of the elite Political Economy Club from 1831 to 1872, Loyd was appointed an exchequer bill commissioner in 1831 and appeared before a parliamentary committee the following year to discuss renewal of the charter of the Bank of England. This led, eight years later, to his book *Thoughts on the Separation of the Departments of the Bank of England*, which heavily influenced the passing of the Bank Charter Act of 1844.

In his book, Loyd argued that the role of the Bank of England was to provide a safe place of deposit for government and public money and to ensure the strength of the British currency. He strongly opposed other banks issuing their own notes, believing that the central bank's control of the country's money supply would prevent the economy from entering a period of inflation or slipping into a destructive period of deflation— either of which would lead to economic instability and contraction.

In 1850, Loyd became First Baron Overstone, with his seat at Wolvey Hall, Warwickshire; with peerage came permanent membership in Parliament's House of Lords. The London branch of Jones, Loyd & Co. was taken over by the London and Westminster Bank in 1864, which left him no longer directly involved in the banking industry. Nevertheless, Lloyd continued to influence the country's financial policy. Through the 1860s and 1870s, the government regularly consulted him on banking-related matters, especially during financial crises and when issues involving monetary policy came up for consideration by Parliament.

At his death on November 17, 1883, Loyd's personal fortune was valued at about £5.2 million, making him one of the richest people in England. He is remembered for recognizing the importance of central banks to strong national economies.

Justin Corfield

See also: Banking School/Currency School Debate; Banks, Central.

Further Reading
Clapham, Sir John. *The Bank of England: A History*. London: Cambridge University Press, 1970.
Loyd, Samuel Jones. *Tracts and Other Publications on Metallic and Paper Currency*, ed. J.R. McCulloch. Englewood Cliffs, NJ: A.M. Kelley, 1972 (reprint of 1857).
O'Brien, D.P., ed. *The Correspondence of Lord Overstone*. Cambridge, UK: Cambridge University Press, 1971.

Luminent Mortgage Capital

Luminent Mortgage Capital, Inc., was a real-estate investment trust with mortgages centered in San Francisco that relied on investor money from California, and gradually elsewhere throughout the United States, to buy mortgages and related instruments. Formed in 2003 to invest in highly rated mortgage-backed securities, Luminent is an example of a company that was born and thrived in the real-estate boom of 2003 to 2006 and died in the bust that followed.

A publicly traded company, Luminent took in money to fund the boom in property development in the San Francisco Bay area. While its base of operations was located in Philadelphia, the company incorporated in Maryland. At the height of the property boom in the new century's first decade, it gained a triple-A rating and enjoyed rapidly rising investments, earnings, and share prices.

With the downturn in the property market in early 2007, however, investors began to pull back their funds, causing the flow of new capital into the company to slow. Also, fewer and fewer borrowers applied for or were granted new loans. With a number of Luminent's clients failing financially, it was not long before the company faced severe financial difficulty. In the first half of 2007, the company sold only $31 million of its mortgage securities, compared to sales of $3.1 billion the previous year. Luminent was able to buy only $1.26 billion in loans to be held for investment in the first half of 2007, compared to $3.14 billion in the first half of the previous year.

With the advent of the full-blown subprime

mortgage crisis, Luminent faced continued devaluation of its assets and a lack of new business. Finally, when the markets opened on Monday, August 6, 2007, the company announced that it was forced to suspend dividend payments to investors and seek fresh sources of capital to alleviate what it hoped would be a short-term cash-flow problem.

Later in August 2007, a major attempt was made to salvage the business by offering the San Juan–based investment company Arco Capital Corp. a majority stake in the company, including about half its stock and control over four seats on the board, in exchange for a loan of $60 million and a sale of some of the investments at a massively reduced price of $65 million. Arco became the major secured creditor, followed by Washington Mutual's WaMu Capital Corporation, which also provided funds to keep Luminent solvent. Ultimately, however, these agreements did not bring in sufficient capital to keep the company afloat.

On September 8, 2008, Luminent Mortgage Capital filed for Chapter 11 bankruptcy protection. As of July 31, 2008, it had debts of $486.1 million and assets of $13.4 million. Its shares reached a low of 7.7 cents, and the firm became, through restricting, a publicly traded partnership rather than a publicly traded real-estate investment trust.

Justin Corfield

See also: Mortgage Markets and Mortgage Rates; Mortgage, Subprime; Recession and Financial Crisis (2007–); Shadow Banking System.

Further Reading

Colter, Allison Bisbey. "Pipeline." *American Banker*, September 11, 2008, p. 12.

"Problems Mount for 2 Mortgage Firms." *New York Times*, September 27, 2007, p. C4.

"Speculation on Asset Cap Boosts Freddie, Fannie." *Los Angeles Times*, August 7, 2007. Available at http://articles.latimes.com/2007/aug/07/business/fi-mortgage7. Accessed February 2010.

"Two U.S. Companies Involved in Mortgages Move to Raise Cash." *New York Times*, August 21, 2007. Available at www.nytimes.com/2007/08/21/business/21lend.html. Accessed February 2010.

Lundberg, Erik Filip (1907–1987)

Swedish economist Erik Lundberg was one of the foremost thinkers in what became known as the Stockholm school of economics, which included such other notables as Nobel laureates Gunnar Myrdal, Bertil Ohlin, and Dag Hammarskjöld. The Stockholm school—of which Lundberg was the last surviving member—was known for laying the theoretical underpinnings of the northern European welfare state and, among economists, for pioneering sequence, or process, analysis. Although Lundberg spent his entire career in Sweden and was the only member of the group to remain in academia, his work proved influential around the world, in policy as well as in theory.

Erick Filip Lundberg was born on August 13, 1907, in Stockholm, Sweden. He earned his doctorate in economics in 1937 and was appointed director of Sweden's National Institute of Economic Research, a post he held for the next eighteen years. In 1946, he accepted a chair in economics at Stockholm University, where he lectured until 1965. From the mid-1960s to his retirement in 1974, Lundberg was a professor at the Stockholm School of Economics. In addition to his academic posts, Lundberg served as an economic adviser to a large Swedish bank beginning in the 1950s. He also served as president of the Royal Swedish Academy of Sciences (1973–1976) and as a member of the academy's Economics Prize Committee, which selects the winners of the Nobel Prize in Economic Sciences (1969–1979, chairman 1975–1979).

As a working theoretical economist, Lundberg became known for formulating models of macroeconomic fluctuations, which helped the Swedish government, among others, devise resource allocation policies. His first major work, *Studies in the Theory of Economic Expansion* (1937), appeared a year after John Maynard Keynes's *General Theory of Employment, Interest, and Money*. By the time a second edition of *Studies in the Theory of Economic Expansion* was published in 1955, Lundberg had become well known and widely regarded for his writings on business cycles and economic growth, notably *Business Cycles and Economic Policy* (1953) and *Instability and Economic Growth* (1968).

In his research, Lundberg expanded the methods that economists used to analyze business cycles. He incorporated a "multiplier" into his models that took into consideration the effects of changes in exports and investment on business fluctuations. He also demonstrated how to apply price mechanisms and their time lags when adjusting for changes in demand to an understanding of business cycles. Lundberg died in Stockholm on September 14, 1987.

Justin Corfield

See also: Stockholm School.

Further Reading

Baumol, William J. "Erik Lundberg 1907–1987." *Scandinavian Journal of Economics* 92:1 (March 1990): 1–9.

Laursen, Svend. "Lundberg on Business Cycles and Public Policy." *Quarterly Journal of Economics* 69:2 (May 1955): 221–234.

Lundberg, Erik Filip. *The Development of Swedish and Keynesian Macroeconomic Theory and Its Impact on Economic Policy.* Cambridge, UK: Cambridge University Press, 1996.

———. *Instability and Economic Growth.* New Haven, CT: Yale University Press, 1968.

Luxemburg, Rosa (1871–1919)

Rosa Luxemburg was a Marxist economist, philosopher, and revolutionary who, in the study of economic cycles, became best known for developing theories of overproduction/underconsumption and the need for imperialist capitalist economies to move production to their colonies. She also is remembered for cofounding, with Karl Liebknecht, Die Internationale, which became the Spartakusbund (Spartacist League), and later—in collaboration with independent socialists and the international communists of Germany—the Communist Party of Germany.

Luxemburg was born on March 5, 1871, in Zamość, in Russian Poland, and educated in Warsaw. At the age of fifteen, she joined the Proletariat Party, a left-wing Polish political group, and took part in strikes that they organized. A crackdown by Russian authorities forced her to flee to Switzerland in 1889, where she attended the University of Zurich. There, her studies included philosophy, mathematics, and economics—with a particular interest in stock exchange crises. In Switzerland, she met other exiled Russian socialist revolutionaries, including Leo Jogiches, with whom, in 1893, she founded *Sprawa Robotnicza* (Workers' Cause), a newspaper that opposed the nationalist policies of the Polish Socialist Party and advocated socialist revolution in Germany, Austria, and Russia to ensure Polish independence.

Luxemburg married the German Gustav Lübeck in 1898 and became a German citizen, settling in Berlin. As a member of the left wing of Germany's Social Democratic Party, she worked with Karl Kautsky to expel from the party those who supported Eduard Bernstein's revisionist theory, which called for trade union activity and parliamentary politics as a means to achieve socialism. She opposed Germany's establishment of a colonial empire in Africa and China, arguing against its involvement in China in 1900, and against the increasingly expensive arms race, which she believed would lead inevitably to war. At the same time, she wrote articles about European socioeconomic issues for a variety of newspapers. Luxemburg and Jogiches were arrested in Warsaw during the failed 1905 revolution in that city. Meanwhile, with revolutionary activism rising in less developed parts of Europe, Luxemburg was coming to the conclusion that socialism was more likely to arise in an underdeveloped country such as Russia than in more industrialized countries. She published *The Mass Strike, the Political Party, and the Trade Unions* in 1906, in which she advocated a general workers' strike.

Marxist theoretician and firebrand Rosa Luxemburg addresses a 1907 gathering of the Internationale, a precursor of the Communist Party of Germany she helped found. Steady equilibrium growth, Luxemburg argued, is not possible in a closed capitalist economy. *(ullstein bild/The Granger Collection, New York)*

Vladimir Lenin, exiled from Russia, met Luxemburg in Munich in 1907 while she was attending the Russian Social Democrat's Fifth Party Day. Luxemburg taught at Berlin's Social Democratic Party school from 1907 to 1914, and in 1913, she published *The Accumulation of Capital*, a book about economic imperialism.

Luxemburg became more internationalist in her thinking, working with, among others, Liebknecht, Jogiches, and French socialist politician Jean Jaurés to unify European socialist parties and workers' groups to stop World War I, which she believed would be fought over imperialism and nationalism. Although she had predicted it, she was devastated by the onset of the war, particularly when the Social Democratic Party supported Germany's invasion of France and French socialists supported the French war effort. In 1916, Luxemburg was imprisoned for her efforts to organize antiwar demonstrations and a general strike and to encourage young men to refuse the draft. During this time, she wrote *The Russian Revolution* (1922), a book critical of Lenin and the methods of the Russian Bolsheviks, which she saw as a move toward dictatorship. In it, she famously declared, "Freedom is always the freedom of the one who thinks differently."

After Luxemburg was freed from prison in November 1918, she and Liebknecht founded the newspaper *Red Flag*, which supported amnesty for political prisoners. The Spartacist League joined with other groups to become the Communist Party of Germany, led by Luxemburg and Liebknecht, who favored violent revolution. Although Luxemburg supported the formation of the Weimar Republic, she was outvoted, by other members of the party, and in January 1919, the Communists tried to seize power in Berlin. Luxemburg and Liebknecht joined the attempted revolution and were captured and killed by the anti-Communist Freikorps (Free Corps), under the direction of Social Democratic leader Friedrich Ebert.

Justin Corfield

See also: Marxist Cycle Model.

Further Reading

Basso, Lelio. *Rosa Luxemburg, A Reappraisal.* London: Deutsch, 1975.

Bronner, Stephen Eric. *Rosa Luxemburg: A Revolutionary for Our Times.* University Park: Pennsylvania State University Press, 1997.

Ettinger, Elzbieta. *Rosa Luxemburg: A Life.* London: Pandora, 1988.

Hudis, Peter, and Kevin B. Anderson, eds. *The Rosa Luxemburg Reader.* New York: Monthly Review, 2004.

Nettl, J.P. *Rosa Luxemburg.* London: Oxford University Press, 1966.

Shepardson, Donald E. *Rosa Luxemburg and the Noble Dream.* New York: Peter Lang, 1996.

Madoff, Bernard (1938–)

An influential securities industry executive on Wall Street, Bernard Madoff became a prominent symbol of corporate corruption in December 2008, when he confessed to running the largest Ponzi scheme in history, said to have bilked investors of more than $50 billion. For decades, Madoff had run a successful brokerage firm alongside a secretive investment management business that billed itself as a hedge fund. On March 12, 2009, Madoff pleaded guilty to eleven federal counts of fraud, and on June 29 of that year, he was sentenced to 150 years in prison.

Born on April 29, 1938, Madoff grew up in Laurelton, a small town in Queens, New York. He married Ruth Alpern in 1959 and graduated from Hofstra College the following year. In 1960, he founded a broker-dealer firm, Bernard L. Madoff Investment Securities, with a $50,000 loan from Ruth's parents. At first working alone, and later with his brother Peter and other family members, Madoff ran this legitimate brokerage firm until his arrest in December 2008.

Although Madoff likely will be remembered for the illegal Ponzi scheme that he operated, he was an influential figure on Wall Street for years before he became a household name. His early adoption of computerized trading helped his firm gain a reputation as an efficient provider of quick trades. Madoff also helped popularize the nascent Nasdaq stock market, which was founded in 1971 as an alternative venue for stock trading.

Madoff's promotion of the Nasdaq won him favor with the Securities and Exchange Commission (SEC). During the 1970s, he essentially was running a "third market" for stock trades. SEC regulators, attempting to crack down on monopolies, were glad to take advantage of the competition and transparency that this new market offered. Madoff also popularized the now-standard practice of paying customers a nominal amount in return for their business (paying for "order flow"), served on several self-regulation boards within the securities industry, donated to both Republican and Democratic politicians, and lobbied for restructuring of the stock market.

The early success of Madoff Investment Securities was aided by the support of Madoff's father-in-law, Saul Alpern. Managers at Alpern's accounting firm acted as unlicensed money managers for their clients, sending business to Madoff in return for commissions. From the 1960s to 1992, when the SEC intervened, workers at Alpern's firm gener-

New York financier Bernard Madoff, charged with running a Ponzi scheme that cost investors an estimated $50–$65 billion, was seen as a symbol of the greed and corruption endemic in the American financial community. *(Hiroko Masuike/Stringer/ Getty Images)*

ated more than half a billion dollars for Madoff Investment Securities through referrals.

These referrals also provided a steady stream of potential clients for the investment management business that Madoff had begun running on the side. Madoff offered an improbably high rate of return on investments, but he was extremely private about the details of his investment strategies. The secretive nature of Madoff's operation lent it the appeal of an elite club, and Madoff soon built a large network of satisfied and loyal clients. Meanwhile, his brokerage business offered a convenient cover for his unregulated investment management activities. Madoff moved money between the firms as needed, using profits from one operation to cover cash shortages in the other.

At the start of his career, Madoff seems to have invested his clients' money legitimately. At some point, however, he began operating a Ponzi scheme. Madoff testified that he began the scheme in 1991; others charged that it actually began sometime

around the stock market crash of 1987, possibly earlier. Ponzi schemes use money received from new investors to pay "returns" to current investors. This allows the operator to simulate huge returns, when in fact those returns are just money borrowed from future investors. Ponzi schemes are difficult to get out of once they are begun, because all investors eventually will demand to be paid. Because the operator is promising more money than he actually has, he can never make good on all of the promises and must keep taking in more money from new investors in order to fund payouts to current investors.

By 2008, Madoff's Ponzi scheme was falling apart. The tight capital market, fueled by the financial crisis, prompted many of his investors to withdraw their money, and Madoff could not keep up with the demand. In addition, regulatory changes had reduced the profitability of brokerage activities, meaning that Madoff could no longer use excess profits from his legitimate broker-dealer business to pay out promised returns.

On December 10, 2008, Madoff's sons, Andrew and Mark Madoff, contacted the Federal Bureau of Investigation, saying that Madoff had confessed to them that he had been running a Ponzi scheme for years. On March 12, 2009, Madoff pleaded guilty to eleven federal charges of fraud, and on June 29, U.S. District Court Judge Denny Chin sentenced him to serve 150 years in prison and forfeit $170 billion in assets.

Madoff's Ponzi scheme was unprecedented in scale. The actual dollar amount of the fraud likely will never be known, but some estimate that Madoff went to prison owing investors more than $50 billion (including fabricated returns). Pension funds, university endowments, charities, and individual investors lost millions to the scheme. Exactly how Madoff managed to operate the scam on such a large scale and for so long remains unknown. It is also unclear to what extent other executives in the firm knew about his illegal activities. Madoff's guilty plea meant that he was not required to cooperate with investigations into others' involvement.

Many observers regarded the Madoff case as symptomatic of inadequate regulation in the financial sector. Regulatory agencies failed to investigate his operations despite many red flags. For instance, many of Madoff's family members held key positions in Madoff Investment Securities—an unusual arrangement for a financial firm. Madoff also reported suspiciously high returns in his investment management business, but the SEC never scrutinized these investment activities. Beginning in 2000, former financial industry executive Harry Markopolos repeatedly went to the SEC with accusations and evidence that Madoff was engaging in illegal activities, but his warnings went unheeded.

For many observers, Madoff became a symbol of rampant greed and corruption on Wall Street, and his scheme came to light in the midst of a national reassessment of the U.S. financial system. Against a backdrop of corporate wrongdoing and crumbling financial institutions, Madoff's actions fueled public cynicism about the financial sector in the United States. The Madoff scandal, remarkable for its magnitude, likely will remain an enduring symbol of the worst excesses of the financial system of the early twenty-first century.

Suzanne Julian

See also: Hedge Funds; Ponzi Scheme (1919–1920).

Further Reading

Arvedlund, Erin. *Too Good to Be True: The Rise and Fall of Bernie Madoff.* New York: Portfolio, 2009.

Kirtzman, Andrew. *Betrayal: The Life and Lies of Bernie Madoff.* New York: HarperCollins, 2009.

Strober, Deborah H. *Catastrophe: The Story of Bernard L. Madoff, the Man Who Swindled the World.* Beverly Hills, CA: Phoenix, 2009.

Malthus, Thomas Robert (1766–1834)

Thomas Robert Malthus was a British demographer and economist best known for his belief that unchecked population growth always exceeds the means of subsistence or support. This theory was important to Malthus's concept of economic crises within the business cycle, such as it was understood in the early nineteenth century. He extended this theory—and his inquiries into economic processes in general—to formulate the famous theory of classical economics, which became the basis, directly or indirectly, of later business-cycle theory.

Early Years

Malthus was born on February 14, 1766, near Guildford, Surrey, England. He first was home-schooled, then attended Jesus College, Cambridge University, graduating in 1784; he received a master's degree from Cambridge in 1791 and became a fellow in 1793. He was ordained in 1797 and briefly served as a country parson. He married in 1804, and in 1805, he was named a professor of history and political economy at Haileybury, where he remained until his death on December 29, 1834, near Bath, England.

Theory of Population Growth and Economic Survival

Malthus was a product of the Age of Enlightenment, a period when intellectual pursuits and rational discourse were encouraged as a way to unlock the secrets of nature. His views, first articulated in *An Essay on the Principle of Population* (1798), contradicted those of such eighteenth-century notables as Jean-Jacques Rousseau, William Godwin, and Benjamin Franklin, who believed that high fertility rates caused economic booms by increasing the number of available workers. In Malthus's view, high growth rates led to serious economic problems, as a country's population continued to grow at a much faster rate than its food supply. Such an imbalance in

Thomas Malthus's theory of human demography—that population unchecked by disease, war, or famine increases much faster than food supplies—has had an enduring influence on the study of history and economics, including the business cycle. *(The Granger Collection, New York)*

the growth rates of population and food supply would lead to a scarcity of food, resulting in starvation, poverty, disease, and war. He believed that the only way to avoid such terrible consequences was to slow population growth through "moral restraint" (including late marriage and abstinence) and the use of contraception.

Malthus's theory, advanced for its day, provoked resistance within the Church of England as well as in more conservative sectors of society. He was reviled by many contemporaries as hard-hearted, a prophet of doom, and an enemy of the working class. More forward-looking thinkers recognized his work as the first serious economic study of the welfare of the lower classes. Later, many twentieth-century economists, including Julian Simon, dismissed Malthus's prophecies of disaster on empirical grounds. In their view, massive population growth had not led to catastrophe in more developed economies, primarily because the industrial and technological revolutions of the late nineteenth and early twentieth centuries had increased productivity across economic sectors, including agriculture. However, twentieth-century social scientists researching economic development pointed to Malthus's theory as a good predictor of what could happen in economically underdeveloped countries.

Trade

Malthus believed that international trade policy, especially regarding food, was necessary to delay the dire economic and social consequences anticipated by his theory of population growth. However, his views on international trade were inconsistent. He started out as a "free-trader," supporting, in 1814, free trade in corn (i.e., grain) by eliminating tariffs because the cultivation of the British variety of corn was increasingly expensive. He supported free-trade economists—most notably Adam Smith and David Ricardo—who believed that it was economically beneficial for a country (Great Britain) to rely on foreign sources for food if other nations could produce food more efficiently and cheaply.

At first, Malthus saw free trade in food as a way to alleviate the burden of feeding a rapidly growing population. However, he changed his position in 1815 when he threw his support to the protectionists, thus acknowledging the realities of international trade. He argued that other countries often prohibited the import of British goods, or raised taxes on imported goods (corn) to make it too expensive to buy. If Britain were to continue accepting imports of foreign corn from uncooperative countries, it would be at a trade disadvantage and its food supply would be held captive to foreign politics, potentially leading to food shortages in England. Malthus encouraged the support of domestic food production to guarantee that Britain would remain self-sustaining.

Other Economic Inquiries

Malthus was interested in other economic issues as well. In a pamphlet published in 1800, *The Present High Price of Provisions,* he advanced a theory that linked price levels with the rise and fall of an economy's money supply, arguing that rising prices were followed by increases in the money supply. He also investigated the causes of fluctuations in property values (such as the price to purchase or rent land). He determined that such fluctuations resulted from the combined factors of agricultural yields and the availability (or scarcity) of land.

Economist David Ricardo, a contemporary, incorporated Malthus's theory of "rents" with his own theory of "profits" to create an early version of the classical theory of economics, which linked optimal prices with supply conditions. But Malthus was not entirely comfortable with Ricardo's theory. In his own treatise, *Principles of Economics* (1820), Malthus took an important step beyond Ricardo—and a major stride toward formulating the complete theory of classical economics—by introducing the idea of a "demand" schedule, in

which supply and demand together determine the optimal pricing of goods.

Abhijit Roy

See also: Classical Theories and Models; Demographic Cycle.

Further Reading
Brander, James A. "Viewpoint: Sustainability: Malthus Revisited?" *Canadian Journal of Economics* 40:1 (February 2007): 1–38.
Brown, Lester R., Gary Gardner, and Brian Halweil. *Beyond Malthus: Sixteen Dimensions of the Population Problem.* Washington, DC: Worldwatch Institute, 1998.
Dixon, Robert. "Carlyle, Malthus and Sismondi: The Origins of Carlyle's Dismal View of Political Economy." *History of Economics Review* 44 (Summer 2006): 32–38.
Hollander, Samuel. *The Economics of Thomas Robert Malthus.* Toronto: University of Toronto Press, 1997.
Sachs, Jeffrey D. "The Specter of Malthus Returns." *Scientific American* 299:3 (September 2008): 38.
Turner, Michael, ed. *Malthus and His Time.* Houndmills, UK: Macmillan, 1986.

Manufacturing

In economics, manufacturing refers to the application of capital goods, labor, and resources to the production of goods. These goods can be divided into two basic categories: consumer goods, such as appliances and clothes, that are destined largely for consumers, and capital goods, such as machines, tools, and equipment, that are used in the manufacture of other goods and purchased by businesses. Manufacturing represents one of the main pillars of activity in any economy, along with agriculture, extractive industries (such as timber or mining), service industries, and the financial sector. Manufacturing, which both affects the business cycle and is affected by it, has undergone a long-term transformation, rising to importance in the developed, or industrialized, countries of Europe, North America, and Japan from the late eighteenth to the mid-twentieth century, before undergoing a slow decline in those areas and an increase in regions of the developing world, most notably East Asia.

History

Traditionally, manufacturing was the province of skilled craftsmen, who usually worked by themselves or in small shops, employing hand-held tools. While this model still survives in both the developed world (usually for highly specialized and often elite goods, such as concert-quality violins or haute couture fashion) and the developing world (for many simple and inexpensive products, such as basic clothing or utensils), it gradually has been replaced—beginning with the first industrial revolution of the late eighteenth and early nineteenth centuries—by a very different model of production. The industrial model of manufacturing utilizes new sources of energy (primarily coal and oil) to run machines in order to mass-produce goods.

Besides making goods cheaper and more plentiful, industrialization deeply affected the labor force as well. Workers no longer labored in small shops but in factories with many employees. Moreover, workers were de-skilled after a fashion, as they no longer had to learn the complex tasks of hand manufacturing; instead, they only needed to be trained in the relatively simple tasks associated with operating machinery and performing assembly line work.

While the technology involved in manufacturing has undergone countless improvements and innovations over the past 250 years, the manufacturing process itself was based on two revolutionary ideas. The first was the concept of interchangeable parts, developed in the late eighteenth century. With components made to set specifications, complex goods could be manufactured more cheaply, as the same kind of part would always fit in the same finished good. The second innovation—the assembly line—came in the late nineteenth and early twentieth centuries, beginning in the American meat-packing industry but perfected, most famously, by American auto manufacturer Henry Ford. By breaking down the process of building highly complex products, such as automobiles, into simple tasks and bringing the materials to the worker, rather than having the worker fetch them, Ford dramatically reduced the amount of time—and hence labor costs—necessary for the manufacture of automobiles, putting these once elite consumer goods into the hands of working- and middle-class purchasers.

These innovations—new forms of energy, new technologies, and new production models—could only fully be realized by those who had—or had access to—large amounts of capital. Industrialization, then, removed the means of production from the hands of workers and put it into the hands of those who owned the capital, that is, the factory owners. Unable to compete—both because machine manufacturing produced goods cheaper than workers could by hand and because ordinary workers could not afford to buy the machines—workers were forced to sell their labor to the highest bidder. Thus, the modern wage system of employment was born. At the same time, innovations in manufacturing steadily lowered the prices of goods, making it possible for ordinary people to afford them, thus ushering in the modern consumer age.

De-Industrialization

England was home to the first industrial revolution, but the technologies and methods pioneered there soon were adopted in other parts of the world during the nineteenth century—notably in continental Europe, North America, and Japan. In the years since World War II, however, industrialization has spread to all parts of the world, most notably East Asia and, to a lesser extent, the more economically advanced countries of Southeast Asia and Latin America.

This has led to a phenomenon known as de-industrialization in parts of the older industrialized countries of Europe, North America, and Japan, where economies have become more dependent on the provision of services rather than the production of goods. Whereas roughly one in three employed Americans worked in manufacturing in 1950, by the first decade of the twenty-first century, that figure had declined to about one in eight. This decline is attributable to several factors, among them new technologies that improved productivity—that is, allowed each worker to produce more output in a set period of time—and the outsourcing of manufacturing to low-wage countries such as Mexico, India, Southeast Asia, Taiwan, and, eventually, mainland China.

While the decline undoubtedly has hurt those areas that once were centers of manufacturing—such as the so-called rust belt states in the Midwest and Northeast or the Midlands and north of England—economists vigorously debate the impact of de-industrialization on the U.S. economy as a whole and whether that impact has been good or bad. Some argue that the loss of high-paying manufacturing jobs has hollowed out the middle class and contributed to the stagnation of real wages (i.e., wages accounting for inflation) since the 1970s, despite growth in real gross domestic product per capita of more than 50 percent. They also point to the huge trade deficits that the de-industrialization process has contributed to as dangerous to the country's long-term economic health, as they require large influxes of capital to finance, undermining the country's ability to set its own monetary policy.

Others, however, argue that the shift of manufacturing to low-wage countries has benefited Americans in several ways. Most importantly, they say, the shift of manufacturing to low-cost countries has brought down the price of goods, making Americans better off in material terms, even if wages have remained stagnant. As for trade deficits, they maintain that these have more to do with the imbalance of savings and investment at home. If domestic capital can be utilized more profitably in other sectors, such as housing or finance, then this necessitates borrowing from abroad. Of course, the recent shift of large sums of capital into these two sectors has been blamed for both the housing bubble and the financial crisis of the late 2000s. Moreover, those who say that de-industrialization is not necessarily a bad thing contend that services are an ever more critical ele-

ment in advanced economies and, here, the United States runs a significant surplus.

How an economist or economic policy maker views de-industrialization and trade often determines what he or she thinks should be done—or not done—about them. Virtually all experts and policy makers agree that the free flow of capital at the heart of this globalization process is, in sum, a positive force, enriching both developing and developed economies. But those who worry about de-industrialization—particularly labor unions and union-oriented economists (unionized workers in the private sector are highly concentrated in manufacturing)—say that the United States should strictly enforce international wage and environmental standards, so that developing-world countries do not have an unfair advantage over the United States.

Business Cycle

Along with these long-term trends, manufacturing is deeply affected by the business cycle. When consumer demand flags and business inventories build up, manufacturing output usually goes into decline, leading to increased unemployment, which can contribute further to waning demand. In addition, because manufacturing is so dependent on financial capital—most industries need steady flows of credit to meet payroll, purchase raw materials, and purchase capital equipment—the tightening credit markets that often are associated with—or that trigger—recessions can make it difficult for manufacturers to operate at full capacity or expand, leading to reductions in investment and hiring.

For example, during the 1930s, when manufacturing represented a much greater component of the American economy, the collapse in the credit markets and weakening consumer demand led to a massive drop in industrial production, roughly 37 percent between the peak of August 1929 and the trough of March 1933. By comparison, during the most recent recession, industrial production in the United States was off by about 15 percent between the onset of the downturn in the fourth quarter of 2007 and its end in the second quarter of 2009.

James Ciment

See also: Bethlehem Steel; Chrysler; Fleetwood Enterprises; General Motors; Industrial Policy; Production Cycles.

Further Reading

Beatty, Jack, ed. *Colossus: How the Corporation Changed America.* New York: Broadway, 2001.

Bluestone, Barry, and Bennett Harrison. *The Deindustrialization of America: Plant Closings, Community Abandonment, and the Dismantling of Basic Industry.* New York: Basic Books, 1982.

Kenton, Lawrence V., ed. *Manufacturing Output, Productivity, and Employment Indications.* New York: Novinka/Nova Science, 2005.

Whitford, Josh. *The New Old Economy: Networks, Institutions, and Organizational Transformation of American Manufacturing.* New York: Oxford University Press, 2005.

Market Trends

Usually referring to the valuation of corporate securities as listed on key market indices, such as the Dow Jones Industrial Average (DJIA), market trends—that is, the direction of key market indices—fall into two basic categories: "bull" and "bear." A bull market is a period in which the value of corporate securities, or stocks, is collectively trending upward; a bear market is a period in which those stocks are collectively trending downward. The identification of a trend is based on real money terms, accounting for inflation. In other words, if stock prices remain flat for an extended period of time, inflation is actually lowering their value, producing what is, in effect, a bear market. Although market trends are widely reported in the media, the whys and hows of their connection to the real economy are disputed among economists.

Since bull and bear markets concern collective market trends, it is possible that a specific stock or even an entire stock sector, such as technology, may decline in an overall bull market or rise in an overall bear market. Even in the strong bull markets, there may be particular companies or sectors of the economy that are suffering; conversely, even in the bleakest bear markets, companies and sectors may be found that are doing quite well. Moreover, a bull market or bear market does not necessarily mean that the overall price index will go up or down every trading day—only that it is trending in one direction or the other over time.

(The origins of the terms "bull" and "bear" are obscure and disputed. "Bull" may derive from the German word *buellen*, meaning "to roar." "Bear" may have come from the pessimistic attitudes of bearskin wholesalers on the European exchange in the eighteenth and nineteenth centuries. Others suggest that "bull" and "bear" reflect the animals' methods of attack—a bull thrusts upward with its horns; a bear swipes downward with its claws.)

Relationship to General Economy

The relationship between market trends and the performance of the actual economy—productivity, output, growth, employment, and other such factors—is complicated and not always synchronous. That is because market trends are driven more by expectations of economic performance than by the real-time performance of the overall economy. Stock market investing is, after all, a form of gambling, albeit one based on informed decision rather than guessing. In other words, bull markets are driven by an expectation that the economy—or a sector of it, in the case of a more selective investment—will turn around or continue to expand. In addition, market trends are based on changes in corporate profitability that may not be indicative of the overall economy if, for example, profits rise or fall because of changes in conditions in other countries, or because of changes in tax laws. Finally, the market trends may not indicate overall well-being of the typical citizen if, for example, corporate profits increase while take-home pay falls.

Thus, bull markets are often related to overall business cycles but generally not in real time. Bull

The two great symbols of trends in the financial marketplace—bulls and bears, captured in this 1879 painting by William H. Beard—are of uncertain origin. According to one explanation, a bull throws you up in the air and a bear knocks you down. *(The Granger Collection, New York)*

markets begin when indices begin to trend upward from a trough or a low point in overall securities valuations. Conversely, bear markets begin when market indices begin to trend downward from a plateau or a high point in overall securities valuations. Thus, bull markets tend to begin during periods in which the overall economy is doing badly but investors come to believe that an economic turnaround is imminent. For example, despite mass layoffs in 2009 and anemic or negative economic growth, the Dow Jones Industrial Average (DJIA) increased by some 50 percent between March and October. In such a scenario, investors have come to believe that a period of corporate profitability is about to begin, even if companies are losing money at that particular time. By this reasoning, stocks are seen as undervalued. Alternatively, bear markets begin when investors come to believe that stock prices are overvalued and that profits are likely to decline in the future. In this respect, bull and bear markets presage general trends in the economy. It remains true, of course,

that an extended period of economic expansion is likely to be accompanied by a bull market, and an extended period of economic contraction is likely to be accompanied by a bear market.

"Efficient Market Theory"

Mainstream economists invoke the concept of "efficient market theory" to explain stock prices and overall market trends. According to this view, securities markets are highly proficient at absorbing the kinds of financial information that affects stock prices. In other words, new information affects a given stock price or index value but is quickly absorbed. Thus, at any given time, the stock market is likely to have acknowledged all relevant information and factored it into the price of a given security or index. According to the efficient market theory, a theory of market behavior dating from the 1960s, current prices include all past information so that new information is unpredictable and arrives "unannounced," causing prices to rise as often as it causes prices to fall. As a result, price changes look random, resembling the pattern of somebody rambling without a specific destination (hence the name "random walk" for this phenomenon). In other words, there is no magic formula for beating the market. Especially in the long term, an investor can only do as well as the overall market by absorbing and correctly analyzing relevant information. At any given time, of course, an investor can beat the market by predicting or guessing at the random movements better than others. (This ignores the possibility of "insider trading," whereby an investor acts on knowledge not available to the investment community at large; such unfair practices undermine faith in the markets and are punishable by severe criminal penalties.)

Nevertheless, economists also observe that certain anomalies undermine efficient market theory. These anomalies derive from the fact that investors are human beings and their decisions subject to emotion, personal psychology, or sheer impulse. It has been long noted, for example, that certain characteristics of stocks—such as high dividends or a high earnings-to-price ratio—attract investors, pumping their perceived value beyond the level suggested by other indicators.

Herd Mentality

The herd instinct—another human trait—plays an important role as well. If a given investor has come to believe that, in a bull market, others are likely to buy a particular stock, the investor is likely to pay more for the stock than the available information indicates it is worth. In other words, all indicators may suggest that the stock is worth $10 per share, but if an investor comes to believe—based on past performance or future expectation—that others are willing to pay more than $10, he or she may pay $20 for the stock in the hope that its price will rise to, say, $30.

This mentality is precisely what causes bubbles, such as the one that drove stock prices to dizzying heights in the 1920s, far above their intrinsic value.

The DJIA soared 150 percent between 1925 and 1929, far in excess of the rise in corporate earnings. The same mentality, in reverse, pertains in bear markets, where investors sell shares below their intrinsic value because others are selling. Thus, in the aftermath of the Great Crash of 1929, the DJIA fell by more than 80 percent—also well in excess of the decline in corporate earnings.

A more recent example of the herd mentality and market bubbles occurred in the dot.com boom and bust of the late 1990s and early 2000s. With incessant talk of the Internet "changing business as we know it," investors rushed to buy shares in companies exploiting the new technology, even if those companies were losing money and had business models that left management experts shaking their heads. High-tech stock prices soared on this herd mentality, as investors came to believe in "first mover advantage"—that the first company to exploit an Internet niche was likely to thrive. In other words, with investors wanting to get in on the ground floor, they flocked to every initial public offering (IPO) of shares in a high-tech firm. Federal Reserve Board chairman Alan Greenspan characterized the phenomenon as "irrational exuberance." Inevitably, as in the crash of the 1930s, the crash in Internet stocks that began in early 2000 sent the price of even tried and tested Internet companies plummeting. The herd of investors hastened the sell-off just as aggressively as they had fueled the buy-up, fearful that they would lose even the meager remains of their initial investment. In short, investors in bubble and bust markets tend to base their buy and sell decisions on what other investors are doing rather than on the intrinsic value of the stock or the market generally.

Economists also debate the cause-and-effect relationship between market trends and real economic performance overall. In other words, they question whether market trends merely reflect overall performance or play a role in shaping it. Most economic historians have come to the conclusion, for example, that the stock market crash of 1929 was a contributing factor to the Great Depression but not the most important one.

That is because so few people—about one in ten Americans—actually had money in the markets at the time and because other factors, such as growing inequalities in wealth and income and lagging sectors such as agriculture, played a more important role in the economic collapse of the 1930s. In the early 2000s, however, far more people have a financial stake in the equities market, particularly for their retirement savings. If people come to believe that their retirement is in jeopardy, say economists, they may curtail current spending, thereby dampening or reversing economic growth. In such cases, market trends can affect real economic performance in a significant way.

James Ciment

See also: Confidence, Consumer and Business; Financial Markets; Stock Markets, Global.

Further Reading

Cassidy, John. *Dot.con: The Greatest Story Ever Sold.* New York: HarperCollins, 2002.

Galbraith, John Kenneth. *The Great Crash, 1929.* Boston: Houghlin Mifflin, 1997.

Gross, Daniel. *Pop! Why Bubbles Are Great for the Economy.* New York: Collins Business, 2007.

Spencer, Roger W., and John H. Huston. *The Federal Reserve and the Bull Markets: From Benjamin Strong to Alan Greenspan.* Lewiston, NY: Edwin Mellen, 2006.

Marshall, Alfred (1842–1924)

The theories of Alfred Marshall dominated British economic thought from the late nineteenth century to the late 1930s, when the views of John Maynard Keynes gained prominence. As one of the founders of the "neoclassical school," Marshall made enormous contributions to the development of the field of economics, including its establishment as a separate academic discipline.

Born in London on July 26, 1842, Marshall studied mathematics and political economy at the University of Cambridge. He became professor of political economy at the University of Bristol in 1882, before accepting the position of professor of political economy at Cambridge in 1885. During his time there, he published his major work, *Principles of Economics* (1890), which became the leading British textbook in economics for decades; it ran to eight editions between 1890 and 1920. Marshall was also a tutor to Keynes and active in creating a separate degree for economics within the university. Although he retired early in 1908, his work provided the foundation for much British economic thought throughout the 1920s and 1930s. Marshall died in Cambridge on July 13, 1924.

The centerpiece of Marshall's work was what economists refer to as partial equilibrium analysis. His theories focused on individual commodity markets, ignoring the influence that changes in these markets had on other markets, and vice versa. In other words, he considered individual commodity markets in isolation.

In his research on economics, Marshall applied the methodology of a physical scientist by isolating physical systems from external influences to better analyze selected critical variables. This allowed him to study in detail how the economic "laws" of supply and demand worked within a particular market, and to better understand the relationships between the two critical economic variables: price and quantity.

The law of supply states that as prices rise, producers will increase output to get more of their goods on the market. The law of demand states that as prices fall, consumers will buy greater quantities of a good. In microeconomic textbooks, this simplified system is represented by a graph with an upward-sloping supply curve and a downward-sloping demand curve—the famous "scissors" model of supply and demand. The interaction of supply and demand, therefore, determines both market prices and quantities. Market equilibrium (the point at which producers will sell all their goods) occurs when the supply curve and the demand curve intersect (since this is the only point at which the conditions of both laws are satisfied). Market competition (influenced by the wants and incomes of consumers) is assumed to drive actual prices to their equilibrium price. This model is also used to explain other economic and historical phenomena.

Another of Marshall's contributions to economics, which grew out of his research on the laws of supply and demand within markets, was the idea of price elasticity. Now a fundamental concept for economists, price elasticity relates to the relative responsiveness (or sensitivity) of one variable, such as demand, to changes in price. For example, if the price elasticity of demand for X is given as 3.1, a 1 percent increase in price will, if all other factors remain constant, generate a 3.1 percent reduction in the quantity demanded. In this example, the relationship is defined as elastic because the change in price has a significant effect on the quantity demanded. If, however, the price elasticity of demand for good Y is given as 0.7, the same 1 percent increase in price will generate only a 0.7 percent reduction in the quantity demanded. In this example, the relationship between price and demand is "inelastic" because the change in price has a relatively minor effect on the quantity demanded.

Principles of Economics was initially intended as a two-volume work, but Marshall never completed the second volume. However, material that was to have been included in Volume 2 found its way, in a somewhat fragmented fashion, into his last two works, *Industry and Trade* (1919) and *Money, Credit and Commerce* (1923). Marshall's discussion of the business cycle, for example, was noticeably disjointed. It provided more of a description of the sequence of a cycle than an explanation of the various forces that are at work in the cycle. In his model of the business cycle, Marshall describes the following sequence: Rising business confidence leads to increased borrowing from banks, and hence an increase in the price level. The growing demand for loans pushes interest rates very high. Borrowers must sell goods in order to pay their debts. Prices fall, and business failures increase. Nevertheless, Marshall's contributions to economic analysis continued to influence the teaching of the subject throughout the world well into the twentieth century.

Christopher Godden

See also: Classical Theories and Models; Hawtrey, Ralph George; Lerner, Abba P.; Neoclassical Theories and Models.

Further Reading

Groenewagen, Peter. *A Soaring Eagle: Alfred Marshall, 1842–1924.* Cheltenham, UK: Edward Elgar, 1995.

Marshall, Alfred. *Industry and Trade.* London: Macmillan, 1919.

———. *Money, Credit and Commerce.* London: Macmillan, 1923.

———. *Principles of Economics.* Amherst, NY: Prometheus, 1997. First published 1890.

Reisman, David. *The Economics of Alfred Marshall.* London: Macmillan, 1986.

Marx, Karl (1818–1883)

Karl Heinrich Marx was a highly original thinker whose writings on the nature and limitations of the capitalist system were fundamental to the rise of socialist thought and government—including the communist state—in the twentieth century. His writings continue to provide essential insights for students of economics, philosophy, history, politics, and law. Within the realm of economics, Marx's analysis of the exploitation of labor in the capitalistic system served as the basis for political theories of business cycles.

Born on May 5, 1818, in Trier, Germany, Marx was educated at the University of Bonn and the University of Berlin, where he received a doctorate in philosophy in 1841. He became the editor of a radical newspaper, *Rheinische Zeitung*, which was shut down by the Prussian government in 1843 for promoting dangerous viewpoints. Marx fled to Paris, where he became involved with a number of early socialist and communist groups. His friendship and working association with German social scientist Friedrich Engels led to the publication of the *Communist Manifesto* in 1848, a work that develops the political and governmental implications of his fundamental ideas, calling for a workers' revolution. After being expelled from Paris for such incendiary work, Marx and his family settled in London in 1849.

Through his growing interest in political economy, which focuses on the role of the state in economic matters, Marx came to the belief that in order to change the institutional framework of the capitalist system, it was first necessary to develop a solid understanding of how capitalism functioned. After much study in the reading room at the British Library, he produced the first volume of his famous critique of capitalism and political economy, *Das Kapital*, in 1867. Two further volumes, left incomplete at the time of his death, were edited by Engels and eventually published in 1885 and 1894.

The Marxist interpretation of history emphasizes the importance of, and the close link between, social and economic relationships. Marx focused on the exploitation of one group by another, especially of labor by capitalists. Within the capitalist system of commodity production and exchange, in Marx's view, workers (the "proletariat") are forced to sell their labor to capitalists (the "bourgeoisie"). Given that the capitalists are the sole owners of land and capital—the critical factors of production—workers possess no means of support other than to offer themselves as wage labor. The large pool of readily available labor places downward pressure on wage rates, which reduces worker income. This increases the profits of factory owners, which come through extracting surplus value, or the value created by the worker minus the amount paid to the worker. Capitalists can also increase surplus value by utilizing capital equipment or speeding up the rate of production, while keeping wages at the same level. At the same time, these capitalist forces further immiserate the working classes. Marx considered this to be exploitation of the worker, pure and simple. In his view, the capitalist system is founded at its core upon the vulnerability of the laboring classes.

A central element of Marx's economic philosophy was his theory of the trade cycle and economic

For Karl Marx, business cycles in the capitalist system are predicated on the exploitation of labor. Because business-owners profit by exploiting workers, he said, shifts in the balance between capital and labor in the production process cause profits to rise or fall. *(Time & Life Pictures/Getty Images)*

development. During the upswing of the cycle, he maintained, competition between entrepreneurs for labor—due to increased economic activity—leads to sharp increases in wages. The rise in costs to capitalists causes them to modify the production process, incorporating more capital equipment and allowing them to cut back on labor. This was precisely the trade-off that occurred during the industrial revolution. However, Marx observed, given that capitalists derive profit from the exploitation of labor, any change in the relative size of capital and labor in the production process will cause the rate of profit to decline (because there would be less labor to exploit).

Because this tendency would be associated with the downswing of the cycle, it would lead to an increase in unemployment. The resulting downward pressure on wages—given the lower demand for labor—would counteract the tendency of profits to decline by reducing the costs of production. This, in turn, would constitute an incentive to expand production once again and thereby trigger a new upswing of the cycle.

The repetition of these cycles, Marx argued, would cause the growing misery of the working class and the increasing concentration of economic and political power in the hands of a few capitalists. Rising social unrest, he argued, would eventually lead to the collapse of the capitalist mode of production. Although Marx detailed what he believed to be the long-term "laws of motion" associated with capitalism, he provided little analysis of the economic structure that would eventually replace it.

Despite the obvious limitations of Marx's analysis—most noticeably his failure to anticipate the flexibility of capitalism and the rigidity of socialist governments—his work continues to generate a vast literature, and Marxist theory continues to provide important insights into the global nature of modern-day capitalism.

Christopher Godden

See also: China; Classical Theories and Models; Eastern Europe; Marxist Cycle Model; Russia and the Soviet Union.

Further Reading

Berlin, Isaiah. *Karl Marx: His Life and Environment.* Oxford, UK: Oxford University Press, 1978.

Marx, Karl. *Das Kapital.* 3 volumes. London: Penguin, 2004.

Marx, Karl, and Frederick Engels. *The Communist Manifesto.* London: Longman, 2005.

McLellen, David. *Karl Marx: His Life and Thought.* London: Macmillan, 1973.

Sweezy, Paul. *The Theory of Capitalist Development: Principles of Marxist Political Economy.* New York: Monthly Review, 1970.

Marxist Cycle Model

Although he was trained in the classical tradition, the nineteenth-century German political economist Karl Marx, whose ideas inspired social-ist parties around the world as well as communist revolutionaries from Moscow to Beijing to Havana in the twentieth century, offered a radical reinterpretation of the classical understanding of the business cycle. Rather than establishing a stable equilibrium of supply and demand, as classical economic thinkers asserted, capitalist economies in Marx's view are characterized by periodic crises and a secular trend toward diminishing profits and increasing exploitation of workers. A political thinker as well as an economist, Marx argued that such tendencies would inevitably lead to revolutionary upheaval, as workers rose up and overthrew the capitalist system, replacing it with a socialist model of economics. Marx's most developed theory of capitalist economic crisis exists only in sketchy form in Volume 3 of *Capital*, published after his death based on incomplete manuscripts.

Marx's life corresponded in time with the rapid expansion of the industrial revolution from its birthplace in England—where Marx spent many years working out his theories—to continental Europe. Technological advances, he noted, permitted capitalists (those who owned the means of production) to replace workers (those who were forced to sell their labor) with machines. While this process allowed for increased profits at the microeconomic level of individual firms, it came with great macroeconomic costs for society in general.

Rising profits provided the capital for further investment. But as more capitalists invested, competition rose and profits fell, leading to periodic economic busts until new advances allowed the process to begin again. Meanwhile, all of the capital investment in equipment put more and more workers out of a job, creating what Marx called "the reserve army of the unemployed." The masses of desperate people inevitably drove down wages, as workers competed with each other for the dwindling supply of available jobs. Moreover, working conditions would become more onerous as capitalists, desperate to preserve profits in the face of competition, accelerated the pace of work and imposed conditions that made workplaces ever more dangerous and unpleasant.

The general trend in capitalism, then, would be toward a smaller and richer capitalist class, as those able to survive the periodic busts in the business cycle bought up smaller firms and the capital equipment of failed firms at fire sale prices even as they captured ever greater shares of the market. Meanwhile, an expanding working class would become poorer and more immiserated. Impoverished laborers would no longer be able to buy the goods produced by capitalists, leading to ever more volatile swings in the business cycle.

There was a way out of this vicious circle, argued Marx. Capitalists could invest abroad in new markets, where profits were higher. Vladimir Lenin, Marx's early-twentieth-century disciple and leader of the Russian Revolution of 1917, elaborated on this idea, using it to explain why great economic powers seized colonies and then exploited their surplus value of labor and resources. But it was only a temporary solution, Lenin argued, as the same "contradictions" of capitalism in the metropolis inevitably would spread to other exploited countries and colonies.

Ultimately, Marx argued, there was no way to save capitalism from itself. Like other economic systems before it, he contended, capitalism contained the seeds of its own destruction. As workers became poorer, they would also become more politicized, recognizing that their condition could only improve with the overthrow of both the capitalist class and the capitalist system. The latter's replacement would come with socialism, where the means of production are owned by the workers themselves, thereby ending class tensions and the periodic crises of capitalism.

Marx never went very far into the specifics of how the socialist system would operate, and those who sought to put it into practice generally instituted command-style economies that failed to provide the carrots and sticks necessary to promote economic innovation, effective management, worker productivity, responsiveness to consumer needs and demands, or sustained economic growth. Moreover, Marx's critique of capitalism has also proved less than accurate; technological innovation has created unprecedented wealth, and workers, at least in industrialized countries, have seen their standards of living generally rise and their working conditions improve since the dark days of the industrial revolution of Marx's time. Still, Marx's idea that economic interests inform people's political and social values—a variation on the classical precept of self-interest driving economic growth—has become a bedrock of political science and sociological thought.

James Ciment

See also: China; Classical Theories and Models; Eastern Europe; Marx, Karl; Russia and the Soviet Union.

Further Reading

Glombowski, Jörg. "A Marxian Model of Long Run Capitalist Development." *Journal of Economics* 43:4 (December 1983): 363–382.

Hollander, Samuel. *The Economics of Karl Marx: Analysis and Application.* New York: Cambridge University Press, 2008.

Maksakovsky, Pavel V. *The Capitalist Cycle*, trans. Richard B. Day. Chicago: Haymarket, 2009.

Marx, Karl. *Capital: A Critique of Political Economy*, trans. Ben Fowkes. New York: Vintage, 1976–1981.

Merrill Lynch

Now an investment banking and wealth management division within Bank of America, Merrill Lynch was once the largest commercial brokerage house in the world and a major independent investment bank. Heavily exposed to mortgage-backed securities and other financial instruments whose value was undermined by the collapse in housing prices during the late 2000s, Merrill Lynch nearly went bankrupt before being acquired by Bank of America in September 2008, in a controversial deal brokered by Secretary of the Treasury Henry Paulson and Federal Reserve chairman Ben Bernanke.

From its origins in the late eighteenth century through the early years of the twentieth, the stock market was largely the domain of wealthy businessman and financiers in New York City and other financial centers in the Northeast and Midwest. Charles Merrill, the company's founder, and his partner Edmund Lynch, who joined a year later, realized that the American middle class represented a major pool of potential investors in corporate and other forms securities.

Drawing on the reserves of these modest investors, as well as major investors on Wall Street, Merrill Lynch capitalized on the newly emerging retail chain store industry, purchasing a controlling interest in Safeway in 1926, then a small group of local grocery stores in the West, and turning it into the nation's third-largest supermarket chain. Merrill Lynch prospered mightily on the deal and on gains from the stock market boom of the 1920s. Fearing that a bubble was emerging, however, the company began to urge its clients to divest themselves of risky investments in 1928 and shifted its own investments to low-risk financial instruments.

Despite these prudent moves, the company was hard hit by the stock market crash of 1929, and sold its retail brokerage business in 1930 to E.A. Pierce and Company in order to concentrate on investment banking. Throughout the 1930s and 1940s, Merrill Lynch—which joined with E.A. Pierce in 1940 and then with the New Orleans–based commodities trading and branch stock brokerage firm of Fenner & Beane in 1941—perfected its strategy of offering investors what it called a "department store of finance." In other words, the firm did not just buy and sell securities for investors, but also provided small investors with advice, education, seminars, and literature on how to buy, hold, and sell securities wisely. In 1959, the firm—now known as Merrill, Lynch, Pierce, Fenner, and Smith, after Beane dropped out of the firm and financier Winthrop Smith became a partner—became the first brokerage house to incorporate, and went public (sold ownership shares to the public) in 1971.

During the 1950s and 1960s, the company prospered by establishing a network of branch offices across the country, operated by more than 15,000 brokers. This allowed the company to place, or sell, the securities it underwrote directly, rather than having to go through independent brokers, as was the case with most investment banks. At the same time and into the 1970s and 1980s, the company also expanded aggressively abroad.

Its growth to become the largest investment bank in the world by the mid-1990s did not come without embarrassments and setbacks, however. In 1986, its reputation was besmirched when one of its brokers was arrested in a major securities fraud operation and its finances took a huge blow in the stock market crash of 1987. On Black Monday—October 19—the company lost $377 million, largely in mortgage-backed securities, the biggest single-day loss of any investment bank in U.S. history. In 1994, Merrill Lynch was implicated for having advised Orange County, California, treasurer Robert Citron to invest in high-risk securities, in violation of state law. The company ultimately settled with the county for $400 million, though it did not admit any wrongdoing, in 1998. But all of these problems would pale in comparison to the events of 2008.

By the early twenty-first century, Merrill Lynch had become Wall Street's number one underwriter of collateralized debt obligations—complex financial instruments that are backed by other securities, often mortgage-backed ones. Many of the collateralized debt obligations underwritten by Merrill Lynch were backed by subprime mortgages. These securities offered huge potential profits, but, as is the case with all such securities, they came with high risk—in this case, the potential that the low-income, poor-credit-history mortgage holders would default on their loans.

As housing prices collapsed in 2007, taking the secondary mortgage market with them, the company began to hemorrhage money. In January 2008, Merrill Lynch reported a fourth-quarter loss for 2007 of nearly $10 billion, most of it attributable to writing down subprime mortgage-related assets. Between mid-2007 and mid-2008, the company lost a total of nearly $20 billion, as its

ing panic in the global financial markets. But in subsequent months, details about the deal emerged that cast doubt on the motives and methods of mediators Paulson and Bernanke. Both, it was alleged, had strong-armed Bank of America's chairman, Kenneth Lewis, into making the deal, threatening him with increased regulatory scrutiny and action if he did not comply. Nor did Bank of America come off well. In early 2010, the Securities and Exchange Commission charged the bank's executives with hiding the huge losses sustained by Merrill Lynch in order to get shareholders to approve the merger.

James Ciment

See also: Bank of America; Banks, Investment; Recession and Financial Crisis (2007–).

Further Reading

Perkins, Edwin J. *Wall Street to Main Street: Charles Merrill and Middle-Class Investors.* New York: Cambridge University Press, 1999.

Story, Louis, and Julie Creswell. "For Bank of America and Merrill, Love Was Blind." *New York Times,* February 7, 2009.

U.S. Securities and Exchange Commission. *Securities and Exchange Commission v. Bank of America Corporation,* Civil Action no. 09-6829 (JSR) (S.D.N.Y.). Litigation Release no. 21371, January 11, 2010. Available at www.sec.gov/litigation/litreleases/2010/lr21371.htm. Accessed February 2010.

Bank of America CEO Ken Lewis (right) shakes hands with Merrill Lynch president John Thain after BoA's takeover in September 2008. Lewis and BoA later faced charges of failing to disclose key merger-related information to shareholders. *(Mario Tama/Getty Images)*

stock price plummeted. By late summer, financial analysts were predicting more losses and even bankruptcy for the firm.

Meanwhile, in mid-September, other investment banks were reeling from the subprime mortgage crisis. Lehman Brothers was forced to declare bankruptcy—the largest in U.S. history. To avoid the same fate, Merrill Lynch opened acquisition talks with Bank of America, the nation's largest commercial bank, with Paulson and Bernanke acting as mediators. The two policy makers feared that the collapse of the world's largest investment bank would spur panic in the financial markets and plunge the global economy into depression. To use a phrase that grew in popularity during the crisis, Merrill Lynch was an institution that was simply "too big to fail."

On September 15, the same day Lehman Brothers declared bankruptcy, Bank of America announced that it was acquiring Merrill Lynch in a $50 billion, all-stock deal. At the time, the merger was hailed for helping to ease the grow-

Metzler, Lloyd Appleton (1913–1980)

The American economist Lloyd Appleton Metzler made notable contributions to several areas of economics but is best remembered for his studies of international trade. Paul Samuelson called him one of the half-dozen most important economists in the world during the 1940s and 1950s.

Metzler was born in Lost Springs, Kansas, in 1913. He attended the University of Kansas, receiving a bachelor's degree in 1935 and a master's in business administration in 1938. He was awarded a PhD from Harvard University in 1942. His doctoral thesis, "Interregional Income Generation," dealt with the foreign-trade multiplier in a theoretical two-country world, from a Keynesian perspective. The first chapter, which examined the stability properties of the two countries, was published in the April 1942 issue of *Econometrica*; the second chapter, exploring inter-country transfers, was published in the June 1942 issue of the *Journal of Political Economy*. Both articles were well received in the academic community, and Metzler was heralded as one of the bright young scholars in his field.

After a year in Washington as a government economist during World War II, and another year as an assistant professor at Yale University, Metzler joined the faculty of the University of Chicago in 1947. On a faculty that included Milton Friedman, Franco Modigliani, and Kenneth Arrow, Metzler stood as a self-described "token New Dealer," comfortable with Keynesian and neoclassical economics and decidedly not a member of the Chicago school. There was no tension or friction between Metzler and his colleagues, however, and much of his work was accessible to and respected by all, regardless of school of thought.

In 1949, Metzler articulated what came to be called the "Metzler paradox." Although it rarely occurs in practice, he identified the phenomenon as a potential factor in the Heckscher-Ohlin (H-O) general equilibrium model of international trade, developed by Swedish economists Eli Heckscher and Bertil Ohlin of the Stockholm school. The H-O model was designed to predict patterns of production and trade according to the theory of comparative advantage. In other words, it is based on the assumption that a country will find it advantageous to export products that involve its most abundant or least expensive resources (natural resources, domestic expertise, or cheap labor, for example); and, conversely, that it will import products that, if produced domestically, would consume the country's scarcest or most expensive resources. Within this model, according to the Metzler paradox, if the exporting country's offer curve is sufficiently inelastic (inflexible), a tariff on imports by the importing country can result in a reduction of the relative price. Even though the paradox is rarely if ever seen in real-world situations, its theoretical validity has proved useful in economic analyses of international trade based on the H-O model. Also in 1949, Metzler compiled an extensive survey of international trade theory that not only popularized his own theories about stability in the foreign exchange market, but also influenced a generation of graduate students who were able to benefit from access to a broad array of theories in one place.

Outside the realm of international trade theory, Metzler's 1951 essay "Wealth, Saving, and the Rate of Interest" addressed arguments on the "neutrality of money" and examined various monetary policies to demonstrate their effects on interest rates and relative prices. Although this was not Metzler's primary area of study, the essay became one of the most important in the debate over monetarism—the school of thought, advocated by Samuelson and others, that controlling the money supply is the most effective way of controlling short-term demand and economic activity.

Although he continued to teach, Metzler took a hiatus from publishing after discovering he had a brain tumor upon his return from a lecture tour of Scandinavia in 1952. When he resumed writing in the 1960s, he focused on an earlier area of interest—mathematical economics, specifically the unification of comparative static stability and dynamic stability analysis. The Social Science Research Council funded his work on *The Mathematical Basis of Dynamic Economics*, which explored the relationship between differential and difference equations in price theory and the analysis of business cycles. Lloyd Metzler died on October 26, 1980.

Bill Kte'pi

See also: Balance of Payments; Business Cycles, International; Capital Account; Current Account; Exchange Rates.

Further Reading

Horwich, George, and Paul Samuelson, eds. *Trade, Stability, and Macroeconomics: Essays in Honor of Lloyd A. Metzler*. New York: Academic, 1974.

Metzler, Lloyd A. *Collected Papers.* Cambridge, MA: Harvard University Press, 1973.

Tvede, Lars. *Business Cycles: History, Theory, and Investment Reality.* New York: John Wiley & Sons, 2006.

Weintraub, E. Roy. *How Economics Became a Mathematical Science.* Durham, NC: Duke University Press, 2002.

Mexico

The largest Spanish-speaking country in the world, with more than 110 million people, Mexico is located between the United States to the north, Central America to the south, the Pacific Ocean to the west, and the Gulf of Mexico and Caribbean Sea to the east. The country is highly diverse ecologically, ranging from the deserts of the northwest to the rain forests of the south, though most of its people inhabit a belt of states across the central part of the country.

Humans first began inhabiting what is now Mexico during the Paleolithic Period, and the country is believed to be home to the first great civilization of the Americas, the Olmecs, beginning in the middle of the second millennium BCE. In the early 1500s, the central part of the country was conquered by the Spanish, a process that resulted in the loss of up to 90 percent of the indigenous people.

The colonizers imposed a feudal order known as the *encomienda* system, whereby Spanish landlords were given vast land grants or control of the country's valuable mines and then allowed to employ peasants in serf-like conditions. Frustration with Spanish policy led to a revolt by the local elite and independence in the early 1820s, though economic conditions changed little. Thus, political turmoil and insurrection recurred sporadically through the early twentieth century, culminating in the Mexican Revolution (1910–1920), which resulted in widespread land reform.

Throughout much of the twentieth century, Mexico was ruled by a single party—the Partido Revolucionario Institucional, or Institutional Revolutionary Party (PRI), which nationalized the vital oil industry in the 1930s and generally pursued a policy of economic autarky (self-sufficiency), with high tariffs, nationalized industries, subsidies for basic consumer goods, and heavy government involvement in the economy.

Falling energy prices in the 1980s forced Mexico to seek international financial assistance and helped promote a transition to more free-market, trade-oriented policies, culminating in the 1992 signing of the North American Free Trade Agreement (NAFTA), which sought to create closer economic ties between Mexico, Canada, and the United States. The new reforms created a more dynamic and wealthier economy, but one that saw increased divisions between rich and poor. More integrated into the world economy, Mexico was hard hit by the 2007–2009 financial crisis and recession, which saw demand for Mexican exports contract in their biggest market, the United States.

Economic History Through World War II

Mexico was home to some of the most vibrant civilizations in the pre-Columbian history of the Americas and, at the time of first contact with Europeans in the late 1400s and early 1500s, had two major centers of urban civilization: that of the Aztecs in the Valley of Mexico in the central part of the country, and that of the Maya in the Yucatan Peninsula region in the south. Both controlled widespread trading networks that linked them to regions as far away as what is now the southwestern United States and Central America.

In 1519, the first Spanish conquistadores arrived in the Valley of Mexico. With the help of superior weapons, the pathogens they carried, and indigenous allies—who resented harsh Aztec rule—the Spanish quickly defeated the Aztecs and established dominion over the region. While Spanish authorities quickly outlawed slavery of indigenous peoples, the *encomienda* system imposed working conditions not unlike those of slavery. Under the Spanish labor system, the peasantry could not leave their employers, who had virtually total control over their lives both on and off the job. Many land-owners and mine owners worked these quasi serfs to death with long hours and harsh conditions. In the century following the conquest, it is estimated that the indigenous population of the Valley of Mexico fell from about 25 million to 1 million.

Initially, the Mexican economy under the Spanish was based chiefly on the export of precious metals, particularly silver. Gradually, commercial agriculture—including sugar plantations along the Gulf of Mexico and livestock raising in the Valley of Mexico—became important components. What barely changed was the social order, in which a handful of very powerful ethnic Spanish ranchers and mine owners ruled over a vast peasantry and mining proletariat consisting primarily of *mestizos*, or people of mixed Spanish and indigenous heritage.

Spain was a relatively weak colonial power and, for much of the period in which it ran what was then called New Spain, it imposed little control over the economic and political life of the colony. To counter the rising power of Britain and France, and the trade inroads those countries were making in its American colonies, Spain in the mid-eighteenth century began to impose tighter mercantilist rule, attempting to direct more of the colonies' trade to the mother country. But when the French Revolution and the Napoleonic wars of the late eighteenth and early nineteenth centuries once again weakened Madrid's control, local elites—many inspired by the revolutionary rhetoric and ideas of France—broke free and established an independent Mexico in 1821.

For the first half-century of independence, Mexico's economy remained rooted in large-scale agriculture and mining, with modernization stunted by political turmoil. Under dictator Porfirio Díaz, who ruled the country from 1876 to 1911, Mexico embarked on a modernization program that included high tariffs to protect local industries but also increased foreign investment, particularly from the United States, to modernize mining and commercial agriculture industries and build the beginnings of a railroad and communications network. The policies worked, but created great discrepancies in wealth and did little to address the most contentious of domestic economic issues—landlessness among the peasantry. The Mexican Revolution that ensued in the second decade of the twentieth century saw Díaz overthrown and a massive redistribution of land.

Renewed unrest developed as a result of the Great Depression, during which the Mexican economy, increasingly dominated by the United States, was dealt a heavy blow from the downturn north of the border. Thousands of Mexican workers who had migrated to the United States during the prosperous years of World War I and the 1920s were forced to return home, as unemployment rose and per capita income fell. The result was a political turn to the Left under the PRI and the initiation of more autarkic economic policies, including nationalization of the oil industry in 1938 and an emphasis on import-substitution industrial development.

Oil Boom and Bust

The policies initiated in the 1930s paid dividends in the immediate post–World War II era, with the government using rising oil revenues to expand education and build a heavy industry infrastructure. Still, by the 1960s, those revenues were shrinking as existing oil fields went into decline. By 1966, Petróleos Mexicanos (Mexican Petroleum, or Pemex) was barely producing enough to meet domestic demand.

Between 1971 and 1973, however, oil and natural gas were discovered in the areas near Tampico, Reynosa, and Poza Rica, and the first discoveries were made in the states of Tabasco and Chiapas. These areas, together with the Cantarell field discovered in 1976 near Campeche in the Gulf of Mexico, have become the country's highest crude producers. Since 1978, this region has provided 79 percent of Mexico's total production and is the principal source of the nation's hydrocarbon reserves.

In the mid-1970s, Pemex undertook an aggressive strategy to accelerate the export of crude oil and bring in more foreign currency. In this way, the government hoped to finance new industrial and commercial development. The decision would prove disastrous. Throughout the world, the early 1970s was characterized by extreme volatility in both finance and production. The decision of U.S. president Richard Nixon to end the Bretton Woods monetary system in 1971, precipitated in large part by a growing tendency toward the deregulation of global finance, threw a relatively orderly international system of trade and finance into disarray. That situation was exacerbated by the oil embargo of 1973. World oil prices skyrocketed in deregulated markets, and the financial windfall of oil exporters flooded the eurodollar market. U.S. and European international banks, seeking to recycle so-called petrodollars, looked to Latin American countries as potentially lucrative new markets.

With international funding, Mexico experienced a second oil boom from 1974 to 1982. Crude

The Mexican oil industry, vital to the country's economy, was nationalized in 1938. Through the state-owned company Pemex, petroleum accounts for about one-third of government revenues. Declining capacity has been a problem in the twenty-first century. *(Steve Northup/Time & Life Pictures/ Getty Images)*

exports during this period jumped from 5.8 million barrels per day to 544 million per day. Once again, the movement of international markets determined the fate of the Mexican economy. As the effects of the 1979 energy crisis began to recede and oil prices began to decline, the U.S. economy continued to suffer from stagflation—sluggish economic growth along with rising inflation. In response, the U.S. Federal Reserve raised interest rates to unprecedented levels—over 19 percent by July 1981. Faced with lower oil prices and drastically higher interest rates on international loans, Mexico declared a moratorium on its loan payments. Other Latin American nations quickly followed suit, and the 1982 debt crisis was born, with profoundly negative consequences for the region.

Increased exports during the boom were not matched by equally ambitious goals in domestic refining and the production of petroleum-based products. In 1974, almost 800,000 barrels were refined daily, and the construction of new refineries pushed refining capacity to 1.5 million barrels per day in 1981. This relatively modest increase ended with the debt crisis, and no new capacity has been added in the years since. Likewise, petrochemical production reached its highest point in 1982—14.5 million tons (13.2 metric tons)—and has held constant at that level ever since.

With the collapse in oil prices in the early 1980s, however, Mexico experienced a growing balance-of-payments shortfall, resulting in massive capital flight abroad. By 1982, the country had virtually depleted its foreign-capital reserves in an effort to shore up the peso and to prevent rapid inflation. Fears that the government could not pay its debts and would have to raise taxes only exacerbated the problem, forcing the government to devalue the peso several times. These moves resulted in inflation rates approaching 100 percent annually in the middle and latter years of the decade. Both domestic and foreign investment faltered, and the economy went into a period of stagnation that Mexicans call the "lost decade."

Market Reforms, Foreign Investment, and the Crisis of 1994

To improve the economy's performance and comply with the strictures of international lending institutions, which the country's finances had come to rely on, Mexico embarked on a program of pro-market reforms, including privatization of state enterprises—though never in the politically sensitive oil industry—and deregulation. The government also established a policy of encouraging U.S. corporations to establish assembly factories, or *maquiladoras*, which were largely free of Mexican taxes and regulations on the repatriation of profits. Soon, large zones along the northern border were filled with such assembly plants, which manufactured everything from clothing to automobiles.

By the early 1990s, when Mexico signed NAFTA, which put it on the road to fuller integration with the economies of Canada and the United States, the economic outlook had improved and the country was once again experiencing growth, though on a modest scale. But 1994, the year in which NAFTA went into effect, proved rocky for the Mexican economy. The situation looked good at the start of the year, with inflation slowing, the currency stable, and the overall economy growing steadily since 1988. The trade deficit caused some concern about the balance of payments, but this situation was eased with significant foreign investment coming into the country. The foreign capital inflows, stimulated by expectations about NAFTA, took the form of both direct investment (ownership of companies and factories) and portfolio investment (stocks, bonds, and such). The result was a boom in Mexican securities, and the stock market was one of the best performers in the world.

As the year unfolded, however, Mexico experienced a number of political shocks that had devastating economic consequences. In January, an uprising broke out among the indigenous population in the southern state of Chiapas—the first armed revolt in the country since the Mexican Revolution of the 1920s. In March, the leading candidate in the presidential election, scheduled for that summer, was assassinated. In September, the general secretary of the ruling PRI was also assassinated. In November, the chief investigator of the murder resigned, charging a cover-up. And in December, there were reports of renewed fighting in Chiapas. Meanwhile, there was a spate of kidnappings of foreign businessmen in Mexico City.

Not surprisingly, confidence among foreign investors plummeted. Since stocks and bonds can be sold much more quickly than physical assets like factories, portfolio investment is more volatile than direct investment. Thus, portfolio inflows, which had reached $9 billion in the fourth quarter of 1993, began to dry up. Then, with investors pulling out of the country in droves, the inflow turned into an outflow of almost $6 billion in the fourth quarter of 1994. This served once again to weaken the peso.

Initially, the Mexican Central Bank tried to support the currency with U.S. dollar reserves, selling dollars and buying pesos to prop up the value of the latter. But the reserves were quickly depleted, falling from $26 billion in the first quarter of the year to $6 billion in the fourth quarter. After losing $2 billion in a week, the government stopped supporting the peso on December 20, 1994. The currency fell from 3.5 pesos per dollar to 3.9 pesos immediately, and to 5.2 pesos by December 31, 1994.

To make matters worse, the government had been borrowing in the form of *tesobonos*, short-term bonds linked to the dollar, where bondholders did not have any currency risk; interest rates on these bonds were lower than for *cetes*, the normal Mexican government bonds. This transformed the currency crisis into a debt crisis, since the government did not now have enough dollars to repay *tesobono* holders.

International financial markets reacted immediately and violently. The sharp fall in the peso after seven years of stability fundamentally altered expectations of currency traders, who had come to believe that sudden devaluations in Mexico were a thing of the past. As they withdrew funds, the peso (and Mexican securities) fell further. Moreover, the shock waves provoked by the devaluation reached well beyond Mexico. In the two weeks after the devaluation, other Latin American financial markets collapsed as well because of the capital being pulled out—what became known as the "Tequila effect." Emerging markets in Asia were hit too, as were European markets.

To prevent Mexico from defaulting, and to protect the rest of the world from the contagion effect of such a default, an international loan package of $50 billion was put together. The United States committed $20 billion, the International Monetary Fund (IMF) $17 billion, and other countries and international institutions $13 billion. The loan was secured by revenues from Mexico's oil exports, which were put into an escrow account in New York.

Mexico also undertook an IMF-approved stabilization program, with severe belt-tightening in government spending and bank lending. This reduced the purchasing power of Mexicans, and the fall in the peso made foreign products much more expensive. Imports shrank, and exports, now more competitive, increased; by the second quarter of 1995, the nation's trade deficit had turned into a surplus. Portfolio investment returned by the end of 1995, and the currency, now allowed to float freely—it was no longer pegged to the dollar or any other currency—stabilized at between 6 and 7 pesos per dollar. Mexico repaid the entire amount of the emergency loan, with interest, before it was due. Thus, one might conclude that the crisis was dealt with effectively and quickly.

The resolution, however, came at a high price. Due to reduced bank lending, interest rates rose sharply, exceeding 100 percent on consumer loans. Business investment plunged, and there was a wave of bankruptcies and bank failures. The unemployment rate almost doubled, and the gross domestic product (GDP) fell by 7 percent, a very large decline for a modern economy.

Growth and Crisis

By 1996, the Mexican economy was once again on the mend, buoyed by exports to a surging U.S. economy and the rising powers of Asia, especially China. Helping the situation was a renewed interest by the Mexican government—which, since the late 1990s, was no longer under the exclusive control of the PRI—in establishing fiscal probity. The government replenished its foreign reserves and abandoned its policy of supporting a strong peso, all the while implementing tight controls on wage and price increases. All of this resulted in a new wave of foreign investment and a surge in exports, helping the country avoid the massive balance-of-payments problems in Argentina and Brazil that triggered the South American economic crisis of 2002.

By the mid-2000s, Mexico had emerged as the second-largest economy in Latin America, after that of the far more populous Brazil. It had the highest per capita income in the region, which by 2007 reached nearly $8,000 annually, placing Mexico among the top middle-income countries in the world. Still, the nation's economy was plagued with problems. The high per capita income masked significant wealth and income gaps, not just between classes but between regions, with the north and Mexico City doing far better than other parts of the country. Continuing poverty continued to plague about 40 percent of the country, and the unemployment rate even in the best years rarely fell below 25 percent. Millions migrated north, legally or not, to seek work in the United States. Their remittances home, valued at some $20 billion annually in the mid-2000s, provided the second-largest source of foreign capital into Mexico, after petroleum exports.

While Mexico's increased integration with the economy of the United States since the 1980s has brought substantial economic growth, it has made the country far more vulnerable to fluctuations north of the border. Although the government imposed a number of measures in the wake of the 1994 financial crisis to ensure that its banks were not over-leveraged with speculative investments, and the country avoided the kind of housing price bubble experienced in the United States, Mexico's financial sector was nevertheless highly exposed to the latest global financial crisis because so many of its banks were owned by institutions in the United States and Spain, two countries hard hit by the mortgage and housing problems at the heart of the crisis.

Even more devastating, according to economists, was the subsequent recession in the United States, which led to falling exports, higher unemployment, declining petroleum prices, lackluster foreign investment, reduced income from tourism, and diminishing remittances from Mexicans working north of the border. After posting an average 4 percent growth rate through the mid-2000s, the Mexican economy expanded by just 1.3 percent in 2008 and declined by 6.8 percent in 2009.

James Ciment, Animesh Ghoshal,
and Wesley C. Marshall

See also: Central America; Latin America; Tequila Effect.

Further Reading

Moreno-Brid, Juan Carlos, and Jaime Ros. *Development and Growth in the Mexican Economy: A Historical Perspective.* New York: Oxford University Press, 2009.

Lustig, Nora. *Mexico: The Remaking of an Economy.* Washington, DC: Brookings Institution, 1998.

Organisation for Economic Co-operation and Development (OECD). "Economic Survey of Mexico 2009: Overcoming the Financial Crisis and the Macroeconomic Downturn." July 30, 2009. Available at www.oecd.org/document/2/0,33 43,en_2649_33733_43394050_1_1_1_1,00.html. Accessed September 28, 2009.

Schlefer, Jonathan. *Palace Politics: How the Ruling Party Brought Crisis to Mexico.* Austin: University of Texas Press, 2008.

Servín, Elisa, Leticia Reina, and John Tutino. *Cycles of Conflict, Centuries of Change: Crisis, Reform, and Revolution in Mexico.* Durham, NC: Duke University Press, 2007.

Teichman, Judith A. *Policymaking in Mexico: From Boom to Crisis.* New York: Routledge, 1988.

Middle East and North Africa

An expansive geographic area that stretches across northern Africa and Southwest Asia, from Morocco in the west to Iran in the east, from the Sahara Desert and Indian Ocean in the south to the Mediterranean Sea, Turkey, and the states of the former Soviet Union to the north, the Middle East and North Africa (hereinafter referred to as the Middle East) share a common faith, Islam, and, with some major exceptions, a common language and culture, Arabic.

The Middle East, the birthplace of Western civilization, was under the rule of Rome for centuries (with the exception of Persia, modern-day Iran). The region came under the rule of various Arabic caliphates through the middle ages, before being incorporated into the Ottoman Empire in the fifteenth and sixteenth centuries. Over the course of the nineteenth century and following the collapse of the Ottomans, the region was colonized by European powers, largely Britain and France.

Independence came to most of the Middle East immediately before and after World War II, a period that also saw the emergence of a modern economic order throughout much of the region, built on its vast oil and natural gas reserves. Unevenly distributed, these reserves have provided great wealth to some national economies, leaving much of the rest of the region struggling to modernize and develop. Political turmoil has also been a hallmark of the region, some because of the conflict with Israel but much due to conflicts between and within Arab states and with Iran.

Economic History Before the Oil Boom

After Africa, the Middle East was the first place to be inhabited by human beings several hundred thousand years ago. Its great river valleys—the Nile in Egypt and the Tigris and Euphrates in Iraq—were home to humanity's first major civilizations. By the latter centuries of the first millennium BCE, much of the region had come under the sway of the Roman Empire, which remained dominant until the fifth century CE.

The event that shaped the region's subsequent

history was the birth of Islam in the early seventh century CE in what is now Saudi Arabia, and the impetus the faith gave to the tribes of the Arabian Peninsula to unify and conquer much of Southwest Asia and Africa north of the Sahara from 633 through the early eighth century. The region was unified politically for several centuries under successive caliphates, or states ruled by a caliph (an Arabic term that combines leader and prophet), before gradually breaking apart into several caliphates in the ninth and tenth centuries.

Still, even after the collapse of a central authority, the region remained unified by faith (virtually all people in the region converted to Islam), a common Arabic language and culture (with large pockets of indigenous language and culture surviving), great centers of learning and science, and an interwoven, trade-based economy.

Islam, the dominant cultural element in the region, differed from medieval Christianity on issues of money. While the latter frowned upon the acquisition of wealth beyond a person's basic needs, Islam emphasized the importance of using one's wealth for the common good—in charity, a central tenet of the faith, and good works. As the founder Prophet Muhammed himself was a merchant, so trade was seen as a godly activity, especially when it resulted in the spread of the faith. And indeed, Islam's spread had as much to do with merchants as it did with armies.

Under both unified and separate caliphates, the region was interwoven by a vast trading network of land routes and sea lanes that linked its various parts with each other and with regions as far away as China, India, West Africa, and Christian Europe. Merchants, often doubling as government representatives, facilitated the trade in a vast array of products, including precious and nonprecious metals, oil, dyes, textiles, and drugs. Arab traders also introduced a number of financial innovations, including the check, the bill of exchange, and the joint stock company. Great cities emerged, such as Cairo in Egypt and Baghdad in Iraq, as centers of trade, with vast marketplaces known as souks where almost any product or service available in the medieval world could be obtained.

Even the onslaught of the Mongols, which led to the sacking of Baghdad in 1258, only served to reroute the intricate trading networks of the region. Still, assaults by Mongols and Turkic peoples undermined the stability in the region and began the long-term decline in its economic and political fortunes. By the late sixteenth century, virtually all of the region, with the exception of Persia, had come under the suzerainty of the Ottoman Turks, who shared a common faith but spoke a different language and possessed a different culture than their Arab subjects.

At the same time, the rise of European maritime power and the discovery of the Americas shifted the Middle East from the center of world trade to its periphery by the late 1600s and led to its economic and technological decline vis-à-vis Europe and the West. From the seventeenth through the nineteenth centuries, the region languished under Ottoman rule, leaving it vulnerable to Western colonization. In 1830, France occupied Algeria—later expanding its conquests to include much of northwest Africa, while Britain seized possessions along the periphery of the Arabian Peninsula.

Other parts of the Ottoman Empire—most notably, Egypt—broke free of the sultan's rule. Under the breakaway governor Muhammad Ali, Egypt developed the beginnings of industrial infrastructure and instituted land reforms in the mid-nineteenth century, a process that drew in large numbers of European traders, professionals, and capital—some of it to build the Suez Canal. Under Ali's successor and grandson Ismail, however, Egypt fell into debt to European financiers and came under the control of European colonizers by the 1880s.

With the collapse of the Ottoman Empire after World War I, much of the rest of the region, from Iraq in the east to Palestine in the west, also came under British and French rule, though under the League of Nations mandate system this was expected to be temporary. By World War II, Egypt, Iraq, and Saudi Arabia had all achieved nominal independence, though they continued to be ruled by pro-British regimes.

Oil Boom

It was also during this period that the first great oil discoveries in the region were made, with vast reserves being found and exploited in Iran, Iraq, Saudi Arabia, and other Gulf territories from the 1910s through the 1930s—reserves that would later be found to be the largest in the world by a significant margin.

The exploration and exploitation of this carbon wealth was conducted by Western oil companies, who also took the lion's share of the profits, fueling nascent nationalist movements both in colonized and noncolonized countries and territories in the region—movements that would see the toppling of many pro-Western regimes after World War II, including those in such key countries as Egypt (1952) and Iraq (1958). Efforts to politically unify the Arab world came to naught, however, partly because of differences between countries with great oil resources and those with little or none.

Over the course of the 1950s and 1960s, the region participated in the global economic boom, though not nearly as much as Europe or East Asia. Led by nationalist leaders, many of the countries, such as Algeria, Egypt, and Iraq, promoted autarkic economic development, whereby national economies were to be made self-sufficient through centralized planning and state-led development of heavy industry. Such policies met with mixed success, achieving better results in countries where large oil revenues could fund the development.

The event that utterly transformed the region economically, however, came in the early 1970s. Through much of the 1950s and 1960s, two trends could be seen in the region's key oil and natural gas industries. The first was the increasing control national governments asserted over Western oil companies, with many regimes nationalizing their local industries and others demanding ever greater percentages of the revenues those resources provided.

At the same time, however, a glut in world energy supplies kept prices low, so that even where Middle Eastern oil-producing countries had come to control more of the revenues, these remained relatively small. By the early 1970s, however, ever greater energy demand in the West had eliminated the supply surplus. Thus, when various Arab oil exporters united to punish the West for its support of Israel during the Arab-Israeli War of 1973, the price of crude oil surged, from roughly $3 a barrel to $12. Six years later, during the Islamist revolution in Iran, disruptions in supply and panic on world markets would again send oil prices soaring, to more than $40 a barrel (over $100 in 2009 dollars).

These "oil shocks" and the "energy crisis" they triggered helped end the post–World War II economic boom in the West, creating a decade of "stagflation," a period of slow or negative growth combined with inflation. For the Middle East, the picture was more mixed. Like other developing countries around the world, oil-poor Middle Eastern countries were hit with dramatically higher prices that undermined economic growth. But for those countries with huge oil and natural gas reserves, the spike in oil prices produced an unprecedented economic boom.

Resource-rich countries around the Middle East, and particularly in the Persian Gulf region, spent huge sums of money building modern housing, schools, manufacturing infrastructure, and transportation and communications networks in an effort to join the ranks of the developed nations in a single bound. Even non-resource-rich Middle East countries benefited somewhat from the boom in the form of increased aid from oil-rich countries and, even more so, from the remittances of nationals who went to work in those countries. But there was also a great deal of conspicuous consumption in the oil-rich countries, as much of the wealth accrued to elites with close connections to the royal families or dictatorial regimes that ruled them. Speculative excess also ensued, especially in Kuwait, where the unregulated Souk al-Manakh stock market saw securities valuations inflate to unsustainable levels before crashing in 1982.

Leaders of the Gulf Cooperation Council nations—the six Arab states of the Persian Gulf—held the group's thirtieth annual summit in Kuwait City in December 2009. Discussions focused on the global economic downturn, which did not spare the region. *(Yasser al-Zayyat/Stringer/AFP/Getty Images)*

Boom-and-Bust Cycle

Inevitably, the boom led to bust, however, as the oil industry responded to high prices by bringing new fields in other parts of the world into production. The huge run-up in oil prices in the 1970s was followed by a collapse in the 1980s and 1990s. While the reserves of the region were so vast that revenues continued to pour in, many countries had to scale back some of their most ambitious development projects and their social welfare networks. In non-resource-rich countries, economic stagnation set in, as corruption, a lack of skilled workers, and overspending on arms stunted economic growth.

The situation helped foster a new militancy in the region. Whereas in the 1950s and 1960s, the calls for political and economic reforms had been promoted by those with a socialist, Pan-Arabist, or nationalist agenda, now the activism was coming

from Islamists, many of whom called for a return to Koranic economic principles. With the exception of Iran, where an Islamist revolution overthrew a free market–oriented dictator in 1979, the Islamist militancy did not succeed in toppling the largely pro-Western regimes of the region. But it did result, among other changes, in an effort within the business community of the Islamic world to create financial instruments that adhered to religious principles, including bans on interest-bearing loans, bonds, and other securities.

By the early 2000s, the economies of many oil-rich Middle Eastern countries were rebounding, as rising demand from newly emerging industrializing countries in Asia put upward pressure on energy prices. In the Persian Gulf region, there was a new spate of construction and infrastructure expansion as some states, most notably in the semi-independent principalities of the United Arab Emirates, including Dubai and Abu Dhabi, which attempted to turn themselves into centers of finance.

But the new boom did not survive the global financial crisis of 2008–2009, which deflated the real-estate and finance bubbles that had been inflating in the Persian Gulf region since the 1990s, largely based on loose credit and the inrush of oil revenues. In addition, the recession that followed the crisis reduced economic output around the world and lowered demand for oil, bringing down energy prices and reducing revenues in oil-rich countries.

For non-resource-rich Middle Eastern countries, the recession of the late 2000s has resulted in lowered exports, tighter credit, stagnating domestic economies, and a drop in remittances from nationals who once worked on the vast construction projects of the Persian Gulf region. Although down, oil revenues will continue to bolster Middle Eastern economies—at least, those with significant reserves—but growth rates for the region as a whole are expected to fall below 4 percent for 2009, down by nearly one-half from the boom years of the early and middle 2000s.

James Ciment

See also: Africa, Sub-Saharan; Israel; Oil Shocks (1973–1974, 1979–1980).

Further Reading

Lewis, Bernard. *The Middle East: A Brief History of the Last 2,000 Years.* New York: Scribner, 1995.

Ochsenwald, William, and Sydney Nettleton Fisher. *The Middle East: A History.* 7th ed. Boston: McGraw-Hill, 2010.

Pappé, Ilan. *The Modern Middle East.* New York: Routledge, 2005.

Safadi, Raed, ed. *MENA Trade & Investment in the New Economy.* New York: American University in Cairo Press, 2003.

Mill, John Stuart (1806–1873)

Through his penetrating and comprehensive study of economics and political economy, the English economist, philosopher, and reformer John Stuart Mill had a great influence, albeit in-directly, on thinking regarding the nature of free markets, the equilibrium condition of supply and demand, and the various forces underlying the rise and fall of business cycles.

At the time of his death on May 8, 1873, the sixty-six-year-old Mill (born May 20, 1806) was regarded as the greatest British philosopher of the nineteenth century. A Renaissance man, he wrote prolifically and on a wide range of subjects, including politics, social issues, economics, women's rights, civil rights and slavery, and religion. He also served for a time as a member of Parliament, held an academic position, and worked in commerce for the British East India Company.

Mill regarded economics as a separate science, a self-contained and complete discipline that did not rely on other fields to make sense. Yet he also referred to economics as an inexact science in which not all laws governing the phenomena being studied could be known. The result, he acknowledged, was that any conclusions economists might draw can only be approximate and must always leave room for doubt. Finally, Mill saw economics as a discipline that relies on deduction to reach valid conclusions—even if his own methods, according to some commentators, could at times be inconsistent. In that deductive method, as defined by Mill, the first step was the statement of a law or laws by induction. Once the law was stated, the next step was to deduce the laws by means of observation. The final step was verification. Although various elements of Mill's approach have been superseded, some economists believe that his view of economics as a separate discipline has aided in the development and interpretation of both microeconomic and macroeconomic equilibrium models.

Mill's background was unique in that he was a child prodigy who was purposefully and specifically trained to become a genius. He was the son of a Scottish philosopher and historian, James Mill. His father sent him to be educated by the English philosopher and social reformer Jeremy Bentham, whose ideas on utilitarianism formed the basis of much of Mill's thought for several years. Under Bentham's curriculum, Mill read Roman which had kept agricultural prices artificially high. Mill wrote that a laissez-faire policy on the part of the government should be a general practice, as any departure from it was bound to bring evil consequences in the form of a reduction in aggregate social welfare. Nevertheless, Mill did accept the use of government intervention on certain occasions and, like many intellectuals of the nineteenth century, looked for economic means to alleviate poverty that arose from inequalities in the demand for labor.

While Mill did not write as extensively on business cycles as his contemporary, French economist Clément Juglar, he did explore the dynamics of supply and demand, the two major forms of money (currency that circulates and credit), and some of the causes and consequences of financial booms and busts. Mill believed that an excess of credit creates a temporary state of overproduction, that overproduction ends when prices fall, and that a steady-state equilibrium is eventually reached in the labor market—a classical economic paradigm that has survived into the twenty-first century.

Robert N. Stacy

See also: Classical Theories and Models.

Further Reading

Balassa, Bela A. "John Stuart Mill and the Law of Markets." *Quarterly Journal of Economics* 73:2 (May 1959): 263–274.

Harris, Abram L. "John Stuart Mill: Government and Economy." *Social Service Review* 37:2 (June 1963): 134–153.

Hausman, Daniel M. "John Stuart Mill's Philosophy of Economics." *Philosophy of Science* 48:3 (September 1981): 363–385.

Hollander, Samuel. *The Economics of John Stuart Mill.* Toronto: University of Toronto Press, 1985.

Mill, John Stuart. *Principles of Political Economy.* New York: Oxford University Press, 1998.

British philosopher and economist John Stuart Mill believed in the classical, free-market paradigm. In his view, disruptions in the equilibrium of supply and demand—economic cycles—are caused by the overreaction of traders to unexpected market shocks. *(The Granger Collection, New York)*

and Greek classics and studied mathematics intensively. His study of economics focused on the works of Adam Smith, whose practical approach he admired, and David Ricardo, who extended Smith's theories on free markets.

Mill's own great work in the field, *Principles of Political Economy*, was published in 1848; another seven editions would appear during his lifetime, the last in 1871. The book was used as the principal economics text at Oxford University until 1919, nearly fifty years after Mill's death. The work that replaced it, written by Alfred Marshall, was strongly influenced by Mill and his views.

Like Smith and Ricardo, Mill was a believer in free markets and, therefore, free trade and no or low tariffs between nations. That economic philosophy had begun to predominate in England during the mid-1840s with the abolition of the Corn Laws,

Mills, Frederick Cecil (1892–1964)

Economist and statistician Frederick Mills, a colleague of Wesley Clair Mitchell and Willard

Thorp, was a leading researcher at the National Bureau of Economic Research (NBER) from 1925 to 1953, and a faculty member at Columbia University from 1919 to his death in 1964. In professional circles, he is best known for his use of statistics to analyze economic data, his work on the cyclical behavior of production and prices, and as a leading authority on inflation.

Mills was born on March 24, 1892, in Santa Rosa, California. He attended the University of California, from which he received a bachelor's degree in 1914 and a master's in 1916. During that same period he worked as an investigator for California's Commission of Immigration and Housing and served on the U.S. Commission on Industrial Relations. His work focused on issues of unemployment, migratory labor, and immigration. From 1916 to 1917, he was a Garth fellow in political economy at Columbia University in New York, where he studied under such notable scholars as Wesley Clair Mitchell (economics), John Dewey (philosophy), and Franz Boas (anthropology). He received a PhD from Columbia in 1917, publishing his dissertation that year under the title "Contemporary Theories of Unemployment and Unemployment Relief."

Mills's book *Statistical Methods*, published in 1924, described the use of quantitative techniques to analyze problems in business and economics. It provided insights into the specific types of data gathering and analysis—including such methods as time-series studies—that were performed at the NBER in the early 1920s. In the highly regarded book, which demonstrated the advantages of using statistics in economic analysis, Mills also explained cases in which the methodology was not ideal. Nevertheless, it formed the basis for the methodology he would employ consistently for his entire career.

Another of Mills's well-known studies, *The Behavior of Prices* (1927), presented data on the prices of 200 items. Although the work was criticized for presenting data in isolation without taking into consideration outside factors, Mills had stated at the outset that the study was only preliminary and

would eventually include a fuller examination of prices in a broader context. His work on prices and business cycles, based on statistical research and an empirical foundation, led him to conclude that there were certain regularities in cycles that could be identified. From that proposition, he believed a larger set of conclusions could be drawn.

Despite the development of econometrics and the increased use of statistics in economic analysis in the early twentieth century, Mills's approach was not universally accepted. Many disagreed with his methods—including his very use of statistics to derive meaning from economic and business events. Mills served as president of the American Statistical Association (1934) and the American Economic Association (1940).

Robert N. Stacy

See also: Mitchell, Wesley Clair; National Bureau of Economic Research; Thorp, Willard Long.

Further Reading

Bye, Raymond T. *An Appraisal of Frederick C. Mills' The Behavior of Prices.* New York: Social Science Research Council, 1940.

Mills, Frederick C. *The Behavior of Prices.* New York: Arno, 1975.

———. *Productivity and Economic Progress.* New York: National Bureau of Economic Research, 1952.

———. *Statistical Methods Applied to Economics and Business.* 3rd ed. New York: Holt, 1955.

———. *The Structure of Postwar Prices.* New York: National Bureau of Economic Research, 1948.

Woirol, Gregory R. "The Contributions of Frederick C. Mills." *Journal of the History of Economic Thought* 21:2 (June 1999): 163–185.

Minsky, Hyman (1919–1996)

American economist Hyman Minsky proposed influential ideas about the workings of national economies that touch directly on business cycles in general. His research and theories on financial crises received much attention during the financial meltdown of the early 2000s.

Minsky was born in Chicago on September 23, 1919. He received his bachelor's degree from the University of Chicago and his master's and doctorate degrees from Harvard University, where he studied under Joseph Schumpeter and Wassily Leontief and was influenced by, among others, Irving Fisher and Jacob Viner. Widely viewed as the outstanding financial Keynesian of the last quarter of the twentieth century, Minsky taught at Brown University, the University of California at Berkeley, Washington University in St. Louis, and the Jerome Levy Economics Institute at Bard College in New York. Although he was not as familiar to the general public as some other economists, he was well known and highly influential in the academic and financial communities.

Minsky believed that capitalism was inherently fragile and that the back-and-forth movement from fragility to robustness created business cycles. The behavior of bankers and businesspeople—particularly their uncertainty about financing and investing during booms and busts—also influences the cycle. According to Minsky, these financial uncertainties and the responses to them "called the tune for aggregate demand and employment." In times of prosperity, more money is available than is needed to meet obligations, leading to increased speculation. Lending increases until it exceeds what borrowers can pay. At that point, lenders decrease the amount of available money (sometimes referred to as a "Minsky moment") and the economy contracts. Thus, how well the financial world performs has much to do with how the business world performs. Minsky called this approach "financial Keynesianism." In the 1960s and 1970s, when he was advancing these arguments, such connections were not well established. Minsky also suggested that the prices of outputs and capital assets are separate entities that are determined differently and not completely linked in an economy. He argued that there is a connection between business decisions and financial relationships, although the connection might not always be well understood or optimally coordinated.

Minsky believed that business cycles, with their extreme swings from boom to bust, will always occur in a free-market economy. Furthermore, he maintained, government intervention can do a great deal to counteract the violent swings, and that regulation, the use of the Federal Reserve, and other government actions are the best means to accomplish this end. He supported government-created deficits, as Franklin D. Roosevelt's administration instituted in the 1930s, believing that a large debt would provide a safe investing haven for cautious investors. While Minsky's work was generally seen as pioneering, not all economists agreed with his ideas.

Minsky died in Rhinebeck, New York, on October 24, 1996, but his theories have remained influential. His notion that debt accumulation drives an economy toward the brink of disaster received especially wide attention during the financial crisis of the early 2000s. He also identified three types of borrowing that contribute to a situation marked by crippling, insolvent debt—specifically, borrowing related to hedging, or selling short and buying long to balance investment risk; speculating; and Ponzi schemes, in which earlier investors are paid high returns with money from new investors. And, indeed, the financial meltdown that began in 2007 was largely precipitated by the collapse of the housing and subprime mortgage markets in which there were poorly understood hedges, speculation, and even Ponzi schemes.

Robert N. Stacy

See also: Fisher, Irving; Kindleberger, Charles P.; Minsky's Financial Instability Hypothesis; Post Keynesian Theories and Models; Viner, Jacob.

Further Reading

Bellofiore, Riccardo, and Piero Ferri. *The Economic Legacy of Hyman Minsky, Volume 1: Financial Keynesianism and Market Instability.* Northampton, MA: Edward Elgar, 2001.

———. *The Economic Legacy of Hyman Minsky, Volume 2: Financial Fragility and Investment in the Capitalist Economy.* Northampton, MA: Edward Elgar, 2001.

Dymski, Gary, and Robert Pollin, eds. *Monetary Macroeconomics: Explorations in the Tradition of Hyman P. Minsky.* Ann Arbor: University of Michigan Press, 1994.

Minsky, Hyman P. *Can "It" Happen Again? Essays on Instability and Finance.* Armonk, NY: M.E. Sharpe, 1982.

———. *Inflation, Recession and Economic Policy.* Brighton, UK: Wheatsheaf, 1982.

———. *John Maynard Keynes.* New York: Columbia University Press, 1975.

———. *Stabilizing an Unstable Economy.* New Haven, CT: Yale University Press, 1986.

Taylor, Lance, and Stephen A. O'Connell. "A Minsky Crisis." *Quarterly Journal of Economics* 100, Supplement (1985): 871–885.

Minsky's Financial Instability Hypothesis

Minsky's financial instability hypothesis is a theory of financial market instability named for its originator, twentieth-century American economist Hyman Minsky. According to classical economic equilibrium theory, the forces of supply and demand inevitably lead to a price equilibrium in which there are no shortages or surpluses of goods—in other words, where quantity demanded equals quantity supplied. Moreover, efficient market theory states that the values assigned to assets and liabilities by financial markets cause efficient use of resources because known information is always reflected in prices and new information is absorbed instantly. By contrast, Minsky's financial instability hypothesis rejects both of these views, arguing instead that capitalist economies are fundamentally unstable, exhibiting periods of inflation and debt deflation that have the potential to spin out of control.

Minsky was not the first economist to explore the idea of financial instability, but while similar ideas were developed by earlier theorists, today's theories about financial instability are most closely associated with the ideas he presented in his 1986 book *Stabilizing an Unstable Economy* and elaborated on in a 1992 paper titled "The Financial Instability Hypothesis." In the two works, Minsky discussed the impact of debt on the behavior of economic system as a whole. In his view, a prolonged period of tranquility, when the system is stable and returns are normal, leads financial innovators (whether banks or brokers or dealers) on a quest for higher returns. This, in turn, leads to a period of high risk-taking, financial innovation, and unsustainable levels of debt that ultimately disrupt stability, raise asset prices, and create speculative booms. When the boom finally ends, it is followed by a period of reduced asset valuation, intense credit contraction, and a financial crisis in which the unsustainable levels of debt cannot be serviced. Minsky saw a critical role for government in stabilizing the economy by running sizable deficits during economic downturns and then accumulating a surplus during inflationary booms.

While many economists focus their attention on consumer behavior, understanding it as the core of the "real economy," Minsky focused on Wall Street and the money flows that make investment, production, employment, salaries, and purchases possible, all of them financed in some way by credit. Credit itself is one of the financial innovations that generate wealth and fuel economic growth. However, at the same time, credit creates the instability at the heart of Minsky's hypothesis because it allows businesses and individuals to take advantage of investment opportunities that arise, whether or not they have money available in a savings or checking account.

Credit can take other forms that similarly lead to Minsky-type instability. Other innovations include money market funds, bonds, options, hedge funds, and a wide range of derivatives, including collateralized mortgage obligations (CMOs) and collateralized debt obligations (CDOs), as well as investment financing options—from margin accounts to credit cards, and home equity lines of credit for the individual—that institutional lenders use to reduce their risk and provide cash for lending purposes. Like the businesses and individuals to which they lend, banks seek profits by financing activity. And like all entrepreneurs, bankers are aware that innovation assures profits. Thus bankers, whether they are brokers or dealers, are merchants of debt who strive to innovate in the assets they acquire and the liabilities they market.

Minsky distinguishes three kinds of financing—hedge, speculative, and Ponzi. Hedge financing units are those that can fulfill all contractual payment obligations by their own cash flows. Speculative finance units can meet interest payments on debt but cannot repay the principle out of income cash flows and must issue new debt to meet commitments on maturing debt. Ponzi financing must borrow or sell assets to pay interest on outstanding debts.

Minsky argues that an economy's financing regions can be stable (hedge financing) or unstable (speculative or Ponzi financing). Over periods of prolonged prosperity, the economy makes a transition from financial relations that make for a stable system to financial relations that make for an unstable system. During a protracted period of good times, capitalist economies tend to move from a financial structure dominated by hedge finance units to a structure in which there is a preponderance of units engaged in speculative or Ponzi financing.

Minsky believed that sound fiscal and monetary policies—in particular, public spending to offset reductions in private spending and central bank lender-of-last resort interventions—can steady financial markets and restore stability. In *Stabilizing an Unstable Economy* (1986), he discusses the nine contractions and the even greater number of domestic or international financial crises since 1950 to demonstrate that big government played a significant role in avoiding a repeat of the 1929–1933 macroeconomic collapse. Many economists have used Minsky's hypothesis to help explain the financial crisis of 2008–2009 and to offer solutions to prevent a reoccurrence.

Carol M. Connell

See also: Asset-Price Bubble; Debt; Deflation; Innovation, Financial; Minsky, Hyman; Regulation, Financial; Systemic Financial Crises.

Further Reading

Cooper, George. *The Origin of Financial Crises: Central Banks, Credit Bubbles, and the Efficient Market Fallacy.* New York: Vintage, 2008.

Minsky, Hyman P. "The Financial Instability Hypothesis." *The Jerome Levy Economics Institute*, Working Paper No. 74 (May 1992).

———. *Stabilizing an Unstable Economy.* New Haven, CT: Yale University Press, 1986.

Pressman, Steven. *Interactions in Political Economy: Malvern After Ten Years.* New York: Routledge, 1996.

Whalen, Charles, and Jeffrey Wenger. "Destabilizing an Unstable Economy." *Challenge* 45: 5 (2002): 70–92.

Mises, Ludwig von (1881–1973)

Ludwig von Mises was an economist of the Austrian school who made pathbreaking contributions to monetary (money supply) theory and business-cycle theory. He is credited with developing the Austrian theory of the business cycle. An ardent advocate of free markets, Mises participated in the famous socialist calculation debate, arguing that socialist planners were incapable of efficiently coordinating modern economies. Though Mises's influence on economics diminished with the rise of Keynesianism in the mid-twentieth century, his work received renewed attention as Austrian economics returned to favor in the last decades of the century.

He was born Ludwig Heinrich Edler von Mises on September 29, 1881, in what is now Ukraine but was then part of the Austro-Hungarian Empire. He studied at the University of Vienna and received his Doctor of Laws degree in 1906. Mises was influenced by the founders of the Austrian school of economics, Carl Menger, and Eugen von Böhm-Bawerk. Employed by the Austrian Chamber of Commerce, Mises was also a long-serving, though unpaid, faculty member at the University of Vienna, where his private seminars cultivated the next generation of Austrian economists. Though an influential adviser to the Austrian government, Mises left Austria for Switzerland as the Nazis rose to power. Eventually emigrating to the United States, he was a visiting professor at New York University from 1945 until his retirement in 1969. For virtually his entire adult life, Mises was actively engaged at the highest levels in both the intellectual and policy struggles of Europe. He died on October 10, 1973.

Mises's first important contribution to economics was *The Theory of Money and Credit* (1912), in which he provided the first modern treatment of monetary theory. In doing so, he bridged the gap between microeconomics (economics at the individual, organizational, or company level) and macroeconomics (the economy of a nation or region as a whole) by establishing what determines the value of money. His solution was the *regression theorem*, in which he suggested that the value of money is, and always must be, based on the value that the market gives to money as a commodity.

The most important contribution of *The Theory of Money and Credit*, however, would come to be known as the Austrian theory of the business cycle. Integrating the contributions of such earlier economists as Richard Cantillon, Knut Wicksell, and Eugen von Böhm-Bawerk, Mises developed the theory that economies undergo business cycles primarily due to the policies of the central bank. Easy credit policies on the part of the central bank will be felt first in banking and financial markets, where an artificial increase in loanable funds will reduce the going rate of interest below the natural rate established by natural supply and demand. Lower interest rates, in turn, increase borrowing and investment, which results in decreased saving and increased consumption. The signals of increased consumption, the theory goes, encourage entrepreneurs to invest in processes that change the structure of production and the array of capital goods away from the underlying preferences of consumers. Eventually, it is said, such changes will be revealed as bad investments and will require a painful process of reallocating labor and capital via unemployment and bankruptcy. One of Mises's students, Friedrich August von Hayek was awarded the Nobel Prize in 1974 for his elaborations of the theory.

Mises's other writings made significant contributions on a variety of economic issues. He wrote one of the few economic treatises of the twentieth century, *Human Action: A Treatise on Economics* (1949), which presented a systematic exposition of the principles of economics from methodology to policy conclusions. In addition, he greatly influenced a new generation of American economists who firmly established the Austrian school of economics in the United States. The Ludwig von Mises Institute was founded in 1982 in Auburn, Alabama.

Mark Thornton

See also: Austrian School; Böhm-Bawerk, Eugen Ritter von; Hayek, Friedrich August von.

Further Reading

Hülsmann, Jörg Guido. *Mises: The Last Knight of Liberalism.* Auburn, AL: Ludwig von Mises Institute, 2007.

Kirzner, Israel M. *Ludwig von Mises: The Man and His Economics.* Wilmington, DE: ISI Books, 2001.

Mississippi Bubble (1717–1720)

An episode of speculative excess in early-eighteenth-century France, the Mississippi Bubble made and destroyed fortunes for thousands of investors across Europe, lured by the promise of mineral wealth in the country's imperial holdings along the Mississippi River. More than a mere mining and real-estate boom and bust, the Mississippi Bubble was an early example of how easy credit policies and a lack of hard economic data can run up the market price of an investment far above its real value.

After the War of Spanish Succession of 1701–1714 and as a result of the excessive spending of King Louis XIV, France was in bad financial shape. In 1714, a Scottish economist with connections to the duke of Orleans, nephew of King Louis XIV, arrived in Paris with a scheme to revive the French treasury and economy. John Law was the thinker behind the "real bills doctrine," an economic theory stating that a money supply should grow with the economy, if necessary by allowing banks to issue their own notes. Law insisted this would not fuel inflation because businesses would accept

In 1717, economist and financier John Law set up a joint-stock company in France for reclaiming colonial land in Mississippi. Law issued more and more shares as the share price continued to rise. The bubble finally burst, and Law became a hated figure. *(MPI/Stringer/Hulton Archive/Getty Images)*

of Louisiana. Rumors had swirled through France for some time that the southern reaches of this territory were rich in gold and silver. The rumors, of course, turned out to be false.

To finance his scheme, Law sold shares in the company both for cash and in exchange for state bonds, which offered a way for the French government to finance its debt. The cash was supplied by the Banque Générale; in other words, Law was extending credit to investors from his bank to buy shares in his trading company. As investors, lured by the idea of great mineral wealth, threw their money at Law, who then invested in bonds, the government granted the Scotsman more exclusive trading rights with other imperial holdings, which in turn lured more investors.

In early 1719, the government took over the Banque Générale, renaming it the Banque Royale (Royal Bank), leaving Law in charge, and backing its issues of bank notes, which now became the de facto paper money of the state. Meanwhile, the expanding Compagnie d'Occident was renamed the Compagnie des Indes (Company of the Indies) to reflect its far-flung trade, though most Frenchmen continued to call the whole enterprise the Compagnie du Mississippi (Mississippi Company).

Appointed controller general and superintendent general of France in January 1720, Law emerged as the most powerful economic figure in the country, controlling its finances and, through the Compagnie des Indes, its trade with the non-European world. Just as important, he now held much of the government's debt, which gave him a steady source of interest income to finance his ever-expanding business empire.

Meanwhile, Law's growing wealth and power had attracted investors who sent share prices in the Compagnie des Indes from 500 livres to more than 10,000 livres over the course of the year 1719. Fortunes were made overnight, as the French press coined a new word for those suddenly wealthy individuals: "millionaires."

But there was an underlying flaw in Law's scheme: the questionable value of the notes the Banque Royale was issuing. As long as they were

the notes only as they needed them—that is, as they expanded production.

In 1715, upon the death of Louis XIV, the duke of Orleans became regent to the young King Louis XV. A year later, Law received a royal charter to open the Banque Générale (General Bank), with the power to issue bank notes. This was a major departure for France, which had always placed its faith in specie money (gold and silver). But Law had convinced the duke that an expanded money supply would spur commerce and, hence, taxable revenues for the national treasury.

In 1717, Law organized another chartered enterprise, the Compagnie d'Occident (Company of the West), which was given exclusive rights to trade with France's territories in North America, stretching from Canada to the modern-day state viewed as solid, people would continue to take them and use them to buy stock in the Compagnie des Indes. By early 1720, however, some investors began to grow uneasy, selling their shares to obtain gold and silver. Soon the sell-off was snowballing. Law as banker responded by limiting gold payments to 100 livres; Law as finance minister declared the Banque Royale's notes legal tender, good for all debts public and private. The bank also promised to redeem Compagnie des Indes shares for the going rate of 10,000 livres, thereby flooding the French economy with money and triggering hyperinflation.

In response, the Banque Royale began lowering the amount it would pay for shares, ultimately to 1,000 livres by the end of 1720. Meanwhile, lawsuits burgeoned as Law's growing legion of opponents got the courts to declare null and void the shares of investors who could not prove they actually owned them—that is, the many investors who had purchased shares with notes from Banque Générale and Banque Royale prior to the time Law declared those notes legal tender. Despite the two-thirds reduction in outstanding shares, the value of a single share continued to drop. By late 1721, they fell back to the 500 livres at which they initially had been offered, in the process destroying the fortunes of numerous "millionaires."

Along with a similar scheme in Britain in 1720 known as the South Sea Bubble, the Mississippi Bubble has gone down in history as one of the great speculative episodes of the early modern era in capitalism. Meanwhile, Law—though still respected for his economic theories—has gone down in history as a financial charlatan of the first order, though some economists say his intentions may have been good even if the methods he used were questionable. As for paper money in France, it was buried for another eighty years. This, argue some economists, put the country at a financial disadvantage against its main economic and imperial competitor, Great Britain, which allowed the issue of paper bank notes, though restricting their issue after 1844 to the central Bank of England.

James Ciment

See also: Asset-Price Bubble; South Sea Bubble (1720); Tulipmania (1636–1637).

Further Reading

Fiske, Frank S., ed. *The Mississippi Bubble: A Memoir of John Law; to Which Are Added Authentic Accounts of the Darien Expedition, and the South Sea Scheme.* New York: Greenwood, 1969.

Garber, Peter M. *Famous First Bubbles: The Fundamentals of Early Manias.* Cambridge, MA: MIT Press, 2000.

Gleeson, Janet. *Millionaire: The Philanderer, Gambler, and Duelist Who Invented Modern Finance.* New York: Simon & Schuster, 1999.

Mitchell, Wesley Clair (1874–1948)

American economist and institutionalist Wesley Clair Mitchell was a leading expert on business cycles and a founder, in 1920, of the National Bureau of Economic Research (NBER). Mitchell played a leading role in monitoring and understanding business-cycle activity in the United States.

The second of seven children, Mitchell was born on August 5, 1874, in Rushville, Illinois. His father, a farmer, had been a doctor in the Civil War. In 1899, Mitchell was awarded a doctorate from the University of Chicago, where he studied under Thorstein Veblen and John Dewey. He taught at the University of California, Berkeley, and at Columbia University and was one of the founders and a director of the New School for Social Research in New York City.

Mitchell is best known for his quantitative studies of business cycles in the United States. His 1913 book *Business Cycles* articulated the basic methodology, conditions, and assumptions that he would follow for the rest of his life. In that work, he examined American business from 1890 to 1911, a period marked by an increase in the accuracy and frequency of record keeping. Indeed, prior to 1890, business record keeping in America was so meager, that, as Mitchell noted, there was no real index to indicate whether prices rose or fell. The greater reliance on detailed statistics to analyze business cycles helped define and describe cycles of boom and bust and what came in between.

According to Mitchell, the business cycle follows a track from prosperity to crisis to depression, and back to prosperity. Within each phase, he noted actions and triggers that move the cycle from one stage to the next. For example, an increase in business activity leads to general prosperity, but as profits rise, costs begin to increase as well. This leads to declining profits and tightening restrictions on credit. This phase is followed, in turn, by decreased production, prices, and costs as businesses struggle to remain solvent. The cycle then continues from depression to prosperity.

Mitchell's influential work at the NBER included gathering data from hundreds of areas and subjecting it to time-series studies. These studies—based on the collection of data at relatively uniform points in time—became the means by which Mitchell and the NBER could identify business cycles, quantitatively measure and explain their characteristics, and predict future occurrences. Thus, Mitchell's conclusions were based on empirical rather than theoretical principles.

In addition to teaching and research, Mitchell served on numerous government committees. He served as chair of the President's Committee on Social Trends (1929–1933), as president of the American Economic Association (1923–1924), and, in 1941, as a member of the original standing committee of the Foundation for the Study of Cycles.

Mitchell's book *What Happens During Business Cycles,* published posthumously in 1951, was described by one reviewer as a contribution to the study of business cycles, but not a major one. Mitchell's method, which by then was being replaced by models, econometrics, and deductive rather than inductive approaches, perhaps had gone as far as it could go. Mitchell's method could identify business cycles, but could not give a "Newtonian" set of rules about them, which became the backbone of modern economic analysis. Nevertheless, Mitchell's work continued to have an enormous influence on later economists who studied business cycles, including Simon Kuznets and Arthur Burns. Mitchell died on October 29, 1948, in New York City.

Robert N. Stacy

See also: Burns, Arthur; Kuznets, Simon Smith; National Bureau of Economic Research.

Further Reading

Burns, Arthur F. *Wesley Clair Mitchell: The Economic Scientist.* New York: National Bureau of Economic Research, 1952.

Klein, Philip A. "The Neglected Institutionalism of Wesley Clair Mitchell: The Theoretical Basis for Business Cycle Indicators." *Journal of Economic Issues* 17:4 (December 1983): 867–899.

Mitchell, Wesley Clair. *The Backward Art of Spending Money, and Other Essays.* New York: A.M. Kelley, 1950.

———. *A History of the Greenbacks: With Special Reference to the Economic Consequences of Their Issue, 1862–65.* Chicago: University of Chicago Press, 1960.

———. *What Happens During Business Cycles, a Progress Report.* New York: National Bureau of Economic Research, 1951.

Monetary Policy

Governments utilize monetary policy to make changes in the supply, availability, and cost of money and credit. By effecting such changes, policy makers attempt to stimulate or discourage the consumption of goods and services by households and firms, in hopes of achieving price stability in times of inflation and economic growth in periods of slow or negative economic growth.

Monetary policy is usually decided upon and carried out by central banks, such as the Federal Reserve System (Fed) of the United States, though other agencies and departments in the executive branch, such as Treasury, as well as legislature, may use monetary policy to effect economic change. While the ability of government to pursue monetary policy differs from country to country, the Fed has three main tools at its disposal: changing the interest rates it charges commercial banks; purchasing or selling government securities; and raising or lowering the reserve requirements of commercial banks.

Policy Tools

In the United States, all federally chartered commercial banks—along with major state-chartered banks—are members of the Fed. This arrangement means that they are allowed to borrow funds from the Fed. When the Fed changes the interest rate it charges member banks, the entire financial system can be affected. This is because both member and nonmember banks are continually making short-term loans to each other in order to meet reserve requirements, operational needs, such as restocking automatic teller machines, or sudden payment demands by other institutions. Banks that have excess reserves can loan them out to those that need to increase their reserves.

The Fed sets its own rate—known as the "discount rate"—which can also affect the federal funds rate. When the Fed reduces the discount rate, it often lowers the federal funds rate, since banks will turn to the Fed if they can get money cheaper there. Conversely, by raising the discount rate, the Fed raises the floor for all federal funds rates. Reducing target interest rates enables commercial banks to reduce their lending rates to customers. It is up to the banks, and not the Fed, to determine how much they want to lower those rates, but competition usually dictates that they stay in line with other banks or risk losing customers. In addition, lower discount rates loosen credit, thereby making banks less selective about whom they offer credit to.

The second means by which the Fed can affect monetary policy is through the purchase or sale of government securities, such as long-term Treasury bonds (T-bonds) or short-term Treasury bills (T-bills). (This activity is conducted by the Federal Reserve Bank of New York, the most influential of the twelve regional Fed banks.) When the Fed buys government securities, it increases the money supply because those holding the securities now have cash in hand instead—cash that they can lend out. Conversely, by selling bonds, the Fed takes in cash, lowering the money supply and tightening available credit. As a guide for its purchase and sale of government securities, the Fed uses the federal funds rate, the rate at which banks borrow from each other.

Finally, the Fed can affect the money supply by raising or lowering the reserve requirements of commercial banks, that is, the money a bank must hold against liabilities such as checking and savings accounts. By raising the reserve requirement, the Fed in effect makes less money available for credit, thereby shrinking the available funds in circulation.

When the Fed takes on any or all of these measures to increase the money supply, it is said to be pursuing an expansionary monetary policy; when it takes measures to reduce the supply, it is pursuing a contractionary policy. When the Fed pursues an expansionary policy, it is making money cheaper and hence more available for business investment, operations, and hiring, as well as for household spending. Such a policy is usually pursued during periods of slow or negative economic growth as a means of stimulating the economy. Conversely, the Fed undertakes a contractionary policy during periods when it fears that accelerated economic growth is triggering or threatening to trigger excessive wage and price inflation. In general, Fed policy aims to smooth out the business cycle and achieve sustained economic growth accompanied by low inflation and low unemployment.

Fed monetary policy achieves changes in the economy through a variety of direct and indirect means. By making money cheaper and more available, it can directly affect consumer demand and business investment. It can even affect productivity indirectly by allowing businesses to invest in new and more efficient equipment.

The Fed's interest rate policies can have a major effect on the business cycle, as the events of the late 1970s and early 1980s make clear. As a result of the energy crisis, sagging productivity, and other factors, the U.S. economy suffered from both slow or negative economic growth and

Chairman Ben Bernanke presents an update on the balance sheet of the Federal Reserve Board—the central monetary policy-making authority in the United States—to a board conference in October 2009. (*Mark Wilson/Getty Images*)

Assets: Short-Term Lending Programs for Financial Institutions
(Billions of dollars)

	9/30/09	12/31/08
Short-term lending programs for financial institutions	264	1,159
Discount window	29	94
Term auction facility	178	450
Currency swaps	57	

high inflation during this period. The Keynesian economic consensus for fighting recession, which advocated fiscal and monetary stimulus, was at a loss, since such stimulus would exacerbate the already high rate of inflation. Monetarists, on the other hand, argued that the Fed could return the economy to steady and sustainable growth by slowing the growth rate of the money supply to what economic growth required. These monetarists argued that inflation was the chief bane, since it created uncertainties in the markets and stymied savings and investment.

With newly appointed chairman Paul Volcker at the helm, the Fed decided to wring inflation out of the system by drastically raising interest rates, thereby making it more expensive to borrow and thus shrinking the amount of money in circulation. With money more expensive, consumers spent less and businesses invested less, and wage and price gains fell off dramatically. The end result was that inflation was brought under control by the early 1980s but at the cost of the deepest economic downturn—and highest level of unemployment—of the postwar era. Over the next two decades, the Fed moved toward attaining a more stable and predictable funds rate as a way to grow the money supply in response to growth in the real economy.

Housing Boom

While the decisions undertaken by Volcker in the 1980s to rein in inflation are widely praised, this is not the case with more recent Fed decisions. Mistakes in monetary policy, as economists understand, can also have major negative effects on the economy that cannot always be reversed by changing policy. A recent example of this is the housing bubble of the early and mid-2000s. From late 2001 to late 2004, the Fed set its funds rate at historically low levels of 2 percent or less, partly to revive an economy hard hit by the dot.com bust and the recession of 2000–2001. By making money cheaper and more available, the Fed made it easier for people to obtain low-cost mortgages, spurring a boom in the housing market that drove up prices to unsustainable levels. But the boom continued even after the Fed raised the funds rate. By this point, the upswing was self-sustaining. Even though credit became theoretically more expensive and scarce—which normally should have made banks more careful in their lending—rising house prices reassured lenders that they could always get their money back should a borrower default. From the perspective of the housing bust years of the late 2000s, many economists and policy makers have argued that the Fed kept interest rates low for too long a period, thereby failing to burst the housing price bubble. In doing so, it also created conditions for an inevitable bursting of the housing price bubble, the single most important factor in the deep recession that hit much of the world economy in 2008 and 2009.

In the wake of the financial crisis triggered by the crash in housing prices, the Fed moved aggressively, agree most economists, though not without controversy. It lowered the benchmark rate it charged member banks to near zero, as a way to loosen credit markets and avert a deepening recession. This was a traditional move and did not meet with much criticism. Perhaps its most controversial move was to provide $85 billion in bailout money to troubled insurance giant AIG, which had in effect insured many of the derivatives and other complicated securities at the heart of the crisis, a move Chairman Ben Bernanke justified by pointing to the catastrophic effect the failure of AIG would have on financial markets worldwide. The Fed would later be criticized for focusing on helping the biggest financial institutions while ignoring the economic plight of ordinary borrowers. Moreover, the Fed would also be criticized for steps it did not take, with many in the media and policy-making circles blaming it for exacerbating the growing financial crisis in late summer of 2008 by not bailing out the major investment bank of Lehman Brothers.

International Factors

Monetary policy makers also have to consider international factors in their decisions. And here the currency system of the country plays an important role. If a nation has a fixed exchange rate—usually against the dollar—lower interest rates are likely to reduce international capital inflows as lenders shy away from places where their money brings in lower returns. Lower rates may also produce domestic capital outflows, as financial institutions, investors, and depositors send their money abroad in search of higher returns. These flows can damage a country's balance of payments and reduce foreign currency reserves, as central banks have to supply the foreign currencies demanded by consumers (to buy foreign goods) and investors (to make foreign investments).

To do this, the bank has to reduce the local currency in circulation—or risk inflation—and thus undermine the expansionary policy of lowering interest rates it undertook in the first place. The effects of the contractionary monetary policy are the opposite of the effects of expansionary monetary policy, but again, the economy returns to the state it was in before the central bank launched its policy. In other words, in a system of fixed exchange rates, the total effect of monetary policy—both expansionary and contractionary—can be zero, and it is not effective for influencing the economy.

If a country has a floating exchange rate, then increasing the money supply decreases interest rates but increases bank lending, consumer spending, imports, and capital outflows. This leads to the depreciation of the local currency. The value of the domestic currency decreases while the value of foreign currencies increases, because the demand for foreign currencies increases as they are needed for importing goods and services and investing abroad. This, in turn, may increase local firms' competitiveness on foreign markets—as the new exchange rate causes local goods and services to become relatively cheaper than foreign ones—and once again may lead to economic growth, increased spending, and higher interest rates. Contractionary monetary policy—decreasing the money supply—has the opposite effects. In short, if the country's exchange rate is floating, monetary policy may be more effective than it would be in countries with fixed exchange rates.

Tiia Vissak and James Ciment

See also: Balance of Payments; Banks, Central; Federal Reserve System; Inflation; Interest Rates; Price Stability.

Further Reading

Fleckenstein, William A., and Frederick Sheehan. *Greenspan's Bubbles: The Age of Ignorance at the Federal Reserve.* New York: McGraw-Hill, 2008.

U.S. Monetary Policy: An Introduction. San Francisco: Federal Reserve Bank of San Francisco, 2004. Available at www.frbsf .org/publications/federalreserve/monetary/MonetaryPolicy .pdf. Accessed January 2010.

Woodward, Bob. *Maestro: Greenspan's Fed and the American Boom.* New York: Simon & Schuster, 2001.

Monetary Stability

Monetary stability, one of the central goals of a nation's monetary policy, means that the value of nation's currency—or, in the case of the euro, a region's currency—remains relatively stable over time, both in terms of purchasing power and vis-à-vis other national currencies. By achieving monetary stability, governments hope to assure steady and sustainable economic growth, with low levels of inflation and unemployment.

Role of Central Banks

In most countries, monetary policy is set by central banks—in the United States, the central bank is the Federal Reserve (usually referred to as the Fed)—though in some nations monetary policy is controlled by monetary boards or institutes. In virtually all countries, central banks, while they are government institutions, enjoy relative autonomy from politics. The reason for this is that politicians, eager to be reelected, might unduly influence central banks to pursue dangerously expansive monetary policies in hopes of producing short-term surges in economic activity during election years, even if such policies might endanger the long-term economic health of the nation.

Monetary stability is generally achieved by a set of policy measures undertaken by the central bank of a country. Central banks usually have the power to set interest rate targets, control discount policy by lending directly to commercial banks, and set reserve requirements for commercial banks. In the United States, for example, the Fed has three means to implement monetary policy. It can change the rate it charges member banks—that

is, all federally chartered and many large state-chartered banks—to borrow money, the so-called discount rate. By charging more, it makes money more expensive to borrow, tightening credit, hiking interest rates, and hence contracting the amount of money in the economy. Charging less produces the opposite effect. While widely noted in the media, the discount rate is largely symbolic, indicating the Fed's overall monetary policy.

The Fed can also increase reserve requirements pertaining to the amount of money commercial banks must hold—their liabilities—against their outstanding loans, or assets. By increasing the requirement, the Fed makes it more difficult for banks to lend money, thereby contracting the amount of money in circulation. Again, by doing the opposite, the Fed indirectly puts more money in the system.

But the most important and effective tool at the Fed's disposal is its power to buy and sell government securities, its so-called open-market actions. By selling securities, the Fed, in effect, sops up money; by buying them back, it releases money into the system. Finally, since the financial crisis of 2008–2009, the Fed and other central banks have added a fourth weapon to their monetary policy arsenal—the buying up of bank assets and equity. This latter tool has been used to increase bank liquidity at a time of credit contraction, in the hope that commercial banks lend more money.

Historical Federal Reserve Actions

By hiking the discount rate, pushing up reserve requirements, and selling government securities, the Fed attempts to shrink or slow the growth of the money supply. This is usually done during periods of economic growth, when the Fed fears that too much investment and spending may lead to too much inflation. In the early 1980s, for example, with the nation experiencing high rates of inflation, the Fed moved decisively in the above-noted ways. The effort worked and the consumer price index measure of inflation dropped from around 13.5 percent in 1980 to 3.5 percent in

1985, though at the cost of the highest levels of unemployment and the worst economic downturn since the Great Depression.

This action was inspired, in part, by the monetarist school of economics—its best-known advocate being Nobel Prize–winning economist Milton Friedman—which argued that the best way to assure sustained economic growth was by maintaining monetary stability. Inflation has a crippling effect on economies in two major ways. By creating uncertainties over future prices and profits, it dampens business investment. At the same time, households tend to spend more, since they anticipate higher prices in the future. Weak investment and rising demand created a vicious cycle of inflation that the Fed aimed to stop in the early 1980s.

By making the opposite moves, the Fed attempts to speed up the increase in the money supply. This is usually done in periods of economic contraction, such as during the post-dot.com recession of the early 2000s, when the Fed lowered the discount rate from 6.5 percent in May 2000 to 1 percent in June 2003.

While the Fed changes its monetary policy in response to changes in the economy, and in hope of affecting the economy, the long-term goal is monetary stability, where the money supply grows at the same rate as the economy, thereby assuring that both inflation and unemployment remain low. In both cases, it should be noted the goal is not zero inflation or zero unemployment although, according to economists, both would be the desired goal in an ideal world. There is always some frictional unemployment as people move from job to job. And mild levels of inflation are generally considered beneficial by economists. This is because wages are "sticky," as workers and firms are reluctant to lower them. If there were no inflation, there would have to be no rises in wages, but that is very unlikely as workers expect to receive more in wages for things like seniority, and firms generally have policies to meet this desire. If inflation were zero, then firms would have to lay off workers to keep prices absolutely steady. Monetary stability, then, is about maintaining a growth in the money supply commensurate with economic growth, and taking into account the fact that mild levels of inflation are necessary.

By achieving monetary stability, central banks also hope to maintain a currency's value vis-à-vis other major currencies. By maintaining a steady ratio, the central bank of a country hopes to ensure that the country can export its goods competitively and borrow money from abroad at reasonable interest rates. If a nation's currency becomes too valuable, then the goods it produces become too expensive in comparison to similar goods produced in other countries. If, on the other hand, the value of the currency falls too much, international investors will be hesitant to buy that nation's government securities, forcing that nation's central bank to raise its interest rates to attract capital and thereby putting a damper on economic growth.

Finally, in the wake of the 2008–2009 financial crisis, many central banks moved to buy up troubled assets and to take equity stakes in commercial banks. This was done because many of the latter had large amounts of mortgage-backed securities, derivatives, and other financial instruments whose value dropped dramatically in the wake of the U.S. and global housing crisis. By buying these assets, the Fed was directly pumping money into commercial banks in the hope that they would lend more money, as the sudden and dramatic tightening of credit in late 2008 threatened to push the global economy into a deep recession, if not depression. Such action was intended, among other things, to increase the money supply as a means of countering recessionary forces.

James Ciment and Željko Šević

See also: Banks, Central; Federal Reserve System; Inflation; Interest Rates; Monetary Policy; Price Stability.

Further Reading

Balino, T.J.T., and Carlo Cottarelli. *Frameworks for Monetary Stability: Policy Issues and Country Experiences: Papers Presented at the Sixth Seminar on Central Banking Washington, D.C. March 1–10, 1994,* Washington, DC: International Monetary Fund, 1994.

Cukierman, Alex. *Central Bank Strategy, Credibility, and Independence: Theory and Evidence.* Cambridge, MA: MIT Press, 1992.

Hetzel, Robert L. *The Monetary Policy of the Federal Reserve.* New York: Cambridge University Press, 2008.

U.S. Monetary Policy. An Introduction. San Francisco: Federal Reserve Bank of San Francisco, 2004. Available at http://www.frbsf.org/publications/federalreserve/monetary/MonetaryPolicy.pdf. Accessed January 2010.

Monetary Theories and Models

Business cycle theory aims at explaining the causes of periodic ups and downs in an economy. Some explanations center on the use of money in modern industrial economies. Since the use of money pervades modern economies, the idea that money is deeply involved with industrial cycles might seem obvious. However, some business cycle theories center on actual goods used in production (industrial equipment and labor) rather than on the money used in buying and selling real goods.

Nineteenth-Century Theories

Several prominent nineteenth-century economists developed monetary (money-based) theories of business cycles. Thomas Malthus explained business cycles in terms of an oversupply of money followed by underspending. Malthus thought that rising prices in a booming economy cause the total supply of money to expand. Booms could therefore be self-financing by inducing more money to be injected into the economy. Conversely, Malthus maintained, booms lead to underconsumption and, due to excessive saving by capitalists, economic busts. By saving money, he argued, capitalists reduce the demand for goods. Reduced spending on goods (or underconsumption) will cut profit rates and send the economy into a crash.

John Stuart Mill offered a different monetary theory of cycles. In his view, business cycles are driven by investor speculation and bank credit expansion. Mill argued that excessive optimism on the part of "rash speculators" causes banks to overextend credit. Excessive bank credit causes a boom, and the economy appears sound during the upswing. However, the undue optimism of rash speculators means that their investment plans are faulty—and that they will ultimately fail. Once speculators start to fail, prices fall, credit contracts, and the economy goes into a downward spiral. And the crisis will affect more than just speculators. Even sound businesses can be caught up in it, leaving many workers unemployed.

In the second half of the nineteenth century, Karl Marx proposed yet a third monetary theory of cycles—one also tightly linked to political forces. According to Marx, the use of money in commerce set capitalism on an unstable path of booms and busts. Capitalists reap profits by investing money (M) in commodities (C), which are then sold for even more money (M'). Since M is less than M', the "capitalist" cycle effectively trades less money for more; the difference between M and M' is defined as "surplus value." Marx maintained that capitalists seek to gain surplus value by exploiting workers.

There are two important factors in Marx's theory of exploitation. First, the existence of some unemployment keeps wages low. And since workers fear becoming unemployed, they will accept wages lower than the value of what they produce. This loss of workers' wages is an important source of surplus value that accrues to capitalists. Second, competition for monetary profit among capitalists causes the rate of profit to decline. Capitalists try to maintain their rate of profit by investing in more capital—including new technology—but they can only invest in capital through further exploitation of workers, and there is a limit to how much they can extract from workers.

Once capitalists have pushed the exploitation to its limits, the economy will crash and many capitalists will become bankrupt. The surviving capitalists will take over capital from those who have failed and start the process all over again.

Thus, the use of money puts capitalism on a boom-and-bust cycle whereby ownership of industry becomes more concentrated over time.

Twentieth-Century Theories

Business cycle theories of the nineteenth century generally lacked a sound theoretical basis and were at best superficially plausible. By 1890, however, basic economic theory had improved and economists were in a position to construct better business cycle theories.

Modern monetary business cycle theory was founded by the Swedish economist Knut Wicksell in the late 1890s and early 1900s. Wicksell maintained that the supply of household savings and the demand for business loans for investment determine the "natural" level of interest rates. Specifically, natural interest rates occur where consumer savings and business investment (and production) are in balance. In such an economy, Wicksell contended, steady growth occurs as households buy more of the output that businesses turn out. Wicksell further maintained that a too-rapid increase in the money supply will drive a wedge between normal consumer saving and business investment, causing a fundamental imbalance that disrupts industry and leads to economic busts.

According to Wicksell's critics, the relationship between an economy's money supply, household savings (and spending), and business investment is not so simple. Among other things, they argue, Wicksell did not sufficiently take into account the possibility of inflation. If households buy more while businesses expand to produce more, then increases in the money supply simply deliver more goods to consumers.

At the same time, however, it is important to remember that industrial production has limits. As businesses and households all try to spend more, prices will rise as too much money chases too few goods. Inflation results from excessive spending by households and businesses. Low interest rates would ultimately cause severe inflation, known as *hyperinflation.* Conversely, artificially high interest rates reduce demand for loans by entrepreneurs and cause price *deflation*, or a general fall in prices and wages.

The twentieth-century Austrian school economists Ludwig von Mises and Friedrich von Hayek took Wicksell's ideas a step further by focusing on the complexities inherent in the relationship among interest rates, business investment, and consumer spending, especially as regards the role of inflation. In the Austrian version of monetary trade-cycle theory, low interest rates cause business investment and consumer spending to rise together. While this is good for short-term growth, such high spending will ultimately cause inflation. The only way to stop this inflation is to raise interest rates by restricting the money supply. But higher interest rates and restricted money supply will force capitalists to liquidate many of their projects. Mises and Hayek therefore advocated preventive measures for the trade cycle. Since creating large amounts of new money causes upswings in the economy that inevitably end in disaster, central banks should be restrained from doing so.

According to the British economist John Maynard Keynes, the main cause of trade cycles has to do with the demand for money rather than the supply of money. With less spending by households and businesses and with more money simply being held by speculators, the money supply will circulate at a slower pace. Thus, a general lack of money demand causes downturns in the business cycle.

The Great Depression: Keynes versus Hayek

The Great Depression of the 1930s provided economists with a prime battleground on which to test their monetary theories of business cycles. Hayek, for one, explained business cycles in terms of variations in the money supply. The fact that the Federal Reserve Bank increased the money supply during the 1920s and pulled back on the money supply in 1929 supports Hayek's case. Indeed, most economists initially subscribed to Hayek's view. Keynes, meanwhile, explained business cycles in terms of variations in money demand. In his view, crises are caused by low spending and speculative cash hoarding. According to Keynes, the persistence of the Great Depression supported that argument. By 1931, the Federal Reserve had tried to lower interest rates to stimulate investment, but the economy slid further into depression. By the late 1930s, most economists accepted Keynes's business cycle theory.

If Keynes is right, the remedy for the trade cycle is for government to boost its spending whenever private spending falls short. The government can then close the gap between private saving and private investment and in so doing restore steady circulation of the money supply. Keynes's followers also believe that the government can make limited use of its control over the money supply to counteract business cycles.

Milton Friedman

University of Chicago economist Milton Friedman challenged post–World War II supporters of Keynes, arguing that business cycles are caused by changes in the money supply. According to Friedman, money demand is relatively stable and consumption does not rise and fall exactly with current income. When people lose current income, he argued, they try to maintain most of their planned consumption. They do so by either liquidating past savings or by borrowing. As the economy slows, consumers will automatically close any gap between saving and investment. Friedman, like Hayek, blamed businesses cycles on manipulation of the money supply by central banks. His solution to radical swings in the economy was to grow the money supply at a slow and steady rate. Friedman's policy of constant money supply growth might not eliminate the trade cycles entirely, he recognized, but it would make them less severe.

Although many economists today still accept

modified versions of Keynes's theory, the academic and policy-making community in the late twentieth century began discounting the role of money in trade cycles. Many insisted that money has no real effect on the economy and that the business cycle is caused by technological or regulatory shocks or by problems in labor markets.

Financial Crisis of 2008–2009

The most recent financial crisis has renewed interest in the original ideas of Keynes and Hayek. Some economists view the subprime mortgage crisis of 2007–2008 and its economic repercussions as another example of a Keynesian collapse of private spending. Other economists blame the Federal Reserve for funding the subprime boom in the years leading up to the crisis. Although economists would continue to disagree as to which monetary theory of trade cycles is correct, the general idea that money is central to explaining trade cycles was back in vogue.

D.W. MacKenzie

See also: Austrian School; Friedman, Milton; Hayek, Friedrich August von; Monetary Policy; Monetary Stability.

Further Reading
Friedman, Milton. *Studies in Quantity Theory.* Chicago: University of Chicago Press, 1956.
———. *A Theory of the Consumption Function.* Princeton, NJ: Princeton University Press, 1957.
Garrison, Roger. *Time and Money: The Macroeconomics of Capital Structure.* New York: Routledge, 1999.
Hayek, Friedrich August von. *Monetary Theory and the Trade Cycle.* New York: Harcourt, Brace, 1933.
———. *The Pure Theory of Capital.* London: Macmillan, 1941.
Keynes, John Maynard. *The General Theory of Employment, Interest and Money.* New York: Harcourt, Brace, 1936.
———. *A Treatise on Money.* New York: Harcourt, Brace and Company, 1930.
Malthus, Thomas R. *Principles of Political Economy: Considered with a View to Their Practical Application.* London: Longman, Hurst, Rees, Orme and Brown, 1820.
Marx, Karl. *Capital: A Critique of Political Economy,* trans. Ben Fowkes. New York: Vintage, 1976–1981.
Mill, John Stuart. *The Collected Works of John Stuart Mill,* ed. J.M. Robinson. Toronto: University of Toronto Press, 1963–1991.

Mises, Ludwig von. *The Theory of Money and Credit*. London: J. Cape, 1934.

Sandelin, Bo, ed. *Knut Wicksell: Selected Essays in Economics*. New York: Routledge, 1999.

White, Lawrence H. *A Theory of Monetary Institutions*. New York: Wiley-Blackwell, 1999.

Money Markets

Money markets are financial markets for short-term financial instruments in various countries in which different types of short-term debt securities, including bank loans, are purchased and sold. Money market instruments are highly liquid and marketable; companies that would like to have a high degree of liquidity prefer to invest in money market securities because they are easy to convert into cash.

Characteristics and Availability

Money market investments are also called cash investments because of their short maturities. Large corporations or governments need to keep sufficient cash to manage their daily operations. These daily operations comprise paying back their short-term debts and tax obligations and the ability to acquire their daily purchases to run their day-to-day business. As money markets are short term and less risky, their return is lower than the longer-term debt instruments such as bonds and equities. The difference between the money market and the capital market is that the money market utilizes short-term debt securities. Money market securities must have a maturity of less than one year, thus money market instruments are less risky than other financial market instruments. Therefore, the default risk is very small. Remembering the golden rule of risk and return in finance, the less risky the investment, the less profitable it is, so their return is relatively small, too.

In sharp contrast to investments made in money markets, investments made in capital markets are long term (more than one year). Market participants in capital markets are also expected to invest in some money market securities for their short-term liquidity needs. Money market instruments are traded in large denominations (often in units of $1 million to $10 million). Because of these high denominations, money markets are not available for small individual investors. However, individuals can still participate in money markets through their bank accounts or mutual funds.

Participants prefer to invest in money markets for their requirement of urgent cash and to fight against the opportunity cost of holding monetary assets such as demand deposits or cash. Even if the interest return is small in money markets, it is better than keeping excess cash on hand. Keeping cash under a mattress does not have any return but has an opportunity cost, namely the interest rate offered for that amount in money markets.

Because money market transactions involve relatively large amounts, participants are generally large institutions or government institutions, such as the U.S. Treasury, central banks (e.g., the Federal Reserve), commercial banks, brokers, dealers, and large financial and nonfinancial corporations.

Instruments and Securities

Money market instruments are investment securities that have a maturity of not longer than one year, bear low credit risk (default risk), and are well known for their ready marketability.

Certificates of deposit (CDs) are debt instruments issued by banks and other depository institutions (savings associations and credit unions) to investors. In other words, CDs are time deposits at a bank with a specific maturity date. Like all time deposits, the funds may not be withdrawn on demand. The main advantage of CDs is their safety and the ability to know what the return will be in advance. As for the disadvantages to CDs, the money is attached to the maturity of the CD and to withdraw it prior to the maturity date results in a loss for the investor.

Negotiable certificates of deposit are time deposits issued by banks and other depository institutions whose terms are negotiable. They are like CDs, but with a secondary market whereby the buyer can resell the security if the funds are needed before maturity. Thus, if an investor purchases a 90-day negotiable CD and finds out that the funds are needed in 30 days, there is a secondary market where the CD can be resold to another investor with 60 days remaining, and the original purchaser can get the funds back before the maturity date.

Treasury bills (T-bills) are short-term government securities that are issued with original maturities of one year or less. T-bills are the most marketable and safest money market securities as they are issued by governments. The reason behind their attractiveness is their simplicity and safety. Basically, T-bills are used by governments to collect money from the public. T-bills have a par value (face value), but are sold for a lower price than the par value; those who buy T-bills make a profit from the difference between the par value and the payment they made for purchasing the T-bill. The only disadvantage of T-bills is that investors do not earn a very high return because treasuries are extraordinarily safe and liquid.

The federal (fed) funds market is the financial market where banks and other depository institutions borrow and lend reserves among themselves. The loans are unsecured and usually overnight. Thus, a bank with excess reserves can loan them to another bank for interest. Likewise, a bank that is short of reserves can borrow from another bank. The fact that the Federal Reserve now pays interest on excess reserves may limit the supply of fed funds since banks can earn interest from the Fed rather than lending their excess reserves to another bank.

Repurchase agreements (repos) are agreements whereby government securities are sold with the simultaneous agreement to buy the securities back at a higher price on a later date (usually the next day). In reality, the buyer of the repo has made a loan to the seller of repo and the government se-

curity serves as collateral. The difference between the selling price of the securities and what they are bought back for is the interest on the loan. Hence, repos are very short-term borrowing instruments backed by government securities. The maturities are usually overnight but may be up to thirty days or more.

Commercial paper is a short-term, privately issued, and unsecured promissory note issued by a large corporation to raise short-term cash, most of the time to finance accounts receivable and inventories. Commercial paper has a fixed maturity of no longer than 270 days and is usually sold at a discount rate from the face value. Face value is the value of a security written on the security, but when sold at a discount rate, the difference between the face value and the discounted cost gives the investor his/her income from this transaction. Commercial paper is considered a very safe investment because the financial situation of a corporation can easily be foreseen for the next few months. Additionally, the creditworthiness and credit ratings of the corporation are usually very high; therefore, the investment is not very risky. Commercial paper is frequently issued in denominations of $100,000 or more. Smaller companies have also found their way into the commercial paper market by getting a backup letter of credit or guarantee from a bank stating that the bank will pay the investor if the issuer of the commercial paper defaults.

Bankers' acceptances are time drafts issued by a bank guaranteeing to a seller of goods that the payment to be made is guaranteed by a bank.

Eurodollar deposits are U.S. dollar–denominated deposits placed in foreign banks outside the United States. This market developed in Europe, but the name has nothing to do with the euro or European countries. A eurodollar deposit is very large in scale and has a maturity of less than six months. Because eurodollar CDs are less liquid, they are more likely to offer higher earnings in comparison to the other money market instruments. They can also pay a higher interest rate, because the deposits are not insured (and hence a deposit insurance premium does not have to be paid) and they are not subject to reserve requirements. Therefore, they are subject to less costly regulation than domestic deposits would be. Large banks in London have organized an interbank eurodollar market. This market is now used by banks around the world as a source of overnight funding. The rate paid on these funds is known as the London interbank offered rate (LIBOR).

Money market deposit accounts are short-term deposit accounts issued by depository institutions (banks, savings associations, and credit unions) that pay a competitive interest rate. These deposits have limited check-writing privileges and are insured up to the deposit insurance limit.

Money market mutual funds are shares that collect small sums from individuals and small corporations, pool them together, and invest them in short-term marketable debt instruments on behalf of the customers. For individuals, the best way to exist in the money markets is through money market mutual funds or through a money market deposit account. The development of money markets is unavoidable because the opportunity cost of keeping cash on hand can be quite high.

While money market funds are considered one of the most secure investments, the financial crisis of the late 2000s shook investor confidence in them somewhat when they experienced severe strains. Money market funds seek a net asset value of at least one dollar. That is, investors can expect that even in troubled economic times, their investment of one dollar will return at least one dollar and, ideally, one dollar plus a small gain. But in the wake of the collapse of Lehman Brothers and the severe crisis that struck the global credit markets in September 2008, two key money market funds fell below one dollar—or, in market parlance, they "broke the buck"—an unprecedented occurrence. As a result, the Federal Reserve stepped in to allow money market funds to purchase deposit insurance for their deposits. This was done to avoid a crisis in this market and a run on these funds. To many analysts, this event was one of the many signs that the financial crisis of 2008–2009 was of a ferocity unmatched since the Great Depression of the 1930s.

Asli Yuksel Mermod

See also: Banks, Commercial; Capital Market; Collateral; Debt Instruments; Depository Institutions; Financial Markets; Stock Markets, Global; Treasury Bills.

Further Reading

Cecchetti, Stephen G. *Money, Banking and Financial Markets.* Boston: McGraw-Hill/Irwin, 2006.

Fabozzi, Frank J., Franco Modigliani, and Michael G. Ferri. *Foundations of Financial Markets and Institutions.* Upper Saddle River, NJ: Prentice Hall, 2009.

Moffett, Michael, Arthur I. Stonehill, and David Eiteman. *Fundamentals of Multinational Finance.* Boston: Pearson Prentice Hall, 2009.

Rose, Peter S., and Sylvia C. Hudgins. *Bank Management and Financial Services.* New York: McGraw-Hill, 2008.

Saunders, Anthony, and Marcia Millon Cornett. *Financial Markets and Institutions: An Introduction to the Risk Management Approach.* New York: McGraw-Hill, 2007.

Money, Neutrality of

Neutrality of money is a controversial concept in economics that bears directly on economists' policy recommendations for controlling economic fluctuations. "Neutrality" refers to the belief that changes in the money supply effect only nominal economic variables, such as prices, wages, and exchange rates, but have no effect on the actual level of output—that is, on real values, or prices corrected for inflation. If money neutrality exists, then efforts to control economic fluctuations through monetary policy will be ineffective, whereas if money is not neutral, then monetary policy has much greater potential to influence economic indicators such as gross domestic product and employment.

For example, if the stock of money is increased by 3 percent, then, according to the neutrality of money theory, prices also should increase by 3 percent, while production levels—and, as a result, the number of employees needed to produce these amounts—should remain exactly the same. Likewise, if the stock of money is decreased by 5 percent, then prices and wages also should decrease by 5 percent, and production levels and employment should not change at all. Some economists argue that a permanent change in the *rate of growth* of money, not just in the size of the money supply, likewise has no effect on long-term real output. This concept is called the superneutrality of money.

Both neutrality and superneutrality of money are based on the assumption that consumers, firms, public institutions, and others active in the markets for goods, labor, and capital are fully aware of all changes in the stock of money. Furthermore, these economic actors adjust prices based on what economists call "rational expectations" about the economy's future. As a result, real values—that is, prices adjusted for the inflationary impact of the growing money supply—remain unchanged. Although this scenario may seem far-fetched, it is supported by some empirical studies.

On the other hand, many economists, in particular those in the Keynesian tradition, maintain that money is not fully neutral—that is, increases in the money supply may affect real variables. Consequently, monetary policy can be used to increase output during economic busts by increasing the stock of money and to cool overinflated booms by decreasing the stock of money. According to these economists, money is not fully neutral because market players have imperfect information and an insufficient understanding of the consequences of making changes in the stock of money. After all, in the real world, all people are not trained economists—even if an individual is informed that additional money has been printed or that banks' reserve requirements have been lowered or strengthened, he or she may not fully understand what those changes mean and, consequently, may not act as rationally as classical economists would expect.

In addition, not only can real variables be affected by changes in the stock of money, but also nominal variables in a real-world economy may not be responsive to changes in the stock of money.

For example, wages tend to be sticky—it is not easy to lower them, especially if trade unions are strong and unemployment is very low—and thus, even if the stock of money is reduced, wages do not always drop. Likewise, as all employers are not enthusiastic to increase wages if unemployment is high and trade unions are weak, wages do not always increase after the stock of money is expanded. Both phenomena run counter to the concept of neutrality of money.

Moreover, many companies do not make minor upward or downward price changes when the stock of money changes slightly because of so-called menu costs: they would have to print and attach new price tags, which is quite time-consuming and costly, especially if they sell a large number of goods (as in a supermarket). In addition, some prices are also sticky—for instance, during economic recessions, all homeowners do not lower the prices of their houses, even if the stock of money is reduced considerably. Indeed, some may not even be aware of such a change.

Research on the neutrality of money is contradictory; the results depend on the country, the level of inflation, and the length of time studied. Most economists conclude that money is not perfectly neutral, at least not in the short run, and therefore monetary policy can influence real output and employment.

Tiia Vissak

See also: Gross Domestic Product; Inflation; Keynes, John Maynard; Monetary Policy.

Further Reading

Hayek, Friedrich A. "On 'Neutral Money.'" In *Money, Capital, and Fluctuations: Early Essays,* ed. Roy McCloughry. 1933. Chicago: University of Chicago Press, 1984.

Lucas, Robert E., Jr. "Expectations and the Neutrality of Money." *Journal of Economic Theory* 4:2 (1972): 103–124.

Saving, Thomas R. "On the Neutrality of Money." *Journal of Political Economy* 81:1 (1973): 98–119.

Serletis, Apostolos, and Zisimos Koustas. "International Evidence on the Neutrality of Money." *Journal of Money, Credit and Banking* 30:1 (1998): 1–25.

Siegel, Jeremy J. "Technological Change and the Superneutrality of Money." *Journal of Money, Credit and Banking* 15:3 (1983): 363–367.

Tyran, Jean-Robert. *Money Illusions and the Strategic Complementarity as Causes of Monetary Non-Neutrality.* New York: Springer, 1999.

Money Store, The

A pioneer in offering subprime home mortgages, the Sacramento-based Money Store became a major lender in the 1990s, before being purchased by First Union, a North Carolina banking corporation, in 1998 and then shut down because of sustained losses two years later.

Opened in 1967 by entrepreneur Alan Turtletaub, The Money Store originally focused on providing second mortgages to persons whose poor credit history made them ineligible for financing by traditional banks. While the second mortgage offered by the company usually came with interest rates several points higher than the traditional loan, the funds could be used by mortgage holders to pay off higher interest credit card debt, making such financing popular.

In 1989, son Marc Turtletaub took over from his father, presiding over the company's boom years in the 1990s. By 1998, The Money Store had revenues of more than $800 million and some 5,000 employees in offices around the country. But with success came the inevitable competition. As profit margins declined, the company began to experience cash-flow problems and started to sell its portfolio of loans to secondary markets to get the money necessary to lend to new clients. The Money Store bundled the loans and sold them as mortgage-backed securities.

For a time, the strategy worked, largely through aggressive marketing to win new customers. Some $40 million in ads in its last years—featuring pitches by baseball icon Phil Rizzuto—made it simple for potential borrowers to obtain a loan through a national 800 number. With the advent of the Internet in the late 1990s, the company took its publicity online in a major way, eventually developing an interactive site where the customer could pick the terms he or she wanted.

But even as the company was selling itself to potential customers, investors in the late 1990s remained wary of mortgage-backed securities and the company found itself facing liquidity problems. With the Asian and Russian currency crises of 1997 and 1998 further freezing up the markets for risky securities, the company was forced to sell itself to First Union for $2.1 billion.

While the infusion of cash from First Union, then the sixth-largest bank in the United States, helped The Money Store remain solvent, it still sustained losses in 1999 and 2000 as new players entered the subprime and second mortgage markets. First Union tried to cut costs by halving its workforce, but to no avail. In 2000, First Union closed down The Money Store, paying out some $1.7 billion in severance pay to employees.

In 2004, former company chairman Morton Dean, now head of MLD Mortgage, purchased the name The Money Store and reopened it for business as a mortgage financer, with a check-cashing operation that allows people to get short-term loans, or advances—usually at very high interest—against future paychecks.

John Barnhill and James Ciment

See also: Mortgage, Subprime; Shadow Banking System.

Further Reading

"First Union to Acquire Money Store for $2.1 Billion." *New York Times*, March 5, 1998. www.nytimes.com/1998/03/05/business/first-union-to-acquire-money-store-for-2.1-billion.html. Accessed August 24, 2009.

"First Union to Shut Down Money Store." *New York Times*, June 27, 2000. www.nytimes.com/2000/06/27/business/first-union-to-shut-down-money-store.html. Accessed August 24, 2009.

Moral Hazard

Moral hazard occurs when people or institutions take greater risks than they ordinarily would because they know that they are not going to be held fully accountable—or even accountable at all—for the costs of their risky behavior. Moral hazard is a critical factor in the insurance business, as underwriters must take into account the fact that the policies they offer may encourage risky behavior. For example, if someone has an auto insurance policy that provides full coverage for theft, the policy holder may be lackadaisical in locking his or her car. Indeed, if the owner is interested in replacing the old car with a new one, he or she may even feel the incentive to behave in a risky fashion.

A similar situation applies to depository institutions with deposit insurance that might act in inordinately risky ways if they know they (or their depositors) are not going to suffer the full consequences of that behavior. For example, a bank may be enticed to take on high levels of risk with its depositors' funds because the bank knows its depositors will not lose if the investments turn sour. Depositors do not worry about the risky investments the banks make because they know their deposits are insured. Banks get to keep the higher return if the risky investments pay off but depositors are shielded from the losses if they do not.

Moral hazard has also been a concern of economists and policy makers for several decades with regard to the international financial system. Many analysts worry that developed countries are encouraged to borrow recklessly because they know that the International Monetary Fund (or a government) would step in to rescue them should they be on the verge of bankruptcy during a financial crisis. Moreover, moral hazard encourages international banks and other financial institutions to make such loans in the developed world for the very same reason.

The financial crisis of 2008–2009 brought the dangers of moral hazard to the attention of the public at large and highlighted a type of moral hazard relating to mortgage securitizations. The securitization of mortgages—the bundling and reselling of mortgages to investors as securities—

encouraged greater risk taking among mortgage originators. Prior to when the securitization of mortgages became widespread, lenders were careful about whom they offered mortgages to, since they would be responsible should the borrower default. But by passing on the risk to others, lenders could act in less responsible ways. At the same time, the originators were more aware of the risks than those assuming them, since the latter did not have specific information about the original mortgagors. Such moral hazard also applied to the many derivatives taken out against securities investments, as these derivatives acted like insurance policies on those investments, shifting some of the risk from one set of investors to another.

Then, in the wake of the financial crisis of late 2008 came the massive $700 billion federal bailout of banks and other financial institutions—a move replicated by central banks and governments in many other countries afflicted by the global credit crisis. Many economists have since theorized that major financial institutions acted in riskier fashion than they should have because they knew that their governments would never allow them to become insolvent or collapse. They were—to use a contemporary financial turn of phrase—"too big to fail." In other words, they knew that their sheer size and involvement in so many aspects of the global financial markets created a situation in which their failure would create economic and political consequences so dire that no government would risk such an occurrence. They had more information than the party who would bear the brunt of their risky behavior—the government and ultimately the taxpayers.

The costs of moral hazard were borne out by the cascade of events in 2008 that led up to the global financial crisis. When the investment bank Bear Stearns became insolvent in March 2008, the government quickly moved in to arrange its rescue by offering guarantees to its ultimate purchaser, fellow investment bank JPMorgan Chase. This, say economists, sent a signal to the markets that the government would come to the rescue should a major investment bank risk going under.

With the impending collapse of the far bigger Lehman Brothers in September 2008, however, Treasury Secretary Henry Paulson and Federal Reserve chairman Ben Bernanke were loathe to step in, fearing that they were encouraging moral hazard throughout the financial sector. As it turned out, the reluctance to rescue Lehman Brothers sent shock waves through the financial markets and contributed to the crisis of late 2008 and early 2009 that prompted the $700 billion bailout. In other words, according to some economists, fears of encouraging moral hazard led to a response that greatly exacerbated the financial crisis and pushed the global financial system to the brink of collapse. In other words, it seemed that the failure of government to bail out Lehman Brothers in order to discourage moral hazard led to a worse outcome than if the government had bailed out the excessively leveraged institution, which had taken on excessively high levels of risk.

James Ciment

See also: Risk and Uncertainty; Troubled Asset Relief Program (2008–).

Further Reading

Fenton-O'Creevy, Mark, Nigel Nicholson, Emma Soane, and Paul Willman. *Traders: Risks, Decisions, and Management in Financial Markets.* Oxford, UK: Oxford University Press, 2005.

Ferguson, Niall, and Laurence Kotlikoff. "How to Take Moral Hazard Out of Banking." *Financial Times,* December 2, 2009. Available at www.ft.com/cms/s/0/34cd41e4-df77–11de-98ca-00144feab49a.html. Accessed January 2010.

Kamin, Steven. "Identifying the Role of Moral Hazard in International Financial Markets." *International Finance* 7:1 (Spring 2004): 25–59.

Lane, Timothy, and Steven Phillips. *Moral Hazard: Does IMF Financing Encourage Imprudence by Borrowers and Lenders?* Washington, DC: International Monetary Fund, 2002.

Stern, Gary H., and Ron J. Feldman. *Too Big to Fail: The Hazards of Bank Bailouts.* Washington, DC: Brookings Institution, 2004.

Morgan Stanley

One of America's most successful investment banks from the 1930s through 2008, Morgan Stanley was hit hard by the financial crisis of the late 2000s, as many of its investments in securitized debt obligations lost value and uncertainty in the markets brought down its share price by nearly half. Nevertheless, Morgan Stanley was one of two major firms that survived the winnowing of the U.S. investment banking industry during the crisis, along with Goldman Sachs, though not before transforming itself into a traditional bank holding company with commercial bank operations.

Morgan Stanley's story begins with the Glass-Steagall Act of 1933, which required that the investment and commercial banking operations of a financial holding company be separated into separate entities. Morgan Stanley grew out of J.P. Morgan and Company, the wealthiest and most powerful financial institution of the late nineteenth and early twentieth centuries, operating both investment and commercial banking operations. In the wake of the 1929 stock market crash and amid the Great Depression that followed, many economists and many in the public came to believe that investment banks and commercial banks should be separated, as the risky behavior of the former jeopardized the solvency of the latter when they were part of the same company. This, it was argued, had caused the sell-off in securities values to lead to an overall collapse of the country's banking system in the early 1930s.

With passage of Glass-Steagall, J.P. Morgan and Co. was forced to split off its investment bank into a new company, headed by Henry S. Morgan (J.P. Morgan's grandson) and Harold Stanley, two former partners at J.P. Morgan. Although Morgan Stanley was largely funded by J.P. Morgan and Co., the split was still in compliance with Glass-Steagall because the company was issued only nonvoting preference shares in Morgan Stanley. At least on paper, J.P. Morgan and Co. could not decide the policies or practices of Morgan Stanley.

From the time it opened its doors on September 16, 1935, Morgan Stanley prospered, aided by the fact that it had acquired much of its parent company's investment banking business. In its first year,

Morgan Stanley handled approximately one-quarter of all the securities issued in the United States. From the outset, Morgan Stanley was so successful that it could demand to be the lead underwriter for all of its client offerings. At the same time, the company benefited from the collegial investment banking atmosphere of the times, whereby rival firms rarely poached clients from each other.

By the early 1940s, however, competition began to increase, as some clients would request bids from various investment banks before making a purchase. Still, most of Morgan Stanley's blue-chip clients continued to find comfort in the prestige and cachet of the Morgan name. In the 1950s, Morgan Stanley's client roster was the envy of Wall Street and included such giants as General Electric, U.S. Steel, and General Motors. The firm did not need to trade or distribute securities or even resort to advising newly formed companies. This allowed it to avoid undue market exposure or company risk. Major financial innovations had not yet arrived, and competition was not overly intense. Issuing securities was a relatively straightforward process, so clients saw little benefit in having the investment banks fight over business.

The 1960s brought significant changes both at Morgan Stanley—as it expanded into Europe—and in the investment banking business generally. At the prompting of clients, the industry took on a new aggressiveness, and firms began to arrange company takeovers. In addition, competitors such as Salomon Brothers and Goldman Sachs began to gain ground on Morgan Stanley by setting up securities trading departments.

At first, Morgan Stanley looked down on what it regarded as the huckstering of securities. By the 1970s, however, the company realized that it needed to participate in order to keep up with competitors, so Morgan Stanley set up trading and sales desks of its own. Securities trading brought increased risk and fundamentally changed the culture of investment banking. Once dominated by a small group of individuals from top families, investment banking became more of a meritocracy, with traders from all walks of life soon dominating the business.

The 1970s and the 1980s also saw Morgan Stanley move aggressively into the mergers and acquisitions (M&A) business. Initially, the M&A department would provide advice to clients interested in acquiring other companies. But the business proved so lucrative that Morgan Stanley soon began pitching its own ideas to clients in order to ignite further M&A activity. M&A continued to flourish through the 1980s and into the 1990s, expanding through the issue of high-risk ("junk") bonds. Because such activities required considerable capital, Morgan Stanley in 1986 sold 20 percent of its shares to the public.

As with much of the rest of the investment banking community, success followed upon success for Morgan Stanley through the mid-2000s,

Morgan Stanley, with headquarters in New York's Times Square, survived the financial cataclysm that struck down so many other U.S. investment firms in 2008, but reconstituted itself as a bank holding company, which meant tighter federal regulation. *(Bloomberg/Getty Images)*

though the company lost more than a dozen employees in the terrorist attacks of September 11, 2001. In 2004, Morgan Stanley handled the highly successful initial public offering (IPO) of the Internet search engine company Google and traded in the flourishing collateralized debt obligation instrument market, whereby home mortgages were bundled and sold to investors.

With the meltdown of the subprime mortgage market in 2007, Morgan Stanley found itself forced to write down a number of bad investments, requiring a $5 billion cash infusion from a Chinese investment company in exchange for nearly 10 percent equity. The financial crisis of 2008 continued to batter the firm, which saw its share price fall nearly 50 percent by the early fall. As other "too big to fail" investment banks did exactly that, there was talk that Morgan Stanley would merge with a major commercial bank. Instead, the company sought to reconstitute itself. On September 22, 2008, it announced that it would be doing business as a bank holding company, bringing it full circle to the structure of the original J.P. Morgan back before Glass-Steagall. (The law's stipulations against combining investment and commercial banking under one firm had been overturned with passage of the 1999 Financial Services Modernization Act.)

While the new Morgan Stanley would be subjected to the much tighter federal regulation surrounding commercial banks, directors felt that the benefits outweighed the risks, especially in an era of financial volatility. As a bank holding company, it would have access to far greater assets and a more diversified business, thereby reducing its exposure to the risks of being an investment bank only. Morgan Stanley was not alone in making this decision; Goldman Sachs did the same. With other investment banks having collapsed or been taken over by commercial banks, the decision of Morgan Stanley and Goldman Sachs to become bank holding companies ended an era of stand-alone investment banks on Wall Street.

Patrick Huvane and James Ciment

See also: Banks, Investment; Troubled Asset Relief Program (2008–).

Further Reading

Chernow, Ron. *The House of Morgan: An American Banking Dynasty and the Rise of Modern Finance.* New York: Grove Press, 2010.

Gordon, John Steele. *The Great Game: The Emergence of Wall Street as a World Power, 1653–2000.* New York: Simon & Schuster, 1999.

Morgan Stanley Web site: www.morganstanley.com.

Morgenstern, Oskar (1902–1977)

German economist Oskar Morgenstern, together with Hungarian economist John von Neumann, is known as the co-founder of game theory, the branch of applied mathematics that translates situations in the social sciences into game-like strategic scenarios. Morgenstern and von Neumann co-authored *Theory of Games and Economic Behavior* (1944), the first book-length treatment of the subject.

Morgenstern was born on January 24, 1902, in Gorlitz, Germany, to the illegitimate daughter of German emperor Frederick III. He attended the University of Vienna, Austria, earning a PhD in 1925. He became the director of the Austrian Institute for Business Cycle Research in 1931 and a professor at the University of Vienna in 1935. Three years later, he received a Rockefeller Foundation fellowship to study in the United States, where he chose to remain when the Nazis invaded Vienna and forced his dismissal from the university. He took a teaching position in economics at Princeton University in New Jersey and soon joined the staff of its Institute for Advanced Study. By this time, the institute had become home to a number of scholars who had emigrated from troubled Europe, including Albert Einstein and Morgenstern's future research partner, von Neumann.

In the kind of collaboration promoted by the

institute, von Neumann's strength was his expertise in mathematics, while that of Morgenstern—who had already written a book on the science of economic predictions—was economics. In *Theory of Games and Economic Behavior*, Morgenstern and von Neumann discussed competition, utility, domination, and standards of behavior in mathematical terms; explained how economic situations could be modeled as games; and discussed what could be learned by "solving" these games. The work was revolutionary. Although World War II was the overwhelming focus of public attention in 1944, the book and its authors received widespread acclaim and attracted a level of public interest unlike that of any other publication on the mathematics of economics—and unlike no mathematician other than Einstein.

Theory of Games also reformulated the expected utility hypothesis, which had been originally described in 1738 by Dutch-Swiss mathematician Daniel Bernoulli. The hypothesis concerned human behavior during gambling and other situations in which the outcome is uncertain, when the size and probability of risk (the consequence of losing) and reward (the consequence of winning) influence the likelihood of someone making a wager. Morgenstern and von Neumann modernized the hypothesis to describe mathematically a rational decision maker according to four axioms. According to the first axiom, completeness, the decision maker prefers one outcome to another; the second axiom, transitivity, holds that the individual's preferences are consistent (for example, if he likes vanilla better than strawberry and strawberry better than pistachio, then he likes vanilla better than pistachio); the third, independence, says that adding an equal amount to each of the two outcomes does not change their order of preference; and the fourth, continuity, says that there is a possibility that a combination of the individual's second and third choice will be equal to his first choice. If these four axioms are true, then the individual's behavior is rational and can be represented mathematically. The resulting mathematical function takes into account the individual's risk aversion;

in other words, the suggestion is not that all individuals will make the same choices, but rather that the traits determining how an individual makes choices can be mathematically modeled.

The expected utility hypothesis has been applied to economics, politics, psychology, and other social sciences. Researchers have explored its ramifications in such areas as consumer behavior, decisions about medical care, and investing. Toward the end of his career, Morgenstern explored the economics of defense, among other fields. He died in Princeton on July 26, 1977.

Bill Kte'pi

See also: Risk and Uncertainty; Von Neumann, John.

Further Reading

Henn, R., and O. Moeschlin, eds. *Mathematical Economics and Game Theory: Essays in Honor of Oskar Morgenstern.* New York: Springer, 1977.

Morgenstern, Oskar. "The Collaboration Between Oscar Morgenstern and John von Neumann on the Theory of Games." *Journal of Economic Literature* 14:3 (1976): 805–816.

von Neumann, John, and Oskar Morgenstern. *Theory of Games and Economic Behavior.* Princeton, NJ: Princeton University Press, 2007.

Mortgage-Backed Securities

A mortgage-backed security (MBS) is a debt instrument whose value is based on a pool of mortgages. Investors in MBSs buy an undivided share of a pool of specific mortgages. MBSs derive their cash flows from the underlying mortgages in the pool. The most basic form of MBS simply passes the cash flows from the pool of mortgages to investors.

The U.S. MBS market was jump-started and has been sustained by the activities of three government-sponsored enterprises (GSEs): the Government National Mortgage Association (GNMA, or Ginnie Mae), the Federal National Mortgage Association (FNMA, or Fannie Mae), and the Federal Home Loan Mortgage Corporation (FHLMC, or Freddie Mac). Fannie Mae and Freddie Mac issue MBSs directly from pools of mortgages they have purchased from private lenders. Fannie Mae and Freddie Mac are publicly traded, government-sponsored companies, the stocks of which are traded on the New York Stock Exchange. Their securities were always assumed to have an implicit guarantee from the government since they were issued by a government-sponsored enterprise, even though there was no explicit guarantee. This proved to be correct when Fannie Mae and Freddie Mac were put into receivership by the federal government in late 2008 due to the unprecedented crisis in the mortgage market. Although shareholders in Fannie Mae and Freddie Mac saw the value of their stock decline, Fannie Mae and Freddie Mac securities were indeed fully guaranteed by the government. Ginnie Mae, which is part of the Department of Housing and Urban Development, guarantees the timely payment of interest and principal of MBSs issued by private lenders who purchase the Ginnie Mae guarantee. The private MBSs with the Ginnie Mae guarantee are known as Ginnie Mae securities and are backed by the full faith and credit of the U.S. government. Fannie Mae, Freddie Mac, and Ginnie Mae MBSs make up the core of what is known as the agency/GSE for MBSs. They were valued at a massive $5.3 trillion on March 31, 2009, compared to $7.5 trillion of outstanding, publicly held debt owed by the U.S. government on the same date.

Background

In 1970, Ginnie Mae launched an important financial innovation that was to set the credit and banking markets on a new path. The innovation was the Ginnie Mae–guaranteed pass-through certificate, issued by private lenders but with the Ginnie Mae guarantee, commonly referred to as the Ginnie Mae MBS. In 1981, Fannie Mae launched the Fannie Mae–guaranteed pass-through certificate, which significantly expanded the scale and scope of the MBS by directly buy-

ing mortgage pools from private lenders. Freddie Mac soon followed with its own pass-through MBS product. GSE involvement greatly expanded the scale of the MBS market and propelled its growth. Fannie Mae and Freddie Mac expanded the secondary market for mortgages by buying pools of mortgages that did not qualify for the Ginnie Mae guarantee. Fannie Mae and Freddie Mac have their own underwriting standards with which borrowers and originators must comply. Fannie Mae and Freddie Mac buy qualifying mortgages—also called conforming fixed-rate and variable-rate mortgages—from approved originators. Fannie Mae exchanges MBSs in the form of pass-through certificates for pools of conforming mortgages originated by financial institutions. Freddie Mac does the same, but its basic guaranteed MBS is called a participation certificate, which operates like a pass-through certificate. The other option for originators of mortgages that conform to GSE underwriting standards is to sell the mortgages to Fannie Mae and Freddie Mac for cash. Note that Fannie Mae and Freddie Mac issue their own securities, called agency securities, to get the funds to buy the mortgage pools from private lenders. With Ginnie Mae, private lenders sell their own MBSs but with the Ginnie Mae guarantee.

Mortgages that do not conform to the underwriting standards of the two GSEs or qualify for the Ginnie Mae guarantee are used as collateral for private-label MBSs, issued by private institutions with no government involvement. Subprime mortgages are a subsegment of the private label market. Not all nonconforming mortgages are subprime. Loans over a certain limit, called jumbo loans are not subprimes, for instance. In 2009, that limit was up to $625,250, depending on the area. Underwriting standards constrain how much a homeowner can borrow, what percentage of the value of a home (called the loan-to-value ratio) the person can borrow, and what percentage of the person's income is available to pay interest and principal on the mortgage loan. In addition, the credit profiles of prospective mortgagors are examined.

The MBS market is important because it facilitates the flow of capital from investors all over the world to families that would like to finance the purchase of a home. Banks originate mortgage loans that supply the capital needed by prospective homebuyers. The mortgage loans are then transformed into MBSs by a process known as securitization. MBSs are sold to investors such as mutual funds, hedge funds, pension funds, corporate treasuries, insurance companies, banks, and private individuals all over the world. Funds invested in MBSs flow back to the banks, which can then originate more mortgage loans. Without the ability of financial institutions to securitize and sell their mortgages, the amount of loans they can make becomes constrained.

Interest payments are determined by taking the product of the contractual monthly interest rate of the mortgage loan and the outstanding mortgage balance. There are two components of principal payments. The first is scheduled repayment of principal. This is the amortized amount necessary to pay off the mortgage loan in equal monthly payments of principal and interest over the life of the loan, typically thirty years (360 months). Note that as the principal declines each month, the level payment consists of slightly larger amounts of principal and a smaller amount of interest since the outstanding balance is falling. The other component of principal payments is unscheduled payments, which come from borrowers who pay off more than is required in a given month so that the loan is paid off before the final maturity date. When a mortgagor defaults and the foreclosed home is sold by the lender, the proceeds from the sale count as unscheduled repayment of principal. In the declining real-estate market of the late 2000s, the sale of foreclosed properties from subprime borrowers who were unable to make their mortgage payments were often insufficient to cover the outstanding loan balance. The loss must be borne by the investors in the MBS or by a financial institution that has agreed to guarantee the payments to MBS investors.

Risks

Mortgage-backed securities expose investors to interest rate risk, prepayment risk, liquidity risk, and credit risk. When market interest rates increase, such as rates on new mortgages, the value of outstanding MBSs will fall. This happens because competing newly issued MBSs backed by higher-yielding mortgages will offer higher interest rates than will outstanding MBSs. The only way investors will be willing to buy the MBS that pays a lower interest rate is if the price of the MBS declines. Indeed, the price must fall to a level that compensates investors for the lower income from interest the MBS will generate.

The prepayment risk on MBSs derives from the mortgagor's option to prepay the loan before it matures. Most mortgage loans have original maturities of either fifteen or thirty years. The prepayment option gives the mortgagor the right to prepay all or part of the mortgage principal before its final maturity date, and the unscheduled principal payment must be distributed to owners (investors) of the MBS. Prepayments also result when homeowners sell the home and pay off the mortgage. Investors are then forced to reinvest the prepaid mortgage balance. If these funds cannot be invested in securities that yield the same as the MBS did, then the investor is worse off due to the mortgagor's prepayment.

Liquidity risk refers to the possibility that an investor in MBSs or any security cannot sell his or her position for a reasonable price because few if any competing bids are being offered. In 2007, the private-label market became extremely illiquid and nearly shut down due to the crisis in the mortgage market.

Credit risk refers to the possibility that the principal value of an MBS is not repaid to investors. This would occur if the mortgages backing the pool default and the proceeds from foreclosure sales are insufficient to cover the balance of the mortgage loan.

The fundamental difference between the agency market and the private market for MBSs is how credit risk is managed and distributed. In the agency market, credit risk is absorbed by the guarantor—Fannie Mae, Ginnie Mae, or Freddie Mac. The credit risk embedded in a pool of nonconforming mortgages financed with a private-label MBS is typically shifted onto the investors of the MBSs.

Private-label MBSs generally divide the greater risks of the securities they issue into various classes, depending on the degree of risk. The simplest case is for one class of MBS to be placed in a subordinated position with respect to another security that takes a senior position. The subordinated note is designed to protect the investors in the senior security position from credit losses. As long as losses are below the principal amount of the subordinated class, the senior class will not expect any losses. For example, a mortgage loan pool of $1 million is divided into a $900,000 senior class and a $100,000 subordinated class. If $90,000 of mortgage principal is not repaid, the subordinated class will lose $90,000 (90 percent of its principal) while the senior class will not lose any principal. This is called the senior/subordinated structure. It enables the senior class of MBSs to attain a very high credit rating, perhaps AAA. The subordinated class will receive a much lower credit rating, perhaps BBB, because it is more likely to experience losses of principal. The only way investors are willing to buy a subordinated class of MBSs is if the security offers a high enough return to compensate for the additional risk. It is possible to pay the subordinated security a higher yield only if the senior class receives a lower yield. The pool of mortgages backing an MBS generates only so much interest each period. It can be redistributed but not increased.

Credit ratings are evaluations performed by private companies that assess the quality of securities. The three principal rating agencies in the United Sates for MBSs are Moody's, Standard & Poor's, and Fitch. The rating is a quantitative measure of the reliability of the security according to the particular agency. Triple A (AAA) is the highest rating, indicating that the security is unlikely to experience delays or defaults in repayment. D is the lowest rating, indicating that a security has already defaulted and remains in default.

Types

The basic MBS, whose cash flow has the same profile as the underlying mortgages, is called a pass-through security. The pass-through security is the building block of more complex MBSs created by bankers. It is called a pass-through security or pass-through certificate because the interest and principal payments are passed through to investors.

Another significant financial innovation expanded the secondary market in mortgage loans. Freddie Mac issued the first collateralized mortgage obligation (CMO) in 1983, backed by a pool of thirty-year fixed-rate mortgages. A collateralized mortgage obligation redirects the cash flows (principal and interest) of MBSs to various classes of investors, thus creating financial instruments with varying prepayment risks and varying returns. A CMO is a multi-class or multi-tranche issue of MBS to finance a single pool of mortgage collateral. (The terms "tranche" and "class" are used interchangeably.) Each class of the CMO is a separate security. The classes of securities in a CMO each have the right to receive a different portion of the monthly interest and principal payments of a pool of mortgages or pass-through securities. Investors who are most risk averse can choose any instrument wherein the principal will soon be repaid. Those who are willing to bear more risk can choose an instrument wherein the principal will not be repaid until later and, hence, is subject to a greater prepayment risk. In exchange for the greater prepayment risk, the investor receives a higher return. Needless to say, such provisions make attractive choices available to a wider range of investors. CMOs thus create instruments with varying prepayment risks and varying returns, so that investors can choose the risk/return combination they are most comfortable with.

On a final note, an interesting phenomenon has occurred in the MBS market due to the financial crisis of 2008–2009. The outstanding amount of private-label securities has decreased from just over $4.5 trillion at the end of 2007 to just under $3.7 trillion on March 31, 2009. During the same period, Fannie Mae, Freddie Mac, and Ginnie Mae MBSs increased from just over $4.4 trillion to just under $5.3 trillion—despite the fact that Fannie Mae and Freddie Mac were put into receivership in September 2008 due to their insolvency. Notwithstanding the government takeover, they still purchased large quantities of previously held private-label securities, which in reality is an attempt by the government to lend support to the crisis-ridden mortgage market.

Charles A. Stone

See also: Collateralized Debt Obligations; Collateralized Mortgage Obligations; Debt Instruments; Housing Booms and Busts; Mortgage Lending Standards; Mortgage Markets and Mortgage Rates; Mortgage, Subprime; Recession and Financial Crisis (2007–); Real-Estate Speculation.

Further Reading

Fabozzi, Frank J., ed. *The Handbook of Mortgage-Backed Securities.* New York: McGraw-Hill, 2006.

Federal Home Loan Mortgage Corporation (Freddie Mac). "Mortgage Securities Products." Available at www.freddiemac.com/mbs/html/product.

Federal National Mortgage Association (Fannie Mae). "Mortgage-Backed Securities." Available at www.fanniemae.com/mbs/index.jhtml?p=Mortgage-Backed+Securities.

Government National Mortgage Association (GinnieMae) Web site: www.ginniemae.gov.

Lucas, Douglas J., Laurie S. Goodman, Frank J. Fabozzi, and Rebecca Manning. *Developments in Collateralized Debt Obligations: New Products and Insights.* Hoboken, NJ: John Wiley & Sons, 2007.

Spotgeste, Milton R., ed. *Securitization of Subprime Mortgages.* Hauppauge, NY: Nova Science, 2009.

Stone, A. Charles, and Anne Zissu. *The Securitization Markets Handbook: Structures and Dynamics of Mortgage- and Asset-Backed Securities.* New York: Bloomberg, 2005.

Mortgage, Commercial/Industrial

Investments in commercial or industrial real estate are normally financed by borrowing. There are many types of commercial and industrial real estate, including multifamily rental housing, office buildings, retail properties, warehouses, hotels, medical office facilities, student housing, recreational facilities, and so on. The acquisition of any of these types of properties involves a "capital stack," in which a primary mortgage loan rests at the bottom, the equity of the investors rests at the top, and a mezzanine loan may fill any gap between the primary loan and equity.

Leveraging

Real-estate investors use borrowing to increase financial leverage, defined as the ratio of the total investment to the equity invested. For example, suppose that an investor has $1 million to invest in real estate, and conventional primary loans are available to finance 60 percent of the purchase price. This means that an investor can purchase real estate worth $2.5 million with the equity of $1 million (since $2.5 million x 60 percent = $1 million). However, suppose that mezzanine financing is also available and that the investor finances 20 percent of the total real-estate investment from this source. Combining this amount with the 60 percent primary loan, the investor now can borrow 80 percent of the purchase price of the investment property, and therefore can purchase real estate in the amount of $5 million (since $5 million x 80 percent = $1 million). The total value of the real-estate investment is sensitive to the degree of leverage in this range. Use of leverage increases the expected return to the $1 million in equity, provided that money for the mezzanine finance can be borrowed at an interest rate (after tax) that is less than the after-tax return to equity. However, a greater expected return to equity comes at the cost of greater risk.

The main sources of loans for commercial/industrial real estate are commercial banks, life insurance companies, and investors in asset-backed securities (pension funds, insurance companies, and other long-term investors). As of December 31, 2009, the institutions listed in the following table held

Outstanding Commercial Mortgage Debt, United States (December 31, 2009)

Commercial banks	$1,296.4 billion
Savings institutions	$123.9 billion
Life insurance companies	$237.5 billion
Asset-backed securities holders	$582.3 billion
Other sources	$245.4 billion

Source: Board of Governors of the Federal Reserve System, *Flow of Funds Accounts of the United States*, Z1, March 11, 2010, 97.

outstanding commercial mortgage debt of $2,485.5 billion in the United States.

Primary mortgages for commercial/industrial properties differ substantially from residential mortgages granted to homeowners. These loans are less standardized, require extensive and detailed documents upon submission of an application, and often involve a lengthy approval process. No consumer protection laws apply in this loan market. The loans are of shorter duration—usually 5 to 10 years—and are not fully amortizing (i.e., require a balloon payment at maturity). Therefore, if the investor intends to hold the property for a longer period, a new loan must often be obtained. Borrowers face a prepayment penalty with real teeth. Often that penalty is sufficient to ensure that the yield for the lender is the same whether the loan is held to maturity or paid back before maturity. This is known as the yield maintenance penalty. Furthermore, because investors in commercial or industrial property often view defaulting on a loan simply as a business decision based on financial costs and benefits, the loan-to-value (LTV) ratio is lower than with residential mortgages. LTV is normally 60 to 70 percent for primary mortgages, but can be as high as 80 percent. Lastly, the ability of the borrower (and the property) to pay the debt service on the loan is based on a detailed analysis of the income stream that the property can be expected to generate. This point requires some detailed discussion.

The relevant income stream is the annual cash flow called net operating income (NOI). NOI is the actual gross income of the property (gross rents and other income sources such as parking fees and so on) minus operating expenses, local property taxes, leasing expenses, and funds set aside as reserves for replacement or repair of capital equipment. Estimation of the gross income of the property involves detailed analysis of the existing leases and their expiration dates. Operating expenses include fixed expenses (e.g., insurance) and variable expenses (utilities, management fees, janitorial service, and so on). Leasing expenses included commissions to leasing agents and incentives to tenants (moving allowances, upgrades to their space, months of free rent, and so on). As defined, NOI has only two uses—debt service and before-tax return to equity. Lenders require that NOI exceed debt service payments (interest and reductions in principal); debt service coverage ratio (DCR) is defined as NOI divided by debt service payments. DCR often is set at 1.25 to 1.4, and depends upon the type of property involved and the amount of risk that is perceived.

Mezzanine loans stand after the primary mortgage loan in priority, and thus are much riskier. Mezzanine loans involve higher interest rates and substantial fees. As commercial real-estate experts note, while the interest rate on a first mortgage is usually well below 10 percent, the mezzanine rates can easily rise above 10 percent. A mezzanine loan sometimes is secured by voting stock in the company of the borrower. The mezzanine loan is separate from the primary loan, with a separate promissory note, loan document, and collateral. The loan normally is nonrecourse (the lender cannot sue for any asset beyond the collateral). Prepayment terms are comparable to those for the primary mortgage loan and are constructed so that the lender's rights terminate with repayment.

An alternative to borrowing at arm's length is an equity participation loan. The lender offers a lower interest rate in return for a share in the income of the property or a share in the appreciation in the value of the property. The lender receives a portion of the income or appreciation in value if it exceeds some base amount. In effect, the lender is providing both debt and equity. The larger equity component is shared between owner and lender. An equity participation loan that involves sharing current income means that the debt service coverage ratio is increased.

The conduit loan became increasingly important in the United States in the first decade of the 2000s. The conduit loan is a mortgage that becomes part of a pool of mortgages that is sold as a commercial mortgage-backed security (CMBS). Underwriting standards are set by the secondary market—the CMBS market—and conduit loans must be structured and documented for easy sale to the agent that buys up the loans, holds them, and sells securities based on the cash flows provided by the loans. Those agents are called real-estate mortgage investment conduits (REMIC) or financial asset securitization investment trusts (FASITs). Rating agencies such as Standard & Poor's, Moody's, or Fitch assign credit ratings to the various classes of bonds. Fannie Mae and Freddie Mac issue these securities for small residential rental properties, but otherwise the CMBS market is private.

A simple version of a CMBS would divide the returns to the pool of mortgages equally among those who purchase shares in the pool. However, since the preferences of investors differ, the returns to the mortgage pool are divided into "tranches." The collateralized mortgage obligation (CMO) is a version of the CMBS in which several tranches are formed with different return characteristics. For example, the top tranche (Tranche A) is of short maturity and would receive interest, amortization, and any prepayments for a certain number of years. The next tranche (Tranche B) would be of longer duration and receive only interest payments until Tranche A is paid off, and so on. Any residual after payments are made to the tranches accrues to the equity interest of the issuer. The CMBS is a complex instrument, and the market collapsed completely in the financial crisis of 2008–2009.

Market Trends in the United States

Commercial real-estate markets in the United States experienced rising market values after the recession of 2001, with an increase in prices of 50 to 60 percent (depending upon the type of real estate) from 2002 to the peak in 2007. Many economists attribute these increases largely to a decline in the capitalization rates applied to the net income streams of the properties as loans became increasingly available at lower rates.

Commercial real-estate markets in the United States began to experience sharp declines in rents and prices with the onset of the recession in December 2007. The immediate cause of the recession was the drop in housing construction that resulted from the end of the housing market bubble—a topic covered in other entries in this volume. Commercial real-estate prices had been inflated by the easy availability of credit and the attendant high degrees of leverage. As noted above, many of the loans for commercial real estate remained on the balance sheets of lenders. Sharp declines in market values reduce asset values in banks and other financial institutions, placing them in danger of insolvency. Since these loans tend to be of shorter maturities than housing loans, a major problem of refinancing (or default) of these properties is expected to arise in the years 2011–2015.

The sources of the sharp decline in market values can be examined in a basic model of commercial real-estate price. The value of a commercial property is estimated by industry professionals as

$$\text{Value} = \text{NOI} / \text{Capitalization rate}$$

The capitalization rate (or cap rate) is risk-adjusted cost of capital minus the expected percentage increase in value over the coming year. Some economists have found that cap rates (for office buildings in downtown Chicago) depend upon the borrowing rate, the implicit cost of equity, and recent changes in local market conditions— changes in the vacancy rate and office employment. In other words, market participants were found to use recent changes in local market conditions as predictors of the changes in market value. An increase in the vacancy rate of one percentage point was associated with an increase in the cap rate of 67 basis points. The average capitalization rate in this particular market during 2006–2007 was 6.7 percent. Since then, the vacancy rate has increased by 2.8 percent, which means that the cap rate has increased by 1.9 to 8.6 percent. Also, NOI has declined as rents have declined and vacancies have increased. For example, an office building with NOI of $1 million in 2007 might have had a value of:

$1,000,000 / 0.067 = $14.93 million

Suppose that NOI is now $900,000. The current value of that same building is estimated to be:

$900,000 / 0.086 = $10.465 million

This demonstrates a decline of 30 percent. A decline in value of this magnitude likely puts the building "underwater," meaning that the building is worth less than the balances on the outstanding loans. Recent reports indicate that market values for commercial real estate have dropped by larger amounts in other locations. One study notes a 50 percent decline in office building values in Phoenix, Arizona, for example.

Ultimately, commercial real estate depends upon employment and the overall level of economic activity. Commercial real-estate markets will recover as the general level of business activity recovers. In the meantime, property owners and their lenders will undergo the painful process of deleveraging.

John F. McDonald

See also: Fixed Business Investment; Mortgage Markets and Mortgage Rates; Savings and Investment.

Further Reading

Bergsman, Steve. *Maverick Real Estate Financing.* Hoboken, NJ: John Wiley & Sons, 2006.
Clauretie, Terrence, and G. Stacy Sirmans. *Real Estate Finance: Theory and Practice.* Mason, OH: Cengage Learning, 2010.
Downs, Anthony. *Real Estate and the Financial Crisis.* Washington, DC: Urban Land Institute, 2009.
Grubb & Ellis. "Office Trends Report—Fourth Quarter 2009: Chicago, IL." Chicago: Grubb & Ellis, 2010. Available at www.grubb-ellis.com/SitePages/GetFileFromDB .ashx?type=9&id=475. Accessed April 2010.
McDonald, John. "Optimal Leverage in Real Estate Investment with Mezzanine Lending." *Journal of Real Estate Portfolio Management* 13:1 (2007): 1–5.
McDonald, John, and Sofia Dermisi. "Office Building Capitalization Rates: The Case of Downtown Chicago." *Journal of Real Estate Finance and Economics* 39:4 (2009): 472–485.
Rudolf, John, "Phoenix Meets the Wrong End of the Boom Cycle." *New York Times*, March 17, 2010, B6.

Mortgage Equity

Mortgage equity, also referred to as home equity, is the value of the unencumbered part of a homeowner's mortgaged property—in other words, the market value of the home (including building, land, or other assets) minus the outstanding balance of the mortgage owed. This is the amount the property owner could expect to recover if the property is sold; it is sometimes called "real property value."

Mortgage equity represents hypothetical liquidity—it is not a liquid asset itself—and is considered to have a rate of return (profit) of zero. Home equity loans, or second mortgages, provide a way of "extracting" liquid equity from the illiquid equity of a mortgage property. Homeowners may use such loans to cover a variety of expenses, such as renovations to the property, paying down debts, paying for a child's college, and other major expenses. Investors may use home equity loans to extract equity from their properties in order to make other investments with high enough rates of return to pay the interest on the loan and still make a profit. In such loans, the equity of the property—rather than its full value—is used as collateral; thus, the amount available to be borrowed will be limited to the former. Home equity loans are usually for a shorter term than the first mortgage.

Home equity loans are often used to pay down bills that have accumulated over time and that carry significant interest rates or penalty fees, such as medical bills, student loans, or credit card debts. This strategy, according to personal finance experts, has both pros and cons. On the one hand, because it is a secured loan where the lender has a lien on the property, a home equity loan will usually carry a lower interest rate than other interest-bearing debts, thus effectively reducing the amount of money needed to pay off the debt. Moreover, in the United States, interest paid on home equity loans is an income tax deduction that reduces tax liabilities. Interest payments on most other loans, such as credit card and automobile loans, are not. However, home equity loans are secured recourse debts, meaning that if they are not paid off, the lender can seize (foreclose on) the property used as collateral. Furthermore, "recourse" means that the borrower is personally liable for the debt if there is insufficient equity to pay off the loan after the property has been seized by the lender. By contrast, a first mortgage (as long as the original mortgage has not been refinanced) is typically a nonrecourse debt; thus, foreclosure of the property may discharge the debt of the initial mortgage (even if the lender does not recoup the full amount owed) but does not affect any remaining debt on the home equity loan if there are insufficient funds to pay off the home equity loan issuer. Note also that when a property is foreclosed upon, the first or original mortgage issuer has first claim on the proceeds from the sale of the property before the issuer of the home equity loan is entitled to be repaid.

State laws govern how much homeowners can borrow against their property. Most states allow loans of up to 100 percent of the property's equity; some place the limit lower; and still others permit "over-equity loans," which extend a sum greater than the value of the equity serving as collateral. Over-equity loans have become much less common as banks tightened credit standards in the wake of the subprime mortgage crisis and credit crunch of 2007–2009. The amortization period of a home equity loan is usually ten to fifteen years if the loan is for the full amount available; it

may be much shorter if a smaller loan is needed. (In the case of emergency home repairs, a home equity loan is considered by financial counselors to be much smarter than using a credit card, as it carries a lower interest rate; moreover, the interest expense may be offset by tax benefits.) Shorter amortizations usually include a balloon payment at the end of term.

Open-ended home equity loans are also called home equity lines of credit—meaning that the borrower can draw funds on an as-needed basis; these typically carry a variable interest rate. Although they can be useful when the exact amount necessary is not known in advance, the interest rate will often be higher than that of a traditional home equity loan. Because the interest rate is variable, it is not possible to "lock in" a favorable percentage when applying for the credit, as it is with a second mortgage. Whether on a second mortgage or line of credit, a home equity credit incurs a variety of transaction fees in addition to the interest on the loan, such as appraisal fees, originator fees, title fees, closing costs, and so forth.

The rate of mortgage equity withdrawal—the amount of equity collectively extracted by means of home equity loans in a given country in a given period—is a telling macroeconomic statistic that economists monitor carefully. During the U.S. housing market boom from the 1990s through part of the first decade of the twenty-first century, for instance, the contribution of mortgage equity withdrawals to total personal consumption expenditures nearly tripled.

Mortgage equity can also have a significant, if indirect, effect on economic growth. Many economists believe that rapidly rising U.S. housing values in the early and mid-2000s—which, of course, meant rising levels of equity—spurred a burst of consumer spending. And since consumer spending represents about two-thirds of all economic activity, this contributed to the solid economic growth experienced in the United States and many other countries during this period. There were two reasons for this. First, rising equity levels allowed homeowners to take out home equity loans, which they could then use to purchase big-ticket consumer items, such as cars and appliances. Second, many homeowners saw their rising equity levels as a way to finance retirement, meaning that they could save less and spend more. Of course, when housing prices began to fall in 2007, so too did equity levels, contributing to a significant drop-off in consumer spending and higher savings rates.

Bill Kte'pi and James Ciment

See also: Consumption; Housing Booms and Busts; Mortgage Lending Standards; Mortgage Markets and Mortgage Rates; Mortgage, Subprime; Recession and Financial Crisis (2007–); Savings and Investment.

Further Reading

Guttentag, Jack. *The Mortgage Encyclopedia: An Authoritative Guide to Mortgage Programs, Practices, Prices, and Pitfalls.* New York: McGraw-Hill, 2004.

Kratovil, Robert, and Raymond Werner. *Modern Mortgage Law and Practice.* Englewood Cliffs, NJ: Prentice-Hall, 1981.

Morris, Charles R. *The Trillion Dollar Meltdown: Easy Money, High Rollers, and the Great Credit Crash.* New York: PublicAffairs, 2008.

Mortgage Lending Standards

Mortgage lending standards are used by banks and other lending institutions to determine the fitness of a potential borrower for a prospective loan. The structure of a mortgage loan—its principal, interest rate, amortization, and term—affects the level of risk the bank is willing to take on, as do the financial health and future prospects of the borrower, and the effects of the real-estate market on the value of the home that serves as collateral. When housing prices are on the upswing, lenders balance the risk of a loan by the prospect of recouping or even profiting through foreclosure. This process and that of collateralization—the bundling and sale of mortgages as securities—were key in lowering mortgage standards during the housing boom that led to the subprime mortgage crisis of 2007–2008.

Risk-Based Pricing

Loan approval is not a binary, "yes" or "no" process. The applicant's creditworthiness determines not simply whether or not he or she is approved for a mortgage, but which mortgage terms are approved. Applicants who present a greater risk but still fall within acceptable credit standards are given less favorable terms—generally higher interest rates. Sometimes condemned as a predatory lending practice, risk-based pricing is defended by the banking industry as a compromise measure that makes credit available to those to whom it would not otherwise be extended.

Subprime mortgages are an obvious example of risk-based pricing. These mortgages were historically offered to individuals with poor credit ratings but high incomes. Over time, however, especially during the early twenty-first-century housing boom, the "high income" part of the requirement was increasingly overlooked or disregarded. For example, NINA loans—No (declared) Income, No (declared) Assets—had been offered to applicants with a high credit score and some explanation for the lack of income (such as being self-employed or prohibited from disclosing their compensation), but the housing bubble saw the popularization of NINJA loans—No (declared) Income, No (declared) Job, No (declared) Assets—which could be repaid only by selling the house.

Credit Scores

One of the criteria used to evaluate a potential mortgage loan, especially for a residential property, is the borrower's credit score. Although awareness of credit scores has been raised in recent years, they are still widely misunderstood. A credit score is based on a statistical analysis of information in the subject's credit report. In the United States, there are three major credit bureaus—Equifax, Experian, and TransUnion—and a number of third-party scoring systems. The major credit rating bureaus make use of the FICO model, offered since 1958 by a consumer credit scoring company called Fair Isaac. The information in a person's credit report includes past borrowing and credit accounts, bank information, outstanding debts, payment delinquencies, and so on. The various pieces of information are weighted differently, according to proprietary and secret formulas. While the consumer can obtain access to his or her credit report, there is no transparency to the credit score itself, nor any way to reverse it. Subjects cannot learn how many points they may have lost for one reason or another, and there is no disclosure regarding which pieces of information have been weighted most heavily in calculating the overall credit score. Specific reasons will be given if and when credit is denied, but the exact scoring mechanism is not disclosed.

According to Fair Isaac, the FICO score is calculated according to the following broad formula: 35 percent is punctuality of payment; 30 percent is amount of debt (specifically, how close the subject is to meeting his or her credit limit); 15 percent is length of credit history; 10 percent is types of credit used; and 10 percent is recent activity, such as credit card applications. However, each of these elements is based on multiple factors, and the relative percentages apply only in "typical" cases. In the many atypical cases, the weighting is affected by a variety of unusual circumstances, such as a court judgment or bankruptcy filing.

For decades, the use of credit scores as a mechanism for determining creditworthiness was praised for being blind to gender, ethnicity, or an interviewer's personal preferences. In theory, at least, items that pertain most to credit risk are weighted most heavily. In practice, credit scoring systems have come under critical scrutiny, especially as their use has broadened in recent years. Insurance companies have started using credit scores to set premiums for homeowner insurance, and some employers have begun running credit checks on job applicants as an indication of character and responsibility. The increasing reliance on credit scores has focused attention on a variety of problems with the systems of information gathering and calculation. To begin with, creditors do not always update information in a timely manner, so

old debts may continue to be reported after they have been resolved. In addition, because credit limits can be increased in order to impact the 30 percent debt limit, third-party agencies sell "credit boosting services" that artificially improve the customer's credit score by opening an unusable account with a high credit limit. More importantly, credit scores are simply inaccurate as predictive measures. Studies indicate that the accuracy of credit scores in predicting whether or not the subject will be delinquent has been steadily declining since at least the turn of the century.

Redlining

Redlining is the discriminatory and illegal action whereby financial institutions limit or eliminate the credit they offer to borrowers in impoverished urban neighborhoods, usually those inhabited by ethnic minorities. Legally, mortgages cannot be denied on the basis of ethnicity, just as discrimination is outlawed in other contexts. In practice, however, there is a disproportionate rate of foreclosure in the United States on black- and Hispanic-owned homes, even relative to those owned by poor whites. Furthermore, the practice of redlining has made it more difficult for middle-class nonwhites to obtain a mortgage than for lower-class whites. A perennial issue, pervasive redlining has come to light again in the aftermath of the subprime mortgage crisis. In certain parts of the country, high-risk subprime mortgages were disproportionately issued in black neighborhoods. Within a certain median-income bracket, it has been alleged, race was a greater determining factor in the issuance of subprime mortgages than median neighborhood income. Several class-action discrimination claims have been filed against lending institutions for discriminatory predatory practices.

Redlining itself began in 1935, when the new Federal Home Loan Bank Board (FHLBB) commissioned color-coded maps of American cities, with the colors of various neighborhoods indicating relative credit risk. "Declining neighborhoods," for example, were outlined in yellow, while affluent suburbs and newly developed neighborhoods were outlined in blue; those deemed too risky for standard mortgages were outlined in red. These maps were made by a variety of groups and experts, with no overarching guidance as to the standards that should be used in determining what distinguishes a creditworthy neighborhood from a risky one. A number of the maps were constructed with race as a factor in assessing credit risk. In the East and the industrial cities of the Midwest, this generally meant that black neighborhoods, and many immigrant precincts, were redlined. In the Southwest, Mexican-American neighborhoods were so identified.

The result was to discourage loans to nonwhite neighborhoods in many parts of the country, contributing significantly to urban decay and the difficulty of maintaining a healthy nonwhite middle class. The same kind of discrimination applied to small business loans as well as residential mortgages. A practice analogous to redlining—not using FHLBB-commissioned maps per se, but still using neighborhood boundaries as indicators of race—has been alleged in the credit card industry as well, with worse credit terms offered to nonwhites than to whites of equal income. Realtors are sometimes accused of practicing unofficial redlining by steering prospective homebuyers toward one neighborhood or another in order to preserve a racial status quo.

Bill Kte'pi

See also: Housing Booms and Busts; Mortgage-Backed Securities; Mortgage Markets and Mortgage Rates; Mortgage, Subprime; Recession and Financial Crisis (2007–); Real-Estate Speculation.

Further Reading

Dennis, Marshall W., and Thomas J. Pinkowish. *Residential Mortgage Lending: Principles and Practices.* Mason, OH: South-Western, 2003.

Koellhoffer, Martin. *A Mortgage Broker's Guide to Lending.* New York: Mortgage Planning Solutions, 2003.

Morgan, Thomas A. *The Loan Officer's Practical Guide to Residential Finance.* Rockville, MD: QuickStart, 2007.

Mortgage Markets and Mortgage Rates

The residential mortgage market in the United States consists of two components: the market in which loans are originated, called the primary mortgage market, and the market in which loans are bought and sold, known as the secondary mortgage market. Mortgage loans are originated by commercial banks, savings and loan associations, savings banks, credit unions, mortgage companies with lines of credit, and mortgage brokers that prepare applications (but are not lenders). The first four types of originators are depository institutions that make loans to homebuyers. Mortgage companies with lines of credit are not depository institutions, but have lines of credit with major financial institutions. Mortgage brokers do not make loans themselves, but work with real-estate brokers and buyers to prepare loan applications that are forwarded to commercial banks, thrifts, and mortgage companies.

Primary Mortgage Market

There are many types of mortgage loans available. The standard loan has a fixed interest rate, a long term (usually fifteen or thirty years), and equal (level) monthly payments. The monthly payment is equal to the principal of the loan multiplied by a mortgage constant. The formula for the mortgage constant is as follows:

$$MC = r/\{1 - [1/(1 + r)^n]\}.$$

In this equation, r is the monthly interest rate and n is the number of time periods (months). For example, if the annual interest rate is 6 percent and the term is thirty years, then $r = 6$ percent$/12 = 0.005$ and $n = 360$. The mortgage constant is 0.0059955, and the monthly payment on a loan of $100,000 is $599.55 ($100,000 $\times$ .0059955), which is sufficient to pay the interest on the loan and the principal in exactly thirty years. This type of loan is fully amortized because the principal is paid off over the term of the loan. The first payment is made at the end of the first month. The interest on the loan for the first month is $500 (0.005 x $100,000 = $500), leaving $99.55 to go toward reducing the principal of the loan. The borrower enters the second month with a balance of $99,900.45 ($100,000 – $99.55 = $99,900.45), pays interest of $499.50 (0.005 x $99,900.45 = $499.50), and reduces the principal by $100.05 ($599.55 – $499.50 = $100) at the end of the month, and so on. The mortgage constant is the stream of monthly payment for 360 months that has a present value of $1 when discounted at an annual rate of 6 percent. The mortgage constant increases as the interest rate rises and as the term of the loan becomes shorter (smaller n). If the term of the loan is infinite, then the mortgage constant is simply the interest rate, and the principal is never repaid.

One difficulty with the standard fixed rate mortgage is interest rate risk. Financial institutions are in the business of "borrowing short and lending long." For example, the major liabilities of a bank are deposits, and most deposits are held in the form of short-term certificates of deposit (CDs) that mature in six months, one year, and so on. If interest rates increase, then banks must increase the rates they offer on CDs in order to keep their deposits. However, the income from their assets— the fixed rate mortgages—will not increase. If the increase in interest rates is sufficiently large, a bank will discover very quickly that it is losing money because it is paying more for its liabilities than it is earning on its assets.

Lenders can avoid this problem by offering adjustable rate mortgages (ARMs), which became popular with borrowers during the housing boom of the late 2000s, as they offer lower initial monthly payments. The interest rate on an ARM is tied to an index and adjusts after a specified period of time. The lender bears less risk because the income from its assets will increase as interest rates rise. Because an ARM involves less interest rate

risk for the bank, the initial interest rate is lower than the rate charged for fixed rate mortgages. The standard terms for ARMs include a periodic adjustment (annual, semi-annual, or monthly, as defined in the contract) of the interest rate that is tied to an index, such as the cost of funds index provided by the Federal Home Loan Bank, the one-year Treasury bill rate, or the London Interbank Offered Rate (known as the LIBOR). The contract rate normally equals the index rate plus a margin that is set at 150 to 275 basis points (i.e., 1.5 percent to 2.75 percent). The terms usually include a cap on the size of the annual adjustment and a cap on the total adjustment that can occur over the life of the loan. Some ARMs have an initial-period discount ("teaser" rate), during which time the initial rate is less than the index rate plus the margin. These mortgages switch to the index rate plus the margin after an initial period of two to three years. Some ARMs include a provision stipulating that the loan can be converted to a fixed rate mortgage within a certain time period (for a fee). Also, a few ARMs have a cap on the size of the monthly payment. Such a cap can lead to what is called negative amortization—the size of the outstanding loan balance increases because the monthly payment is less than the interest on the loan after adjustment.

Most lenders offer a menu of mortgages that may include fixed rate mortgages with thirty-year terms, with different combinations of interest rates and discount points; fixed rate mortgages with fifteen-year terms; and adjustable rate mortgages with annual interest rate adjustments and a lifetime cap. The interest rate is highest on thirty-year fixed rate mortgages, lower on fifteen-year fixed rate mortgage, and lowest on adjustable rate mortgages.

Because of the risk of default, lenders must evaluate both the creditworthiness of the borrower and the quality of the property. A mortgage is a type of contract in which the property serves as collateral for the loan. In the event that the borrower does not meet his or her payment obligations—that is, the borrower defaults—the lender has the right to initiate foreclosure proceedings. In the United States, foreclosure procedures are determined by state law, and differ in procedures, redemption rights, and deficiency judgments. The basic procedure in some states is a judicial procedure. The lender files in court for a judgment against the borrower. In other states, the seizure and sale of the property can take place without a court order if the terms of the mortgage include this right for the lender. In all states, the borrower (mortgagor) has the right, called equitable right of redemption, to prevent a foreclosure sale by making full payment (including penalties). In addition, some states provide for a statutory right of redemption in which the mortgagor can regain the property after it has undergone foreclosure sale. This right has a time limit, and the cost to redeem the property typically is the price paid plus interest and expenses.

The decision to default is the choice of the mortgagor to exercise a "put" option—that is, the right to sell an asset at a specified price, in this case the outstanding balance on the mortgage. Mortgagors typically default for two reasons: a change in their ability to pay, and/or a decline in the value of the property. A household may experience a decline in income, or may suffer from a family member's illness or other unexpected difficulty or expense. These changes may mean that the household is unable to meet its mortgage payments. A lender does not automatically initiate the foreclosure process, but instead may decide to work with the household to modify the payment schedule or other terms of the loan. A decline in the value of the property reduces the mortgagor's equity. If the decline in the property value is greater than the mortgagor's equity, the property is worth less than the amount of the loan, and the mortgagor, who is said to be "underwater," may decide to default. The most important variable in the default decision is the original loan-to-value ratio, but other variables, such as a change in the unemployment rate, also are important. Some mortgages are nonrecourse loans, meaning that the lender cannot go after the mortgagor's private assets in the event of a default. Depending on state

law, other mortgages may be recourse loans, meaning that the lender can sue the mortgagor for the mortgage balance in the event of a default.

Lenders guard against default risk by qualifying the borrower and evaluating the property. When qualifying a borrower, most lenders compare a household's monthly housing expenses—which include interest payments, payments to reduce the principal of the loan, property taxes, and insurance—to its verifiable monthly income. The ratio should not exceed some amount, usually estimated at 31 percent. Lenders also examine the borrower's credit rating, total assets, and other debts. In recent years, borrowers with low credit ratings often were approved for subprime loans, which carried higher interest rates—and higher risk of default. Lenders also require an appraisal of the property. The basic appraisal method is to find three comparable properties that are located near the subject property and that were sold recently. The lender evaluates whether the property is really worth the amount that the buyer and seller have agreed upon in order to determine the size of the loan that can be approved.

Mortgage default insurance provides protection for the holder of the mortgage. In the United States, the first public mortgage insurance program was created by the Federal Housing Administration (FHA) in 1934. The borrower pays an insurance premium that is used to build up the FHA insurance pool. The lender is insured for the full amount of the loss incurred in the event of foreclosure. The FHA program permits borrowers to obtain loans that are fully amortizing and that have low down payments and long maturities (thus reducing their monthly payments). After World War II, the U.S. Veterans Administration (VA) created a mortgage insurance program for military veterans in which the lender is insured for a portion of the property value, allowing the borrower to make a very low down payment. Private mortgage insurance is supplied by private firms. The typical policy covers a portion of the loan when the down payment is less than 20 percent of the price of the property.

Secondary Mortgage Market

The secondary mortgage market is the market in which mortgages are bought and sold. The market consists of two parts: a larger portion that is operated by two government-sponsored enterprises, and a smaller portion that is operated by private firms.

The Federal National Mortgage Association (Fannie Mae) was created as a government agency in 1938 to purchase FHA-insured mortgage loans and VA loans. In 1968, Fannie Mae became a private company, with the implicit backing of the U.S. government. Its original purpose was to purchase loans at face value (even if the current value was below face value) so that lenders could increase lending. Fannie Mae sold the mortgages to investors when interest rates fell and their values increased. Its activities were financed by issuing bonds, and the agency relied on the U.S. Treasury to cover its losses. Beginning in 1970, Fannie Mae was permitted to purchase conventional mortgages as well as FHA and VA mortgages. In the 1970s, Fannie Mae held most of the mortgages in its portfolio, and issued some mortgage-backed securities. During the 1980s, Fannie Mae issued more mortgage-backed securities and began to purchase adjustable rate mortgages to reduce interest rate risk.

The Federal Home Loan Mortgage Corporation (Freddie Mac) was chartered in 1970 as a government-sponsored enterprise with the mission of purchasing conventional, FHA, and VA loans. It specialized in the purchase of conventional loans. Its initial capital came from the sale of stock to the Federal Home Loan Banks, the federally chartered system of banks that issues bonds and lends to thrift institutions. Freddie Mac issues a variety of mortgage-backed securities. Both Fannie Mae and Freddie Mac provide guarantees for the purchasers of their mortgage-backed securities.

Fannie Mae and Freddie Mac expanded in the 1990s and 2000s, but began to experience large losses in 2007 as a result of a sharp decline in housing prices that precipitated a massive wave of mortgage defaults throughout the nation. At that time,

the two agencies together owned or guaranteed $5 trillion in home mortgages—approximately 50 percent of all outstanding home loans. By summer 2008, it was clear that Fannie Mae and Freddie Mac soon would be bankrupt, with negative consequences for the housing market and the entire financial system. In July 2008, federal legislation created the Federal Housing Finance Agency to oversee the two agencies; it placed Fannie Mae and Freddie Mac into conservatorship in September of that year. This effectively made Fannie Mae and Freddie Mac federal agencies. The government provides up to $100 billion to each firm to take care of any shortfalls in capital. Subsequently, the Federal Reserve System initiated a program to purchase the mortgage-backed securities issued by Fannie Mae and Freddie Mac.

Until 2008, the private portion of the mortgage-backed securities market was driven by major investment banks such as Goldman Sachs, Morgan Stanley, Merrill Lynch, Lehman Brothers, and Bear Stearns. These financial institutions were not depository institutions (with deposit insurance from the Federal Deposit Insurance Corporation), but rather concentrated on underwriting financial instruments such as stocks and bonds for major corporations and issuers of mortgage-backed securities.

The process of creating an MBS begins when an individual mortgage is funded by a lender, which then sells the mortgage to one of these major investment banks, or to an intermediary that then sells mortgages to the major institutions. The mortgages are accumulated and packaged as securities, which are offered to investors such as pension funds, insurance companies, Federal Home Loan Banks, and other domestic and international financial institutions.

Mortgage-backed securities can take a variety of forms. The simplest type is the pass-through security, in which the investor receives a share of the cash flow from the pool of mortgages, which consists of interest payments, principal payments, and prepaid loans. The mortgages are held by a trustee. A more complex pass-through security is called a senior or subordinated pass-through. In this case, the senior pass-through has first priority on cash flows, and the subordinated pass-through is held by the issuer as equity. Mortgage-backed bonds promise semi-annual payments of principal and interest until maturity. Mortgage-backed bonds have maturity dates that are considerably shorter than the terms of the underlying mortgages because most mortgages are not held to term.

Collateralized mortgage obligations are the most complex form of mortgage-backed securities. These instruments restructure the cash flows from a pool of mortgages. The idea of the collateralized mortgage obligation is to rearrange the cash flows into a number of different securities with different maturities. These different classes are called tranches; a typical collateralized mortgage obligation has three or four tranches, but may have many more. Because the cash flows are uncertain, the bottom tranche often is owned by the issuer as equity. An example of a collateralized mortgage obligation structure is as follows:

Assets	Liabilities	Maturity	Coupon Rate	Amount
Mortgages $70 Mil.				
	Tranche A	5–7 yrs.	8.25%	$20 Mil.
	Tranche B	7–9 yrs.	8.5%	$20 Mil.
	Tranche C	9–10 yrs.	9.0%	$15 Mil.
	Tranche Z	10–11 yrs.	9.5%	$10 Mil.
	Equity			$ 5 Mil.
$70 Mil.				$70 Mil.

Payments to Tranche A have the highest priority and come from interest, principal, and prepayments. Payments in excess of the coupon rate serve to retire Tranche A. If prepayments are made at a faster rate than expected, the maturity of the tranche is shortened. Tranche B receives only interest payments until Tranche A has been retired. Once Tranche A has been retired, Tranche B receives payments that go toward retiring this tranche. This pattern is followed for the other tranches.

Other forms of collateralized mortgage obligations exist. For example, some tranches are based only on interest payments, and others are based on principal payments. These tranches are known as interest-only and principal-only strips.

The Government National Mortgage Association (Ginnie Mae), a U.S. government agency, specializes in providing insurance for mortgage-backed securities (typically pass-through securities) that consist of FHA or VA loans. Private institutions create these pass-through securities, known as Ginnie Mae securities, but the securities are guaranteed by Ginnie Mae in the event of default.

The secondary mortgage market serves several purposes. As noted earlier, traditional mortgage originators such as banks and thrift institutions face default and interest rate risk when they hold on to the mortgages in their portfolios. Fannie Mae was created to provide these institutions with a secondary market for FHA loans so that they could provide more of these insured loans to the public. The secondary market enables capital to flow more readily from regions with a capital surplus to regions with a capital shortage. And the secondary market provides investment vehicles for institutions such as pension funds and other institutions that wish to earn good returns in the long term.

Crisis in the Secondary Mortgage Market

It is now understood, however, that the secondary mortgage market system that expanded rapidly in the 2000s was flawed as a result of "asymmetric information," which can take two forms. Adverse selection occurs before a transaction is consummated—in this case, it means that borrowers who are bad credit risks seek loans most diligently. Moral hazard occurs after the transaction takes place, meaning that the borrower engages in behavior that is undesirable from the lender's point of view. In both cases, the lender has less information than the borrower about the borrower's qualifications and behavior.

Consider the following sequence involved in the creation of a mortgage-backed security: A mortgage broker prepares an application for a borrower, but earns a fee only if the mortgage application is approved—and earns a larger fee for higher loan amounts or higher interest rates. Thus, the broker has an incentive to exaggerate the quality of both the applicant and the property and to push the applicant into a subprime loan with a higher interest rate. Indeed, there is an incentive for fraud in representing both the qualifications of the borrower and the value of the property. The mortgage broker has more information than the lender. If the mortgage is approved by the lender, then the lender has an incentive to convince the issuer of a mortgage-backed security to buy the mortgage. The mortgage-backed security issuer packages mortgages into a security and pays a rating agency to give the security a rating of investment grade. The rating agencies face a conflict of interest. Higher ratings make customers happier, and mean that more business will be forthcoming. Finally, the issuer wishes to sell the tranches to investors. All of these examples involve asymmetric information with adverse selection. In addition, once the loan has been granted, the borrower may decide not to make the required payments and to live in the house until evicted—moral hazard.

These problems became particularly acute in the subprime mortgage market during the early 2000s. This market provided mortgage loans to households that otherwise would not have qualified for standard mortgages because of their low or unstable incomes and/or low credit ratings. Many of these mortgages were ARMs with low initial interest rates that adjusted upward in two or three years. Indeed, a sizable number of these mortgages were known as variable payment ARMs, in which the borrower could choose to make a payment that was less than the interest on the loan. Furthermore, the bubble in housing prices that had emerged in 2003 began to deflate in mid-2006. Housing prices in the United States had increased by 60 percent to 90 percent. Households that had purchased homes near the end of boom in housing prices soon found that they were underwater (i.e., owed more than the value of their home).

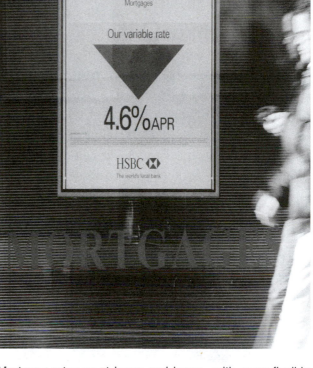

Mortgage rates went lower and lower—with more flexible terms and looser qualification standards—during the housing bubble of the early 2000s. When property values declined, variable mortgages were reset at higher rates and foreclosures skyrocketed. *(Graeme Robertson/Getty Images)*

Mortgage defaults increased rapidly in 2007 and 2008. In all, 2.3 percent of all mortgage loans were delinquent or in foreclosure as of the second quarter of 2006; this percentage increased to 3.1 percent in the second quarter of 2007 and to 5.7 percent in the second quarter of 2008. During this same time, the percentage of subprime loans that were delinquent or in foreclosure increased from 8.0 percent to 12.0 percent to 22.5 percent.

The sudden increase in mortgage defaults on subprime loans meant that many of the mortgage-backed securities based on these loans lost value (some became completely worthless). Particularly hard hit were the financial institutions that retained the equity tranche of the collateralized mortgage obligation. These institutions included Fannie Mae, Freddie Mac, and the major investment banks, such as Bear Stearns, Lehman

Brothers, Merrill Lynch, and Morgan Stanley. In addition, insurance giant AIG (American International Group) had sold a form of insurance called credit default swaps to the holders of collateralized mortgage obligations—but failed to hold enough reserves to cover the losses.

All of these institutions faced bankruptcy in 2008. In September of that year, Bear Stearns was sold to JPMorgan Chase (after the Federal Reserve provided a $30 billion loan to cover its losses), and Lehman Brothers went bankrupt. Merrill Lynch was purchased by Bank of America, and Morgan Stanley narrowly escaped bankruptcy. Fannie Mae and Freddie Mac were put under conservatorship by their federal oversight agency. All of the problems had come home to roost, creating a massive dilemma for the financial system of the United States and, indeed, most of the world.

John F. McDonald

See also: Housing Booms and Busts; Mortgage-Backed Securities; Mortgage Lending Standards; Mortgage, Subprime; Real-Estate Speculation.

Further Reading

Barth, James. *The Rise and Fall of the U.S. Mortgage and Credit Markets: A Comprehensive Analysis of the Market Meltdown.* Hoboken, NJ: John Wiley & Sons, 2009.

Clauretie, Terrence M., and G. Stacy Sirmans. *Real Estate Finance: Theory and Practice.* Mason, OH: Cengage Learning, 2010.

Downs, Anthony. *Real Estate and the Financial Crisis: How Turmoil in the Capital Markets Is Restructuring Real Estate Finance.* Washington, DC: Urban Land Institute, 2009.

Mortgage, Reverse

A reverse mortgage—also called a lifetime mortgage, reverse equity mortgage, or reverse home mortgage—enables U.S. homeowners age sixty-two or older who live in their homes for more than six months every year to create the potential for tax-free income from the value of the homes without selling them, renting them out, or taking on new monthly mortgage payments. In a reverse mortgage, the payment stream is "reversed": the homeowner receives regular monthly payments rather than making them. Reverse mortgages apply to single-family homes, two- to four-unit properties, condominium units, townhouses, and even mobile homes if they are less than thirty years old and the homeowner owns the land and pays real-estate taxes.

A reverse mortgage is not a gift, of course, but a low-interest loan against the equity in the home. If the owner moves out, dies, or sells the property, the loan has to be repaid (the interest is tax deductible) in a single lump sum one year later; the owner or his heirs may also convert the reverse mortgage into a traditional mortgage in order to repay the former. If neither is possible, the home may be foreclosed. However, the homeowner will never owe more than the property is worth, no matter how much its value decreases or how long the borrower lives. Thus, the owner will never have to use assets other than the home itself to repay the reverse mortgage. (One exception to this rule is that homeowners have to pay mortgage insurance premiums that reduce the lenders' risks in such cases.) Moreover, if the sale proceeds of the home are larger than the amount owed on the reverse mortgage, the homeowners or their heirs will receive the difference.

The maximum sum homeowners can borrow under a reverse mortgage depends on several factors: their age (or the age of the youngest spouse in a couple); the appraised home value; the selected program; current interest rates (fixed or adjustable), usually pegged to U.S. Treasury bonds; the lending limit in the area; and whether or not there is a mortgage on the property. The sum is larger if the homeowner is older, if the property is a more valuable home, and if there is already a mortgage on it. If the property is already mortgaged, the owner can often qualify for a reverse mortgage if he or she has paid off at least 40 percent of the loan or has the funds to do so. Homeowners can also use the cash advance from the reverse mortgage to pay off the mortgage.

Homeowners can choose from a variety of plans

to receive the funds from a reverse mortgage: (1) as a line of credit—the most popular option, in which borrowers receive the proceeds as installments at times and in amounts they choose, or as unscheduled payments; (2) as fixed monthly payments—whether for a designated time period (term) or for as long as they live and occupy the home (tenure); (3) as a combination of 1 and 2, above; or (4) as a lump sum (though this carries the highest interest fees). Generally, borrowers can change the payment plan at a later time if they wish.

Homeowners themselves are free to decide how to spend the proceeds from a reverse mortgage—to make other investments, cover their daily living expenses, repair or modify their home, pay off existing debts, take a vacation, buy a car, or any other way they choose. As ever, of course, they must still cover all expenses associated with owning the property, such as real-estate taxes, utilities, and routine maintenance. As long as they pay for these, they cannot be evicted from the home.

Before applying for a reverse mortgage, homeowners typically go through a forty-five-minute face-to-face interview or third-party telephone consultation with a counseling firm approved by the U.S. Department of Housing and Urban Development (HUD) and receive a "certificate of counseling." This requirement protects consumers and their family members by ensuring that they understand the different types of reverse mortgages available to them, the financial consequences of assuming one, and the effects on taxes and Medicaid and other need-based government assistance payments. For example, these can be affected if the borrower withdraws too much from the reverse mortgage line of credit—if the total liquid assets at the end of any month are greater than $2,000 for a single person or $3,000 for a couple.

Many financial counselors advise against reverse mortgages, or at least argue that they should be used only as a last resort to keep seniors in their homes. There are several reasons for this. Origination fees for reverse mortgages can be steep, often double those for standard mortgages. If the value of the house—and hence the owner's equity—declines significantly, a reverse mortgage can cause their heirs to lose the right to own or live in the property. (The original mortgage holder may not be evicted, but upon his or her death, the house could become the property of the lender.) Finally, reverse mortgages might increase the borrower's income to a level that makes the borrower ineligible for Medicaid or other need-based social programs.

Tiia Vissak

See also: Mortgage Equity; Mortgage, Subprime; Retirement Instruments.

Further Reading

"Home Equity Conversion Mortgages. Handbook No. 4235.1." Available at www.hud.gov/offices/adm/hudclips/handbooks/hsgh/4235.1/. Accessed February 2009.
"Reverse Mortgage." Available at www.reversemortgage.org. Accessed February 2009.
"Reverse Mortgage Guides." Available at www.reverse mortgageguides.org. Accessed February 2009.

Mortgage, Subprime

A subprime mortgage is a home mortgage offered to an individual with low income or with a minimal or weak credit history—in other words, someone who would not be eligible for a standard, or prime, mortgage. Because they involve higher risk, subprime mortgages usually come with higher interest rates than standard mortgages. Lenders charge different interest rates for different subprime mortgages, depending on the income and creditworthiness of the borrower, as well as the size of the loan and the loan-to-asset ratio (the size of the home loan compared to the market value of the home being purchased). The degree of risk associated with a subprime mortgage is rated by letter—A to D in ascending order of risk (descending order of quality).

To make it possible for low-income individuals to afford a mortgage, lenders offer different payment schemes on subprime loans. In adjustable-rate mortgages (ARMs), the interest rate starts out low and then climbs (or falls) depending on the index—such as the federal rate to members banks—to which it is linked. In interest-only mortgages, the borrower defers paying back the principal until a later date. Both of these allow for lower initial monthly payments before higher interest rates kick in or before a balloon payment against the principal comes due. During the housing boom of 2003 to 2006, about 80 percent of subprime mortgages issued in the United States were of the adjustable-rate variety.

Borrowers take out subprime loans either to purchase a home or to refinance one. In the latter case, several factors may be considered in making the decision. When interest rates are falling, homeowners may decide that they can reduce their monthly payments by taking out a new mortgage, especially one with an initial low interest rate. Instead, homeowners may decide to refinance their homes in order to convert their equity into cash—so-called cash-out refinancing—and use the money for any number of purposes.

Virtually nonexistent prior to the 1990s, subprime mortgages remained a small part of the overall mortgage market through the end of the millennium. A variety of factors, including low interest rates, the increasing securitization of mortgages and, most importantly, rising home prices (themselves set in motion, in part, by the proliferation of subprime lending), encouraged lenders to offer more subprime mortgages during the housing boom that began roughly in 2003. With the collapse in housing prices beginning in late 2006, however, and especially with the tightening of credit during the recession and financial crisis of 2007–2009, the subprime mortgage market has contracted significantly.

Credit, Income, Ethnicity, and Neighborhood Factors

A number of factors, individually or in combination, may make a mortgagor a candidate for a subprime mortgage. Most important is the person's FICO score, a credit-risk rating established by the Fair Isaac Corporation. Individuals with a FICO score below about 650, on a scale of 300 to 850, are usually required to take out a subprime mortgage. Factors that go into setting a person's FICO score include their history of paying back loans on time (or not), the amount of outstanding debt they owe, the length of their credit history, the types of credit they use, and their recent borrowing activity.

Even borrowers with a FICO score of above 650, however, may be required to take out a subprime mortgage if their current debt service-to-income ratio is above 50 percent or if the mortgage itself will push the ratio above that level. In addition, if the applicant has had a foreclosure, repossession, or judgment within the past two years, or a bankruptcy within the past five years, they are likely to be required to take out a subprime mortgage. In addition, even someone with a relatively high income and excellent credit history could be required to take out a subprime mortgage if the value of the property—and hence the mortgage they are taking out—is so large that the lender feels it may be an undue burden on the mortgagor's finances. In general, subprime mortgages do not meet the standards set for conforming loans by the Federal National Mortgage Association (FNMA, or Fannie Mae) and the Federal Home Loan Mortgage Corporation (FHLMC, or Freddie Mac), the two government-sponsored enterprises (GSEs) that insure the bulk of the country's prime home mortgages.

Finally, such nonfinancial factors as race, gender, and the location of the property may also come into play in deciding who is required to take out a subprime mortgage—even if lenders who take any of these factors into consideration are in violation of federal antidiscrimination laws. Beginning in 2007, the National Association for the Advancement of Colored People (NAACP) began filing lawsuits against about a dozen major financial institutions, charging that they steered black and Hispanic homebuyers who might otherwise have been eligible for prime mortgages into subprime mortgages. Legal and discriminatory issues aside, subprime borrowers tend to be poorer or have sketchier credit histories than borrowers who qualify for prime loans. Thus, subprime lending tends to be concentrated in marginal neighborhoods or in exurban areas where land costs, and hence housing prices, are cheaper.

History

Traditionally, mortgages in American history were hard to come by. Through the 1920s, most people taking them out were required to put 50 percent down and expected to make a balloon payment on the rest of the principal after a relatively short period of time. To encourage homeownership, the federal government began to move into the business of insuring mortgages in the 1930s with the creation of Fannie Mae. However, the Depression and World War II stifled the mortgage market until the late 1940s. As late as 1940, just 44 percent of American families lived in homes they owned.

With government-sponsored enterprises such as Fannie Mae and Freddie Mac (after 1970) insuring mortgages, banks and savings and loans began offering home loans that were more affordable for working-class and middle-income households. These were generally fifteen- or thirty-year fixed-rate mortgages requiring an initial down payment of 20 percent of the value of the property. This type of mortgage, along with low-cost loans through the GI Bill for returning World War II veterans, expanded homeownership dramatically to about 65 percent in 1970. It remained at that level through the mid-1990s, despite some dramatic fluctuations in housing prices and interest rates. Meanwhile, the federal government prodded commercial financial institutions to lend to low- and moderate-income neighborhoods through the Community Re-Investment Act of 1977, making such lending a factor in the government's approval of acquisitions, expansions, and mergers.

A more important factor in the origination

and growth of the subprime market was, in effect, its legalization. Only with the easing of usury laws in the early 1980s did it become possible for financial institutions to charge the higher rates of interest that made subprime mortgages acceptable from a risk point of view. In addition, in 1982, Congress passed the Alternative Mortgage Transaction Parity Act, which allowed for the variable interest rates and balloon payments at the heart of most subprime mortgages. On the demand side, passage of the Tax Reform Act of 1986 allowed for deductions on mortgage interest but not on consumer loan interest. This made even mortgages with higher interest rates a relative bargain compared to other kinds of loans, and it prompted homebuyers and homeowners to increase mortgage indebtedness relative to other forms of indebtedness.

Market factors also came into play. In the mid-1990s, interest rates began to rise, which undermined the prime mortgage market. Lenders, particularly those specializing in mortgages, otherwise known as monoline lenders, began to offer subprime mortgages as a way to increase business. Much of the capital for this lending was raised through the sale of mortgage-backed securities (MBSs). But because subprime mortgages were a new kind of business, many lenders miscalculated profit potential and risk. That, combined with the higher rates of borrowing in the wake of the Asian financial crisis of the late 1990s, led to a shrinking and then a consolidation of the business, though both came to be reversed during the housing boom of the following decade.

Housing Boom

By the early years of the new millennium, the subprime market was on the rebound, especially as housing prices took off. Between 2000 and 2006, at the height of the housing market boom, outstanding debt on subprime mortgages more than tripled—from just under $200 billion to about $600 billion, or 20 percent of the overall new mortgage market. A number of factors fed the growth in subprime lending. Most important was the jump in housing prices, though here a case of chicken-and-egg causality comes into play. Rising house prices reassured lenders that they could recoup losses on the inevitable foreclosures that would result from lending to higher-risk borrowers, allowing them to increase the number of subprime loans. At the same time, by making more people eligible to finance a home purchase, lenders increased the demand for homes, which contributed to the rise in prices.

The increase in subprime lending helped push up new housing starts from about 1.4 million annually in the 1990s to more than 2 million annually by 2005. In addition, the percentage of households living in owner-occupied housing jumped from its 1970s–1990s average of 64 percent to nearly 70 percent. Meanwhile, housing prices rose across the nation at an unprecedented pace. During the bull market in housing from 1994 to 1999, the median home price in America rose from about $130,000 to $160,000 in non-inflation-adjusted dollars, an increase of about 23 percent. By comparison, during the boom of 2001–2006, the median price shot from about $160,000 to $250,000, an increase of roughly 56 percent. The increase was not equal in all areas of the country, of course. On the West Coast, the urban Northeast, and Florida, home prices skyrocketed as much as 20 percent a year, doubling or more in the five years from 2001 to 2006.

With home prices rising steadily, lenders felt reassured that they could sell homes financed with riskier subprime loans should they go into foreclosure; lenders thus began to lower their standards, no longer even requiring borrowers to provide documentation of their income or their assets, leading to so-called NINA (no-income, no-assets) loans. There were even increases in the number of so-called NINJA loans, in which the borrower was not asked for documentation regarding their income, assets, or *job.* What began to emerge was a kind of race to the bottom among lending institutions. More conservative lenders found themselves losing business to more

aggressive ones, forcing the former to adjust or risk going out of business.

In addition, the increase in subprime lending was fueled by the securitization process, in which subprime loans were bundled and sold to investors as financial instruments—mortgage-backed securities (MBSs). Securitization meant that mortgage originators were no longer financially liable should the mortgages go into default, since the risk had been transferred to investors. This process, known to economists as "moral hazard," encouraged mortgage originators to lend more recklessly. Thus, while securitization of mortgages had existed prior to the housing boom of the new millennium's first decade, it became commonplace during this period. In 2000, financial institutions created an estimated $70 billion in mortgage-backed securities. By 2006, the figure had climbed to more than $570 billion—an increase of more than 800 percent.

With the rapid expansion of the subprime market and the lowering of lending standards came the inevitable fraud. This occurred at both ends of the transaction. Lenders claimed that they expected people to report their financial status honestly even if they were not required to provide documentation—yet NINA and NINJA applications encouraged deceit. But in the burgeoning subprime market, it was just as likely that borrowers would fall victim to unscrupulous lenders. Increasingly complex mortgages often came with complicated documentation that hid the high origination fees, the size of the bump in interest rates, and therefore the increase in monthly payments once the upfront rate period was over. As long as home prices were rising and credit was flowing easily, this was not a problem. Mortgagors could readily refinance with a new, lower ARM before the interest rates jumped, since the rising equity in their homes lowered the default risk for lenders. Moreover, many people who might have been eligible for prime mortgages were pushed into subprimes because these loans often carried higher generation fees for the lender.

Housing Bust

In the end, of course, housing prices could not climb at the unsustainable rate of the period between 2003 and 2006. That rate had risen steadily faster than the rate of inflation and had pushed median home prices to ever-higher percentages of median income. By late 2006, there were signs that the housing bubble was beginning to deflate, especially as interest rates climbed. The latter was a result of credit tightening credit by the Federal Reserve, which was concerned about the size of the bubble and about inflation generally in a booming economy. As home prices fell and credit markets tightened, mortgage originators began to cut back on lending and increase documentation requirements. Along with tighter credit—partly a result of financial institutions' concern about the value of the MBSs on their balance sheets and therefore their own liquidity— falling home prices put a damper on consumer spending, which helped push the economy into recession by late 2007. The unemployment rate doubled from 5 percent in 1997 to more than 10 percent in late 2009.

Joblessness and the inability to refinance sent foreclosure rates skyrocketing across the country, from 240,000 in the first quarter of 2007 to more than 930,000 in the third quarter of 2009. And subprime mortgages played an important role in this increase. While subprime ARMs represented just 6.8 percent of all outstanding mortgages in the United States as early as the third quarter of 2007, they accounted for 43 percent of the foreclosures being initiated. All of these factors—the decline in home prices, rising joblessness, tightening credit, and securities valuation questions—led to a near collapse in subprime lending and the market for MBSs, which fell from $570 billion in 2006 to less than $25 billion in 2008. Meanwhile, many housing market experts say that the foreclosure situation was still a growing concern, as many ARMs would still be reset upward. Higher monthly payments would be due from people who had either lost their jobs or whose income would not be sufficient, creating a new wave of foreclosures and a further drag on home prices.

In addition, with house prices falling so dramatically from their 2006–2007 peak, many subprime borrowers found themselves owing more than their houses were worth. Many homeowners in that situation—said to be "upside down" or "underwater"—simply abandoned their homes rather than go through the lengthy and costly process of foreclosure. This was more than a headache for lending institutions, who now found themselves with ever greater numbers of unsold properties worth less than the loans on their books.

Foreclosure Mitigation Efforts

To offset the rising level of foreclosures and loan abandonments, the Barack Obama administration initiated a mortgage foreclosure mitigation plan in early 2009. Mortgagees (lenders) were offered government incentives to maintain monthly payments at no more than 31 percent of the mortgagor's income. In addition, the U.S. Treasury Department increased the capitalization of Fannie Mae and Freddie Mac so that these GSEs could purchase mortgages worth up to 105 percent of the value of a home.

By late that year, it had become clear that many mortgagees were failing to make the adjustments fast enough, prompting the administration to announce in late November that it would be cracking down on slow-moving lenders. Many experts, however, said that upward-shifting ARMs were no longer the main problem facing the housing finance market. Instead, it was joblessness. According to that view, simply adjusting mortgage payments to less than 31 percent of income offered little help to someone who had no job and hence no income. Only by cutting into historically high jobless rates could the government make sure that a mortgage mitigation plan would achieve its aims of keeping people in their homes.

Meanwhile, other economists began to ask deeper questions about whether homeownership was even a smart and economically rational choice for lower-income families. This called into question decades of government efforts to encourage homeownership across the economic spectrum—including the mortgage interest deduction on personal income taxes.

James Ciment

See also: Housing Booms and Busts; Mortgage-Backed Securities; Mortgage Lending Standards; Mortgage Markets and Mortgage Rates; Recession and Financial Crisis (2007–).

Further Reading

Bitner, Richard. *Confessions of a Subprime Lender: An Insider's Tale of Greed, Fraud, and Ignorance.* Hoboken, NJ: John Wiley & Sons, 2008.

Chomsisengphet, Souphala, and Anthony Pennington-Cross. "The Evolution of the Subprime Mortgage Market." *Federal Reserve Bank of St. Louis Review* 88:1 (January/February 2006): 31–56.

Goodman, Laurie S., Shumin Li, Douglas J. Lucas, Thomas A. Zimmerman, and Frank J. Fabozzi. *Subprime Mortgage Credit Derivatives.* Hoboken, NJ: John Wiley & Sons, 2008.

Muolo, Paul, and Mathew Padilla. *Chain of Blame: How Wall Street Caused the Mortgage and Credit Crisis.* Hoboken, NJ: John Wiley & Sons, 2008.

Shiller, Robert J. *The Subprime Solution: How Today's Global Financial Crisis Happened and What to Do About It.* Princeton, NJ: Princeton University Press, 2008.

Zandi, Mark. *Financial Shock: A 360° Look at the Subprime Mortgage Implosion, and How to Avoid the Next Financial Crisis.* Upper Saddle River, NJ: FT Press, 2009.

Myrdal, Gunnar (1898–1987)

Swedish economist and sociologist Gunnar Myrdal is best remembered for his critique of the United States' "separate but equal" policy in his book *An American Dilemma: The Negro Problem and Modern Democracy* (1944). A recipient, with Friedrich Hayek, of the 1974 Nobel Prize in Economic Sciences, Myrdal was also a successful politician.

Gunnar Myrdal was born on December 6, 1898, in Dalarna County, Sweden. He attended Stockholm University, receiving a law degree in 1923 and a doctorate in economics in 1927. His thesis on the role of expectations in price formation, published in 1927, influenced the development of the Stockholm school of economics. He continued his studies in Germany and Great Britain and was a Rockefeller Fellow in the United States in 1929–1930, during which time he published *The Political Element in the Development of Economic Theory.* Myrdal taught for a year at the Graduate Institute of International Studies in Geneva, Switzerland, before being granted the Lars Hierta Chair of Political Economy and Public Finance at the University of Stockholm.

In 1934, Myrdal was elected to the Swedish parliament as a Social Democrat. Then, in 1938, he was commissioned by the Carnegie Foundation in New York to direct a study on race relations in the United States. Published in 1944, the product of his study, *An American Dilemma: The Negro Problem and Modern Democracy,* was one of the first works to expose the gap between the American "ideal" and the grim reality of racial segregation and discrimination. The controversial publication appeared during an era when racial segregation still was enforced in the United States under the doctrine of "separate but equal," derived from the U.S. Supreme Court's 1896 decision in *Plessy v. Ferguson.* Myrdal's book was said to have had a major influence on the landmark Supreme Court decision in *Brown v. Board of Education* (1954), which prohibited racial segregation in public schools.

Myrdal's research—often informed by his experiences with Sweden's welfare state—took into account a variety of data (sociological, anthropological, and legal) in its examination of the crippling effects of President Franklin D. Roosevelt's New Deal policies on the African American population, particularly the minimum wage and restrictions on agricultural production. Myrdal was among the first to suggest that the minimum wage tended to price the marginal worker out of the market. He also contended that by giving farmers incentives to cut production in order to raise prices, the Roosevelt administration actually had caused farmers, particularly in the South, to cut out their black and white sharecroppers and

Swedish economist and public official Gunnar Myrdal served as a member of parliament, minister of commerce, and secretary of a UN commission. He shared the 1974 Nobel Prize for "pioneering work in the theory of money and economic fluctuations." *(The Granger Collection, New York)*

cash and share tenants, adding to agricultural unemployment.

Myrdal resumed his work in the Swedish government in 1942, chairing the Post-War Planning Commission. A year after the publication of *An American Dilemma,* even as the controversy surrounding it continued, Myrdal was named Sweden's minister of commerce, serving from 1945 to 1947. He joined the United Nations in 1947 as executive secretary of the Commission on Europe, a post he held for ten years. In 1957, he directed a Twentieth Century Fund study of economic trends and policies in South Asia that culminated in the 1968 publication of *Asian Drama: An Inquiry into the Poverty of Nations,* which became required reading for would-be development specialists. In that work, Myrdal contended that in order to solve its economic development problems, Southeast Asia must control its population growth, institute land reform to broaden ownership, and commit resources to education and health care.

Myrdal shared the Nobel Prize in Economic Sciences with Friedrich Hayek for "their pioneering work in the theory of money and economic fluctuations and for their penetrating analysis of the interdependence of economic, social, and institutional phenomena." Myrdal died on May 17, 1987, in Danderyd, Sweden. His wife, Alva Reimer Myrdal, who predeceased him in 1984, won the Nobel Peace Prize in 1982.

John Barnhill

See also: New Deal; Stockholm School.

Further Reading

Jackson, Walter. *Gunnar Myrdal and America's Conscience: Social Engineering and Racial Liberalism, 1938–1987.* Chapel Hill: University of North Carolina Press, 1990.

Lankester, Tim. "'Asian Drama': The Pursuit of Modernization in India and Indonesia." *Asian Affairs* 35:3 (November 2004): 291–304.

Lindbeck, Assar, ed. *Nobel Lectures: Economics, 1969–1980.* Singapore: World Scientific, 1992.

Nasdaq

Nasdaq is one of the largest stock markets in the world, second only to the New York Stock Exchange (NYSE) in terms of the monetary volume of transactions and the market capitalization of listed firms. In fact, if measured by the number of firms listed or the number of transactions, Nasdaq is the largest stock market worldwide. More than 3,200 firms, including 335 from 35 foreign countries, are listed on Nasdaq. Since its establishment in 1971, the market has evolved from an electronic service listing price quotes into a bone fide stock exchange and the main rival of the NYSE.

"Nasdaq" also refers to a variety of stock-price indices, the most important of which are the Nasdaq Composite, a value-weighted index of all firms listed and traded on the Nasdaq stock market, and the Nasdaq-100, an index of the 100 largest firms traded on the Nasdaq by market capitalization. Fluctuations in the former were quite dramatic during the late 1990s and early 2000s as a result of the dot.com bubble and bust, and during the financial crisis of 2008–2009. From a base value of 100 when it was launched on February 5, 1971, the Nasdaq Composite grew to 1,000 by July 17, 1995, and reached a peak of 5,132.52 on March 10, 2000. On October 10, 2002, it fell to a low of 1,108.49. After rising again to over 2,800 in October 2007, then falling again below 1,300 in March 2009, it had risen above 2,200 by early 2010.

Being listed on the NYSE "Big Board" is more prestigious and more costly than being listed on the Nasdaq. Many small firms first listed with Nasdaq, then switched to the NYSE when they became large enough. As of 2010, Nasdaq's entry and listing fees were approximately $75,000 and $27,500 per year, respectively, while comparable figures for the NYSE were $250,000 and up to $500,000 per year. In the past, Nasdaq-listed companies tended to be disproportionately small, young technology companies, but now a wider variety of firms are listed, including large companies such as Apple Computer, Intel, and Microsoft, which easily could choose to be listed on the NYSE.

Historically, trades on the NYSE took place at a physical location in New York City, whereas Nasdaq was used by securities dealers at various locations who were connected only electronically. This lack of a central physical location slowed the market's acceptance of Nasdaq as a financial exchange as real as those with trading floors in historic buildings. In 2000, Nasdaq opened its MarketSite

NASDAQ, established in 1971, is the second most active equities trading market in the United States after the New York Stock Exchange. The world's first exchange to conduct trading electronically, NASDAQ is relatively heavy in technology stocks. *(Bloomberg/Getty Images)*

in Times Square. This provides a physical location for Nasdaq's public relations events and serves as a center for financial and business news. Its visually impressive high-tech exterior contrasts markedly with the traditional look of its cross-town rival, the NYSE.

Origins

Nasdaq was an outgrowth of the National Association of Securities Dealers (NASD), which was established in response to the Great Depression. In the aftermath of trading abuses that contributed to the stock market crash of 1929, the Franklin D. Roosevelt administration wished to increase oversight of the financial markets. But effectively regulating smaller, geographically dispersed markets posed an even greater challenge than centralized exchanges such as the NYSE. Self-regulation was seen as a viable option, and in 1939, the NASD was founded in response to

amendments to the Securities Exchange Act of 1934.

The NASD was given the authority to regulate trading in equities, corporate bonds, securities futures, and options, and to license individual members and write rules governing their activities. It also examined members and was sanctioned by the U.S. Securities and Exchange Commission to discipline those that failed to comply with securities laws or with the NASD's rules and regulations.

On February 8, 1971, the NASD launched a method for viewing real-time quotes for "over-the-counter" stocks transacted, called the National Association of Securities Dealers Automated Quotation (NASDAQ) system. This was the first time dealers across the country could see real-time quotes for the over-the-counter securities that they bought and sold. This was not really a stock market, but rather a sophisticated information resource. Originally, only select "market makers" could use the system to trade securities, and until 1987, most NASDAQ trading occurred by telephone. During the October 1987 stock market crash, market makers often refused to answer their phones. This provided the impetus to expand access to screen-based trading and to develop the Small Order Execution System, which provided a method for brokers and dealers to enter into contractually binding trades. Over time, more and more securities dealers purchased dedicated terminals to engage in transactions and to view electronically disseminated screen-based quotes. The development of this system predated, and likely had a significant influence on, the development of the Internet.

The NASD's ability to regulate the Nasdaq impartially was a concern from the start. In the early 1990s, prices still were quoted in eighths. Academic researchers focused attention on the fact that very few prices were quoted in "odd eighths." Prices listed in fourths were much more common than 1/8, 3/8, and so on. This led to greater scrutiny of the wide spreads between bid and asking prices, as well as other practices that seemed to benefit dealers and brokers at the expense of their customers. The NASD's response, which seemed to be directed at protecting members rather than customers, highlighted the conflict of interest in having members regulate themselves. By 2001, the NASDAQ quotation system had become the Nasdaq stock market. The NASD divested its ownership interest in the Nasdaq but continued to act as the market's regulator. In July 2007, the NASD merged with the NYSE's member regulation, enforcement, and arbitration functions to form the Financial Industry Regulatory Authority, or FINRA, Nasdaq's current regulator.

First Electronic Stock Market

Since its inception, Nasdaq has been in direct competition with the NYSE. Over time, the two stock markets have become more similar, but differences still remain. Nasdaq began as a "dealer market" in which market participants buy and sell multiple orders to "market makers." In con-

trast, the NYSE is described as an "auction market" in which buyers and sellers typically transact with one another, with the highest bidding price matched to the lowest asking price. On the NYSE, each security has one market maker who acts as an auctioneer and may or may not act as a principal, buying or selling securities out of inventory. On the Nasdaq, each security has multiple market makers, and, in theory, competition between them should lower transaction costs.

The NYSE has responded to the Nasdaq challenge by purchasing technologically advanced competitors and automating transactions. Nasdaq, in turn, has responded by developing a physical presence and burnishing its brand name, while touting its ability to trade in NYSE-listed stocks through its broker-dealer, Nasdaq Execution Services.

Demutualization, Acquisitions, and Future Direction

Three fundamental forces have had a great impact on stock markets: demutualization, diversification, and globalization. Nasdaq (and the NYSE) are excellent examples of the impact of these forces. From its origins as an over-the-counter market with transactions made and information disseminated between individual dealers over the phone, Nasdaq evolved beyond a sophisticated electronic bulletin board to become the world's most advanced online trading system. It continually added to the information reported by its automated systems and increased the speed at which transactions can be consummated, but still lacked an impressive physical location. In 1992, Nasdaq joined with the London Stock Exchange to link securities markets across the continents for the first time. In 2000, NASD members voted to demutualize, and Nasdaq became an investor-owned corporation.

There were several reasons for this decision. First, it would permit Nasdaq to merge and make cooperative arrangements with other exchanges more readily. Second, the additional capital derived from a public offering would allow the system's infrastructure to be upgraded. Third, the change in ownership structure would eliminate the conflict of interest between the long-term interests of the exchange (a faster, more direct, and technologically advanced trading platform) and the short-term interests of its members (to continue a system that would require use of brokers for transactions and allow them to maintain their informational advantage, with an ability to benefit from the spread between bid and ask prices). Going public would allow member and owners to benefit from changes that would increase the stock price of the Nasdaq but reduce their trading profits. Shares of Nasdaq ownership began trading publicly on July 2, 2002.

In 2005, Nasdaq increased its ownership in the London Stock Exchange to just under 30 percent, but was thwarted in its effort to obtain a controlling interest. In 2007, Nasdaq purchased old, established, but small regional exchanges in Philadelphia and Boston, and in 2008, it purchased the financial company that controls seven Nordic and Baltic stock exchanges, OMX, forming the NASDAQ-OMX Group. In this same year, Nasdaq formed a strategic alliance with the large and dynamic Middle Eastern exchange, Bourse Dubai Ltd., and purchased a one-third stake.

In 1998, the NASD merged Nasdaq with the American Stock Exchange (AMEX) to form the Nasdaq-Amex Market Group. AMEX's historically important trading location in Manhattan near Wall Street may have been a factor. But AMEX remained an independent entity under the NASD parent company, and conflicts arose between the two. In 2004, NASD spun off AMEX, allowing its members to purchase independent ownership, thereby ending its relationship with Nasdaq. (In October 2008, AMEX was purchased by NYSE Euronext, itself a merger of the NYSE and a consortium of European exchanges.) Although mergers have reduced the number of exchanges, competition seems to have intensified among those that remain, reducing fees and spurring advances in technology and international linkages.

Bruce Brown

See also: Dot.com Bubble (1990s–2000); Information Technology; Stock Markets, Global; Technological Innovation.

Further Reading

"Battle of the Bourses." *The Economist,* May 25, 2006. Available at www.economist.com/business-finance/displaystory.cfm?story_id=11455085. Accessed March 2010.

Burton, Maureen, Reynold Nesiba, and Bruce Brown. *An Introduction to Financial Markets and Institutions.* 2nd ed. Armonk, NY: M.E. Sharpe, 2010.

Ingebretsen, Mark. *NASDAQ: A History of the Market That Changed the World.* Roseville, CA: Forum, 2002.

NASDAQ. www.nasdaq.com. Accessed February 2010.

Wright, Russell. *Chronology of the Stock Market.* Jefferson, NC: McFarland, 2002.

National Bureau of Economic Research

The National Bureau of Economic Research (NBER) is a private, nonprofit organization that undertakes a broad array of economic and financial analyses. It operates in a number of program areas, one of which focuses specifically on economic fluctuations and growth. The NBER has had an important role in the dating and understanding of business cycles through data monitoring and analysis for almost ninety years.

The NBER was founded in January 1920. It is located in Cambridge, Massachusetts, but also has branch offices in New York City and Stanford, California. The NBER has seven officers, including, as of this writing, its chairman, John Clarkeson, and president and chief executive officer James Poterba. In addition, it has 25 directors-at-large, 15 directors by university appointment, 11 directors by appointment of other organizations, and 10 directors emeriti. The NBER is the leading private nonprofit research organization in the United States: its roster of contributing experts includes 16 of the 31 American Nobel Prize winners in economics, including Paul Krugman who won the Nobel in 2008, as well as earlier Nobel winners Joseph E. Stiglitz, Robert E. Lucas, Jr., Milton Friedman, and Simon Kuznets. Six of the past chairmen of the president's Council of Economic Advisers either have worked or are currently working as research associates there. More than 1,000 university professors, most of them specializing in business or economics, are also part-time NBER researchers at the same time.

Since its foundation, the NBER has followed five principles: (1) concentrate on facts important for dealing with major economic problems and the connections between them; (2) focus on the collection and analysis of quantitative data, but do not ignore qualitative data; (3) follow scientific principles; (4) stay impartial in presenting results and inform the public of this impartiality; (5) and do not make policy recommendations. For these reasons, and to avoid even a hint of partiality, the NBER has sought financial support from a wide range of sources—including public and private institutions, firms, and individuals, all with diverse ideologies.

The NBER disseminates its economic research among businesspeople, academics, and policy makers. It has studied various issues: national income and its distribution, savings, expenditures, prices (including stock prices and exchange rates), interest rates, wages, employment, pensions, education, health, migration, production, energy, credit, bank assets, financial instruments, business cycles and their measuring and forecasting methods, and the economic and political environment. The NBER publishes time series and other macro, industry, international trade, hospital, demographic, and patent data. (For instance, it has calculated the U.S. Industrial Production Index with the earliest value from 1790 and U.S. foreign trade data from 1879.) It has published annual reports, working papers, books and conference proceedings, the *NBER Digest* (summarizing four or more most recent newsworthy NBER working papers), the *NBER Reporter* (providing reviews of the NBER's research and activity, including reviews of recent NBER conferences and a list of recent NBER working papers), and the *NBER Bulletin on Aging and Health.*

The NBER has eighteen major programs, each of them involving at least twenty NBER research associates and also some faculty research fellows: (1) aging, (2) asset pricing, (3) children, (4) corporate finance, (5) development of the U.S. economy, (6) economics of education, (7) economic fluctuations and growth, (8) environmental and energy economics, (9) health care, (10) health economics, (11) industrial organization, (12) international finance and macroeconomics, (13) international trade and investment, (14) labor studies, (15) law and economics, (16) monetary economics, (17) political economy, and (18) productivity and public economics. All of these programs have a director and publish program working papers. Most of these programs include several primary projects with ten to twelve economists and also some smaller projects focusing on more specialized research areas. An economist may participate in several programs at the same time.

The NBER also has fifteen working groups: (1) Behavioral Finance, (2) Chinese Economy, (3) Cohort Studies, (4) Economics of Crime, (5) Economics of National Security, (6) Entrepreneurship, (7) Higher Education, (8) Insurance, (9) International Trade and Organization, (10) Market Design, (11) Market Microstructure, (12) Organizational Economics, (13) Personnel Economics, (14) Risks of Financial Institutions, and (15) Urban Economics. These groups meet regularly.

In doing research, the NBER cooperates with universities, private and public research organizations, independent researchers, and governments. Eleven organizations (the Agricultural and Applied Economics Association, the American Economic Association, the American Federation of Labor and Congress of Industrial Organizations, the American Finance Association, the American Institute of Certified Public Accountants, the American Statistical Association, the Canadian Economics Association, the Committee for Economic Development, the Conference Board, the Economic History Association, and the National Association for Business Economics) have appointed their own directors for the NBER's board of directors, but the NBER also cooperates with other groups. Some NBER working groups offer travel grants for graduate and doctoral students interested in attending professional meetings or for postdoctoral students studying certain issues while not in residence at the NBER. Such calls for proposals are available for the public at the NBER's home page, www.nber.org/callforpapers/callpapers.html.

Naturally, the NBER is not the only institution offering economic policy analyses or making economic forecasts. The Congressional Budget Office, the U.S. Treasury Department, and the National Economic Council also perform similar tasks.

Tiia Vissak

See also: Congressional Budget Office; National Economic Council; Treasury, Department of the.

Further Reading

Fabricant, Solomon. "Toward a Firmer Basis of Economic Policy: The Founding of the National Bureau of Economic Research." Available at www.nber.org/nberhistory/sfabricantrev.pdf. Accessed March 2009.

National Bureau of Economic Research. "NBER Information." Available at www.nber.org/info.html. Accessed March 2009.

National Economic Council

The National Economic Council (NEC) was founded in 1993 for the purposes of advising the U.S. president on domestic and global economic policy. The NEC is a part of the Executive Office of the President, which includes the Council of Economic Advisers, the Domestic Policy Council, the Office of Management and Budget, the Office of the United States Trade Representative, as well as other agencies. In 2009, President Barack Obama appointed former Treasury secretary Lawrence Summers as NEC director.

The NEC is a White House–led policy council charged with four main tasks: (1) to coordinate domestic and international economic policy making, (2) to coordinate the offering of economic policy advice for the president, (3) to ensure that U.S. policy decisions and programs coincide with the president's economic goals, and (4) to oversee the implementation of the president's economic policy agenda. Basically, the NEC serves as an honest broker (not an advocate) among viewpoints and agencies. At the NEC, the president's top advisers can present, test, and improve their ideas and seek support for them. Although the NEC was established in 1993, this does not mean that the previous presidents did not have any structures for economic policy coordination, but this specific form did not exist before. Nor did the NEC achieve instant success. However, President Bill Clinton still stated that the NEC was the most significant organizational innovation made in the White House during his administration. The NEC's strong procedural norms were modeled after the ones of the National Security Council (NSC), but the NEC remains smaller and slightly more informal than the latter. The NEC cooperates with the NSC as well as with the Council of Economic Advisers (CEA), which is responsible for economic forecasting and general economic analyses.

The director of the NEC and the two deputy directors cooperate actively with top officials and those departments and agencies within the administration whose activities strongly impact the nation's economy: the vice president, the secretary of state, the secretary of the Treasury, the secretary of agriculture, the secretary of commerce, the secretary of labor, the secretary of housing and urban development, the secretary of transportation, and the secretary of energy. Others who can be present at NEC meetings are the administrator of the Environmental Protection Agency, the chair of the Council of Economic Advisers, the director of the Office of Management and Budget, the U.S. trade representative, the assistant to the president for domestic policy, the assistant to the president for national security, the assistant to the president for science and technology policy, and other senior White House staff, because these officials and the heads of these departments and agencies are also considered members of the NEC. Together, the director of the NEC and the officials of these agencies and departments aim to implement the president's economic policy objectives, including the ones related to financial markets, fiscal policy, commerce, agriculture, labor, energy, health care, and Social Security. Advancing the American recovery and reinvestment plan is also among their responsibilities.

Naturally, the NEC is not the only institution in the United States analyzing the state of the economy. The U.S. Treasury Department, the Congressional Budget Office, and the National Bureau of Economic Research, among others, are also active in this task.

Tiia Vissak

See also: Congressional Budget Office; National Bureau of Economic Research; Treasury, Department of the.

Further Reading

Executive Office of the President home page: www.whitehouse .gov/administration/eop/. Accessed March 2009.

National Economic Council home page: www.whitehouse.gov/ administration/eop/nec/. Accessed March 2009.

Peterson Institute for International Economics. "White House National Economic Council Needs More Regular Procedures and More Consistent Presidential Support." Available at www.petersoninstitute.org/publications/newsreleases/ newsrelease.cfm?id=28. Accessed March 2009.

Rosen Wartell, Sarah. "The White House: National Economic Council." In *Change for America: A Progressive Blueprint for the 44th President*, ed. Mark Green and Michele Jolin. Washington, DC: The Center for American Progress Action Fund, 2008.

Neoclassical Theories and Models

First developed toward the end of the nineteenth century, neoclassical economics is a set of theories and models that applies the concept of marginality to the basic precepts of classical economics. Marginality represents the additional benefit or cost that firms and individuals receive through the consumption or production of an additional unit of goods or services.

From Classical to Neoclassical Economics

According to the central paradigm of classical economics, established by thinkers such as Adam Smith, David Ricardo, Thomas Robert Malthus, John Stuart Mill, and Karl Marx in the late eighteenth and mid-nineteenth centuries, the value of a good or service is determined by the labor and material costs that go into making or providing it. If demand for a good or service outstrips supply, then the cost of that good or service will go up. At a certain point, rising costs depress demand, bringing it back into equilibrium with supply. The same process works for wages. If there is a surplus of laborers, then wages decline, lowering the cost of production. As the cost of production goes down, demand goes up, leading employers to hire more workers, thereby lifting wages. Once again, an equilibrium between the demand for and supply of laborers is reached through market mechanisms. In short, according to classical economics, the value of a good or service—or the value of labor—is inherent in that good or service based on the inputs necessary to create or provide it. As for the value of labor, its value is based on the skills, brains, or brawn of the worker—that is, how much value he brings to the production process.

The problem with the classical theory of value was that it focused on the object—the good or service or the worker—while leaving the subject—the buyer of the good or service, the employer who hired the laborer, or even the worker himself—out of the equation. This was evident in the fact that people often paid more (or less) for a good than an objective measurement of the inputs would dictate. For example, a very hungry person will pay a premium for her first potato, regardless of what it objectively cost to grow, harvest, process, distribute, and market that potato. But as her appetite is satiated, she will be willing to pay less and less for each additional potato, regardless of the fact that, objectively speaking, every potato cost the same to produce.

A similar process works for wages as well as prices. A firm will hire workers based not only on the value they produce, but also on their marginal utility. That is, a firm will hire a new worker only so long as the value that the new worker creates matches or exceeds the cost of employing that worker. From the worker's perspective, he sells his labor not only based on what the market says he is worth, but also on what he determines to be the marginal utility of that wage. That is, the wage paid must exceed the disutility—the loss of leisure, the discomfort, the absence from family—of the work itself. Finally, a firm will produce an additional good only if the revenue that good provides exceeds the cost of producing that good. In this way, the firm is maximizing profit. The development of this set of principles is known to economic historians as the "marginal revolution," and it laid the basis for the neoclassical economic paradigm to come.

Emphasizing the behavior of economic agents—as opposed to the objects of production—neoclassical economics rests on three core concepts. First, people act rationally when making their preferences about different economic outcomes. Second, individuals try to maximize utility and minimize disutility, just as firms try to maximize profit and minimize cost. And for all this to work, it is assumed in neoclassical economics that people and firms make their decisions independent of coercion and with full knowledge of all necessary and relevant information.

In short, economic value is determined by consumers, workers, and firms all attempting to maximize their utility or profit within the constraints of the market. That is, a worker naturally would like to be paid far more than the market may determine, and a firm would like to charge far more for its products than consumers may pay. But both cannot, of course, because firms will not hire overpaid workers, and consumers will not pay too high a price. Value, then, is determined by the conflict between desire and constraint, with the market serving as the arena for this battle. When a price or wage is set, a truce is, in effect, called

between these economic combatants, signaling that desire and constraint are in balance, or equilibrium. But, of course, such truces are temporary, as constraints and desires are ever changing. What the neoclassical economics model has in common with its classical antecedent is the concept of an ever-adjusting equilibrium.

Neoclassical Economics and the Business Cycle

With the work of the mid-twentieth-century American economist Robert Solow—who won a Nobel Prize for his efforts—the neoclassical paradigm was applied to the business cycle. According to neoclassical thought, output is produced by means of two inputs: labor and capital. Assuming that labor growth is a given, the main factor that leads to growth comes through capital deepening—that is, the growth of capital in relation to labor. More capital equipment per worker means more output per worker, but only up to a point. That is because the most productive increases are made first. For example, a new railroad line will be constructed where demand is greatest. As new lines are added, they tend to be located in less profitable markets. Thus, the marginal utility of increased capital diminishes. At the same time, new capital equipment raises output per worker, assuming that the addition outpaces labor growth, leading to an increase in wages as the marginal product of labor rises. But, at a certain point, the return from capital deepening diminishes to the point at which it no longer makes sense to invest, leading to diminished economic activity and then recession. Eventually, however, natural growth in labor and consumer demand increases the marginal utility of capital deepening, leading to more investment and economic recovery.

Neoclassical theory dominated the field of economics in the West during much of the twentieth century, for two reasons. First, it is an all-encompassing set of ideas. One can apply the neoclassical critique to just about any aspect of economic life, from employment to production to consumption, and even to such social phenomena as getting married and having children, choosing the location of shelter (e.g., the marginal utility of housing costs versus commuting time), and leisure (e.g., going to a ball game versus earning overtime pay for working over the weekend).

The second reason for the dominance of neoclassical economics is that it lends itself to mathematical modeling. For example, the foregoing description of capital deepening assumes an absence of technological change, as improvements in the quality of capital equipment also would have as much—or perhaps more or less—of an impact on marginal utility and profit as the quantity of capital equipment. Neoclassical economics does not ignore such an obvious fact of modern life as technological change, but instead allows economists to factor it out—or in—as the mathematical modeling of inputs requires. In short, neoclassical models and theories allow economics to become more of a science than a social science, which is what the modern profession aspires to.

Not all modern economists agree with the neoclassical approach. Critics point out that by focusing on marginal decisions, neoclassical economics misses important institutional and historical factors. Furthermore, the mathematical rigor of neoclassical economics requires assumptions about individual rational decision making that blinded mainstream neoclassical economists to the irrational group behavior that caused the economic meltdown of the late 2000s.

James Ciment

See also: Classical Theories and Models.

Further Reading

Arnold, Lutz G. *Business Cycle Theory.* New York: Oxford University Press, 2002.

Hollis, Martin, and Edward J. Nell. *Rational Economic Man: A Philosophical Critique of Neo-Classical Economics.* New York: Cambridge University Press, 1975.

Milonakis, Dimitris, and Ben Fine. *From Political Economy to Economics: Method, the Social and the Historical in the Evolution of Economic Theory.* New York: Routledge, 2008.

Solow, Robert. "A Contribution to the Theory of Economic Growth." *Quarterly Journal of Economics* 70:1 (1956): 65–94.

Yonay, Yuval P. *The Struggle over the Soul of Economics: Institutionalist and Neoclassical Economists in America Between the Wars.* Princeton, NJ: Princeton University Press, 1998.

Neo-Keynesian Theories and Models

Developed in the decades immediately following World War II, neo-Keynesian, or New Keynesian, economics is the modern revival of Keynesian "neoclassical synthesis" economics. That is, it shares with neoclassical economics the idea that, in the long run, economies gravitate toward a price equilibrium where there is low unemployment and high output, but accepts John Maynard Keynes's ideas that, in the short run, such an equilibrium is often elusive. In other words, the main difference between neoclassical economists and the neo-Keynesians rests on their respective views of the short run. Neo-Keynesian theory should not be confused with Post Keynesian theory, the latter being more explicitly tied to Keynes's original ideas.

Much of neo-Keynesian theory focuses on why the economy gets stuck in a position of less than full employment, and on the possible policy responses to this situation. As such, the neo-Keynesian model can be labeled an "imperfectionist" model because short-run disequilibrium positions are the result of some imperfection in how markets operate in the real world, such as the inability of prices to adjust quickly. But if policy makers could somehow remove this imperfection, the economy would slowly gravitate toward full employment on its own. In other words, shocks that lead to economic disturbances can arise on either the demand or supply side. But imperfections in market response create a situation in which the economy cannot adjust instantaneously to such shocks—or may, indeed, amplify the shocks—and thus gets stuck in an equilibrium where there is high unemployment and less than optimal output.

Assumptions

The general neo-Keynesian model is based on three assumptions. The first is that, in the short run, money is non-neutral—that is, the money supply affects both nominal variables such as prices and wages, and real variables such as employment, inflation-adjusted gross domestic product (GDP), and inflation-adjusted consumption The second is that markets may not work perfectly, and these imperfections in real-world markets explain macroeconomic fluctuations in output, such as sticky prices and wages. The third is that aggregate demand dominates in the short run while aggregate supply constraints exist in the long run.

The first assumption is related to the conduct of monetary policy. Breaking from mainstream economics, which argues that central banks control the money supply, neo-Keynesians argue that central banks control the rate of interest, setting it according to some policy objective, such as combating inflation. Non-neutrality means that changes in the rate of interest will have an impact, in the short run, on output and economic fluctuations. In the long run, however, neo-Keynesians agree with the neoclassical assumption of money neutrality—that is, that money supply affects only nominal variables (e.g., prices and wages).

The second assumption says that if wages and prices (among other imperfections) do not adjust quickly enough to changes in output (that is, they are "sticky"), then the economy will be slow to move to its new equilibrium position. In other words, the price mechanism breaks down. This will translate into a disequilibrium position with high unemployment that may persist for some time because nominal wages will fail to adjust downward in a timely fashion. The third assumption simply states that, in the short run, changes in aggregate demand dominate: positive changes in aggregate demand will have positive effects on output and employment. In the long run, however, the economy is constrained by aggregate supply.

New Consensus Model

Over the years, there have been many different versions of the neo-Keynesian model, although they all share the three fundamental assumptions discussed above. Since the 1990s, a new model has emerged that has received considerable attention from economists as well as central bankers and policy makers because of its potential usefulness, especially to central bankers, who control monetary policy. The new model is called the "New Consensus" model or the "Taylor Rule" model, because it is based on a monetary policy theory developed by economist John Taylor. Indeed, the New Consensus model is currently the most widely cited iteration of the neo-Keynesian model, in which the three assumptions from above are clearly implicit. And although there are many variations of this model, the basic model can be summarized by three fundamental assumptions that are expressed as equations.

The first equation is an aggregate demand equation, stipulating that changes in output (or rather the output gap, defined as deviations in actual output from potential or long-run output) are caused largely by changes in the rate of interest. In other words, whenever the central bank changes the rate of interest, output will change accordingly: this is the basic principle of monetary non-neutrality. For example, an increase in the rate of interest will cause output to fall. This result holds because of nominal wage rigidity, allowing monetary policy to have an impact in the short run.

The second equation is a Phillips curve, a formula based on the work of New Zealand economist Alban William Phillips that shows the inverse relationship between the unemployment rate and the rate of inflation. It stipulates that inflation is largely explained by changes in aggregate demand. Whenever aggregate demand is greater than potential output, or the theoretically highest level of GDP attainable by an economy at a given moment in time, prices will tend to rise, and inflation rises above the target rate set by the central bank. The third equation represents the monetary policy position of the central bank. According to this equation, the rate of interest is set by the central bank according to its policy objectives.

The New Consensus model is representative of many countries' current monetary policy stance. Indeed, in many countries, the central bank targets a very specific level of inflation, or a corridor, and uses interest rates to reach it. In many versions of the New Consensus model, control over inflation is the only—or, at least, the overreaching—objective of the central bank.

In practical terms, the model works in the following matter. Assume that a central bank has an inflation target of 2 percent per annum and that actual inflation approaches or surpasses the target. In such a case, the central bank will raise the interest rate. According to the first of the New Consensus model equations, the increase in the rate of interest should therefore decrease output, since a higher rate of interest will deter investment and hiring. In turn, this should lower inflation, according to the second equation. But if this fails to bring inflation down to the target rate or below, the central bank will continue to raise the rate of interest until the inflation target is reached. Yet because this adjustment is not instantaneous, the economy can spend some time in slumps with lower output and higher unemployment. This is considered only temporary, however, as the economy will eventually, or should, gravitate toward a low-unemployment, high-output equilibrium.

Critique of the Neo-Keynesian Model

Post Keynesian economists have noted a number of possible weaknesses in the New Consensus approach. First, and most notably, Post Keynesians point out that the New Consensus model is overly concerned with inflation. They also believe that neo-Keynesians give too little consideration to unemployment or unequal income distribution. Indeed, according to neo-Keynesians, only

inflation is an economic scourge for policy makers. Moreover, say the Post Keynesians, this bias is exacerbated by the neo-Keynesian tendency to focus on demand shocks as the cause of inflation. For Post Keynesians, inflation is, rather, the result of excess costs and of conflicts between workers and firms (and finance).

By focusing on a wrong interpretation of inflation, then, policy prescriptions will only tend to exacerbate the problem, say these critics. In fact, if costs determine prices, then an increase in the rate of interest could lead to an increase in prices in the short run, given the increased cost of borrowing credit. This is known as Gibson's Paradox. It suggests that interest rates and prices may not move in opposite directions. At the very least, their precise correlation is unknown.

Second, Post Keynesians criticize the New Consensus model because its policies to fight inflation result in a weaker economy. The New Consensus argues that unemployment beyond structural unemployment is necessary in order to lower inflation. While in the long run, repeated increases in the rate of interest will eventually lower inflation, doing so may cause a severe recession.

Third, Post Keynesians object to the New Consensus model's conclusion that fiscal policy is ineffective, or at best inflationary. In the New Consensus view, monetary policy is considered the only credible policy and the central bank the only credible institution. Fiscal policy is not considered an effective tool to fight unemployment. Post Keynesians, on the other hand, maintain that fiscal policy is needed to achieve policy goals that include full employment and more equal income distribution.

For Post Keynesians, then, the emphasis on inflation and the exclusive use of monetary policy pose a definite problem for macroeconomic stability. They propose shifting the focus away from inflation and monetary policy dominance in favor of policies aimed at fighting unemployment. And while aggregate demand does play an important role, the focus is rather on income distribution and fiscal policy.

Neo-Keynesian Economics and the Recession of 2007–2009

Critique of the neo-Keynesian model has gained influence since the 2007–2009 recession undermined faith in the theories and policy prescriptions of mainstream economists, who relied too heavily on the self-regulating ability of the economy to gravitate instantly or slowly to a position of equilibrium, or rest. One thing has become clear: the economy does not gravitate on its own toward a predetermined position of equilibrium. On the contrary, what this severe crisis has taught us, say Post Keynesians, is that if left unconstrained, markets can be exuberant and irrational, and prone to periodic excesses. Markets need help to generate employment and to grow and maintain some sort of order.

In the end, numerous policy makers and economists alike have come to appreciate once again some of the insights of John Maynard Keynes, especially his belief that markets need to be regulated to prevent them from becoming too speculative and unstable. This suggests that new financial regulations are needed and that more attention should be paid to maintaining steady growth and aggregate demand, both in the short run and in the long run. In this sense, fiscal and regulatory polices are an integral component of well-functioning markets.

Louis-Philippe Rochon

See also: Keynes, John Maynard; Keynesian Business Model; Neoclassical Theories and Models; Post Keynesian Theories and Models.

Further Reading

Gordon, Robert J. "What Is New-Keynesian Economics." *Journal of Economic Literature* 28: 3 (September 1990): 1115–1171.

Mankiw, N. Gregory. 1990. "A Quick Refresher Course in Macroeconomics." *Journal of Economic Literature*, American Economic Association 28:4 (December 1990): 1645–1660.

Rochon, Louis-Philippe, and P. Nicholas Rowe. "What Is Monetary Policy? Should Central Banks Be Targeting Inflation?" In *Introducing Macroeconomic Analysis: Issues, Questions, and Competing Views*, ed. H. Bougrine and M. Seccareccia. Toronto: Emond Montgomery, 2009.

Taylor, John B., ed. *Monetary Policy Rules.* Chicago: University of Chicago Press, 2001.

Netherlands, The

The Netherlands, also known as Holland, is a small country of about 16.5 million people, located in northwestern Europe, between Germany and Belgium, on the North Sea coast. The nation is flat and low-lying, with about one-quarter of its landmass situated below sea level, made habitable for about 60 percent of the population through land reclamation and an extensive network of dikes.

The Netherlands has a long and illustrious economic history, having become a major center of finance and trade in the seventeenth century and an innovator in the development of modern capitalist institutions. Although slow to industrialize and historically eclipsed by larger neighbors, the Netherlands reemerged at the front ranks of economic innovation and prosperity in post–World War II Europe. A member of the European Union and the eurozone, contemporary Netherlands has a free-market economy based on manufacturing, services, trade, and financial activities.

Economic History to World War II

Settled by Germanic tribes in the first millennium BCE, the Netherlands was conquered by the Romans in the first century BCE. During the Middle Ages, the Low Countries (the Netherlands and Belgium) became a major commercial center, where goods from the Mediterranean were exchanged with those from the Baltic region.

By the 1400s, the Dutch city of Antwerp had emerged as one of the largest marketplaces in Europe, where Italian silks, marbles, and mirrors were exchanged for English woolens, German iron and copper, Spanish fruit, French wines and dyes, and Baltic wheat, fur, and timber. At the beginning of the sixteenth century, the region came under the dominion of Charles V, the Hapsburg emperor of Spain and other parts of Europe. The acquisition came just as Spain was beginning its conquest of the Americas, an event that led to a flood of precious metals and currency flowing into the Hapsburg dominions. Much of the money went to the Low Countries, where it paid for all of the goods marketed there and turned Amsterdam into a leading financial center of Europe.

In the late sixteenth century, the seven provinces of what would become the Netherlands united and began their nearly century-long struggle for independence from the Hapsburg Empire. Even as the conflict continued in the 1600s, the Dutch Republic, which had declared independence in 1581, emerged as the center of a global trading system that ultimately stretched from the Americas to West Africa to the East Indies. Spearheading that network was the Vereenigde Oost-Indische Compagnie (VOC, or Dutch East India Company), often called the world's first international corporation, established in 1602.

In the succeeding decades, armed VOC merchant ships pushed the Portuguese from Ceylon (now Sri Lanka) and the East Indies (Indonesia), establishing Dutch control over the lucrative trade in spices and other tropical goods from the east. With the founding of the Geoctroyeerde Westindische Compagnie (GWIC, or Dutch West India Company) in 1621, merchants in the Netherlands helped steer some of the valuable trade in silver and other products of Spanish America to Dutch ports. At the same time, Dutch merchants emerged as some of the most aggressive slave traders, establishing trading posts along the West African coast.

The abundance of trade, combined with Amsterdam's role as the financial center of Northern Europe, made the Netherlands the richest country on the continent (on a per capita basis) and produced the so-called Golden Age of Dutch history, including its outpouring of artistic masterpieces. A financial innovator as well, the Netherlands had been identified by some economic historians as the first fully capitalist state in human history, where merchants held sway over government and freed business from the often onerous restrictions set by royal authorities in such nominally mercantile

states as England. It was in Amsterdam that the first modern stock exchange was established in the 1600s, while Dutch merchants created the modern insurance industry and pension system. Holland was also home to the first great speculative bubble in modern capitalist history, tulipmania—a wild frenzy over exotic tulip bulbs that created and destroyed fortunes overnight in the mid-1630s.

Despite the end of the Eighty Years' War for independence in 1648, the days of Dutch commercial supremacy were numbered. For with all their wealth and innovation, what the merchants could not do was make Holland militarily competitive with rising powers such as Britain and France, both of which used their greater populations and military resources to challenge Dutch maritime supremacy. By the eighteenth century, the Netherlands had lost its place as a world power, though it still remained an important financial and trading center.

Under French dominion during late revolutionary and Napoleonic eras, the Netherlands emerged as a kingdom in 1814 and briefly united with Belgium, which would become independent in 1830. While Belgium would become one of the leading centers of the industrial revolution in continental Europe during the nineteenth century, Holland lagged behind, held back by the difficulty of building a modern industrial and transportation infrastructure in a country laced with waterways and dependent on wind power.

Post–World War II Boom

Occupied by Germany in World War II, and losing its valuable East Indian colonies just after the conflict, the Netherlands emerged from the war eager to reestablish itself as a trading and financial center in a unified Europe. Toward that end, it was a founding member of both the North Atlantic Treaty Organization (NATO) and the European Coal and Steel Community, the predecessor of the European Union. Indeed, in the first decades after the war Holland participated in the "economic miracle" of Western Europe, aided

An economic power in the seventeenth century on the strength of maritime trade and financial innovations, the Netherlands today boasts one of the most stable economies in Europe. Shipping is still a mainstay, and the port of Rotterdam is one of the world's busiest. *(Bloomberg/Getty Images)*

first by billions of dollars in postwar U.S. funds under the Marshall Plan and then by rising demand from a growing middle class. In the 1950s and 1960s, the country followed the Western European model of combining free markets with strong state direction of major industries and a generous social welfare system.

For two decades, the policies worked well, raising Dutch standards of living to some of the highest levels in the world. But with the oil crisis of the 1970s, which hit the Netherlands particularly hard—it had almost no indigenous forms of energy, aside from that produced by its abundant windmills—the country entered a period of economic stagnation. In response, the government embarked on one of the most aggressive sets of free-market reforms in continental Europe during the 1980s, while retaining its extensive social welfare system.

By the 1990s and 2000s, the Netherlands was consistently posting some of the best economic numbers in the European Union, with unemployment levels below those of other member countries and consistently higher annual gross national product (GDP) growth. By 2008, the country was ranked by the World Bank as having the tenth-highest GDP per capita in the world; overall the economy ranked sixteenth in size. The contemporary Dutch economy rests on several pillars, including finance, shipping and transportation (the port of Rotterdam is the busiest in Europe), and agriculture, including food processing.

With so much of its economy tied to finance and insurance, the country was hard hit by the global financial crisis of 2008–2009. The collapse of the Belgian financial giant Fortis Bank in September 2008—one of the largest bank failures in Europe, with major effects in the Netherlands—forced the government to purchase the bank's Dutch banking and insurance divisions for more than $23 billion.

In addition, the global recession that followed the crisis had a major impact on the country's port and shipping sector. Together, the financial crisis and recession undermined economic performance. GDP growth had consistently exceeded 3 percent annually through the early and middle 2000s, but the Dutch economy was expected to shrink by roughly 0.75 percent in 2009. Unemployment was expected to climb above 6 percent, relatively low for continental Europe but high by Dutch standards.

James Ciment

See also: Belgium; Tulipmania (1636–1637).

Further Reading

Arblaster, Paul. *A History of the Low Countries.* Basingstoke, UK: Palgrave Macmillan, 2005.

CPB Netherlands Bureau for Economic Policy Analysis. "The Credit Crisis and the Dutch Economy 2009–2010." No date. Available at http://74.125.155.132/search?q=cache:dp2NfhHp6BoJ:www.cpb.nl/eng/pub/cepmev/cep/2009/pdf/summary_uk.pdf+netherlands+economy+2009&cd=2&hl=en&ct=clnk&gl=us. Accessed September 29, 2009.

Schama, Simon. *The Embarrassment of Riches: An Interpretation of Dutch Culture in the Golden Age.* New York: Alfred A. Knopf, 1987.

New Deal

The New Deal was the informal name for a set of programs initiated by the Franklin Roosevelt administration in the 1930s to lift the U.S. economy out of the Great Depression and to provide social welfare benefits to lower- and middle-income Americans. Historians actually refer to two "New Deals." The first, dating from the years 1933–1934, was aimed at reversing the worst economic downturn in U.S. history and providing immediate relief to hard-hit individuals, families, farms, and businesses. The second, launched in 1935, established more long-term social welfare and economic programs, many of which continue to the present day.

Background

The background to the New Deal was, of course, the unprecedented economic catastrophe known as the Great Depression. Between the stock market crash of October 1929—the triggering event for the downturn in the public's eye—and the inauguration of the Democrat Roosevelt in March 1933, the nation's economy experienced a contraction of epic proportions, as gross domestic product (GDP) fell by one-third and the official unemployment rate soared to 25 percent.

After some hesitation, Roosevelt's predecessor, Republican Herbert Hoover, had attempted to address both the high unemployment and drop in economic output through limited public works programs, government loans to major financial and industrial institutions, and appeals for private contributions to help the unemployed. But Hoover's efforts were limited by his philosophy that government relief encouraged dependency and by the prevailing economic wisdom that government deficits contributed to recession by drying up the funds available for private investment. Notably, both Hoover and Roosevelt subscribed to this conventional view, though the latter would jettison it for much of his first term.

When Roosevelt took office—with large Democratic majorities in Congress to back him up—the most immediate problem was the collapse of the nation's financial system, as interbank lending dried up and thousands of smaller institutions failed. To protect their savings, depositors had panicked, making runs on still solvent banks, forcing many of them to fail because they did not have the liquid funds to meet all of the depositors' withdrawals. Roosevelt immediately declared a bank holiday, giving the Treasury Department time to certify solvent institutions and reorganize insolvent ones, and reassuring customers that banks were now safe places to put their money. Several months later, in June 1933, Congress passed the Glass-Steagall Act, which, among other things, established the Federal Deposit Insurance Corporation (FDIC), guaranteeing deposits and separating commercial and investment banking, the latter activity advancing the financial speculation that had contributed to the stock market crash. These measures stabilized the banking system.

Farms were in equally bad shape, with crop prices having dropped below the cost of growing the products. The Agricultural Adjustment Act encouraged farmers to limit their output, since overproduction was a major cause of falling prices, and offered them payments that brought their income up to sustainable levels. To provide jobs, the administration launched the Civilian Conservation Corps, which ultimately put some 2.5 million young people to work restoring the environment; the Public Works Administration, which appropriated $3.3 billion (about $55 billion in 2009 dollars) to hire unemployed adults on infrastructure projects; and the Tennessee Valley Authority, which put thousands to work building dams and electrical power systems across a wide swath of the Appalachian South, a particularly hard-hit region of the country.

But the most important program of the so-called First Hundred Days was the National Recovery Administration (NRA), which attempted to limit the cutthroat competition in various industries that had driven down prices, profits, wages, and employment. The NRA did this through committees of businessmen and labor and consumer representatives that drafted codes to limit production and set prices. At the same time, the law guaranteed workers the right to organize unions and bargain collectively.

While the various programs of the First New Deal helped stabilize the economy, they were only partially effective against the most pernicious problem of the Depression—unemployment, which lingered above 17 percent into 1935. Meanwhile, Roosevelt's New Deal policies faced growing criticism from both the Right and the Left. With the economy somewhat recovered, business groups and Republicans spoke out against excessive government interference. In 1935, they won a victory when the U.S. Supreme Court—in the case of *Schecter v. United States*—overturned the enabling legislation for the NRA as an unconstitutional federal involvement in intrastate trade. From the Left came demands for more radical measures to address social inequities. Among these was a popular plan by California public-health advocate Francis Townsend for public pensions for old people and demands from Louisiana politician Huey Long for a radical redistribution of the nation's wealth.

Second New Deal

Concerned that leftist opposition and lingering high unemployment might undermine his reelection chances in 1936—and angry with what he felt was betrayal by the business interests he felt he had saved with First New Deal legislation—Roosevelt launched a far broader panoply of social welfare and economic legislation in 1935. The first piece was the Emergency Relief Appropriation Act, which set aside billions of dollars for a variety of programs. Among these were the Resettlement Administration, which relocated destitute families into planned communities; the Rural Electrification Administration, bringing electricity to underserved areas; and the National Youth Administration, which provided jobs for young adults and students. However, the biggest program was the Works Progress Administration (WPA), which ultimately hired some 8.5 million workers—including artists and performers—to work on infrastructure and social welfare projects across the country.

Then, in the summer of 1935, came the so-called Second Hundred Days, which introduced legislation with the most lasting legacy for American society. Among the new laws was the National Labor Relations Act, which further strengthened workers' rights to organize and bargain collectively and launched the most far-reaching unionization drive in American history. To steal the thunder of advocates for the elderly, Roosevelt pushed through the Social Security Act, creating a public pension plan. The law also included a new federal-state partnership on unemployment and a program—Aid to Dependent Children (later Aid to Families with Dependent Children, AFDC)—that would lay the groundwork for federally subsidized welfare. The administration also introduced legislation to redistribute wealth through a more progressive income tax through the Wealth Tax Act. However, compared to the other key legislation of 1935, the Wealth Tax Act was a modest effort.

The initiatives proved so popular that, despite continued double-digit unemployment, Roosevelt won reelection in 1936 in the biggest landslide in American presidential history to that date, having forged what political experts called a New Deal coalition of white Southerners (Southern blacks were largely debarred from voting) and urban Northerners. But with the victory under his belt, Roosevelt made two costly errors. To fend off conservative Supreme Court efforts to undermine New Deal legislation, he contrived a plan to increase the number of high court justices—with his own appointees. While constitutionally legal, the move struck many Americans, including Roosevelt supporters, as a power-grabbing effort not unlike those being made by fascist and Nazi governments in Europe. Second, having never dropped his commitment to balance the federal budget, Roosevelt scaled back many of the economic stimulus programs introduced during his first term. Mean-

First Lady Eleanor Roosevelt visits a construction site of the Works Progress Administration in 1936. The central New Deal program to combat joblessness, the WPA provided jobs to some 8.5 million Americans—many on public works projects—over eight years. *(The Granger Collection, New York)*

while, fearing inflation in a recovering economy, the Federal Reserve raised interest rates.

The two measures sent the economy into a new downward spiral in 1937 and 1938—the so-called "Roosevelt Recession"—forcing the administration to return to deficit spending. While Roosevelt also introduced some new legislation in 1937 and 1938—including measures to build housing for low-income families, another farm bill, and legislation banning child labor and establishing a minimum wage and forty-hour workweek for many employees—the energy of the New Deal had been largely spent, especially after a turn to the right by voters in the congressional midterm elections of 1938 and as the administration shifted its focus to the growing threat of global conflict.

Impact and Legacy

Economists and historians in the decades since have debated the effectiveness and legacy of the New Deal. Most agree it was effective, within limits. It did turn the economy around somewhat and prevented the kind of political upheaval experienced in Europe. But many students of the era also say that it did not go far enough. While the administration did adopt some of the countercyclical ideas of John Maynard Keynes—that is, deficit spending to spur aggregate demand—Roosevelt was too concerned about government spending and thus too timid in the jobs and social welfare programs he launched. That is why, critics say, unemployment remained in the double digits into 1938. Only with the massive defense spending of the late 1930s and early 1940s—that is, government spending on a scale urged by Keynes to address a downturn as steep as the Great Depression—did unemployment fall to pre-Depression levels. Meanwhile, some conservative historians and economists in recent years have resurrected contemporary arguments that New Deal programs actually prolonged the

Depression by absorbing capital that might have been used by the private sector and creating a sense of uncertainty in the business community that stifled investment.

Few students of American history and economics, however, would deny the immense legacy of the New Deal, with supporters arguing that it laid the foundation for the prosperity of the post–World War II era. Countercyclical deficit spending became a standard tool in the recession-fighting arsenal of the federal government while the New Deal's social legislation laid the groundwork for the limited social welfare state of recent decades. And the New Deal coalition assembled by Roosevelt dominated the country's politics through the 1970s. Only with the economic crises of that latter decade—and the conservative resurgence they triggered—did the New Deal coalition begin to come apart and some of the New Deal policies begin to be reversed, though Social Security remains largely untouched to this day.

James Ciment

See also: Great Depression (1929–1933); Keynes, John Maynard; Keynesian Business Model; Public Works Policy.

Further Reading

Barber, William J. *Designs Within Disorder: Franklin Roosevelt, the Economists, and the Shaping of American Economic Policy, 1933–1945.* New York: Cambridge University Press, 1996.

Bernstein, Michael A. *The Great Depression: Delayed Recovery and Economic Change in America, 1929–1939.* Cambridge, UK: Cambridge University Press, 1989.

Leuchtenburg, William. *Franklin Roosevelt and the New Deal.* New York: Harper & Row, 1963.

Rosen, Elliot A. *Roosevelt, the Great Depression, and the Economics of Recovery.* Charlottesville: University of Virginia Press, 2005.

New York Stock Exchange

Measured by both the dollar value of its listed company securities and by the annual dollar total of shares traded, the New York Stock Exchange (NYSE) is the world's preeminent stock exchange. Founded in 1792, it has been owned and operated since 2007 by NYSE Euronext, Inc., a holding company that controls or owns an interest in a number of securities exchanges in Europe, the United States, and the Middle East.

Operations

As a stock exchange, the NYSE offers facilities for the sale and purchase of various kinds of financial instruments, most notably, corporate securities for companies that are listed on the exchange. The NYSE is located in two buildings in the financial district of Lower Manhattan, with the main trading floor situated in a National Historic Landmark building at 11 Wall Street.

The total capitalization of the roughly 2,700 companies listed on the exchange is about $10 trillion, and the value of share trades on the exchange exceeds $20 trillion annually. To be listed on the NYSE, a company must have at least 1 million shares valued at a minimum of $100 million. By comparison, the second-largest exchange, the National Association of Securities Dealers Automated Quotations, or NASDAQ, has about half the annual share trades, by value, of the NYSE; the largest non-U.S. exchange, the London Stock Exchange, does about $7.5 trillion in annual trades.

The value of stocks listed on the NYSE is indicated by various indices. The most widely watched index is the Dow Jones Industrial Average, which comprises thirty of the largest and most representative companies listed on the NYSE. The NYSE Composite is an index of all stocks traded on the exchange. With an original value of 50 points, based on the market closing at the end of 1965, the NYSE Composite stood at about 7,300 at the beginning of 2010, down from its highest closing figure of 10,387 on October 31, 2007.

Corporate securities are bought and sold through the exchange during operating hours—9:30 a.m. to 4:30 p.m., Eastern Standard Time—

A neoclassical building at 18 Broad Street in Lower Manhattan has been home to the New York Stock Exchange—the world's largest—since 1903. The trading floor is located on nearby Wall Street, where the exchange originated in 1792. *(Henny Ray Abrams/Stringer/AFP/Getty Images)*

History Through World War II

The history of the NYSE encapsulates the financial history of the United States itself. In 1790, the federal government began refinancing the debt it and the thirteen states had accrued during the Revolutionary War, offering the first major issues of publicly traded securities. Two years later, three of these government bonds, along with shares in two banks, were traded in New York City. At the same time, to facilitate such trades, twenty-four brokers and merchants signed the Buttonwood Agreement, named after a tree of that kind that grew on Wall Street, establishing the basic rule that securities would be traded on a commission basis.

With the economy reviving in the wake of the War of 1812 and, along with it, the number of corporate securities, members of the organization of brokers that had signed the Buttonwood Agreement drafted a constitution of rules in 1817, adopting the name New York Stock & Exchange Board (the exchange's name would be changed to its current one in 1863) and renting their first offices in a room on Wall Street. The exchange would move several times to larger headquarters over the years, finally establishing itself in its current Wall Street location in 1922.

Virtually all of the major economic endeavors of the early republic, including the Erie Canal and many of the first railroad stocks, were financed through various forms of bonds and securities bought and sold on the New York exchange. With the development of the telegraph in the 1840s, shares in distant companies could now be traded, leading the exchange to establish more stringent requirements, including detailed financial statements, for a company to be listed. The development of the stock ticker in 1867, which instantaneously transmitted share-price information across the country and via undersea cable to Europe, also contributed to the NYSE's growing influence over U.S. financial markets.

To create more expedited exchanges, the NYSE adopted continuous trading in the 1870s, abandoning the old practice of allowing trades at

by traders who work for investment banks and brokerage houses. To trade on the floor, each of the several thousand traders must own a "seat," which can cost upward of several million dollars and requires that the trader pass certain competency and ethical tests. Activity on the floor can be frenzied, as traders jockey to have their purchase or sale orders registered. However, the days of this kind of activity are probably numbered, as the NYSE is expected to follow other exchanges, such as NASDAQ, in converting to all-electronic trading. Moreover, many brokerage houses and investment banks have been reducing the number of workers manning the trading posts on the floor, preferring to have them work at computer terminals in company-owned trading floors and offices.

set times. To facilitate this new practice, brokers dealing in specific stocks—known as specialists—manned set trading posts on the trading floor.

Despite setbacks, including several financial panics, the exchange continued to grow through the late nineteenth and early twentieth centuries. In 1886, it posted its first million-share day, and in 1892, it organized the New York Stock Exchange Clearing House to expedite trades between brokers. In 1896, the *Wall Street Journal* began to publish its Dow Jones Industrial Average (DJIA), with an initial value of 40.74. The listing came on the eve of a vast expansion in the value and volume of securities listed on the exchange, as the U.S. economy underwent a wave of corporate mergers that crested in the early years of the twentieth century.

World War I represented a milestone in the history of the NYSE. With the United States emerging from the war as the leading creditor nation in the world, New York supplanted London as the world's financial center, with the NYSE becoming the world's largest exchange. By the late 1920s, the NYSE was the center of frenzied speculation in corporate securities that drove up the DJIA to nearly 400. But the crash of 1929 and the Great Depression that followed reduced that figure to just over 40 in 1932, about where it had been when the index was created 36 years before. (The DJIA would not return to its 1929 high until 1954.) At the same time, the federal government, through the new Securities and Exchange Commission, began to regulate the sale of corporate securities and became more vigilant in preventing securities fraud.

History Since World War II

As trading on the NYSE expanded in the post–World War II period, the exchange instituted a number of reforms and innovations. These included new recommendations of transparency for listed companies, asking them to bring in outside directors and to stop transactions between the officers and directors. There were also internal changes. In 1971, the exchange was reorganized as a not-for-profit corporation, with policy-making decisions shifted to the twenty-one-member board of directors, including ten outside directors, the following year. Technological innovation, including new data-processing computers and the development, in 1978, of the International Trading System, providing electronic links with other exchanges around the world, facilitated the global securities trade. A year later, the NYSE organized the New York Futures Exchange, offering trading in financial derivatives.

In the wake of the largest single-day percentage drop in the NYSE on October 19, 1987, the exchange instituted what were known as "circuit breakers," which would automatically halt trading in the event of huge price swings. Many experts blamed computerized trading—in which sell orders on large blocks of shares held by institutions automatically went through when prices hit a certain figure—for the massive sell-off in stocks that day. On October 27, 1997, a 554-point drop in the DJIA triggered the circuit breaker for the first time.

Much of this innovation came under the leadership of Chief Executive Officer Richard Grasso, who had risen through the NYSE's ranks from clerk. Grasso was also widely credited with maintaining the NYSE's reputation as the world's leading stock exchange. But when it was revealed in 2003 that he had received a compensation package worth nearly $140 million, it created a firestorm, the revelation coming as it did in the wake of a series of corporate pay scandals. In the end, Grasso was forced to resign but ultimately kept the compensation, after New York State's appeals court overturned a lower court ruling that he return much of the compensation.

Still, under Grasso's leadership, trading on the exchange had continued to grow. In 1992, the NYSE had its first billion-share day and the DJIA topped 10,000 for the first time in 1999. The exchange also modernized, introducing expanded forms of electronic trading and going public as the now for-profit NYSE Group, Inc., with a share offering of its own in 2006. A year later, the NYSE Group, Inc., merged with Paris-based Euronext, which owned several major exchanges in Europe. Not only did the merger create what management called the "first global stock exchange," but it gave the NYSE access to Euronext's expertise in electronic trading.

The financial crisis and recession of 2007–2009 had a major impact on the corporate securities markets. From its peak of more than 14,000 in October 2007, the DJIA fell by more than half, to less than 6,500, in March 2009. At the height of the crisis, in the late summer and early fall of 2008, the NYSE Composite and the DJIA experienced some of the wildest fluctuations in their history. None of this, of course, dampened overall trading. More important for the exchange's future than temporary rises and falls in securities prices are two other factors—whether all electronic trading will eliminate the need for a trading floor, and whether the shift in global economic power to East Asia will eventually eclipse the NYSE's position as the world's leading stock exchange.

James Ciment

See also: Dow Jones Industrial Average; Stock Markets, Global.

Further Reading

Geisst, Charles R. *Wall Street, a History: From Its Beginnings to the Fall of Enron.* New York: Oxford University Press, 2004.

New York Stock Exchange Web site: www.nyse.com.

Sorkin, Andrew Ross. *Too Big to Fail: The Inside Story of How Wall Street and Washington Fought to Save the Financial System from Crisis—and Themselves.* New York: Viking, 2009.

New Zealand

New Zealand, an island nation located in the South Pacific, is home to roughly 4.3 million people. A relatively new nation, its economic history is shorter than that of most countries around the world. Significant European settlement only began in the 1840s, and for much of the country's existence, the economy was based upon agricultural exports. The collapse of the commodities markets around the world during the Great Depression had a profound impact on New Zealand, leading to an insulated economy that stressed employment over growth. The eventual lifting of restrictions led to considerable hardships for many New Zealanders, but also resulted in real economic growth during the 1990s and the beginning of the twenty-first century.

The original inhabitants of New Zealand were the Maoris, whose tribal society saw little trade between different groups. The first Europeans to settle in New Zealand came mostly from Great Britain. Their goals at first were to exploit the natural resources of the two principal islands, which resulted in an export economy. Whale oil, sealskins, and timber were among the earliest products and required little or no processing before being shipped to foreign markets. During the 1850s, gold was discovered in several parts of New Zealand, attracting many settlers. Within a decade or two, many of the readily exploitable resources had been depleted.

During the 1850s, however, sheep were introduced to New Zealand. Grasslands were created by partially clearing some forest areas; this in conjunction with the suitable climate proved favorable for large-scale livestock production. Wool from New Zealand found a ready market in British mills, thanks to free trade between the two countries. Many immigrants were attracted to New Zealand, thanks to the relatively high living standards. British capital allowed the New Zealand government to begin building an infrastructure of railroads and manufacturing in the last half of the nineteenth century.

Between the mid-1870s and the mid-1890s, the economy of New Zealand stagnated. Flat prices for wool and the need to pay off loans for the creation of infrastructure slowed New Zealand's growth. The invention of refrigeration in the 1890s, however, opened British markets to new products. Mutton, beef, cheese, and butter could be preserved and shipped halfway around the world. The need to process New Zealand's exports remained minimal. Land prices increased, and most New Zealanders worked directly or indirectly in agriculture. The outbreak of World War I in 1914 led to a boom for New Zealand. Great Britain remained its main trading partner, and food products were in great demand. In return, manufactured products were imported in large amounts, and New Zealand's economy remained undiversified.

The end of the war resulted in a downturn in the commodity markets. Many New Zealand farmers had difficulty paying back the loans they had taken to buy additional land. By 1931, farm income was negative in New Zealand and unemployment was rising. As the rest of the world suffered through the Great Depression, New Zealand's exports fell dramatically. The demand for imports fell as well, since few people had money to spend. The government forced the banks to reduce interest rates and devalued the New Zealand pound. It also began to exert more direct control over the economy, including creating a central bank to stabilize the economy. Confidence began to return, along with markets for commodities.

In 1938, a balance-of-payments crisis threatened to throw the New Zealand economy back into a recession. To deal with the problem, the government introduced direct control of imports. The goal was to prevent unemployment such as that suffered in the Depression. Known as "insulationism," the policy was intended to protect New Zealand's developing industry and to provide full employment for workers. Domestic demand for products was met by domestic production, even if the cost was greater than for imports. The government also hoped to diversify New Zealand's economy, to prevent dependence on the agricultural sector.

Other countries also limited imports during and immediately after World War II, but New Zealand was unique in continuing the policy for decades. The commodity market collapsed after the Korean War, slowing the export of New Zealand's products. In addition, many countries, including the United States, subsidized their farmers to keep food prices below those of New Zealand. Even Great Britain, whose market remained open to New Zealand's imports, could not absorb the islands' production. In 1973, even that market was closed when Britain joined the European Economic Community.

Although unemployment remained low during this time, New Zealand's economy fell behind those of most other developed countries. Real income failed to increase as much as expected, and consumers were deprived of goods available in other countries. A crisis took place in 1973, when oil-producing countries agreed to raise the price of oil. New Zealand, like all other oil-importing nations, was hard hit. Unemployment grew, as did inflation. The government responded with a costly program known as "Think Big," intended to make New Zealand more self-sufficient. Government controls over wages and prices, as well as other parts of the economy, were instituted. Large-scale investments were made in different industries, including chemical and oil refining. These policies were unsuccessful and failed to reverse the decline of New Zealand's economy.

In 1984, the Labour Party came to power with the goal of deregulating New Zealand's economy. Import controls and tariffs were lifted. Credit was made available, and many speculative investments were made in the late 1980s. The stock market crash in October 1987 forced many companies into bankruptcy, and unemployment remained high. Market forces, however, made their effect known in the 1990s. Inefficient industries were forced out of business, and only those that could compete internationally remained. Throughout most of the 1990s, New Zealand's economy grew at a healthy rate. Despite a recession in 1998, this trend continued into the twenty-first century. Unemployment fell and the economy became more diversified, with significant agricultural and industrial sectors.

A growing level of external debt through the early and middle years of the 2000s—as local banks borrowed from abroad to finance a housing and construction boom—exposed the New Zealand economy to the financial crisis of 2008–2009, leading to a severe recession that lasted from late 2008 through much of 2009, with the GDP shrinking in 2009 by 1.3 percent. Many likened the country's economic situation to that of Iceland, which nearly went bankrupt when investors took their money out of local financial institutions during the credit crisis of 2008. However, New Zealand was better situated economically, as many of its banks were owned by larger and better-capitalized institutions in nearby Australia. Still, the country was expected to post anemic growth in 2010, as weak external demand continued to drag down exports and a limping world economy slowed tourism.

Tim J. Watts

See also: Australia.

Further Reading

Callaghan, Paul T. *Wool to Weta: Transforming New Zealand's Culture and Economy.* Auckland, NZ: Auckland University Press, 2009.

Gould, Bryan. *Rescuing the New Zealand Economy: Where We Went Wrong and How We Can Fix It.* Nelson, NZ: Craig Potton, 2008.

Robinson, G.M., Robert Jude Loughran, and Paul J. Tranter. *Australia and New Zealand: Economy, Society and Environment.* New York: Oxford University Press, 2000.

Northern Rock

The British bank Northern Rock, once a major player in that nation's mortgage market, went into government ownership on February 22, 2008, several months after the Bank of England granted it an emergency loan to help it achieve sufficient liquidity. Northern Rock was the first major British financial institution to collapse in the face of the global financial crisis, and the first to go into government ownership in response. The bank's condition stabilized after its nationalization, and on January 1, 2010, it was restructured into two separate entities, both of which remained in "temporary public ownership."

The Northern Rock Building Society was formed in 1965 and became Northern Rock in 1997, when it made its initial public offering on the London Stock Exchange. The bank eventually became one of the five-largest mortgage lenders in the United Kingdom. Northern Rock's somewhat high-risk investment model featured a strong reliance on short- and medium-term wholesale funding. Beginning in 2006, Northern Rock also made subprime mortgage loans. When the global capital and credit markets tightened in 2007, Northern Rock was hit with a liquidity crisis. Although the bank had adequate assets, it could not access enough capital to honor maturing money-market loans and other liabilities. A House of Commons Treasury Committee later found that Northern Rock had not had adequate insurance to cover its holdings and that its investment strategies had been unnecessarily risky.

In September 2007, the government-owned Bank of England, in its role as "lender of last resort," granted an emergency loan of £26.9 billion to Northern Rock. News of the loan sparked a run on the bank, and share prices plummeted. In an effort to control public anxiety, Chancellor of the Exchequer Alistair Darling announced that the government would guarantee all deposits held with Northern Rock; the British government thus took responsibility for £29 billion in liabilities, in addition to the cost of the outright loan.

In the months after the Bank of England loan, several private companies bid unsuccessfully to take over Northern Rock. Darling announced in November 2007 that, in order to protect both taxpayers and Northern Rock depositors, any takeover bid offers would have to be approved by the UK government. By the February deadline for bid submission, more than ten groups had made bids, including such major financial institutions as Olivant, Cerebus, JC Flowers, Lloyds TSB, Lehman Brothers, and Bradford & Bingley. The largest of the private bids came from a coalition consisting of Virgin Group, AIG, WL Ross, and First Eastern Investment.

Northern Rock, however, declined all bids, declaring them too far below the bank's previous trading value. The UK government agreed, and on February 17, 2008, Darling announced that Northern Rock would be taken into temporary public ownership and that shareholders would be offered compensation for their shares. The next day, trading in Northern Rock shares on the London Stock Exchange was suspended; the bank was formally nationalized on February 22, 2008. Government-appointment chairman Ron Sandler took over its interim leadership, later transitioning to a nonexecutive chairman role when Gary Hoffman (formerly of Barclays) became chief executive in October 2008. The government set up the UK Financial Instruments Limited in November 2008 to manage the government's investments in financial institutions, including Northern Rock.

In an attempt to cut costs and speed repayment of Northern Rock's debts, the bank initiated the first of several rounds of job cuts in July 2008, eliminating 800 positions. The bank planned to cut about one-third of all jobs—about 2,000—by 2011. By March 2009, the bank had repaid two-thirds of the initial loan of £26.9 billion and seemed likely be able to repay the government loan in full by the end of 2010. Other strategies to cut costs included reducing the bank's loan book by selling off its mortgage assets and not issuing new mortgages to existing customers.

Northern Rock was restructured on January 1, 2010, into two separate entities: Northern Rock plc, which holds all customer savings and about £10 billion of the Northern Rock mortgage book; and Northern Rock (Asset Management) plc, which holds the remainder (about £50 billion) of the mortgage holdings, the remaining government loan, and the firm's riskier assets, including unsecured loans and subordinated debt. The asset-management company does not accept deposits or make any new mortgage loans. Both of the new entities remained in temporary government own-

ership as of early 2010, though an eventual return to the private sector was still expected.

Northern Rock was the first major financial institution in the UK to experience problems severe enough to trigger a government takeover. Since the takeover, however, the UK Treasury has taken on full or partial ownership of several other major financial entities, including Bradford & Bingley, Royal Bank of Scotland, and Lloyds Banking Group. The nationalization of Northern Rock generated some controversy in the UK, and critics have argued about where the blame should fall for Northern Rock's failure. In retrospect, it seemed that government intervention helped bolster confidence in the bank as a safe place to deposit money, especially amid the turbulence of a nationally struggling economy. Nonetheless, the Northern Rock experience remains relevant to the ongoing debate in the United Kingdom as well as the United States about the proper role of government in financial markets.

Suzanne Julian

See also: Banks, Commercial; Recession and Financial Crisis (2007–); United Kingdom.

Further Reading

Brummer, Alex. *The Crunch: The Scandal of Northern Rock and the Escalating Credit Crisis.* London: Random House Business, 2008.

Walters, Brian. *The Fall of Northern Rock: An Insider's Story of Britain's Biggest Banking Disaster.* Petersfield, UK: Harriman House, 2008.

Norway

While Norway, like other European countries, felt the impact of the economic crisis of 2008–2009, it has fared better than many other European Union (EU) countries. Its economic performance during this time is in part due to its reliance on natural resources—especially oil and natural gas—for exports and the government's prudence in saving the revenues from these exports. Also, like Sweden, Norway's situation illustrates the advantages of remaining outside of the European Monetary Union and of the policies the EU Central Bank. Norway's greater freedom in promoting fiscal and monetary policies designed specifically for its economy has allowed it to avoid a heavier impact from the global economic downturn.

Norway is a northern European country that includes over 50,000 islands. Along with Sweden, Denmark, Finland, and Iceland, it is considered to be one of the Nordic countries. Norway has a population of approximately 4,730,000, with just over 10 percent of the population living in the capital of Oslo. The country is governed by a constitutional monarchy with a unicameral parliament. Norway has a highly developed social welfare system, a literacy rate of 100 percent, and a high standard of living for its citizens. Government expenditure in the economy for the years 1999 to 2008 constituted an average of 43.96 percent of the nominal gross domestic product (GDP; nominal GDP is the value of goods and services during a given year measured in current prices), compared to 42.54 percent for the euro-area countries.

Compared to most of its neighbors, the Norwegian economy is relatively small. However, in terms of GDP per capita, Norway ranks second in the world, after Luxembourg, with a GDP per capita that is two-thirds greater than that of the United States. Norway has the second-largest sovereign wealth fund after Abu Dhabi. For 2006, Norway placed second among EU and European Free Trade Association (EFTA) countries for contributions to official development assistance (ODA) to developing countries, exceeding the United Nations' target of 0.7 percent of donors' gross national product (GNP).

North Sea Riches

Norway has immense offshore oil and natural gas deposits. As of 2006, it was the third-largest net oil exporter in the world and the second-largest supplier of natural gas to continental Europe.

However, production has begun to decline and plans are afoot for petroleum exploration in other regions. The revenues from oil and gas exports are used to support state ownership of companies and to underwrite the social welfare networks. For domestic consumption, Norway relies almost entirely on domestically generated hydropower as its source of electricity. Norway is one of the world's largest exporters of fish, and this sector employs many of the inhabitants of its remote coastal regions. Norway has little arable land and has to import most of its food.

The country's external debt was eliminated in the mid-1990s. Cognizant of the fact that its reserves will ultimately be depleted, Norway prudently keeps a sizable amount of revenue from oil and gas export earnings. With the increased demand and consequent price increases for petroleum, Norway's economy flourished, particularly during 2004–2007. An indicator of Norway's economic health is its unemployment rate, which was 2.6 percent in 2008, the lowest among the Scandinavian countries and comparing favorably with both the euro-area average of 7.4 percent and the Organisation for Economic Co-operation and Development (OECD) average of 5.9 percent.

Norway has been a member of North Atlantic Treaty Organization (NATO) since its inception in 1949. Primarily driven by possible threats to its sovereignty and control over the petroleum and fisheries industries in the region, Norway has twice rejected EU membership in referenda, in 1972 and 1994. However, as a member of the EFTA's European Economic Area (along with Iceland and Liechtenstein), Norway participates in the EU market and contributes to its funds and activities.

Between 1995 and 2000, real GDP grew at an average rate of 3.78 percent, which is high relative to the euro-area and OECD averages of 2.68 percent and 3.23 percent, respectively, for the same period. (Real GDP is the market value of all the goods and services produced within a country during a given year, measured in constant prices, so that the value is not affected by changes in the prices of goods and services.) With the onset of the recession in 2001, real GDP grew at an average rate of 1.50 percent over 2001–2003, returning to a healthier 3.03 percent over 2004–2006, concomitant with the construction boom related to private residence construction. The rate of growth of real GDP increased to 3.7 percent in 2007, but started a downward trend in 2008, with a rebound anticipated by 2010.

Although, like any other resource-based economy, Norway's oil revenues have fluctuated with the externally determined price of oil, the government's fiscal conservatism has somewhat insulated its economy from the world financial turmoil that began in 2008. Nonetheless, toward the end of that year, a number of factors began to affect the country's economy: high inflation, high interest rates, accelerating decline in house prices, weakening demand for exports, moderate increases in unemployment (with the manufacturing and construction sectors being hardest hit), and a drop in consumer spending. In the third quarter of 2008, real house prices decreased by 6.8 percent, a substantially greater change than the average decline of 1.8 percent for the euro area.

Norway's financial sector has not been as hard hit by the economic downturn as that of other northern countries and Western European nations, partly due to the fact that the Norges Bank (Norway's central bank) is independent of the European Central Bank. The Norges Bank is taking action to ensure that this sector remains relatively stable by reducing key interest rates. New banking funds were also set up, one to provide capital for banks and another to buy company bonds.

Because of its foresight in saving funds from oil revenues and the proactive measures taken by its central bank, it is unlikely that Norway will be affected to the same extent as its neighbors by the decade's financial and economic turbulence.

Marisa Scigliano

See also: Denmark; Finland; Iceland; Sweden.

Further Reading

Central Intelligence Agency. *The CIA Factbook—Norway.* Available at https://www.cia.gov/library/publications/the-world-factbook/geos/no.html. Accessed March 2009.

Economist Intelligence Unit (EIU). *Country Report—Norway.* London: EIU, 2009.

———. *ViewWire—Norway.* London: EIU, 2009.

Eurostat. "Eurostat Yearbook 2008." Available at http://epp.eurostat.ec.europa.eu/. Accessed March 2009.

———. "Key Figures on Europe, 2007/08 edition." Available at http://epp.eurostat.ec.europa.eu/. Accessed March 2009.

Organisation for Economic Co-operation and Development (OECD). *OECD Economic Outlook* no. 84. Paris: OECD, 2008.

Statistics Norway. "Minifacts About Norway 2008." Available at www.ssb.no/english/subjects/00/minifakta_en/en/. Accessed March 2009.

U.S. Government Department of Energy. "Energy Information Administration: Norway." Available at www.eia.doe.gov/cabs/Norway/Background.html. Accessed March 2009.

Oil Industry

One of the largest and wealthiest industries in the world, the oil industry influences virtually all other sectors of the economy, given how reliant modern business and civilization itself is on petroleum as an energy source. While immensely powerful and profitable, the oil industry has been notoriously volatile, going back to its earliest days in the Pennsylvania oil fields of Civil War–era America. Indeed, two of the hallmarks of its history have been the sudden swings from shortage to glut and back to shortage. Through much of the history of the oil age, the product has existed in abundance, leading to low prices and fierce competition, though since the oil shocks of the 1970s, there have been periodic shortages that have led to much higher prices and profits. Throughout this history, oil companies have tried to respond to this volatility—sometimes successfully, sometimes not—through consolidation and other measures to limit what they consider destructive competition and overproduction.

Before considering the industry's history, it is useful to understand what it comprises. The oil industry includes three basic activities: (1) exploration, drilling, and pumping of crude oil from beneath the earth's surface; (2) the refining of that crude into useful petroleum products—everything from tar to home heating oil to gasoline to aviation fuel; and (3) the distribution of those products to industry and consumers, through gasoline stations, home oil-heating suppliers, and so forth. Major international oil companies may have operations in all three areas, though the first is often done in cooperation with the national oil companies of petroleum-exporting countries while the third is shared with many independent operators.

Birth of an Industry

The oil industry did not spring from nothing—it was an event waiting to happen. It was an accepted fact in the nineteenth century that anyone who discovered an abundant and cheap source of oil would "strike it rich," as kerosene was already the preferred source of lighting fuel. In 1859, the event happened, but not before the Pennsylvania Rock Oil investors backing Edwin Drake, a retired railroad conductor, had given up hope on drilling rather than digging for oil. Prior to Drake, most people in the nascent industry believed that oil could best be obtained by digging into the ground, much in the way coal was exploited. Drake's decision to drill led to the first great oil strike in world history.

Immediately, the area around Titusville, Pennsylvania, became a boomtown, as a dollar invested in a producing well could yield thousands of dollars in profits. But there was an inherent problem in the economic model of oil at the outset—a problem the industry shared with much commodity and agricultural production. That is, revenue is price multiplied by volume. Since there is nothing one can do about price, the secret of producing untold wealth was to maximize production before the price fell or the oil field went dry. Drillers either made their fortunes or went broke trying. Wells were drilled with wild abandon, pumping "full out," and soon the market was flooded with unwanted oil.

Maximizing revenue by maximizing volume works well when quantity demanded exceeds quantity supplied, but when that maximizing strategy leads to overproduction and supply exceeds demand, prices drop, sometimes precipitously. Indeed, oil prices plunged from $10 to 10¢ per barrel in less than a year, making the container more valuable than the oil inside it. Pumping oil continued unabated as prices spiraled downward because individual drillers could still maximize revenue by maximizing production as long as the price of crude oil exceeded the cost of extraction. One driller showing restraint and slowing his rate of production only meant less revenue for him as others pumped with all their might. Drillers collectively seemed unable to sense the repercussions of what maximizing production today would do to price tomorrow; but even if they did, there was nothing they could do about it. As boom went bust, overnight fortunes evaporated into a spate of bankruptcies, since money was entirely reinvested in drilling rigs, which had lost all their value. Collapsing oil prices were not all that brought on the bad times; too many wells operating full out were sucking oil fields dry in no time.

Consolidation and Cartel

Ohio businessman John D. Rockefeller was the first to come up with a solution to the problem of overproduction. Rockefeller recognized that it was impossible to control drillers, so he focused instead on the refining end of the business. Drilling had a low barrier of entry whereas refining posed a higher barrier both financially and technologically. Through a series of acquisitions, rarely ceded voluntarily, and by cutting deals with railroads to transport his oil for less cost than his competitors, sometimes skirting law and regulations, Rockefeller in ten short years was able to gather 90 percent of the refining industry under his corporate umbrella, the Standard Oil Trust.

With such a commanding control of the refining business, Rockefeller controlled the market for oil products and the drillers. To his defenders, Rockefeller was a trust maker who brought an industry from disorder to order, thereby eliminating wasteful booms and busts in the oil patch and guaranteeing to customers a plentiful supply of standard products (products that the public could rely on) at a reasonable price. But much of the public and the government saw him in a different light. In 1911, the U.S. Supreme Court forced the breakup of Standard Oil, which meant that Rockefeller had to exchange his shares in Standard Oil for a group of companies. The Rockefeller family fortune expanded after Rockefeller retired, as these companies set out on their individual paths to develop new businesses that the Standard Oil Trust, as a single corporate entity, had been slow in doing. The value of some of these companies, individually, was more in five years after the breakup than the entirety of Standard Oil at the time of the breakup.

With the passing of the Standard Oil monopoly, stability in the oil patch was maintained on a global scale by the oil power brokers of the day, including Walter Teagle, of Standard Oil of New Jersey (later Exxon) and Henri Deterding, of Shell. Along with other oil magnates, they established a system of global pricing of oil at a social affair held in a Scottish castle in 1928, calling for cooperation in production and the sharing of incremental demand increases among a cartel of supposedly competing oil companies. Their system stabilized the price at a healthy level for the oil companies as long as others joined, which they did. With a mechanism in place for allocating incremental production to meet growing demand among the participating oil companies, the global oil business, with the exception of Soviet oil, was under the control of a cartel of oil companies. Of course, the involvement of U.S. oil companies in this arrangement to fix pricing and production was in direct violation of the Sherman Antitrust Act. The Rockefeller dream of world control over oil, for the most part, had finally come true, although not with domination vested in the hands of an individual, but in a small group of executives who, in the aggregate, controlled most of the world's oil. The success of this agreement hinged on all these individuals cooperating, which was difficult to achieve except during times of falling oil prices.

East Texas Oil Boom

In 1930, only two years after the system was set up, price stability was threatened by yet another mammoth oil discovery of the kind that continued to plague the oil companies until the oil crisis in the 1970s. The East Texas oil boom, coming at the time of the Great Depression, created a glut, and oil prices collapsed locally to 10¢ per barrel. Teagle and Deterding were powerless to stop the flood of oil coming into the market because they did not control the East Texas oil fields. But those involved in the boom sought a solution of their own by requesting federal and state intervention. The state governments of Texas and Oklahoma obliged, declaring martial law on the grounds that the independents were squandering a valuable natural resource, particularly at 10¢ per barrel.

Using conservation to justify their actions and the local militia to enforce their will, states succeeded in slowing oil production significantly. Through the Texas Railroad Commission, a rationing system to control production was established, and oil prices rose. Government action to protect and conserve a natural resource served the interests of the global oil cartel. Thus, capitalism and conservation joined hands with a common

objective, but different goals. Deterding's pooling arrangement among the oil cartel members and the Texas Railroad Commission's rationing of production stabilized the world price of oil. Both actions were valuable lessons for the Organization of Petroleum Exporting Countries (OPEC) when it gained control over oil prices and production in the 1970s.

Birth of OPEC

In 1960, Saudi Arabia, Iran, Iraq, Kuwait, and Venezuela created OPEC, not necessarily to raise oil prices but to prevent further reductions in posted prices being forced on them by the major oil companies. The original unity of purpose was gone by the second OPEC meeting in 1961, when a rough-and-tumble battle broke out among OPEC members as each sought to garner a larger export volume at the expense of others. OPEC was behaving no differently than the earliest oil drillers; it was every producer for itself.

By no measure could OPEC be considered a success prior to the oil crisis in 1973. There was little coordination among the members, and politics kept getting in the way of negotiations. Meanwhile, new sources were coming on stream, such as Nigeria, putting more pressure on OPEC's approach of maximizing revenue by maximizing production, another reminder of the oil industry's early days. In 1965, OPEC failed at an attempt to gain control over future increases in production just as it failed to gain control over current production. The major oil companies, meanwhile, were trying to restrain production to prevent further declines in oil prices. The irony is that in only ten years, OPEC would take over the oil companies' role of restraining production to control prices. The role reversal would not be complete, as the OPEC idea of what the market could and should pay for oil in the 1970s would be radically different than that of the oil companies in the 1960s.

The 1967 Six-Day War between Israel and Egypt sparked the first Arab boycott. The war was over before the boycott had any effect, and the boycott was doomed anyway when Venezuela and Iran refused to join. Even the formation of the Organization of Arab Petroleum Exporting Countries (OAPEC) within OPEC in 1968 did not succeed in strengthening the resolve of OPEC to bring order to the oil market. Order, of course, meant maximizing the respective production volume of each member to maximize revenue. Oil company attempts to rein in production to maintain prices, which varied for each member of OPEC, irritated the oil producers, who now had to contend with new oil production from Qatar, Dubai, Oman, and Abu Dhabi.

The 1973 oil crisis was not caused by a shortage of oil. In fact, the greatest worry right up to the eve of the crisis was how to keep new production from flooding the market and further weakening oil prices. The producers were worried about anything that would shrink their export volumes. But a series of crises—including the 1973 Arab-Israeli War and subsequent boycott by Arab oil producers of perceived pro-Israeli Western countries, including the United States, followed by the 1979 Iranian Revolution—led to cuts in production even as demand remained strong. The result was spot shortages and a dramatic run-up in crude prices, from around $4 to $40, in non-inflation-adjusted dollars, between 1973 and 1980.

Oil Crises and Responses

From the birth of the automobile age in the early twentieth century, oil consumption has doubled about every decade. Even the Great Depression did not dampen growth in oil consumption, but the age of oil did not begin in earnest until after the Second World War. In 1960, OPEC was supplying 38 percent of world oil; this increased to 47 percent in 1965 and 56 percent in 1973, meaning that OPEC exports were growing faster than world oil demand. During this time, the United States was emerging as a major world importer as its production began a long-term decline.

With the rise of OPEC, the world no longer had to face a cartel of oil companies, but instead a cartel of oil-producing states. The greatest transfer of wealth in history—from oil-consuming to oil-producing states—would occur with the quadrupling of oil prices in the 1970s. But changes in the world of energy were at work that would come back to haunt the oil producers. Among these was a worldwide economic decline that reduced overall energy demand. High oil prices instigated a desperate search for alternative sources to oil, leading to a resurgence of coal, an accelerated pace in building nuclear power plants, a greater reliance on natural gas and anything else not called oil, including wood-burning electricity-generating plants.

There were also great gains in energy efficiency, whereby cooling a refrigerator, heating a home, and running an automobile, truck, locomotive, marine, or jet engine could be achieved with significantly less energy. Conservation of energy took the form of keeping indoor temperatures higher in summer and lower in winter, driving the family car fewer miles, and recycling energy-intensive products such as glass, aluminum, and paper. Companies set up energy managers to scrutinize every aspect of energy use in order to identify ways to reduce consumption.

In addition to slashing demand, high-priced oil caused an explosion in non-OPEC crude supplies, best exemplified in the North Slope of Alaska and in the North Sea. The North Slope of Alaska is an inhospitable place to develop and operate an oil field and necessitated the construction of an 800-mile-long pipeline to the port of Valdez in southern Alaska over mountain ranges and tundra. North Slope production peaked at 2 million barrels per day (bpd) a few years after the pipeline started operating in 1977. The North Sea was an even greater challenge, with its hundred-knot gales and hundred-foot seas. Floating oil-drilling platforms explored for oil in waters a thousand feet (304.8 meters) deep. "Oceanscrapers," structures taller than the Empire State Building in New York City, were built on land, floated out to sea, and flooded (carefully) to come to rest on the ocean bottom as production platforms. North Sea oil started with

45,000 bpd of output in 1974 and grew to over 500,000 bpd in 1975, to 1 million bpd in 1977, to 2 million bpd in 1979, to 3 million bpd in 1983, eventually peaking at 6 million bpd in the mid-1990s. Every barrel from the North Slope and North Sea was one barrel less from the Middle East OPEC producers.

Oil exporters dictated prices after the 1973 oil crisis, but continually changing prices implied that OPEC could not control the price as well as the oil companies had. When oil prices fluctuate widely, no one knows, including the oil producers, what tomorrow's price will be. This provides speculative opportunities for traders who try to outwit or outguess oil producers. All they needed was a place where they could place their bets. Once the traders started placing bets, buyers and sellers of oil had an opportunity to hedge their investments against adverse price changes. In the early 1980s, the New York Mercantile Exchange (NYMEX) started trading futures in heating oil, then gasoline, and finally crude oil. First attracting primarily speculators, soon oil companies as buyers and oil producers as sellers started trading. The development of a cash and futures market, with contracts that could be settled in monetary or physical terms, eventually eroded the oil producers' control over price. Since the early 1980s, the primary determinant of oil prices has been the relationship between supply and demand. The oil producers (OPEC) attempt to influence price by cutting back or expanding production, and in this indirect way to affect the price of oil. But they no longer dictate price as they had in the years immediately following the 1973 oil crisis.

Collapsing Prices

With consumers doing everything they could to reduce oil consumption, and with every OPEC and non-OPEC producer operating full out, taking advantage of the price bonanza to maximize revenue, it was becoming increasingly difficult to maintain price. There had to be a swing producer to maintain a balance between supply and demand in order to keep prices high, and that swing producer was Saudi Arabia.

Saudi Arabia's production was initially boosted as replacement crude during the Iranian Revolution in 1978 and 1979 and during the early years of the Iran-Iraq war. After production in Iran and Iraq was restored, Saudi Arabia had to cut back sharply to maintain price. With OPEC members producing full out, Saudi Arabia had to cut production again to keep prices from eroding further. Saudi Arabia was now playing the same historical role played by the United States when the Texas Railroad Commission had the authority to control oil production to maintain oil prices. (The United States ceased being a swing producer in 1971 when the commission authorized 100 percent production for all wells under its jurisdiction.) This meant that it would not allow production to meet demand but would allow producers to pump as much as they wanted, when they wanted.

Being a swing producer means that one has excess capacity that can be released onto the market if prices get too high for consumers of a product or that can be cut back when prices fall too low for producers. While at first glance it would seem in Saudi Arabia's interest to maintain the highest possible prices it could get, there were other factors that led to it wanting more stability. First, sky-high oil prices might encourage development of alternative forms of energy that would ultimately hurt the oil industry or lead to exploration for new sources of oil, which is indeed what happened after the oil shocks of the 1970s. There was also a financial component. Saudi Arabia invested large chunks of its oil revenue in Western securities; if oil prices went so high as to cripple those economies, Saudi finances would suffer.

In 1985, with cessation of exports just over the horizon, Saudi Arabia was at the end of its tenure as swing producer. Something had to be done. Saudi Arabia again unsheathed the oil weapon, not against the consuming nations but against its fellow OPEC members. Saudi Arabia opened the oil spigot and flooded the market with oil, causing oil prices to collapse below $10 per barrel and threatening to financially wipe out OPEC. Saudi Arabia then forced its fellow producers to sit around a table and come to an agreement on production quotas and a mechanism for sharing production cutbacks whereby Saudi Arabia would cease to be the sole swing producer. The cartel would now act as a cartel.

Price Hikes of 2007–2008

The second period of high oil prices was from 2007 to late 2008, with the all-time record price of $147 per barrel set in 2008. Economic growth, fueled by enormous personal debt acquisition by U.S. consumers, resulted in higher crude oil growth in both the United States and Asia, particularly China, as manufacturer for the world. Spare capacity for the OPEC producers fell to about 1–2 million barrels per day, a far cry from the late 1970s and early 1980s, when Saudi Arabia could make up for the cessation of exports from Iran of nearly 6 million barrels per day and still have capacity to spare. A low level of excess capacity is just another way of saying that quantity demanded is getting too close to the quantity supplied, which can cause huge jumps in price as buyers start bidding up to ensure supplies.

The spiking of prices in 2007 and 2008 was not the same as in 1973, when buyers and sellers struggled with each other to control prices. The cause of the second era of high oil prices was simply a lack of spare capacity: demand getting too close to supply. In 2009, oil prices were restored to the $60–80 per barrel range, propped up by the continuing growth of oil demand in China and India despite the economic collapse blanketing the rest of the world. As such, oil prices reflect a continuing tightness in the relationship between supply and demand. Any resurgence in demand in the United States would cause a surge in oil prices again and potentially another round of boom and bust. However, if the supply of oil is constricted from lack of discoveries below ground and governments above ground prohibiting drilling, we might be entering

an era of perpetual high prices. Oil production does not have to peak for prices to act as though peaking is occurring. A lack of major discoveries to compensate for aging oil fields and continuing growth in demand will keep spare capacity too anemic to induce a bust in the oil patch.

Roy Nersesian

See also: Middle East and North Africa; Oil Shocks (1973–1974, 1979–1980).

Further Reading

Barsky, Robert B., and Lutz Kilian. "Oil and the Macroeconomy Since the 1970s." *Journal of Economic Perspectives* 18:4 (2004): 115–134.

Feldman, David Lewis, ed. *The Energy Crisis: Unresolved Issues and Enduring Legacies.* Baltimore, MD: Johns Hopkins University Press, 1996.

Nersesian, Roy. *Energy for the 21st Century.* Armonk, NY: M.E. Sharpe, 2010.

Verleger, Philip K. *Adjusting to Volatile Energy Prices.* Washington, DC: Institute for International Economics, 1993.

Yergin, Daniel. *The Prize: The Epic Quest for Oil, Money, and Power.* New York: Touchstone, 1992.

Oil Shocks (1973–1974, 1979–1980)

During the mid- and late 1970s, the U.S. and global economies were hit by two so-called oil shocks, in which shipments of petroleum from the Middle East underwent dramatic curtailments because of war and political upheaval, resulting in price spikes and supply shortages in many oil-importing countries.

The oil shocks had both immediate and long-term consequences for the United States and the world. The sudden and dramatic rise in prices, particularly in the aftermath of the first oil shock in 1973–1974, accelerated a global economic downturn that was marked by inflation and high unemployment, a situation that defied the traditional understanding of and remedies for recessions. The inability of governments to deal with such a recession led to dramatic political realignments in the United States and some industrialized countries, with liberal governments giving way to conservative ones.

In addition, the two oil shocks undermined one of the pillars of the post–World War II global industrial boom: cheap energy. At first, governments responded with measures to conserve energy and find alternatives to petroleum. Ultimately, however, it was market forces that solved the "energy crisis" ushered in by the oil shocks, at least temporarily. High petroleum prices encouraged new exploration and the development of new extraction technologies, which flooded the market with cheap oil from the mid-1980s through the early 2000s. One effect of this was to undermine conservation and alternative energy efforts, until more systemic shortages—a result of stagnant production and soaring demand in emerging economies such as China and India—surfaced in the mid-2000s.

Long used for lighting, petroleum emerged as a major source of energy in the early twentieth century, a result of major new finds—in the United States, Russia, and the Middle East—and major new markets, most notably motor vehicles and electric generating plants. By the early post–World War II era, petroleum vied with coal to become the world's most important source of energy. The dramatic rise in consumption was balanced by increases in production, mostly in the Middle East, keeping prices low. In the early 1960s, for example, a gallon of gas in the United States sold for roughly the same price, adjusted for inflation, that it had sold for in the 1920s.

1973–1974

Just as it is today, the Middle East—the source of much of the world's oil exports—was a volatile region in the 1950s and 1960s, as rising Arab nationalism challenged both Western interests and the existence of Israel, a nation founded in 1948 on land that many Arabs believed was rightfully theirs. Fearing an onslaught, Israel launched a preemptive attack on three of its Arab neighbors—Jordan, Syria, and Egypt—in June 1967, quickly defeating them and seizing parts of their territories. In response, three of the largest Arab oil exporters—Kuwait, Libya, and Saudi Arabia—hastily imposed an oil embargo on the United States and other Western countries, both as punishment for supporting Israel and as way to shift their foreign policy away from the Jewish state in the future. The embargo not only failed in this regard, but also was largely a nonstarter, as a result of a lack of coordination among the three governments and an oversupply of oil on the world market.

Three key changes took place between 1967 and the next Arab-Israeli War of 1973. The first, and perhaps more important, change had to do with world oil supplies. By the late 1960s, global consumption of oil was beginning to approach production capacity, leaving little slack in the event of a disruption in supply. Second, oil exporters had enjoyed little of the gains that such a tight market should have produced. This was because the United States had pulled out of the Bretton Woods Accord in August 1971, a World War II–era agreement that pegged the world's major currencies to the U.S. dollar and the U.S. dollar to the price of gold. Pulling out of Bretton Woods led to a devaluation of the dollar, and because virtually all international oil purchases were made in dollars, this meant less money in the coffers of oil-exporting states. The third change had to do with Arab politics. In 1968, several conservative Arab oil exporters founded the Organization of Arab Petroleum Exporting Countries (OAPEC), originally a kind of antiboycott group dedicated to politically leveraging their oil output in more moderate ways than a boycott. But the inclusion of more Arab nationalist regimes, such as Algeria, Egypt, and Syria—as well newly radicalized Libya—led to a radicalization of the organization.

Soon after the 1967 Arab defeat, leaders in Egypt and Syria began to plot their response to Israel's seizure of Arab territories, which they took in a coordinated surprise attack on October 6, 1973. In support of its fellow Arab governments

Motorists line up for gas in Vienna, Austria, during the oil shortage of 1973–1974. Triggered by an OAPEC embargo in response to U.S. policy in the Middle East, the crisis had enduring economic consequences across the industrialized world. *(Rue des Archives/ The Granger Collection, New York)*

and to punish the West for its supposedly pro-Israeli policies, Saudi Arabia—the world's greatest petroleum exporter—along with fellow Islamic exporters Iran, Iraq, Kuwait, and the United Arab Emirates, posted a unilateral price hike of 17 percent, to nearly $4 a barrel. Then, on October 16, they imposed a sales boycott on the United States, to punish it for supporting Israel in the war. In early November, OAPEC announced a 25 percent cut in production, with a further 5 percent cut threatened. By early 1974, the boycott—as well as the subsequent panic over oil supplies—had driven up prices by some 400 percent over prewar levels, to about $12 per barrel. Shortages began to be felt in the United States and other oil-importing countries, leading to long lines at gasoline stations, a rationing system for the sale of gasoline in many countries, and unpopular conservation measures in the United States, including a new national speed limit of 55 miles per hour (88.5 kilometers per hour) and year-round daylight savings time.

The boycott was called off by all participants except Libya in March 1974, but the move had little effect on oil prices, as the tightening of the ratio between supply and demand allowed the Organization of Petroleum Exporting Countries (OPEC)—a larger group that included most of the noncommunist world's largest producers at that time—to continue to dictate high prices.

Throughout much of the mid-1970s, prices remained at a new plateau of $10 to $20 per barrel, contributing to sluggish growth in the U.S. and global economies. Normally, economic weakness translates into stable or even lower prices and wages. But not this time—the dramatic hike in oil prices rippled through the economy in the form of higher prices for the many goods whose production and distribution depended on significant inputs of energy. Thus, the standard Keynesian remedy used by Washington, D.C., and other governments since the Great Depression—deficit spending to increase aggregate demand and thereby boost investment, production, and employment—was largely off the table, as it would only increase already crippling inflation rates.

1979–1980

With the Iranian Revolution of 1979, which disrupted production for the world's second-largest oil exporter, came yet another blow to world oil supplies and the price of petroleum. Although this was not a concerted effort by oil producers, OPEC took advantage of the situation by posting two price hikes that together yielded more than a one-third increase in the price of a barrel of oil, to nearly $17. A panicked world market—responding to the revolution and to Iraq's invasion of Iran in 1980—sent prices to the stratospheric level of nearly $40 a barrel (roughly $100 in 2009 dollars). Once again, Americans experienced lines at the gas station and rampant inflation. The administration of President Jimmy Carter responded by deregulating the price of domestically produced oil—in the hope that this would spur production and bring prices down—and by offering a plan to wean America from its dependence on foreign oil by promoting conservation and the development of alternative energy sources.

The twin oil shocks of the 1970s also provided a windfall for the OPEC countries. Between 1972 and 1980, net oil-export revenues for OPEC soared from less than $40 billion annually to nearly $300 billion in non-inflation-adjusted dollars (or from about $100 billion to nearly $600 billion in 2009 dollars). Particularly in the Persian Gulf states, the influx of money resulted in a sudden upswing in prosperity rarely seen before in world history. Massive construction projects were soon under way, with unprecedented consumption on the part of ordinary citizens. The rise in prices also led to flush economic times in such oil-producing American states as Texas and Oklahoma.

But the good times were not to last. While energy conservation helped drive down demand to a degree, increased production—spurred by high prices—ultimately undid the same dramatic upswings. High prices prompted aggressive exploration of new oil fields (e.g., in the North Sea off Great Britain and Norway) and the development of new technologies that allowed for the more efficient extraction of oil from existing fields. All of the new supply led to a dramatic decline in price. Between the mid-1980s and the early 2000s, the price of a barrel of oil hovered between $10 and $30. Adjusted for inflation, oil prices hit a post–World War II low in 1998.

The dramatic decline helped ease the United States through a steep recession in the early 1980s and contributed to an economic boom that would continue through the rest of the decade and, following another brief recession in the early 1990s, into the early twenty-first century. At the same time, OPEC producers experienced a dramatic decline in revenue, to between $100 billion and $150 billion annually, until the end of the century, that severely crippled their economies, as well as those of Texas and Oklahoma. The organization also lost much of its geopolitical clout, as non-OPEC members, such as Angola (which joined in 2007), Mexico, Canada, Great Britain, Norway, a newly free-market Russia, and the United States (with its vast new oil fields in Alaska), began to outproduce OPEC member states.

But just as the market undermined OPEC's efforts to drive up oil prices in the 1980s and 1990s, so market forces contributed to a dramatic upswing in the middle to late 2000s. This time, however, the impetus came from consumption rather than production, as developing countries—most notably China and India—industrialized rapidly. Between early 2003 and July 2008, when the benchmark price on the New York Mercantile Exchange hit a record high, the price of a barrel of crude oil soared from just under $30 to $147.30. Because the rise was so much steeper than the increased demand seemed to warrant—even taking into account such shocks as Hurricane Katrina's impact on the oil industry in the Gulf of Mexico in 2005 and upheavals in the Middle East such as the Israeli-Hezbollah War in 2006—there was much talk in the media and among experts about the influence of oil speculators on crude prices. Whatever the case, by late 2008, the market once again was exerting its influence, as a demand-reducing global recession—to which the spike in prices had contributed—brought prices back down to $40 to $60 per barrel.

Aside from the impact of oil-price fluctuations on the global economy—and vice versa—the effects are more lasting, because of two virtually incontrovertible facts about oil production and consumption. The first, often referred to as "peak oil theory," is that oil is a finite global resource and, more controversially, that the world is now reaching a point at which reserves and production gradually will diminish. The second is that the burning of oil and other carbon-based fuels leads to climate change and a host of cataclysmic effects, including massive flooding in coastal areas and prolonged drought in more arid regions. Both of these forces impel humanity to find alternative sources of energy, and with each upturn in prices, efforts are made to do so. Still, the fluctuating nature of oil prices often undoes such efforts, undermining the long-term strategies necessary to build a global economy that relies less on fossil fuels.

James Ciment and Nuno Luis Madureria

See also: Middle East and North Africa; Oil Industry; Recession, Stagflation (1970s).

Further Reading

Barsky, Robert B., and Lutz Kilian. "Oil and the Macroeconomy Since the 1970s." *Journal of Economic Perspectives* 18:4 (2004): 115–134.

Bohi, Douglas R., and Michael A. Toman. *The Economics of Energy Security.* Norwell, MA: Kluwer, 1996.

Feldman, David Lewis, ed. *The Energy Crisis: Unresolved Issues and Enduring Legacies.* Baltimore: Johns Hopkins University Press, 1996.

Verleger, Philip K. *Adjusting to Volatile Energy Prices.* Washington, DC: Institute for International Economics, 1993.

Yergin, Daniel. *The Prize: The Epic Quest for Oil, Money and Power.* New York: Touchstone, 1992.

Over-Savings and Over-Investment Theories of the Business Cycle

Over-savings and over-investment theories of the business cycle are distinct theoretical models that explain the cyclical behavior of the economy. While there are overlapping connections between these two theories, they usually are treated as distinct from one another.

Over-Savings Theories

In a macroeconomic context, over-savings means that households are saving a greater proportion of their income. The aggregate effect of greater savings is a decrease in aggregate consumption, which leads to a decline in aggregate expenditures, or demand. In essence, the decision by households to save more leads to a decrease in aggregate demand with a corresponding decrease in national income. This fall in aggregate demand triggers a business cycle downturn.

The question of over-savings, also referred to as underconsumption, has a long history in economics. In *The Wealth of Nations* (1776), Adam Smith identified parsimony, or saving, as the source of capital, or investment by entrepreneurs in business. One of Smith's followers, Jean-Baptiste Say, established a fundamental law of markets: supply creates its own demand. Say's law asserted that it was impossible for over-production to occur in an economy. There could never be underconsumption or over-savings, Say wrote in his *Treatise on Political Economy* (1803).

Debate over Say's Law

One of the most famous debates about the over-savings/underconsumption theory of the business cycle took place between Thomas R. Malthus and David Ricardo, both classical economists. Ricardo supported Say's law, arguing that all savings become investment expenditures—hence, there could be no over-savings. Malthus put forth the over-savings doctrine that not all savings become investment; therefore, there could be an over-production of goods and services. In the twentieth century, John Maynard Keynes, the most famous economist of that century, said that it was unfortunate that Ricardo had won the debate. He believed that Malthus's theory helped explain the business cycle, which industrial economies had experienced periodically beginning early in the era of industrial capitalism, starting around 1750.

Nearly two centuries later, Keynes constructed a more complete and comprehensive theory of the business cycle that encompassed the potential of aggregate over-savings. His theory of the business cycle took into account the disequilibrium between planned savings and actual savings, as well as a disturbance between planned business investment and realized business investment. This was the first comprehensive, modern model of the business cycle, and it had a role for underconsumption/over-savings.

Over-Investment Theories

Over-investment theories of the business cycle explain the role of aggregate investment in the cyclical process of the economy. There are several modern approaches to the over-investment theory of the business cycle. These theories do not accept the assumption that financial markets are consistently efficient and tend toward stability. These considerations are key aspects of modern financial economics. However, alternative approaches to the business cycle identify a variety of factors that can destabilize financial markets. These include central bank policies that inject additional liquidity into the economy; sudden increases in prices that lead business to a belief that revenues are rising unexpectedly; innovations that stimulate significant business investment; and the opportunity to create new types of financial securities. In any of these situations, businesses will increase their level of investment beyond the previous equilibrium level of aggregate investment in the economy.

One theoretical explanation of the over-investment approach to the business cycle holds that a central-bank expansion of the money supply will create a cycle of price movements. The money supply increase leads to price increases, which stimulate businesses to increase investment. This is the core of the Austrian theory of the business cycle. The economy experiences over-investment, which expands production capacity. As a result, there is inadequate aggregate demand for the supply of goods and services, and price levels begin to decrease. The deflation leads to a cyclical downturn in the economy, and the economy moves to a depressed state.

A second over-investment approach to the business cycle was put forth by Hyman Minsky, who argued that an increase in financial liquidity in markets would spur a process of securitization. In essence, new financial securities would be created. A speculative surge would grow in response to the new securities, and financial asset inflation would begin. Eventually, a financial bubble would emerge in the broader securities markets. The bubble inevitably would burst, causing a wave of uncertainty in these markets. This uncertainty would cause business investment to fall, and the economy would begin a downturn in the business cycle.

The so-called Great Recession of 2007–2009 drew attention to heterodox theories of economic crises. In the mid-2000s, Ben Bernanke, chair of the Federal Reserve Board of Governors, stated that excess liquidity in financial markets resulted from a "glut" of global savings—a clear reference to the over-savings theory. However, the economic problems that led to the financial crisis of the first decade of the twenty-first century were caused by over-investment. The Post Keynesian theory of the business cycle associated with Minsky underscored the increased securitization and creation of a speculative bubble. The growth of the derivatives markets from the mid-1990s to the late 2000s had created a new set of financial securities that allowed excess liquidity to flow into the housing markets in a highly speculative fashion—high-risk mortgages bundled as derivatives and sold as creditworthy investments. By 2008, the derivatives market was valued at $660 trillion, at a time when the global economy had a gross domestic product of approximately $60 trillion ($14 trillion in the United States). The speculative fever broke, setting off worldwide panic in financial markets.

The response of many central banks was to place large amounts of monetary reserves and capital funds into the private-sector financial system to prevent the collapse of major financial institutions. In the United States, the Federal Reserve also provided guarantees against losses to encourage mergers of banks and brokerage firms. All of this may form the foundation of an even greater wave of excess liquidity and create the potential for a new round of securitization, which may create a future financial bubble.

William Ganley

See also: Balance of Payments; Savings and Investment.

Further Reading

Clarke, Peter. *The Keynesian Revolution in the Making: 1924–1936.* Oxford: Clarendon, 1988.

Colander, David C., and Harry Landreth. *History of Economic Thought.* 4th ed. Boston: Houghton Mifflin, 2002.

Garretson, Roger. "The Austrian Theory of the Business Cycle." In *Business Cycles and Depressions: An Encyclopedia,* ed. David Glasner. New York: Garland, 1997.

Glasner, David, ed. *Business Cycles and Depressions: An Encyclopedia.* New York: Garland, 1997.

Hayek, Friedrich A. *Prices and Production.* 2nd ed. New York: Augustus M. Kelley, 1935.

Hunt, E.K. *History of Economic Thought.* 2nd ed. Armonk, NY: M.E. Sharpe, 2002.

Kates, Steven. *Say's Law and the Keynesian Revolution.* Cheltenham, UK: Edward Elgar, 2009.

Keynes, John M. *The General Theory of Employment, Interest, and Money.* London: Macmillan, 1936.

Malthus, Thomas R. *Principles of Political Economy.* Edited by John Pullen. Cambridge, UK and New York: Cambridge University Press, 1989.

Minsky, Hyman P. *Can "It" Happen Again?* Armonk, NY: M.E. Sharpe, 1982.

———. *John Maynard Keynes.* New York: Columbia University Press, 1975.

Ricardo, David. *Principles of Political Economy and Taxation.* 1821. Cambridge, UK: Cambridge University Press, 1973.

Overvaluation

Overvaluation occurs when the price of an asset does not reflect the asset's intrinsic or fundamental value, or when the selling price exceeds its "buy" value. The intrinsic or fundamental value of an asset would reflect all information, which is complete and understood by all, including factors that have a direct effect on the expected value of the income streams of the assets. Any asset subject to a financial valuation (such as a stock, bond, or currency) can be subject to overvaluation—that is, it is trading at a price higher than

its intrinsic value. An asset can be overvalued for many reasons, including overconfidence of superior potential returns, market scarcity, emotional attachment, and market hype. Overvaluation can also pressure companies to falsify or overstate current earnings, and can lead to an economic meltdown if multiple assets are greatly overvalued and then, when doubts about the overvaluation spread through society, are corrected all at once.

A full understanding of overvaluation must begin with the deeper concept of valuation. Valuation is the process of evaluating the market value of an asset, usually obtained by assessing the current value as well as potential returns through different financial models such as discounted cash flows. Market valuation may also include intangibles. For example, when an inventor acquires a patent for a new device it will increase its value compared to a similar product without patent protection; the patent confers upon the invention an added value: market monopoly for a certain number of years. Also, two individuals making an evaluation can assign different values to the same item because of different perceptions—correct or not—of the item's utility. Market consensus is reached when multiple individuals reach comparable valuations.

Hence, an asset will have two values: a buy value (the value agents in the market are willing to pay to acquire it) and a sell value (the value for which the agents are ready to sell the asset). When the sell value is superior to the buy value, one can infer that the good is overvalued. By the same reasoning, when a sell value is inferior to the buy value, an asset is said to be undervalued.

To better understand this concept, it is useful to examine a basic financial asset such as a share of company stock. Assume that an individual decides to purchase shares at a price of $10. Using a valuation model, the individual estimates that the stock is worth $12 (based on expected market growth and dividends, for example), meaning it is either undervalued by the market or overvalued by the buyer. A year later, the individual tries to sell the stock for $14—making this the sell value—but the best buy value he can find is $13. Hence, one can say either that he is overvaluing the stock or the market is undervaluing it.

A good can be overvalued for many different reasons. This can occur when a person overestimates the potential returns of an asset; for example, he could overvalue the potential dividends that will be paid. It can also occur when market scarcity is overestimated (the market believes the item is more rare than it actually is), or when there is an emotional bond to the particular asset. For example, entrepreneurs will often overvalue their start-up companies because of their own emotional involvement.

Another frequent source of overvaluation is market hype. In this case, the overestimation of potential returns is shared by multiple individuals simultaneously, leading to a rapid inflation of the asset price. Market hype can be generated by rumor, conjuncture, or even deceit. Such overvaluations last a relatively short period of time and are subject to drastic market corrections.

If many financial assets are continually bought and sold at an overvalued price, the result can be an economic bubble. This happens when an asset is continually traded at an upward value but the basics of its valuation (present and future earnings) do not change. At some point, the buy and sell values are too extended and no one is willing to purchase the asset at its sell price. This can lead to a rapid readjustment of the asset's value, as buyers bring the value back to a more rational level.

In addition, the constant overvaluation of company stock can exert undue internal pressure to meet the sell price, sometimes with disastrous results. In some cases, overvaluation by the market has led companies to misstate financial earnings and resort to accounting fraud. Recent decades have witnessed a number of cases in which a major corporation padded or even faked earnings in order to match market expectations. Consequences for a national economy can be equally drastic. If too many goods are overvalued, the competitiveness of the local economy may be compromised. General consumption might then decline, and economic adjustments slow. Debt burdens could also increase if the company uses debt to buy back its own stock to keep the stock trading at the overvalued price.

A market correction occurs when multiple parties conclude that one or more assets are overvalued and that the prices of the goods should be reduced to a more rational level. This is not a formal process (nobody declares a market correction), but rather an informal group consensus in which the price of an asset is quickly adjusted. In a conventional open market, where only a few goods are overvalued, the market is able to correct itself adequately and at regular intervals. Although the impact can be catastrophic for a few companies, the overall effects can be limited.

Where many goods are overvalued simultaneously, however, the danger to the overall economy is much greater. In that situation, there is a greater risk of economic crash should multiple investors try to leave the market at the same time. This can be especially dangerous when mass psychology prompts a wave of irrational selling, even dragging down assets that are not overvalued. For example, if the market decides that many companies in the real-estate sector are overvalued, there may be a mass movement to sell the stock of these companies, even if some companies are fundamentally sounds and fairly valued. This has occurred time and again in economic downturns, such as the subprime mortgage crisis of 2008–2009.

Jean-Francois Denault

See also: Asset-Price Bubble.

Further Reading

Damodaran, Aswath. *The Dark Side of Valuation: Valuing Young, Distressed and Complex Businesses.* 2nd ed. Upper Saddle River, NJ: FT Press, 2010.

Marciukaityte, Dalie, and Raj Varma. "Consequences of Overvalued Equity: Evidence from Earnings Manipulation." *Journal of Corporate Finance* 14:4 (September 2008): 418–430.

Pacific Rim

Pacific Rim is a term widely used to describe countries that border the Pacific Ocean. The term Pacific Rim was used during the late 1980s by journalists in the United States to symbolize informally the common political and economic interests of the countries in this region. Such countries include Brunei, China, Hong Kong, the Republic of Korea (South Korea), Malaysia, the Philippines, Singapore, Taiwan (Chinese Taipei), and Thailand. Russia is geographically a Pacific Rim country, but its traditional political and economic links have been with Europe. Other countries that border the Pacific are Australia, Indonesia, Japan, New Zealand, Papua New Guinea, Canada, the United States, and some countries in Central and South America. The description of the Pacific Rim region and countries has been expanding geographically over time. Today, Pacific Rim means all the countries of Northeast Asia, Southeast Asia, Oceania, North America, and Latin America that are geographically connected to the Pacific Ocean. The Pacific Rim thus comprises a large number of countries with great linguistic, religious, historical, cultural, economic, political, and other differences. It comprises advanced industrialized countries, newly industrialized countries, and developing countries with diversified opportunities for trade, investment, and movement of people.

Economic Growth Experience

The "East Asian Miracle" has contributed substantially to the economic boom of the Pacific Rim. In Asia, while about half the economies had high growth rates in the 1950s, 1960s, and 1970s, there were some "miracle" economies that experienced not only high growth but also consistent growth for three continuous decades, from the 1960s through the 1980s. These are the four newly industrialized economies (NIEs) —Hong Kong, South Korea, Singapore, and Taiwan, also known as the "Asian Tigers." Taiwan, in particular, had an overall (four-decade) average annual growth rate of 5.8 percent. Studies have shown that in the second half of the twentieth century there is no growth rate comparable to that of the four NIEs anywhere else in the world. Factors contributing to such high growth include high rates of investment in physical and human capital, rapid growth of agricultural productivity, export orientation, a decline in the fertility rate, and the role of government in promoting the development of specific industries and efficient economic management. The economies of Indonesia, Malaysia, and Thailand have also achieved reasonably high growth rates. China has witnessed phenomenal success as a Pacific Rim region economy, experiencing sustained average growth of over 9.5 percent since 1981. Another economic power in the Pacific Rim region, Japan, is one of the top three wealthiest nations in the world and is a leading global exporter and importer. Since 1982, transpacific trade has exceeded transatlantic trade.

Economic Organizations

The Pacific Rim region contains several regional, subregional, transpacific, and international organizations that play critical roles in addressing the economic, political, geopolitical, security, and strategic interests of the countries in this region, namely: ASEAN (Association of South East Asian Nations), APEC (Asia-Pacific Economic Cooperation), East Asia Community (EAC), East Asia Summit (EAS), and the Asia-Europe Meeting (ASEM). APEC and ASEAN are the two prominent arrangements for economic cooperation in the region.

ASEAN was established in 1967 in Bangkok by five countries (now known as the original members)—Indonesia, Malaysia, Philippines, Singapore, and Thailand. Brunei Darussalam joined in 1984, Vietnam in 1995, the Lao People's Democratic Republic (Laos) and Myanmar in 1997, and Cambodia in 1999. In 2007, the ASEAN region had a population of 560 million, a combined gross domestic product (GDP) of almost US$1.1 trillion, and a total trade of about US$1.4 trillion. Export-oriented industrialization is the key driver of economic growth of ASEAN. The organization has expanded to ASEAN+3, which includes the ten member states of ASEAN and the three East Asian nations of Japan, China, and South Korea. ASEAN+3, with a total population of about 2 billion, has a combined GDP of $9.09 trillion and foreign reserves of $3.6 trillion. The ASEAN+3 region not only represents one-third of the world's population and 16 percent of the world's GDP, but also holds more than half of the world's financial reserves. Trade and investment relations between ASEAN countries and Japan, China, and South Korea have facilitated economic growth in the region.

APEC

Asia-Pacific Economic Cooperation (APEC) is a forum of twenty-one Pacific Rim countries described as "member economies." Unlike ASEAN, APEC stands as an example of an "open regionalism" forum. Generally, regional or subregional trade agreements are made based on geographic proximity, such as the European Union, NAFTA, and ASEAN. In that sense, APEC is a different kind of economic-cooperation arrangement. The process for the formation of APEC began in 1989 with the involvement of twelve member economies (the other members joined later), namely the six ASEAN countries (Brunei Darussalam, Indonesia, Malaysia, the Philippines, Singapore, and Thailand), South Korea, and the five Pacific OECD (Organisation for Economic Co-operation and Development) countries (Australia, Canada, Japan, New Zealand, and the United States). At a 1994 meeting held in Bogor, Indonesia, APEC put forth the Bogor Goals of free and open trade and investment in the Asia Pacific. APEC's 21 member economies, with a population of more than 2.7 billion (approximately 40 percent of the world's population), represent about 55 percent of world GDP and 49 percent of world trade. The term APEC is now sometimes used synonymously with the Pacific Rim, and the organization is sometimes referred to as the Pacific Rim group. A complete list of ASEAN, ASEAN+3, and APEC members can be found in the table that follows.

Pacific Rim in the 1990s and Early Twenty-first Century

The 1990s saw economic boom and bust cycles in the Pacific Rim countries. Unprecedented growth in several countries of the region was followed by

Regional Economic Cooperation in the Pacific Rim

ASEAN Member countries (year joined)	APEC Member economies (year joined)
1. **Indonesia** (1967)	1. Australia (1989)
2. **Malaysia** (1967)	2. **Brunei Darussalam** (1989)
3. **Philippines** (196	3. Canada (1989)
4. **Singapore** (1967)	4. **Indonesia** (1989)
5. **Thailand** (1967)	5. **Japan** (1989)
6. **Brunei Darussalam** (1984)	6. **Republic of Korea** (1989)
7. **Vietnam** (1995)	7. **Malaysia** (1989)
8. Laos (1997)	8. New Zealand (1989)
9. Myanmar (1997)	9. **Philippines** (1989)
10. Cambodia (1999)	10. **Singapore** (1989)
	11. **Thailand** (1989)
	12. United States of America (1989)
	13. Chinese Taipei (1991)
ASEAN+3 includes	14. Hong Kong, China (1991)
China	15. **China (People's Republic of China)** (1991)
Japan	
South Korea	16. Mexico (1993)
(Republic of Korea)	17. Papua New Guinea (1993)
	18. Chile (1994)
	19. Peru (1998)
	20. Russian Federation (1998)
	21. **Vietnam** (1998)

Note: The countries/economies in bold hold membership in both ASEAN/ASEAN+3 and APEC.

the Japanese recession and the 1997–1998 Asian financial crisis. Some of the countries affected by the Asian financial crisis, such as Indonesia, Malaysia, the Philippines, the Republic of Korea, and Thailand, started reviving soon after. Between 1999 and 2006, average per capita income in these countries grew by more than 8 percent. Japan, in spite of her sluggish economy, continues to rank as the world's second-largest economy. The economically dynamic China and rising India are the largest contributors to global growth since 2000. China was responsible for 32 percent of world GDP growth in 2001–2004 and has seen a nearly sevenfold increase in its trade; it is now the world's third-largest trading economy. All economies in East and North-East Asia, except China, saw a marginal slowdown in 2007, and China's relatively better performance is due to the generation of domestic consumer demand. Hong Kong, China, Taiwan, and South Korea saw higher levels of consumption and investment during 2007. Slowing demand in the United States and the European Union, major destinations for exports, is eventually reducing export revenues in export-oriented econ-

omies across the region. It is predicted that overall economic growth in the Pacific Rim will slow down in line with the global economic slump, and that the leading economies of India and China will continue to remain relatively strong as a result of growing domestic demand and their demographic advantage. The recovery of the Asia Pacific region from the global economic crisis of 2008–2009 has started. However, the region faces serious problems of unemployment and government interventions, as well as a need for structural policies to stimulate sustainable economic growth.

M.V. Lakshmi

See also: Asian Financial Crisis (1997); Australia; Canada; Central America; Chile; China; Colombia; Indonesia; Korea, South; Latin America; Mexico; New Zealand; Russia and the Soviet Union; Southeast Asia; United States.

Further Reading

Collinwood, Dean W. *Japan and the Pacific Rim.* New York: McGraw-Hill Higher Education, 2007.

Houseman, Gerald L. *America and the Pacific Rim: Coming to Terms with New Realities.* Lanham, MD: Rowman & Littlefield, 1995.

McDougall, Derek. *Asia Pacific in World Politics.* New Delhi: Viva, 2008.

Miller, Sally M., A.J.H. Latham, and Dennis O. Flynn, eds. *Studies in the Economic History of the Pacific Rim.* Routledge Studies in the Growth Economies of Asia. London and New York: Routledge, 1998.

Rao, Bhanoji, *East Asian Economies: The Miracle, a Crisis and the Future.* Singapore: McGraw-Hill, 2001.

Ravenhill, John, ed. *APEC and the Construction of Pacific Rim Regionalism.* Cambridge, UK: Cambridge University Press, 2002.

Panic of 1901

The panic of 1901 was a severe stock market crash. It was felt most strongly on the New York Stock Exchange (NYSE). This was one of the first significant crashes on the NYSE and came at the end of a five-year period of rapid expansion and increased interest in stock trading. During this period, the volume of activity had increased to 600 percent of what it had been in 1896. (That increase in trading required the exchange to relocate to its cur-

In a 1901 cartoon titled "Wall Street Bubble—Always the Same," financier J.P Morgan is caricatured as a Wall Street bull blowing bubbles of inflated stock—in this case, of Northern Pacific Railroad—for eager investors. The result was a broad market collapse. *(The Granger Collection, New York)*

rent main building at 18 Broad Street, though the trading floor is at 11 Wall Street.)

Background

The 1901 crisis was precipitated by a fight among bankers and tycoons over control of the Northern Pacific Railroad. The Northern Pacific (NP) operated throughout northwest North America, particularly from Minnesota to Washington, with tracks covering Manitoba and British Columbia in Canada. The railroad was chartered in 1864 to connect the Great Lakes with the Puget Sound in Washington State, thus granting access to Pacific shipping to the northern United States. It had largely been financed by Jay Cooke, an Ohio lawyer who was best known for helping to finance the Union's Civil War efforts. NP continued to expand throughout the late nineteenth century, avoiding most of the serious financial hardships that befell many of the country's other railroads—that is, until the Panic of 1893. This was

yet another recession caused by a burst railroad "bubble"; in this case, the crisis brought about the NP's bankruptcy. From the start, multiple parties fought for control of the company, and three individual courts asserted their own claims to jurisdiction over the bankruptcy proceedings.

Enter J.P. Morgan

Financier J.P. Morgan was given the task by the bankruptcy court of straightening out the NP. An adept banker, Morgan became increasingly effective at merging and consolidating firms and business interests. He was one of the first to recognize that railroads worked more effectively and were better investments when they were consolidated into a larger financial unit, as economies of scale kicked in and competition was removed in various markets. Morgan acquired and reorganized a number of regional rail lines and organized industry-wide conferences to discuss the ramifications of legislation like the 1887 Interstate Commerce

Act. He also arranged in 1892 the merger that created General Electric, and in 1901 consolidated various steel businesses with the Carnegie Steel Company to form the United States Steel Corporation, thus enlarging even on the work of his fellow nineteenth-century tycoons.

His practice of taking over distressed assets, reorganizing them, and making them profitable was widely known as "Morganization," even though the work was usually done by men he appointed to the task. With this track record under his belt, the legendary financier was now called upon to Morganize the NP, and he began to buy up stock.

Morgan, Hill, and NP

The reason for those stock purchases was that Morgan was responding to Edward Henry Harriman, the head of the Union Pacific Railroad, who wanted to expand his line. Harriman, the NP, and the Great Northern railroad run by James Hill, had all simultaneously sought access to Chicago, a major industrial city that had the potential to serve as a hub for all of them, as well as a funnel of railroad traffic, and to which none of them yet had a route. When the price of another railroad that did offer easy access to Chicago—the Chicago, Burlington, and Quincy railway—was set at $200 a share, Hill and the NP swept in and bought it up, sharing the route between them. Harriman, left completely out of the cold in this deal, responded by attempting to buy a controlling interest in the NP, which in 1901 was still trading for a relatively low price because of its years in receivership. Once he controlled the NP, Harriman intended to use that power as leverage for gaining Chicago access for his railroad—the Union Pacific—at favorable terms.

The Crisis

Harriman's rapid stock purchases of NP, starting on May 3, 1901, caused James Hill to do the same, urged on by Morgan, along with other Morgan-owned companies, all in order to keep the stock out of Harriman's hands. As a result of all this buying, the price of the stock inflated rapidly, trading for as much as $1,000 a share. But this price had little to do with the worth of the company and far more to do with the extent to which Harriman wanted Chicago for the Union Pacific and how far Hill and Morgan would go to stop him. Moreover, these mostly private issues had little to do with the concerns of the everyday investors who owned NP shares or the speculators who took advantage of the sudden upswing. So great was the rise that when the crash came, as a correction to inflated stock prices that had spread from NP to other stocks as investors panicked and moved their money out of all kinds of corporate securities, it came hard: railroad stocks, as well as mining stocks and U.S. Steel, crashed severely.

Unable to gain control of NP, and thus of Chicago, Harriman organized a National Securities Company (NSC) as a trust with which to buy up railroad stocks and managed to win Hill's loyalty away from Morgan. However, the NSC did not last long before it was shut down by government antitrust regulators. In the meantime, investors returned to the market, lured by stock bargains, and the exchange rebounded, fueled by strong growth in the real economy.

Bill Kte'pi

See also: Panic of 1907; Panics and Runs, Bank.

Further Reading

Bruner, Robert F., and Sean D. Carr. *The Panic of 1907: Lessons Learned from the Market's Perfect Storm.* New York: John Wiley & Sons, 2009.

Linsley, Judith Walker, Ellen Walker Rienstra, and Jo Ann Stiles. *Giant Under the Hill: A History of the Spindletop Oil Discovery at Beaumont, Texas.* Denton: Texas State Historical Association, 2008.

Morris, Charles R. *The Tycoons: How Andrew Carnegie, John D. Rockefeller, Jay Gould, and J.P. Morgan Invented the American Supereconomy.* New York: Holt, 2006.

Strouse, Jean. *Morgan: American Financier.* New York: Harper, 2000.

Wolff, David. *Industrializing the Rockies.* Boulder: University Press of Colorado, 2003.

Panic of 1907

A major financial crisis that precipitated a dramatic drop in U.S. stock prices and set off a mild recession, the Panic of 1907 was triggered by a failed effort of speculators to corner part of the market in copper, which, in turn, set off a liquidity crisis at key New York banks. The panic is best remembered for being the last time a U.S. financial crisis was largely remedied by the efforts of private bankers, and was led by financier J.P. Morgan. The panic renewed calls among economists and policy makers for the United States to follow major European countries by setting up a central bank that could both prevent and respond to crises in the financial markets by regulating bank credit and providing liquidity.

As in the case of most financial crises, the Panic of 1907 resulted from a number of contributing factors beyond the immediate one. By the fall of 1907, when the cornering effort failed, the securities markets and the financial sector had already taken a number of blows. Among these were the great San Francisco earthquake of 1906, which led to market instability as capital flowed out of New York to the West Coast, and the passage of the Hepburn Act that same year. The Hepburn Act gave the Interstate Commerce Commission increased powers, including the authority to set maximum railroad rates, which sent railroad stock prices dramatically downward. Finally, and perhaps most importantly, the powerful Bank of England raised its interest rates at the end of 1906, drying up capital in the U.S. markets as British and other investors sought to take advantage of higher returns in London. All of these factors contributed to the volatility of U.S. financial markets and a tightening of credit in 1907.

That same year, Otto Heinze, brother of United Copper Company founder Augustus Heinze, came up with an elaborate scheme to gain control of the company and make a fortune in the process. Otto believed that a major portion of the company's publicly traded shares had been bought "short," a financial practice whereby the purchaser borrows money to buy shares in hopes that the share price will then go down. The borrower can then sell the shares, repurchase them at a lower price, pay back the loan, and pocket the difference. Otto planned to aggressively purchase shares so as to drive up the price. This would force the short buyers to dump their shares in order to pay back their loans, at a much higher price. Otto would then sell his shares and reap a large profit.

Otto began his buying scheme in October, but he miscalculated on two fronts. He had underestimated the amount of money he would need

Commenting on the schemes and manipulation that lay behind the Panic of 1907, this contemporary cartoon shows "common honesty" erupting from a volcano and people fleeing with "stocks," "secret rate schedules," "rebates," and "frenzied accounts." *(Library of Congress)*

to effect the corner, and he overestimated the number of shares that had been bought "short." In other words, there were plenty of shares available for short sellers to buy in order to cover their position. Otto was successful at first, driving up the price of United Copper stock from under $40 to over $60 a share. Within days, however, short sellers dumped their holdings in the company, which caused a drop in the share price to under $10. Otto and his brokerage firm, Gross and Kleeberg, were unable to meet their obligations and were forced to declare bankruptcy. A number of banks and financial trusts with major holdings in United Copper stock suddenly saw their assets shrink, made worse as panicky depositors withdrew their money. More importantly, other banks and trusts became fearful, refusing to lend money to the troubled institutions. The credit markets soon began to freeze up, triggering a recession that gripped the country for the rest of 1907 and much of 1908. The national unemployment rate rose from 3 percent to 8 percent, with industrial production falling by more than 10 percent.

Even before the recession kicked in, however, the financial panic was being addressed by some of the richest and most influential financiers on Wall Street. Their actions were coordinated by the most powerful banker of the age, John Pierpont Morgan. Meeting in the library of his mansion on Manhattan's Madison Avenue, the bankers came up with a scheme to shore up the assets of key banks with tens of millions of dollars while at the same time liquidating those of the most troubled institutions in order to pay depositors. Despite these actions, many New York banks refused to make the short-term loans to each other that would lubricate the credit markets. The financial markets responded with panic selling of securities, as stock prices plunged. This time Morgan assembled an even larger group of bankers and got them to provide more than $20 million in short-term loans. Still, the markets continued downward until the New York Clearing House, a consortium of city banks, came up with $100 million to shore up the credit

markets. Meanwhile, Morgan and other bankers persuaded the city's major newspaper editors and clergymen to urge calm.

In the end, the panic was quelled. While the value of shares traded in the various New York markets fell by 50 percent, they recovered quickly. Beyond the few institutions immediately affected by the collapse of United Copper stock, there was no great wave of bankruptcies in the financial industry. The recession triggered by the panic proved short-lived, representing a slight dip in an ongoing upward trend in economic growth and securities valuation that lasted from the late 1890s through the far worse recession of 1921–1922.

And while Morgan was praised around the world for his deft handling of the crisis, many on Wall Street and beyond became more convinced than ever that the United States needed a central bank to regulate credit and lending and to provide liquidity during periods when private money dried up. The country had no such institution since President Andrew Jackson vetoed the rechartering of the second Bank of the United States in the 1830s. Six years after the Panic of 1907 came passage of the Federal Reserve Act and the founding of the Federal Reserve Bank.

James Ciment

See also: Panic of 1901; Panics and Runs, Bank.

Further Reading

Chernow, Ron. *The Death of the Banker: The Decline and Fall of the Great Financial Dynasties and the Triumph of the Small Investor.* New York: Vintage, 1997.

Strouse, Jean. *Morgan: American Financier.* New York: Random House, 1999.

Panics and Runs, Bank

Bank runs are episodes in which depositors at a given financial institution lose confidence in that institution's ability to meet its obligations, specifically, its ability to produce the funds it holds on behalf of depositors. Many such runs occurring simultaneously produce a bank panic. A common occurrence in the United States through the early twentieth century, bank runs and panics have largely been eliminated since the creation in 1933 of the Federal Deposit Insurance Corporation (FDIC), a federal agency that insures deposits up to a specified amount of money.

An eerie echo of old-style bank runs occurred as a result of the subprime mortgage crisis of the late 2000s. In June 2008, panicked clients withdrew more than $1.5 billion in deposits from the California-based bank IndyMac, a financial institution highly exposed to subprime mortgages either by originating them or investing in subprime mortgage-backed securities. But while scenes of depositors lining up outside the doors of IndyMac branches evoked images from the early 1930s, the FDIC quickly moved in to secure deposits, making sure insured depositors did not lose money and quieting the alarm.

"Fractional Reserve Banking"

Virtually all banks maintain only a small amount of the assets entrusted to them by depositors in their vaults, a system known as "fractional reserve" banking. This is done because much of the profit that banks generate comes out of the "spread," the difference between the lower interest they pay depositors and the higher interest they collect on loans to businesses and individuals, or the return they earn on the securities they purchase with those depositor assets.

Beyond keeping only a small amount of depositors' funds on hand, fractional reserve banking presents another risk, known as "asset-liability mismatch." That is, a bank's liabilities (the funds it technically owes depositors) are usually more short-term in nature. Even if depositors do not regularly close their accounts, they draw upon them frequently, taking some or most of their money out for any number of immediate needs on an ongoing basis. A bank's assets (loans and securities), however, are less liquid. A mortgage or a business loan, for example, is usually paid back in installments over a long period of time while the securities a bank invests in often have fixed maturity dates, such as government or corporate bonds. In short, a bank cannot readily meet sudden liabilities by liquidating long-term assets.

While seemingly a risky practice, "fractional reserve" banking is, in fact, the way in which banks always operate, allowing them to make loans. Usually, banks are able to function smoothly because of the "law of large numbers." That is, holding the funds of thousands or even millions of depositors assures a great degree of safety for a bank since it is highly unlikely that, barring some emergency, all or even a large number of depositors would withdraw their funds at once. And even should such an unlikely event occur, banks have several backstops to protect them: they can borrow funds on a short-term basis from other banks through interbank lending, or, if they are members of the Federal Reserve System (the Fed)—which all nationally chartered and most larger state-chartered banks are—they can secure funds directly from the Federal Reserve Bank, the so-called "lender of last resort." And, as noted earlier, modern depositors enjoy a final protection, that of the FDIC, though FDIC intervention to protect deposits usually entails placing the troubled institution into receivership, which can often lead to the sale of its assets and the formal dissolution of the bank.

Panics Through the Great Depression

A run may occur on an individual bank because of something specific to that institution, or a run can occur against many banks at once. When the latter occurs, it is known as a "bank panic," or simply "panic." Panics were common in nineteenth-century U.S. economic history, especially with the liberalization of state bank chartering laws before the Civil War. During that period, banks not only lent out money against deposits, but also issued their own currency in the form of bank notes. Lightly regulated, if at all, such banks often held little specie, or coinage with an intrinsic value in the precious metal they contain, to back up the bank notes they issued. Indeed, the assets of many banks, particularly in rural areas, were in the land deeds they held, a very illiquid asset indeed and one that fluctuated wildly in value.

The notes banks issued against depositor assets varied in value as well, depending on the institution's reputation and location. Usually, bank notes depreciated in value the farther they circulated from the issuing bank, since the reputation of that bank and the ability to submit the banks for specie became more attenuated with distance. Unscrupulous individuals would often establish banks in very remote locations, making it almost impossible for holders of notes to redeem them. Indeed, so far into the wilderness were they located that people called them "wild cat" banks because they existed where wild cats roamed.

But even more reputable banks could be victims of bank runs, especially at times when real-estate bubbles burst and the land deeds held by the bank became worth much less. Panicky depositors or holders of bank notes would then descend on banks to withdraw their money or turn their notes into specie, creating a panic that brought the nation's financial system to its knees and triggered a general downturn in the economy. Such was the case in 1819, 1837 and 1857. By the late nineteenth and early twentieth centuries, bank panics—such as those of 1873, 1893, and 1907—were more likely to be triggered by a collapse in corporate securities valuations—often those of railroads—an asset held by many banks at the time. In most of these cases, the panic began with a run on a major bank in New York or a regional financial center, which usually produced a general lack of confidence in the solvency of other banks. This pattern illustrates that both bank runs and bank panics tend to feed on themselves. As more depositors withdraw their funds, the banks become less solvent, triggering fears in other depositors who then demand their money.

To prevent such panics, in 1913, Congress established the Fed, which not only served as a lender of last resort to member banks but set rules for the amount of assets a member bank had to keep on hand to pay depositors. Still, this protection did not prevent the worst bank panic in American history, that of the early 1930s, from occurring. As the economy reeled from the Great Depression, bank deposits dried up as people withdrew their money to live on, to put into safer assets such as gold, or to stash away under the proverbial mattress. At the same time, bank assets declined, either because individuals and businesses could no longer pay back their loans or because the securities a bank held lost value. Many larger banks, for example, had invested in corporate securities, whose values declined precipitously as a result of the Great Wall Street Crash of 1929.

By late 1932, some 9,000 banks had failed. As newly elected president Franklin Roosevelt waited to take office—which, in those days, occurred in March—panic spread through the system, as depositors made runs on banks across the country. The nation's financial system was collapsing. As one of his first acts in office, Roosevelt declared a "bank holiday," ordering the closure of the nation's banks for several days. While they were shut down, Roosevelt signed the Emergency Banking Relief Bill, which allowed the Treasury Department to reopen banks that were solvent and reorganize and manage those that were not. This move reassured depositors and ended the panic. Later that year, Congress passed the Glass-Steagall Act, legislation that enabled the FDIC and prevented commercial banks—that is, the ordinary banks that held deposits and issued loans—from engaging in such investment bank activities as the underwriting of corporate securities and other high-risk investments.

The FDIC and Glass-Steagall effectively stabilized the U.S. banking system, kept bank runs to a minimum, and ended traditional bank panics. Over the years, the amounts the FDIC insures have risen—from $2,500 to the current, albeit temporary, limit of $250,000 per depositor—to keep pace with inflation and overall economic growth. At the same time, however, Glass-Steagall's firewall between commercial and investment banking was torn down by the Gramm-Leach-Bliley Act of 1999, a reform that many economists say contributed to the financial crisis of 2008–2009.

Financial Crisis of the Late 2000s

Indeed, the late 2000s crisis has tested the safeguards established under Roosevelt's New Deal legislation of the 1930s. As the housing boom took off in the early 2000s, many banks began to drop their lending standards, allowing less qualified applicants—or subprime borrowers—to take out a mortgage. Rapidly rising home prices reassured financial institutions that even should a borrower go into default, the bank would recoup its losses and then some by selling off the repossessed home at a price well above the outstanding debt on the mortgage. In addition, the securitization of mortgages appeared to spread the risk of default to many investors so that the bank originating the mortgage was no longer 100 percent liable for the default.

But as the housing market collapsed and prices declined, a number of banks found themselves holding very large quantities of nonperforming subprime loans. By June 2008, rumors began to spread that IndyMac Bank, a California-based institution that had aggressively marketed subprime mortgages, might become insolvent. As noted above, despite assurances from the FDIC, depositors lined up and demanded the right to remove their money. While the images evoked the bank runs of the early 1930s, in fact, the system worked; the FDIC placed the bank into receivership and ensured that depositors did not lose a dime of their money and did not face any significant delays in gaining access to it. Three months later came the collapse of Washington State–based Washington Mutual (WaMu), another victim of the subprime mortgage collapse. This time, however, the FDIC moved more quickly and a bank run was avoided, with the FDIC putting the bank into receivership and then orchestrating the purchase of its assets by JPMorgan Chase.

While such federal-government action served to foreshorten and avoid bank runs during the financial crisis of the late 2000s, another problem looms, say some economists—that of banks whose assets are worth less than zero but which remain propped up by the promise of support from the Fed. Such banks are popularly known as "zombie banks"—the financial equivalent of the walking dead. Zombie banks are often the victim of "silent runs" in which potential depositors avoid putting their money into the bank rather than existing depositors pulling theirs out. To assure potential depositors, the zombie bank might offer higher interest rates, putting the squeeze on healthy banks. This allows zombie banks to grow but not enough to return themselves to financial health. And because of their straitened circumstances, they do not lend as much money, thereby curtailing investment and economic activity. Moreover, their very existence undermines confidence in the banking system as a whole, since depositors and other banks do not know which institutions are likely to become insolvent, thereby curtailing deposits and interbank lending. Many economists cite the existence of such banks as a major factor behind the prolonged slump in the Japanese economy following the real-estate collapse there in the early 1990s, and they worry that a similar scenario might play out in the United States and other economies hard hit by the real-estate collapse of the late 2000s.

James Ciment

See also: Federal Deposit Insurance Corporation; Great Depression (1929–1933); IndyMac Bancorp; Panic of 1901; Panic of 1907; Savings and Loan Crises (1980s–1990s).

Further Reading

Cecchetti, Stephen G. *Money, Banking, and Financial Institutions.* Boston: McGraw-Hill/Irwin, 2006.

Chorafas, Dimitris N. *Financial Boom and Gloom: The Credit and Banking Crisis of 2007–2009 and Beyond.* New York: Palgrave Macmillan, 2009.

McGrane, Reginald. *The Panic of 1837: Some Financial Problems of the Jacksonian Era.* New York: Russell & Russell, 1965.

Wicker, Elmus. *Banking Panics of the Gilded Age.* New York: Cambridge University Press, 2000.

———. *The Banking Panics of the Great Depression.* 2nd ed. New York: Cambridge University Press, 2000.

Paulson, Henry (1946–)

Henry Paulson, an investment analyst who occupied senior management positions at the investment firm Goldman Sachs for many years, was appointed U.S. secretary of the Treasury in 2006 by President George W. Bush. The appointment was the culmination of Paulson's many years in public service. In his new capacity, Paulson worked with Chairman of the Federal Reserve Ben Bernanke and Director of the Federal Reserve of New York Timothy Geithner (who would later succeed Paulson as Treasury secretary) on managing the early stages of the global financial crisis of 2008.

Henry Merritt Paulson, Jr., was born March 28, 1946, in Palm Beach, Florida. He grew up in Barrington Hills, Illinois (outside Chicago), as the son of a wholesale jeweler. He graduated from Dartmouth College in 1968, where he majored in English and was a member of Phi Beta Kappa. While at Dartmouth, Paulson played varsity football as an offensive lineman and was nicknamed "Hank the Hammer" for his determination and aggressive play; he earned All Ivy and All East honors, as well as an honorable mention for All American. He continued his education at the Harvard Business School, earning an MBA in 1970.

Moving to Washington, D.C., Paulson began his career as a staff assistant to the assistant secretary of defense at the Pentagon from 1970 to 1972. He then moved on to the position of staff assistant to President Richard Nixon, working under adviser John Ehrlichman from 1972 to 1973 as a member of the White House Domestic Council. Paulson joined Goldman Sachs in 1974, rising rapidly through the ranks to become a partner in 1982. From 1983 to 1988, he headed Goldman's Investment Banking Services for the Midwest Region, and in 1988 became the managing partner in the Chicago office. Paulson's meteoric rise in Goldman Sachs continued in the 1990s, as he was appointed co-head of the

U.S. Treasury secretary Henry Paulson, a former chairman and CEO of Goldman Sachs, played a key role in the government's response to the financial meltdown of 2007–2008. He was the chief architect and promoter of the $700 billion TARP bailout. *(Bloomberg/Getty Images)*

Investment Banking Division (1990), president and chief operating officer (1994), and co-senior partner (1998). With the firm's initial public offering (IPO) in 1999, he was designated chairman and chief executive officer of the Goldman Sachs Group, Incorporated.

Paulson had been dubbed "Mr. Risk," in part because he was one of the first on Wall Street to recognize the profit potential for investment banks that take leveraged positions with their own capital in addition to acting as intermediaries. Under his leadership, Goldman Sachs's strategy focused on identifying profitable risks, determining how to control and monitor them, and avoiding catastrophic missteps in investing. During his thirty-two-year career at the firm, Paulson accumulated an equity stake worth an estimated $700 million.

After an intense recruitment effort by the White House, Paulson left Goldman Sachs in early July 2006 to become President Bush's third Treasury secretary (after John Snow and Paul O'Neill). He had been reluctant to accept the nomination but agreed after receiving assurances that he would be an active participant in economic-policy formulation. Paulson was described by some as the ideal person to deal with the U.S. economic and fiscal situation because of his understanding of debt and risk taking. As the U.S. economy had come to resemble a giant venture-capital fund drawing money from global capital markets and investing it in high-risk, high-return projects, the importance of understanding and managing risk, global imbalances, and capital flows had become central to virtually every economic issue faced by the government.

As Treasury secretary, Paulson came face-to-face with the financial crisis that began to emerge in the early months of 2008. Working closely with Bernanke and Geithner, he helped arrange emergency funding and other measures to save such former financial giants as Bear Stearns, AIG, Merrill Lynch, and Citigroup. The controversial decision to let Lehman Brothers fall into bankruptcy set off a wave of fear and uncertainty within the U.S. and international financial markets that, many believe, catalyzed the global economic meltdown. Paulson was also the architect and chief manager of the Troubled Assets Relief Program (TARP), a Bush administration plan that provided some $700 billion in federal funds to ailing financial institutions.

In December 2008, reflecting on the lessons of the financial crisis and government intervention in the markets, Paulson declared, "We need to get to a place in this country where no institution is too big or too interconnected to fail . . . because regulation alone is never going to solve the problem. There's no regulator that's going to be so good they're going to be able to deal with or ferret out all of the problems. So it takes a balance between the right regulatory system and market discipline. . . . Only if we have the freedom to fail, is there really going to be the freedom to succeed."

Following the election of Barack Obama in November 2008, Paulson worked with the incoming administration's economic team, including Geithner, Obama's nominee to head the Treasury Department, to ease the transition at a time of great economic peril. After leaving office in January 2009, Paulson accepted a teaching and research position at the Johns Hopkins School of Advanced International Studies in Washington. An avid environmentalist, he also remained active in various conservation causes.

Frank L. Winfrey

See also: Stimulus Package, U.S. (2008); Treasury, Department of the; Troubled Asset Relief Program (2008–).

Further Reading

Altman, Alex. "Henry M. Paulson, Jr." *Time,* September 18, 2008.

Bhushan, Amarendra. "Henry M. Paulson, Jr." *CEOWORLD Magazine,* September 25, 2008.

"Mr. Risk Goes To Washington." *BusinessWeek,* June 12, 2006.

Paulson, Henry. *On the Brink: Inside the Race to Stop the Collapse of the Global Financial System.* New York: Business Plus, 2009.

Penn Central

The bankruptcy of the Penn Central railroad in 1970 was the largest bankruptcy in U.S. history to date. The corporation's failure was symptomatic of the decline of railroads after World War II, and illustrated how some institutions had overextended themselves. The Penn Central crisis also highlighted the continuing disagreement in the United States over whether poorly run corporations should be bailed out by the federal government, a discussion that continues to the present.

Since its beginning in the nineteenth century, the American railroad industry has been plagued by overcapacity and mismanagement. Between 1876 and 1970, railroad bankruptcies and receiverships totaled more than 1,100. During the Great Depression, nearly one-third of the country's railroads sought bankruptcy protection from creditors. In 1933, Congress added Section 77 to the federal Bankruptcy Act, to be applied specifically to railroads. Under this section, railroads were allowed to declare bankruptcy and then continue operations while being protected from creditors. The section allowed rail traffic to continue, which was important to the economic life of the United States, while the railroad was reorganized to pay off creditors.

Railroads joined most other industries in a financial resurgence during the 1940s. War production and the massive movement of people across the country provided additional revenues. With the end of the war, however, railroads began a slow decline, particularly in terms of passenger travel and freight being hauled over short distances. The main competitors of the railroads were the automobile and the truck. Both provided greater flexibility than the train. The development of interstate and multi-lane highway systems increased the advantages of motor vehicles over trains. In 1956, the Federal-Aid Highway Act provided additional federal monies for constructing additional highways.

Railroads that served the northeastern United States faced particular difficulties by the end of the 1950s. This densely populated, but relatively small, region turned away from the railroads to a greater extent than other areas. On November 1, 1957, two of the largest railroads in the region, and of the United States as a whole, announced that they were studying a merger. Pennsylvania Railroad and New York Central both provided a combination of freight and passenger service, and both suffered from declining revenues. Merger talks dragged on for years, hampered by the suicide of New York Central's chief executive officer. The Interstate Commerce Commission approved the merger on April 27, 1966, but court hearings took another two years. On February 1, 1968, the two railroads formally merged to become the Pennsylvania New York Central Transportation Company, better known as the Penn Central.

The goal of the merger was to create a railroad more economically sound than its two predeces-

sors. The planners hoped that they could consolidate services and equipment, but their efforts were unsuccessful. Railroads were highly regulated at the time by the Interstate Commerce Commission (ICC). The ICC prevented Penn Central from ceasing operations on lines that were not economically viable, in order to prevent a loss of service to those who lived along the lines. Rates charged by the railroads were also regulated by the ICC, so Penn Central could not raise revenue that way. Efforts to save money by consolidating operations were unsuccessful because the computer systems used by the railroads were not compatible. Operational savings were also hampered by different signal systems and other equipment. Even labor costs could not be cut. Contracts with strong railroad unions prevented Penn Central from eliminating unneeded positions or firing surplus personnel.

Realizing the railroad industry was in trouble, Penn Central's managers tried to diversify the corporation's interests. Large investments were made in industries as different as pipeline networks, real estate, and land development. These ventures, however, failed to bring in much additional income. They also drained much of the railroad's cash. Efforts to raise additional money to pay interest on short-term debts were unsuccessful, thanks to a tight credit market in the late 1960s.

By June 1970, Penn Central was unable to pay its debts. Although the corporation had assets of nearly $7 billion, most were pledged as security for $2.6 billion in loans. On June 21, Penn Central filed for bankruptcy under Section 77. The announcement sent shock waves through the American financial system. An effort by the Nixon administration to underwrite $200 million in loans came under fire from Democratic congressmen. The bailout was viewed by most Americans as a favor for the administration's friends in big business. Penn Central continued to operate, although debts continued to accumulate. The corporation's leadership was criticized for poor business decisions and was fired.

Legislation followed to prop up the railroad industry. On May 5, 1971, Amtrak was created to operate rail passenger service throughout the country under the federal government's control. Because passenger service was the least profitable railroad operation, most railroads were willing to turn operations over to Amtrak. Other railroads faced bankruptcy, leading Congress to national-ize Penn Central on April 1, 1976. Five smaller railroads were consolidated with Penn Central, resulting in the Consolidated Rail Corporation, better known as Conrail.

Penn Central's collapse, followed by that of other railroads, caused Congress to deregulate the railroads in 1980. Cost-cutting steps like closing down some unprofitable rail lines followed. Surviv-ing railroads were able to concentrate on the most profitable freight lines, and the industry became more prosperous in the 1990s.

Tim J. Watts

See also: Debt.

Further Reading

Daughen, Joseph R., and Peter Binzen. *The Wreck of the Penn Central.* Boston: Little, Brown, 1971.

Salsbury, Stephen. *No Way to Run a Railroad: The Untold Story of the Penn Central Crisis.* New York: McGraw-Hill, 1982.

Sobel, Robert. *The Fallen Colossus.* New York: Weybright and Talley, 1977.

Philippines

Situated off the coast of Southeast Asia, the Phil-ippines consists of an archipelago of more than 7,000 small and large islands between the Pacific Ocean and the South China Sea. While its more than 92 million people make it the twelfth most populous country in the world, it ranks only forty-seventh in gross domestic product (GDP), classifying it among middle-income nations.

Settled for tens of thousands of years, the islands were occupied by the Spanish in the six-teenth century and remained a colony of Madrid until 1898, when they were seized by the United States in the Spanish American War. Following occupation by the Japanese in World War II, the Philippines gained independence in 1946. Its post-independence history was marked by political turmoil and dictatorship until the 1980s, when true democracy was established.

A largely poor and agricultural country for most of its history, the Philippines emerged from American colonialism as the second wealthiest nation in Asia, after Japan, but corruption and mismanagement reduced its fortunes consider-ably until a rapid industrialization period began in the 1990s. Despite the vagaries of modern global economics, including the Asian financial crisis of 1997–1998 and the global downturn of 2008–2009, the Philippines has shown consis-tently strong growth, even if it lags behind other East and Southeast Asian economies.

Economic History Before the Marcos Era

The first humans are believed to have arrived in the archipelago around 40,000 BCE, though the dominant Malay people did not begin settling there until about 6,000 BCE. By the first mil-lennium CE, the islands were integrated into a trade network that linked them with Southeast Asia and China. Because the country consists of thousands of islands, it was never unified until the arrival of the Spanish, though various states emerged around Manila Bay as early as the tenth century.

In 1521, Portuguese-born explorer Ferdinand Magellan, a naturalized Spaniard, arrived in the is-lands on his historic voyage around the world. Ma-gellan was killed in a battle there with indigenous peoples while attempting to claim the islands for Spain. Over the course of the sixteenth century, Spain completed its conquest of the islands, which were governed from Mexico, and converted most of the people to Catholicism. Thus, the Philippines became the only majority Christian country in Asia, which it remains today.

While far from other colonial possessions, the Philippines became an important link in Spain's global trade network in the sixteenth and seventeenth centuries. Manila emerged as the major exchange port where Chinese goods such as silks and artisan products were traded for American silver. With the decline of the Spanish Empire in the late seventeenth and early eighteenth centuries, the Philippines languished economically until reforms in the mid-1700s opened it up to world trade. This created a wealthy elite of mixed Spanish and Filipino heritage in the nineteenth century who made their fortunes in the commercial production of tropical agricultural products. This landed aristocracy would maintain a stranglehold over the Filipino economy through both the Spanish and U.S. periods and into the post-independence era.

In 1898, the United States—a new global power—went to war with Spain and easily seized the Philippines from the militarily weaker country. More difficult was the suppression of indigenous rebels under independence leader Emilio Aguinaldo, who, angry that the United States would not grant them independence, fought the Americans in a bitter insurgency that resulted in the deaths of hundreds of thousands of Filipinos between 1898 and 1901.

U.S. rule proved a mixed blessing for the Philippines. While the Americans created a modern educational system, they also attempted to impose an alien culture. And while they helped build up the Filipino economy, it became largely an appendage to the U.S. market, exporting tropical agricultural commodities in exchange for manufactured goods. Still, under U.S. tutelage, the rudiments of a modern economy and industrial and transportation infrastructures emerged. By independence in 1946—following a three-year occupation by Japanese forces in World War II—the Philippines had the second-highest per capita GDP in all of East Asia, after Japan, though there remained gross inequalities in wealth among classes and between urban and rural areas. The United States had also attempted land reform but was largely unsuccessful in the effort.

A nominal democracy during the first quarter-century of independence, the Philippines was rocked by political turmoil, including a long-running communist insurgency in the 1950s. The country also prospered economically during the global boom of the 1950s and 1960s as a major exporter of agricultural products and as home to one of the most advanced industrial infrastructures in Asia. With the rise to power of Ferdinand Marcos, who was first elected president in 1965 and then seized dictatorial powers in the early 1970s, the economy languished, a victim of misguided economic policies, corruption, and a crony capitalism in which family members and friends took over most of the country's industries and drove many of them into the ground, either through incompetence or plunder.

Economy Under Marcos

Marcos, the president of the Philippines from 1966 to 1986, pushed through several initiatives that shaped the Philippine economy into the 1980s, increasing agricultural productivity, building roads, developing alternative sources of energy, and building hotels in the capital, Manila, to attract tourists. With the momentum of the country's ambitious undertakings, overseas lenders continued to grant loans to banks, businesses, and the government.

In the latter part of the 1970s, economic indicators in the Philippines showed definite progress, as well as less positive signals. The economy was expanding—the gross national product (GNP) grew by an average of 6 percent throughout the 1970s—but the unemployment rate rose. Throughout the decade, the country imported far more than it exported, leading to a rapidly expanding trade deficit. By the end of the decade, the foreign debt was overwhelming economic activity. These negative indicators began to alert international investors that the country was on the verge of severe economic problems.

In the early 1980s, several developments took place in the Philippines that would further erode the economy. Still reeling from the oil shock of the 1970s and the global recession it unleashed, the country continued to rely heavily on foreign borrowing and international trade. While the price of oil (and of oil imports) soared, the prices of the Philippines's major exports—sugar, lumber, copper concentrate, and coconut products—declined sharply. This meant an accelerating trade deficit and reduced investments in the country by wary businesses and financial firms in the West.

In January 1981, after being reelected to another six years as president through fraudulent balloting, Marcos appeared to make new efforts to move the country toward economic stability. He ended martial law, which had hampered domestic commerce and foreign investment in the country since 1972, and continued with his development plans, including the construction of new plants for steel, phosphate, cement, diesel engines, and petrochemicals. He also sought to reduce dependence on foreign oil by building nuclear and geothermal electric power plants. But many of the projects proved to be overly ambitious, at once poorly planned and economically unsupportable. The major source of funding was foreign borrowing, but misallocations, reckless spending, and the unsound economic policies of the Marcos regime made foreign banks wary of lending to the Philippine government. As foreign investments tightened up and interest rates skyrocketed, many of the projects were abandoned, and the Philippines was mired in rising debt.

On top of the looming crisis, a major financial scandal erupted in 1981 that would further disrupt the plans for progress. Textile magnate Dewey Dee fled the country after scamming several government and private banks, leaving behind approximately $70 million in debt to various financial institutions. His disappearance provoked a financial crisis that sent major investment houses and finance companies into turmoil.

Amid the mounting debts, fleeing investors, and declining popular support for the regime, political agitation mounted. On August 21, 1983, Benigno Aquino, Marcos's chief political rival, was assassinated upon returning from political exile in the United States. The airport shooting triggered renewed political turbulence, which in turn caused a crisis of confidence in the investment community. Capital fled the country at an alarming rate. By October, the Central Bank of the Philippines was forced to notify creditors that it was unable to pay its debts. The country was essentially bankrupt. President Marcos again turned to foreign lenders, but his dismal economic performance in the past and the mounting political sentiment against him made overseas investors distrustful and unwilling to lend.

In February 1986, after another fraud-riddled election, a popular uprising variously referred to as the People Power Revolution and Yellow Revolution forced Marcos to flee the country and installed Corazon Aquino, widow of Benigno, as president. After two decades of Marcos's dictatorial rule, the Philippines was getting a fresh start politically. The reforms that ensued brought an end to some of the worst corruption and cronyism of the era and encouraged foreign investors, setting the stage for a period of renewed growth.

Post-Marcos Economy

At first, foreign investors and lenders, including the United States and Japan, remained reluctant to put their money into the Philippines. With the promising signs of reform, however, President Aquino was eventually able to garner more than $1.2 billion in foreign loans and grants—over half of it coming from the United States. In moving the economy forward, the Aquino administration focused on debt repayment as its top priority, economic growth driven by exports, and less government regulation. As a result, the nation's annual GDP rose from 4.3 percent in 1986 to 6.7 percent in 1998, with economic expansion continuing through most of the 1990s.

The 1997–1998 Asian financial crisis, which began in Thailand and spread throughout Southeast Asian and Japan, had a major impact on the Philippines. Foreign investors, whose capital had been key to the country's export-led growth in the 1990s, began to pull out, which sent the value of

In metropolitan Manila, the Philippines, high-rise construction was suspended and shantytowns spread during the Asian financial crisis of 1997. Unequal distribution of wealth remains a chronic problem as the nation struggles for growth and stability. *(Romeo Gacad/AFP/Getty Images)*

the Philippine currency, the peso, plummeting. After growing by more than 5 percent in 1997, the Filipino economy fell into negative growth the following year, even as the government tried to bolster employment by raising tariffs on imported goods.

The late 1990s and early part of the next decade were a period of slow recovery, with the economy dragged down by the aftermath of the crisis, a series of natural disasters, a major bank failure, and scandals that led to the impeachment and ouster of President Joseph Estrada in 2001. By mid-decade, however, the Philippines was once again enjoying robust growth, driven by strong prices for mineral exports and a burgeoning manufacturing sector, supported by U.S., Japanese, and other firms building electronics and other assembly plants in the country to take advantage of the Philippines's relatively low labor costs. Between 2000 and 2007, per capita GDP, measured on a purchasing-power parity basis, which allows for differences in the values of various currencies, rose from $3,600 to $5,000.

The 2008–2009 financial crisis did not affect the Filipino economy as badly as it did those of the United States and much of the West. For one thing, the Philippines continued to lag behind many East Asian and Southeast Asian countries as a destination for foreign capital. Moreover, much of the capital that had been invested in the country went into building manufacturing and service infrastructure, not into securities or other financial instruments that could be easily liquidated. In addition, the Asian financial crisis of the late 1990s had led the government to impose higher capital requirements on banks, leaving them less leveraged and less vulnerable to the declines in financial instruments that had caused so much damage elsewhere, such as mortgage-backed securities.

Still, the global recession that followed the financial crisis hit the Philippines on several fronts. First, the drop in prices of raw materials hurt the nation's mining sector, while the overall decline in global demand undermined growth in manufactured exports. On the bright side, many multinational companies, eager to pare costs, maintained their operations in the country because of its low labor costs, helping offset the drop in remittances sent back by the millions of Filipino nationals working in economically ailing Persian Gulf and Western countries. Thus, the country was expected to follow its East and Southeast Asian neighbors into a rapid recovery from what turned out to be a relatively short-lived recession. Many economists predicted a growth rate of between 4 and 7 percent for 2009.

James Ciment and Berwyn Gonzalvo

See also: Asian Financial Crisis (1997); Indonesia; Southeast Asia.

Further Reading

"Avoiding Recession." *The Economist*, August 28, 2009.

Bresnan, John, ed. *Crisis in the Philippines: The Marcos Era and Beyond.* Princeton, NJ: Princeton University Press, 1986.

Calit, Harry S., ed. *The Philippines: Current Issues and Historical Background.* New York: Nova, 2003.

Karnow, Stanley. *In Our Image: America's Empire in the Philippines.* New York: Random House, 1989.

Nadeau, Kathleen. *The History of the Philippines.* Westport, CT: Greenwood, 2008.

PNC Financial Services

PNC Financial Services is a Pittsburgh-based financial services corporation and regional banking franchise operating in the mid-Atlantic and Midwest. It has become one of the largest banks in the United States, ranked fifth by deposits and third by the number of off-site ATMs. The case of PNC offers an example of how a severe economic crisis provides opportunities for fundamentally sound financial institutions.

PNC began as the Pittsburgh Trust and Savings Company in Pittsburgh, Pennsylvania, in 1852, and opened its current corporate offices in 1858. Growing gradually but steadily over the course of the twentieth century, the PTSC was renamed the Pittsburgh National Corporation in 1959. In 1982 it merged with the Provident National Corporation—another descendant of a nineteenth-century Pennsylvania bank, this one in Philadelphia—and called itself the PNC Financial Corporation. The new PNC quickly expanded its holdings through acquisitions of smaller banks, until its coverage extended from New York City to Kentucky. By the start of 2008, acquisitions of the Riggs National Corporation, Mercantile Bankshares, Yardville National Bancorp, and the Sterling Financial Corporation had put it among the top ten American banks.

The Global Economic Crisis of 2008–2009

Like other reasonably healthy banks, PNC was in a position to benefit from the widespread bank failures of the 2007–2009 financial meltdown and subsequent crisis while at the same time using its financial health to help stabilize the economy. In October 2008, it was chosen by federal regulators to acquire the failing National City Bank, a Cleveland institution and one of the ten-largest banks in the country. Founded as the City Bank of Cleveland in 1845, its history had largely paralleled that of PNC and other moderately successful nineteenth-century banks. National City had gone on an acquisitive binge from 2004 to 2008, spending billions of dollars to acquire the Provident Financial Group, Allegiant Bancorp, Fidelity Bankshares, Harbor Florida Bankshares, and MAF Bancorp (the holding company of MidAmerica Bank).

The acquisitions proved too much to digest, and National City suffered as it expanded into the period when the credit markets were about to freeze up and investments were beginning to fail. By the middle of 2008, federal regulators put National City Bank on probation. The exact terms of the agreement reached with the Office of the Comptroller of the Currency were confidential. National City did disclose to the public that the problems had revolved around the bank's overextension and its liberal risk-management practices—the two areas of concern for so many of the banks that failed in the aftermath of the subprime mortgage crisis.

The PNC acquisition of National City was called a "takeunder" because the purchase price of $5.58 billion was below National City's nominal value. Moreover, taking over the bank allowed PNC to receive $7.7 billion of federal money from the 2008 Emergency Economic Stabilization Act, which allowed PNC to make a significant profit. On the other hand, the exact nature of that profit depended on the accuracy of value estimations of the bank's holdings—a less than sure thing in the fourth quarter of 2008, given how many banks had overestimated the value of their investments and made other accounting errors.

Acquiring National City made PNC the fifth-largest bank by deposits, and it will remain so even after selling off at least sixty-one of the National City branches, as required by the Justice Department's antitrust division (the sales will take place in areas where the acquisitions have given PNC too much control over local banking, i.e., those places where PNC was competing with National City).

Bill Kte'pi

See also: Banks, Commercial; Recession and Financial Crisis (2007–).

Further Reading

Boselovic, Len. "PNC Acquiring National City." *Pittsburgh Post-Gazette*, October 24, 2008. www.post-gazette.com/pg/08298/922560–100.stm. Accessed August 24, 2009.

O'Hara, Terence. "Riggs, PNC Reach New Merger Agreement." *Washington Post*, February 11, 2005.

PNC Financial Services Web site: www.pnc.com.

Political Theories and Models

The political theory of businesses cycles asserts that politicians cause upswings and downturns in the economy for political reasons. According to this view, politicians and political trends can influence the business cycle under specific conditions.

Ideally, politicians pursue economic policies that promote prosperity for all. Nor is it hard to imagine how such an ideal situation might arise, at least hypothetically. If political candidates compete against each other openly and honestly, if voters are fully informed about the policies and programs proposed by office seekers, and if elected officials carry out the promises they made as candidates, the people are likely to get policies that best serve their interests (or that they think will do so). Thus, under ideal political conditions, national leaders will do their best to make the ups and downs of the business cycle less severe. In reality, however, there is great potential for—and a long history of—abuse of government powers that cause large swings in economic performance. Elections are not always open and candid, voters are often not well informed, and elected officials frequently alter their policies after taking office. In

the popular view, government leaders are notorious for misusing the public trust in this way, often under pressure from special-interest groups.

Elections and Economic Policy

One underlying cause of political business cycles is the timing of elections. Specifically, incumbent politicians may be inclined to alter policy so as to exaggerate economic growth during election years, while accepting slower growth rates, or even recessions, when not facing reelection. If this is indeed the case, political business cycle theory underscores the destabilizing effects of governmental influence on the economy as a whole. Underlying the possibility that the election cycle affects the business cycle are several facts of political and economic life. First, voters strongly oppose higher taxes and inflation. Second, voters like increased government spending and more jobs in their districts. Yet if elected officials try to keep taxes low and spending high, the government will face a growing budget deficit, which can backfire as interest rates rise and choke off private spending. If the deficit is accommodated by central bankers, then higher inflation will be the result.

Similarly, if politicians try to reduce inflation during an election year by raising interest rates, this can increase the unemployment rate and cost them votes. Incumbent politicians may thus conclude that it is advantageous to run larger deficits and accept higher inflation rates—policies that may trigger a boom—during election years, particularly if a large part of the inflation (which lags output growth in the boom) does not emerge until after the election. When the election is over, the officials can then implement policies to reduce deficits and inflation. This means that politicians are more likely to cut spending and fight inflation in the early phases of their terms than in the latter years. The result will tend to be economic slowdown in the period just after elections, followed by economic acceleration as politicians rely on inflation and deficit spending to win votes in boom years.

The election cycle will affect the business cycle only to the extent that voters are shortsighted. An informed electorate will not be swayed by an artificial election-year upswing if they know that it will be followed by a post-election recession. Moreover, if voters remember that a politician fooled them with an artificial boom in the previous election year, they will not fall prey to the same manipulation. According to several statistical studies, however, economic conditions during an election year have a greater influence on voting outcomes than do economic conditions for a presidential candidate's full term in office.

Historical Examples

History provides numerous examples of economic policy being used to political advantage. During the first term of President Franklin D. Roosevelt (1933–1937), for example, political motivations were part and parcel of the New Deal programs instituted to combat the Great Depression. Even though the South was the poorest region of the United States, a disproportionate amount of New Deal spending went to Northeastern and Western states, where incomes were 60 percent higher. Why did Roosevelt direct federal spending toward wealthier states rather than to the poverty-stricken South? One explanation is that the Southern states could be relied on to vote Democratic no matter their circumstances. Voters in the West and Northeast, meanwhile, were more open to voting Republican. Because Roosevelt was a Democrat, it made political sense for his administration to spend more money in states where they needed to win votes.

Federal spending by the Roosevelt administration totaled $4.5 billion per year in 1932 and again in 1933, jumping to $6.5 billion in 1934 and the election year of 1935. In 1933, the U.S. gross national product (GNP) was $55.6 billion and the unemployment rate was 24.9 percent. In 1935, the GNP stood at $72.2 billion and the unemployment rate at 20.1 percent. Roosevelt won reelection after a large increase in federal spending and a modest improvement in economic conditions. Economic conditions deteriorated with the crash of 1937, but began to improve during the election year of 1939. In short, the Roosevelt administration gives every appearance of having structured and timed federal spending based on electoral considerations, which suggests that at least part of the economic oscillation of the Great Depression was due to the election cycle.

During the postwar era, the election of 1972 presents an especially interesting case in point. In that year, President Richard Nixon undertook a rather obvious effort to create a political business cycle, and it worked. Blaming Republican election losses in 1954 and 1958, as well as his own defeat in 1960, on bad economic conditions, Nixon pursued an anti-inflation policy in 1969, which led to a recession. As the 1972 election approached, Nixon appointed Arthur Burns as Federal Reserve chairman. Burns injected an extra $51 billion into the economy, and Nixon added an additional $63.6 billion through the Treasury Department. The result was an election-year boom. The economy grew at an unsustainable rate of 7.3 percent during the twelve months leading to the November 1972 balloting. At the same time, Nixon directed federal money to key voting groups in states he needed to win, funding state aid projects, veterans' benefits, and Social Security payments. Nixon's landslide victory—he won reelection with 60 percent of the vote—suggests that voters forgot about the high unemployment during the early part of his first term and rewarded him for the election-year boom.

Parties

The idea of a purely election-driven political business cycle suggests that the two major U.S. parties follow the same policies and deliver the same results. While election-driven business cycles find considerable support in the historical record, party affiliation is another political factor in the upswings and downturns of the economy. It has been suggested, for example, that Republican politicians are relatively more concerned with preventing inflation, and that Democratic politicians are generally more concerned with preventing unemployment. That being the case, the ascendancy of one party or another may contribute to a change in the business cycle. If Democrats are in power, they will tend to allow a higher inflation rate while they try to minimize unemployment; consumers thus grow accustomed to higher inflation. Conversely, in a Republican administration, economic policy may shift toward fighting inflation, and unemployment will therefore rise, at least temporarily; in this case, the public comes to expect slower price increases.

The result is a tendency toward inflationary booms during Democratic administrations and recessions during the early phases of Republican administrations. In the early years of a Democratic administration, after people have come to expect low inflation (as a carryover from GOP policy), inflation may cause the economy to grow faster and achieve lower unemployment, at least temporarily. Once these temporary gains are realized, however, there will be little the Democratic administration can do to realize further reductions in unemployment. People will get used to higher inflation, and the economy will return to "normal," at least until an anti-inflation Republican administration is elected.

While the proposition that political parties implement different policies for different purposes carries theoretical plausibility and appears to be supported by statistical evidence, a closer look at history weakens the case for partisan political business cycles. In support of the theory, economic statistics for the 1980s do indicate that Republican president Ronald Reagan was more concerned with inflation than with unemployment. Moreover, inflation rates did fall during the first term of the Reagan administration, and unemployment rates were high in 1981 and 1982. But the anti-inflation policies of the early Reagan years were implemented by Federal Reserve chairman Paul Volcker, who was appointed by Reagan's Democrat predecessor, Jimmy Carter, in August 1979. Volcker

had been preceded as Federal Reserve chairman by G. William Miller, appointed by Carter early in the previous year. Miller, out of character for a Democratic administration, was far more concerned with inflation than with unemployment. By 1979, as rising prices became a serious problem—both economically and politically—Carter replaced Miller with the anti-inflation Volcker. Thus, by contrast with Nixon, who would fight inflation first and switch to fighting unemployment as he approached reelection—which he won in a landslide—Carter took on unemployment first and then fought inflation during the election year—and he lost. What these examples suggest, therefore, is not that Democrats and Republicans pursue different policies that determine the economic cycle, but rather that Nixon knew how to use the political business cycle to his advantage and Carter did not.

Interest Groups

Still another explanation of political business cycles focuses on special interests. As a general principle, business owners can earn more profits by keeping wages low, provided that workers maintain high productivity for less pay. Because workers will find it easier to demand higher wages when there is full employment, businesses may find advantage in economic instability. An occasional crisis might make workers so fearful of unemployment that they will work hard even at relatively low wages. The special-interest-group version of political business cycle theory is hard to substantiate. While individual interest groups certainly do have influence in politics, it is not clear that all businesses can work together as a group against labor. On the business side, special-interest groups split up by industry and cannot work together easily. Moreover, the labor movement continues to have a major influence on politics even as union membership has declined over previous decades. The idea that business interests can consistently beat out labor interests on the unemployment issue is far from proven, and the reverse could easily be true. Labor unions might well be more influential when it comes to the business-cycle issue than are businesses. Overall, the case for the interest-group theory of political business cycles is weaker than for the election-cycle theory.

Stability and Instability

Finally, the political stability or instability of a country may be a vital factor in the business cycle and the expansion or contract of the economy. While the United States has been blessed by one of the most stable political systems in world history—with the major exception of the Civil War, political conflict in America has always been resolved through the electoral system—most other countries around the world have not been so lucky. Economists generally assert that stability is good for the economy for a number of reasons. First, it provides the kind of predictable political environment that the private sector needs to make investment decisions. Political stability also tends to assure a relatively stable monetary policy, maintaining inflation at a level that encourages a healthy level of consumption as well as a useful degree of savings. Finally, political stability reassures foreign interests that a particular country is a good place to invest.

Some economists argue, however, that the relationship between political stability and economic prosperity is a more complicated matter, and that, in some cases, instability can be more beneficial to the economy, at least in the long-term. While politically destabilizing events such as revolution and war often interrupt economic activities in the short run, they can also set the stage for more rapid growth in the medium- and long-term. This is especially the case when revolutionary forces are set in motion by an existing government's inability to deal with economic issues. If a revolution overthrows such a system and installs one that is more capable of managing the economy, the event can be seen as a boon to the economy.

The major example of political instability in U.S. history—the Civil War—offers a useful example. The waning years of the antebellum era saw a political stalemate as the slaveholding states maintained a veto in the Senate that blocked the interests of free states, despite the fact that the latter represented a large majority of the population and economic output of the country. While this veto power was most notable in preventing antislavery legislation, it also had an impact on other economic policy issues. For a variety of reasons, Southerners opposed the tariffs that Northern industrial interests viewed as essential, they blocked homesteading legislation, and they insisted that a transcontinental railroad run through their region of the country. Southern secession freed up the legislative logjam, allowing a Northern-dominated Congress to pass an agenda that, say economic historians, helped pave the way for the expansion of the industrial revolution in the latter half of the nineteenth century and the emergence of the United States as the world's great industrial economy.

D.W. MacKenzie, Bing Ran, and James Ciment

See also: Fiscal Policy; Monetary Policy; Public Works Policy; Tax Policy.

Further Reading

Ake, Claude. "A Definition of Political Stability." *Comparative Politics* 7:2 (January 1975): 271–283.

Alesina, Alberto, and Jeffrey Sachs. "Political Parties and the Business Cycle in the United States, 1948–1984." *Journal of Money, Credit and Banking* 20:1 (February 1988): 63–82.

Beck, Nathaniel. "Elections and the Fed: Is There a Political Monetary Cycle?" *American Journal of Political Science* 31:1 (1987): 194–216.

Golden, David G., and James M. Poterba. "The Price of Popularity: The Political Business Cycle Reexamined." *American Journal of Political Science* 24:4 (1980): 131–143.

MacRae, Duncan. "A Political Model of the Business Cycle." *Journal of Political Economy* 85:2 (April 1977): 239–263.

Mevorach, Baruch. "The Political Monetary Business Cycle: Political Reality and Economic Theory." *Political Behavior* 11:2 (1989): 175–188.

Nordhaus, William D. "The Political Business Cycle." *Review of Economic Studies* 42:2 (1975): 169–190.

Olson, Mancur Lloyd, Jr. *The Rise and Decline of Nations: Economic Growth, Stagflation, and Social Rigidities.* New Haven, CT: Yale University Press, 1982.

Richards, Daniel J. "Unanticipated Money and the Political Business Cycle." *Journal of Money, Credit and Banking* 18:4 (1986): 447–457.

Ponzi Scheme (1919–1920)

A Ponzi scheme is a financial scam in which existing investors are paid inordinately high returns, not from any increase in the value of their investment but out of the funds provided by new investors. Named for Charles Ponzi, an Italian-American immigrant who conceived and ran one of the most notorious of such schemes in the early part of the twentieth century, Ponzi schemes are fraudulent, illegal, and fated to collapse once the pool of new investors dries up, usually resulting in widespread losses. Ponzi schemes have occurred periodically in U.S. history, with the biggest to date being that run by New York financier Bernard Madoff from the early 1990s through the mid-2000s, which bilked investors of tens of billions of dollars.

An impoverished immigrant from Sicily, Ponzi came to the United States in 1903 at the age of nineteen. After working at various jobs in the United States and Canada—and running afoul of U.S. law for illegally smuggling immigrants into the country—Ponzi in 1919 discovered a loophole in the international postal system that seemed to guarantee substantial and assured profits for an investor. International postal-reply coupons (IPRCs) were a form of prepaid postage in which a sender could pay for a recipient's reply. IPRCs were popular in the Italian-American community because they allowed relatively well-off immigrants to cover the cost of postage for poorer relatives and friends back home.

The purchase price of an IPRC was the cost of a letter's postage in the sender's country. This created a discrepancy in value if similar postage in the recipient's country was worth more or less than that in the sender's country. For example, if sending a letter cost 5 cents in the sender's country and 10 cents in the recipient's country, the IRPC was undervalued. The coupon could then be exchanged for stamps in the recipient's country, which in turn could be redeemed for cash, yielding a 5 cent, or

Italian-American immigrant Charles Ponzi bilked investors of some $5 million in a scam involving international postal reply coupons in 1919–1920. The eponymous—and illegal—pyramid scheme reached a new level with the Bernard Madoff case decades later. *(The Granger Collection, New York)*

50 percent, profit. This was exactly the situation between Italy and the United States in 1919. With Italy's currency undergoing rapid devaluation against the U.S. dollar after World War I, IPRCs could be bought relatively cheaply in Italy and redeemed for stamps in the United States; these could then be sold for a hefty profit.

Based in Boston, Ponzi used his own and borrowed funds to make a test run. The results were less than encouraging. Delays in the system and the large administrative expenses of buying and redeeming large numbers of IPRCs ate up all of the profits and more. Yet Ponzi was not deterred. A talented salesman, he convinced people—despite what he had learned—that the scheme was foolproof, promising investors major returns in ninety days. So many flocked to his scheme that he was able to pay the original investors the same spectacular returns in a mere forty-five days.

As the news spread, more and more people brought their money to Ponzi—many of them previous investors who plowed their profits back into the enterprise. This not only allowed him to continue paying high returns, but to hire a large staff to run the business and to live the life of a millionaire—at least for a time, in 1919 and early 1920.

Another term for a Ponzi scheme is a "pyramid scheme." As the term suggests, a pyramid scheme requires an exponentially larger base of new investors to pay off the growing number of earlier investors at the top. Sooner or later, the pool will run out—sooner if the scheme is exposed, which is exactly what happened when the *Boston Post* ran an exposé on July 26, 1920.

Thousands in Boston showed up at Ponzi's offices demanding that he return their money. With investments still pouring in from his operations in other cities, he was able to make good on their demands, reaffirming his reputation and keeping the scheme alive. But time was running out. On August 10, auditors where he banked announced that Ponzi did not have sufficient funds to redeem all of his obligations. This time the flood of investors demanding money back overwhelmed his resources. Three days later, Ponzi was arrested by federal authorities and charged with mail fraud. Tried and found guilty that November, he was sentenced to five years in federal prison. It took almost a decade to untangle the finances of Ponzi's scheme, with later investors recovering just 30 cents on the dollar. After serving several years in prison, Ponzi was eventually deported, dying in poverty in Brazil in 1949.

Charles Ponzi did not invent the scheme that was named for him, nor did such scams cease occurring after he had been exposed. In the decades since, law-enforcement authorities have exposed dozens of major Ponzi schemes in the United States. The most spectacular was the one run through Bernard L. Madoff Investment Securities, a New York City financial services firm run by a prominent Wall Street trader and philanthropist. Facilitating over-the-counter, or nonexchange stock and bond trades directly between investors, Madoff and his company for years gave investors consistently higher returns than other firms. By late 2008, however, with the stock market in rapid decline and more and more investors wanting to withdraw their money, Madoff had trouble meeting his obligations and keeping the scheme alive. With the firm already under federal investigation, Madoff admitted publicly that his operation was a Ponzi scheme with liabilities of tens of billions of dollars. He was arrested in December 2008, pled guilty to all charges in March 2009, and was sentenced to 150 years in prison in June 2009.

As in Ponzi's case, Madoff's scheme required an operator capable of winning people's confidence and a pool of investors gullible enough to overlook the oldest adage of the marketplace: if a deal is too good to be true, it probably is. The differences between Ponzi and Madoff were in the sophistication of the latter's operation and the scale and duration of the fraud. Whereas Ponzi's roughly year-long scheme bilked investors of about $5 million, Madoff's scheme—which investigators say operated from the 1960s through the 2000s—cost them an estimated $65 billion, making it the largest financial fraud in history.

James Ciment

See also: Madoff, Bernard.

Further Reading

Dunn, Donald. *Ponzi: The Incredible True Story of the King of Financial Cons.* New York: Broadway, 2004.

Zuckoff, Mitchell. *Ponzi's Scheme: The True Story of a Financial Legend.* New York: Random House, 2005.

Portugal

A small nation situated on the Iberian Peninsula in southwestern Europe, Portugal, with a current population of about 10.6 million, traditionally had one of the poorer and least developed economies in Western Europe. Modernization in the post–World War II era, however, has brought it closer to European living standards and per capital gross domestic product (GDP).

One of the first nation states to emerge in Western Europe in the Middle Ages, Portugal became a pioneer in overseas exploration, conquest, and trade in the fifteenth and sixteenth centuries as mariners brought back spices and other exotic goods from Asia while establishing colonies there, as well as in Africa and South America. But the country was soon outpaced by larger and more economically advanced competitors and went into economic decline from the seventeenth century through the early twentieth century.

As late as 1950, half of Portugal's active population was still employed in agriculture and the GDP per capita was similar to those of Greece, Bahrain, Colombia, and Namibia. Yet, as the decade of the 1950s unfolded, a strong industrialization push—buoyed by technological transfers, by new projects melding private and public capital, and by a controlled but progressive openness of the economy—sent the country toward the front ranks of growing European economies, with 5.8 percent of annual growth in the GDP per capita for the period of 1950–1973.

Following a pattern later trod by successful NICs (newly industrialized countries) in the developing world, Portugal added exports of light industrial goods to its traditional agricultural exports, which benefited from the comparative advantage of cheap labor in the final value added. But just as plans for the development of heavy industry were under way, the country was hit by a double shock: the international energy and economic crisis that spread from oil upheaval in the Middle East and the military coup of April 25, 1974, known as the "Carnation Revolution," which ended forty-one years of authoritarianism and personal dictatorship without bloodshed.

The 1974 revolution unleashed a revolutionary process marked by new democratic freedoms, as well as street confrontations between Left and Right. Among the most important changes brought on by the change in regimes was the decision to dismantle Portugal's overseas empire and end costly anti–national liberation wars in Angola, Mozambique, and Guinea-Bissau. Decolonization saved the state a lot of resources but it also led to a wave of returning Portuguese nationals from the overseas colonies. Around the same time, Portuguese emigration to other European nations began to wane.

The revolution also wrought significant changes in economic policy, including a nationalization program that brought the largest enterprises in banking, manufacturing, transportation, and services under government control. This led to what economists call a dual economy—large, capital-intense sectors became public monopolies and oligopolies, while small and medium-sized enterprises, as well as foreign-owned companies, remained in private hands. At the same time, agrarian reform led to the redistribution of the large landed estates of the northern part of the country but left the small land holdings in the center and south in the hands of existing owners.

This transformation led to much economic disruption. The large industrial enterprises underwent a swift depreciation in capitalization and posted large losses. Price distortions, decreased competitiveness, and the crowding out of private investment slowed economic growth. Moreover, Portugal's troubled macroeconomic situation, with public debt and inflation rising to crippling levels, combined with a general slowdown in the world economy in the late 1970s and early 1980s, led to two International Monetary Fund interventions in 1978–1979. Structural reforms eased the macroeconomic problems while a policy shift helped spur economic growth. Internal consumption rose, and despite the austerity measures, a broader social welfare network was established.

By the mid-1980s, however, things were beginning to change. A strategic consensus of Left and Right led to Portugal's accession to the European Union (EU) in 1986. To harmonize its economic policies with those of the EU, the government eased restrictions on the movement of capital in and out of the country and, under the Center-Right government of President Aníbal Cavaco Silva, initiated a privatization agenda in 1998, all part of a general trend toward increasing economic competitiveness.

The liberalization cycle, along with increased flows of foreign capital (balanced between direct foreign investment and structural fund transfers from the EU), the largest privatization effort in the EU per capita, closer economic ties with neighboring Spain, a strong revival in the all-important tourist sector, and an increase in construction, led to dramatic economic growth. By the early 1990s, Portugal had pulled its GDP per capita up to roughly 75 percent of the average for the EU.

At this point, many economists had come to believe that Portugal's economic development was self-sustaining. But in the late 1990s and early 2000s, new problems arose. Existing structural problems, weak productivity, a poorly educated workforce, and new imbalances in public finances combined with the competitive pressures of globalization led to a decade of anemic growth, political stalemate, and an inability to tackle structural problems. This economic weakness left Portugal unprepared for the crisis that swept world financial markets in 2008. By early 2010, public sector debt had risen so much—to more than 9 percent of GDP—that investors were beginning to question the country's very solvency. The Portuguese crisis—along with those in Greece and Spain—sent global financial markets into panic and prompted talk of the EU guaranteeing the country's debt.

Nuno Luis Madureira and James Ciment

See also: Greece; Ireland; Spain.

Further Reading

Confraria, João. "Portugal: Industrialization and Backwardness." In *European Industrial Policy*, ed. James Foreman-Peck and Giovanni Frederico, 268–294. Oxford: Oxford University Press, 1999.

Corkill, David. *The Portuguese Economy Since 1974*. Edinburgh, UK: Edinburgh University Press, 1993.

"Europe Watches as Portugal's Economy Struggles." *New York Times*, February 9, 2010. Available at www.nytimes.com/2010/02/10/world/europe/10portugal.html. Accessed March 2010.

Syrett, Stephen. *Contemporary Portugal: Dimensions of Economic and Political Change*. Aldershot, UK: Ashgate, 2002.

Poseidon Bubble (1969–1970)

The Poseidon bubble—a brief speculative episode involving Australian mining stocks in late 1969 and early 1970—illustrates the severe economic fluctuations in the form of bubbles and busts that can occur in the absence of regulatory controls over a country's natural resources.

The Poseidon bubble was one of the biggest booms in the history of the Australian stock market, if only for a brief time. Fueled by rampant speculation, shares in Poseidon NL (No Liability) rose from $0.80 in September 1969 to $12.30 the following month, rocketing to $280 in February 1970 before finally crashing. Millionaire investors were created overnight, only to be returned to the rank and file just as abruptly.

Poseidon NL was a mining company that discovered a potential new source of nickel in September 1969. The price of nickel had been rising steadily because of the manufacturing demands of the Vietnam War and because work stoppages at Inco, a major Canadian supplier of the metal, had sharply reduced the available supply. Poseidon's discovery of a major mining site in western Australia resulted in the first month's leap in share price. Mining in general, an inherently risky business, had been especially healthy and profitable during Australia's "long boom" since the end of World War II. Across the country, growth was strong, and unemployment and inflation were low. The mining sector expanded rapidly, as venture capital was increasingly available to fund explorations of the vast continent and its many natural resources.

From the 1950s to the time of Poseidon's nickel find, fortunes had already been made from a succession of explorations—the Mount Tom Price iron mine, the Bass Strait oil fields, the Weipa bauxite mine, and the Mary Kathleen uranium mine. From 1958 to 1968, the ASX All Mining Index, tracking the performance of mining stocks on the Australian Exchange, experienced an average growth of 25 percent per year. The price of nickel was spiraling almost out of control at the time of the Poseidon find, nearly tripling from January 1968 to October 1969. The company had been doing poorly in recent years, accounting for its low share price at the time of the discovery. The mere announcement on September 29, 1969, that nickel had been found, with no indication of how big the find was, was enough to more than double the price of the stock in one day. The big jump came after October 1, 1969, when Poseidon's directors announced that the find was a major one.

Poseidon's previous struggles may have contributed to the speculative bubble that followed. A minor company suddenly faced with a windfall after years of fruitless exploration made for a good story—and good stories capture the public's imagination and excite speculation. The ASX All Mining Index leaped 44 percent from October to December on the strength of Poseidon's performance and the general excitement over Australian mining; other companies took out exploration leases near Poseidon's. But hard information about the quantity and quality of the nickel find was difficult to come by. Prices rose so quickly that Poseidon's more detailed drilling report on November 19, 1969, did not affect already inflated share prices. There was still no reasonable estimate of how much or how good the ore was, other than it constituted "a major find."

The Poseidon bubble, like many others, took on a life of its own. The rising cost of nickel propelled prices in the early weeks, which only began declining back to more reasonable levels after the November peak. Poseidon broke $100 per share, then $200. Even more remarkable was the rise in share prices for mining companies that had not made any new finds. As long as they were in the nickel business and had a lease to drill near Windarra, the location of Poseidon's find, investors were interested. The value of the Poseidon find itself was still uncertain, but speculators assumed the entire area was rich in nickel, with plenty for everyone. New companies found buyers for their stock just by declaring an intent to drill near Windarra, even before any prospecting had been done.

Shares of the Tasminex Mining Company rose from $2.80 to $16.80 in two trading days, based on rumors that it had found a nickel site. The stock price rose as high as $96 after the publication of an interview with the company chairman about Tasminex's high hopes. Tasminex never did find nickel, and the company chairman sold his shares before the price fell.

Nevertheless, brokerage houses continued to recommend Poseidon stock, with a London-based broker suggesting in early 1970 that as much as $382 per share would be a reasonable price for a stock that had sold for $0.80 barely three months earlier. Poseidon share prices peaked in February 1970, after which both it and the ASX All Mining Index began to fall rapidly. Just as the skyrocketing prices had been only tenuously connected to any real cause, there is no clear indication of what caused the fall. When some investors started selling, others followed. Given the number and magnitude of assumptions inherent in investors' behavior during the bubble, it was inevitable that confidence would eventually fall. Continuing to buy Poseidon and other Australian mining stocks required that an investor believe the price of nickel would remain high (despite two temporary events— that had inflated the price—the Vietnam War and the strike in Canada), as well as that the Poseidon find was a major one or that other companies would make significant finds, and that the ore was of high quality. Moreover, because mining is not a fast-paced activity, these assumptions would have to be held for a long time while waiting for the companies to turn profits. As it turned out, none of the assumptions proved correct.

The price of nickel drifted down to reasonable levels. Few other mining companies discovered nickel in Windarra. And Poseidon's own find did not actually produce any of the ore until 1974, five years after the bubble. Even at that, the find turned out to be smaller than expected, yielding relatively low-quality nickel ore that cost more to mine than the company had planned. The mine was soon taken over by Western Mining, and basically broke even over the course of its lifetime.

Poseidon, at least, had a viable mine; many of the other companies in the bubble never even had mining leases.

After the bubble burst, enough investors had lost money that the Australian government took up an investigation. It came to the conclusion that trading activity in the country's stock exchanges had too little oversight and too little regulation. The Poseidon bubble thus led to a reform of Australia's securities trading regulations over the course of the 1970s.

Bill Kte'pi

See also: Asset-Price Bubble; Australia; Commodity Markets.

Further Reading

Adamson, Graeme. *Miners and Millionaires: The First One Hundred Years of the People, Markets and Companies of the Stock Exchange in Perth, 1889–1989.* Perth, Australia: Australian Stock Exchange, 1989.

Chancellor, Edward. *Devil Take the Hindmost: A History of Financial Speculation.* New York: Farrar, Straus and Giroux, 1999.

Kindleberger, Charles P. *Manias, Panics, and Crashes: A History of Financial Crises.* Hoboken, NJ: John Wiley & Sons, 2000.

Post Keynesian Theories and Models

Post Keynesian theory explicitly develops concepts of British economist John Maynard Keynes's "general theory" that often were only implicitly or obliquely mentioned in Keynes's revolutionary 1936 book, *The General Theory of Employment, Interest and Money.* Moreover, Post Keynesians explain why early post–World War II economists who labeled themselves as "Neoclassical Synthesis Keynesians" and their student progeny who call themselves "New Keynesians" never understood Keynes's analytical framework. Instead, these "Keynesians" merely adopted classical theory, larded it with some Keynesian words, and attributed unemployment to the truculence of workers who would not let the market wage decline suf-

ficiently to generate full employment. Of course, this sticky wage argument was the backbone of nineteenth-century classical economists' explanation of the significant unemployment observed to occur in the world in which we live.

Keynes's paradigm-shifting economic text, *The General Theory of Employment, Interest and Money,* attempted to overthrow orthodox classical theory, which said that rigid wage rates and government policies interfering with the operation of a "free" market caused recessions and depressions. Keynes claimed that he provided a revolutionary analytical way for economists to think about the economy.

Perhaps Keynes's most radical assertion was that the three axioms underlying classical theory were not applicable to a modern, money-using, entrepreneurial economic system. Once Keynes challenged the three fundamental classical theory axioms, his resulting economic theory could explain the operation of a money-using, market-oriented capitalist economy. However, these three classical axioms remain central to today's mainstream economic thinking. Only Post Keynesians have discarded them.

Rejected Axioms of Classical Economics

An axiom is defined as a statement accepted as a universal truth, without proof, that is used as the basis for argument. The classical axioms that Keynes rejected are (1) the *ergodic axiom,* which, in essence, assumes that past history is a reliable basis for predicting future outcomes; (2) the *gross substitution axiom,* which asserts that every item on the market is a good substitute for every other item on the market; and (3) the *neutral money axiom,* which asserts that any increases in the quantity of money will always be inflationary. (More technical definitions of these axioms are given below.)

Only if these three axioms are rejected can a model be developed that has the following characteristics: (1) money matters in the long and short run; that is, money affects real decision making, as the economic system moves from an irrevocable past to an uncertain future; (2) economic decision makers recognize that they make important, costly decisions in uncertain conditions where reliable rational calculations regarding the future are impossible; (3) monetary contracts are a human institution developed to efficiently organize time-consuming production and exchange processes in modern capitalist economies, with the money-wage contract being the most ubiquitous of these contracts; and (4) unemployment, rather than full employment, and an arbitrary and inequitable distribution of income, are outstanding faults in a modern, market-oriented, capitalist economy. These faults can be corrected only when government policies, in cooperation with private initiatives, are aimed at eliminating these flaws in our economic system.

The ergodic axiom postulates that all future events are actuarially certain—that is, the future can be accurately forecasted from the analysis of existing past and current market data. Consequently, income earned today at any employment level is entirely spent either on produced goods for today's consumption or on buying investment goods that will be used to produce goods for the (known) future consumption of today's savers. In other words, orthodox theory presumes if the future is knowable (i.e., ergodic) then all current income is always immediately spent on producibles, so there is never a lack of effective demand for things that industry can produce at full employment. The proportion of income that households save does not affect aggregate demand for producibles; it only affects the composition of demand (and production) between consumption and investment goods. Thus, savings creates jobs in the capital goods–producing industries just as much as consumption spending creates jobs in the consumer goods–producing industries. Moreover, in this classical theory, savings is more desirable than consumption since the resulting assumed investment projects have positive returns such that, when financed by today's savers, today's investment will automatically increase tomorrow's total income.

In Post Keynesian theory, however, people recognize that the future is uncertain (nonergodic) and cannot be reliably predicted. Consequently, people decide on how much of their current income they will spend on consumer goods and how much they will save. Current savings are then used to purchase various liquid assets. These liquid assets are, in essence, time-machine vehicles that savers use to store and transport their saved purchasing power to an indefinite future date. Unlike savers in the future, known (ergodic) classical system, real-world savers in a world with an uncertain (nonergodic) future do not know exactly what they will buy or what contractual obligations they will incur at any specific future date.

In an entrepreneurial economy, money is that thing that discharges all legal contractual obligations, and money contracts are used to organize production and exchange activities. Accordingly, the possession of money—and other liquid assets that have small carrying costs and can be easily resold for money in a well-organized and orderly market—means that savers possess the liquidity to enter into money contracts to demand products whenever they desire in the uncertain future and/or in order to meet a future contractual commitment that they have not foreseen. Liquid assets are also savers' security blankets, protecting them from the possibility of hard times. For as Nobel Prize winner John Hicks stated, income recipients know that they "do not know just what will happen in the future."

Keynes argued that money (and all other liquid assets) have two essential properties: First, money (and all liquid assets) does not grow on trees, and hence labor cannot be hired to harvest money when income earners reduce consumption to save more and thereby increase their demand to hold money or other liquid assets. Accordingly, the decision to consume versus to save income in the form of liquid assets, including money, is a choice between an employment-inducing demand for producible goods and a non-employment-inducing demand for liquid assets, including money. When savings increase at the expense of the demand for consumption producibles, sales and employment decline in the consumption-production sector without any offsetting employment increases in the money- (or liquidity-) providing sector.

Second, Keynes argued that liquid asset prices will increase as new savings increases the demand for such assets relative to the supply of liquid assets. Because of high carrying and high resale costs, reproducible durables are not gross substitutes for liquid assets as a means of storing contractual settlement power to be carried forward into an uncertain future. Consequently, since producibles are not good substitutes for storing liquidity, higher liquid asset prices do not divert this demand for liquidity in the form of nonproducibles into a demand for producibles. If, however, the gross substitution axiom were applicable, then producibles would be gross substitutes for nonproducible liquid assets. Accordingly, if savings increases the relative price of liquid, nonproducible assets, then savers would be induced to substitute producibles, thus inducing entrepreneurs to hire more workers, and there would never be a lack of effective demand for the products of industry.

In the real world, however, investment spending is constrained solely by entrepreneurs' expectations of profits, relative to their cost of obtaining financing and funding to pay for real investment in plants and equipment. If the future is uncertain, these expectations of future profits cannot depend on a statistically reliable calculation of future profit income. Instead, these expectations depend on the "animal spirits"—of a spontaneous (entrepreneurial) desire for action rather than inaction, as Keynes wrote in *The General Theory*. In an economy where money is created by banks, if entrepreneurs have high animal spirits and therefore borrow from banks to finance the production of additional working-capital goods, then the resulting increases in the quantity of money as entrepreneurs borrow to expand production will be associated with increasing employment and output. The classical neutral money axiom, however, asserts that if the money supply increases in response to borrowing from the banking system, this increase in the money quantity will not alter the level of employment or output. In other words, the classical neutral money axiom asserts that if banks create additional money in response to any increased demand for borrowing, the result must be that this increase in money will be more money chasing the same level of output, thereby causing prices to inevitable increase—inflation.

Finally, in the political realm, classical economists especially associate this neutral money axiom with any government borrowing (deficit spending). Thus, government deficit spending causes money to be "printed." This newly printed money means, given the neutral money axiom, that more money is chasing fewer goods. Consequently, classical theory's assertion that financing government deficits by increasing the money supply always creates inflation is merely an assertion, and not a proven fact.

Anti-Inflation Policy

Post Keynesians identify two types of inflation and therefore suggest two different policies to fight inflation. These two types of inflation are (1) commodity inflation and (2) incomes inflation.

Commodity inflation is identified with rising prices of durable, standardized commodities such as agricultural products, oil, and so forth, that are typically traded on well-organized public markets where the prices are reported daily in the media. These markets tend to have prices associated with specific dates of delivery—either today (spot market price) or on a specific date in the future. The markets for future delivery are typically limited to dates only a few months in the future. Since most commodities take a significant amount of time to be produced, the supply available for these near-future dates is relatively fixed by existing stocks plus semifinished products expected to be available on a specific future date. If there is a sudden, unexpected increase in demand or fall in supply for a future date, this change will inflate the market price for future delivery. The proper anti–commodity inflation policy is for the government to maintain a buffer stock, that is, a commodity inventory that can be moved into or out of the market to prevent the commodity market price from inflating (or deflating). For example, the U.S. government maintains a Strategic Petroleum Reserve (SPR) in caves on the Gulf Coast. During "Desert Storm," the short Iraq war in 1991, in order to prevent disruption of oil supplies from causing commodity inflation, the U.S. government made oil from the SPR available to the market. It is estimated that this prevented the price of gasoline at the pump from increasing by 30 cents per gallon.

Incomes inflation is associated with rising money costs of production per unit of goods produced. These rising money costs of production reflect increases in money income to owners of inputs used in the production process that are not offset by increases in productivity. Post Keynesians advocate anti–incomes inflation policy that would limit wage and other money income payments to increases in productivity. Such a policy is called an "incomes policy," and if effective, it will assure stable prices without depressing the economy and creating any unemployment. For example, the Kennedy administration in the early 1960s instituted a wage-price guideline policy that used publicity to limit union wage demands and/or industrial profit increases per unit of output.

On the other hand, the conventional wisdom that accepts the neutral money axiom believes inflation is caused by government printing money. Consequently, it is argued that the central bank should institute a tight monetary policy to fight incomes inflation. The central bank's tight money policy can be successful only if the resulting rise in interest rates and so forth reduces aggregate demand sufficiently to seriously threaten profits in the private sector of the economy. The resulting slack in production and increased unemployment are expected to stiffen the backbone of entrepreneurs sufficiently so that they will refuse to agree to any money wage and/or other production costs increases. In other words, the conventional wisdom of anti-inflationary policy involves depressing the economy sufficiently to constrain inflationary income demands. The cost is a large increase in unemployment and loss in profits and output.

Employment

In accepting Keynes's ideas, Post Keynesians reject the classical neutral money axiom when they argue that changes in the money supply due to borrowing from banks to finance the production of investment goods affects the level of employment and output in both the short run and the long run.

In arguing that his "general theory" is more applicable to the world of experience than is classical economic theory, Keynes wrote: "The classical theorists resemble Euclidean geometers in a non-Euclidean world who, discovering that in experience straight lines apparently parallel often meet, rebuke the lines for not keeping straight—as the only remedy for the unfortunate collisions which are occurring. Yet, in truth, there is no remedy except to throw over the axiom of parallels and to work out a non-Euclidean geometry. Something similar is required today in economics."

In the above analogy, unemployment is the "unfortunate collision," while "rebuking the lines" is classical economic theory's claim that unemployment is due to workers' refusing to accept a market wage low enough to encourage firms to hire all workers, that is, to create full employment. In other words, classical theory blames the unemployed victims of unemployment for the problem.

At the time that Keynes wrote, not all of the three fundamental axioms of classical theory were explicitly recognized by professional economists. Consequently, Keynes implicitly threw out these three classical axioms, without knowing and therefore specifically spelling out which classical axioms were required to be overthrown to provide the equivalent of a non-Euclidean economics for the world of experience in which the unemployed are not responsible for the unemployment that occurs.

As a result, when, immediately after World War II, economists such as Paul Samuelson and his followers wanted to explain Keynes's economic analysis, Samuelson's "Neoclassical Synthesis Keynesianism" was based on the same three classical axioms that Keynes had implicitly thrown over. Accordingly, these economists who called themselves "Keynesians" had no real theoretical connection to Keynes's general theory. Instead, these Keynesians explained unemployment to be the result of labor unions and workers refusing to accept a market wage that assured full employment and/or government setting a minimum wage above the full-employment market wage and/or monopolistic firms refusing to lower product prices to more competitive levels in order to sell all that a fully employed labor force could produce.

The fundamental contribution of Post Keynesians, then, was to explicitly explain which axioms Keynes had to overthrow to provide a general theory of employment, interest, and money applicable to the world we live in. In this world or experience, money, money contracts, and the desire for liquidity are the major institutional forces that make the real economic world go round. The classical theory that still dominates mainstream economic thought and policy recommendations, whether labeled Neoclassical Synthesis Keynesian, "New Keynesian," classical theory, efficient market theory, rational expectations theory, or something else, on the other hand, is still constructed on a foundation of the three classical axioms that Keynes overthrew. Consequently the mainstream economic theory that has dominated economics analysis and policy decisions both domestically and internationally in recent decades created economic conditions that resulted in the so-called "Great Recession" that began in 2007.

Why? If, for example, the future were knowable (ergodic), then all decision makers today would "know" their future income stream and future contractual outlays. Consequently, in an ergodic world, no rational person today would enter into a mortgage contract unless they knew they could meet all future mortgage contractual payments. Nor would anyone have bought a house with a mortgage loan since today many a homeowner is "underwater"—that is, the outstanding mortgage debt exceeds today's market price for the house. Consequently, classical theory argues that government should remove all restrictions and government protection of consumers on mortgage loans,

credit cards, banking lending policies, and so on. As a result, beginning in the 1970s, financial market deregulation was adopted by most governments.

Today, most "experts" agree that a basic cause of the Great Recession was the large number of defaults in the subprime mortgage market, and that the inability of the economy to recover is in large part due to many homeowners still "underwater" and therefore spending less on goods and services. Yet, such an outcome would not be possible in a classical world in which the future was known ergodically.

When Keynes labeled his analysis a general theory, he meant it was more general than classical theory because it was based on fewer restrictive axioms. When the three classical axioms are added to Keynes's general theory, classical theory becomes a special case of Keynes's more general theory. Keynes explicitly notes that "the postulates [axioms] of classical theory are applicable to a special case only and not to the general case. . . . Moreover, the characteristics of this special case assumed by classical theory happen not to be those of the economic society in which we actually live, with the result that its teaching is misleading and disastrous if we attempt to apply it to the facts of experience."

The policy prescriptions of Keynes's general theory are quite different from the "special-case" conventional classical theory wisdom of mainstream economists as far as policies to create a fully employed society and encourage a prosperous global economic system without causing inflation.

Paul Davidson

See also: Galbraith, John Kenneth; Keynes, John Maynard; Keynesian Business Model; Neo-Keynesian Theories and Models.

Further Reading

Davidson, Paul. *The Keynes Solution: The Path to Global Economic Prosperity.* New York: Palgrave Macmillan, 2009.

Hicks, John R. *Economic Perspectives.* Oxford: Clarendon Press, 1977.

Keynes, John Maynard. *The General Theory of Employment, Interest and Money.* New York: Harcourt, Brace, 1936.

Poverty

Poverty is generally defined as the condition of being unable to afford the basic necessities of life, including food, potable water, clothing, and shelter. Beyond lacking the absolute minimum to keep body and soul together on a daily basis, the term becomes trickier to define. Depending on the general standard of living and social values in a particular country, the inability to obtain a primary education and basic health care for oneself and one's family, for example, might also be counted among the defining characteristics.

Poverty is also time and space specific. What constitutes poverty for one generation in a particular society might not for another. Indoor plumbing was a luxury in the nineteenth century but is considered a necessity to even the most impoverished household in the United States in the twenty-first. More importantly, poverty is defined very differently in the developed and developing worlds. Someone living in a two-room shack with electricity, running water, and enough to eat, but little else, might live well above the poverty line in Africa but would be considered extremely impoverished in Europe or North America.

Measuring Poverty

For much of the developing world, the World Bank—the world's leading multilateral development institution—sets the income threshold not to be in poverty at $1.25 per person, per day. An income below that level makes it almost impossible to provide the basic necessities of life, including 2,000 to 2,500 calories for an adult male per day. By this standard, about 1.4 billion people—or one in four persons in the developing world—live below the poverty level. At the same time, the U.S. government officially sets the poverty threshold for an individual at $10,991 per person per year—or about $30 per day—and $22,025 for a family of four in 2008. While the U.S. standard has been updated regularly to account for inflation since it was first conceived in the early 1960s, it remains a controversial figure, since it is based on what many experts regard as an outmoded premise.

Specifically, the figure assumes that people spend about one-third of their income on food, which was the case for poor people in the early 1960s. Today, however, with dramatically lower food prices in the United States, the figure is closer to one-sixth. In other words, the government assumes that if the head of a household of four is spending a $7,341.67 a year on food (one-third of $22,025), the household is living right on the poverty line. In reality, however, if food represents one-sixth of the average poor person's budget, then a person really needs six times that amount, or $44,050 annually, to lift a family of four out of poverty. Moreover, with exceptions for costlier Alaska and Hawaii, the government does not differentiate between locations, even though data and common sense point to the fact that it is far more expensive to live in urban areas than in small towns. (Moreover, the government measures income at pre-tax levels—even though the money going for taxes cannot be used to buy food, shelter, and other necessities—and does not include various governments benefits, such as food stamps and childcare subsidies, that help families obtain necessities.)

Because poverty is so difficult to define in absolute terms, most scholars argue for a relative definition. In 1995, the National Academy of Sciences argued that poverty should be defined in income-relative terms. That is, a family would be considered poor if its household income falls below 50 percent of the median household income. This definition, of course, makes poverty a phenomenon independent of the overall business cycle. Thus, as economies expand and prosperity increases—likewise the median income—the number of poor people will not change significantly; nor would times of contraction, when median income falls, bring a change in the number living in poverty.

In these relative terms, poverty is defined as inequality of income. To measure this, as opposed to absolute deprivation, economists use a statistical tool known as the Gini coefficient. On the Gini scale of inequality, a zero represents absolute equality (everyone in the measured group has exactly the same amount of income), while a one represents absolute inequality (one person in the group has all of the income). Based on data from 2007–2008, the United Nations determined that the country with the most equally distributed income was Denmark, with a Gini coefficient of .247, while Namibia was the most unequal, with .743. The United States fell in roughly in the middle of all countries, with a Gini coefficient of .408, though this placed it among the most income-unequal of industrialized nations. Thus, measuring poverty in relative terms puts the United States at a high level of poverty among industrialized nations.

In the course of U.S. history, long-term declines in poverty generally have coincided with periods of rising equality—whether caused by rising levels of productivity in the private sector or by government initiative—regardless of fluctuations in the business cycle. Thus, American inequality and poverty levels fell dramatically in the period between 1929 and 1975, while poverty levels have gone up slightly between the mid-1970s and the late 2000s, a period of greatly increased income inequality.

Causes and Cures

Perhaps even more difficult than measuring poverty is determining its causes, which can differ widely among individuals and nations. For impoverished nations, many factors play a critical role: a poor natural environment, overpopulation, war, corruption, misguided government policies, or a colonial past. Whatever the combination of causes, poverty is typically a vicious cycle for poor nations. Where people have little income, they save even less, if at all. The lack of savings means a dearth of capital to invest in equipment and human resources (education and health care). The lack of investment means that productivity remains low, which, in turn, means that people cannot be paid more and thus cannot save, perpetuating the cycle.

Nevertheless, many countries in the post–World War II era have lifted themselves out of poverty, rising from developing-world to developed-world status. The best-known examples are found in East Asia. In 1981, the region was the world's poorest, with some 80 percent of the population living below $1.25 a day (in inflation-adjusted terms). By the late 2000s, the figure had fallen to well under 20 percent. Meanwhile, sub-Saharan Africa has languished, with about 50 percent of its population living in poverty during the early 1980s and up to 2009.

While each nation has a unique history to explain its climb out of poverty, the key factor is breaking the vicious cycle of low productivity, low savings, and low investment through large investments in education and basic health care. By doing so, governments lift productivity and savings, which in turn increases investment. With rising levels of productivity come rising profit margins, often because wages lag due to the pro-business, anti-union policies of the government. Higher profit margins encourage foreign investment as well, contributing to incomes, savings, and domestic investment.

The causes of poverty among cohorts of the population in relatively wealthy nations have many causes as well: discrimination, high unemployment, inadequate education and health care, crime, substance abuse, and what some sociologists refer to as a "culture of poverty," whereby children growing up in poor families with a high dependency on government relief tend to end up in the same situation when they become adults. In recent years, there has been an effort in the United States and other industrialized countries to break that culture of poverty by shifting from cash transfers in the form of welfare to in-kind vouchers for education and childcare, as well as the old standby of food stamps. In addition, tougher work requirements have been imposed in the hopes that this would create a home environment in which work, rather than idleness, becomes the cultural norm. An especially popular program in the United States is the Earned Income Tax Credit, which provides refundable tax credits to people whose wages alone are unable to lift them out of poverty, the so-called "working poor."

James Ciment and Donna M. Anderson

See also: Employment and Unemployment; Income Distribution; Wealth.

Further Reading

Burtless, Gary. "What Have We Learned About Poverty and Inequality? Evidence from Cross-National Analysis." *Focus* 25:1 (2007): 12–17.

Danziger, Sheldon, and Robert Haveman, eds. *Understanding Poverty.* Cambridge, MA: Harvard University Press, 2001.

Fisher, Gordon M. "The Development and History of the Poverty Thresholds." *Social Security Bulletin* 55:4 (1992): 3–14.

Harrington, Michael. *The Other America: Poverty in the United States.* New York: Collier Books, 1994.

Moffitt, Robert. "Four Decades of Antipoverty Policy: Past Developments and Future Directions." *Focus* 25:1 (2007): 39–44. Madison, WI: Institute for Research on Poverty.

Sachs, Jeffrey D. *The End of Poverty: Economic Possibilities for Our Time.* New York: Penguin, 2005.

Schiller, Bradley R. *The Economics of Poverty and Discrimination.* 10th ed. Upper Saddle River, NJ: Pearson/Prentice Hall, 2008.

Price Stability

Price stability refers to the condition in which inflation is low and average prices remain relatively unchanged for a given period of time even though some prices rise and others fall. Since the beginning of the 1990s, price stability was the primary objective of monetary policy in many countries. Although central banks are not always explicit about what exactly price stability means to them, most seem to have accepted that inflation is considered low when it is kept at about a 2 percent year-over-year increase in the average price of a representative basket of goods and services such as food, clothing, housing, and other items that typical consumers buy. For this purpose, the most commonly used measure of inflation is the consumer price index (CPI). Other measures include the producer price index (PPI), which gives the average change in prices received by producers for their products. The GDP deflator, yet another widely used indicator, measures the average change in the price of all the goods and services included in the gross domestic product (GDP), as opposed to the CPI, which omits some goods and services included in the deflator while including others not in the deflator.

Causes of Inflation

Inflation is the sustained increase in a price index, often the CPI, over a period of time. Therefore, economists do not consider a one-time increase in prices when calculating inflation; increases must be continuous and must affect the general or average price of items included in the basket—and not only a few items. For instance, the inflation rate would be zero if increases in the prices of some commodities were offset by decreases in the prices of other items in the basket. Thus, even if individual consumers experience inflation when the goods they happen to purchase cost more, the overall inflation is low if the basket of goods includes items with small or no price increases.

This discrepancy is only one of many limitations on the measure of inflation. All measures of inflation must confront the limitation of changing goods and services over time. As new products are introduced, for example DVD players, the inflation measure needs to include items that simply did not exist in a prior measurement period. In addition, altered buying habits—either because of new tastes or because of higher or lower prices—mean that the relative weight given to products needs to change. Economists take these complications into account, making adjustments that are sometimes controversial. Even small adjustments, compounded over time, can alter measurement of important economic statistics related to the business cycle. For example, disagreement about whether or not the typical U.S. worker is better off today than in the past is based on which inflation measurement in used.

Although there is general agreement among economists about what causes inflation in theory, there often are debates about what has caused inflation in practice. Economists agree that inflation can occur when there is an increase in the aggregate demand (or total spending) relative to the productive capacity of the economy. Increase in demand can be caused by various factors, such as an increase in government spending, a fall in the rate of interest, a cut in the income tax rate, or an improvement in business and consumer confidence. Demand side inflation can also occur when, according to the common expression, "too much money is chasing too few goods." This may result from an increase in the money supply by the central bank, which led the Nobel Prize–winning economist Milton Friedman to remark, "Inflation is always and everywhere a monetary phenomenon."

Some economists point to the pricing methods of monopolistic firms as a source of inflation. A standard method used in pricing products is known as "markup pricing," in which firms add a profit margin to their cost of production. If the cost of production rises, firms try to preserve their profit margins and pass on the increase to customers. If markets were sufficiently competitive, no firm would dare attempt increasing its prices for fear of losing customers or market share. Because firms do have power over the market, however, they often end up increasing prices, and buyers generally accept living with inflation.

Consequences of Inflation

Why is price stability desirable? Most economists and policy makers conclude that inflation has negative consequences for an economy, including the arbitrary redistribution of assets and distorted decision making. The most obvious negative effect of high inflation is on people with fixed incomes that do not appreciate with rising prices. Thus, some retirees (but not Social Security recipients), people depending on social welfare programs, and workers without cost-of-living adjustments, lose to inflation. Overall economic growth can be slowed by inflation if it creates uncertainty for consumers and investors, thereby making it difficult to plan for long-term projects. There is debate about the impact of inflation on undesirable speculative activities. Some economists maintain that inflation tends to encourage speculative activities at the expense of real investments that expand the productive capacity of the economy. On the other hand, Nobel laureate James Tobin argues that inflation lowers the return on monetary assets relative to real assets and that the reaction of investors is to hold more of their assets in real

capital projects. Finally, borrowers benefit from high inflation because the real rate of interest, the interest rate adjusted for inflation, is lower than the nominal interest rate, the amount they actually pay. If the cost of borrowing is lower (due to high inflation), consumers may buy more houses, cars, and other assets. Firms then have the incentive to supply these items, which benefits the whole economy.

Policy Options

Most central banks have made inflation targeting an essential element of their monetary policy. The inflation target is usually set at an annual rate of 2 percent, achieved through a combination of monetary policies. If the aggregate demand is considered too strong, the central bank will raise interest rates in order to depress demand and keep inflation from rising. Similarly, when demand is weak and there is a risk of deflation, the central bank will lower interest rates to stimulate the economy. In this way, many of the recessions in recent times appear to have been engineered by policy makers.

Because it generally takes a long time for an economy to recover from a recession, some economists argue against what they regard as an obsessive preoccupation with inflation at the expense of employment. They argue that full employment should be the overriding objective of economic policy, and propose models that show that full employment is compatible with price stability. In this view, relatively low levels of inflation, say below 4 percent, are an acceptable trade-off for the more devastating impact of unemployment and slow economic growth. In addition, some economists maintain that low levels of inflation are desirable because they give business firms flexibility in setting wages and salaries. They point out that cutting an employee's pay could lead to disgruntlement and lower productivity. However, a bit of inflation allows employers to give all employees a nominal wage increase while actually cutting the real pay of poorly performing workers by raising their pay less than the inflation rate.

Galloping Inflation and Hyperinflation

When inflation rises to excessive rates, however, great damage can be done to an economy. Galloping inflation, the informal term economists and policy makers use in referring to rates in the 20–1,000 percent per year range, can significantly distort economic behavior. Galloping inflation occurred in a number of Latin American economies from the 1970s to the 1990s, where individuals tended to hold onto minimal sums of the national currency, just enough for daily purchases. The rest was sold for hard currencies; this capital flight caused local financial markets to collapse, making it difficult for businesses to access capital for operations and expansion. During galloping inflation, consumers also spend their money rapidly on larger purchases, and the increased demand fuels further inflation. Contracts get written with prices hikes in mind, making it difficult to calculate the costs involved in fulfilling contracts, thereby slowing business activity.

Even worse is hyperinflation, where the value of the currency virtually collapses over a very short period of time, usually a few months or years. The most famous case of hyperinflation was in Germany in 1922 and 1923, where inflation reached 10 billion percent. Unable to raise taxes enough to meet its war reparations commitments, the German government opted instead to inflate its way out of the crisis by printing money in unsustainable amounts. As the inevitable hyperinflation kicked in, consumers dumped their money as quickly as they could while wages climbed precipitously. Price and wage instability created gross economic inequities and distortions, which left workers in poverty and many businesses, particularly small ones, reduced to penury and bankruptcy. Many historians cite this bout of hyperinflation as a prime factor in the rise of the authoritarian Nazi Party, which came to power a decade later. A more recent example is Zimbabwe, where the government's policy of printing quantities of money far in excess of what the economy can support has led to a collapse in production and exports, as well as a mass exodus of people to neighboring countries in search of work and economic stability.

Hassan Bougrine

See also: Deflation; Inflation; Monetary Policy.

Further Reading

Mosler, Warren. B. "Full Employment and Price Stability." *Journal of Post Keynesian Economics* 20:2 (1997–1998): 176–182.

Wray, L. Randall. "The Social and Economic Importance of Full Employment" In *Introducing Macroeconomic Analysis: Issues, Questions and Competing Views*, ed. Hassan Bougrine and Mario Seccareccia, 219–228. Toronto: Emond Montgomery, 2009.

———. *Understanding Modern Money: The Key to Full Employment and Price Stability.* Aldershot, UK: Edward Elgar, 1998.

Production Cycles

The production cycle for a firm is the period over which a product is created, or a service is provided, until payment is received from the customer. For example, a custom-furniture manufacturer, when responding to a customer order, will need to order materials and hire labor to manufacture the product. In this case, the production cycle begins at the moment that these materials and labor arrive on the scene, and it doesn't end until the product is finished and paid for. For a service organization such as a restaurant, purchases of food and materials used to provide meals, as well as the labor to prepare and serve the meals, all need to be in place prior to the commencement of operations. The production cycle begins when they are put in place. The end of the cycle occurs the moment the customers pay.

With the continued development of the Internet and fiber-optics communications infrastructure and related techniques, such as just-in-time production methods and bar-coding control of warehousing operations, the management of the operations cycle has become much more time efficient. The growing importance of service-based industries might also imply that operation cycles are becoming more compressed as services are less dependent on the flow from raw materials to final service. The modern science of operations management and financial management are devoted to understanding the nature of this cycle, forecasting and optimizing product and service flow, and minimizing costs and financial resources involved in the process.

Long-Term Production Cycles

There are still many important industries in the economy that will continue to experience very long production cycles. Organizations in the residential and nonresidential construction industry, for example, face very long production periods due to the nature of the business. Construction firms need to purchase and assemble land, seek zoning approvals from local governments, and install and connect to basic services like water, sewer, and roads before building construction can begin. Accurately forecasting demand is extremely difficult, and the timing of completion could unfortunately coincide with a downturn in the overall economy and slack demand.

Firms that manufacture large, complex capital goods such as aircraft and oceangoing ships also require substantial periods of time to design and manufacture products. If an increase in capacity to manufacture is required, a large-scale investment in plant and equipment will also add time to the production cycle. Firms that provide utilities (infrastructure) such as fiber-optic cable service are assembling right-of-way agreements and permits, and laying cable well in advance of any customer sales.

Such firms must live with the long time lags from project inception to receiving payments from customers. These time lags create considerable risk for the firm. Will future economic conditions support sales at a time when products or services are actually available? These risks tend to be attenuated or perhaps underappreciated upon the introduction of a new technology, or the early part of a business expansion when the outlook for the future is favorable and current sales are brisk. Decisions are made to proceed within an environment of optimism. Longer-term negative implications are not as readily apparent. These could include the possibility of a downturn in

the economy, changes in technology that might negatively affect the competitive advantage of the firm's product or service, and the consideration of marketplace impacts of potential overcapacity relative to demand.

Keynesian Economics and Production Cycles

The Keynesian aggregated-expenditures model captures this potential mismatch of planned activity versus results upon market delivery as the cause of cycles of expansion or contraction of the overall economy. The model starts with the plans of businesses (in the aggregate, over all businesses in the national economy) to produce at the beginning of the period. A production plan ensues that is based upon the best forecast of sales by management during the period. If this plan is realized by the end of the period, in that planned production equals sales, the process is repeated and the economy is in equilibrium. If planned production is less than sales, unintended inventory reduction occurs, and businesses plan to increase production the next period. If planned production is greater than sales, unintended inventory increases, and production plans are reduced for the next period. During the period, unanticipated changes in household income, business investment, government expenditure, and changes in foreign trade (aggregate demand) or changes in credit (banking) conditions can affect the end of period reconciliation of production and sales, and thus can change plans for the following period.

The uncertainty about the planning period, unanticipated changes in aggregate demand, and adjustments to production plans set up the potential for an economy to experience periods of economic expansion and contraction. Against this backdrop, government fiscal policy, monetary policy, credit and banking conditions, and technological change all interact to amplify or attenuate the natural fluctuations of production cycles.

Historical Examples of Production Cycles

Historically, the production cycle for capital goods and infrastructure, given its large size and impact on the economy, has contributed to upward and downward swings in economic activity. Early large-scale infrastructure projects such as the Erie Canal were commercially successful, but similar projects in the second wave of expansion after the 1830s were not, due to the competition of more efficient railroads, a new technology whose impact was unanticipated by those financing and building canals. State financial support was important during this second phase as states sought canal investment to promote economic development. Along with the growth of rail competition, excessive debt made the canal companies, and their state backers, subject to financial stress and bankruptcy during downturns in economic activity such as the economic depression or panic of 1837.

Economic theorists and historians have extensively examined the effect of large-scale expansion of the railroad network upon the long-term development of the U.S. economy. The network stretched approximately 30,000 miles (48,300 kilometers) and was confined to east of the Mississippi prior to 1860. By 1910, 351,000 miles (565,110 kilometers) of track were in place within a transcontinental system. Business-cycle theorist Joseph Schumpeter attributed a long upward swing in economic activity after 1875 to the railroads. Other economists, including Robert Fogel and Albert Fishlow, have argued that the quantitative impact of the railroads on the overall economy and the business cycle was relatively small (less than 5 percent of gross domestic product, or GDP). Additionally, economist Jeffrey Williamson maintained that the indirect effects of railroads, in terms of promoting technical change in industry and agriculture, induced higher rates of investment and productivity growth in the overall economy. Overcapacity, high debt, and poor management made many railroads vulnerable to economic downturns by the 1890s. Some 153 railroads filed for bankruptcy during the economic depression of 1893 alone.

Between 1899 and 1929, electric-power generation expanded by almost 300 percent. The new technology greatly increased manufacturing production efficiency over steam power methods and introduced a whole new lifestyle on the consumer side, based upon electric lighting and appliances in the home. Although the provision of electric power required large-scale investment in plant and equipment and supportive financing, electric power utility stocks were the most prized on Wall Street during the euphoria of the roaring 1920s economic expansion. These companies suffered some of the worst financial outcomes after the stock market crash in 1929 and the onset of the Great Depression from 1929 to 1932.

During the 1990s economic expansion, Internet technology companies and fiber-optic utilities that invested in the infrastructure to support the Internet played the same role. The industry is broadly defined as the telecommunications industry, which includes wholesale carriers of fiber-optic Internet traffic, such as AT&T and Verizon, and equipment manufacturers such as Cisco Systems. Business investment in new equipment and structures rose nearly one-third as a share of GDP from 1995 to 1999, as business had high and rising expectations of profits for the decade ahead from the applications of new technology. A large share of the investment increase appeared directly within the telecommunications industry. Its share of the economy doubled, providing two-thirds of the new jobs and one-third of the new investment during the expansion. The expansion of the network eventually outpaced the growth of Internet traffic. By 2002, the industry lost $2 trillion in market capitalization, and 25 major companies in the industry were in bankruptcy. By 2007, the imbalance between capacity and demand had in large part been attenuated. Falling prices for Internet service and productivity gains by equipment suppliers have stimulated demand such that capacity utilization levels similar to 2000 have been reattained.

Housing Boom and Bust

The expansion of the U.S. economy after November 2001, deceleration of growth since 2006, and decline since December 2007 have all in part been driven by the expansion and contraction of the production cycle for residential housing. The contribution of housing to the 2007–2009 recession has been particularly spectacular and unprecedented, with spillovers to the global economy.

The surge in demand and production actually started before the 2001 recession in the mid-1990s. The 2001 recession had just a minor impact on the strong upward trend in housing prices and production that ended in 2006 and 2007, respectively. The ensuing decline in prices and production from 2006–2007 was a major drag on the economy, which eventually went into a recession in December 2007. From the first quarter of 2006 through the first quarter of 2008, the decline in residential housing investment was the leading negative contributor to overall economic performance. During the economic expansion from 2002 through 2003, the expansion of residential housing investment was the second or third leading sector in contributing to growth, after household consumption and nonresidential investment. Note that part of the increase in household consumption was fueled by homeowners' refinancing or taking home equity lines of credit that extract part of the inflated equity in their homes due to the large increases in housing prices. The funds taken out could then be used for consumer purchases.

During 2005 and 2006, a number of events initiated an end to the long-term increase in housing construction and house prices. By August 2006, housing starts were down by 20 percent from the 2005 peak. Rising home prices reduced the number of households that could qualify for a mortgage to buy a home. Sales and inventories peaked at 1.1 million units and 536,000 units during 2006. Both series entered a steep decline until May of 2009, with sales and inventories falling to 342,000 and 292,000 respectively, levels comparable to the pre-expansion levels of the early

1990s. Prices surged in real terms by 33 percent over the cycle, from 1996 to 2006, and then declined by 15 percent to early 2009.

From 2006 to 2009, foreclosures on mortgages doubled, which made the reduction of inventories more difficult for the home-building industry. Many homebuyers, at the margin in terms of ability to make mortgage payments, were enticed by low initial interest-rate arrangements during the early 2000s that required refinancing at higher interest rates within three to five years. Many of these households were not able to pay the higher payments or to refinance because their homes had declined in value and they now owed more than what the homes were worth. Many were forced into foreclosure. Consequently, the home-building industry cut back new construction to extremely low levels. At the peak of the cycle during the first quarter of 2005, 448,000 units were started. By the first quarter of 2009, housing starts were reduced to 78,000 units, a reduction of 83 percent.

The financial crisis and recession, beginning in late 2007 in the United States but in 2008 in many other countries, are widely considered the worst since the Great Depression. The upward thrust of the business cycle during the early 2000s and the eventual collapse in late 2007 have their origins in the production cycle of residential housing and related factors and events.

A number of factors that were unique to the early 2000s contributed to the rapid growth in residential construction. There was a large flow of foreign saving into the United States, and financial institutions were eager for new customers, particularly in mortgage lending. Much of the lending was poorly managed in terms of evaluating client risk. Domestically, the supply of savings to the mortgage market was no longer constrained by regulations, as these had been removed by deregulation during the mid-1980s. Since that time, the housing-construction sector has had a much stronger and sustained impact on the overall economy.

On the demand side, the surge of demand actually started in 1997 and continued through the 2001 recession to peak in 2006. This has been linked to a strong upward shift in the long-term trend in labor productivity after 1997, which continued until a deceleration in 2004. Researchers have discovered a strong link between growth in labor productivity, growth in labor income, and a positive outlook by consumers, which spurred interest in investment in housing. A number of other factors supercharged this demand, including interest by households in second homes as an investment, and the availability of financing to lower-income households.

Innovations in financial markets also allowed for a freer flow of savings into mortgage markets. Since the 1990s, securitization of mortgages allowed financial institutions to package and sell mortgages and receive new funds to make more mortgages. Financial institutions no longer held mortgages to maturity. The negative side of this process was that the quality of the mortgage-backed securities was not known, and many investors relied on equally irrational ratings by services such as Moody's, Standard & Poor's, and Fitch Rating Services. Additionally, some of the buyers of mortgage-backed securities bought them for their higher yield, by borrowing less expensive funds in short-term financial markets, such as the commercial paper market. These negative aspects would eventually become influential in the collapse of the housing market, the market for new housing, and impacts on financial markets and the economy in general.

It was after September 2007, when home-price appreciation stopped, that events cascaded through financial markets to start a broader downturn in the overall economy. This negatively affected public confidence in the value of mortgage securities, which suddenly no longer had a viable market. Short-term sources of lending such as the commercial paper market virtually disappeared as suppliers of capital became concerned that borrowers holding mortgage-backed securities who were intending to refinance portfolios containing mortgage-backed securities might not be able to repay loans. This triggered the failure and near-failure of many prominent financial institutions. Credit markets froze and stock prices fell, initiat-

ing a national and global economic contraction. The U.S. economy officially entered a long-lasting recession in December 2007.

Production cycles have played an important role in the history of business cycles in the United States. Production cycles will continue to be important in the modern economy. With growing integration of the world economy, production cycles could take on new meaning domestically as foreign customers and suppliers participate in the cycle. International financial aspects such as exchange rates and interest rates will become involved in the interaction between the production cycle of an industry and the overall business cycle.

Derek Bjonback

See also: Inventory Investment; Manufacturing.

Further Reading

Bernanke, Ben. "Four Questions About the Financial Crisis." Board of Governors of the Federal Reserve System, April 14, 2009.

Emmons, William A. "Housing's Great Fall: Putting Households' Balance Sheets Together Again." *The Regional Economy*, Federal Reserve Bank of St. Louis, October 2009.

Gorton, Gary. "The Panic of 2007." Remarks delivered at the Federal Reserve Bank of Kansas City's Annual Economic Symposium, Jackson Hole, Wyoming, August 25, 2008.

Hughes, Jonathan, and Louis P. Cain. *American Economic History.* 8th ed. Boston: Addison-Wesley, 2010.

Kahn, James A. "Productivity Swings and Housing Prices." *Current Issues in Economics and Finance* 15:3 (July 2009): 1–8.

Katz, Jane. "Running in Cycles." *Regional Review*, Federal Reserve Bank of Boston, 14:2 (2nd/3rd quarter): 22–30.

McConnell, Campbell R., and Stanley L. Brue. *Economics: Principles, Problems, and Policies.* 17th ed. New York: McGraw-Hill/Irwin, 2006.

Miles, William. "Housing Investment and the U.S. Economy: How Have the Relationships Changed? *Journal of Real Estate Research* 31:3 (2009): 329–350.

Phelps, E.S. "The Boom and the Slump: A Causal Account of the 1990s/2000s and the 1920s/1930s." *Policy Reform* 7:1 (March): 3–19.

Samuelson, Robert J. "The Worrying Housing Bust." *Newsweek*, October 16, 2006.

Schoonover, Eric. "Wholesale Bandwidth: The Price Is Still Right." *Business Telecommuncations Review* (July 2007).

Schwiekart, Larry, and Lynne Doti. *American Entrepreneur.* New York: Amacom Books, 2010.

Stiglitz, Joseph E. *The Roaring Nineties.* New York: W.W. Norton, 2003.

Productivity

Productivity is a measure of how efficiently an economy produces goods and services. Labor productivity equals the national output divided by the number of workers needed to produce this output. Productivity growth, the percentage change in productivity from one year to another, measures the *additional* output per worker that we get this year compared to last year. A broader notion, total factor productivity, seeks to combine labor and capital inputs in the denominator of the productivity measure. Because of the difficulties adding together such diverse factors as labor and various kinds of capital, most economists focus on labor productivity.

National well-being mainly depends on productivity. The more each worker produces, the more a nation has to consume; and the faster productivity grows, the faster average living standards rise. To take a simple example, U.S. productivity grew around 3 percent per year from 1947 to 1973. Since then it has grown only 2 percent per year. Had productivity growth not fallen, the average standard of living in the U.S. would have been nearly 50 percent greater in 2010 than it actually was. Productivity growth can also help tame inflation by offsetting higher input costs with a need for fewer inputs by business firms.

There are three main economic approaches to analyzing the determinants of productivity and productivity growth—the neoclassical, the Post Keynesian, and the behavioral-social.

The Neoclassical Approach

The neoclassical approach emphasizes the importance of new technology, capital investment, and economic incentives. Capital investment takes place when firms expand, purchasing new plants and equipment. This contributes to productivity growth because new machinery helps workers produce more efficiently. In addition, when firms expand and invest, they usually adopt new technologies and therefore can produce goods more efficiently. Robots on an automobile assembly line make automobile workers more productive; a computerized inventory system that automatically orders goods when store shelves are low makes salespeople more productive.

According to the neoclassical view, savings are necessary for new investment to take place; they are what finance business investment. The rewards for saving are the interest, dividends, and capital gains earned from income that is saved rather than spent. For this reason, neoclassical economists support large incentives to save, particularly low taxes on these forms of income.

Other economic incentives also affect productivity growth. Incentives spur people to work hard so that they can become wealthier. If businesses and workers get to keep the gains from productivity growth, they will have greater incentives to produce more efficiently. This means that income taxes and taxes on corporate profits must be kept low.

Neoclassical economists also emphasize the need for labor discipline, to make sure people seek work rather than seeking to increase their leisure time. If lack of effort leads to low income, and maybe even poverty, there is a greater incentive to work hard. Consequently, government programs that help people survive with little or no income from work (such as unemployment insurance and food stamps) provide disincentives to work hard and be productive. In addition, these government programs must be financed, so they require a tax increase, further hurting productivity.

Finally, the neoclassical approach to productivity demands that inflation be kept firmly under control. Prices provide important information to the firm. They signal how to produce goods efficiently, and what resources are cheaper and better to use in production. During inflationary times, when all prices are rising, firms usually have a hard time figuring out the most efficient way to produce goods; as a result, productivity growth suffers. In addition, in times of inflation, managers must focus on controlling inflation and reducing costs rather than producing goods more efficiently.

The Post Keynesian Approach

The Post Keynesian approach emphasizes the importance of demand in promoting productivity growth. Three mechanisms operate here. The first comes from Adam Smith, who noted that goods can be produced more efficiently when firms can divide tasks, when individuals can specialize and develop expertise in narrow areas, and when machinery can be employed to assist workers. This is possible only when sales are large enough to justify capital investment and a restructuring of production. Robust sales let firms take advantage of economies of scale, or the gains that come from specialization and investment in new machinery.

A second reason why productivity depends on demand stems from the characteristics of a service economy. The productivity of a symphony orchestra does *not* depend on how fast musicians play a piece of music. Rather, its productivity (the value of its output divided by the number of players) depends on ticket sales. When the economy stagnates, people are reluctant to go to the symphony. The productivity of the orchestra thus falls. In a booming economy, the concert hall is full and the productivity of the orchestra grows rapidly. The orchestra may also produce CDs, a manufactured good. Again, demand determines productivity. The value of the output in this case depends on how many CDs get sold. When demand is high and sales boom, productivity soars; when people are not buying CDs, productivity declines.

What is true of the symphony orchestra is true of most service occupations and even industries that produce physical goods (as the CD example shows). The productivity of the sales force in a store, of real-estate agents, and of newspaper reporters all depend on sales. For example, when home sales fall due to poor macroeconomic conditions, the productivity of realtors declines.

Finally, productivity is just an average of the productivity in different industries. It will change with changes in the industrial composition of the nation. When demand shifts to goods and services produced by more productive economic sectors, productivity will increase. In an expanding economy, growing sectors are likely to be more productive and labor can shift there. Conversely, in a stagnant economy, people tend to stay put rather than move to more productive sectors.

In the eighteenth century, François Quesnay pressed French policy makers to support agriculture, believing this was most productive economic sector. He argued that greater demand for agricultural goods would move workers from other sectors to agriculture, where they would be more productive, and let French farmers employ more advanced production techniques to meet the additional demand. In the twentieth century, Nicholas Kaldor looked at the manufacturing sector as the most productive sector, but his argument parallels Quesnay—some sectors are more productive than other economic sectors, and the government should aid more productive economic sectors.

For these reasons, Post Keynesians look to government policies to promote full employment and support high-productivity industries as a means of boosting productivity.

The Behavioral-Social Approach

The final approach to productivity growth focuses less on macroeconomic factors and more on microeconomic ones such as relative pay and the treatment of workers. In this view, people matter; how they are treated and how they work together affect productivity. In many jobs, individual effort is at the discretion of each employee. Unhappy employees can reduce productivity to the detriment of all. They may even quit or have to be fired, requiring both time and effort in order to find and train a replacement.

Behavioral and social economists see the excellent employee relations at Japanese firms as a major reason for the large productivity growth in Japan after World War II. To improve productivity growth, they advocate following many Japanese labor practices—increased employee participation in firm decision making, rewarding all employees for improvements in productivity, treating employees better, and putting greater effort toward improving job satisfaction. In contrast, an adversarial relationship between management and workers, rather than a cooperative one, hurts productivity. Attempts to control workers more, to prevent and break unions, and to squeeze more out of each employee while reducing pay, benefits, and job security, will lead to lower productivity growth.

Behavioral and social economists also point out that people care about relative pay as much as absolute pay. The ultimatum game examines this issue. Two people have a fixed sum of money to divide. The first person can propose any division she chooses; the second person can only accept or reject this division. If accepted, each person receives the amount of money proposed by the first subject; if the division is rejected, each person receives nothing. From a neoclassical perspective, assuming rational and self-interested individuals, dividers should propose that they get almost all the money; the second subject should then accept this offer, rather than receiving nothing. In many experimental settings, individuals have played this game for real stakes. Daniel Kahneman found that dividers tend to make substantial offers and that most people reject unequal offers. These results have been replicated many times, including in cases where people rejected offers equal to one month's pay because they felt the split was unfair.

According to the behavioral approach, the ultimatum game better approximates what goes on in the real world than the neoclassical model of self-interested individuals. Large firms propose a division of the revenues they receive from selling goods. Workers can ill afford to reject this offer outright, since they need a job and an income to survive. But workers can *quasi-reject* a proposal they regard as unfair by working less hard, by sabotaging production and firm efficiency, and by causing firm resources to be used in setting rules and monitoring workers rather than in producing goods and services.

There is some empirical evidence that large pay differentials do hurt productivity when productivity depends on team effort. This is true for sports teams, academic departments, and business organizations.

An Assessment of the Theories

No consensus exists among economists regarding the most important determinants of productivity growth or the reasons why U.S. productivity growth slowed beginning in the 1970s. In addition, the main theories face great difficulty explaining the rise in productivity growth in 2009 during what has been called "the Great Recession." Since there was little new investment taking place and no new technology adopted into new production processes, the neoclassical perspective cannot help explain this change, though some economists argue that the productivity gains have something to do with employed workers carrying more of the load that had been performed by laid-off workers. The increase of productivity growth during this time goes counter to the Post Keynesian prediction. And since income inequality likely rose (as usually occurs during a recession), the behavioral perspective also fails to explain the anomaly.

Overall, these three theories, plus the many other hypotheses that have been put forward, explain but a small part of changes in productivity growth over time and across nations. Given the importance of productivity for national well-being, this area of economics will surely receive greater attention and study in the near future.

Steven Pressman

See also: Growth, Economic; Wages.

Further Reading

Altman, Morris. "A High Wage Path to Economic Growth and Development." *Challenge* 41 (January/February 1998): 91–104.

Blinder, Alan, ed. *Paying for Productivity: A Look at the Evidence.* Washington, DC: Brookings Institution, 1990.

Bloom, Matt. "The Performance Effects of Pay Dispersion on Individuals and Organizations." *Academy of Management Journal* 42 (February 1999): 25–40.

Gordon, David. *Fat and Mean.* New York: Free Press, 1996.

Levitan, Sar, and Diane Werneke. *Productivity: Problems, Prospects and Policies.* Baltimore, MD: Johns Hopkins University Press, 1984.

Pressman, Steven. *Fifty Major Economists.* 2nd ed. London and New York: Routledge, 2006.

———. "The Efficiency of Nations: A Post Keynesian Approach to Productivity." *Journal of Post Keynesian Economics*, forthcoming.

Profit

Profit is defined as the excess of revenues over costs. The term has roots in Latin words meaning to advance, progress, grow, or increase. It is generally applied in two different ways, one for economics and one for accounting.

Accounting Profit

Accounting profit is the difference (excess) between revenues and costs incurred. The costs are incurred during the process of bringing to market whatever goods and services are documented as a productive enterprise (whether by harvest, extraction, manufacture, or purchase) and represent expenditures on the components of delivered goods and/or services plus any operating or other expenses. These costs are typically divided into fixed costs and variable costs. Fixed costs do not change in proportion to production levels or sales and include items such as rent, salaries (of permanent, full-time workers), property taxes, and interest expense. Variable costs are those that increase directly in proportion to the number of units produced or sold; they can include outlays for goods sold, sales commissions, shipping charges, delivery charges, direct materials or supplies, and wages of part-time or temporary employees.

The revenue portion of the profit calculation is relatively straightforward. Revenues represent the value, in dollars, of the items sold. One potential ambiguity is the determination of which period the revenue should be recognized, or "booked." Costs, however, can be significantly more challenging to represent accurately, due to accounting definitions and guidelines. Items such as depreciation, amortization, and overhead are often open to interpretation and changing rules and regulations. Depreciation is defined as a deduction for the wearing down and/or obsolescence of capital, such as vehicles, buildings, and machinery, used in the production of an enterprise's goods and services. Amortization is the consumption of the value of assets—usually intangible ones, such as a patent or a copyright—over a period of time. Overhead expenses are production and nonproduction costs that are not readily traceable to specific jobs or processes. Overhead expenses encompass three general areas: indirect materials, indirect labor, and all other miscellaneous production expenses, such as taxes, insurance, depreciation, supplies, utilities, and repairs.

Accounting profit can be expressed by a few different calculations, each defined by a different technical term:

1. *Gross profit* is the amount received from sales minus the costs of goods included in those sales, called "Cost of Goods Sold." On a unit basis, this represents the profit margin represented by each item sold. The profit should be enough to pay for all other expenses associated with managing the business, such as salaries, advertising, depreciation, and interest, among others.

2. *Net profit* is the amount received from sales, minus all the expenses incurred in operating the business, including the opportunity cost of using all of the resources in their next best alternative. Thus, net profit includes the foregone wages and interest that an owner/investor could have earned in the next best alternative to this business. Net profit always represents a positive number. Net income is calculated

by the same method, but can be positive or negative. If it is negative, the term used is *net loss*.

3. *Operating profit* is the amount derived from core business activities and does not include revenue from other sources, such as return on investments or interest on loans.

4. *EBIT (earnings before interest and taxes)* also represents core business earnings, but is calculated prior to deductions for loan interest and tax payments.

Economic Profit

Economic profit refers to the surplus funds generated by an enterprise over and above net profit. The calculation of net profit includes all costs incurred in producing and selling the goods of the firm, including the implicit costs of the owner's foregone income to do this business. These costs also include any associated with capital investment, including loan principal and interest. Economic profit can be viewed as a bonus or reward for the owner/investor, in consideration of their willingness to take the risk of funding and/or operating the business enterprise. In this context, net profit is sometimes referred to as "normal profit." The calculation of normal profit includes (as a cost) the rate of return required by a potential investor to make or continue their investment in the enterprise. Economic profit occurs when the revenue level is sufficient to exceed all costs, including the cost of capital investment and any other opportunity costs.

In a purely capitalistic society, profits and losses are the primary concern of the business owner, investors, and management. Those who own firms (capitalists) undertake the task (personally or through their appointed representatives) of organizing and performing production efforts so as to optimize their income and profitability. The quest for profits is guided by the famous "invisible hand" of capitalism, as conceived by Adam Smith. When profits are above the normal level, they attract additional investment, either by new firms or by existing firms looking to maximize their return. The investment seeks only the highest reward and is not concerned with the underlying vehicle or venue that produces the profits. Additional competitors generally drive prices (and then profits) down. New investment continues to enter until profit levels no longer exceed the return available elsewhere. This "free-market" system drives investment in areas where consumers provide demand. With technological innovation, consumer demand shifts to new industries and investment follows. Over time, that market becomes crowded, prices and profits fall, and there is demand for new innovation—repeating the cycle. In a market economy, economic profits can exist for a long time only if the firms in the industry can keep other firms from entering. If new firms can enter because the existing firms are earning a return over and above a "normal" rate of return, the economic profit will be driven out by the increased competition.

Social Profit

The social profit from a firm's activities is the normal profit plus or minus any externalities that occur in its activity. A firm may report relatively large economic profits, but by creating negative externalities, its social profit can be rendered relatively small.

An externality is any effect not directly involved in the transaction. When this occurs, market prices do not reflect the full costs or benefits in production or consumption of a product or service. A positive impact is called an external benefit, while a negative impact is called an external cost. Producers and consumers in a given market may either not bear all of the costs or not reap all of the benefits of the economic activity. For example, a manufacturing or chemical company that causes air or water pollution imposes costs on the entire society, in the form of cleanup efforts that will be needed later or in the form of taxes and regulatory restrictions on operations or the consumption of products in that market. On the other hand, a homeowner who takes care to maintain his house and property creates value not only for his own home, but also for the other homes and owners in the neighborhood. For these neighbors, increased home values come without effort or expenditure on their part but yield a higher price when they choose to sell their house.

In a competitive market, the existence of externalities causes either too much or too little of the good to be produced or consumed in terms of overall costs and benefits to society. In the case of external costs, such as environmental pollution, the goods often will be overproduced because the producer does not take into account the external costs. If there are external benefits, as in the areas of education or safety, private markets may well produce too little of the goods because the external benefits to others are not taken into account. Here, overall cost and benefit to society is defined as the sum of the economic benefits and costs for all parties involved.

Early champions of capitalistic principles focused on economic profit, with little regard to social profit. As the industrial revolution gained momentum, however, technological progress brought new challenges. Few, if any, foresaw the cost of advances in technology, especially as American society was embracing a more materialistic, consumption-oriented lifestyle. The quest to maximize profits rewarded short-term thinking and policies. The focus on corporate earnings led to "creative" accounting practices, and ultimately outright fraudulent and criminal activity.

In the early years of the twenty-first century, the dubious practices of a number of major corporations were brought to light. At Enron, Tyco, and WorldCom, to name just a few, senior managers were found to have committed accounting fraud and sent to prison. The impact of their actions led to financial ruin for many stockholders and employees, a general loss of confidence in the nation's corporate infrastructure, and the introduction of regulatory guidelines to prevent future occurrences. Laws such as the Sarbanes-Oxley Act—officially

the Public Company Accounting Reform and Investor Protection Act of 2002—were passed to establish new or enhanced standards for the boards of directors, management, and accounting firms of all publicly traded U.S. companies.

Despite these experiences—both the fraudulent practices and the efforts to enact remedies—the year 2008 found the country facing similar profit-driven challenges. This time, the culprits were bad lending practices and complicated investment strategies designed to maximize profits but understood by few investors, traders, or lenders. The impact of these practices was found to be far more damaging and widespread than those earlier in the decade, affecting companies across industries from banking to manufacturing and damaging national economies around the globe. Given the depth and scope of the crisis, the world's government leaders and economic policy makers responded with Keynesian force, intervening with large bailouts and buyouts.

The global financial crisis and recession of the late 2000s gave impetus, at least in some quarters, to a new paradigm for the conduct of business, particularly as it pertains to the definition and pursuit of profits. In the new formula, social and environmental values were added to the traditional economic measures of corporate or organizational success. Triple bottom line (TBL) accounting—measuring people, planet, profit—is a methodology that quantifies the social and environmental impact of an organization's activities relative to its economic performance, for the purpose of targeting and achieving improvements. The phrase was coined by John Elkington in his 1998 book *Cannibals with Forks: The Triple Bottom Line of 21st Century Business* and has been elaborated by others, most notably Andrew Savitz in *The Triple Bottom Line* (2005).

With the ratification of new standards for urban and community accounting by the United Nations and ICLEI (International Council for Local Environment Initiatives) in 2007, the triple bottom line became the dominant international approach to public-sector, full-cost accounting. Similar UN standards apply to natural and human-capital measurement to assist in measurements required by TBL, such as the ecoBudget standard for reporting ecological footprints. In 2003, the ICLEI was officially renamed ICLEI–Local Governments for Sustainability. In the private sector, a commitment to corporate social responsibility implies a commitment to some form of TBL reporting.

Corporate social responsibility (CSR) is an obligation of the organization to act in ways that serve both the interest of stockholders and those of its many stakeholders, both internal and external. It consists of three essential components:

- Doing business responsibly
- Taking a leadership position in community investment and social issues relevant to the business
- Transparency and public reporting of the social, environmental, and financial effects and performance of the business.

Ideally, CSR policy would function as a built-in, self-regulating mechanism whereby businesses would monitor and ensure their adherence to law, ethical standards, and international norms. Essentially, CSR is the deliberate inclusion of public interest in corporate decision making and respect for the triple bottom line.

The practice of CSR has been subject to considerable debate and criticism. Proponents argue that there is a strong case to be made in pure business terms, in that corporations benefit from operating with a broader and longer perspective than their own immediate, short-term profits. Critics argue that CSR distracts from the fundamental economic role of businesses. Others argue that there is no proven link between CSR and financial performance. And many question its relationship to the fundamental purpose and nature of the business enterprise—inevitably entailing higher expenses and risking lower profits. Even the most ardent supporter of CSR will admit that the financial advantages are hard to quantify and that the benefits are not always visible, at least not in the short term.

Nonprofits

A nonprofit organization (NPO, or not-for-profit) is any organization that does not aim to make a profit and is not a public institution. Whereas for-profit corporations exist to earn and distribute taxable business earnings to shareholders, nonprofit corporations exist solely to provide programs and services of public benefit. Often these programs and services are not otherwise provided by local, state, or federal entities. While they are able to earn a profit—called a surplus in the case of nonprofits—such earnings must be retained by the organization for the future provision of programs and services. Earnings may not benefit individuals or stakeholders. Underlying many effective nonprofit endeavors is a commitment to management. NPO leaders have learned that nonprofit organizations need effective management just as much or even more than for-profit businesses do, precisely because they lack the discipline of the bottom line.

In the United States, nonprofit organizations are formed by incorporating in the state in which they expect to do business. The act of incorporating creates a legal entity that enables the organization to be treated as a corporation under law and to enter into business dealings, form contracts, and own property as any other individual or for-profit corporation may do. The two major types of nonprofit organization structure are membership and board-only. A membership organization elects its board, holds regular meetings, and has power to amend its bylaws. A board-only organization typically has a self-selected board and a membership whose powers are limited to those delegated to it by the board. One major difference between a nonprofit and a for-profit corporation is that the former does not issue stock or pay dividends, and may not enrich its directors.

Charles Richardson

See also: Corporate Finance.

Further Reading

Albrecht, William P. *Economics.* Englewood Cliffs, NJ: Prentice-Hall, 1983.

Ammer, Christine, and Dean Ammer. *Dictionary of Business and Economics.* New York: Free Press, 1977.

Drucker, Peter. *What Business Can Learn from Nonprofits.* Boston: Harvard Business Review Press, 1989.

Hillstrom, Kevin, and Laurie Collier Hillstrom. *Encyclopedia of Small Business.* Farmington Hills, MI: Gale Cengage. 2002.

Pyle, William W., and Kermit D. Larson. *Fundamental Accounting Principles.* Homewood, IL: Richard D. Irwin, 1981.

Public Works Policy

A government's public works policy derives from the fact that certain economic goods and services are deemed "public goods." Public goods provide economic benefit to society and cannot be obtained in efficient quantities through the regular workings of the profit-based free market. That being the case, they are difficult to price according to the law of supply and demand. The most common example of a public good is national defense. Although defense is considered essential to any country, it is not always clear when defense is needed nor how much people are willing to pay for it. What is clear is that if left to the provision of markets, the quantity of national defense provided would be too small and not be socially optimal. This is because markets provide goods and services as long as private benefits to the individual exceed private costs. However, with national defense, the social benefits (total benefits to society) are much greater than the private benefits. Also, there is a "free-rider problem" since you cannot exclude others from being protected. If one group voluntarily pays for national defense, even those who do not pay cannot be excluded from being protected. Hence, everyone has an incentive to let others pay. Thus, national defense like other public goods, is deemed to be best provided by government.

Public works—usually large infrastructure projects such as roads, bridges, dams, power systems, and the like—are generally viewed by economists as public goods as well. Perhaps the best example of a public works project in the United States is the Interstate Highway System built in the 1950s and 1960s. The congressional act authorizing the federal, as opposed to local, funding of roads is known as the National Interstate and Defense Highways Act of 1956. The highway system was deemed necessary for national defense, to facilitate troop and armament movements throughout the country during the cold war. In addition, it was recognized, an interstate highway system would also provide important commercial benefits to the private sector, as it would enable the producers and suppliers of goods to reduce transportation costs. In economics, this is known as a positive "spillover effect" from the provision of a public good.

Absent the profit motive of a market that determines the supply and demand of a good or service, governments need to plan for and budget for the provision of public goods. How public goods policy is devised, implemented, and paid for naturally varies by country and political system. In the United States, for example, public works planning is largely decentralized, carried out by cities and states across the country; funding may be provided directly or indirectly by the federal government, which may also play a role in regulatory oversight. In Japan, by comparison, the national government views public works as a part of national industrial policy and plays a much larger, direct role in planning and development.

Public Works, Natural Monopolies, and Government Control

Another economic rationale for collective action, whether by government or voluntary self-organization, is that some economic goods are deemed to be "natural monopolies." A natural monopoly is a project that requires large up-front investment in physical capital, such as an electrical plant. It does not make economic sense to build more than one plant in a given geographical location that could be served by one plant. Some economists believe that the concept of natural monopoly provides the economic rationale for government to make policy for public works, which usually entail large costs and long periods of time to build. The most commonly known public works projects, in addition to roads, are canals, water and sewer systems, shipping ports, dams, airports, bridges, and mass transportation systems. In addition to the large upfront costs of public works projects, infrastructure can also be expensive to maintain over long periods of time. For this reason, public works policy is also part of the fiscal policy-making process of the government authority at any level.

Economists, planners, public administrators, and politicians do not agree on an exact definition of public works. Many economists believe that, if a natural monopoly can provide a revenue stream, then it is best for profit-making entities to provide the good or service because this will create an incentive for efficiency. Moreover, some economists point out, governments may have an incentive to overprovide public goods because doing so tends to enhance their power, increase their budgets, and help garner political favor through targeted spending. Other economists contend that it is best for government to control public works to exert quality control and to ensure that the public interest is fully served. In the United States, at least, public works policy is generally driven by both economic reasoning and political benefit, usually combining both private and public interests.

Public Works and Regulation Economics

Because of the natural monopoly and the public goods nature inherent in public works (the positive spillover effect), many economists agree that there is a role for government in ensuring that the public good is provided at a level that ensures the greatest net societal benefit. Net societal

benefits are total societal benefits less total costs. The economic analysis of natural-monopoly implementation is called "regulation economics." The purpose of such analysis is to ensure that providers of public goods and natural monopolies charge a fair and reasonable price for the good or service, meet the public demand at that price, and that the government regulatory framework provides the right incentives to allow this to happen. Regulation economics seeks to find the best policy for regulating natural monopolies.

The chief argument for private provision of public goods is that it put less of a strain on public finances. For example, many states in the United States have privatized parts of their road systems, usually those that link multiple population centers and are used by a large number of people. This ensures that only those using the roads are actually paying for them, thereby generating revenue and reducing congestion. The private provision of public works is usually implemented through concessions, whereby private companies bid for the right to operate and maintain the public roads and highways for a period of time in return for an upfront fee or a percentage of the profits. Because of the large sums of monies involved in many of these projects, privatization of roads is a politically charged issue.

Public Works and Economic Development

Some economists recommend the private provision of public goods in underdeveloped nations because the tax base is not large enough to publicly finance the building and maintenance of public works. Yet public works with positive spillovers are important for economic growth. For example, the government might grant a private company the right to build and operate a public work (such as a shipping port, road system, or hydroelectric dam) that will, through spillover, encourage and facilitate economic activity. Ownership of the public work may either be transferred to the private operator or remain with the political authority. Thus, the success or failure of privately constructed public goods depends on the strength of the political institution and the way the bid process and private-public contractual agreement are structured. The overriding goal should be to provide the greatest public benefit at the least cost. In this sense, public works policy should be part of a larger economic development policy for a given political entity.

Other economists believe that anything that generates revenue and can exclude "free riding" is neither a public good nor a public work and should not be provided by government. Examples of public goods that are natural monopolies include public utilities like gas and electricity. The provision of electricity for homes and businesses and gas for heating, cooking, and manufacturing necessitates extensive outlays of capital and requires that gas lines and electrical cables be built throughout a given area. The construction, maintenance, and repair of this infrastructure can be disruptive to the day-to-day lives of citizens, so it is important that they are regulated and managed by public officials. Although there are exceptions, in general, public works such as water and sewage systems are publicly owned and operated so as to ensure public health and safety. Regulatory economics attempts to answer the trade-off between efficiency and competition versus ensuring adequate provision of services with the least disruption of public life.

Public Works and the Business Cycle

Beyond the basic need for infrastructure or to pursue a common purpose such as national defense, public works policy may be influenced by the business cycle. That is, governments will sometimes engage in public works projects during periods of economic contraction as a means to increase employment, income, and aggregate demand. Perhaps the most well-known public works program of this type in U.S. history was the Works Progress Administration (WPA), a centerpiece of President Franklin Roosevelt's New Deal to combat the Great Depression.

The federally financed Interstate Highway System of the 1950s and 1960s was the largest public works project in history. The nationwide network, featuring innovative design and engineering, was conceived for both civil defense and economic development. *(Topical Press Agency/Stringer/ Hulton Archive/Getty Images)*

During the lifespan of the WPA (1935–1943), 25 percent of all American families had a member of their family employed by the agency. In 1938 alone, more than 3 million people were employed by the program. During the eight years of its existence, the WPA employed 8 million people, who had 30 million dependents. With a budget of approximately 6 percent of national income, the WPA built or repaired some 120,000 bridges, 80,000 miles (128,800 kilometers) of city streets, 540,000 miles (869,045 kilometers) of rural highways, 25,000 miles (40,233 kilometers) of sewers, 1,100 water-treatment plants, 18,000 parks and recreational buildings, 16,000 athletic fields, 500 airports, 36,000 schools, and 6,000 administrative buildings.

Historians and economists have debated whether the WPA was essentially a public works agency or a relief program. It was certainly a way to reduce the suffering of mass unemployment (which averaged 17 percent in the United States from 1930 to 1940). Political scientists have also shown that WPA projects tended to be built in areas where it was expected that votes would do President Roosevelt the most good in gaining reelection. The Roosevelt administration did attempt to institutionalize public works policy into the federal government, with a proposed cabinet-level department, but Congress rejected the idea.

Keynesian economists believe that government can and should use fiscal stimulus to create demand in an economy during times of recessionary crisis and that public works programs are a good way to do this. The WPA is often cited as a successful example of this approach, though some economists question whether the WPA was actually a stimulus or only provided temporary employment. Indeed, it was not until the United States joined World War II and geared up military manufacturing that unemployment fell below 10 percent.

In summary, public works policy makes up part of the fiscal, development, natural resources, public health, and transportation policy of a given political entity. Public works, by their nature being public goods and natural monopolies, require a give-and-take between the private sector and between differing layers of government within a nation. How a public works policy is made depends on the type of political system and institutions involved. Nevertheless, public works are an important and indispensable part of an economy.

Cameron M. Weber

See also: Employment and Unemployment; Fiscal Policy; New Deal.

Further Reading

Buchanan, James M., and Gordon Tullock. *The Calculus of Consent: Logical Foundation of Constitutional Democracy.* Ann Arbor: University of Michigan Press, 1965.

Button, Kenneth, Jonathan Gifford, and John Petersen. "Public Works Policy and Outcomes in Japan and the United States." *Public Works Management and Policy* 7:2 (2002): 124–137.

Darby, Michael R. "Three-and-a-Half Million U.S. Employees Have Been Mislaid: Or, an Explanation of Unemployment, 1934–1941." *Journal of Political Economy* 84:1 (1976): 1–16.

Howard, Donald S. *The WPA and Federal Relief Policy.* New York: Russell Sage Foundation, 1943.

Jasay, Anthony de. *Social Contract, Free Ride: A Study of the Public-Goods Problem,* New York: Oxford University Press, 1989.

There are no entries for the letter Q.